General Editor

Michael Ryan teaches in the Department of Film & Media Arts at Temple University. He is co-editor (with Amitava Kumar) of *Politics and Culture* (www.politicsandculture. org). His books include *Marxism and Deconstruction* (1982), *Camera Politica* (with Douglas Kellner, 1986), and *Politics and Culture* (1989). He is the editor of *Literary Theory: An Anthology* (with Julie Rivkin, 2nd edn. Wiley-Blackwell, 2004) and *Cultural Studies: An Anthology* (Wiley-Blackwell, 2008). His textbooks include *Literary Theory: A Practical Introduction* (2nd edn. Wiley-Blackwell, 2005), *Cultural Studies: A Practical Introduction* (Wiley-Blackwell, 2009), *An Introduction to Criticism* (Wiley-Blackwell, forthcoming), and *An Introduction to Film Analysis* (forthcoming).

Volume Editors

Gregory Castle is Professor of English at Arizona State University. His publications include *Postcolonial Discourses: A Reader* (Wiley-Blackwell, 2001), *Modernism and the Celtic Revival* (2001), *Reading the Modernist Bildungsroman* (2006), and *The Blackwell Guide to Literary Theory* (Wiley-Blackwell, 2007).

Robert Eaglestone is Professor of Contemporary Literature and Thought at Royal Holloway, University of London. His books include *Ethical Criticism: Reading after Levinas* (1997), *Doing English* (3rd edn., 2009), *The Holocaust and the Postmodern* (2004), *Derrida's Legacies* (with Simon Glendenning, 2008), *J. M. Coetzee in Theory and Practice* (with Elleke Hoehmer and Katy Iddiols, 2009). He is series editor for *Routledge Critical Thinkers*.

M. Keith Booker is the James E. and Ellen Wadley Roper Professor of English and Director of the Program in Comparative Literature and Cultural Studies at the University of Arkansas. He is the author of more than 30 books, including *The Science Fiction Handbook* (with Anne-Marie Thomas, Wiley-Blackwell, 2009).

The Wiley-Blackwell Encyclopedia of Literature
www.literatureencyclopedia.com

The *Wiley-Blackwell Encyclopedia of Literature* is a comprehensive, scholarly, authoritative, and critical overview of literature and theory comprising individual titles covering key literary genres, periods, and sub-disciplines. Available both in print and online, this groundbreaking resource provides students, teachers, and researchers with cutting-edge scholarship in literature and literary studies.

Published:

The Encyclopedia of Literary and Cultural Theory, General Editor: Michael Ryan

The Encyclopedia of the Novel, General Editor: Peter Melville Logan

The Encyclopedia of Twentieth-Century Fiction, General Editor: Brian W. Shaffer

Forthcoming:

The Encyclopedia of English Renaissance Literature, General Editors: Garrett A. Sullivan, Jr. and Alan Stewart

The Encyclopedia of Romantic Literature, General Editor: Frederick Burwick

The Encyclopedia of the Gothic, General Editors: William Hughes, David Punter, and Andrew Smith

The Encyclopedia of Postcolonial Studies, General Editors: Sangeeta Ray and Henry Schwarz

The Encyclopedia
of Literary and Cultural
Theory

General Editor: Michael Ryan

Volume II

Literary Theory from 1966 to the Present

Edited by Robert Eaglestone

A John Wiley & Sons, Ltd., Publication

This edition first published 2011
© 2011 Blackwell Publishing Ltd

Blackwell Publishing was acquired by John Wiley & Sons in February 2007. Blackwell's publishing program has been merged with Wiley's global Scientific, Technical, and Medical business to form Wiley-Blackwell.

Registered Office
John Wiley & Sons Ltd, The Atrium, Southern Gate, Chichester, West Sussex, PO19 8SQ, United Kingdom

Editorial Offices
350 Main Street, Malden, MA 02148-5020, USA

9600 Garsington Road, Oxford, OX4 2DQ, UK

The Atrium, Southern Gate, Chichester, West Sussex, PO19 8SQ, UK

For details of our global editorial offices, for customer services, and for information about how to apply for permission to reuse the copyright material in this book, please see our website at www.wiley.com/wiley-blackwell.

The right of Michael Ryan to be identified as the author of the editorial material in this work has been asserted in accordance with the UK Copyright, Designs and Patents Act 1988.

Wiley also publishes its books in a variety of electronic formats. Some content that appears in print may not be available in electronic books.

Designations used by companies to distinguish their products are often claimed as trademarks. All brand names and product names used in this book are trade names, service marks, trademarks or registered trademarks of their respective owners. The publisher is not associated with any product or vendor mentioned in this book. This publication is designed to provide accurate and authoritative information in regard to the subject matter covered. It is sold on the understanding that the publisher is not engaged in rendering professional services. If professional advice or other expert assistance is required, the services of a competent professional should be sought.

Library of Congress Cataloging-in-Publication Data

The encyclopedia of literary and cultural theory / general editor, Michael Ryan.
v. cm.
Includes bibliographical references and index.
Contents: v. 1. Literary theory from 1900 to 1966 / edited by Gregory Castle – v. 2. Literary theory from 1966 to the present / edited by Robert Eaglestone – v. 3. Cultural theory / edited by M. Keith Booker.
ISBN 978-1-4051-8312-3 (hardcover : alk. paper) 1. Criticism–Encyclopedias. 2. Literature–History and criticism–Theory, etc.–Encyclopedias. I. Ryan, Michael, 1951- II. Castle, Gregory. III. Eaglestone, Robert, 1968- IV. Booker, M. Keith.
PN81.E435 2011
801′.9503–dc22

2010029411

A catalogue record for this book is available from the British Library.

Set in 10/12.5 Minion by Thomson, Noida, India
Printed and bound in Singapore by Fabulous Printers Pte Ltd

03   2011

Contents

List of Entries

Volume I: Literary Theory from 1900 to 1966

Volume II: Literary Theory from 1966 to the Present

Volume III: Cultural Theory

Notes on Contributors to Volume II

Marian Aguiar is an associate professor in the Literary and Cultural Studies Program, Department of English at Carnegie Mellon University. Her forthcoming book, *Tracking Modernity: India's Railway and the Culture of Mobility* (2011), explores cultural representations of modernity by looking at images of railway space in colonial, nationalist, and postcolonial South Asian contexts. Her articles have appeared in *Cultural Critique*, *Modern Fiction Studies*, *Journal of Modern Literature*, and *Rethinking Marxism*, as well as in edited book collections.

Frederick Luis Aldama is Arts and Humanities Distinguished Professor of English at the Ohio State University and Director of Latino Studies. He is the editor of five collections of essays and the author of seven books, including *Postethnic Narrative Criticism* (2003), *Brown on Brown* (2005), and the MLA-award winning *Dancing With Ghosts: A Critical Biography of Arturo Islas* (2005), *Why the Humanities Matter: A Common Sense Approach* (2008), *Your Brain on Latino Comics: From Gus Arriola to Los Bros Hernandez* (2009), and *A User's Guide to Postcolonial and Latino Borderland Fiction* (2009). He has published numerous articles, co-edits the series "Cognitive Approaches to Literature and Culture" (UTexas Press), and sits on the board for the Americas book series (Texas Tech University Press).

Eva Aldea obtained her PhD from Royal Holloway, University of London in 2009. She is currently teaching at Goldsmith College, University of London and Westminster University. She is the author of *Magical Realism and Gilles Deleuze: The Indiscernibility of Difference* (2010) and co-editor (with Geoff Baker) of *Realism's Others* (2010).

Shahidha Bari is a lecturer in English and philosophy at Queen Mary University of London. She works in the fields of literature, philosophy, and politics, with particular interests in Heidegger, Derrida, and Nancy. She has a literary specialism in the romantic poetics. She is the author of *Keats and Philosophy* (2011), is a co-founder (with Nemonie Craven Roderick) of *How to Live* (www.htlblog.com) and is a co-author of the *How to Live* guidebook to modern life.

Oliver Belas has taught at the University of London, where he completed his PhD, and now teaches in London. His research interests include genre writing (particularly crime and science fiction, and science writing), literary and cultural theory, African American literature, and pedagogy. He has contributed to the *Journal of American Studies*, and is currently co-editing and contributing to a volume provisionally entitled *Rethinking Genre*.

Arthur Bradley is a senior lecturer in literary and cultural theory in the Department of English and Creative Writing at Lancaster University. He is the author of *Negative Theology and Modern French Philosophy* (2004); *Derrida's "Of Grammatology": A Philosophical Guide* (2008) and *The New Atheist Novel: Fiction, Philosophy and Polemic After 9/11* (2010). He is currently working on a book on the philosophy of technology from Marx to Stiegler.

Gabriel Noah Brahm, Jr. is an assistant professor of English at Northern Michigan

University and a research fellow in Israel studies at Brandeis University. His published works have appeared in *Critical Studies in Media Communication*, *Democratiya*, *Nineteenth-Century Literature*, *Poetics Today*, *Rethinking History*, and elsewhere. He was one of the founding associate editors of the journal *Politics and Culture*.

Daniel Burgoyne is a professor at Vancouver Island University. He is the co-author (with Christine Hult and Richard Gooding) of *The New Century Handbook* (2005) and an associate author of Janet Giltrow's *Academic Writing: An Introduction* (2nd edn. 2009). He co-directs the Literary Theory Research Group at VIU and is editing the Broadview Press edition of James De Mille's *A Strange Manuscript Found in a Copper Cylinder*. He has published and given talks on romanticism, the gothic, literary theory, and hoaxes. His research focuses on scientific romance.

Joseph Carroll is Curators' Professor of English at the University of Missouri-St Louis. He is the author of *The Cultural Theory of Matthew Arnold* (1982), *Wallace Stevens' Supreme Fiction: A New Romanticism* (1987), *Evolution and Literary Theory* (1995), and *Literary Darwinism: Evolution, Human Nature, and Literature* (2004). He has produced an edition of Darwin's *On the Origin of Species*. He is a co-editor (with Brian Boyd and Jonathan Gottschall) of *Evolution, Literature, and Film: A Reader* (2010), and he co-edits an annual journal, *The Evolutionary Review: Art, Science, Culture*. A collection of his recent essays, *Reading Human Nature: Literary Darwinism in Theory and Practice*, is in press.

Andrew Clark is a PhD student and part-time lecturer in European thought at the University of Portsmouth. His doctoral thesis considers the idea of the autobiographical in the work of the French philosopher

Jacques Derrida. His research interests include the essence of argument, of history, of ethics, of personal identity, and of psychological problems.

Claire Colebrook is Edwin Erle Sparks Professor of Literature at Penn State University. She has published books and articles on literary theory, feminist theory, continental philosophy, and the poetry of John Milton. Her most recent book is *Deleuze and the Meaning of Life* (2010).

G. Thomas Couser is a professor of English and founding director of the Disability Studies program at Hofstra University. He is the author of *American Autobiography: The Prophetic Mode* (1979), *Altered Egos: Authority in American Autobiography* (1989), *Recovering Bodies: Illness, Disability, and Life Writing* (1997), *Vulnerable Subjects: Ethics and Life Writing* (2004), and *Signifying Bodies: Disability in Contemporary Life Writing* (2009), as well as about 50 articles or book chapters. He is currently writing a book about contemporary American "patriography" (memoirs of fathers by sons and daughters) and a memoir of his own father.

Marcel Danesi is a professor of semiotics and anthropology at the University of Toronto. Currently, he is the editor-in-chief of *Semiotica*, the official journal of the International Association for Semiotic Studies. Among his many books are *Vico, Metaphor and the Origin of Language* (1993), *Cool: The Signs and Meanings of Adolescence* (1994), *Understanding Media Semiotics* (2002), *The Quest for Meaning: A Guide to Semiotic Theory and Practice* (2007), and *X-Rated: The Power of Mythic Symbolism in Popular Culture* (2009). He was elected a Fellow of the Royal Society of Canada in 1998 for his work in semiotics.

Anne Donadey is a professor of European studies and women's studies at San Diego State University. Her research area is francophone and anglophone postcolonial feminist writers. She is the author of *Recasting Postcolonialism: Women Writing between Worlds* (2001), co-editor (with H. Adlai Murdoch) of *Postcolonial Theory and Francophone Literary Studies* (2005), and editor of a special issue of *L'Esprit créateur* on the works of Assia Djebar (Winter 2008).

Lisa Downing is founder and director of the Centre for the Interdisciplinary Study of Sexuality and Gender in Europe (CISSGE) at the University of Exeter, where she is a professor of French discourses of sexuality. Her research specialisms include sexuality studies, critical theory, and modern French literature and film. She is the author and editor of numerous books, including *Desiring the Dead: Necrophilia and Nineteenth-Century French Literature* (2003) and *The Cambridge Introduction to Michel Foucault* (2008).

Robert Eaglestone is a professor of contemporary literature and thought at Royal Holloway, University of London. He is the author of four books, including *Ethical Criticism: Reading after Levinas* (1997), *The Holocaust and the Postmodern* (2004), *Doing English* (3rd edn. 2009), and the editor or co-editor of a further four books, including (with Simon Glendinning) *Derrida's Legacies* (2008), and (with Elleke Boehmer & Katy Iddiols) *J. M. Coetzee in Theory and Practice* (2009). He has published widely on contemporary philosophy, contemporary literature, literary theory, and historiography, and on the Holocaust and genocide. He is the series editor of *Routledge Critical Thinkers*.

Claire Feehily teaches cultural memory, humanities, and literary studies at Birkbeck College, and at the School of Advanced Studies, University of London. She is currently working on a book about the British New Right's cultural politics and has pub-lished in the fields of European contemporary culture and war memory.

Finn Fordham is a lecturer at Royal Holloway, University of London. He specializes in James Joyce, twentieth-century literature and theory, and has written two books: *Lots of Fun at "Finnegans Wake"* (2007) and *I Do, I Undo, I Redo: The Textual Genesis of Modernist Selves* (2010). An edited volume, *James Joyce and the 19th Century French Novel*, is due out in 2011.

Anthony Fothergill is a senior lecturer at the University of Exeter, where he teaches English literature and cultural theory. He has also taught at the University of Heidelberg and at Kenyon College, Ohio. He has written widely on modernism and modernity. His most recent book is *Secret Sharers: Joseph Conrad's Cultural Reception in Germany* (2006). He has published a book-length study on Conrad's *Heart of Darkness* (1989; 2000) and has edited works by Conrad and Oscar Wilde.

Monica Francioso obtained her PhD in 2005 from Royal Holloway, University of London. She has taught at several UK universities, as well as at University College Dublin. She has published on the development of narrative theory in postwar Italy, the Italian literature of migration, postmodern novels and theories, and on the works of Enrico Palandri and Gianni Celati.

Katie Garner is a PhD student and postgraduate tutor in English literature at Cardiff University. Her doctoral thesis looks at women writers' imaginative and scholarly responses to the medieval revival in the late eighteenth and early nineteenth centuries.

Greg Garrard is Chair of the Association for the Study of Literature and the Environment (UK) and author of *Ecocriticism* (2004). He was awarded a National Teaching Fellowship in 2005 for his work on education for sustainable development, and is a senior teaching fellow at Bath Spa University.

Anna Gething lectures part time in English at Bath Spa University. Her research falls into four overlapping areas: contemporary women's writing, gender studies, postcolonial writing, and the senses in literature. Current work focuses on the writing of Kate Grenville. She has also published on the abject and grotesque in Angela Carter and Jonathan Swift, rites of passage in the fiction of Jamaica Kincaid, the gendering of smell in literature, women and violence in *The Sopranos*, and domestic dystopias in popular culture.

Mrinalini Greedharry is an assistant professor in the Department of English at Laurentian University. She is a graduate of the University of London and has taught in universities in Finland, the UK, and Canada. Her most recent book, *Postcolonial Theory and Psychoanalysis* (2008), examines how we might turn from psychoanalytic readings of colonial culture to an interrogation of psychoanalysis as a colonial discourse. Her current research focuses on questions of methods in interdisciplinary scholarship and how theoretical approaches can be realized as new pedagogical practices.

Gavin Grindon is postdoctoral research fellow in visual and material culture at Kingston University, and has previously taught at Manchester and Goldsmiths universities. He has published articles in *Third Text*, *Art Monthly*, and the *Journal of Aesthetics and Protest*, and is currently writing a history of art and activism in the twentieth century which orients itself around the theory of revolution-as-festival.

Nicole M. Gyulay is currently publications editor at the Institute of Education, University of London. She obtained her PhD in postcolonial literature in 2007

from Royal Holloway, University of London. Her publications include "Writing for the West: V. S. Naipaul's religion," in the *South Asian Review*, and "Multiplicity destroyed by singularity: Salman Rushdie and religious hybridity," in *Spiritual Identities: Literature and the Post-Secular Imagination* (2010).

Matthew T. Helmers, candidate for a PhD in English and American studies at the University of Manchester, is currently working on the constructions of gender, sexuality, and temporality that inform the literary, legal, and psychoanalytic understandings of homosexual panic.

Jonathan Hensher is a researcher in French studies at the University of Manchester, specializing in text–image relations and the illustrated book. His publications include "From innocent to indecent: Eroticism and visual punning in Cochin's illustrations to *Roland furieux*," in S. Donachie & K. Harrison (eds.), *Love and Sexuality: New Approaches in French Studies* (2005) and "Engraving difference: Pierre-Clément Marillier's oriental illustrations in the *Cabinet des Fées*," *Journal for Eighteenth-Century Studies* 31 (2008).

Ken Hirschkop is an associate professor of English at the University of Waterloo, Ontario. He is the author of *Mikhail Bakhtin: An Aesthetic for Democracy* (1999) as well as many articles on Bakhtin, and he co-edited (with David Shepherd) the collection *Bakhtin and Cultural Theory* (2005).

Joe Hughes is a lecturer at the University of Minnesota. He is the author of *Deleuze and the Genesis of Representation* (2008) and *Deleuze's Difference and Repetition* (2009).

Ian James is a fellow in modern languages at Downing College and a lecturer in the Department of French at the University of Cambridge. He is the author of *Pierre*

Klossowski: The Persistence of a Name (2000), *The Fragmentary Demand: An Introduction to the Philosophy of Jean-Luc Nancy* (2006), and *Paul Virilio* (2007).

John J. Joughin is a professor of English literature and is Pro Vice-Chancellor (Research; Acting) at the University of Central Lancashire, Preston. He is editor of *Shakespeare and National Culture* (1997) and *Philosophical Shakespeares* (2000), and joint editor (with Simon Malpas) of *The New Aestheticism* (2003).

Jane Kilby teaches in the School of English, Sociology, Politics and Contemporary History at the University of Salford. She specializes in the interdisciplinary question of violence, trauma, and testimony, and, more generally, the politics of feminist theory and methodology. Her publications include *Violence and the Cultural Politics of Trauma* (2007), *The Future of Memory* (co-edited with Antony Rowland and Rick Crownshaw, 2010), as well as articles on violence, trauma, the body, and feminism.

Koonyong Kim is a James B. Duke Fellow and PhD candidate at Duke University. He has published on critical theory and postmodern global culture. He is also the Korean translator of Fredric Jameson's work.

Jennifer Lewis was awarded a PhD by the University of Warwick in 2001 for her work on Zora Neale Hurston. She is currently writing a book on place and the body in African American literature. She teaches English and American literature at Bath Spa University.

Simon Malpas teaches English Literature at Edinburgh University. He the author of *The Postmodern* (2005) and *Jean-François Lyotard* (2003), editor of *Postmodern Debates* (2001) and *William Cowper: The Centenary Letters* (2000), and co-editor (with John Joughin) of *The New Aestheti-*

cism (2003) and (with Paul Wake) of *The Routledge Companion to Critical Theory* (2006). He has also published work on aesthetics, romanticism, continental philosophy, twentieth-century literature, and Victorian nonsense.

Anita Mannur is an assistant professor of English and Asian/Asian American Studies at Miami University, Ohio. She is the author of *Culinary Fictions: Food in South Asian Diasporic Cultures* (2010) and co-editor of *Theorizing Diaspora* (2003). She has published articles on the cultural politics of Asian American literature in *Amerasia Journal*, *MELUS*, and several anthologies.

Nick Mansfield is a professor in critical and cultural studies at Macquarie University in Sydney. His books include *Subjectivity: Theories of the Self from Freud to Haraway* (2000), *Theorizing War: From Hobbes to Badiou* (2008), and *The God Who Deconstructs Himself: Subjectivity and Sovereignty Between Freud, Bataille and Derrida* (2010). He is one of the general editors of the journal *Derrida Today*.

Martin McQuillan is Dean of the Faculty of Arts and Social Sciences at Kingston University, London. His publications include *Paul de Man* (2001) and *Deconstruction After 9/11* (2009), and the edited volumes *The Politics of Deconstruction: Jacques Derrida and the Other of Philosophy* (2007) and *Deconstruction Reading Politics* (2008).

Kaye Mitchell is a lecturer in contemporary literature at the University of Manchester and course director of the MA in Contemporary Literature and Culture. Her research covers twentieth-century and contemporary literature, critical theory, and gender and sexuality. She is the author of *A. L. Kennedy* (2007) and *Intention and Text* (2008), and has published various articles on contemporary literature and theory. Recent projects include articles and chapters on 1950s lesbian pulp fiction, on contemporary erotic memoirs by women, and on the figure of the archive in twentieth-century gay fiction.

Gerald Moore is a lecturer in French at Wadham College, Oxford, having previously taught at Université Paris-12 (Val de Marne). His book on poststructuralist politics, *Politics of the Gift*, is forthcoming (2011). He has also published on Michel Houellebecq and translated works by Henri Lefebvre, Michel Foucault, and Georges-Didi Huberman, among others.

Simon Morgan Wortham is a professor of English at Kingston University, London. His recent books include *Counter-Institutions: Jacques Derrida and the Question of the University* (2006), *Experimenting: Essays with Samuel Weber* (co-edited with Gary Hall, 2007), *Encountering Derrida: Legacies and Futures of Deconstruction* (co-edited with Allison Weiner, 2007), *Derrida: Writing Events* (2008) and *The Derrida Dictionary* (2010).

Stephen Morton is a senior lecturer in English at the University of Southampton. His publications include *Gayatri Spivak: Ethics, Subjectivity and the Critique of Postcolonial Reason* (2007), *Salman Rushdie: Fictions of Postcolonial Modernity* (2008), *Terror and the Postcolonial* (co-edited with Elleke Boehmer, 2009), and articles in *Textual Practice*, *Interventions*, and *New Formations*.

John Mowitt is a professor in the department of Cultural Studies and Comparative Literature at the University of Minnesota. He is the author of numerous texts on the topics of culture, theory, and politics, including *Re-Takes: Postcoloniality and Foreign Film Languages* (2005) and the co-edited volume, *The Dreams of Interpretation: A Century Down the Royal Road* (with Catherine Liu, Thomas Pepper, & Jakki Spicer,

2007). In 2009 he collaborated with the composer Jarrod Fowler to transpose his book *Percussion: Drumming, Beating, Striking* (2002) from a printed to a sonic text. His current project, *Radio: Essays in Bad Reception*, is forthcoming. He is also a senior co-editor of the journal *Cultural Critique*.

Aris Mousoutzanis is a sessional lecturer at the Faculty of Arts and Social Sciences, Kingston University. He has researched and published on areas such as critical and cultural theory (especially psychoanalysis and trauma theory), technoculture and cyberculture, media and globalization, popular culture, science fiction, and the gothic.

Ankhi Mukherjee is a CUF lecturer in the Faculty of English Language and Literature at the University of Oxford and a fellow of Wadham College. Her specialisms include Victorian and modern literature, critical and cultural theory, particularly psychoanalysis, and postcolonial studies. She is the author of *Aesthetic Hysteria* (2007), co-editor (with Laura Marcus) of *A Companion to Literary Criticism and Psychoanalysis* (2011), and has several articles in refereed journals such as *PMLA*, *MLQ*, and *Textual Practice*. Her latest book project, *What is a Classic?* (2011), examines canon wars and other contestations of literary value in twentieth- and twenty-first-century English literature and literary criticism.

Rebecca Munford is a lecturer in English literature at Cardiff University. She is the co-editor (with Stacy Gillis and Gilliann Howie) of *Third Wave Feminism: A Critical Exploration* (2007), and special issues of *Literature Interpretation Theory* (2009) and *Women: A Cultural Review* (2009). Her forthcoming work includes the book *Decadent Daughters and Monstrous Mothers: Angela Carter and the European Gothic*.

Alex Murray is a lecturer in twentieth-century literature at the University of

Exeter. He is the author of *Recalling London* (2007) and *Giorgio Agamben* (2010), and he is one of the founding editors of *Parrhesia: A Journal of Critical Philosophy*.

Mary Orr is a professor of French at the University of Southampton. Her monograph, *Flaubert's Tentation: Remapping Nineteenth-Century French Histories of Religion and Science* (2008), reflects her current research interests in the "intertextuality" of scientific writing of the period, whether by women in science prior to Marie Curie, or by writers of fiction and poetry.

Lisa Otty is a postdoctoral research fellow at the University of Dundee, working on an AHRC-funded project entitled "Poetry Beyond Text." She has published articles on aesthetics and the relationship between literature and visual art in journals such as *Litteraria Pragensia* and *Interdisciplinary Humanities*.

Robert Dale Parker is James M. Benson Professor in English at the University of Illinois. He has written *How to Interpret Literature: Critical Theory for Literary and Cultural Studies* (2008) as well as books on American literature and American Indian literature.

Jason D. Price is a teaching associate and a candidate for a PhD in literature at Arizona State University. He received his MA from Seton Hall University after receiving a BA from the College of New Jersey.

Abigail Rine is a PhD candidate and ORSAS scholar at the University of St Andrews, as well as a visiting assistant professor of English at George Fox University. A recent participant in the doctoral seminar of Luce Irigaray, her work on women's writing and feminist theory appears in Forum for Modern Language Studies, as well as the forthcoming book collections *Sex, Gender and Time in Fiction and Culture* and *Mortified: Representing Women's Shame*.

John Paul Riquelme is a professor of English at Boston University. His work on literary theory, the gothic tradition, and literature of the long twentieth century includes guest edited issues of *New Literary History* and *Modern Fiction Studies*, editions of *Dracula*, *Tess of the d'Urbervilles*, and *A Portrait of the Artist as a Young Man*, and books and essays on Wilde, Yeats, Joyce, Eliot, Beckett, Iser, and postcolonial theory. He is currently writing a study of Wilde and early modernism.

Adam Roberts is a professor of nineteenth-century literature at Royal Holloway, University of London. He has published a number of studies of Romantic and Victorian topics, as well as a *History of Science Fiction* (2005), an introductory *Fredric Jameson* (2000) and more than a dozen science-fictional, postmodern-ish novels.

Mark Robson is an associate professor of English at the University of Nottingham, where he founded and directs the Analysis of Democratic Cultures Research Group. He is the author of *Stephen Greenblatt* (2008) and *The Sense of Early Modern Writing* (2006), co-author (with Peter Stockwell) of *Language in Theory* (2005), editor of *Jacques Rancière: Aesthetics, Politics, Philosophy* (2005) and co-editor (with Joanne Morra and Marquard Smith) of *The Limits of Death: Between Philosophy and Psychoanalysis* (2000).

Nemonie Craven Roderick holds a Westfield Trust Interdisciplinary Studentship at Queen Mary, University of London, where she is completing a PhD thesis on the work of Emmanuel Levinas. Her essay "Subject to memory? Thinking after *Caché*" is published in David Sorfa and Ben McCann (eds.), *The Cinema of Michael Haneke* (2010). With Shahidha Bari, she is creator and co-founder of *How to Live* (www. htlblog.com) and co-author of the *How to Live* guidebook to modern life.

Deirdre Russell is a film studies lecturer at the University of Glamorgan. She received her PhD in French studies from the University of Manchester. Her thesis, "Narrative identities in contemporary French autobiographical literature and film," explores the social dimensions of European autobiographical identity. She has published book chapters on autobiographical film.

Michael Ryan teaches in the School of Communications at Temple University. His most recent essay, "Are liberals mutants? Human history as evolutionary history," appeared in *Politics and Culture* (2010). He has written several scholarly monographs, including *Marxism and Deconstruction* (1982) and *Politics and Culture* (1989), and edited several university textbooks, including *Literary Theory: An Anthology* (co-edited with Julie Rivkin; 2nd edn. 2004), *Literary Theory: A Practical Introduction* (2nd edn. 2007), *Cultural Studies: An Anthology* (2008), and *Cultural Studies: A Practical Introduction* (2010).

Laura Salisbury is RCUK Research Fellow in Science, Technology and Culture and a lecturer at Birkbeck, University of London. She has published on various topics, including Samuel Beckett and neuroscientific conceptions of language; Beckett, poststructuralist ethics and comedy; and the philosophy of Michel Serres and science fiction. With Andrew Shail, she is the editor of *Neurology and Modernity* (2010). Her major research project is on the relationships between aphasiology, modernism, and modernity.

Danielle Sands is completing a PhD on Derrida at Royal Holloway, University of London. Her publications include an article in *Textual Practice* entitled "Thinking through *Différance*: Derrida, Žižek and religious engagement."

Michael Snyder is a professor of English and humanities at Oklahoma City Community College and has taught at the University of Oklahoma, where he received his PhD. His work focuses on twentieth-century American and Native American literature and culture and his dissertation is entitled "Mixedblood metaphors: Allegories of Native America in the fiction of James Purdy." His essays on Gerald Vizenor appear in book collections for Broadview Press and the University of New Mexico Press, and other pieces have appeared in *Studies in American Indian Literatures*, *American Indian Culture and Research Journal*, and *Critique: Studies in Contemporary Fiction*.

Robin Stoate is a doctoral candidate in English literature at Newcastle University. His research focuses on technocultures and wider issues relating to theorizing the subject in cultural and critical theory, along with literature, film, and on the internet. He has published on such topics as fictional representations of nanotechnology, and relationships of care between human beings and machines. He is the co-author (with Andrew Shail) of the BFI classics book *Back to the Future* (2010).

Khachig Tölölyan is a professor of comparative literature and cultural theory at the College of Letters at Wesleyan University (Middletown, Connecticut). He is the founding editor of *Diaspora: A Journal of Transnational Studies*, and has published on a wide range of topics, ranging from narratology and the American novel to diasporic nationalism and terrorism.

Ben Trott is a doctoral candidate at the Free University of Berlin.

Anastasia Valassopoulos teaches postcolonial fiction and film in the School of Arts, Histories and Culture at the University of Manchester. She has published articles in *Research in African Literatures*, *Popular Music and Society*, and *Critical Survey*, and has contributed to numerous collections on postcolonial literature and cinema. She has published *Contemporary Arab Women Writers: Cultural Production in Context* (2007).

Paul Wake is a senior lecturer in English literature at Manchester Metropolitan University. He is the author of *Conrad's Marlow* (2007), editor (with Simon Malpas) of *The Routledge Companion to Critical Theory* (2006), and has published articles on narrative theory, postmodernism, and children's literature.

Melanie Waters is a lecturer in English at Northumbria University and has published work on feminist theory, American poetry, and popular culture.

Allison Weiner is a visiting assistant professor in the Department of Comparative Literature at Cornell University. She received a PhD in comparative literature from Yale University in 2008. She specializes in literary theory, focusing particularly on poststructural theory and contemporary continental philosophy in her scholarship and teaching. She is the co-editor (with Simon Morgan Wortham) of *Encountering Derrida: Legacies and Futures of Deconstruction* (2007). Her current work explores intersections of ethics, the body, and disability.

Anne Whitehead is a senior lecturer in the School of English at Newcastle University. She has published *Trauma Fiction* (2004) and *Memory* (2008). She has also co-edited (with J. J. Long) *W. G. Sebald: A Critical Companion* (2004) and (with Michael Rossington) *Theories of Memory: A Reader* (2007).

Ross Wilson is a lecturer in the School of Literature and Creative Writing at the University of East Anglia. He works on literary theory and philosophical aesthetics, and romantic and Victorian poetry. He is the author of *Subjective Universality in Kant's Aesthetics* (2007), *Theodor Adorno* (2007), and is editor of *The Meaning of "Life" in Romantic Poetry and Poetics* (2009). The book on which he is currently working is envisaged as an extended reading of Percy Shelley's statement that "we live on, and in living we lose the apprehension of life."

Min Wild teaches at the University of Plymouth. She specializes in the eighteenth century and her *Christopher Smart and Satire* (2008) engages with the periodical press and the Enlightenment in Britain. She has also published on Wyndham Lewis and on the personification of words, texts, and literary styles from the Bible to the present day.

Aesthetic Theory

LISA OTTY

Aesthetic theory examines the relationship between perceptual, sensory experience and value judgments and raises questions about taste, art, value, and truth. While aesthetic theory is often held to be synonymous with the philosophy of art, its importance extends far beyond this realm. Indeed, as reflection on a fundamental part of human experience, aesthetic theory has consequences for many different discourses, impacting on notions of subjectivity, politics, and ethics. Having fallen out of fashion in the mid-twentieth century, the field has been brought back to the fore recently and is currently recognized as an area of critical importance in contemporary philosophical inquiry.

To grasp what is at stake in late twentieth-century aesthetic theory, it is important to understand the field as developing out of and reacting against "high" modernist aesthetics. In the American context, the influence of modernist aesthetics reached its zenith in the 1960s but extended well into the 1970s. Formalist critics such as Clement Greenberg (1966[1961]) argued that art is "disinterested" or autonomous from social systems such as history, politics, and economics. This autonomy is grasped positively as freedom from the utilitarian concerns and pragmatic considerations of everyday life. Art is situated as the haven of values which transcend individual concerns and the particular, material conditions of production and reception. In this sense, modernism holds aesthetic values to be superior to those inscribed by "interested" judgments which are made according to the subjective needs and desires of the moment. If art concerns itself with such "interests" it is in danger of being reduced to propaganda, or merely reinforcing the values of the dominant social group. The distance between art and life, between aesthetic values and non-aesthetic values, must therefore be constantly reinscribed in order to preserve a space for values uncontaminated by political or economic concerns. "High" modernism thus appears to depend upon the idea of aesthetic values as universal and timeless rather than historical and contingent. In such a framework, taste is held to be the critic's ability to discern these universal values in the artwork rather than a purely subjective individual judgment.

It has been against the apparent timelessness and universality of aesthetic value and against the authority of critical taste that much "postmodernist" aesthetic theory has been directed. Critics have attacked the narrative of modernism, arguing that aesthetic values, like all other values, are historical and socially constructed (Krauss 1972).

In other words, what has been made to appear as universal is in fact nothing more than the culturally privileged position (Western, bourgeois, white, and masculine) and the idea of good taste is complicit with economic and cultural domination, a means of validating a particular set of norms and of suppressing different kinds of experiences and tastes. One critical project, therefore, has been to give voice to other types of aesthetic theory, articulating, for example, feminist aesthetics (Hein & Korsmeyer 1990) and comparative aesthetic theories, which consider the relation between a specific experience, place, and culture (Van Damme 1996). Another influential argument is the "institutional theory" of art, which argues that aesthetic value does not depend on the quality of the object but rather on the social context (the "art world") in which we experience the work (Danto 1964; Dickie 1974). Different contexts encourage different kinds of aesthetic attitude toward the work and, therefore, value can be understood as something that is attributed by the specific institution (i.e., the gallery) rather than something inherent in the work. Taken to its logical conclusion, the institutional argument suggests that art and aesthetic experience are not autonomous of wider social systems at all but are in fact a form of illusion generated by a specific set of cultural conditions. Some critics have thus asserted that the very idea of aesthetic value is a kind of mystification that masks the real social conditions of the production and consumption of art (Bourdieu 1984[1979]). Such sociological work is important in that it often reveals the assumptions and biases inherent in the aesthetic theories that it rejects.

The sociological approach to art is not without its problems, however, for to deny the validity of aesthetic judgments and to claim that art is no different from any other object is to reduce art to a nexus of social, political, and economic values. It is thus to

deny art and aesthetics as a site of potential freedom and truth. This is a central concern in the work of German Frankfurt School theorist Theodor Adorno, whose *Aesthetic Theory* (2004[1970]) continues to be influential today. For Adorno, the autonomy of art is not a hard-won freedom but rather an exclusion from society, a consequence and so expression of the domination of human experience by the forces of rationalization. History, as Adorno sees it, is a progressive domination of the natural world by technology, science, and capital. Art, he argues, is an "after image" of a lost human capacity for extracting and positing meaning and truth intuitively (through aesthetic experience) rather than logically or conceptually. It is a reminder that the forces of techno-scientific rationalization obscure and repress other types of knowledge and experience and, by reducing thought to logic and value to a system of exchange, operate to suppress difference. Art is important because it is incommensurable with empirical reality and, as a result, it constitutes a space in which critical reflection on society can be articulated and explored. However, while Adorno argues that art is necessarily autonomous, this is not to say that the aesthetic is understood as a realm beyond history nor is aesthetic value considered to be higher than other values. Indeed it is against universalizing aesthetic theories that Adorno positions his Marxist theory, arguing that art, although it appears as something cast out and so different, is essentially sociohistorical and inseparable from the conditions of its production and reception.

Adorno's aesthetic theory is famously pessimistic about the future of art and the potential of aesthetics to maintain an alternative to dominant forms of knowledge and experience. If art provides the last bastion of resistance against techno-scientific capitalism, a field in which the truth potential of aesthetic experience hibernates, it is also an increasingly encroached-upon space and therefore one that is continually under threat of dissolution. Moreover, although it is its distance from society that gives art its power, the exclusion of art means that it is unable to effect any real social change. Thus, as many Marxist critics have argued, while art can be understood as voicing critique of society, that critique is already silenced by the separation of art from other social systems. The autonomy of art is not only its strength but also its weakness.

Such pessimism provoked a sequence of debates about the death or end of art in the 1970s and '80s. For some, late twentieth-century art showed that art and aesthetics were entirely infiltrated by politics and economics (Bürger 1984[1974]). The work of artists like Andy Warhol and Jeff Koons seemed to affirm the logic of late capitalism and to celebrate the artwork as a commodity while the slogans of political artists such as The Guerrilla Girls highlighted the prejudices inherent in aesthetic judgments and art institutions. In this light, it appeared as though the forces of rationalization had encroached so far into the sphere of aesthetics that they had rendered autonomy all but impossible and thus annihilated the critical potential of art. Art's subsumption into the rationality of late capitalism had rendered it nothing more than a commodity, one product among others. If art and aesthetic value were collapsed into life and social values, moreover, not only did it seem to signal the end of a genuinely critical art but also, if it is the case that to have a theory one must have a discrete field, the end of aesthetic theory.

Since the mid-1990s Anglo-American criticism has developed a renewed interest in aesthetics, often referred to as new aestheticism. A key text in this regard is American philosopher Jay Bernstein's *The Fate of Art* (1992) which distinguishes between aesthetics and postaesthetic philosophy:

the former understands art as separated from other spheres of experience, cut off from truth and so effectively silenced, while the latter is the thinking that responds to this silencing at the center of aesthetics, namely the contradiction of art's autonomy. If art is a critique of (but also product of and by no means opposite to) the rationalized, conceptual "scientific" cognition that modernity privileges, then post-aesthetic theory attempts to maximize and highlight this critical potential. It accepts that art relies on some degree of autonomy (thus postaesthetic philosophy is not institutional critique) but denies that it is severed from truth, from politics, from morality. Instead of bemoaning or celebrating aesthetic alienation, such work attempts to understand art in nonaesthetic terms, and thereby to avoid the distinction between art and truth. In other words, post-aesthetic philosophy attempts to preserve the importance of aesthetics by breaking down the frameworks in which aesthetic theory has conventionally been thought. This process is evident not only in Adorno's work, as Bernstein demonstrates, but also in the "paraesthetic" theories of French poststructuralists like Jacques Derrida and Jean-François Lyotard, who allow aesthetics to pervade their writing as well as their thought (Carroll 1987).

Those writing under the banner of new aestheticism must also be understood as postaesthetic theorists for they do not seek a return to the framework of "high" modernist aesthetics and reject the universalizing tendencies associated with earlier aesthetic theories (Eagleton 1990). However, they also reject the sociological approach of schools such as new historicism and institutional theory. Instead new aestheticism proposes an understanding of aesthetics that grasps the specificity and particularity of the work, reading art and literature as fully implicated in society and history yet at the same time as evading or exceeding reduction to mere commodities. Aesthetic value is not the only criteria by which works are judged, but that does not mean that there is no such thing as aesthetic value. For new aestheticism, the importance of aesthetics lies in its intersections with politics and ethics: it is the fact that art and aesthetic experience are different from other types of knowledge and experience that makes them valuable, for they provide a space for an alternative form of truth to that provided by logic or science (Beech & Roberts 2002; Joughin & Malpas 2003). Staking out the potential of this alternative is the task of any future aesthetic theory.

SEE ALSO: Adorno, Theodor; Derrida, Jacques; Lyotard, Jean-François; New Aestheticism

REFERENCES AND SUGGESTED READINGS

Adorno, T. W. (2004). *Aesthetic Theory* (ed. G. Adorno & R. Tiedemann; trans. R. Hullot-Kentor). London: Continuum. (Original work published 1970.)

Beech, D., & Roberts, J. (2002). *The Philistine Controversy*. London: Verso.

Bernstein, J. M. (1992). *The Fate of Art: Aesthetic Alienation from Kant to Derrida and Adorno*. Cambridge: Polity.

Bourdieu, P. (1984). *Distinction: A Social Critique of the Judgment of Taste*. London: Routledge and Kegan Paul. (Original work published 1979.)

Bürger, P. (1984). *Theory of the Avant-Garde*. Minneapolis: University of Minnesota Press. (Original work published 1974.)

Carroll, D. (1987). *Paraesthetics: Foucault, Lyotard, Derrida*. New York: Methuen.

Danto, A. (1964). The artworld. *Journal of Philosophy*, 61 (19), 571–584.

Dickie, G. (1974). *Art and the Aesthetic: An Institutional Analysis*. Ithaca: Cornell University Press.

Eagleton, T. (1990). *The Ideology of the Aesthetic*. Oxford: Blackwell.

Greenberg, C. (1966). Modernist painting. In G. Battcock (ed.), *The New Art: A Critical Anthology*. New York: E. P. Dutton. (Original work published 1961.)

Hein, H., & Korsmeyer, C. (eds.) (1990). *Aesthetics in a Feminist Perspective*. Bloomington: Indiana University Press.

Joughin, J., & Malpas, S. (2003). *The New Aestheticism*. Manchester: Manchester University Press.

Krauss, R. E. (1972). A view of modernism. *Artforum* (Sept), 48–51.

Van Damme, W. (1996). *Beauty in Context: Towards an Anthropological Approach to Aesthetics*. Leiden: Brill.

African American Literary Theory

JASON PRICE

African American literary theory since 1966 has responded to both the Black Arts Movement of the 1960s and '70s and the contemporaneous influx of Western literary theory in the academy. Theoretical arguments in this field address questions of the critic's audience and responsibilities, the use of European theory in reading black texts, and representations of gender, race, and sexuality in African American literature. The theoretical responses to these issues reveal a multiplicity of positions from critics as varied as Henry Louis Gates, Jr., Barbara Smith, and Charles I. Nero and a wide range of theoretical approaches too, including structuralism, poststructuralism, and European feminism.

The Black Arts Movement, led by figures like poet and critic Amiri Baraka and Larry Neal, was a corollary to the Black Power Movement. The movement centered on an assumption of an essential "blackness," or an understanding of an authentic black experience. Consequently, texts written by African Americans during this period were judged by the degree to which they were true to the black experience of everyday life. For example, leaders of the movement championed realistic novels like Richard Wright's *Native Son*, while Ralph Ellison's *Invisible Man* was less highly regarded. While critics like Gates and Houston A. Baker, Jr. voiced their opinion that the Black Arts Movement was limited in its ideological approach to African American literature, several critics acknowledge that the it was successful in securing African American studies and literature programs in the academy.

In his critique of the Black Arts Movement, Gates traces the nonliterary treatment of black texts back to some of the earliest works in the African American literary tradition. In *Figures in Black* (1987) for example, discussing the poems of Phillis Wheatley and the autobiographies of Frederick Douglass, Gates reveals how these works weren't read for their literary merit. Rather, these early African American texts were read by white critics, both slaveholders and abolitionists, as proof of black literacy and therefore of the possibility of black culture and humanity. Gates suggests that such a beginning for the criticism of African American art has had a profound effect on the trajectory of how we read black texts. His critique of the Black Arts Movement, then, is its failure to consider the literary complexity of black texts. Gates's critique is informed by formalist, structuralist, and poststructuralist theories. By using these theories, Gates suggests, we can better appreciate the rich layers of black texts by performing close readings, examining form and content, viewing "blackness" as a trope (rather than as a marker of authenticity), and looking for intertextuality, or the way these texts revise, relate, and respond to previous texts and tropes.

In contrast to Gates's adopting of several European theories, early founding black feminist theorists like Barbara Smith and

Barbara Christian condemn the practice of black critics who incorporate European theories in readings of black texts. In "Toward a black feminist criticism" (1977) Smith calls for a black feminist way of reading, explaining that white feminists have largely disregarded the question of racial politics and that black male critics often ignore sexual politics. In defining this way of reading, Smith argues that the reader should consider the intentions of the writer, focus on representations of black and female identity, and assume that black women have a literary tradition. In addition to Smith's stance against using European male theory to read black women's art, her consideration of the writer's intent is also at odds with the formalist and poststructural theories that Gates draws on, where writer's intent is of no concern. Lastly, Smith calls for an analysis of sexuality in African American texts that would also lead to a black lesbian way of reading, pointing out that heterosexuality is often privileged in black texts.

Like Smith's theory of reading, Alice Walker's "In search of our mothers' gardens" (1983[1974]), a precursor to Smith's essay, addresses the shortcomings of white feminist theory for black feminists. Walker takes issue with Virginia Woolf's feminist essays, arguing that black women under slavery produced art even though they were remarkably more oppressed than white women. Under the institution of slavery and racial oppression, the question of "a room of one's own" (the title of one of Woolf's feminist essays) was not a plausible consideration for African American women artists, as Walker reveals. Walker argues that, as black women were denied the opportunities of the fine arts, they expressed themselves in other media like their gardens, as her essay's title suggests. Walker's critique of the blindness of white feminist criticism was essential in founding a black feminist criticism.

Drawing on Smith's essay and discussing Walker's texts, Barbara Christian critiques the use of theory in reading black texts, arguing instead that the goal of criticism should be to recover texts that remain silenced or receive little treatment in critical circles. Like Smith, Christian sees European theory dominating the current critical discourse. She also argues that black writers have always theorized in their art like the theories implicit in Toni Morrison's novels, for example. In addition, she suggests that the language of European theory confuses the position of black feminist critics. Christian further warns against the power of European theory, emphasizing that critics who use these theories largely ignore texts by African American writers. She also suggests that readings informed by theory are proscriptive, offering the Black Arts Movement as an example of theory simplifying the world and limiting the possibilities for interpretations of texts. In her reading of the Black Arts Movement, Christian suggests that the leaders of the movement tried to replace a white center of power with a black center, a problematic and perhaps equally oppressive move that Morrison also critiques in *Playing in the Dark*.

While Christian does not specifically name those critics who practice European theory, it is generally assumed that she targets Gates and Baker. Michael Awkward, a poststructuralist and self-identified black male feminist critic, disagrees with Christian's dismissal of theory. Awkward argues that Christian's portrayal of black critics as natives colonized by white poststructural theory is too simplistic and fails to acknowledge the possibility that black critics choose to use it. In addition, Awkward points out that Barbara Smith's call for a black feminist criticism is theoretical, although Smith doesn't draw on contemporary theory. Awkward also takes issue with Christian for assuming that black

males and whites can't do the kind of work she describes. Dismissing theory, Awkward contends, would also be to dismiss the important work of Gates, Baker, Mary Helen Washington, and Hortense Spillers (who uses Lacanian psychoanalysis) – theoretically informed critics who, Awkward suggests, have greatly enriched our knowledge of African American texts and their production.

Continuing the discussion concerning the appropriation of European theory in the reading of black texts, Joyce A. Joyce also argues against theory. Joyce offers a position similar to Smith, Christian, and theorists of the Black Arts Movement as she sees a connection between black lives or black realities and black literature. Focusing more on the question of the critic's responsibility and audience than on previous theorists, Joyce argues that theoretical critics like Gates no longer write for the black community, but for a small audience. She also posits that poststructural theory isn't useful in discussing black American literary works as the poststructural challenge to the idea of a stable identity, one that is finite and knowable, and the arbitrary relation between sign and signifier seems to ignore black American history. In contrast to Gates who suggests that he is attempting to defamiliarize black texts to help him appreciate their literary value, Joyce argues that black creative art is an "act of love" which brings people together, preventing "estrangement" rather than promoting elitism. Joyce's position is ultimately informed by class and a recognition of the critic's responsibility to black people.

Both Gates and Houston Baker's responses to Joyce challenge her reading of literature and point out what they see as several flaws in her essay. While early on Baker was more aligned with the Black Arts Movement, his and Gates's theoretical stances have become increasingly similar in their use of poststructural theory. In his response to Joyce, Baker points out that poststructuralist theory performs a powerful critique of Western philosophy, especially its forms of privileging, which has been a major source of oppression for black culture and black people. Gates responds similarly, however, suggesting that the richness of black texts demands that readers work harder to do justice to the writer. Responding to Joyce's critique of the poststructuralist idea of language as play, Gates argues for the usefulness of this concept as he contends that black people have been reading white language as systems of play since 1619. Gates also describes how black literature inhabits spaces of difference, and suggests that it is the critic's responsibility to identify formal difference in black texts as revision through close reading. In addition, Gates argues that black critics must form their own language of criticism, a practice he attempts later in *The Signifying Monkey* (1988). In response, Joyce later points out where Gates and Baker misread her essay and she accuses them of being dismissive and abusive in their treatment of her writing.

Deborah McDowell, a black feminist critic, also weighs in on the theoretical debate between Gates, Baker, Joyce, and Awkward. In reviewing their arguments McDowell comments on the nature of the relationship between theory and practice, challenging their division and arguing that theory is too often privileged in that ostensible binary. She also points out that often in the arguments over theory the concept of theory is synonymous with poststructuralist theory. Thus, critics like Gates and Baker accuse black feminists of being conservative and resistant to theory, whereas McDowell disagrees. McDowell argues for the importance of considering recent historical developments in this debate, especially the recent second renaissance of black women writers being read.

Such a consideration is important for McDowell because it highlights how poststructural assumptions – the death of the author, and the challenging of history, tradition, and authority – were contesting many of the assumptions of black feminist criticism that were developing in response to this new trend of a prevalent reading of black women's texts. For example, black feminist critics called for recovering and describing a literary tradition in the face of the poststructuralist challenge of the very idea of tradition. McDowell explains how, despite the differences, black feminists and poststructuralists have key concerns in common. The focus on analyzing the relationship between the margins and the center in terms of hierarchies is pivotal to both theoretical schools. While both groups have this common focus, they are often viewed as antithetical, and McDowell posits that this view stems largely from the general perception of black feminist criticism as lower class in terms of a theoretical hierarchy in the academy.

Amid critiques of their adoption of European poststructuralist theory, both Gates and Baker attempted theoretical projects with a more African American theoretical basis. Baker's theorization of the blues as a matrix in *Blues, Ideology, and Afro-American Literature* (1984) seeks to develop an approach to most African American and American literature based in the vernacular, or everyday language, and music of black people. Drawing on the poststructuralist and Derridean idea of a decentered subject, Baker views the blues singer as being always at the crossroads, portraying the way in which experience is always multiple and varied. Thus, for Baker the blues singer and his experience serve as codifiers that cannot be pinned down to any final significance or meaning. He also points out that the blues are always on the move to further support this inability to contain them in any one account. He suggests that a single interpretation can seem to bring order to experience but single readings are always disturbed by "remainders."

Henry Louis Gates's project in *The Signifying Monkey* assigns a similar importance to vernacular in identifying a particularly African American tradition of literary theory, as he draws on figures from Yoruban myth to rename current theoretical concepts in the vernacular of African Americans. In this book, Gates attempts to read black texts in terms of their own tradition rather than merely borrowing European theories. Thus, the goal in this book is markedly different from the earlier *Figures in Black*, in which he admittedly reads black texts and their criticism in light of European theories. In a similar way to McDowell, Gates attempts to debunk the idea that theory is only a Western exercise. To accomplish this task, he selects two trickster figures, Esu-Elegbara and the signifying monkey (which he sees as particularly Afro-American), for the basis of his project of identifying a theory of reading existent in the black tradition. Gates posits that Esu is a figure for the nature and function of interpretation, while the signifying monkey serves as a figure of figures.

Discussing the signifying monkey, Gates argues that the monkey's language of signifyin' indicates intertextuality or black formal revision and repetition, indicating a black difference. For example, Gates reads the repetition of situations from William Wells Brown's *Clotel* in Frances E. W. Harper's *Iola Leroy* as an example of this repetition and revision. Gates defines the task of the African American literary theorist as the responsibility to name the tradition and its antecedents (both black and white), and then to rename and thus revise and signify upon these antecedents. In *The Signifying Monkey*, Gates contends that he uses European theories only as analogies

and points out the differences between them and the theories of the black vernacular. Gates proceeds to define different types of textual relations and explains the two ways in which texts can signify: motivated or unmotivated signifyin'. Motivated signifyin' is intertextuality that attempts to be corrective or to offer a negative critique of a previous text. In contrast, unmotivated signifyin' pays homage to a previous text or texts.

The theoretical conversation involving Gates, Baker, Joyce, and others continued to evolve as in "The crisis in black American literary criticism and the postmodern cures of Houston A. Baker, Jr., and Henry Louis Gates, Jr." (1994) Sandra Adell addresses several problematic theoretical maneuvers in Baker's *Blues, Ideology, and Afro-American Literature* and Gates's *The Signifying Monkey*. Adell views Baker's and Gates's attempts to identify an authentic African American tradition through blues and signifyin' as contradictory because the methods they employ render the concept of authenticity dubious. In contrast to previous critiques of the work of Gates and Baker, Adell argues that she finds no fault with their use of poststructuralist and deconstruction theories in their writings, as for Adell the question of theory as it relates to African American literature is one that demands investigation, and using European theories seems to be for her a necessary evil of being a literary critic.

In treating Baker's text, Adell suggests that his attempt to argue for a non-Eurocentric approach to African American literature is somewhat contradictory seeing how his writing is greatly informed by European theorists. She also comments that the connections he makes between various theoretical concepts and paradigms is often uncritical and misguided. Similarly, she points out contradictions in Gates's text, like the manner in which he posits black literature to have a black signifying difference, only to assert later that all texts signify. Another contradiction that she points to is Gates's idea that to signify is to revise in a formal way but signifyin' is also playful and ambiguous. While critiquing the theoretical underpinnings beneath several of Gates's and Baker's claims, Adell also responds to previous critiques of their work, suggesting that they are as interested in the political and social implications of African American literature as they are in increasing the appreciation of its literary richness. Adell's essay concludes that for all their attempts to be non-Eurocentric, Baker and Gates, ultimately, are perhaps more so in the final analysis.

bell hooks and Cornel West have also communicated their positions on the relevance of postmodernism for African American literary and cultural theory. While hooks advocates the value of postmodernism for black cultural theory, she does so with an acknowledgment that postmodernism has often been exclusionary and the theoretical territory of white males. hooks critiques current postmodern theoretical endeavors, suggesting that postmodernism can be more than merely theoretically attractive or fashionable if it engages its politics of difference with the politics of racism. Of particular relevance for hooks is the postmodern challenge of essentialism as it relates to the critique of an essential or authentic "blackness." Her critique is akin to Gates's in this regard in that she acknowledges that the black experience is multiple and, along with the critique of a fixed identity, postmodernism offers new constructions of self and possibilities of agency. Like Joyce with her concern about elitism, hooks advocates a strong relationship with the black community and encourages black critics to engage in dialogue both within academic arenas and with the poor and undereducated classes. Cornel West, on the other hand, refutes the relevance of postmodernism, especially as it is expressed in the academy and literary arts, as he sees its current practice as marginalized from black life. This lack of a connection with the black community, in West's view, renders postmodernism's value for black resistance negligible. While hooks asserts that West's view of black life seems essentialist, he argues that black music is ultimately the best arena for black postmodern resistance in popular culture. West deems literary critics to be too easily tempted by material interests to make postmodernism relevant for black life, suggesting that they will instead merely appropriate Eurocentric theory.

Ann duCille also touches on the issue of poststructuralism by making use of it in her critique of the state of relations between black women and men. Citing critiques of black women authors like Morrison, Gayl Jones, and Alice Walker by black male critics, she reveals how these novels are often accused of male bashing and putting the question of gender before that of race by male critics. DuCille objects to the authority of black male critics like Addison Gayle and Ishmael Reed who suggest that the representations of male–female relationships in the novels of black women are inaccurate and misleading. Using poststructuralist theory, duCille challenges their assumptions of an essential black experience, an absolute historical truth, and that art must tell the truth. She posits that these critiques are phallocentric and just one truth in a plurality of truths. Therefore, the gynocentric truth she sees these authors portraying is also another, equally valid truth. DuCille seeks to challenge the trend where male texts are often regarded as true history and master narratives while women's texts are judged only in relation to them. In addition, she acknowledges that male critics can be gynocentric and that female critics can be phallocentric in their readings as well.

If for black feminist critics their position of alterity is doubled because they are unprivileged in Western metaphysics in terms of both gender and race, the position black homosexuals occupy is also, in some ways, doubly marginal. Black queer theorists, like Charles I. Nero and Marlon B. Ross, articulate the oppression experienced by gay black males and explore black homosexual ways of reading. Nero reveals the prevalent assumption in the African American community and in literature that homosexuality is a European phenomenon forced on Africans, and challenges this idea with close readings of some early African American texts. Describing the position of black homosexual men, Nero explains how gay culture is thought to be comprised of white males and how early attempts to improve the race and the Black Power movements often excluded gays or positioned homosexuality as antithetical to their movements.

Ross describes the media's representation of the black community's relationship with white gays, suggesting that the media distorts it and pits the one against the other. Ross also points out that black homosexuality was tolerated in black communities because of notions of racial solidarity; white homosexuals didn't receive the same treatment in the black community. Describing the difference in "coming out" for gay men in terms of race, Ross explains that white gay men left their communities to move to urban areas, whereas gay black men remained in their communities. He concludes that Eurocentric notions of gay culture existing autonomously fail to translate to the gay experience in black culture. Thus, while the idea of an autonomous gay culture is liberating for white gay males, for black homosexuals, as Ross argues, the concept caused distancing and intolerance from their communities.

More recent African American theory continues to expand, challenge, and revise these earlier theories. In addition, the move to cultural studies, a practice of reading cultural phenomena as texts, toward the end of the 1990s by critics like Wahneema Lubiano, Hazel Carby, and Karla Holloway continues to influence the course of African American literary theory. Lubiano's warning that we must prevent oversimplification of Afro-American cultural production during the increased world interest in African American literature is significant for cultural and literary theorists alike. More contemporary works continue theorizing cultural studies like bell hooks's *Homegrown* (2006), while others pick up the study of vernacular like Alfonso W. Hawkins's *The Jazz Trope* (2008). Black feminists continue to theorize about black literature like Cheryl Wall in *Worrying the Line* (2005) and black queer theorists carry on investigations of sexuality as does Marlon Ross in *Manning the Race* (2004).

SEE ALSO: Derrida, Jacques; Gates, Henry Louis; hooks, bell; Poststructuralism; Smith, Barbara H.

REFERENCES AND SUGGESTED READINGS

Adell, S. (1994). The crisis in black American literary criticism and the postmodern cures of Houston A. Baker, Jr., and Henry Louis Gates, Jr. In *Double-Consciousness/Double Bind: Theoretical Issues in Twentieth-Century Black Literature*. Urbana: University of Illinois Press.

Awkward, M. (1995). *Negotiating Difference: Race, Gender, and the Politics of Positionality*. Chicago: Chicago University Press.

Baker, H. A., Jr. (1984). *Blues, Ideology, and Afro-American Literature: A Vernacular Theory*. Chicago: Chicago University Press.

Baker, H. A., Jr., & Redmond, P. (1989). *Afro-American Literary Study in the 1990s*. Chicago: Chicago University Press.

Christian, B. (2007). *New Black Feminist Criticism, 1985–2000*. Urbana: University of Illinois Press.

Gates, H. L., Jr. (1987). *Figures in Black: Words, Signs, and the "Racial" Self.* New York: Oxford University Press.

Gates, H. L., Jr., (1988). *The Signifying Monkey: A Theory of Afro-American Literary Criticism.* New York: Oxford University Press.

Hawkins, A. W. (2008). *The Jazz Trope: A Theory of African American Literature and Vernacular Culture.* Lanham, MD: Scarecrow.

Holloway, K. (2002). *Passed On: African American Mourning Stories: A Memorial.* Durham, NC: Duke University Press.

Hooks, B. (2006). *Homegrown: Engaged Cultural Criticism.* Cambridge, MA: South End.

Mitchell, A. (ed.) (1994). *Within the Circle: An Anthology.* Durham, NC: Duke University Press.

Napier, W. (ed.) (2000). *African American Literary Theory: A Reader.* New York: New York University Press.

Parham, M. (2009). *Haunting and Displacement in African American Literature and Culture.* New York: Routledge.

Richter, D. H. (ed.) (2007). *The Critical Tradition.* Boston: Bedford.

Ross, M. B. (2004). *Manning the Race: Reforming Black Men in the Jim Crow Era.* New York: New York University Press.

Smith, B. (1977). Toward a black feminist criticism. *Conditions*, 1 (2), 25–44.

Walker, A. (1983). In search of our mothers' gardens. In *In Search of Our Mothers' Gardens.* Orlando, FL: Harcourt, Brace, pp. 231–244. (Original work published 1974.)

Wall, C. (2005). *Worrying the Line: Black Women Writers, Lineage, and Literary Tradition.* Chapel Hill: University of North Carolina Press.

Agamben, Giorgio

ALEX MURRAY

The work of Giorgio Agamben (b. 1942) has been influential in political philosophy, legal theory, and cultural studies, with his critique of the Western political and juridical traditions gaining him a wide readership in the past 10 years. Yet his work is much broader in scope and his more than 15 book-length projects have explored a diverse range of areas. His early education saw the influence of Martin Heidegger, whose understanding of the relationship between language and being profoundly influenced Agamben's early work.

Agamben's reading of Heidegger focuses on the problem of the negative foundation of the human through the question of language. As human beings we are forced to conceptualize ourselves linguistically – language mediates our very consciousness. Yet language is an imposed and abstract system, and Agamben argues that there is something more primary than language – a voice – that we cannot have access to. We are then condemned to living through a negative relation to language in which we experience our linguistic essence as a loss. Agamben's work then proceeds as an investigation of how this irreducible negativity is played out in many different ways.

First, Agamben is interested in the ways languages of power and control are utilized in politics. In particular he is interested in the ways in which legal means are utilized to draw the boundaries of political systems and the privileges they bestow. Political community is usually measured by creating a binary between us and them, citizens and noncitizens. Here the political rights of one group are dependent upon them being excluded from another. Yet Agamben argues that this process works upon an inclusive exclusion. Here he explores the figure of *homo sacer* (sacred or holy man) who in ancient Roman law could be killed without the offender being punished by law. The *homo sacer* was considered to be sacred, in that he had been sacrificed and cast out of the political system, being left without rights. Agamben claims that the sovereign has the same place of being both within and outside of the laws that he is able to control. A sovereign also has the potential to suspend the rule of law, as happens in a "state of exception." For

Agamben the position of the sovereign and *homo sacer* reveal the limit point of politics, namely that any member of a political community has the potential to be excluded from that community and reduced to what he calls "bare life," which is the product of the distinction between life and politicized life which, following Aristotle, he names *zoē* and *bios*. Agamben then traces a genealogy of the production of bare life in the political and legal systems of the West, drawing a line that connects the foundational principles of those systems with the Holocaust perpetrated by the National Socialists in Germany in World War II.

Yet Agamben's critique of Western politics is made with an eye toward what he terms the "community that comes." This community is a rejection of all forms of identity, a community made of "whatever being" which will have no form of commonality except being in common. This community is, importantly, not futural; it is not going to come, but is always coming. The means by which the coming community will emerge are related to the inoperativity that Agamben explores within the political, social, and cultural structures of the present. Inoperativity refers to the ways in which these structures fail to work, that they are characterized by paradoxes and tensions that produce figures such as *homo sacer* in the case of politics. The inoperativity of the system and the sites become the focus for Agamben, and it becomes necessary to force them to breaking point. One of Agamben's favorite figures who produces greater inoperativity in a system is Melville's "Bartleby, the Scrivener" who, when asked to perform tasks in the legal office in which he is employed responds, "I would prefer not to." His preference, which is importantly not a refusal, suspends the logic upon which a series of ideas, such as work, law, action, etc. are based and becomes instead an instance of potentiality. This is a key idea for Agamben, for whom human potentiality is not strictly a question of passing through into actuality, of a potential to do, but also to not do. The idea of not doing, of rendering inoperative is the driving force behind Agamben's community.

Agamben's work extends beyond questions of ontology and politics and enters into other domains, such as literature, art, and religion. Yet in all of these cases they should not be seen as secondary. As with the case of Bartleby Agamben finds philosophy everywhere and seeks to erode the distinction and difference between politics, philosophy, and poetics. Agamben's idea of poetics is of a general schema of representation which stretches across the arts. Poetics, to summarize, are works that draw attention to their own form: artworks that expose the artist; literature that exposes language; films that expose the mechanics of cinema. An example of this is in poetry in which Agamben explored enjambment as the key feature of poetry, that which distinguishes it from its other, prose. Enjambment is the name for the sentence, or syntactical construction that carries over beyond a rhyme. It is therefore a tension between the meaning (syntax) and form (rhyme), a "hesitation between sound and sense." Agamben therefore reads poetry as having an anxiety about the end of the poem, the point where poetry must fall back into prose as the tension between meaning and form collapse back into one another. Agamben's interest is in how this manifests itself, and in particular how certain sorts of poetry seek to push the tensions to the point of disintegration.

Agamben's work has in recent years moved toward a greater articulation of his own "method," which he gives the name of an "archaeology," an exploration of the tensions and structures of the past as they manifest themselves in the contemporary. Agamben sees the exploration of these structures and their erosion as the "political task of our generation."

SEE ALSO: Deleuze, Gilles; Derrida, Jacques; Foucault, Michel; Poststructuralism; Semiotics

REFERENCES AND SUGGESTED READINGS

Agamben, G. (1991). *Language and Death: The Place of Negativity* (trans. K. Pinkus with M. Hardt). Minneapolis: University of Minnesota Press. (Original work published 1982.)

Agamben, G. (1993a). *The Coming Community* (trans. M. Hardt). Minneapolis: University of Minnesota Press. (Original work published 1990.)

Agamben, G. (1993b). *Stanzas: Word and Phantasm in Western Culture* (trans. R. L. Martinez). Minneapolis: University of Minnesota Press. (Original work published 1979.)

Agamben, G. (1998). *Homo Sacer: Sovereign Power and Bare Life* (trans. D. Heller-Roazen). Stanford: Stanford University Press. (Original work published 1995.)

Agamben, G. (1999a). *The End of the Poem: Studies in Poetics* (trans. D. Heller-Roazen). Stanford: Stanford University Press. (Original work published 1996.)

Agamben, G. (1999b). *Potentialities: Collected Essays in Philosophy* (trans. and ed. D. Heller-Roazen) Stanford: Stanford University Press.

Agamben, G. (2000). *Means without End: Notes on Politics* (trans. V. Binetti & C. Casarino). Minneapolis: University of Minnesota Press. (Original work published 1996.)

Mills C. (2008). *The Philosophy of Giorgio Agamben.* Durham: Acumen.

Althusser, Louis

JOE HUGHES

Louis Althusser (1918–90) was a Marxist philosopher whose work exercised an enormous influence on the evolution of French Marxism and on the course of literary theory. Althusser always thought of his work as providing Marxism with a *philosophy*. For this reason, with the exception of his late work on "aleatory materialism," almost all of Althusser's theoretical writings take the form of a commentary on Marx.

Althusser's two central works – *Reading Capital* and *For Marx* – identify, describe, and draw the consequences of an "epistemological break" in Marx's work. Marx's "scientific discovery," according to Althusser, lies in his break with humanism. The "early Marx" was still caught up in the problems of humanism. He still believed, for example, that "only the essence of man makes history, and [that] this essence is freedom and reason" (2005: 224). To understand history and to understand the state one must first understand human nature and its potentials. In an early essay, Marx himself wrote that the ideal state would be the one in which "the individual citizen, when he obeys the State's laws, is only obeying the natural laws of his own reason, of human reason" (224).

Althusser argues that in 1845, the year of Marx's *The German Ideology* and the *Theses on Feuerbach*, "Marx broke radically with every theory that based history and politics on an essence of man. . . . This rupture with every *philosophical* anthropology or humanism is no secondary detail; it is Marx's scientific discovery" (2005: 227). Marxism can no longer be founded on a philosophy of the concrete subject, materialist or idealist, from this point on. The individual subject simply cannot function as its starting point. Rather than finding a middle ground between Locke and Kant, Althusser will argue that Marx staked out an entirely new vantage point with a new set of concepts, a "new way of asking questions about the world, new principles, and a new method" (227).

These new concepts are those of the "mature Marx." Althusser lists the following: "the concepts of social formation, productive forces, relations of productions, superstructure, ideologies, determination in the last instance by the economy, specific determination of the other levels, etc." (2005: 227). In other words, Althusser has in mind the entire conceptual apparatus supporting Marx's theory of "social formation" that we know from *Capital*. In what has become his most well-known work, "Ideology and ideological state apparatuses: Notes toward an investigation," Althusser goes to the foundation of this new set of nonhumanist concepts by submitting Marx's theory to the "ultimate condition of production": "the reproduction of the conditions of production" (2001: 85). Most of Marx's concepts can be easily reconciled with this ultimate condition. Althusser has relatively little trouble accounting for the reproduction of the "means of production" (the raw materials and tools of production). The reproduction of "forces of production" (the workers who use the tools) is settled through a mix of wages, biological reproduction, and education (spiritual, technical, or otherwise). What Althusser cannot immediately account for is the reproduction of the "relations of production" or those social structures which organize production.

In "classic Marxism" this role was given to the "state apparatus," the set of institutions which regulate social order: the police, the courts, the army, and so on. Althusser's innovation was to complicate this notion of the state apparatus by dividing it into two forms (which were already there in practice, he argues): the "State Repressive Apparatus" and the "State Ideological Apparatus." The repressive state apparatuses (RSAs or SAs) are those which act by force (the police and the army) but also by "mere administrative commands and interdictions" and even by

"tacit censorship." As the name suggests, their function is primarily repressive. Althusser's main interest is in the "ideological state apparatuses" (ISAs) of which he provides a long list including the family, churches, radio programs, television shows, literature, trade unions, and, the most influential of them all, the educational system. It is these apparatuses that ultimately secure the reproduction of the relations of production. The only question is how.

This raises the prior question however of ideology – a concept whose meaning is not at all clear and has been the subject of considerable debate. This is in part because what we know about Althusser's conception of ideology is drawn from diverse sources, several of the most important of which are qualified by the appendage "notes." "Very schematically," Althusser writes, "an ideology is a system (with its own logic and rigor) of representations (images, myths, ideas, or concepts, depending on the case) endowed with a historical existence and role within a given society" (2005: 231). This system of representations is not optional. It is not a false consciousness that criticism can break through. It is an essential component of society in general. Human societies "secrete ideology as the very element and atmosphere indispensable to their respiration and life.... *historical materialism cannot conceive that even a communist country could ever do without ideology*" (2005: 232; emphasis original). As he puts it somewhat provocatively in *Lenin and Philosophy*, "ideology has no history" (2001: 107).

This system of representations is not floating out there in an imagined heaven of ideas. Nor is it something created and controlled by a "group of individuals (Priests or Despots) who are the authors of the great ideological mystification" (2001: 112). Althusser confronts these two conspiracy theory interpretations of ideology with two theses of his own. First, ideology is "material." By this Althusser means that it lives not in our heads but in the everyday actions of subjects: "the 'ideas' of a human subject exist in his actions" (114). Althusser quotes Pascal to make this point rather dramatically: "Kneel down, move your lips in prayer, and you will believe" (114). Second, there is no hidden operator of the system. It works only in and through the "ideological state apparatuses," those rituals or structured *activities* in which we engage every day at the dinner table, at school, in telephone conversations with our friends. Thus Althusser's statement that "[t]he subject acts insofar as he is acted" (114) contains both theses in condensed form. Ideology, then, is the set of those institutional structures, or apparatuses, however mundane or serious, which structure or "govern" our everyday actions. As he puts it in *For Marx*, the "representations" that constitute the system of ideology "are usually images and occasionally concepts, but it is above all as *structures* that they impose themselves on the vast majority of men" (2005: 233).

We become incorporated into these structures through a process Althusser calls "interpellation" or "hailing." He gives a famous example of the police shouting, "Hey! You there!" In this situation "the hailed individual will turn around. By this mere one-hundred-and-eighty-degree physical conversion, he becomes a *subject*" (2001: 118). This example clarifies, first of all, the material nature of ideology. In the *act* of turning around, the individual is immediately incorporated into the structure of a particular ritual or ISA. The very structure of this apparatus instantly defines and even "governs" the subject's possible actions. What *I* can do is determined by the particular apparatus in which I find myself engaged. Second, it shows in a concrete way how the hailing or interpellation works. Interpella-

tion is an address to individuals which incorporates them into a ritual in which they will take up a determinate subject position. In this case, the act of hailing is particularly flagrant and the subject position is well defined, but there are many other ways to interpellate, from the overly vigorous handshake of a "type-A" business exec to a birthday card from your mother. Each of these acts brings us into a structure in which we occupy a more or less determinate subject position, whether that be "suspect" or "mom's little boy." Interpellation, then, is the act that welcomes us into the various "rituals" or ISAs which govern our everyday actions and thus ensures the reproduction of the relations of production.

An examination of the various subject positions created in interpellation gave rise to one of the more interesting applications of Althusser's thought in the late 1970s and early 1980s. One of the ISAs Althusser listed in his essay was literature. Althusser himself, however, did not develop the way in which literature functioned in the structure of ideology. Several literary critics, such as Catherine Belsey and Colin McCabe, thus developed Althusser's claims by describing the subject positions created by the "classic realist text" and the modernist text. After this brief Golden Age Althusser's thought slowly receded from the public eye. Recently, however, there have been several calls for a return to Althusser. These calls are inspired primarily by the recent appearance of an entire corpus of late writings by Althusser in which he outlines the fundamental premises of his philosophy which he now describes as an "aleatory materialism" or a "philosophy of the encounter." In these writings Althusser emphasizes the role of pure chance in conjunctures and the radically undetermined nature of change.

SEE ALSO: Ideology; Marx, Karl; Marxism

REFERENCES AND SUGGESTED
READINGS

Althusser, L. (1975). *Reading Capital* (trans. B.
Brewster). London: New Left Books.
Althusser, L. (1999). *Writings on Psychoanalysis:
Freud and Lacan* (trans. J. Mehlmen).
New York: Columbia University Press.
Althusser, L. (2001). *Lenin and Philosophy, and
Other Essays* (trans. B. Brewster). New York:
Monthly Review Press.
Althusser, L. (2005). *For Marx* (trans. B. Brewster).
New York: Verso.
Althusser, L. (2006). *Philosophy of the Encounter:
Later Writings, 1978–1987* (trans. G. M. Gosh-
garian). New York: Verso.
Anderson, P. (1983). *In the Tracks of Historical
Materialism*. London: Verso.
Belsey, C. (1980). *Critical Practice*. London: Methuen.
Eagleton, T. (2006). *Criticism and Ideology: A Study
in Marxist Literary Theory*. London: Verso.
Elliot, G. (1983). *Althusser: The Detour of Theory*.
New York: Verso.
MacCabe, C. (1989). *James Joyce and the Revolution
of the Word*. London: Macmillan.
Montag, W. (2003). *Louis Althusser*. New York:
Macmillan.

American Indian Literary Criticism and Theory

ROBERT DALE PARKER

The criticism of American Indian literature
began earlier and has a longer history of
theoretical engagement than is ordinarily
recognized. Before European writing systems reached what are now known as the
Americas, the people now known as Indians
or Native Americans had their own writing
systems of various kinds, from Mayan glyphs
to wampum and petroglyphs. Moreover,
American Indians, like all peoples, have
always had an extensive oral literature and
a history of thinking about their own and
their neighbors' oral literature. That history
continues into contemporary times, both
through oral tradition and through the dialogue between oral and written traditions.

Beginning with the European invasion,
then, and the introduction of European
writing systems, Europeans changed and
were changed by Native American literary
thinking of many kinds. Euroamericans
were slow to recognize the presence as
well as the breadth and intricacy of Indian
oral literature, but in the nineteenth century
Henry Rowe Schoolcraft, Daniel Brinton,
and many other Euroamericans began to
write about Indian oral literature, usually
without much acknowledging the extent of
their dependence on the critical thinking
of individual American Indians who taught
them – or taught their sources – about
Indian languages and traditions. These early
accounts of Indian literature influenced
mainstream literary writing, most famously
in Henry Wadsworth Longfellow's *The Song
of Hiawatha* (1855), the most popular
American poem of its time. With the growth
of professional anthropology in the late
nineteenth and early twentieth centuries,
the massive project of writing down Indian
oral literature grew in sophistication and
breadth. While the published anthropological studies from that time usually reflect
colonialist perspectives and draw on varying
degrees of familiarity with the languages and
cultures they record, they also vary in the
ways they included, relied on, and recognized Indian scholars. Nevertheless, anthropologists gathered a vast archive of primary
texts and interpretation of those texts.
Working under the assumptions of what
has come to be called salvage anthropology,
they usually supposed, for the most part
inaccurately, that Indian cultures were
about to disappear and that anthropologists
needed to write down Indian cultures before
Indians and their traditions and languages
faded away. Still, as a record, however
imperfect, of the storytelling and other
oral literature of particular times and places,
the legacy of such late nineteenth- and
early twentieth-century anthropologists as

Washington Matthews and Franz Boas, along with Boas's many students, remains invaluable.

In later years, anthropologists began to reconsider how early Euroamerican anthropologists imposed their own culture's ideas of storytelling onto the stories that they transcribed and recorded. Dennis Tedlock studied how the process of transcribing and translating changed the stories that it recorded, and Tedlock and others sought new ways to make the transcription and translation of stories faithful to oral performances. Barre Toelken and others showed how stories are integrated into the culture, rituals, and beliefs of the people who tell and listen to the stories. Meanwhile, as Native scholars and writers increasingly joined the scholarly discussion of traditional Indian oral narrative, or spoke and wrote back to it, or incorporated it into their own experience of oral traditions and their own literary writing, scholars and writers called attention to the close relation between land, so often central to Indian self-definition, and the stories that grow out of the land and hold the people and the land together.

Growing in part from these emerging discussions as well as from broader changes in American and American Indian culture and education, including the response to the African American Civil Rights Movement, the published body of written Indian literature grew dramatically in the years following N. Scott Momaday's (Kiowa) *House Made of Dawn* (1968). Kenneth Lincoln dubbed the new outpouring of Indian literature the Native American Renaissance. Soon, as the scholarly criticism of American literature expanded beyond its traditional bounds, scholars began to study and theorize about the new Indian writing. They often drew heavily on the long tradition of anthropological scholarship that they found ready and previously relatively unaddressed by literary scholars.

In the early years of this new body of literature and scholarship, many poet-scholars played a leading role, inspired partly by Tedlock's experiments with rendering the orality of storytelling in the form of printed poetry and the experiments of the anthropologist Dell Hymes, who turned to poetry for ways to make the printed page express the patterns and structures of oral storytelling. Led by Jerome Rothenberg and others, an "ethnopoetics" movement emerged. The ethnopoets often searched through anthropological transcripts of Indian stories, songs, and rituals and rewrote them as English-language poetry. While much of the poetry showed great inventiveness and power, it also came under attack as falsifying the oral traditions that it sought to represent by rewriting them and transforming them onto the page. Gradually, the influence of the ethnopoetics movement waned, in part from the criticism it provoked and in part because the desire for non-Indian poets to imagine ways to represent a Native oral poetry diminished in the face of the increasing recognition won by contemporary Indian poets themselves. Nevertheless, the ethnopoetics movement also influenced the writing of Indian fiction in such influential early novels as *House Made of Dawn* and Leslie Marmon Silko's *Ceremony* (1974), which integrated poetic versions of oral prayer and storytelling into their prose narratives. For both fiction writers and critics, an ongoing dialogue with or even dependence on oral storytelling came to seem like a defining feature of the new Indian writing and a way of connecting it to Indian traditions and history.

Another poet, fiction writer, and critic, Paula Gunn Allen (Laguna), called for the emerging literary study of Indian writing to take heed of the defining role of women in Indian cultures and stories and proposed as well that the central role of ceremony in Indian cultures and writing defines the difference between Indian writing and non-Indian writing. Other critics joined the growing effort to define a distinguishing difference in Indian literature. William Bevis noted that Indian novels take a different approach from the novels previously central to the study of American literature. While such novels as *Moby-Dick*, *The Adventures of Huckleberry Finn*, *The Great Gatsby*, or those of Henry James, tell of characters leaving home, Indian novels, by contrast, such as the acclaimed early works of Momaday, Silko, and James Welch (Blackfoot and Gros Ventre), tell of characters who return home. In seeing Indian writers as centered on their homelands, Bevis's argument anticipated many later arguments, even as Indian writing itself diversified after the boom of attention and excitement surrounding the flurry of new Indian writing in the 1970s and 1980s.

As a consensus emerged that Indian writing centered on place, on home, on orality, and on storytelling, that consensus produced competing reactions. On the one hand, some critics, including Allen and the poet Kimberly Blaeser (Anishinaabe), came to see such features as definitional of what makes Indian writing distinctive. They see orality as opposed to what they see as the linear patterns of Euroamerican writing, and they celebrate the distinctiveness of Indian difference from Euroamerican traditions. Such ideas had enormous influence on Indian writers and the theory and criticism of Indian writing, even while many critics came to believe that Allen tended to generalize too broadly and to underestimate the variations and differences within Indian cultures. The novelist and critic Greg Sarris (Pomo and Coast Miwok), for example, characterizes Pomo culture and intellectual life by writing about Pomo oral storytelling, and lets the circuitous wiles of storytelling influence the structure of his critical writing. The novelist and critic/historian LeAnne

Howe (Choctaw) makes the focus on storytelling into a theory of Indian imagination and Indian–white relations, a theory she calls "tribalography."

The desire to define the distinctiveness of Indian writing made sense in a world where the dominant culture has done and continues to do so much to take away, even to steal, Indian distinctiveness, taking Indian land, making Indian religion illegal, fostering the myth that Indians were supposedly disappearing (the last of the Mohicans), forcing Indian children into colonialist boarding schools that often sought to destroy Indian languages and cultures, and trying desperately to assuage the colonialists' guilt by converting Indianness into the romanticized nostalgia of commercial products, from toy headdresses and tomahawks to toy Indians, to movies, to advertising images and sports mascots. In the same way, and at more or less the same time, some African Americans developed the Black Arts Movement, some Chicanas and Chicanos defined their history through the legend of Aztlán, and some feminists sought to establish a special and distinct difference that defines women's or feminine writing.

Each of those movements in turn provoked counterarguments. In the theorizing of Indian culture and literature, the counterarguments have taken many forms. Perhaps the most prominent counterargument has come from the writer and theorist Gerald Vizenor (Anishinaabe). Vizenor spoofs fixed ideas of Indianness – the clichés of the savage warrior, the stoic wooden Indian, the romantic Indian princess, and the natural Indian ecologist – calling them "terminal creeds." Instead of valorizing images of Indianness, Vizenor valorizes tribal history and heritage. Through humor and satire, he models his theoretical and literary writings on the irrepressible playfulness of tribal tricksters and trickster stories, and he revalorizes the sometimes derogatory terms "mixedblood" and "crossblood" as models for the unpredictable combinations of ideas and histories in what he calls "postindian" life and writing. The term "postindian" evokes Vizenor's engagement with poststructuralist theory and with the flamboyant eclecticism of contemporary postmodernism. In response to Vizenor, some critics have seized on the idea of the trickster as a defining characteristic of Indian writing, though that might seem to go against Vizenor's skepticism about defining characteristics. Others, notably the novelist and critic Louis Owens (Choctaw and Cherokee), have celebrated Vizenor's focus on postmodernist multiplicity, taking the metaphor of the mixedblood as a representative signifier for Indian writing. For Owens, the metaphor of the mixedblood resonates in an age of cultural and genetic mixing, and in a context where the racial prejudices of the dominant culture exoticize the routine of mixed Indian heritages. Often, from the perspective of the dominant culture, mixed heritages seem to compromise Indian authenticity, as if only the dominant culture were allowed to change and still remain true to itself, and as if changes in Indian culture signify, once again, the myth of Indian disappearance. On the other hand, some critics have rejected the metaphor of the mixedblood as overly biological and thus reincorporating the myth of biological authenticity that the metaphor sets out to spoof. And some critics fear that the focus on tricksters can oversimplify Indian traditions and go too far to celebrate disruption and disrespect, thus reducing the role of the sacred and the role of respect for history, tradition, and practicality.

Thus while some critics see Vizenor's ideas as a club to beat up other critics for oversimplifying Indian literature by trying to define it, others respond to Vizenor by seeking new strategies of definition that might not succumb to the oversimplifications that Vizenor critiques. After all, critics observe, no other American ethnic or racial group has a land base. No other American ethnic or racial group has a literature and culture emerging from distinct nations that have their own governments and sovereignty. Indeed, Indians do not form an ethnic group or a race in the usual sense of those terms in American English. They are instead a wide variety of peoples that have emerged through the cultural heritage of hundreds of different Indian nations, many of them recognized by the federal government, some recognized by state governments, and some not governmentally recognized at all. Elizabeth Cook-Lynn (Crow Creek Lakota) thus asks Indian writing – and theory and criticism about Indian writing – to attend first to what good it can do for the sovereignty, land, and languages of Indian nations. Robert Warrior (Osage) challenges critics to attend to the intellectual sovereignty that he sees as underlying the history of Indian writing, instead of letting Indian specificity dissipate into the assimilating perspectives of non-Indian literary history. Taking up that challenge, Craig Womack (Muskogee Creek and Cherokee) invites critics to reshape questions about the definition of Indian literature by thinking less in terms of Indianness in general and more in terms of the specific histories of particular Indian nations, an invitation that Womack himself takes up in his history of Muskogee literature and that Daniel Heath Justice (Cherokee) takes up in a history of Cherokee literature. With a related focus on the centrality of Native communities, Jace Weaver (Cherokee) proposes what he calls "communitism" as a value that defines the distinctiveness of Indian traditions and Indian literary writing. Robert Dale Parker looks to changing, rather than consistent, cultural patterns and histories to characterize Indian literature. Meanwhile, in a variety of ways across a long and diverse series of writings, Arnold Krupat stands out among critics who work to integrate the criticism and theory of Indian literary studies into the broader debates across the theory and politics of literary studies in general, while also attending to the specific qualities of Indian literary history.

Some critics, carrying the torch of Vizenor's postindianism, have looked skeptically on the challenges put forth by Cook-Lynn, Warrior, and Womack. In response, Womack, Weaver, and Warrior have argued for the centrality and value of national self-consciousness in Indian literary writing and in critical writing about Indian literature. Their argument coheres with an increasing attention to the historical centrality of sovereignty in American Indian politics and in Indian studies more generally, owing to an increasing recognition of the key role of sovereignty in Indian political and intellectual history and in the current struggles faced by Indian nations, as well as by indigenous peoples across the world. Indeed, in recent years, Indian studies within and beyond literary studies has begun to engage more largely with international indigenous studies, including the call by such scholars as the Maori Linda Tuhiwai Smith for scholars, indigenous and nonindigenous, to make their scholarship serve indigenous communities rather than simply asking what use they can make of the indigenous peoples they study. Drawing on similar dialogues, and calling attention to the frequent conflations of nationalism with masculinity and to the increasing movement of Native people into cities and away from their national homelands, Shari Huhndorf (Yup'ik) calls for a broader, international indigenous dialogue, combined with an attention to feminist questions, to reinflect and supplement the focus on local nationalism.

Recent scholars have also called attention to the way that contemporary writing dominates the study and teaching of Native American literature. Increasingly, scholars are turning to the literary detective project of recovering forgotten Indian writing from before the Native American Renaissance. Such scholarship has brought readers to Jane Johnston Schoolcraft (Anishinaabe), William Apes (or Apess, Pequot), Sarah Winnemucca (Paiute), Alex Posey (Muskogee Creek), Zitkala-Sa (Gertrude Bonnin, Yankton Sioux), John Joseph Mathews (Osage), D'Arcy McNickle (Confederated Salish and Kootenai, Cree), and a growing number of other once forgotten writers from the nineteenth and early twentieth centuries. Scholars have thus begun the task of testing, corroborating, and revising their models and theories against a longer history of Indian literature as well as against the continually evolving experiments of new generations of contemporary Indian writers.

SEE ALSO: Postcolonial Studies and Diaspora Studies; Vizenor, Gerald

REFERENCES AND SUGGESTED READINGS

Allen, P. G. (1986). *The Sacred Hoop: Recovering the Feminine in American Indian Traditions*. Boston: Beacon.

Bevis, W. (1987). Native American novels: Homing in. In B. Swann & A. Krupat (eds.), *Recovering the Word: Essays on Native American Literature*. Berkeley: University of California Press, pp. 580–620.

Blaeser, K. M. (1997) Like "reeds through the ribs of a basket." *American Indian Quarterly*, 21(4), 555–565.

Cook-Lynn, E. (1996). *Why I Can't Read Wallace Stegner and Other Essays: A Tribal Voice*. Madison: University of Wisconsin Press.

Cook-Lynn, E. (2007a). *Anti-Indianism in Modern America: A Voice from Tatekeya's Earth*. Urbana: University of Illinois Press.

Cook-Lynn, E. (2007b). *New Indians, Old Wars.* Urbana: University of Illinois Press.

Krupat, A. (1992). *Ethnocriticism: Ethnography, History, Literature.* Berkeley: University of California Press.

Krupat, A. (1996). *The Turn to the Native: Studies in Criticism and Culture.* Lincoln: University of Nebraska Press.

Krupat, A. (2002). *Red Matters: Native American Studies.* Philadelphia: University of Pennsylvania Press.

Krupat, A. (2009). *All That Remains: Varieties of Indigenous Expression.* Lincoln: University of Nebraska Press.

Owens, L. (1992). *Other Destinies: Understanding the American Indian Novel.* Norman: University of Oklahoma Press.

Owens, L. (1998). *Mixedblood Messages: Literature, Film, Family, Place.* Norman: University of Oklahoma Press.

Parker, R. D. (2003). *The Invention of Native American Literature.* Ithaca: Cornell University Press.

Sarris, G. (1993). *Keeping Slug Woman Alive: A Holistic Approach to American Indian Texts.* Berkeley: University of California Press.

Tedlock, D. (1983). *The Spoken Word and the Work of Interpretation.* Philadelphia: University of Pennsylvania Press.

Toelken, B. (1987). Life and death in the Navajo coyote tales. In B. Swann & A. Krupat (eds.), *Recovering the Word: Essays on Native American Literature.* Berkeley: University of California Press, pp. 388–401.

Toelken, B., & Scott, T. (1981). Poetic retranslation and the "pretty languages" of yellowman. In K. Kroeber (ed.), *Traditional Literatures of the American Indian: Texts and Interpretation.* Lincoln: University of Nebraska Press, pp. 65–116.

Vizenor, G. (1994). *Manifest Manners: Postindian Warriors of Survivance.* Hanover, NH: Wesleyan University Press.

Warrior, R. A. (1995). *Tribal Secrets: Recovering American Indian Intellectual Traditions.* Minneapolis: University of Minnesota Press.

Weaver, J. (1997). *That the People Might Live: Native American Literatures and Native American Community.* New York: Oxford University Press.

Womack, C. S. (1999). *Red on Red: Native American Literary Separatism.* Minneapolis: University of Minnesota Press.

Appiah, Kwame Anthony

ANASTASIA VALASSOPOULOS

Kwame Anthony Appiah's work is popular and influential across many genres including philosophy, African American studies, and more recently, postcolonial studies. He was born in London in 1954 and lived in Ghana and England. He was educated at Cambridge, where he studied semantics and philosophy. Currently he is Laurance S. Rockefeller University Professor of Philosophy at the University Center for Human Values at Princeton. Appiah is also a crime fiction writer and has written three novels, among which are *Another Death in Venice* and *Nobody Likes Letitia.*

Appiah's ability to move *beyond* seemingly opposing ideas of modernity and tradition in his discussions of contemporary culture has been very prominent. As Rooney has noted, "Appiah avoids falling into the polemical trap of an either/or: *either* modern philosophy of a Western universalist formation *or* traditional thought" (2000: 13). This is a key concept in Appiah's work, elaborated and reformulated in some of his major writings.

In *In My Father's House* (1992), Appiah argues for the necessity of remembering that when "writing about culture … one is bound to be formed, morally, aesthetically, politically, religiously – by the range of lives one has known" (xi). Appiah points to how varying philosophies of the world's cultures are interconnected and how this connectedness can help teach us all about what it means to be part of the human race. For Appiah, any indicator of "race" (apart from the human *race*) is a poor one that tells us nothing about our cultural tendencies. "The truth is that there are no races" (72). The concept of *race* is a barrier to understanding and accommodating cultural difference – it erases the humanity shared by all. Appiah argues for turning "to our advantage the mutual interdependencies history has thrust upon us" and to understand that this interdependence need not be a sign of weakness (115).

In *Color Conscious: The Political Morality of Race* (1996; with Amy Gutman), Appiah eloquently argues that restrictive ideas of race only serve to further restrict ideas on what it means to be human. The concept of race can only provide generic connections between groups of people and cannot hope to explain "social or psychological life" (74). We cannot assume that subcultures share a common culture – for example, that all Asian American or African American subcultures form a specific kind of culture because they arguably share a common history or have been interpolated similarly. In arguing for a move away from labels that accentuate difference, Appiah is aware of the problems this heralds. How do we separate ourselves and construct distinct cultural identities, while at the same time making claims for multicultural sympathies?

Appiah rejects claims for "authentic" cultures of any kind, untouched by other communities or sociopolitical forces (1996: 95). Nevertheless, while Appiah presents reasons for why differences between groups matter, he maintains that groups must understand that relationships exist which *unite* them. He proposes that we "live with fractured identities; engage in identity play; find solidarity, yes, but recognize contingency, and, above all, practice irony" (104).

Thinking It Through: An Introduction to Contemporary Philosophy (2003a) reveals the extent to which philosophical debates around issues such as morality, justice, and the law all influence and are influenced by ideas used to differentiate ourselves from others. Here, Appiah notes how "it is important, in thinking about how we should behave, to bear in mind that each of us has one life to live and that living that life well –

making a success of one's life – is important. And the fact that it is important to make a success of one's life provides a connection between self-regarding and other-regarding considerations" (217). Mutual interdependency is a key factor in Appiah's assessment of contemporary philosophy.

In his influential work *Cosmopolitanism: Ethics in a World of Strangers* (2006), Appiah addresses how considerations of the self and the other may be brought into dialogue. Rejecting globalization and multiculturalism as useful terms, he instead invests in the idea of the cosmopolitan. Putting the idea of cultural imperialism under scrutiny, Appiah asks us why in a post-9/11 world we are witnessing a discourse of the West and the rest. He promotes a conversational model, "in particular, conversation between people from different ways of life" (xxi). To learn, to know, to investigate – not to persuade, win over or force – is what Appiah promotes. "I am arguing that we should learn about people in other places, take an interest in their civilisations, their arguments, their errors, their achievements, not because that will bring us to an agreement, but because it will help us get used to one another" (78). Appiah's arguments overall remind us that we are living in a world where cultural exchange is inevitable. The question is, will this exchange be adversarial or will it be accommodating? (2003a: 341–2).

SEE ALSO: Gates, Henry Louis; Orientalism; Postcolonial Studies and Diaspora Studies; Said, Edward

REFERENCES AND SUGGESTED READINGS

Appiah, A. K. (1992). *In My Father's House: Africa in the Philosophy of Culture*. London: Methuen.

Appiah, A. K. (1994). *Nobody Likes Letitia*. London: Constable.

Appiah, A. K. (1995). *Another Death in Venice*. London: Constable.

Appiah, A. K. (2003a). *Thinking It Through: An Introduction to Contemporary Philosophy*. Oxford: Oxford University Press.

Appiah, A. K. (2003b). *The Ethics of Identity*. Princeton: Princeton University Press.

Appiah, A. K. (2006). *Cosmopolitanism: Ethics in a World of Strangers*. New York: Norton.

Appiah, A. K., & Gutman, A. (1996). *Color Conscious: The Political Morality of Race*. Princeton: Princeton University Press.

Rooney, C. (2000). *African Literature, Animism and Politics*. London: Routledge.

Asian American Literary Theory

ANITA MANNUR

The term "Asian American literary theory" describes collective concerns about, on the one hand, aesthetics, literature, and the construction of "Asian American" identity, and on the other, the racial and ethnic politics of Asian American cultural formation. Since its inception, it has systematically problematized the dominant way in which race is understood, especially in the US, by questioning the binary opposition of black and white.

The playwright Frank Chin was an early theoretician in this field, and his work was rooted in 1960s "Yellow Power" cultural nationalism. In addition to his dramatic work, he was the coeditor of the pioneering Asian American literary anthology *Aiiieeeee!* He argued that it was the materiality of race that defined Asian American literature and he showed how anti-Asian racism was embodied in stereotyped characters in popular culture like Charlie Chan and Fu Manchu. Chin became well known in Asian American literary studies for extending this critique to the representation of Asian American men in the work of writers such as David Henry Hwang, Amy Tan, and Maxine Hong Kingston, which he argued were emasculating. His "cultural nationalism" often emerged at the expense of feminist concerns and his stance on gender and race has been very controversial, but his continued analysis of Asian American subjectivity grants him an important place early place within Asian American studies.

Following from, and developing in response, to Chin's critique, the next generation of Asian American literary theorists – including Amy Ling, Elaine Kim, King-Kok Cheung, and Sau-Ling Wong – laid further groundwork. Not only responding to debates over gender in Asian American literature, these theorists underscored the primary features of the Asian American literary tradition, initiating a critical conversation about neglected works by Asian American authors. For Kim, establishing the social context of Asian American literature was a necessary first step in orienting critics to Asian American texts. Ling's work recovered the "lost" writings of early Chinese American authors. Cheung argued that the intersecting forces of nationalism and feminism were mutually constitutive Asian American critics. Sau-Ling Wong's work furthers these scholars' work by reading Asian American literature alongside frameworks of race, food, psychoanalysis, and gender. Collectively, the early theorists integrated gender into the extant narrative about Asian America, paving the way for several feminist analyses to emerge.

However, as a greater awareness of newer immigrant groups in the US arose in literary criticism, cultural nationalism as a critical paradigm gave way to a focus on diasporic connections with Asia. This turn to diasporic and postcolonial studies in the early 1990s broadened the scope of Asian American theory, which now turned to consider the role of immigration, neocolonial expansion into Asia, and the movement of capital, labor, and commodities between Asia and the United States. Sau-Ling Wong's "Denationalization reconsidered" (1995) prompted an important inquiry into where Asia fits into conceptualizations of Asian America. Wong argued for a definition of Asian American studies as distinct from Asian studies. Works by Lisa Lowe and David Palumbo-Liu have been instrumental in providing critical tools for negotiating the connection between Asia and America in sociopolitical and economic terms. Lowe's landmark *Immigrant Acts* (1996) ushered in a new phase in Asian American literary theory. Rather than considering theory as a Western construction, Lowe embraced a theoretical foundation for Asian American literary studies. For her, "history and historical necessity" (41) fuel articulations of citizenship in American culture. Central to Lowe's work is a critique of the myths of American citizenship, its inherent contradictions and implications for understanding the increased economic and political dominance of the US in Asia. Lowe offers greater nuance to conceptualizing Asian American difference; through the vectors of heterogeneity, hybridity, and multiplicity, one can negotiate historically and politically inflected forms of difference in Asian American cultural production that more systematically engage with the forms of US imperialism. Palumbo-Liu (1999) maintains that the development of the American nation was tied to an expansion across the Pacific in tandem with the movement of Asians into the borders of the US nation-state. This duality foments a tension between "Asian" and "American," disallowing a complete fusing of the two. This explains the logic of inclusions and exclusions that have kept Asians in the United States from being viewed as fully American. The use of the slash in his title *Asian/American* addresses the tenuous sep-

aration of Asian and American while acknowledging their undeniable connections.

In the early 2000s, the field of Asian American theory had come to recognize its broad multiplicities and heterogeneities (to borrow Lowe's phrase). It has given rise to new and exciting work that considers changes in global economic structures, the effects of post-1965 immigration, while engaging marginalized forms of analysis sensitive to sexuality, gender, and class.

Often considered to be blind to inequities of race and ethnicity, psychoanalysis provided rich, fertile ground for theoretical work: Anne Cheng's *Melancholy of Race* (2002) and David L. Eng's *Racial Castration* (2001) are texts that attend to the possibility of understanding racial formation, sexuality, and gendered performance in terms of affect and psychoanalysis. Both suggest that literary analyses of the psychic lives of immigrants and populations of color can propel conversations about race, psychoanalysis, gender, and sexuality. One of the foremost theoretician of psychoanalysis in Asian American literary studies, Eng is also a pioneer in theorizing sexuality. Focusing on masculinities and Asian American queerness, Eng locates gay Asian men in Asian American studies. Gayatri Gopinath's (2005) articulation of queer diasporas in transnational frame brings focus to alternate forms of sexuality and same-sex desire in South Asian public cultures. Key to Asian American queer theory in general is an understanding of sexuality and queerness as central to the project of defining race and ethnicity. Even as Asian American studies occasionally considers queerness to be structured by a kind of impossibility, queer theory revisits the archive of Asian American literature to attend to the complexities of sexuality. Susan Koshy's *Sexual Naturalization* explores the imbrications of sex and race in the US imagination. Anti-miscegenation legislation, Koshy argues, reproduced America as a white nation while the expansion of the US into Asia allowed white American men to have sexual liaisons with women in Asia.

Because it developed in tandem with ethnic studies, Asian American literary studies has long engaged comparative ethnic/racial perspectives. James Lee (2004) situates Asian American racial formation alongside other US ethnic and racial minorities; Allan Isaac's (2007) concept of "American Tropics" and critical empire studies reads 1898, the year of the Spanish-American war and the official inauguration of US imperialism in the Philippines, the Pacific, and Puerto Rico as a culturally significant moment requiring a comparative reading of Filipino American, Puerto Rican, and Hawaiian literatures; Crystal Parikh (2009) theorizes the connections between Asian American and Chicano/a literatures; Bill Mullen (2004) theorizes Afro-Orientalism; Daniel Kim (2005) considers black–Asian connections while Song (2005) examines the racial politics of the LA riots. Comparative analyses of Jewish Americans (Schlund-Vials, in press) and Arab Americans figures into comparative ethnic literary studies.

If the debate set in motion by Frank Chin's polemics is any indication, Asian American studies has negotiated the thorny terrain of recognizing the "proper" objects of study since its earliest days. As Viet Nguyen (2002) argues, the idea of Asian America is one in which Asian American intellectuals remain invested, both materially and intellectually. Extending this line of inquiry, Kandice Chuh's *Imagine Otherwise* (2003) engages the question of epistemology in Asian American studies. Chuh proposes replacing identity politics with what she calls Asian Americanist critique. This shift away from the question of objects and subjects of Asian American inquiry and toward a "subjectless discourse" allows for strategic attention to be placed on the critiques rather than on subjectivities. As Lowe's work ushered in a new era of theoretical work in the late 1990s, Chuh's work stands poised to inspire the next generation of theorists. Chuh's call for a new form of Asian Americanist critique paves the way for closer attention to literary aesthetics. A renewed emphasis on literary form and poetics informs new work (R. Lee 1999; Lye 2005; Park 2008; Yu 2009) which strategically reads Asian American literature alongside canonical works of American literature. Park's *Apparitions of Asia*, for instance, provides a literary genealogy for Asian American avant-garde poetry, tracing its origins to American Orientalisms in modernist poetics.

While many consider Asian American cultural formation in pan-ethnic or comparative racial terms, several important developments have taken place in single ethnic studies. South Asian and Filipino American studies contends with being a part of, yet apart from, Asian America. Srikanth (2004) maps the centrality of the diasporic imagination to South Asian American literary studies. Analogously, Filipino empire studies has oriented the field to US imperialism in Asia while also, as in the work of Campomanes (1995), examined the discrepancies between the Filipino American literature of exile and the prevailing ethos of Asian American literature, thus expanding the field's theoretical scope.

At the close of the first decade of the twenty-first century, Asian American literary theory continues to think through history, politics, and relations of power extending the scope of Asian American critique. Intersectional analysis and cultural studies has led to new work, with vital connections being fomented to environmental studies (Hayashi 2007); food studies (Xu 2008; Mannur 2010); disability studies (Wu 2008). The field has moved beyond negotiating inclusions/exclusions, recognizing that to transform the varied logics of inequities requires systematic engagement with forms of power and domination that structure Asian America and America's global reaches in Asia.

SEE ALSO: Orientalism; Postcolonial Studies and Diaspora Studies

REFERENCES AND SUGGESTED READINGS

Bow, L. (2001). *Betrayal and Other Acts of Subversion: Feminism, Sexual Politics, Asian American Women's Literature*. Princeton: Princeton University Press.

Campomanes, O. (1995). Filipinos in the United States and their literature of exile. In V. Rafael (ed.), *Discrepant Histories: Translocal Essays on Filipino Cultures*. Philadelphia: Temple University Press, pp. 159–192.

Cheng, A. (2002). *The Melancholy of Race: Psychoanalysis, Assimilation and Hidden Grief*. New York: Oxford University Press.

Cheung, K.-K. (1990). *The Woman Warrior* versus *The Chinaman Pacific*: Must a Chinese American critic choose between heroism and feminism? In M. Hirsch & E. F. Keller (eds.), *Conflicts in Feminism*. New York: Routledge, pp. 234–251.

Chin, F., & Chan, J. P. (1972). Racist love. In R. Kostelanetz (ed.), *Seeing through Shuck*. New York: Ballantine.

Chuh, K. (2003). *Imagine Otherwise: On Asian Americanist Cultural Critique*. Durham, NC: Duke University Press.

Eng, D. L. (2001). *Racial Castration: Managing Masculinity in Asian America*. Durham, NC: Duke University Press.

Gopinath, G. (2005). *Impossible Desires: Queer Diasporas and South Asian Public Cultures*. Durham, NC: Duke University Press.

Hayashi, R. (2007). *Haunted by Waters: A Journey through Race and Place in the American West*. Iowa City: University of Iowa Press.

Isaac, A. (2007). *American Tropics: Articulating Filipino America*. Minneapolis: University of Minnesota Press.

Kim, D. (2005). *Writing Manhood in Black and White: Ralph Ellison, Frank Chin, and the Literary Politics of Identity*. Stanford: Stanford University Press.

Kim, E. (1984). *Asian American Literature: An Introduction to the Writings and Their Social Context*. Philadelphia: Temple University Press.

Koshy, S. (2004). *Sexual Naturalization: Asian Americans and Miscegenation*. Stanford: Stanford University Press.

Lee, J. (2004). *Urban Triage: Race and the Fictions of Multiculturalism*. Minneapolis: University of Minnesota Press.

Lee, R. (1999). *The Americas of Asian American Literature: Gendered Fictions of Nation and Transnation*. Princeton: Princeton University Press.

Ling, A. (1990). *Between Worlds: Women Writers of Chinese Ancestry*. New York: Pergamon.

Lowe, L. (1996). *Immigrant Acts: On Asian American Cultural Politics*. Durham, NC: Duke University Press.

Lye, C. (2005). *America's Asia: Racial Form and American Literature*. Princeton: Princeton University Press.

Mannur, A. (2010). *Culinary Fictions: Food in South Asian Diasporic Culture*. Philadelphia: Temple University Press.

Mullen, B. (2004). *Afro-Orientalism*. Minneapolis: University of Minnesota Press.

Nguyen, V. (2002). *Race and Resistance: Literature and Politics in Asian America*. Oxford: Oxford University Press.

Palumbo-Liu, D. (1999). *Asian/American: Historical Crossings of a Racial Frontier*. Stanford: Stanford University Press.

Parikh, C. (2009). *An Ethics of Betrayal: The Politics of Otherness in Emergent US Literatures and Culture*. New York: Fordham University Press.

Park, J. (2008). *Apparitions of Asia: Modernist Form and Asian American Poetics*. Oxford: Oxford University Press.

Schlund-Vials, C. (in press). *Modeling Citizenship: Jewish and Asian American Writing*. Philadelphia: Temple University Press.

Song, M. (2005). *Strange Future: Pessimisms and the 1992 Los Angeles Riots*. Durham, NC: Duke University Press.

Srikanth, R. (2004). *The World Next Door: South Asian American Literature and the Idea of America*. Philadelphia: Temple University Press.

Wong, S.-L. (1993). *Reading Asian American Literature: From Necessity to Extravagance*. Princeton: Princeton University Press.

Wong, S.-L. (1995). Denationalization reconsidered: Asian American cultural criticism at a theoretical crossroads. *Amerasia Journal*, 21 (1–2), 1–27.

Wu, C. (2008). The Siamese twins in late-nineteenth-century narratives of conflict and reconciliation. *American Literature*, 80 (1), 29–55.

Xu, W. (2008). *Eating Identities: Reading Food in Asian American Literature*. Honolulu: University of Hawaii Press.

Yu, T. (2009). *Race and the Avant-Garde: Experimental and Asian American Poetry Since 1965*. Stanford: Stanford University Press.

Authorial Intention

KAYE MITCHELL

Arguments over authorial intention – and the relevance of this to the interpretation of a text – go back many centuries, having a notable force and currency in the discussion of religious texts. However, contemporary debates about authorial intention in the literary sphere can be quite precisely dated to the publication of a seminal article, entitled "The intentional fallacy," by W. K. Wimsatt and Monroe Beardsley, which first appeared in 1946 in the *Sewanee Review*. In that article, Wimsatt and Beardsley, who are generally associated with the school of literary criticism known as new criticism, argue that "the design or intention of the author is neither available nor desirable as a standard for judging the success of a literary work of art" (1962[1946]: 92). Although they are, as the quotation reveals, primarily concerned with questions of value, this article served to initiate a discussion about the relationship between authorial intention and textual meaning that has continued, in different forms, to this day. The debates around intention touch on many of the most fundamental questions in literary criticism: the

determinacy and determinability (or not) of textual meaning; the proper object of literary criticism; the author's authority (and the level of control he/she can wield over the meanings of his/her own work); the functions and methods of criticism; the resolution of interpretative disagreements; the role of the reader; and the nature of literary value. Such debates also, of course, spill over into the contiguous realms of art criticism and art history, aesthetics, philosophy, theology, film and theater studies, translation studies, and any discipline in which interpretation is key.

Wimsatt and Beardsley are keen, above all, to distinguish the task of the literary critic from that of the biographer, historian, or psychoanalyst. The primary object of criticism, according to their argument, should be "the text itself" – divorced from the conditions of its creation and the intentions and desires of its creator. In a separate article – "The affective fallacy" – they proceed to argue that the text should also be divorced from the conditions of its reception, that is, from any emotional effect that it produces in the reader. In identifying both fallacies, they aim to render the discipline of literary criticism more rigorous, focused, and objective, by endorsing "the way of poetic analysis and exegesis" – close reading – rather than "the way of biographical or genetic enquiry" (1962[1946]: 104).

"Intention," on Wimsatt and Beardsley's understanding of it, is "the design or plan in the author's mind" at the time at which he/she is writing the literary work and the premise of their argument is that this prior plan or blueprint is not accessible to the critic (how are we to know what is going on in the mind of the author?), whereas the text itself gives us all the information that we could hope to have (1962[1946]: 92). They therefore seek to specify the direction of inference in criticism: arguing that authorial intentions should be inferred (if at all) from the meanings of the text, rather than the other way around. There is no point, they say, in "consulting the oracle" (104).

Crucially, Wimsatt & Beardsley distinguish between what they class as "internal" and "external" evidence in the interpretation of a literary text. The contents of the author's mind are "external" to the text itself; the poem's use of language and syntax are "internal" features of the text that are easily available to the critic. However, they do complicate this somewhat by introducing the category of "intermediate" evidence, which can include "the use of biographical information" and which concerns "the character of the author" and/or "private or semiprivate meanings attached to words or topics by the author or by a coterie of which he is a member" (1962[1946]: 98).

Wimsatt and Beardsley are the first "anti-intentionalists" and in many ways they set the terms of the debate that has followed, in describing intention as something private and inaccessible (a mental state) and in seeking to shift the focus of criticism from the author to the work. Indeed, they might more accurately be viewed as "anti-authorialists" rather than anti-intentionalists, and it is worth comparing their thesis to the arguments of C. S. Lewis and E. M. W. Tillyard concerning the literary work's relationship to the poet's personality in *The Personal Heresy* (1939). In addition to arguing that intention is neither relevant nor available to the literary critic, the anti-intentionalist generally argues: that the author is not always the best reader of their own work (authors don't always know what they mean or mean what they say); that the author is not the best judge of the work's value; that it is better to analyze and evaluate the finished work rather than the work that the author had in mind during the creative process; that the text is a public object which has a life beyond the intentions that the author may have had for it; and that the text may contain meanings

and produce effects above and beyond those intended by the author (and that this abundance of meaning partly accounts for the cultural value of literary works).

Both Wimsatt and Beardsley returned to the question of intention in their later work – Beardsley in *The Possibility of Criticism* (1970) and in "Intentions and interpretations: A fallacy revived" (1982), and Wimsatt in "Genesis: An argument resumed" (1968), which is included in his *Day of the Leopards* (1976). In this article, Wimsatt reinforces the original thesis with the expanded claim that "the intention of a literary artist *qua* intention is neither a valid ground for arguing the presence of a quality or a meaning in a given instance of his literary work nor a valid criterion for judging the value of that work" (1968: 12).

The anti-intentionalist line of reasoning has been strengthened by a more general "linguistic" turn in late twentieth-century critical theory, which has tended to favor formalist and structuralist analyses of texts, and by an anti-subjective turn which has tended to compound the undermining of the author, perceived as the stable source and determiner of meaning. Thus Roland Barthes lambasts "the image of literature to be found in ordinary culture [which] is tyrannically centred on the author, his person, his life, his tastes, his passions" and argues that writing signals the "birth" of the reader and the "death" of the author (1977: 143). Michel Foucault asserts that "today's writing has freed itself from the domain of expression," it is no longer tied to "the exalted emotions related to the act of composition or the insertion of a subject into language" but is, on the contrary, "a game that inevitably moves beyond its own rules" (1977: 116).

If the tendency within literary criticism and theory in the second half of the twentieth and early twenty-first centuries has been to decry references to authorial intention, this has not been a universal tendency. In fact, there have been notable arguments put forward in favor of intentionalism. The most sustained and decisive rebuttal of the intentional fallacy argument comes from E. D. Hirsch, Jr., in *Validity in Interpretation* (1967) and the later *Aims of Interpretation* (1976). Hirsch defends what he sees as "the sensible belief that a text means what its author meant," and his argument has both ethical and methodological motivations (1967: 1). On the ethical front, he claims that "[w]hen we fail to conjoin a man's intentions to his words we lose the soul of speech, which is to convey meaning and to understand what is intended to be conveyed" (1976: 90). For methodological reasons, he argues that it is necessary to take authorial intention as our interpretative criterion, in order to achieve "validity" in criticism. We should "re-cognize" the author's meaning because such "re-cognitive interpretation" is "the only kind of interpretation with a determinate object, and thus the only kind that can lay claim to validity in any straightforward and practicable sense of that term" (1967: 27). This validity is necessary, in Hirsch's view, if literary criticism is to become a "cognitive," "scientific," serious discipline.

These are, or have become, the main arguments for intentionalism: that the readers have a kind of ethical responsibility to abide by the author's intention in their reading of a literary text, and that authorial intention can offer us an objective criterion for determining the meaning of a literary work (and thus for resolving interpretative disagreements, for example). Intentionalists tend to assert, more generally, that the author has, of necessity, a privileged relationship with the work; in the words of F. E. Sparshott, the author is more than "a bystander at his own performance" (1976: 107). This is part of a way of thinking which views literary works as the unique expression of some unique human subject and which asserts that works of art acquire their value in part because they are deliberately made by human beings (they are artifacts). So Frank Cioffi argues that "there is an implicit biographical reference in our response to literature. It is ... part of our concept of literature" and "the suspicion that a poetic effect is accidental is fatal to the enjoyment which literature characteristically offers" (1976: 66, 68).

In response to the arguments originally offered by Wimsatt and Beardsley, intentionalist critics have claimed that authors generally *do* say what they mean and mean what they say (they are in the business of communication, rather than deliberate obfuscation), and that the mental states of others *are* readable, to some extent, so intention is not absolutely private and inaccessible. Even if we cannot "consult the oracle," we can look at contextual information (such as diaries, letters, or other works by the author) which will tell us something about the author's intentions at the time of writing. (And in fact, as I have suggested, Wimsatt and Beardsley do not rule out such "intermediate," contextual evidence.)

In recent years intentionalist critics such as Gary Iseminger and William Irwin have sought to develop and expand upon Hirsch's arguments. Iseminger actually describes his approach as "Hirschian," as he claims that "if exactly one of two interpretive statements about a poem, each of which is compatible with its text, is true, then the true one is the one that applies to the meaning intended by the author" (1992: 78, 77). Irwin, meanwhile, develops a notion of "urinterpretation" that "seeks to capture the intention of the author, although not necessarily his understanding," and that involves an interrogation and reworking of Foucault's "author-function" (1999: 11).

Much anti-intentionalism has worked from the premise that intentionalism and formalism are incompatible, that an attention to the text's formal qualities precludes an acknowledgment of intention. Yet it is possible (as I have argued at some length in *Intention and Text*) to conceive of other variants of intention which do not attribute it to some extratextual author figure, but rather concentrate on the ways in which the text itself is "intentional"; so intentionalism doesn't have to be authorial intentionalism. In *Art and Intention*, Paisley Livingston (who describes himself as a "partial intentionalist") concludes that he hopes to keep intention "on the research agenda in aesthetics" (2005: ix, 211); arguably, within the fields of literary criticism and theory, it has never really gone away.

SEE ALSO: Anglo-American New
Criticism; Barthes, Roland; Foucault, Michel

REFERENCES AND SUGGESTED
READINGS

Barthes, R. (1977). *Image, Music, Text*. London: Fontana Press.

Beardsley, M. C. (1970). *The Possibility of Criticism*. Detroit: Wayne State University Press.

Beardsley, M. C. (1982). Intentions and interpretations: A fallacy revived. In M. J. Wreen & D. M. Callan (eds.), *The Aesthetic Point of View: Selected Essays*. Ithaca: Cornell University Press, pp. 188–207.

Cioffi, F. (1976). Intention and interpretation in criticism. In D. Newton-de-Molina (ed.), *On Literary Intention*. Edinburgh: Edinburgh University Press, pp. 55–73.

Foucault, M. (1977). What is an author? In D. F. Bouchard (ed. and trans.), *Language, Counter-Memory, Practice*. Ithaca: Cornell University Press, pp. 139–164.

Hirsch, E. D. (1967). *Validity in Interpretation*. New Haven: Yale University Press.

Hirsch, E. D. (1976). *The Aims of Interpretation*. Chicago: Chicago University Press.

Irwin, W. (1999). *Intentionalist Interpretation: A Philosophical Explanation and Defence*. Westport, CT: Greenwood.

Iseminger, G. (1992). *Intention and Interpretation*. Philadelphia: Temple University Press.

Lewis, C. S., & Tillyard, E. M. W. (1939). *The Personal Heresy: A Controversy*. Oxford: Oxford University Press.

Livingston, P. (2005). *Art and Intention*. Oxford: Clarendon.

Mitchell, K. (2008). *Intention and Text: Towards an Intentionality of Literary Form*. London: Continuum.

Sparshott, F. E. (1976). Criticism and performance. In D. Newton-de-Molina (ed.), *On Literary Intention*. Edinburgh: Edinburgh University Press, pp. 104–115.

Wimsatt, W. K. (1968). Genesis: An argument resumed. In *Day of the Leopards (1976)*. New Haven: Yale University Press, pp. 11–39.

Wimsatt, W. K., & Beardsley, M. C. (1954). The affective fallacy. In *The Verbal Icon: Studies in the Meaning of Poetry*. Lexington: University Press of Kentucky, pp. 221–32.

Wimsatt, W. K., & Beardsley, M. (1962). The intentional fallacy. In J. Margolis (ed.), *Philosophy Looks at the Arts*. New York: Scribner's, pp. 91–105. (Original essay published 1946.)

B

Badiou, Alain

ALEX MURRAY

The work of Alain Badiou (b. 1937) has emerged as one of the most innovative and comprehensive philosophical projects in postwar France. Badiou's work is characterized by a desire to bring about the "return of philosophy itself." By this Badiou means to introduce an understanding of both subjectivity and ontology, which seeks its foundation in a return to the basic question of philosophy: What is being? Yet this is not done in the name of some sort of analytic formalism, but for largely political ends. Badiou's Maoist heritage and his commitment to a radical collective politics are never far from the surface. He is not simply an academic philosopher and he routinely engages in French and world politics in an accessible and polemical manner, including an introductory book on *Ethics* (2000 [1993]) and *The Meaning of Sarkozy* (2008b) in which he provides a historicization and anatomization of the Sarkozy phenomenon.

Badiou's research is, to a large extent, driven by the twin problems of ontology and subjectivity. If his work is underpinned by the exploration of mathematics as ontology, it has been in order to explore the problem of the subject of politics. In Badiou's magnum opus, *Being and Event* (2005[1988]), and the second volume *Logics of Worlds* (2008a[2006]), he outlines how, through an articulation of a set theoretical understanding of mathematics, there is within the structure of the universe an underlying potential for transformation which becomes his theory of the subject. Badiou in doing this is neither an analytic philosopher, nor a poststructuralist thinker, but instead attempts to outline a new way of suturing what he sees as the erroneous divisions between the two. He argues that a way to truth can be seen in the four generic conditions of truth that have been severed in twentieth-century thought: love (in particular, the work of Lacan), science (in particular, the mathematics of set theory), art (in particular, modern poetry from Hölderlin and Mallarmé to Celan), and politics (in particular the events of May '68).

Badiou's claim is that philosophy needs to think these four conditions together, and that the way to do this is through the equation mathematics = ontology. Set theory is one of the most important branches of contemporary mathematics, providing something like a metalanguage for mathematics, with any mathematical question being subsumed in set theory. It is not possible to go into Badiou's use of it here, but suffice it to say that Badiou utilizes set theory as it provides him with an innovative means of formalizing ontological questions: he can present ontological questions as set-theoretical equations. This means that he can take features of set theory – namely inconsistent multiplicity and the void – and import them into ontological discussions. This allows him to posit two important claims: that there is something within a given situation that is not limited to the situation, and that there is always a nothing that is both included in the situation yet does not participate in the situation.

While the theoretical apparatus that underpins Badiou's thought is complex, its outcomes are somewhat easier to grasp. The "situation" is the basic name Badiou gives to experience in its broadest sense, or to utilize the mathematical expression they are "indifferent multiplicities." Each situation is a presentation of these multiplicities but that does not mean that it is anything more – there can never be any truth that emerges from a situation. Just because one situation (capitalism and "parliamentarism") is dominant doesn't mean that it is "right" or that it is universal. That there is a void that underpins and escapes the situation means that there is always something within the situation that has the potential to rupture it. Badiou gives this truth the name "event." The event means that philosophy is not to be found in the exploration of structures, as so much of twentieth-century thought has been, but in "emergence," which is incalculable.

So for Badiou the emergence of the event is the basis of subjectivity: a subject must have "fidelity" to the event. So subjectivity is not limited to the conditions of the situation, but must emerge as a militant to the truth of the event. These "militants" can exist not just in politics, but also in any of the generic truth procedures – love, science, art, and politics. It may be useful here to look at some examples to ground our dis-

cussion. St. Paul often stands as Badiou's epitome of the political militant. Badiou locates St. Paul in the legal, racial, and religious conditions of his own situation. Paul begins life as a Roman citizen, a Pharisaic Jew, and an active persecutor of Christians, firmly entrenched in his particular cultural, social, ethnic, and religious hegemony. Then in the year 34 or 35 BC, while traveling on the road to Damascus, he sees a divine apparition and is converted to Christianity. From that moment on Paul pledges his life to becoming a missionary for the nascent religion. For Badiou, the event of Christ's resurrection is a truth-event, and Paul, in experiencing that event and maintaining fidelity to it, undergoes a process of subjectivization, the becoming of the subject.

Another model for Badiou's understanding of fidelity is that of Samuel Beckett. Beckett's work has long been understood to epitomize a modern nihilism, a lack of faith in any possible structure. Yet Badiou refuses to accept that there is despair in Beckett; instead he sees in his work the struggle to maintain fidelity to the event of nothingness. Badiou argues that Beckett's work is about courage, resistance, and action in an indifferent world and that Beckett's poetic fidelity to the event of nothing is a serious and deeply political gesture. Here we see how Badiou is able to transform a writer/artist through an incorporation into his own critical framework, and his *Handbook of Inaesthetics* (2004) offers several examples of his radical rereadings beyond the strictly philosophical.

Badiou's work offers one of the most comprehensive attempts to rethink philosophy since Heidegger and a series of interventions in debates from science to poetics that has as its ultimate goal an awakening of the transformative potential of the present through an understanding of the truth of the event.

SEE ALSO: Deleuze, Gilles; Marxism;
Psychoanalysis (since 1966); Subject Position;
Žižek, Slavoj

REFERENCES AND SUGGESTED
READINGS

Badiou, A. (1999). *Manifesto for Philosophy* (trans.
N. Madarsz). Albany, NY: SUNY Press. (Ori-
ginal work published 1989.)
Badiou, A. (2000). *Ethics: An Essay on the Under-
standing of Evil* (trans. P. Hallward). London:
Verso. (Original work published 1993.)
Badiou, A. (2003a). *Infinite Thought: Truth and the
Return to Philosophy* (trans. and ed. O. Feltham &
J. Clemens). London: Continuum.
Badiou, A. (2003b). *Saint Paul: The Foundation of
Universalism* (trans. R. Brassier). Stanford: Stan-
ford University Press. (Original work published
1997.)
Badiou, A. (2004). *Handbook of Inaesthetics* (trans.
A. Toscano). Stanford: Stanford University
Press. (Original work published 1998.)
Badiou, A. (2005). *Being and Event* (trans. O.
Feltham). London: Continuum. (Original
work published 1988.)
Badiou, A. (2008a). *Logics of Worlds: Being and
Event*, vol 2 (trans. A. Toscano). New York:
Continuum. (Original work published 2006.)
Badiou, A. (2008b). *The Meaning of Sarkozy* (trans.
D. Fernbach). New York: Verso. (Original work
published 2007.)

Bakhtinian Criticism

KEN HIRSCHKOP

Mikhail Bakhtin (1895–1975) was a
twentieth-century Russian philosopher
turned literary critic and theorist. After
the devastation of World War I and the
drama of the Russian Revolution – he was
22 at the time of the latter – Bakhtin
embarked on a search for a new basis for
moral and ethical life. At first he believed
that the key to making ethical life more
compelling and central was philosophy.
Only through a new ethical philosophy
could one demonstrate that sympathy
and ethical action revolved around an in-
eradicable distance between ourselves and
others, a distance that, once acknowledged,
would lead us to appreciate our need for
others and their need for us. But although
Bakhtin would continue to write philosophically throughout his life, from the
mid-1920s onward he began to rework
this argument as a theory of language
and literature, in which "novelistic discourse," rather than philosophy, became
the means by which Europe would regain
its moral and political bearings. In the
course of writing three books, drafts for
several essays, and many, many notebooks
– only a few of his works were finished
during his lifetime – Bakhtin argued for the
power of three elements of this novelistic
discourse: its dialogical language, its carnivalesque imagery, and its chronotopic
narrative. Each of these, in its own way,
contributed to a deep-seated transformation in our sense of the world and our
relations, ethical and political, with others.

Dialogical language acknowledged in its
style that feelings, ideologies, and attitudes
were never expressed directly, but always at
a distance, by the reuse and orchestration of
existing ways of speaking and writing, with
all the contextual flavor and ideological
baggage they carried with them. Carnivalesque imagery destroyed the sphere of sacred spaces and objects, bringing people and
things into a "zone of familiar contact," in
which the pressure of social roles was suspended, hierarchies turned topsy-turvy, and
all was submitted to cycles of perpetual
transformation. Chronotopic narratives
presented the world not as a neutral
backdrop – a society, an environment, a
situation, a sequence of historical events –
within which a heroic protagonist must
act, but as something itself in the process
of "becoming" at the point of possible
transformation.

Together these novelistic techniques transformed a world that had overvalued the past, stood in awe of the sacred, and found itself dominated by the declamatory and bombastic style of "official seriousness." Novelistic discourse, drawing on energies and genres nurtured in popular culture, would make a world fit for those willing to embrace its historical, transitory nature. Bakhtin couched this argument in language that was alternately literary-critical, religious, and political. There were secular forces – variously called the epic, monologism, the poetic – that clearly stood in the way of the novel's project; but his language also touched on problems that were the fate of frail and mortal creatures as such. As a consequence, there has been constant and vigorous dispute over the meaning of Bakhtin's work, which itself seems plagued by ambiguity.

In ordinary circumstances, one could look at the history of a writer's life and at his or her own testimony to resolve such ambiguities. Unfortunately, ordinary circumstances are thin on the ground in the case of Bakhtin. Because his life spans some of the most dramatic and violent events of the twentieth century he found himself, both personally and intellectually, constantly reacting to the sudden and pressing changes of circumstance. Hardly any of his work, therefore, was written or published without an element of calculation and censorship, and research has shown that even Bakhtin himself was not above playing fast and loose with facts when he thought it useful to do so. If the brutal history of the twentieth century left its scars on his work, these remain unhealed even to the present day.

A COMPLICATED LIFE,
A COMPLICATED LEGACY

Bakhtin was born in 1895 to a middle-class Russian family. He moved away from his family in 1914, going to Petrograd, probably to be with his older brother Nikolai (who would later become an academic linguist and classicist in England and a noted friend of Wittgenstein's). After the Russian Revolution, Bakhtin followed the lead of many in search of a more secure existence, moving to the provincial cities of Nevel and Vitebsk, respectively. There he become part of a circle of intellectuals interested in literature and philosophy, which included the pianist Mariia Iudina, the philosophers Lev Pumpianskii and Matvei Kagan, the critic Pavel Medvedev, the then musicologist Valentin Voloshinov, and I. I. Sollertinsky, later director of the Leningrad Philharmonic. Returning to Leningrad in 1924, Bakhtin inevitably became embroiled in the intense debates then taking place over what the culture and literature of a revolutionizing society should look like. His first attempt to contribute in print to this discussion was, however, ominously unsuccessful: a detailed philosophical critique of Russian formalism was accepted by an important journal that was forcibly closed by the Communist Party before the issue with Bakhtin's article appeared (the article was finally published 50 years later). In 1929, Bakhtin published the book, *Problems in Dostoevsky's Art*; but he had been arrested in December of 1928 on the charge of belonging to a counter-revolutionary religious organization. A campaign waged on his behalf (which included support from prominent authors like Maxim Gorky), a favorable review of his book by Anatoly Lunacharsky, then head of the powerful Commissariat of Enlightenment, and Bakhtin's severe osteomyelitis, ensured that his sentence was reduced from time in a labor camp to a period of exile in a rural town.

After serving his six-year term of exile, Bakhtin took up a post at a teaching institute in Saransk, Mordovia, only to have to leave it in 1937 to escape the wrath of the Stalinist purges that were sweeping through the institutions of Soviet society. He spent the war years in and around Moscow, all the while managing to write and defend a dissertation on Rabelais. He returned to Saransk in 1946 and led a relatively peaceful existence as a relatively obscure university professor until 1961, when his work was rediscovered by postgraduate students in Moscow. They vigorously promoted his rehabilitation ands revival as a public figure, and in 1963 a revised version of his book on Dostoevsky was published, to be followed by a revised version of the Rabelais dissertation in 1965. In the years that followed, Bakhtin became a venerated figure, whose past and work remained, nevertheless, somewhat mysterious. Many of his unpublished essays and notebooks, including substantial fragments of an unfinished work of philosophy from the 1920s, finally made it into print.

There were also more controversial additions to the Bakhtin canon. Beginning in 1970 a campaign was waged to have Bakhtin recognized as the author of a series of works published under the names of his friends, I. I. Kanaev (a short article on vitalism), V. N. Voloshinov (the books *Freudianism* and *Marxism and the Philosophy of Language*, and an article) and P. N. Medvedev (*The Formal Method in Literary Scholarship* and the articles that preceded it). The campaign was officially successful in the then Soviet Union, although the evidence for Bakhtin's authorship was limited to reports of conversations with Bakhtin, in which he was said to have admitted writing the so-called "disputed texts." These claims were treated skeptically outside the Soviet Union (and eventually by many inside as well) and research revealed a number of occasions on which Bakhtin denied authorship or refused to assert it in writing, as well as plans and drafts for the works written by Voloshinov and Medvedev themselves.

With Bakhtin's death in 1975 (Voloshinov died in 1936 of tuberculosis and Medvedev was murdered in the purges in 1938), final resolution was doomed, but even those originally committed to Bakhtin's authorship have now hedged their bets considerably.

The dispute over these texts, however, is actually no more than a skirmish in the larger struggle to define the meaning of Bakhtin's legacy. Generally speaking, those who assert Bakhtin's authorship claim he was a religiously inspired philosopher who, at some point after his failure to publish in 1924, decided to translate his concerns into an idiom (Marxist linguistics and literary theory) acceptable to the Soviet authorities. According to this interpretation, Bakhtin's works from 1926 onward should be read as coded discussions of religious and philosophical themes. On the other hand, those suspicious of Bakhtin's claim to authorship tend to see the transformation of his work as inspired by a genuine interest in the literary and linguistic work of his friends and those around him, and they regard the shift of interest and emphasis as ultimately productive. This dispute has, unfortunately, bled into the editorial preparation and publication of Bakhtin's texts, many of which are unreliable, either because references to religion have been deleted owing to Soviet censorship, because references that appear overtly communist have been deleted by those who see them as concessions to the Stalinist dogma of the time, or because reference to foreign scholars have been deleted owing to the Russian chauvinism of editors (such as the deletion of footnotes to German Jewish scholars in the famous essay "Discourse in the novel"). That, excepting the three books published in his lifetime, all of Bakhtin's works are either fragments of uncompleted works, notebooks, or drafts for essays, means that editors have an even greater role than usual in putting together printed, final versions of Bakhtin's work.

THE PROJECT FOR AN ETHICAL PHILOSOPHY (1918–1926)

Of Bakhtin's original project for a grand ethical philosophy several long fragments remain: an introduction titled (by the editors, not Bakhtin himself) "Towards a philosophy of the act," a draft of a long chapter devoted to aesthetics titled "Author and hero in aesthetic activity," notes to two lectures from a series with nearly the same title and a lecture on religion, all delivered in 1924. In these texts, Bakhtin argues that our experience of human life is inevitably and irrevocably split. On the one hand, we perceive our own ideas and feelings as necessarily unfinished and aimed forward, with no possible end in sight; on the other, we experience the ideas and feelings of others as bounded by a context or a background, as part of a physical, creaturely world. When we understand or sympathize with others, therefore, we do not translate their feelings or thought into the categories of our own experience: we understand them by responding in a distanced, sympathetic fashion. If, for instance, another is in pain, understanding means not re-experiencing the pain, but comforting or helping the other who is suffering.

Acknowledging this division was the basis for all genuine responsibility and moral action. We would realize that from within our own resources no sort of satisfaction or conclusion was possible: for that we relied on others, who, in their turn, depended on the charity we extended them by virtue of our "outsidedness" in relation to them. Within this schema, the artwork occupied a privileged position, for there the author achieved a kind of synthesis or balancing between the inner energies of the hero and the author's ability to represent them as part of a creaturely "external" world.

TURN TO THE NOVEL AND THE DIALOGICAL THEORY OF LANGUAGE (1927–1936)

When composing the book *Problems of Dostoevsky's Art*, Bakhtin reframed the problem. To be precise, he reframed it twice. In the first half of the book, the ethical relationship between *I* and *other* is described as the relationship Dostoevsky crafts between the author and the hero. In his prose writings, Bakhtin claims, Dostoevsky found the formal means to represent the hero not as an object or function of the plot, but as a voice with rights equal to those of the author. In the second half of the book, this formal achievement was described as a matter of style: Dostoevsky's discourse was not monological, putting heroes and situations in their place, but dialogical or doubly directed. It had a dual, ambivalent meaning, depending on both the frame of the work as a whole (the author) and the resistant and independent intentions of the hero.

Although this was portrayed as an artistic innovation of Dostoevsky's, Bakhtin anchored dialogism in a philosophy of language he was to develop extensively over the next 45 years. Its fundamental claim was that phenomena like parody, irony, stylization, and the strategic use of language types drawn from other written genres or distinct social groups were all instances of a dialogical orientation toward language. This dialogical orientation understood language not as a tool for the expression of an ego's feelings or intentions, but as an ocean full of the expressions of *others*, at once creaturely – in the sense that they often had distinctive external forms (manifested in spelling, accent, syntax, and so on) – and spiritual, in the sense that each embodied a distinctive point or view or ideology (in the neutral sense of that term). The writer or speaker whose expressions exploited this dialogism created utterances that were "double-voiced," in which one could sense both the original source language and the new – perhaps critical, perhaps not – inflection given to it by the speaker.

Bakhtin's next step was to broaden his argument in dramatic fashion. In what may be his most important essay, "Discourse in the novel" (1934–5) and in a series of shorter essays on the novel written between 1940 and 1945, Bakhtin made dialogism a central feature of novelistic discourse as such, and made novelistic discourse the representative of both modernity itself and its democratic aspirations. From here until the end of his life he associated the denial of dialogism with "official seriousness" and the representatives of repressive institutions and structures. By contrast, the source of dialogical energy was said to be a "heteroglossia," a world of double-voiced, skeptical, and distanced language, that flourished in everyday life and was concentrated in the lower, popular genres of writing and speech.

CHRONOTOPE AND CARNIVAL (1937–1951)

Having identified dialogism with not just Dostoevsky in particular, but with the novel as a radically new kind of writing, Bakhtin went on to elaborate on the novel's other distinctive features and talents. In the mid-1930s he began work on a study of the Bildungsroman (the novel of education or maturation) and of Goethe as its culmination. His argument was that one can witness, from the advent of the ancient Greek novel onward, a gradual change in the way prose represented the intersection of time and space. Whereas in older forms space was rendered as a neutral background

for the adventures and exploits of the hero, and time seemed to have no developmental aspect, artistic prose gradually wove time and space together in an intricate "chronotope," such that each began to exert a kind of forward pressure or movement on the action represented. Space became localized and concrete, and began to carry with it the marks of time; time acquired a irreversible momentum orientated first and foremost to moments of transition and transformation.

In the drafts that have been collected and published as "The Bildungsroman and its significance for the history of realism" Bakhtin described how the hero of artistic prose evolved from a static model, to a collection of traits gradually revealed, and finally to a protagonist that found itself transformed under the pressure of experience; after which, the developing force of the hero itself spread outward into the world beyond it, which became a place never settled in its ways, always poised on the brink of possible change. But Bakhtin cleverly switched horses when it was time to flesh out this idea of a world constantly at the point of transition, exchanging Goethe for the extravagant world of Rabelais.

Initially content to describe Rabelais, too, as a master of the chronotope, Bakhtin quickly ditched this useful concept in favor of the idea of the carnivalesque. In a dissertation first completed in 1940, then revised several times until it was published as *François Rabelais and the Popular Culture and the Middle Ages and Renaissance* in 1965 (the English translation sports the shorter title *Rabelais and His World* [1984b]), Bakhtin presented Rabelais's grotesque, public square imagery as a sophistication of cultural forms derived from the popular culture of medieval and Renaissance Europe. Bakhtin argued that the form and style of Rabelais's imagery was drawn from what he called "festive-popular culture," the apogee of which was the celebration of carnival in the Christian calendar. This festive-popular culture, Bakhtin claimed, had been persistently misunderstood as no more than an opportunity for respite from the everyday toil and piety of medieval Europe, a carefree moment for letting off steam. What had been missed was what Bakhtin called the deep "philosophical" content of carnival and its associated culture, for carnival was not merely a time to relax but a complete alternative model of the world, inhabited by the popular classes on a regular basis.

This alternative world was permeated by a "culture of laughter," through which the individual gained distance not only from his or her individual fate, but from fatedness as such, from the conviction that the rules, roles, and hierarchies that structured medieval social life were permanent and enduring. During carnival, the high was made low, the spiritual was rendered in earthly form, and all rank and hierarchy was either suspended or explicitly reversed. The cycles of human and natural transformation and renewal, embodied in the seasons and the patterns of human birth and death, were applied to the matter of human society and history. Rabelais would take this imagery and spin it in a democratizing and progressive direction, making the emphasis on permanent transformation a weapon of sharp satire and of utopian vision.

THINKING OF THE HUMAN SCIENCES (1952–1975)

During the last 25 years of his life Bakhtin did not pursue an intensive study of literature. Instead, he developed the implications of his dialogical philosophy of language and considered its implications for the work of the human sciences in general. In the 1950s his principal works were two

articles, "The problem of speech genres" (1953) and "The problem of the text" (1959–60). The first of these suggested that we think of genre not only as a literary category, but as a category pertaining to all speech; the second carefully distinguished between a theory of language and a theory of discourse or utterance, in which the dialogical aspect of language, its status as a response, would be the paramount consideration. In these works and the texts that followed until his death, the combative and militant tone typical of his writing on the novel seemed to recede.

If drama receded from the works, though, it intervened in the life. While Bakhtin was living a quiet life in Saransk, three postgraduate students in Moscow had discovered his work in the library. They went to visit him and from then on two of them, Sergei Bocharov and Vadim Kozhinov, devoted themselves to the dissemination of Bakhtin's work and to his rehabilitation in Soviet life. In these last years Bakhtin became well known not just within the Soviet Union, but also internationally.

His writings in these last years consists of notes and jottings, most of a general and philosophical character, devoted to further describing dialogical relations, the role of the dialogical author, and the nature of human responsibility. Some of these were selected by Bocharov and Kozhinov and published as "Notes from 1970–1971" (a misleading title, as it turned out) and "Towards a methodology of the human sciences."

After Bakhtin's death in 1975, previously unpublished texts finally made it into print and information about his life began to be made public, although much of it, as noted above, turned out to be false or dubious. In the 1990s work began on a properly edited, comprehensive *Collected Works*. At the time of writing, five volumes of the expected seven have been published.

LEGACY AND APPLICATIONS

The concepts of dialogism, chronotope, carnival, and outsidedness translate large philosophical concerns into the language of literary analysis. As a consequence, they have a certain grandeur and an enviable range of application. The wide variety of scholars who adopted Bakhtin as their own testifies to just how fluidly these concepts could be applied. Concepts like dialogism and the chronotope have been used to analyze not only literary texts from the Bible to postmodern fiction, but also historical texts, classical and popular music, visual art, digital media, and a number of popular traditions. Bakhtin's vivid account of the philosophy of carnival itself led to a broad and deep reconsideration of the meaning of carnival practices around the world, past and present.

But perhaps even more striking has been the multiplicity of approaches which have seen Bakhtin as an ally or as theoretical ballast for their method. Originally described as formalist or structuralist, Bakhtin soon found himself taken on by critics who saw him as a humanist alternative to structuralism, by proponents of psychoanalytic and poststructuralist approaches like Kristeva, by postcolonial critics, feminists, and Marxist writers.

SEE ALSO: Carnival/Carnivalesque; Kristeva, Julia; Poststructuralism

REFERENCES AND SUGGESTED READINGS

Bakhtin, M. M. (1981). *The Dialogic Imagination: Four Essays* (trans. C. Emerson & M. Holquist). Austin: University of Texas Press. (Original work published 1975.)

Bakhtin, M. M. (1984a). *Problems of Dostoevsky's Poetics* (trans. C. Emerson). Manchester: Manchester University Press. (Original work published 1963.)

Bakhtin, M. M. (1984b). *Rabelais and His World* (trans. H. Iswolsky). Bloomington: Indiana University Press. (Original work published 1965.)

Bakhtin, M. M. (1986). *Speech Genres and Other Late Essays* (trans. V. W. McGee). Austin: University of Texas Press. (Original work published 1979.)

Bakhtin, M. M. (1990). *Art and Answerability: Early Philosophical Essays by M. M. Bakhtin* (ed. M. Holquist & V. Liapunov; trans. V. Liapunov). Austin: University of Texas Press. (Original works published 1975, 1979.)

Bakhtin, M. M. (1993). *Toward a Philosophy of the Act* (trans. V. Liapunov). Austin: University of Texas Press. (Original work published 1986.)

Bakhtin, M. M. (1996). *Sobranie Sochinenii. Tom 5: Raboty 1940x–Nachala 1960x* [Collected Works. Vol. 5: Works from the 1940s–early 1960s]. Moscow: Russkie Slovari.

Bakhtin, M. M. (2000). *Sobranie Sochinenii. Tom 2: Problemy Tvorchestva Dostoevskogo, 1929. Stat'i o Tol'stom, 1929. Zapisi Kursa Lektsii Po Istorii Russkoi Literatury, 1922–1927* [Collected Works. Vol. 2: Problems of Dostoevsky's Art, 1929. Articles on Tolstoy, 1929. Notes for the Course of Lectures on the History of Russian Literature, 1922–1927]. Moscow: Russkie Slovari.

Bakhtin, M. M. (2002). *Sobranie Sochinenii. Tom 6: Problemy poetiki Dostoevskogo, 1963. Raboty 1960x–1970x* [Collected Works. Vol. 6: Problems of Dostoevsky's Poetics, 1963. Works of the 1960s and 1970s]. Moscow: Russkie Slovari.

Bakhtin, M. M. (2003). *Sobranie Sochinenii. Tom 1: Filosofskaia Estetika 1920x Godov* [Collected Works. Vol. 1: Philosophical Aesthetics of the 1920s]. Moscow: Russkie Slovari.

Bakhtin, M. M. (2008). *Sobranie Sochinenii. Tom 4(1): Fransua Rable v Istorii Realizma (1940 g.). Materialy k Knige o Rable (1930–1950 gg.). Kommentarii i Prilozheniia* [Collected Works. Vol. 4(1): François Rabelais in the History of Realism (1940). Materials for the Book on Rabelais (1930s–1950s). Commentary and Addenda.] Moscow: Russkie Slovari.

Brandist, C. (2002). *The Bakhtin Circle: Philosophy, Culture, Politics*. London: Pluto.

Clark, K., & Holquist, M. (1984). *Mikhail Bakhtin*. Cambridge, MA: Belknap.

Emerson, C., & Morson, G. S. (1990). *Mikhail Bakhtin: The Creation of a Prosaics*. Palo Alto, CA: Stanford University Press.

Hirschkop, K. (1999). *Mikhail Bakhtin: An Aesthetic for Democracy*. Oxford: Oxford University Press.

Kristeva, J. (1973). The ruin of a poetics. In S. Bann & J. E. Bowlt (eds.), *Russian Formalism*. Edinburgh: Scottish Academic Press, pp. 102–119.

de Man, Paul (1983). Dialogue and dialogism. *Poetics Today*, 4(1), 99–107.

Medvedev, P. N. (1991) *The Formal Method in Literary Scholarship: A Critical Introduction to Sociological Poetics* (trans. A. J. Wehrle). Baltimore: Johns Hopkins University Press. (Original work published 1928.)

Stallybrass, P., & White, A. (1986). *The Politics and Poetics of Transgression*. London: Methuen.

Stam, R. (1989). *Subversive Pleasures: Bakhtin, Cultural Criticism, and Film*. Baltimore: Johns Hopkins University Press.

Tihanov, G. (2000). *The Master and the Slave: Lukács, Bakhtin and the Ideas of Their Time*. Oxford: Clarendon.

Todorov, T. (1984). *Mikhail Bakhtin: The Dialogical Principle* (trans. W. Godzich). Manchester: Manchester University Press.

Voloshinov, V. N. (1986). *Marxism and the Philosophy of Language* (trans. I. R. Titunik & L. Matejka). Cambridge, MA: Harvard University Press. (Original work published 1929.)

Voloshinov, V. N. (1987). *Freudianism: A Critical Sketch* (trans. I. R. Titunik). Bloomington: Indiana University Press. (Original work published 1927.)

Bal, Mieke

JOE HUGHES

Mieke Bal (b. 1946) is a European scholar of literature and culture who specializes in narrative theory. Her writing is thoroughly interdisciplinary and ranges from literature to visual culture to theology and biblical studies. She has been particularly influential in defining the fields of narratology and cultural analysis. Her early work in narratology informed much of her later work in visual culture, cultural analysis, and what she "somewhat halfheartedly" called "postmodern theology" (2006: xix). It was largely through the conceptual structures developed in *Narratology* (1985[1980]) that Bal began to study non-literary objects.

Like the French literary theorist Gérard Genette, Bal took a rigorously systematic approach to narratology. The system is organized around a distinction, originally Genette's, but here more fully developed and more systematically followed, between three narrative levels: fabula, story, and text. A fabula consists of the basic elements of a narrative text – for example, objects, events, actors, and the chronological and logical relations between them. "Story" refers to the specific ways in which these things and people are viewed. Events may be placed in a non-chronological or alogical sequence, for example. Actors become characters, or specific, human-like individuals. All things, people, and events become "focalized" or seen through a certain character's mode of perception. The last level, that of the text, is the level of the words themselves, the set of "linguistic signs" through which the story is told. Here objects are described in specific ways and, most importantly, the story is narrated.

In addition to simplifying and systematizing Genette's narratology, Bal influentially revised the notion of focalization. Genette distinguished between two types of focalization – internal and external – according to the "knowledge" a focalizer has of its objects (1980: 189). Bal argued that the "functional difference" between internal focalization and external focalization is not a matter of knowledge and its degrees of restriction, but is grounded, rather, in a subject–object distinction. In internal focalization we see the particular, imperceptible opinions of the subject; in external focalization we see a perceptible field of objects (2006: 19).

In *Narratology*, Bal had used a *bas-relief* to explain the concept of focalization – ostensibly to demonstrate that focalization, unlike narration, is nonlinguistic and thus does not belong to the level of the text (1985 [1980]: 103). But this formula is easily reversed: if a drawing could exemplify focalization, focalization and other narratological concepts could equally explain visual phenomena. All those concepts which were not tied to the level of the "text" were capable of "traveling" to other fields of inquiry. As Kaja Silverman (2008) has pointed out, the concept of focalization informed Bal's earliest engagements with visual culture, and in works like *Reading Rembrandt* (1991) and *Quoting Caravaggio* (1999c), Bal both extended narratological concepts to visual art and began developing a repertoire of new, interdisciplinary concepts. One of the more important of these is the notion of a "preposterous history," a concept which extends narratological concepts (anachronism and frame) to historical problems. A preposterous history emphasizes the ways in which the present rediscovers or reinterprets the past, but in doing so allows the past to reshape the present.

Bal was a founding director of one of the major institutional homes of cultural studies: the Amsterdam School of Cultural Analysis. This attention to the complex interaction between past and present – the ways in which the present reshapes the past and the ways in which the past shapes the present – is one of the distinctive features of her conception of cultural analysis. Cultural analysis is not simply the study of everything in our world that is not "high" culture. In her introduction to *The Practice of Cultural Analysis*, she explains:

> Cultural analysis as a critical practice is different from what is commonly understood as "history." It is based on a keen awareness of the critic's situatedness in the present, the social and cultural present from which we look and look back, at the objects that are always already of the past, objects that we take to define our present culture. ... Far from being indifferent to history, cultural analysis problematizes history's silent assumptions in order to come to an understanding of the pas that is different. This understanding is not based on an attempt to isolate and enshrine the past in an objectivist "reconstruction" nor on an effort to project it on an evolutionist line. ... Instead, cultural analysis seeks to understand the past as *part of* the present, as what we have around us, and without which no culture would be able to exist. (1999a: 1; emphasis original)

We study culture, Bal argues, because we want to understand our world (2006: 391). This particular conception of a preposterous history allows us to understand the role of the past in the present. In order to come to terms with the present, however, we need to reach beyond disciplinary boundaries. Throughout Bal's work, there is a constant and careful attention to interdisciplinary methodology, and in her retrospective introduction to *A Mieke Bal Reader*, she identified as the unifying thread throughout her work the concept of the concept.

As early as *Narratology* Bal described a theory as a "systematic set of generalized statements about a particular segment of reality" (1985[1980]: 3). These "generalized statements," concepts, help us describe certain phenomena by providing a common or social (and therefore both political and pedagogical) framework for discussion. They organize phenomena. They determine what questions we ask of phenomena. They structure our observations about them. They do all this, further, without pretending to exhaust or represent the thing they help describe. For all these reasons, it is imperative that we are absolutely clear and rigorous about the nature and extension of our concepts. Later, Bal refined this picture, placing less emphasis on the requirement of systematicity (concepts are "miniature theories" [2006: xxii]) and by arguing that the relationship between concept and object is, at root, metaphorical. A metaphor asks us to compare two terms according to a ground, and this has several consequences: it brings out something both new and specific in the objects compared and it places them in new frames of references. In the same way, theoretical concepts are not meant to coincide with the object they help describe. They pull out new aspects of the object and introduce it into a new frame of reference (Bal 1994). By insisting on the generality of concepts and their heuristic rather than representative function, Bal is able to treat concepts as specific but at the same time nomadic, capable of "traveling" from one discipline to another (2002).

SEE ALSO: Cultural Studies; Genette, Gérard; Narratology and Structuralism

REFERENCES AND SUGGESTED READING

Bal, M. (1985). *Narratology: Introduction to the Theory of Narrative* (trans. C. van Boheemen). Toronto: University of Toronto Press.
Bal, M. (1991). *Reading Rembrandt: Beyond the Word–Image Opposition*. New York: Cambridge University Press.
Bal, M. (1994). Scared to death. In M. Bal & I. E. Boer (eds.), *The Point of Theory: Practices of Cultural Analysis*. New York: Continuum.
Bal, M. (1999a). Introduction. In *The Practice of Cultural Analysis: Exposing Interdisciplinary Interpretation*. Stanford: Stanford University Press.
Bal, M. (1999b). Memories in the museum: Preposterous histories for today. In *Acts of Memory: Cultural Recall in the Present*. Hanover, NH: University Press of New England.
Bal, M. (1999c). *Quoting Caravaggio: Contemporary Art, Preposterous History*. Chicago: University of Chicago Press.
Bal, M. (2002). *Travelling Concepts in the Humanities: A Rough Guide*. Toronto: University of Toronto Press.
Bal, M. (2006). *A Mieke Bal Reader*. Chicago: University of Chicago Press.
Cherry, D. (ed.) (2008). *About Mieke Bal*. Oxford: Wiley-Blackwell.
Genette, G. (1980). *Narrative Discourse: An Essay in Method* (trans. J. E. Lewin). Ithaca: Cornell University Press.
Silverman, K. (2008). Je vous. In D. Cherry (ed.), *About Mieke Bal*. Oxford: Wiley-Blackwell.

Bhabha, Homi

ANKHI MUKHERJEE

Homi K. Bhabha is a foundational figure for postcolonial theory. He was born in Bombay, India, in 1949, educated at the University of Bombay and Christ Church, Oxford, and is at present Professor of the Humanities in the Department of English and American Literature at Harvard University.

Bhabha's most significant book, arguably, is *The Location of Culture*, a collection of writings published in 1994, which includes definitive versions of his influential essays "The other question," "Of mimicry and man," "Signs taken for wonders," and "DissemiNation." *Nation and Narration*, edited by Bhabha, is another central text in his oeuvre, containing a variety of contributions on national narratives. "Foreword: Remembering Fanon: Self, psyche, and the colonial condition," Bhabha's 1986 introduction to the Pluto edition of Frantz Fanon's *Black Skin, White Masks*, played a key role in the 1980s revival of Fanon's work and in the resurgence of critical appropriations of Fanon in the academy, which Henry Louis Gates, Jr., (1991) has termed "critical Fanonism." Bhabha is also the author of several influential critical articles, such as "At the Limits" (1989), a commentary on the aftermath of Salman Rushdie's *Satanic Verses*, "Queen's English" (1997), a study of hybridized speech, "Cosmopolitanisms" (2000), on the pluralistic nature of cosmopolitanism, and "Adagio" (2005), a reflection on the legacy of Edward Said.

Bhabha's work has provided many valuable conceptual leads and catchphrases to postcolonial theory: nation and narration, anticolonial agency, third space or the place of hybridity, ambivalence and uncanny doubles, mimicry, pedagogic and performative nationality. Bhabha formulates a postcolonial method that draws on high European theory – Sigmund Freud and Jacques Lacan, Hannah Arendt, M. M. Bakhtin, Jacques Derrida, Michel Foucault, to name the major influences – and teases and tests it in reappraisals of the phenomenon of colonialism and the quandaries of the postcolonial condition. Bhabha's theoretical formulations engage with literary texts (by Joseph Conrad, Henry James, V. S. Naipaul, Salman Rushdie, Toni Morrison, for example) as well as nonfiction writings by J. S. Mill, Frantz Fanon, and Charles Taylor. Bhabha writes in an eloquent and sometimes difficult style, and famously won the runner-up award in the 1998 "Bad Writing Competition" (from the journal *Philosophy and Literature*) for a line from *The Location of Culture*.

In "Signs taken for wonders," Bhabha examines the role of the English book in the perpetuation of English cultural rule. Bhabha argues that the fetishized English book – the sign taken for wonders, whether it is the Bible or a canonical text – is a site of colonial ambivalence. Bhabha provides two distinct and seemingly contradictory accounts of this ambivalence or "splitting" of the voice of authority. He argues that it is a constitutional undecidability in the very edicts of Englishness that makes possible anticolonial and postcolonial intervention and subversion: the colonized disarticulate the voice of the colonizer at the very point of its splitting. He also suggests, however, that

colonial ambivalence is invented when master texts are subjected to acts of repetition in the "dark unruly spaces of the earth." In "Of mimicry and man: The ambivalence of colonial discourse," Bhabha outlines his view of colonial mimicry as a discursive operation in which the excess produced by the *ambivalence* of mimicry – "almost the same, but *not quite*" – serves to undermine and make uncertain the totalizing discourses of the colonial system. Mimicry, Bhabha says, works like camouflage, not a repression of difference, but a form of resemblance that defers presence by displaying it partially and metonymically. Through his conceptualization of mimicry, Bhabha problematizes the old colonial relationship between a monolithic power and its faceless victims. Bhabha suggests instead that the colonial presence is always ambivalent, split between its appearance as deliberative and its articulation as repetition and difference. Bhabha illustrates this process by first noting the fetishistic marks of European cultural and disciplinary presence in the space of the colony – cricket fields, European clubs, colonial courts, theaters, mock Etons, the English book. The function of these "transparencies of authority," as Bhabha terms them, is not to satisfy the demands of European nostalgia but to exert a normalizing influence over the native, to re-form the African or Indian as a copy of the displaced European "original." This double exercise of power, which acts to authorize the European and civilize the native, gives rise to mimicry. The colonial disciplinary regime fails to produce allegories of Englishness and produces instability and hybridity instead, and colonial subjects "who are almost the same, but not quite, not white," "less than one and double." The colonist's identity is jeopardized by the emergence of the supplement and the counterfeit. The identity of the colonized, in turn, is not simply a mimesis of the European original, but a mask of mimicry that is more menace than resemblance.

Bhabha's terms of exegesis in *The Location of Culture* are "the arbitrariness of the sign, the indeterminacy of writing, [and] the splitting of the subject of enunciation" (1994a: 175–6). His concepts of mimicry and hybridity are a version of Derridean *différance*, the difference within binary terms that supersedes them: it is in the uncanny space between dominant cultural formations that Bhabha finds "the location of culture." Bhabha's organizing principle is a deconstruction of the "sign" and his particular emphasis is on the indeterminacy in cultural and political judgment. He seeks to move from what he calls the "pedagogical" aspect of cultural identifications (fixed, exclusive, discriminatory) to the "performative" aspect of the articulation of identities, or what he calls "the disruptive temporality of enunciation." Enunciation (meaning both speaking and performance) is the scene of creative heterogeneity, of differing and deferring: It is through the vicissitudes of enunciation that the borders between objects or subjects or practices are reconstituted. Bhabha identifies his critical task as postcolonial translation, which seizes upon the contradictory and ambivalent space of cultural statements. Postcolonial agency thus emerges as a politics of relocation and reinscription that rejoices in "representational undecidability."

Bhabha draws heavily on Jacques Lacan's ideas on mimicry in *The Four Fundamental Concepts of Psychoanalysis* (Lacan 1981) to conceptualize a colonial subject who is the same as the colonizer but different. The mimic man, not quite, not white, is a partial representation of the colonizer. Far from being reassured, the colonizer sees a grotesquely displaced image of himself: the familiar, transported to distant parts, becomes uncannily transformed. Bhabha undermines the model of mimicry that locates the other as a fixed phenomenological entity, opposed to the self. The subject of desire, according to Bhabha is never simply a "Myself," just as the Other is never simply an "It-self." In the foreword to Fanon's *Black Skin, White Masks* (Bhabha 1986), Bhabha turns Fanon's idea of the dualistic nature – black skin, white masks – of colonial pathology into an altogether philosophical meditation on the idea of Man as his alienated image, not self and other, but the alienated and othered self as inscribed in the complex of colonial identities. Bhabha lauds Fanon for putting the psychoanalytic question of the desire of the subject to the historical condition of colonial man, though he concedes that this insight into the ambivalences of identification in Fanon's early work is eventually sacrificed to the insurgent political need to name and frame the other in the language of colonial racism. Bhabha's psychoanalytic "remembering" – as distinct from a translation – of Fanon has been criticized as obscuring Fanon's paradigm of colonial condition as one of unmitigated antagonism between native and invader (Benita Parry) and repressing the Manichaean history of colonialism in favor of colonial ambivalence (Abdul Jan Mohamed). Bhabha's "misreading" of Fanon has been used by other commentators as a critical instance to highlight the gap between academic and political anticolonialism, and also between the expatriate postcolonial intellectual floating in global space, and the class- and ethnicity-bound, immobilized postcolonial with no access to interstitial or neutral ground.

Nation and Narration is a source book for postcolonial theory's ongoing interrogation of the idea of nation. Bhabha's unique contribution to the question of nation formation is to link nations with narratives of nations. In sharp contrast with ideas of the nation as a self-identical and consistent community that is untouched by the depredations of history, Bhabha proposes a "double narrative movement." He sees the nation as an object of a nationalist pedagogy, vested with the continuity and accumulated authority of its past, but also as subjects of a process of signification which denies that past history in live performances of a heterogeneous and processual identity. The pedagogic narratives of nationality are revised and rewritten by migrant and marginalized narratives. Bhabha documents how political solidarity is bestowed upon cultural difference and heterogeneous histories by the self-contained idea of nations: he also celebrates the "marks of difference" shored by destabilizing iterations of that idea.

Bhabha sees the distinction between theory and political practice dismantled in a liminal "third space." Theory, he argues in *The Location of Culture*, is not necessarily elitist and Eurocentric. Theory and politics are not disparate entities and are mobilized in the productive matrix of writing, which defines the social and makes it available for action. In an interview titled "The Third Space," Bhabha extends the idea of the third space to imply the opening up of a hybridized space – that allows new positions to emerge – in postcolonial revisions of colonial discourse. He locates the diasporic subject in the borderline place and disjunctive temporality of the third space. In the context of the clash of cultures brought about by the publication of *The Satanic Verses*, Bhabha reinforces Rushdie's vision of emergent social identities that do not respond to either "Islamic fundamentalists" or "Western literary modernists." These subjectivities do not draw upon a pure past or a holistic and unicultural present for authentication, but live in doubt, questioning, and a rich confusion of cultural imperatives. The boundary becomes the place where the terms of cultural engagement, whether antagonistic or collaborative, are continually negotiated and cultural hybridities that emerge in moments of historical transformation are authorized.

Bhabha's current work is around ideas of global citizenship and global discourse, and how aesthetic and ethical experiences influence cultural citizenship. It issues a call to "de-realize" or defamiliarize democracy, so that its occlusions and injustices can come to light, and the democratic ideal can be applied to "other" contexts. In the essay "Democracy de-realized," Bhabha also anticipates a cosmopolitanism "outside the box of European intellectual history," one that privileges circumferences as well as centers, and gives rise to global citizenship. The territorial location of global citizenship, Bhabha says, is "postnational, denational or transnational," and such a community is best constituted through feelings of fragmentedness ("partiality") and through a shared historical sense of transitional time.

SEE ALSO: Bakhtin, M. M.; Derrida, Jacques; Fanon, Frantz; Foucault, Michel; Freud, Sigmund; Gates, Henry Louis; Lacan, Jacques; Postcolonial Studies and Diaspora Studies; Said, Edward

REFERENCES AND SUGGESTED READINGS

Bhabha, H. K. (1986). Foreword: Remembering Fanon: Self, psyche, and the colonial condition. In F. Fanon, *Black Skin, White Masks*. London: Pluto.

Bhabha, H. K. (1989). At the limits. *Artforum*, 27(9), 11–12.

Bhabha, H. K. (ed.) (1990). *Nation and Narration*. London: Routledge.

Bhabha, H. K. (1994a). *The Location of Culture*. London: Routledge.

Bhabha, H. K. (1994b). Signs taken for wonders: Questions of ambivalence and authority under a tree outside Delhi, May 1817. In *The Location of Culture*. London: Routledge, pp. 102–122.

Bhabha, H. K. (1994c). Of mimicry and man: The ambivalence of colonial discourse. In *The Location of Culture*. London: Routledge, pp. 85–92.

Bhabha, H. K. (1997). Queen's English. *Artforum*, 35(7), 25–27.

Bhabha, H. K. (2000). Cosmopolitanisms. *Public Culture*, 12(3), 577–590.

Bhabha, H. K. (2003). Democracy De-realized. *Diogenes*, 50(1), 27–35.

Bhabha, H. K. (2005). Adagio. *Critical Inquiry*, 31(2), 371–380.

Gates, H. L., Jr. (1991). Critical Fanonism. *Critical Inquiry*, 17(3), 457–470.

Hallward, P. (2001). *Absolutely Post-Colonial: Writing Between the Singular and the Specific*. Manchester: Manchester University Press.

Huddart, D. (2006). *Homi K. Bhabha*. London: Routledge.

Lacan, J. (1981). *The Four Fundamental Concepts of Psychoanalysis* (trans. A. Sheridan; ed. J.-A. Miller). New York: Norton.

Seshadri-Crooks, K. (2000). Surviving theory: A conversation with Homi K. Bhabha. In F. Afzal-Khan and K. Seshadri-Crooks (eds.), *The Pre-occupation of Postcolonial Studies*. Durham, NC: Duke University Press, pp. 369–380.

Young, R. J. C. (1990). *White Mythologies: Writing History and the West*. London: Routledge.

Young, R. J. C. (1995). *Colonial Desire: Hybridity in Theory, Culture and Race*. London: Routledge.

Bloom, Harold

CLAIRE FEEHILY

Harold Bloom (b. 1930) is an American academic and one of the most prominent postwar literary critics. Since 1959, in many books, articles, and reviews, he has written about an extensive range of individual writers and genres; more recently his concerns have included religious themes, mysticism, the Bible, and Jewish culture. Bloom's works on Romanticism, poetic influence, and Aestheticism were of significant academic influence. But his international success is also derived from bestselling work for a wider

readership. In particular, Bloom is associated with a spirited and polemical defense of Western canonical literature against the "School of Resentment," his term for the theoretical criticism within English Studies in higher education. Bloom was born in New York City in 1930, the son of working-class Yiddish-speaking parents. After winning a scholarship from the State Department of Education, he graduated from Cornell University in 1951. He gained his PhD from Yale University in 1955 and has continued to work at Yale, holding the title of Sterling Professor of Humanities since 1983. Between 1988 and 2004 Bloom was also Berg Professor of English at New York University. He is a MacArthur Prize Fellow, a member of the American Academy, and a past Charles Eliot Norton Professor at Harvard University.

Bloom's earliest work, in the 1950s and '60s, arose from his doctoral study of Shelley. Bloom has emphasized the influence of two critics upon his work: M. H. Abrams, a prominent scholar of Romanticism at Cornell; and the Canadian literary critic Northrop Frye. Bloom's published studies of both Shelley and Blake, *Shelley's Mythmaking* (1959) and *Blake's Apocalypse* (1963), as well as more general studies, defend the critical profile and reputation of Romantic poetry, which, Bloom argues, had suffered through the influence of T. S. Eliot, neo-Christian formalist criticism, and the new critics. Bloom's revisionism lay in his view that Romanticism's influence had been an enduring one, which could be identified in the work of twentieth-century poets, notably W. B. Yeats.

In the 1970s, notably in *The Anxiety of Influence* (1973), Bloom developed his highly influential analysis of poetic influence and the "intra-poetic" relationships between poets and the work of earlier writers. In work that showed a deepening interest in Freud, Bloom presented the history of Western poetry since the Renaissance as a competitive Oedipal struggle between poets and their precursors. Bloom argues that all poetry is intertextual, and that modern poetry needs to be understood in terms of its relationship to past work. Since Milton, poetry has suffered from an anxiety of influence, "a mode of melancholy," in which there is a fear that the writing of poetry is no longer possible. This anxiety is something far greater than a sense of intellectual awe at the achievement of one's literary predecessors; rather, it is a force that makes poetry happen. Bloom maintains that it is necessary for poets to clear imaginative space if their own work is not to be overwhelmed by earlier poetry, and that "strong" poets arrive at their own vocation and original voice by strongly misreading the work of their precursors.

Bloom is also well known for his emphasis on the cultural primacy of canonical texts and writers, particularly Shakespeare. In *The Western Canon* (1994), Bloom defended traditional reading and pedagogy against what he maintained were those intellectual forces grouped against the cultural authority of canonical literature. The context, in the early 1990s in America, was one of cultural, educational, and political controversy about the nature of university literary curricula. Debate ran high as to which texts should be taught in universities and schools and by what pedagogical methods.

Bloom maintains that literary canons are inevitable; his canonical authors shared a status as exemplars of the sublime that "unifies poetic and religious pathos," a group that included the authors of the Bible, the classics and Dante, and the English literary canon. Greatness in literature, Bloom maintains, arises from such spiritual sublimity and aesthetic intensity. He develops the concept of "canonical strangeness" as a criterion for an individual work's merit. Bloom's own literary canon emerges from various works, but includes the authors of

Genesis, *Jeremiah*, and *Job*, Homer, Dante, Shakespeare, Milton, Blake, Wordsworth, Freud, Kafka, and Beckett.

Bloom has written extensively about the nature of reading, maintaining that its purpose is for solitary pleasure and self-knowledge. His emphasis on aesthetic value, literary hierarchy, and canonicity has put him at odds with increasingly influential developments in literary and cultural theory. Bloom was particularly critical of what he saw as the humanities' retreat into politics in higher education in the 1980s and 1990s, and strongly resisted postcolonialist, feminist, and multiculturalist scholarship that encouraged a social reading of literature. His advocacy of literature's autonomy and timelessness has led him to challenge much contemporary Shakespeare scholarship, notably the readings by new historicist critics.

Bloom has not only made a series of important interventions in academic scholarship, he has achieved great popular success with his publications. He has a highly readable, polemical style that demands attention and courts controversy, and his own opinions about literary merit are unambiguous. In *Genius* (2002) Bloom selected 100 writers of what he called particular writerly genius. In 2003 he selected four contemporary American writers for writing the "Style of the Age": De Lillo, McCarthy, Pynchon, and Roth. There has been great interest in publications that, for example, advise people *How to Read and Why* (2000), and interventions in controversial and popular areas, including that of the literary merit of J. K. Rowling's *Harry Potter* series. Bloom expressed "discomfort" at the "mania" over the Potter literary phenomenon, concluding that, yes, 35 million book buyers can be wrong.

SEE ALSO: Abrams, M. H.; Anglo-American New Criticism; Canons; Eliot,

T. S.; Formalism; Frye, Northrop;
Intertextuality; New Historicism

REFERENCES AND SUGGESTED
READINGS

Bloom, H. (1959). *Shelley's Mythmaking*. New
Haven: Yale University Press.
Bloom, H. (1961). *The Visionary Company: A Read-
ing of English Romantic Poetry*. Garden City, NY:
Doubleday.
Bloom, H. (1963). *Blake's Apocalypse: A Study in
Poetic Argument*. Garden City, NY: Doubleday.
Bloom, H. (1970). *Yeats*. New York: Oxford
University Press.
Bloom, H. (1973). *The Anxiety of Influence: A Theory
of Poetry*. New York: Oxford University Press.
Bloom, H. (1994). *The Western Canon: The Books
and School of the Ages*. New York: Harcourt,
Brace.
Bloom, H. (1998). *Shakespeare: The Invention of the
Human*. New York: Riverhead Books.
Bloom, H. (2000). *How to Read and Why*. New York:
Scribner's.
Bloom, H. (2002). *Genius: A Mosaic of 100 Exem-
plary Creative Minds*. New York: Warner.
Frye, N. (1947). *Fearful Symmetry: A Study of
William Blake*. Princeton: Princeton University
Press.

Body, The

GERALD MOORE

As evidenced in the twisted, inhuman bodies of Francis Bacon, the preserved and
plastinated bodies of Damian Hirst and
Günther von Hagens, and the prosthetically
enhanced performance art of Stelarc, the
embodiedness and materiality of identity
is one of the principal fascinations of
twentieth-century and contemporary artistic discourse. In philosophy and theory, too,
emphases on lived experience, mortality,
and desire represent a substantial break
from the Christian legacy of European
modernity.

In his *Meditations on First Philosophy*
(1997[1641]), frequently cited as the founding text of modernity, the French philosopher René Descartes argued that the ability
of purely rational thought to conceive a
conscious subject without a body served
as proof of mind–body dualism, the sepa-
rability of the mind from the physical
body. Reasoning logical certainty and the
structures of thought to be inexplicable in
terms of the experience of a material
body all too prone to error, Descartes ultimately reasserted the Christian doctrine of
the transcendence of the spirit over the
flesh. It was moreover this transcendence
that was essential to the free will of
human beings. Taken alone, Descartes argued, our bodies are just mechanical objects
governed by cause and effect, simple animal
automata driven by material needs. Only
a transcendent, noncorporeal mind could
escape subordination to the base impulses
of desire.

Only much more recently have academics
begun to emphasize the body as positive, to
be celebrated as the site of singularity, difference, and precisely what enables us to
think, rather than condemned as negative.
Following this, increasing attention has also
been paid to the ways that bodies can be
both manipulated and liberated to change
our thinking, with feminists and other
thinkers associated with post-structuralism
taking a particular interest.

One of the earliest to embark on this new
line of thought, the German philosopher
Friedrich Nietzsche speculated in *On the
Genealogy of Morality* (1994[1887]) that
our entire capacity for abstract rationality
originally resulted from the confinement of
the body, the enclosure of humans in societies where unavoidable mutual proximity
served to make instinct-led behavior pro-
hibitively dangerous. Elaborating an un-
ashamedly speculative history of social relations, Nietzsche imagined a prehistory of

humanity in which the numerous scars on the bodies of the weak had the effect of leaving the victims of violence endowed with memory, unable to forget their suffering. Too frail to live instinctively, they instead used their newfound memory to begin to think in terms of time, to imagine the existence of an immortal soul that lives on beyond the death of the body. Unable to inflict physical suffering on the strong, these "slaves" resorted to mental violence, inventing concepts like sin and morality as ways of denigrating the body and outlawing or regulating the benefits of physical prowess. What we experience as guilt or moral conscience, according to Nietzsche, is nothing other than violent animal instincts turned back against themselves, punishing the body as a site of shame and immorality. A strikingly similar claim comes from Sigmund Freud, whose *Civilisation and Its Discontents* (2001[1930]) argues that such an "introjection of the instincts" is at the origin of the superego, the feeling of shame and moral prohibition Freud describes as the internalized law of father.

This focus on the body by the early critics of modernity was to continue in the work of Martin Heidegger, before taking a decisively French turn and emerging as a defining feature of poststructuralist materialism. Despite containing comparatively little analysis of bodies as such, the principal thrust of Heideggerian philosophy was modernity's refusal to acknowledge mortality, the simple fact that human being is Being-in-the-world, a being that dies and lives in overwhelming fear of death's inevitability. Less than the ability to use reason to escape mortality, Heidegger argued that what defines us is primarily the attempt and desire to escape it.

Following Heidegger and with the additional influence of anthropologists like Marcel Mauss, who wrote of the "techniques" of the body, the antinihilistic affirmation of the mortal body would prove crucial to subsequent generations of writers, including philosopher-novelists like Georges Bataille and Simone de Beauvoir and the philosophers, Maurice Merleau-Ponty and Michel Foucault.

Drawing on fieldwork of the emerging discipline of anthropology to historicize the speculations of Nietzsche, Bataille used theoretical works like *The Accursed Share* (1989, 1991 [3 vols., 1948–57]) to develop an account of "base materialism" already embraced by his novels, most notably the heavily pornographic *Story of the Eye* (1987 [1928]). In a reversal of modern interpretations of the Fall, Bataille locates an experience of the sacred in the bodily experience of sexual transgression and sacrifice that defy the moral taboos and fetishizing of hygiene erected as apparently self-evident ideals by modernity.

In major works like *Phenomenology of Perception* (2002[1945]), Maurice Merleau-Ponty presents the body as the origin and ground all knowledge, an inescapable horizon that cannot be extracted from thought. Along with those of Bataille, this idea influenced one of the founders of modern feminism, Simone de Beauvoir. Writing in *The Second Sex* (1997[1949]), de Beauvoir argues that women are subjected to domination because of their bodies' greater proximity to nature. Frailer, subject to more visible processes of aging, not to mention the radical and mysterious, incomprehensible changes of pregnancy, the female body constitutes our primary point of contact with mortality.

The history of the domination of woman, for de Beauvoir, is thus intimately bound to man's attempts to overcome the predicament of his mortality. Reconstructed through myth and fantasy, makeup and dress, and deprived from participating in the privileged arenas symbolic of transcendence – the worlds of work and thought, art and politics, for example – women are reduced to tools through which nature and death are kept at bay. The male fantasy of feminine mystery, famously illustrated by the medieval rituals of courtly love and the wry but secretive smile of da Vinci's *Mona Lisa*, becomes a self-fulfilling prophecy. Women are culturally alienated from their own physiology, unaware of their ability to transcend the nature to which they are stigmatized as belonging.

The Paris-based Bulgarian feminist philosopher and psychoanalyst Julia Kristeva extends this account into a theory of "abjection," identifying "woman" as one of the classical literary figurations of degradation and impurity. Outlined in *Powers of Horror* (1982[1980]), the abject refers to the unsettling sensation of death infecting life, of corporeality – including feces, sperm, sweat, and menstrual blood – whose stigmatization leaves us unnecessarily alienated from our bodies. Kristeva's reminder that bodily relations are prior to the more abstract exchanges of language is also in agreement with the work of other poststructuralist theoretical feminists, including Luce Irigaray and Hélène Cixous. Irigaray explores the female anatomy and writes of the bodily encounter with the mother prior to all language. Cixous's "The laugh of the Medusa" (1991[1975]) calls for the creation of an *écriture féminine*, a feminine writing not subject to – and which moreover makes explicit – the suppression of the body found in the abstract linguistic exchanges historically privileged by men.

The control exercised over women's bodies has also been linked to the fate of another body, namely the social body or body politic. Against classical (Platonic) and modern (physiocratic, Hegelian) conceptions of the potentially intrinsic harmony of the body politic, other recent theorists have emphasized the artificiality and constructedness of bodies. In *Anti-Oedipus:*

Capitalism and Schizophrenia (1984 [1972]), Gilles Deleuze and Félix Guattari invoke the idea of a "Body without Organs (BwO)" to describe a state prior to and unencumbered by any kind of hierarchical identity. Their argument is that what we regard as the corporeal basis of identity has changed over time, and even once we reject the notion of a metaphysically distinct mind or soul, what we count as a body is still determined by a thinking of transcendence, of metaphysically – as opposed to merely physically – distinct parts. Once again drawing on anthropology to lend weight to the speculative history of Nietzsche, Deleuze and Guattari argue that archaic societies are not defined by aggregations of the individual, privatized, bodies so typical of Western liberal culture. Prior to the onset of monetary and capitalist economies, which are organized first and foremost around the bodies of rulers and the abstract bodies of capital, respectively, what takes precedence is the "body of the earth," the collective body of the tribe, whose members – their tattooed, pierced and painted flesh engraved with the marks of collective identity – have none of the sense of individual self-ownership that comes with capitalism. This is later developed further by Michel Foucault, who argues in works such as the first volume of his *History of Sexuality* (1992[1977]) that our fascination with the body can be traced to the birth of capitalism and the recognition of the profitability of healthy, productive bodies. At the origin of a social body composed of responsible, self-owning individuals, we find (medical) strategies to increase the body's ability to survive and reproduce, thus boosting economic growth, and "governmental" strategies for organizing bodies efficiently in space and time. Wary that bodies be thought passively constructed in this way, Judith

Butler (b. 1956) has examined the multiplicity of transgender and sexual identities to highlight the ways we performatively enact our sexuality by making decisions about what defines us.

These notions of organized and inscribed (social or individual) bodies, bodies that are effectively written into existence, have met with criticism from another French philosopher, Jean-Luc Nancy, who, most notably in *Corpus* (1992), rejects the claim that bodies can be "aestheticized," subjected to unifying narratives of individual or collective identity. Returning to Heidegger's emphasis on finitude and death-bound subjectivity, Nancy denies the implication that the collective identity of a national body politic could ever take precedence over the "singular" experience of one's mortal human body. The finite body is what is constantly expressed in the desire for immortality of writing, but is not what is written and consequently cannot be rewritten. On the contrary, death reverses every attempt to recreate the body as something else. In saying this, he is no doubt influenced by his own experience of undergoing a heart transplant, discussed in *L'Intrus* (*The Intruder*), which has also inspired a film of the same name by the French director Claire Denis.

SEE ALSO: Cixous, Hélène; Deleuze, Gilles; *Ecriture Féminine*; Foucault, Michel; Heidegger, Martin; Kristeva, Julia; Irigaray, Luce

REFERENCES AND SUGGESTED READINGS

Bataille, G. (1987). *Story of the Eye* (trans. J. Neugoschel). San Francisco: City Lights Books. (Original work published 1928.)

Bataille, G. (1989). *The Accursed Share: An Essay on General Economy*. Vol. 1: *Consumption* (trans. R. Hurley). New York: Zone. (Original work published as 1 of 3 vols., 1948–57.)

Bataille, G. (1991). *The Accursed Share: An Essay on General Economy*. Vols. 2 and 3: *The History of Eroticism & Sovereignty* (trans. R. Hurley). New York: Zone. (Original works published as 2 of 3 vols., 1948–57.)

de Beauvoir, S. (1997). *The Second Sex* (ed. and trans. H. M. Parshley). London: Vintage. (Original work published 1949.)

Butler, J. (1990). *Gender Trouble: Feminism and the Subversion of Identity*. New York: Routledge.

Cixous, H. (1991). The laugh of the Medusa (trans. K. Cohen & P. Cohen). In R. R. Warhol & D. P. Herndl (eds.), *Feminisms: An Anthology of Literary Theory and Criticism*. Piscataway, NJ: Rutgers University Press. (Original work published 1975.)

Deleuze, G., & Guattari, F. (1984). *Anti-Oedipus: Capitalism and Schizophrenia* (trans. R. Hurley, M. Seem, & H. R. Lane). London: Continuum. (Original work published 1972.)

Descartes, R. (1997). *Meditations on First Philosophy* (trans. J. Cottingham). Cambridge: Cambridge University Press. (Original work published 1641.)

Foucault, M. (1992). *History of Sexuality*. Vol. 1: *The Will to Knowledge* (trans. R. Hurley). London: Penguin. (Original work published 1977.)

Freud, S. (2001). *The Standard Edition of the Complete Psychological Works of Sigmund Freud*. Vol. 21: *The Future of an Illusion, Civilisation and Its Discontents, and Other Works* (ed. and trans. J. Strachey). London: Vintage-Hogarth. (Original work cited published 1930.)

Heidegger, M. (1962). *Being and Time* (trans. J. Macquarie & E. Robinson) Oxford: Blackwell. (Original work published 1927.)

Kristeva, J. (1982). *Powers of Horror: An Essay on Abjection* (trans. L. S. Roudiez). New York: Columbia University Press. (Original work published 1980.)

Irigaray, Luce (1991). The bodily encounter with the Mother. In M. Whitford (ed.), *The Irigaray Reader*. Oxford: Blackwell.

Mauss, M. (1973). Techniques of the body. *Economy and Society*, 2(1), 70–88.

Merleau-Ponty, M. (2002). *Phenomenology of Perception* (trans. C. Smith & F. Williams). London: Routledge. (Original work published 1945.)

Nancy, J.-L. (1992). *Corpus*. Paris: Metaillié.

Nancy, J.-L. (2000). *L'Intrus*. Paris: Galilée.

Nietzsche, F. (1994). *On the Genealogy of Morality* (ed. K. Ansell-Pearson; trans. C. Diethe). Cambridge: Cambridge University Press. (Original work published 1887.)

Braidotti, Rosi

ROBIN STOATE

Rosi Braidotti is a feminist philosopher and theorist, most widely known for her work on the notion of "nomadic" subjectivity, which responds to and builds upon the theories of Continental philosophers in order to theorize an account of both a politically viable female subject, and a more general notion of positive difference.

Born in Italy in 1954, but growing up in Australia, Braidotti holds dual citizenship. She achieved undergraduate degrees in English literature and philosophy in 1976 and 1977, respectively, at the Australian National University and in 1981 completed her doctorate in philosophy at the University of Paris I (Panthéon-Sorbonne). She holds the post of Distinguished Professor in the Humanities at Utrecht University in the Netherlands, and is founding director of its Center for Humanities. She was foundation chair of Utrecht's Department of Women's Studies (1988–2005), and the Director of the Netherlands Research School of Women's Studies (1995–2005), and has been recognized for her contributions to scholarship and women's studies, receiving an honorary philosophy degree from the University of Helsinki (2007) and being named a Knight in the Order of Nederlandse Leeuw in 2005.

Although Braidotti's work is influenced by several thinkers, including feminist philosopher Luce Irigaray, philosopher and social theorist Michel Foucault, philosopher Gilles Deleuze, and feminist philosopher of science Donna Haraway, she is concerned nevertheless with not tying her approach to one system, and indeed actively interrogating theories even as she uses them.

What Braidotti shares with these thinkers is an understanding that the ways in which we traditionally understand the self (or "subject") are unsustainable. There has long been a basic belief within Western thought that each person is a rational, conscious being, capable of pure thought and in control of its own thoughts and actions; an idea widely associated with the seventeenth-century philosopher René Descartes and the movement of liberal humanism. However, theoretical shifts brought about by things such as psychoanalysis and poststructuralism have suggested that it may be impossible to continue thinking of the subject in this way. The traditional version of the subject has been shown not only to undo itself logically, but to exclude people from its boundaries – anybody who is not white, male, heterosexual, able-bodied, wealthy, and so on – while claiming to be a "universal" human condition.

While Braidotti agrees with this unsustainability in the universal or "unitary" subject, her approach to rethinking it does not subscribe to any one particular model. She believes that theories of the subject should not begin with any concrete set of totalizing rules, or claim to provide a universal structure or set of criteria by which valid subjectivity can be judged. Doing so would only move the boundaries of subjectivity, not erase them. Braidotti's approach to reconciling this problem is to propound a relationship with theories of the subject that remains "nomadic" – negotiating between many different theoretical approaches, but, importantly, ensuring that this process is carried out with intelligence, rigor, and a sense of political responsibility.

The common threads of Braidotti's approach can be observed in four monographs, all available in English. First, *Patterns of Dissonance* (1991) examines a complex relationship between Continental philosophy and women and feminism. Braidotti argues that the "crisis" of the unitary subject is not inherently negative. She believes that the "void" left by the disassembling of that subject – lamented by some critics opposing what they see as an "attack" on rationality – actually represents a space in which alternative philosophies can now be conceived. Braidotti outlines the possibility of creating a positive understanding of a *female* subject within this new space, whose difference from the masculine subject is not predicated on negativity (i.e., being "not-male"). She also argues that what she terms the "question of the feminine" has, in fact, always played a part in thought, disassembling the unitary subject, with the "crisis" taking place alongside the birth of a multitude of feminist theories and practices, even though this relationship is never explicitly enunciated.

Second, *Nomadic Subjects* (1997) is a response to the specific challenges presented by postmodernism to the construction of a feminine subject. The book propounds a strategy of engagement with existing theories to conceive of a version of the subject that is not rooted in any one particular discourse. This "nomadic" approach would provide ways for women and other traditionally marginalized people to be conceived of as viable, and is demonstrated in the book through interconnected readings of theories, cultural practices, and moments of Braidotti's own "nomadic" – literally and figuratively – life history, such as her geographical shifts during her life and career, and her speaking and writing in several languages.

Third, *Metamorphoses* (2002) expands Braidotti's work on nomadic subjects and shows a development in her nonlinear writing style. Like *Nomadic Subjects*, *Metamorphoses* espouses a philosophy that, unlike traditional views of the subject, does not aim to escape the body, but takes it fully into account, in all of its shifting forms. Braidotti concentrates on producing radical accounts not only of gender difference, but of an alternative subject that emerges through contemporary crises of the notions of "human" and "life," such as those brought about by shifting relationships with new technologies, like the Internet or genetic engineering.

Finally, *Transpositions: On Nomadic Ethics* (2006) turns its attention to theorizing an ethics of nomadic subjectivity – that is, on propounding ways in which Braidotti's approach can be sustainable as a way of living a positive life with others. Working on the reconfiguration of the concept of "life" that she begins in *Metamorphoses*, Braidotti uses this model both to defend against criticisms of poststructuralist ethical projects as "relativist" – ethically bankrupt with no stable standard against which to judge ethical behavior – and to critique other attempts to build a poststructuralist ethical model, which she believes to be unsuccessful.

SEE ALSO: Feminism; Postmodernism; Poststructuralism; Psychoanalysis (since 1966); Subject Position

REFERENCES AND SUGGESTED READINGS

Braidotti, R. (1991). *Patterns of Dissonance: A Study of Women in Contemporary Philosophy* (trans. E. Guild). Cambridge: Polity.
Braidotti, R. (1997). *Nomadic Subjects: Embodiment and Sexual Difference in Contemporary Feminist Theory*. New York: Columbia University Press.

Braidotti, R. (2002). *Metamorphoses: Towards a Materialist Theory of Becoming.* Cambridge: Polity.

Braidotti, R. (2006). *Transpositions: On Nomadic Ethics.* Cambridge: Polity.

Butler, Judith

KAYE MITCHELL

BIOGRAPHY AND INFLUENCES

Judith Butler (b. 1956) is one of the leading theorists working in the field of the humanities in the late twentieth and early twenty-first centuries. Having established her international reputation with the publication of *Gender Trouble* in 1990, she is best known for her work in gender and sexuality studies and is often cited as one of the "founders" of queer theory, but her work extends far beyond these fields, and its influence can be felt within philosophy, literary criticism and critical theory, cultural studies, sociology, art theory and criticism, media and communication studies. After completing her PhD at Yale in 1984, Butler taught at Wesleyan University and at Johns Hopkins University; she is currently Maxine Elliot Professor in the Departments of Rhetoric and Comparative Literature at the University of California, Berkeley.

Butler's work is strongly influenced by Continental philosophy, feminism, and psychoanalysis; she has spoken in particular of the influence of Hegel upon her thinking, noting that: "In a sense, all of my work remains within the orbit of a certain set of Hegelian questions: What is the relation between desire and recognition, and how is it that the constitution of the subject entails a radical and constitutive relation to alterity?" (1999b[1987]: xiv). It is notable how these questions (of desire, recognition, subjectivity and subjectivation, and alterity) have informed both Butler's treatment of gender and sexuality, and her recent discussions of terrorism and mourning after 9/11: in the first instance, she has noted how the heterosexual paradigm relies upon an abjection of illicit homosexual desire and how gender is constructed via processes of exclusion (e.g., of those whose bodies and desires are unorthodox or unintelligible); more recently, questions of "alterity" and of the refusal of "recognition" to certain individuals have been central to her consideration of what constitutes both a "livable" life and a "grievable" death.

Hegel's influence is perhaps evident also in Butler's style of questioning, which is influenced by Hegelian dialectics, although it builds to no synthesis. Butler's writing typically proceeds via series of open-ended and interrogative questions, which lends her argument a rhetorical force, but has arguably contributed to negative reviews of her allegedly "difficult" style; along with Homi Bhabha, she was a recipient of *Philosophy and Literature*'s annual "bad writing" prize in 1998. Butler, however, in response to these charges, has drawn attention to the politics of style, asking, in the preface to a new edition of *Gender Trouble* in 1999, "What travels under the sign of 'clarity,' and what would be the price of failing to deploy a certain critical suspicion when the arrival of lucidity is announced? Who devises the protocols of 'clarity' and whose interests do they serve?" (1999[1990]: xx).

This troubling of the workings of language and, in particular, of the ideological underpinnings of logic and clarity, reveals in turn the influence of poststructuralism (especially the work of Derrida and Foucault) upon Butler's thinking, and she is frequently identified as a poststructuralist feminist theorist. Her engagements with the feminist canon have produced illuminating readings of Simone de Beauvoir, Monique Wittig, and Luce Irigaray, among others. Again, her identification with poststructuralism and postmodernism has not always brought her admiration – as she is sometimes held responsible, by her critics, for the "cultural turn" in leftist politics, and for the perceived disadvantages, for feminism, of the social constructivism with which she is associated.

Butler's early interest in psychoanalysis is evident in her provocative rereadings of Lacan and Freud in *Gender Trouble* and *Bodies that Matter* (1993). More recently, in *Giving an Account of Oneself* (2005), she has returned to psychoanalysis – particularly the work of Jean Laplanche – as part of what many have seen as a turn to questions of ethics and politics in her work (arguably, such questions were always motivating factors in her writing), and philosophers such as Levinas and Hannah Arendt have also become central to her thinking.

SUBJECTIVITY

Butler's work is centrally concerned with the ways in which we become subjects (including, but not limited to, the ways in which we become sexed and gendered subjects). This is evident in her first book, *Subjects of Desire* (1999b[1987]), which was first submitted as her PhD thesis in 1984 and later revised as a book. In *Subjects of Desire*, Butler tracks the mutation of Hegel's conception of desire in *Phenomenology of Spirit* within post-Hegelian Western philosophy (specifically, in the work of Alexandre Kojève, Jean Hyppolite, Sartre, Lacan, Deleuze, and Foucault) noting how, for Hegel, desire is "the incessant human effort to overcome external differences," part of the "project to become a self-sufficient subject"; yet by the time of the poststructuralists, desire has increasingly come "to signify the impossibility of the coherent subject itself" (1999b [1987]: 6) And she asks: "How is it that desire, once conceived as the human

instance of dialectical reason, becomes that which endangers dialectics, fractures the metaphysically integrated self, and disrupts the internal harmony of the subject and its ontological intimacy with the world?" (7).

Becoming a subject is, then, for Butler, a necessarily incomplete and fraught process, and much of her work is focused upon the forms of coercion involved in subjectivation (particularly in the imposition of gender and of heterosexuality), the "melancholy" effects of the kinds of abjection and exclusion that subjectivation involves, and the myriad possible "disruptions" to the stability of the subject. In this way, Butler introduces both gender-political questions and psychoanalytic insights into Hegel's account of subjectivity, and thus can be seen as working across (without ever simply synthesizing) quite disparate intellectual traditions.

This is particularly evident in her 1997 work, *The Psychic Life of Power*, which addresses the relationship between the psychic and the social, and is indebted both to Foucault and to psychoanalysis (primarily Freud here), as well as Hegel, Nietzsche, and Althusser. In considering the operations of power in the process of subjectivation, Butler deconstructs any facile opposition between "internal" and "external" forces and influences and explores the extent to which becoming a subject necessarily involves subordination and dependency. She suggests that the subject is formed by power, that power provides "the very condition of its existence," and thus that "power is not simply what we oppose but also, in a strong sense, what we depend on for existence" (1997b: 2). She makes links between childhood dependency (as explored in psychoanalysis) and adult political subjection and uncovers troubling forms of complicity and desires for subordination as central to the experience of being a subject. Unsurprisingly, such an account raises the question of how much power and agency the subject itself possesses; this is a question that haunts much of her work, and her critics have taken her to task for her apparent denial of subjective agency. Here, she asks whether there is "a way to affirm complicity as the basis of political agency, yet insist that political agency may do more than reiterate the conditions of subordination?" so it's clear that whatever agency the subject possesses, it will not amount to transcending or stepping outside these "conditions of subordination" and achieving full autonomy (1997b: 29–30).

In *Excitable Speech: A Politics of the Performative* (1997a), Butler approaches the question of subjectivity in a different way, via an analysis of the relationship between language, speech, and the subject. She discusses performative utterances (i.e., utterances that "do" something, such as "I promise"), which are central to speech act theory but reads speech act theory through the lens of poststructuralism, and politicizes her discussion by considering what words can "do" in the cases of hate speech and pornography/obscenity. Again, agency proves to be a fraught issue here, as Butler asserts that "speech is always in some ways out of our control" and, like Derrida in his reading of J. L. Austin, she stresses the ways in which performative utterances might go awry, failing to enact what they say (1997a: 15).

GENDER AND SEXUALITY

Butler is primarily regarded as a theorist of gender and sexuality and her best-known book, the one with which she is most strongly identified, is *Gender Trouble* (1999a[1990]). *Gender Trouble* introduced her influential but contentious theory of gender performativity and also helped to inaugurate the new discipline of queer theory. If queer theory emerges out of activism (by the likes of Queer Nation in the early 1990s) and the mutations of poststructuralist theory, then it is Butler's theories (along with those of Michel Foucault and Eve Kosofsky Sedgwick) that have been most influential in its development.

In her central claim that gender is performative, Butler is asserting that certain "acts" and "gestures" are not expressive of an already existent, essential, stable, coherent gender, but rather work to "produce the effect" of a coherent gender: "Such acts, gestures, enactments, generally construed, are *performative* in the sense that the essence or identity that they otherwise purport to express are *fabrications* manufactured and sustained through corporeal signs and other discursive means. That the gendered body is performative suggests that it has no ontological status apart from the various acts which constitute its reality" (1999a[1990]: 173).

Elsewhere in *Gender Trouble*, she puts it a little more concisely when she claims that "Gender is the repeated stylization of the body, a set of repeated acts within a highly regulatory frame that congeal over time to produce the appearance of substance, of a natural sort of being" (1999a[1990]: 43–4) The points to note here are, obviously, the non-naturalness of gender and – even more radically – of the gendered *body*, the production of gender via the repetition of certain "acts," gestures, etc., and the "regulatory frame" within which all of this takes place. Gender itself, then, is viewed as one of the ways in which the individual subject is regulated or controlled, but the reliance of gender upon repetition opens up some small possibility of resistance to that system which imposes gender norms upon us all.

Although feminist writers and theorists had for some time been drawing attention to the sex/gender distinction and asserting that the latter was "cultural" rather than "natural" – and Butler references Simone de Beauvoir and Monique Wittig, for example, in the course of her argument – Butler's own work comprises a radical constructivism in its emphasis upon the above points about repetition and regulation, and in its suggestion that even the "corporeal signs" of which she writes are cultural or "discursive" in nature, rather than naturally occurring biological phenomena; the result of this is a kind of collapsing of the sex/gender distinction, where both are viewed as cultural constructions or discursively produced in some way.

Butler proceeds to use drag (cross-dressing) as an example of gender subversion through practices of gender parody, noting how it draws attention to the performative constitution of gender. She claims that "drag fully subverts the distinction between inner and outer psychic space and effectively mocks both the expressive model of gender and the notion of a true gender identity" (1999a[1990]: 174). As she goes on to say, "*In imitating gender, drag implicitly reveals the imitative structure of gender itself – as well as its contingency*" (175). The parodic "imitations" of gender identity that drag artists perform paradoxically reveal that there is no "original" gender to be imitated; indeed, all gender is based on practices of imitation, repetition, and re-enactment.

It's hard to overstate the significance of Butler's account of gender performativity, or its scholarly ubiquity, but there have been problems in the interpretation of performativity which is so often, erroneously, taken as meaning that the subject/individual can choose to "perform" whatever gender identity they like. This is radically at odds with Butler's Foucault-inspired understanding of subjectivity as, like gender, a cultural production/construction. In fact, according to Butler, we do not possess the

necessary agency to make such straightforward choices, and "performativity" should not be confused or conflated with "performance." In this respect, her choice of the notably theatrical practice of drag as an example was not particularly helpful. In an interview in *Radical Philosophy*, Butler (1994) clarified the point that performance "presumes a subject," while performativity "contests the very notion of the subject." In other words, performance requires an already existent stable subject to do the performing, while performativity precedes the subject, and is what brings the subject into being, although this process is an ongoing one which is never fully or successfully completed.

Despite this apparent denial of subjective agency, in describing gender as "contingent" Butler tacitly suggests that it could be experienced and performed "differently," and she raises the possibility of a self-conscious (if not exactly self-directed) troubling of gender – a denaturalizing of gender – that threatens the patriarchal and heteronormative systems with which she is taking issue. She plots this move "from parody to politics" in the last chapter of *Gender Trouble*, arguing there that the reliance of gender norms upon repetition (that is, the fact that gender identity is never absolutely established or achieved, but always in process) opens up opportunities for resistant repetitions. In returning to the topic in the later *Undoing Gender*, Butler describes gender as "a practice of improvisation within a scene of constraint" (2004b: 1) and this is a useful way of summarizing her position, because it stresses the possibility of subversion via "improvisation" but also suggests the limitations of this: in Butler's world agency is always tempered by "constraint."

Aside from the discussion of performativity, another influential feature of *Gender Trouble* is Butler's linking of the production of gender with the production of heterosexuality as part of her discussion of the "heterosexual matrix" (1999a[1990]: 45–100). Butler interrogates Freud's discussion of the Oedipus complex in *The Ego and the Id*, noting the internalization of the lost object which is characteristic of melancholia, and using this reading to address "the melancholic denial/preservation of homosexuality in the production of gender within the heterosexual frame" (1999a[1990]: 73). As far as homosexual desires are concerned, it is not only the object that must be renounced, but also "the modality of desire" (75). Butler's reading of the Oedipus complex suggests that, "In repudiating the mother as an object of sexual love, the girl of necessity repudiates her masculinity and, paradoxically, 'fixes' her femininity as a consequence" (77). Femininity and masculinity, as traditionally conceived, are then consequences of the "effective internalization" of the "taboo against homosexuality"; an orthodox gender identity is established via this renunciation of homosexual desires, but that renunciation is never absolute and so the desire remains as a melancholic trace at the heart of heterosexual identity – simultaneously "denied" and "preserved," impossible yet required for heterosexuality's self-definition (81). Engagements with Lévi-Strauss, Lacan, and Joan Riviere also form part of Butler's analysis of the heterosexual matrix, which emerges, then, as the structure or system within which, and through which, the subject is produced as gendered and through which heterosexuality is constructed as "normal" and "natural."

These arguments concerning heterosexuality and homosexuality complement Butler's theory of performativity, for again gender is being viewed as an effect "of a law imposed by culture," rather than a cause or origin (1999a[1990]: 81) In this instance the "law" is the cultural prohibition of homosexuality, which must be continually reiterated (so again repetition comes into play), and the renunciation of homosexual desires must also be repeatedly enacted, even while it is constitutive of gender itself.

Butler refines and clarifies her theory of performativity in the opening sections of her next book, *Bodies That Matter* (1993), averring that "Performativity is … not a singular 'act,' for it is always a reiteration of a norm or set of norms, and to the extent that it acquires an act-like status in the present, it conceals or dissimulates the conventions of which it is a repetition" (12), and stating that "the agency denoted by the performativity of 'sex' will be directly counter to any notion of a voluntarist subject who exists quite apart from the regulatory norms which she/he opposes" (15).

In addition, Butler's suggestion in *Gender Trouble* that the body is "always already a cultural sign" (1999a[1990]: 90) is developed further in *Bodies that Matter*, where she elaborates a theory of the materialization of sexed bodies, arguing that sex, like gender, is a cultural construction, thus breaking down the sex/gender, nature/culture dichotomies of earlier feminisms. "Sexual difference," she claims, "is never simply a function of material differences which are not in some way both marked and formed by discursive practices," and "sex is an ideal construct which is forcibly materialized through time" (1993: 1). In these arguments, materiality is construed by Butler as the effect of power, rather than as nature/surface/site that is then worked upon, or subjected to the workings of power and as a *process* (of materialization). The material body, for her, is accessible only via discourse and therefore is always already gendered and in this book she asks, "through what norms is sex itself materialized?" and treats sex as "a sedimented effect of a reiterative or ritual practice" (10).

Butler's most recent book dedicated to gender and sexuality is *Undoing Gender*, where she again develops some of her earlier arguments around the regulation of gender, desire, subjectivity, and recognition, but her writing here acquires a more overtly political edge as she touches upon, among other issues, topical questions about the status (as "human" or "intelligible" – or not) of transsexual and transgendered people, about lesbian and gay marriage, and about nonheterosexual family structures.

One outcome of Butler's arguments around gender and sexuality is a kind of suspicion of the viability of identity politics, and this critique of identity has been central to queer theory. In *Gender Trouble*, Butler raises the possibility that identity is "a normative ideal," and thus part of the processes of regulation, rather than "a descriptive feature of experience" (1999a[1990]: 23), and in a 1991 essay entitled "Imitation and gender insubordination," she again warns that "identity categories tend to be instruments of regulatory regimes," while conceding that she is prepared to "appear at political occasions under the sign of lesbian," as long as it can remain "permanently unclear what precisely that sign signifies" (1991: 14). The critique of identity politics, along with the limited agency afforded to the subject by Butler's theories, have led to questions about the possible political utility of her work, but in her recent writings she has focused increasingly and insistently on ethical and political matters.

POLITICS AND ETHICS: RECENT WORK

Much of Butler's work since 2000 has concerned itself with questions around kinship (e.g., in *Antigone's Claim* [2000]), on what it is to be recognized as "human" (or, indeed, refused that recognition), on what constitutes a "livable" life, on the "precariousness" of life, and on questions of terrorism and mourning in the wake of 9/11. *Precarious Life* (2004a) collects together five essays written in response to the "conditions of heightened vulnerability and aggression" following September 11 and emphasizes the vulnerability to death or injury at the hands of others that we all share, using this to stress our necessary interdependency, which often involves a "fundamental dependency on anonymous others" (xi, xii). Engaging more closely with concrete examples than she had done in her previous writings, Butler considers, for example, the forms of "nation-building" (e.g., by the US and Israel) that deny this "primary vulnerability," and the "unlivable lives" of those who are effectively denied subjecthood by having their political and legal rights suspended (such as prisoners in Guantanamo). In doing so, she asserts her right to speak of such matters in a post-9/11 climate of censorship and anti-intellectualism, as well as her right to offer public critiques of Israel without being accused of anti-Semitism (she classes herself as a Jewish anti-Zionist). Referencing Levinas's ethics of nonviolence, she seeks to elucidate the possible political uses of mourning and grief.

This book in particular has been read as indicating a shift in her thinking – away from her more skeptical, poststructuralist-influenced pronouncements and toward a renewed interest in ethics, alterity, the human, political engagement, collectivity, etc. This is evident in her concern, here, with "finding a basis for community" in vulnerability and mourning, and her perhaps unexpected (given her earlier work) preoccupation with "the question of the human" (2004a: 19, 20). Such (broadly speaking) "ethical" questions are taken up again in *Giving an Account of Oneself* (2005), whose arguments are motivated by the question of what it means to lead an "ethical life." Key references here include Levinas, Laplanche, Adorno, and Foucault, and the book develops the idea that moral questions always "emerge in the context of social relations" and that "the form these questions take changes according to context" (3).

Revealing her continuing interest in questions of subjectivation, Butler asks, here, in what the "I" consists – "in what terms can it appropriate morality or, indeed, give an account of itself?" – and asserts that "there is no 'I' that can fully stand apart from the social conditions of its emergence, no 'I' that is not implicated in a set of conditioning moral norms, which, being norms, have a social character that exceeds a purely personal or idiosyncratic meaning" (2005: 7). So, to give an account of oneself requires one to "become a social theorist," to some extent, and the self is understood as relational (8). Yet, Butler adds to this that, "the 'I' is always to some extent dispossessed by the social conditions of its emergence," suggesting that this dispossession "may well be the condition for moral inquiry" (8). Sociality, then, is not altogether a blessing, involving an interdependency that might hint at possibilities of collective action and feeling, but bringing also a dispossession that destabilizes the subject to some degree.

In her latest work, *Frames of War: When is Life Grievable?* (2009), Butler extends the discussion begun in *Precarious Life* of what constitutes a grievable life, and considers specific examples of state rhetoric produced as part of the "war on terror," and the US state's suppression of the humanity of those deemed to be enemies or terrorists. In her accounts of the notorious Abu Ghraib prison photographs, or the situation at Guantanamo, Butler might seem to have moved quite a distance from her earlier Hegelian concerns with desire and subjectivation, but in fact the question of the subject's "relation to alterity" remains central here, revealing

that her preoccupations have remained much the same from her earliest publications to her most recent, even as her frame of reference and the terms of her inquiry have continued to develop – and to enthrall and provoke her readership in equal measure.

SEE ALSO: Feminism; Gender Theory; Poststructuralism; Psychoanalysis (since 1966); Psychoanalysis (to 1966); Queer Theory

REFERENCES AND SUGGESTED READINGS

Butler, J. (1991). Imitation and gender insubordination. In D. Fuss (ed.), *Inside/Out*. London: Routledge, pp. 13–31.

Butler, J. (1993). *Bodies that Matter*. London: Routledge.

Butler, J. (1994). Judith Butler [interviewed by P. Osborne & L. Segal]. *Radical Philosophy*, 67, 32–39.

Butler, J. (1997a). *Excitable Speech: A Politics of the Performative*. London: Routledge.

Butler, J. (1997b). *The Psychic Life of Power*. Stanford: Stanford University Press.

Butler, J. (1999a). *Gender Trouble*. London: Routledge. (Original work published 1990.)

Butler, J. (1999b). *Subjects of Desire: Hegelian Reflections in Twentieth-Century France*. New York: Columbia University Press. (Original work published 1987.)

Butler, J. (2000). *Antigone's Claim: Kinship between Life and Death*. New York: Columbia University Press.

Butler, J. (2004a). *Precarious Life: Powers of Violence and Mourning*. London: Verso.

Butler, J. (2004b). *Undoing Gender*. London: Routledge.

Butler, J. (2005). *Giving an Account of Oneself*. New York: Fordham University Press.

Butler, J. (2009). *Frames of War: When is Life Grievable?* London: Verso.

Kirby, V. (2006). *Judith Butler: Live Theory*. London: Continuum.

Lloyd, M. (2007). *Judith Butler: From Norms to Politics*. Cambridge: Polity.

Salih, S. (2002). *Judith Butler*. London: Routledge.

C

Canons

ANKHI MUKHERJEE

Secular and literary applications of the term "canon" refer to a constellation of highly valued, high-cultural texts that have traditionally acted as arbiters of literary value, determining the discipline of literary studies as well as influencing the critical and cultural reception of literature. In his influential work on the subject, *The Western Canon* (1994), Yale critic Harold Bloom offers several approximate definitions of canonicity. The canon is "the literary Art of Memory," if by memory we mean "an affair of imaginary places, or of real places transmuted into visual images" (17). The canon serves as a memory system, which receives, retains, and orders selective works. It is "the relation of an individual reader and writer to what has been preserved out of what has been written" (17). The canon, Bloom argues, is a standard of measurement that cannot be tethered to political or moral considerations: it should remain instead "a gauge of vitality" (38). Finally Bloom declares that the canon is "Shakespeare and Dante," before proceeding to offer creative readings of 26 of the most prominent canonical authors, and an egregious list of 400 canonical authors or works.

The English word "canon" is derived from the Greek *kanon*, which translates to

"rule," "rod," or "measuring stick." David Ruhnken first used the word in 1768 for selections of authors, a usage that, Rudolph Pfeiffer (1968) notes, was catachrestic. In subsequent uses of the term, its two meanings, selective and regulative, have become increasingly interchangeable; as Wendell V. Harris points out, "selections suggest norms, and norms suggest an appeal to some sort of authority" (1991: 110). The ecclesiastical use of "canon" for definitive books of the Bible reinforces the normative charge of the term, though the literary canon is considerably more flexible than its biblical counterpart. "The desire to have a canon, more or less unchanging, and to protect it against the charges of inauthenticity or low value ... is an aspect of the necessary conservatism of a learned institution," Frank Kermode (1979: 77) observes. Canonicity involves not merely a work's admission into an elite club, but its induction into ongoing critical dialogue and contestations of literary value. The canon is a set of texts whose value and readability have borne the test of time: it is also the modality that establishes "the standards by which to evaluate such texts," to quote Rey Chow (2000: 2037).

It has been a matter of sustained debate in the academy whether the persistence of ideas of canonicity in the twentieth century (as evidenced in the burgeoning market for

The Encyclopedia of Literary and Cultural Theory   General editor: Michael Ryan
© 2011 Blackwell Publishing Ltd

authoritative selections, such as the literary anthology) is a function of cultural conservatism or is simply a validation of enduring aesthetic value. Most notable of these are the disagreements in the 1930s and '40s around F. R. Leavis's highly restrictive "Great Tradition," consisting of the work of just four novelists, and the so-called "canon wars" of the 1980s and '90s in American universities. Defenders of the canon, or the idea of canonicity, argue for the flexibility, adaptability, and enormous variation of the canon. Alastair Fowler (1979) perceives the canon as alive and dynamic, a changeable corpus of works that have achieved transcendental value over time. Fowler lists as many as six differentiations in canons. The *potential canon* includes "the entire written corpus"; the *accessible canon* refers to books that are available at a given time; the *selective canon* is constituted by exclusive lists of authors and texts, as exemplified in anthologies and syllabi; the *critical canon* includes books that have been the subject of critical exegeses; the *official canon* is a composite of the accessible, selective, and critical canons; and, finally, the *personal canon* corresponds to the reading preferences and predilections of individual readers. To Fowler's six definitions, Wendell Harris (1991) adds four more: the *closed canon* of authoritative texts, like the scriptural canon; the *pedagogical canon* (that which is taught in an institution at a given time, and which draws sparingly from the *official* canon); the *diachronic canon*, a group of texts which are prioritized in selection after selection over time, and which constitutes what Harris calls "the glacially changing core" of literature; and, finally, the *nonce canon*, "a rapidly changing periphery . . . only a miniscule part of which will eventually become part of the diachronic canon" (112–13). Fowler's and Harris's categories frequently overlap or change composition, thereby renovating or reconstituting the canon in the very act of con-

stituting it. Christopher M. Kuipers also draws on the productive instability in canonical categories to propose a dynamic concept of the canon: he defines the canon as "*a literary-disciplinary dynamic . . . a field of force that is never exclusively realized by any physical form, just as metal filings align with but do not constitute a magnetic field*" (2003: 51).

If aesthetic value is the key determinant of the various manifestations of canonicity, it is a matter of furious debate whether matters of taste can ever escape ideological determination. Terry Eagleton's Marxist critiques have repeatedly emphasized the liaison between aesthetic value (and the cultural field) and the social order, and the instrumentality of the canon in securing bourgeois hegemony. The leading postcolonial theorist, Edward Said, however, refutes the idea that the canon is a result of a conspiracy, "a sort of white male cabal," and defends the criteria of canon formation: "I think that there is something to be said . . . for aspects of work that has persisted and endured and has acquired and accreted to it a huge mass of differing interpretations" (Said et al. 1991: 52–3). Harold Bloom, too, valorizes canon formation for the agonist formal and aesthetic considerations that mobilize and precipitate canonicity: "Nothing is so essential to the Western Canon as its principles of selectivity, which are elitist only to the extent that they are founded upon severely artistic criteria" (1994: 21). The virtues that warrant canonical status for a literary work, according to Bloom, are as follows: "mastery of figurative language, originality, cognitive power, knowledge, exuberance of diction" (27–8). Most importantly, Bloom asserts, the works possess "strangeness," a singularity that is not easily assimilable into an existing order (3).

A less enchanted view of classical canon formation, as offered by Jonathan Kramnick, shores up both abstract and worldly criteria of selection: "difficulty, rarity, sub-limity, masculinity" (1998: 4). A writer's entry into the canon, anti-canonists argue, reflects his or her ideological conformity with dominant political and intellectual regimes. It is not surprising then that canon debates in the twentieth-century Anglo-American academy have centered on its exclusivity (and dubious inclusiveness) as also its claims of universality. To borrow from Said's formulation on culture, if the canon is, on the one hand, "a positive doctrine of the best that is thought and known, it is also on the other a differentially negative doctrine of all that is not best" (1983: 11–12). In the face of increasing demands for the opening of the canon to women and minority and postcolonial wri-ters, Bloom (1994) argues for upholding the difficulty of canonical literature and its in-accessibility to all but the smallest minority. If rarefied aesthetic value is nothing but "a mystification in the service of the ruling class," he argues, "then why should you read at all rather than go forth to serve the desperate needs of the exploited classes?" (487). Bloom dismisses the attacks on the canon by groups he lumps under "the School of Resentment: Feminists, Marxists, Lacanians, New Historicists, Deconstruc-tionists, Semioticians," adding that "left-wing critics cannot do the working class's reading for it" (492, 36).

It cannot be denied that the canon has historically been a nexus of power and knowledge that reinforces hierarchies and the vested interests of select institutions, excluding the "interests and accomplish-ments, to quote M. H. Abrams, of "Blacks, Hispanics, and other ethnic minorities, of women, of the working class, of popular culture, of homosexuals, and of non-Euro-pean civilizations" (1993: 21). Kramnick's *Making the English Canon* (1998) charts the way in which scholars have composed and shaped English national culture and the

public sphere through canon determination in the eighteenth century. "Literature is not the fragile troping of popular culture so much as it is the instinctive eliting of that culture," Kramnick concludes (100). For Mikhail Bakhtin (1981), canonization is also a process of standardization, in which culture-specific and time-bound norms and conventions, the heteroglossia of a novel, for instance, are normalized and homogenized. In the twenty-first century, however, when the public vocation of humanities faculties is increasingly in doubt, the literary canon "as elite cultural capital" will probably cease to exist anyway, except, as Regenia Gagnier points out, "as a remnant of past bourgeois culture" (2000: 2038). Moreover, the phe-nomenon of global English, related to the circulations of global capital, has dramati-cally altered the monolingual, Eurocentric nature of English studies. However, residual ideas of and a need for canonicity remain. While the high demand for anthologies of minority writing (whether ordered geo-graphically, thematically, or by genre) tes-tifies to a demise of the idea of the canon as "elite cultural capital," it also signals the invention of alternative canons. The emer-gence of other, non-standard, literatures and deconstructive modes of critical exege-sis unsettles the very standards of canonical value assessment, while forming what Patri-cia Waugh calls "an imaginary unity," a new canon (2006: 21).

The opening of the syllabus of canonical works to new contenders is not without controversy and fierce contention. While Bloom vehemently protests a method of selection where aesthetic standards are brushed aside for the cultural contexts and political relevance of a given work, Guillory's more considered response expresses misgivings about the simplistic opposition between dominant and domi-nated cultures: "The very intensity of our 'symbolic struggle' reduces cultural conditions of extreme complexity to an allegorical conflict between a Western cultural Goliath and its Davidic multicultural antagonists" (1993: 42). Guillory cautions against the perils of identity politics in the canon debate that reduces the genius author to "a representative member of some social group" (10), and whereby a canonical author represents a hegemonic group, while the noncanonical author stands for a minority. The production of literary texts, Guillory argues, "cannot be reduced to a specific and unique social function, not even the ideological one" (63). He cautions that the perceived disunities of culture cannot be remedied by forging cultural unities (of gender, race, sexualities, subcultures) at the level of the curriculum, for these often descend into simple allegorical structures of conflict between oppressors and the oppressed, and obscure the historical fact that gender, race, and sexuality are not interchangeable ciphers of marginality. The distinction between canonical and noncanonical – or countercultural - is itself fraught with contradictions: noncanonical works cannot be presented in the academy as equal in importance and value to canonical works and cannot be automatically credentialized as long as the two categories effectively cancel each other. The impasse is as follows: in a heterogeneously constituted university, and in a world of heterogeneously constituted cultural capital, to quote Guillory's terms, noncanonical works should be allowed to enjoy full canonical membership without actually becoming canonical. One way out of the impasse, Guillory suggests, is to imagine the canon not as a set of books but as a "discursive instrument of 'transmission'" (56) of institutional and pedagogic processes that canonical texts are implicated in, but not identical with. It is also important to remember that if canons objectify tradition, they also embody the conflictual history

between educational and social reproduction, which itself critiques and revises tradition. In conclusion, while the limits of the canon are themselves hard to ascertain and subject to perpetual change, both sides of the canon debate are confronted with the reality of the expansion of the canon from Western to worldwide, for, as David Damrosch reminds us in *What Is World Literature* (2003), the world is looking much wider today than it did 25 years ago.

SEE ALSO: Bakhtin, M. M.; Bloom, Harold; Kermode, Frank; Eagleton, Terry; Leavis, F. R.; Marxism; Said, Edward

REFERENCES AND SUGGESTED READINGS

Abrams, M. H. (1993). Canon of literature. In *A Glossary of Literary Terms*. Orlando, FL: Harcourt Brace College Publishers, pp. 19–22.
Bakhtin, M. (1981). *The Dialogic Imagination: Four Essays* (ed. M. Holquist; trans. C. Emerson & M. Holquist). Austin: University of Texas Press.
Bloom, H. (1994). *The Western Canon*. New York: Harcourt Brace.
Chow, R. (2000). Looking backward; Looking forward: MLA members speak. Special Millennium Issue, *PMLA*, 115(7), 1986–2024, 2028–76.
Damrosch, D. (2003). *What Is World Literature?* Princeton: Princeton University Press.
Eagleton, T. (1983). *Literary Theory: An Introduction*. Minneapolis: University of Minnesota Press.
Eagleton, T. (1984). *The Function of Criticism: From the "Spectator" to Poststructuralism*. London: Verso.
Fowler, A. (1979). Genre and the literary canon. *New Literary History*, 11, 97–119.
Gagnier, R. (2000). Looking backward; Looking forward: MLA members speak. Special Millennium Issue, *PMLA*, 115(7), 1986–2024, 2028–76.
Guillory, J. (1993). *Cultural Capital: The Problem of Literary Canon Formation*. Chicago: Chicago University Press.

Harris, W. V. (1991). Canonicity. *PMLA*, 106, 110–21.

Kermode, F. (1979). Institutional control of interpretation. *Salmagundi*, 43, 72–86.

Kramnick, J. B. (1998). *Making the English Canon: Print-Capitalism and the Cultural Past, 1700–1770*. Cambridge: Cambridge University Press.

Kuipers, C. M. (2003). The anthology/corpus dynamic: A field theory of the canon. *College Literature*, 30(2), 51–71.

Pfeiffer, R. (1968). *History of Classical Scholarship from the Beginnings to the End of the Hellenistic Age*. Oxford: Clarendon Press.

PMLA Special Millennium Issue, 115 (2000), 1986–2076.

Said, E. (1983). *The World, the Text, and the Critic*. Cambridge, MA: Harvard University Press.

Said, E., Marranca, B., Robinson, M., & Chaudhuri, U. (1991). Criticism, culture and performance: An interview with Edward Said. In B. Marranca & G. Dasgupta (eds.), *Interculturalism and Performance*. New York: PAJ Publications, pp. 38–59.

Waugh, P. (ed.) (2006). *Literary Theory and Criticism: An Oxford Guide*. Oxford: Oxford University Press.

Caruth, Cathy

JANE KILBY

Cathy Caruth (b. 1955) is Samuel Candler Dobbs Professor of Comparative Literature in the Department of Comparative Literature at Emory University, and her prominence in the field of literary and cultural theory is due to her thinking on trauma. She received her PhD from Yale University in 1988 and taught at Yale from 1986 to 1994, first as Assistant, then as Associate Professor. She then moved to Emory as Associate Professor and was promoted a few years later to Winship Distinguished Research Professor of Comparative Literature and English, before finally taking up her fully endowed Chair. She is the author of *Empirical Truths and Critical Fictions* (1991) and *Unclaimed Experience* (1996); she

edited *Trauma* (1995) and is coeditor, with Deborah Esch, of *Critical Encounters* (1995). Alongside other influential thinkers such as Shoshana Felman and Geoffrey Hartmann, Caruth's early work is most readily understood as a response to the criticism that poststructuralism is politically and ethically paralyzing since it does not allow language the power of referring directly to reality. Taking up the question of experience and history throughout all of her writing, Caruth argues instead that poststructuralism does not deny the possibility that language can give us access to reality, but rather that it refuses a model of reference based on the laws of physical perception. Indeed, according to Caruth (1991), even John Locke's *Essay Concerning Human Understanding*, the founding text of British empiricism, can be read as a narrative complicating its doctrinal status. Influenced in her reading by Paul de Man and the insights associated with deconstruction, Caruth's aim is not then to deny the possibility of accessing reality, but rather to open up the possibility of a rethinking of empiricism in order to attempt to understand anew the critical traditions that are defined in terms of it, such as Romanticism and critical philosophy.

Turning her attention to the question of traumatic history in particular, Caruth's most significant pieces of writing are the editorial she wrote for the *Trauma* collection and her monograph *Unclaimed Experience*. Key to both contributions, and underpinning Caruth's influence on the development of trauma theory, are the ways in which survivors of traumatic events often struggle to believe what has happened to them. In some critical sense, trauma defies comprehension, and if not suffering amnesia, victims nonetheless experience confusing, contrary, and frequently delayed reactions. In other words, and despite having clearly experienced a traumatic event, they struggle to remember and understand with any degree of certainty their experience of it. For survivors, then, the catastrophe or violence occasioning their trauma can be as if it never happened or had any reality. Noting the crisis this generates for the survivor (the subject thought most likely to know the truth or reality of their experience is plagued by uncertainty), Caruth establishes the fundamental enigma of trauma: our most brute, seemingly incontrovertible experience of reality is our least concrete, most enigmatic or evasive. Theorizing this insight as a particularly profound if peculiar paradox, Caruth maintains that trauma is impossible to fully assimilate as an experience or possess as a memory.

For Caruth, this is not to deny the reality of violent events, since the memory of them returns consistently and with a terrifying force to haunt the victim. Drawing on Sigmund Freud's work on trauma, most notably his *Moses and Monotheism* (1920) and *Beyond the Pleasure Principle* (1939), Caruth has gained particular renown for stressing the unique temporal character of trauma. *Moses and Monotheism* and *Beyond the Pleasure Principle* are critical to Caruth in this respect, since they represent Freud's late thinking on the question of the temporality of trauma. But while the question of the temporal structure of traumatic experience runs throughout Freud's corpus, beginning with his work on hysteria, and underpinning some of his key concepts, most crucially repression, Caruth highlights how his later work represents a considerable break with his earlier formulations, which notoriously evolved with an emphasis on the role of dreams, fantasy, and wish fulfillment in the etiology of trauma. The reason for this break is contentious, but for commentators such as Caruth, Freud is forced to revise his understanding of trauma in the wake of World War I and thereby reassess the significance of external events and historical reality to the question of trauma. Of particular importance to Freud, Caruth argues, is his observation that the returning soldiers suffer from nightmares, nightmares which quite literally repeat the horror of war such that the soldiers wake in a state of fright, as if finding themselves once more at the scene of violence. There is, it seems, a compulsion to return and experience the horror as if for the first time. Coupling Freud's insight on repetition compulsion with his reflection on the way in which victims of train crashes would walk away as if unharmed, Caruth's innovation is to stress the belated nature of trauma.

Offering an alternative to repression, Caruth's emphasis on the structural latency of traumatic experience has proved important for scholars engaging with a range of historical, political, and social injustices. In this regard, her intervention is considered particularly vital since it allows an escape from the theoretical deadlocks established by antihumanist and antifoundational critiques of identity politics. The nature of these critiques is manifold, but critically it has been difficult for scholars to mobilize a concept of experience that does not rely on principles of authenticity, immediacy, and transparency. In light of Caruth's work, however, this is no longer an issue, with the concept of traumatic memory allowing not only a mobilization of victim experience and narratives, but an interest in the nature of survival itself. Indeed, for Caruth, the enigma of trauma touches equally and inextricably on the question of destruction and survival, with the future of trauma studies less a question of violence and death than it is of life.

SEE ALSO: Deconstruction; Felman, Shoshana; Freud, Sigmund; de Man, Paul; Poststructuralism; Romance

REFERENCES AND SUGGESTED
READINGS

Caruth, C. (1991). *Empirical Truths and Critical Fictions: Locke, Wordsworth, Kant, Freud.* Baltimore: Johns Hopkins University Press.

Caruth, C. (ed.) (1995). *Trauma: Explorations in Memory.* Baltimore: Johns Hopkins University Press.

Caruth, C. (1996). *Unclaimed Experience: Trauma, Narrative, and History.* Baltimore: Johns Hopkins University Press.

Caruth, C., & Esch, D. (eds.) (1995). *Critical Encounters: Reference and Responsibility in Deconstructive Writing.* New Brunswick: Rutgers University Press.

Cixous, Hélène

ABIGAIL RINE

Hélène Cixous is a highly prolific Francophone theorist, poet, novelist, playwright, philosopher, and literary critic: indeed, she is a writer whose work resists easy categorization. Although the majority of her publications are works of experimental fiction, she is most widely known in the English-speaking world for her contributions to French feminist and literary theory and for formulating the concept of *écriture féminine*, or feminine writing.

Cixous was born in Oran, Algeria, in 1937 of Spanish/French and Jewish/German descent. Coming of age in an atmosphere of lingual and cultural plurality greatly influenced her writing, as did experiencing the death of her father at age 11. When Cixous was 18, she moved from Algeria to Paris, where she passed her *agrégation* in 1959. While teaching at the University of Nanterre in 1968, she received the Doctorat d'État, upon completing an eight-year doctoral thesis on James Joyce. Later that year, in response to the May 1968 student uprisings, Cixous helped found the experimental University of Paris VIII-Vincennes and

was soon granted a professorship in English literature. She published her first novel, *Dedans*, in 1969 and was subsequently awarded the prestigious Prix Médicis. In 1974, Cixous founded a doctoral program in *études féminines* (feminine studies) at Vincennes, which endured a tumultuous relationship with the French government, at times losing accreditation. This program was subsequently expanded into the Centre des recherches en études féminines in 1980 and now offers a range of undergraduate and postgraduate programs, as well as a research seminar led by Cixous.

Cixous first entered the English-speaking literary scene with the publication of "The laugh of the Medusa" (1976[1975]). In this essay, Cixous employs Derridean deconstruction to recast the binary opposition of man/woman. Along with "Sorties," a piece from *The Newly Born Woman* (Cixous & Clément 1986[1975]), "Medusa" introduces and expounds Cixous's notion of feminine writing, a concept still regarded in the Anglo-American world as her most defining contribution to critical theory. Her conceptualization of *écriture féminine* is not limited to her theoretical texts, but continues on the creative front in her experimental fiction and drama. Indeed, her attempts to theorize *écriture féminine* cannot be separated from her practice of *écriture féminine*, which is displayed in all of her writing. Often misunderstood, feminine writing is writing that resists the dominant discourse and, as such, defies any stable codification. Building on Jacques Derrida's analysis of logocentrism and the post-Freudian theories of Jacques Lacan, Cixous envisions a mode of writing that represents what is repressed in the Symbolic order. This order, which she asserts as fundamentally phallocentric, sustains itself through a network of oppositional hierarchies such as man/woman, mind/body, self/other, which inexorably privilege the masculine. In an attempt to challenge and undermine this domineering logic, Cixous calls for a way of articulating nonhierarchical difference and asserts the revolutionary capacity of écriture féminine.

Cixous's ongoing theorization of writing adopts the Lacanian idea that identity and consciousness are conceptualized through language and also reflects Lacan's method of linking language to the body and sexuality. To resist the reductive definitions of "woman" in phallocentric discourse and the exclusion of embodied female experience, Cixous advocates writing that echoes the rhythms and processes of women's bodies, writing that is forceful and fluid, exceeding linear boundaries. She argues that writing, as a physical act, should not repress the reality of the body, but give it a voice. The phenomenon of pregnancy, specifically, provides Cixous with an ample metaphor for selfhood that accommodates, rather than appropriates, the other. In addition to representing female sexuality, she advocates writing that undermines the unitary, authorial "I," opening space for multiple voices and perspectives within a single text. For Cixous, writing is a method of surpassing the opposition of self/other and exploring the capacity for multiplicity within each person.

Though Cixous's concept of feminine writing elicits charges of essentialism for its expression of the sexed body, it is important to clarify that the markers of "masculine" and "feminine" within her work do not denote physical sex, but rather distinct behavioral models. The masculine mode of relation or exchange is marked by censorship, order, and binary logic, while the feminine is characterized by abundance, plurality, and excess. Cixous relates these modes to male and female libidinal economies, to the distinct ways in which each sex experiences jouissance, or pleasure. Though these economies are linked to the sexed

body through the experience of jouissance, they are not irrevocably tethered to it. Women may be predisposed to feminine economy due to their libidinal experiences, capacity for motherhood, and marginal position in society, but men can enter a feminine relational mode, just as woman can participate in masculine economy. Cixous espouses the possibility of bisexuality, using the term in its psychoanalytic context to denote the capacity for both femininity and masculinity within each subject. Through her concept of writing, she seeks a balance of these economies, a coexistence of masculine and feminine that can only be achieved if the feminine is given a voice.

The "sexed" elements of Cixous's theories are perhaps the most misunderstood, due in part to occasional inconsistencies in her terminology. Since her initial works, she has avoided the use of gendered terms, while retaining the key concepts these terms represent. In the essay "Extreme fidelity" (Sellers 1988) Cixous recognizes that her use of the words masculine and feminine at times interferes with her attempts at deconstruction, causing misinterpretations, and recommends a movement away from gendered binary categories. In this vein, her later works have continued to explore the revolutionary potential of writing, without describing such writing as specifically feminine.

In her early works, the writers Cixous presents as exemplary of revolutionary writing are men, such as Shakespeare and Franz Kafka. It is not until Cixous discovers the Brazilian writer Clarice Lispector that she is able to put a female face to her vision of writing. In her capacity as a literary critic, Cixous has devoted much attention to Lispector, whose work embodies Cixous's notion of representing difference without appropriation. In the collection Reading with Clarice Lispector (1990), taken from

Cixous's seminars throughout the 1980s, Cixous enters into dialogue with Lispector's texts, which continually destabilize the borders of the unitary subject and renegotiate the relationship between self and other. More recently, Cixous's work has drawn on numerous women writers, including Marina Tsvetaeva and Ingeborg Bachmann.

During the 1980s, Cixous formed an ongoing collaboration with director Ariane Mnouchkine and began writing theatrical works for the Théâtre du Soleil in Paris. The dramatic technique of speaking through multiple voices granted Cixous new-found freedom as a writer, enabling her to display openly her deconstruction of the closed "I" and assume several identities at once. For Cixous, the format of theater readily lends itself to the exploration of historical events. As such, her plays written for the Théâtre du Soleil reflect a renewed attention to postcolonialism and engage themes of political and ethnic, rather than gendered, alterity.

Throughout the 1990s, Cixous continued to theorize the practice of writing in the context of otherness. A series of lectures published as the book *Three Steps on the Ladder of Writing* (1993) explore in greater detail Cixous's vision of writing praxis. Describing three distinct schools or means of writing – the School of the Dead, the School of Dreams, and the School of Roots – she asserts the need for writing to tap into the unconscious and attempt representation of the repressed. She presents the practice of writing as a descending, inward climb, a continuous struggle to encounter the deepest of human mysteries. Linking writing with death, she describes how the writer, in submitting to the text, suffers a loss of selfhood by leaving behind the familiar and approaching the enigmatic. Cixous asserts the experience of loss as an important resource for writers and relates how the death of her father initiated her own descent into writing. Dream imagery is

also presented as fuel for the writer, by forming a gateway to the unconscious mind. In her rereading of Leviticus, Cixous draws an association between birds, women, and writing in their status as *imund* (unclean) and asserts that writing should reach beyond censorship and societal taboos to approach what is deemed abominable. Her subsequent collection *Stigmata* (1998) resurrects this motif of birds and women and further explores her central ideal that writing should, above all, jar the reader out of complacency. She describes texts that sting and pierce as *stigmatexts*, using the notion of stigmata as that which wounds but also stimulates. Though questions of gender and alterity are featured throughout *Three Steps* and *Stigmata*, within these later works the question of man/woman is largely subsumed in an examination of self/other.

The most recent seam in her oeuvre is a string of autobiographical works. For Cixous, writing as both process and product is able to capture and remember what would otherwise disappear. Her life-writings reveal an endeavor to give expression to the numerous facets of her identity and personal history. *The Day I Wasn't There* (2006a[2000]) and *Reveries of the Wild Woman* (2006c[2000]) recount stories from Cixous's early life while investigating notions of presence and absence, exile and otherness. *Dream I Tell You* (2006b[2003]), addressed to friend and fellow philosopher Jacques Derrida and composed from the fragments of Cixous's dreams, is a collection of meditations that invoke familiar themes of death, friendship, and writing from the unconscious.

The reception of Cixous's work throughout her career has been mixed and primarily centered on her notion of feminine writing. Some feminist theorists, such as Toril Moi (1985), have deemed *écriture féminine* to be essentialist and colored by patriarchal conceptions of femininity. Cixous's work has also been criticized for its reliance upon psychoanalysis, particularly the phallocentric theories of Freud and Lacan, though these criticisms overlook the myriad ways in which she deconstructs and revises psychoanalytic concepts even as she invokes them. Critics of Cixous's theories tend toward literal, rather than metaphorical, readings of her texts and often confuse her markers of "masculine" and "feminine" with physical sex. In response to the overall preoccupation with her earlier publications, critics such as Susan Sellers explore the progression of Cixous's thought throughout her wide range of works. Sellers offers a holistic vision of Cixous, elucidating her thought in its vast diversity by drawing on her fiction, theoretical writings, dream notebooks, and lectures. Such advocates of Cixous's theories seek to redeem *écriture féminine* from its many misconceptions, as well as draw attention to the overlooked and ongoing elements of her work.

SEE ALSO: Deconstruction; Derrida, Jacques; *Écriture Féminine*; Feminism; Gender and Cultural Studies; Gender Theory; Phallus/Phallocentrism; Poststructuralism; Psychoanalysis (since 1966); Subject Position

REFERENCES AND SUGGESTED READINGS

Blyth, I., & Sellers, S. (2004). *Hélène Cixous: Live Theory*. London: Continuum.
Cixous, H. (1976). The laugh of the Medusa (trans. K. Cohen & P. Cohen). *Signs*, 1(4), 875–893. (Original work published 1975.)
Cixous, H. (1990). *Reading with Clarice Lispector* (ed. and trans. V. Conley). Minneapolis: University of Minnesota Press. (Original seminars presented 1980–5.)
Cixous, H. (1993). *Three Steps on the Ladder of Writing* (trans. S. Cornell & S. Sellers). New York: Columbia University Press. (Original lectures presented 1990.)
Cixous, H. (1998). *Stigmata: Escaping Texts*. New York: Routledge.
Cixous, H. (2004). *The Writing Notebooks* (ed. and trans. S. Sellers). London: Continuum. (Original work published 2000.)
Cixous, H. (2006a). *The Day I Wasn't There* (trans. B. B. Brahic). Edinburgh: Edinburgh University Press. (Original work published 2000.)
Cixous, H. (2006b). *Dream I Tell You* (trans. B. B. Brahic). Edinburgh: Edinburgh University Press. (Original work published 2003.)
Cixous, H. (2006c). *Reveries of the Wild Woman: Primal Scenes* (trans. B. B. Brahic). Evanston, IL: Northwestern University Press. (Original work published 2000.)
Cixous, H., & Clément, C. (1986). *The Newly Born Woman* (trans. B. Wing). Minneapolis: University of Minnesota Press. (Original work published 1975.)
Moi, T. (1985). *Sexual/Textual Politics: Feminist Literary Theory*. New York: Routledge.
Sellers, S. (1988). Extreme fidelity. In S. Sellers (ed.), *Writing Differences: Readings from the Seminars of Hélène Cixous*. Milton Keynes: Open University Press.
Sellers, S. (1996). *Hélène Cixous: Authorship, Autobiography and Love*. Oxford: Blackwell.

Cognitive Studies

LAURA SALISBURY

Cognitive studies is a mode of critical analysis of literary texts that takes as its basic premise the belief that the mind and its reasoning processes, alongside its cultural products and affective experiences, can be analyzed systematically in terms of underlying biological and evolutionary frameworks. Cognitive science has its roots in research into theories of mind based upon computational procedures from the 1950s, although it emerged as a field of study in its own right in the mid-1970s. Since that time, work to understand the functional and systematic nature of mental states has developed into a complex intersection of different disciplines, including those of neuroscience, linguistics, psychology, anthropology, the philosophy of mind, computer science (particularly as it is concerned with artificial intelligence), biology, and sociology. As cognitive science has become an increasingly dominant paradigm for understanding the human, using this knowledge to form ways of interpreting cultural products has also become more influential, with cognitive studies being institutionalized as a distinct branch of literary theory after the establishment of a discussion group on the topic at the Conference of the Modern Language Association in the United States in 1998.

In the late 1970s, a "second generation" of cognitive scientists (Lakoff & Johnson 1999) began to move away from the concentration on artificial intelligence and the theories of language and psychology modeled to support it, towards reading the mind as a function of an embodied organism. Using cognitive linguistics, influential researchers such as the linguist George Lakoff and philosopher Mark Johnson produced work accessible to nonspecialist audiences that argued that all conceptual processes are fundamentally grounded in the embodied nature of human experience. This was not simply a way of saying that humans need a body in order to exist; rather, Lakoff and Johnson determined that the very structure of cognition itself is grounded in the specificity of human physiology, our embodiment. They proposed that those neural and cognitive mechanisms that allow us to perceive and orientate ourselves in the physical world fundamentally underpin and structure our conceptual systems, our modes of reason, and our uses of language (Lakoff & Johnson 1999). Every living being categorizes, and animals categorize themselves and their environment according to the specifics of their sensing apparatus and their ability to move their bodies and manipulate objects in the world. This fundamental activity, which is mostly unconscious and

tied to those affective responses drawn from the embodied experience of sensation and perception, provides a template upon which all seemingly "abstract" categories are built, or, more properly, from which they are imaginatively projected. Lakoff & Johnson (1980) thus assert that the metaphors we use to structure our lived experience, those that we live by (such as ones that represent life as a journey that progresses), are universal; they are shared across cultures because of the commonality of the ways in which human minds are embodied.

Such arguments have led the cognitive scientist Mark Turner (1996) to suggest that one might think of the mind itself as fundamentally "literary," given that its basic cognitive operations are forms of metaphorical and metonymic activity. And if fundamental cognitive processes share a family resemblance with the linguistic structures of literature, a study of the workings of literature might, by implication, offer insights for the study of mind. Lakoff & Turner (1989) have themselves extended their analyses of the functioning of the mind into literary studies, offering readings of recurrent metaphors in poetry and describing their effectiveness according to the ways in which they reflect and manipulate fundamentally embodied cognitive metaphors. Turner (1996) has also suggested that narrative, or parable (in his terms), seems to mirror and thus illuminate the operations of meaning making in the human mind that occur as connections are made across and between mental spaces in an onward roll that "blends" seemingly discrete conceptual containers. But the key point for Turner is that it is the everyday human mind that is fundamentally "literary" in its material nature. So although such work places literature and the aesthetic at the heart of the material, neurological functioning of the human – suggesting the importance of analyzing sophisticated literary operations for the insights they might offer into the structural modes of the mind – the readings of texts produced have tended to be less concerned with the particular historical conditions, generic conventions, and what might be thought of as the specifically "literary" character of works, than they have been with the illumination of universal structures of cognition.

Although some critics have sought assertively to distance cognitive studies from evolutionary literary theory (Hogan 2003; Richardson 2004), both approaches share the belief that the structures of mind uncovered and detailed in their analyses are the products of evolutionary development. As a distinct branch of cognitive studies, evolutionary literary theory argues strongly that genes prescribe trends of evolutionary adaptation that determine regular and analyzable modes of human sensory perception and mental development; these, in turn, mold and direct the growth of particular cultural forms. As culture then plays its part in determining which of these prescribing genes will be preserved – which will go on to multiply in succeeding generations – analyzing cultural forms will offer insights into the development of a human organism formed and adapted according to its environment. It is important to draw attention to the fact that evolutionary literary theory is often highly polemical, having determinedly sought to distance itself from the most influential literary theories of the past 40 years. Joseph Carroll, for example, has declared explicitly that his version of evolutionary literary theory, literary Darwinism, will provide modes through which to "analyze and oppose the poststructuralist assumptions that now dominate academic literary studies" (1995: 1). Jonathan Gottschall has also positioned his work as part of a sustained attack on literary and cultural theory and its part in the production of what is dismissively known as the Standard Social Science Model (SSSM), or "social constructivism." According to Gottschall (2008), the SSSM argues that humans are simply blank slates inscribed by social and cultural influences that are wholly unconstrained by human biology. Gottschall indicts Marxism, structuralism, poststructuralism, and Lacanian psychoanalysis, alongside feminist, new historicist, postcolonialist and queer theories, as forms of thought that have contributed to postmodern views of the world and of knowledge. For Gottschall, these theoretical approaches have as their common aim the desire to denaturalize human culture by critiquing its attitudes to gender, sexuality, political ideology, even language itself, revealing them to be fully contingent upon specific historical and social conditions rather than determined by biology. Evolutionary literary criticism, by contrast, finds in biology the determining causes of culture and seeks to describe how cultural manifestations of gender roles, incest taboos, mating strategies, and conflicts offer evidence of our nature as animals that have evolved and adapted to our environment.

The practice of "reverse-engineering," of inferring the function of the whole by examining the operation of the parts, or, in this case, of projecting back a narrative of progressive evolutionary development from a specific contemporary cultural trait, is common within evolutionary psychology and often used in evolutionary literary criticism; however, it bears some analysis. One problem is that the whole process can appear to be somewhat circular: from a present trait a necessary inference is made that it represents the most effective adaptation to the conditions. Nature is seen to produce human culture as its best, most smoothly reflective, mirror. But as John Dupré (2003) has noted in his critique of evolutionary psychology, such readings rarely take account of the complexity and contingency of evolutionary processes themselves, nor do they read in sufficient detail the interactions between nature and culture that offer philosophically and scientifically robust accounts of human behavior. More significantly for literary studies, the traits chosen for analysis by critics working within the evolutionary paradigm, the starting points for their program of reverse-engineering, are often ideologically charged in rather explicit ways, making the presentation of the "naturalness" of particular gendered behaviors, or of selfishness, or of a tendency for humans to wish to organize themselves democratically, worthy of precisely the forms of theoretical critique against which Carroll and Gottschall have explicitly positioned their work. Gottschall (2008) accepts the importance of noting any ideological bias within literary critical analysis, but has recently proposed that such bias is better tackled and removed (rather than critiqued) by implementing the methods used by experimental science to try to produce objective results. Gottschall polemically proposes that scientific method, which foregrounds the rational assessment of evidence, produces tests that are able to prove hypotheses untrue, and reaches conclusions through the quantitative and statistical analysis of data gathered under controlled conditions, is vital if the idea of a criticism that could produce objective, testable, reproducible results is to be upheld. He also suggests that part of the value of a scientific methodology and the empirical study of readers' responses to texts is that it narrows the space of plausible explanations for phenomena. Literary theories based more centrally upon critique, by contrast, expand exponentially the possible interpretations of texts, thus leading readers and a whole discipline toward the posing of ever more complicated questions, but away from offering up robust answers.

Although one might disagree for various reasons with Gottschall's (2008) position that literary studies should be purged of its progressive, leftist ideological bias in favor of scientific attempts to produce ideologically neutral results, it is undoubtedly true that literary studies has learnt in the past and should continue to learn from other fields, as genuine interdisciplinarity offers critics ways of extending, expanding, and seeing the limits of the questions they ask of texts and of their current methodologies. Nevertheless, when Carroll, for example, states that he is analyzing Jane Austen's *Pride and Prejudice* as though it were "the literary equivalent of a fruit fly" (2005: 79), the experimental analogy is perhaps instructive in revealing one of the limits of literary Darwinism. Geneticists use fruit flies in their experiments because they reproduce quickly; fruit flies allow scientists to observe change and to model and analyze hypotheses about adaptation. But as Carroll himself suggests, geneticists do not believe or suggest that genetics only applies to fruit flies. In fact, it is the production and general application of theory rather than the specificity of the fruit fly that is of concern. To use *Pride and Prejudice* as though it were a fruit fly suggests, then, that the historical and generic specificity, and perhaps even what might be thought of as the distinctively literary qualities of Austen's work, are not the main objects of analysis, although they may be drawn on to support the larger thesis. As a result it has been suggested that within such readings the engagement with the existing scholarship on a particular author or field can be minimal (frequently implicitly positioned as partial and methodologically flawed), and the analysis of a particular text's artifactual and linguistic nature sometimes rather slight (Richardson 2004). In Gottschall's search for "literary universals," the explanation offered for the emphasis on the attractiveness of females he finds in narratives and the lack of female protagonists in world folk tales is that the more "active," wandering lives of "traditional culture's males" "are simply better at riveting an audience's attention," than women's "domestic lives" that have traditionally been determined by "gross physical biology, like the necessity of keeping ... lactating mothers and their infants in close proximity" (2008: 154). Leaving aside any feminist critique of this position, in seeking what is deemed to be universal, that which is textually and culturally specific has been sacrificed. By contrast, Hogan's (1997) use of cognitive studies rigorously to identify what might be universal in terms of literary *form* – the shared or common quality of basic generic distinctions, or the cross-cultural appearance of techniques such as symbolism, patterning, paralleling, and particular plot devices – is explicitly framed in terms of a desire to enable critics to illuminate what is also particular to individual literary texts and specific cultures. Hogan's cautious refusal to determine whether universals determined by shared cognitive structures, such as the limits of "rehearsal memory" that proscribe how long a poetic line might become, produce texts that reflect or represent any straightforward universality in non-literary human behavior, is worth noting.

Cognitive studies as a broader discipline has been keen to emphasize that attempts to map higher-level structures (literature) and the mental states central to their production and reception in terms of lower-level structures (biology), without a detailed analysis and understanding of the nature and functioning of that higher level, can lead to accounts of literature that are reductive in terms of their account of aesthetics, and simplistic in terms of the application of scientific theory and evidence (Hogan 2003). By contrast, the form of analysis known as "cognitive poetics," introduced by Reuven

Tsur (1992), seeks precisely to account for the specificity of the higher-level structure of literature in its descriptions of how poetic language and form are determined and constrained by human information processing. Rather as the Russian and Prague schools of semiotics emphasized that defamiliarization is a central aspect of what makes language in some way "literary" or poetic, Tsur suggests that poetry seems to make special use of normal cognitive processes by deforming, disrupting or delaying their functioning. Other approaches that have worked to supplement and engage with existing literary theory rather than to oppose it include Mary Thomas Crane's *Shakespeare's Brain* (2001). Her work is concerned with tracing the continuities and interactions between cultural forms and forces, language, and the material substrate of cognition. Crane describes in detail the particularities of Shakespeare's poetics, suggesting how they may be effective because of the ways in which they are motivated by their origins in the neural systems of a human body that interacts with its environment. In a complex reading of the relationship between the imprints of power experienced through culture, and the constraints and freedoms encoded into "discourse" by cognitive conceptual structures determined by a prediscursive experience of embodiment, Crane brings materialist and poststructuralist concerns with language, subjectivity, and power into a significant dialogue with cognitive studies. In mapping contemporary theories of mind and language on to historical texts, Crane also extends her analysis, suggesting that these new models may offer insights into the Galenic early modern notions of the relationship between the mind and the brain that inform Shakespeare's cultural context and its understanding of the human.

Ellen Spolsky's (1993) work also seeks to engage with new historicist and poststructuralist accounts of literature, offering some neurological support for the emphasis on uncertainty, instability, and cultural contingency, often found in those critical readings. Spolsky suggests a large role for cultural construction in the development of individual minds, but she does this by reading both brain and mind as determined by their modularity. The modularity hypothesis suggests that the brain is composed of various separate and innate structures that have established and distinct functional purposes in relation to mental activity. But because these structures do not quite meet one another, our perceptual and cognitive systems are traced through with gaps. This "genetically inherited epistemological equipment" produces minds structurally determined by their capacity to bridge gaps in multiple ways, to think flexibly, and respond creatively to circumstances. Spolsky's analysis thus suggests a way of reading resistance, dissent, and the reaching after new forms, as fundamental parts of our neuropsychological make-up – a make-up that literature both reflects and assumes its part in producing. Instead of simply passively reflecting reasonably static biological structures determined in the evolutionary past, literature becomes one of the ways that human brains display their plasticity, their capacity to learn and to adapt quickly, and their ability to challenge and reforge modes of understanding the world. Lisa Zunshine (2006) has also suggested that fictional narratives endlessly experiment with, rather than automatically execute, evolved cognitive adaptations. In her argument, cognitive constraints and limits are the very things that are probed, challenged, and explored by literature; as such, Zunshine argues that the aesthetic is a realm that is neurologically determined to be concerned with creativity and dissent rather than consensus and the replication of established norms.

There are many challenges to be faced by cognitive studies as it becomes institution-alized into literary theory. As a broad discipline, it offers fundamentally to reconfigure literary critical methods and to suggest new empirical accounts of what have previously been impressionistic or folk psychological ideas of what happens as literature is being read. But the fact that the poet, gerontologist, and critic Raymond Tallis (2008) has recently suggested that neuroaesthetics appears to him like just another form of academic carpetbagging, to be placed dismissively in the tradition of literary theoretical misappropriations of science, is instructive (although also frustrating in its implied disparagement of measured and thoughtful work in a number of theoretical fields). Tallis claims that much of the neuroscience cited in cognitive readings of literature is hypothetical, often highly speculative. He states that one thing neuroscience knows for certain is that it is still extremely uncertain about how qualia (the experience of things – the sensation of cold, the taste of an apple) relate to observable activities in particular nerve pathways. And it is indeed the extraordinary complexity of these processes that should be recalled every time there is a temptation to imagine that the brain activity seen in an MRI scan or hypothesized from experimental data is fully identical to an experience, an affect, or an orientation toward the world. As the philosopher and one-time student of Derrida's, Catherine Malabou (2008), suggests, most contemporary neuroscience written with the nonspecialist in mind offers accounts of "natural" neurobiological and cognitive functioning that slide too easily over the complexity of the processes by which neuronal activity is translated into mental and representational structures. If there is this process of translation between neuronal and mental at work, then what neuroscience requires is precisely a theory of reading, rather than reduction or passive reflection, to articulate the relations between them.

Such a self-conscious theory of reading would also, Malabou argues, counter the tendency for accounts of brain function simply to reproduce dominant modes of thought – modes that currently seem inevitably to find in the flexible, networked, and modular brain a mirror and support for the naturalness of liberal capitalism. Whether cognitive science is used in readings of literature to support assertions about human universals which remain reasonably static, or whether human nature becomes defined by its capacity to be formed according to innovation, dissent, or creativity, cognitive studies should be thought of alongside those other forms of literary and cultural theory that continue to ask explicitly what it means to read, and what it means to render any activity "natural."

SEE ALSO: Cultural Materialism; Derrida, Jacques; Feminism; Gender Theory; Genre; Marxism; New Historicism; Poststructuralism; Queer Theory; Reader-Response Studies; Social Constructionism

REFERENCES AND SUGGESTED READINGS

Carroll, J. (1995). *Evolution and Literary Theory*. Columbia: University of Missouri Press.
Carroll, J. (2005). Human nature and literary meaning: A theoretical model illustrated with a critique of Pride and Prejudice. In *The Literary Animal: Evolution and the Nature of Narrative*. Evanston: Northwestern University Press, pp. 76–106.
Crane, M. T. (2001). *Shakespeare's Brain: Reading with Cognitive Theory*. Oxford: Oxford University Press.
Dupré, J. (2003). *Darwin's Legacy: What Evolution Means Today*. Oxford: Oxford University Press.
Gottschall, J. (2008). *Literature, Science, and a New Humanities*. Basingstoke: Palgrave.
Gottschall, J., & Sloan Wilson, D. (eds.) (2005). *The Literary Animal: Evolution and the Nature of Narrative*. Evanston: Northwestern University Press.

Hart, F. E. (2001). The epistemology of cognitive literary studies. *Philosophy and Literature*, 25, 314–334.
Hogan, P. C. (1997). Literary universals. *Poetics Today*, 18, 223–249.
Hogan, P. C. (2003). *Cognitive Science, Literature, and the Arts: A Guide for Humanists*. New York: Routledge.
Lakoff, G., & Johnson, M. (1980). *Metaphors We Live By*. Chicago: University of Chicago Press.
Lakoff, G., & Johnson, M. (1999). *Philosophy in the Flesh: The Embodied Mind and Its Challenge to Western Thought*. New York: Basic Books.
Lakoff, G., & Turner, M. (1989). *More than Cool Reason: A Field Guide to Poetic Metaphor*. Chicago: University of Chicago Press.
Malabou, C. (2008). *What Should We Do with Our Brain?* (trans. S. Rand). New York: Fordham University Press.
Richardson, A. (2004). Studies in literature and cognition: A field map. In A. Richardson & E. Spolsky (eds.), *The Work of Fiction: Cognition, Culture, and Complexity*. Aldershot: Ashgate, pp. 1–25.
Spolsky, E. (1993). *Gaps in Nature: Literary Interpretation and the Modular Mind*. Albany: SUNY Press.
Tallis, R. (2008). The neuroscience delusion. *Times Literary Supplement* (April 9).
Tsur, R. (1992). *Toward a Theory of Cognitive Poetics*. Amsterdam: North-Holland.
Turner, M. (1996). *The Literary Mind*. New York: Oxford University Press.
Zunshine, L. (2006). *Why We Read Fiction: Theory of Mind and the Novel*. Columbus: Ohio State University Press.

Core and Periphery

STEPHEN MORTON

The distinction between the core and the periphery is a spatial distinction, which has shaped the mapping of global political and economic power relations from the seventeenth century to the present. This distinction is often associated with the world-systems theory of the Marxist economist Immanuel Wallerstein, who has argued that the global capitalist economy has been expanding since the seventeenth century, and that this expansion has involved massive economic imbalances between the core, or "the West," and the periphery, or "the non-West." Yet this distinction between "the West" and "the non-West" is also an invention of the Western cultural imagination in an attempt to assert the dominance of the core over the periphery.

An interesting example of such a Eurocentric fiction can be found in the German philosopher Hegel's writings on world history. In the appendix to his introduction to the *Lectures on the Philosophy of World History* (first published 1830), Hegel asserted that "*Africa proper* . . . has no historical interest of its own, for we find its inhabitants living in barbarism and savagery" (1975[1830]: 172). In Hegel's view of history, "the African" lives in an "undifferentiated and concentrated unity"; "their consciousness has not yet reached an awareness of any substantial objectivity"; and, as a consequence, the African "has not yet succeeded in making this distinction between himself as an individual and his essential universality, so that he knows nothing of an absolute being which is other and higher than his own self" (177). By defining Africa and Africans in the terms of a racist and Eurocentric model of historical progress, Hegel concludes that Africa is "an unhistorical continent, with no movement or development of its own" (190).

What Hegel's account of Africa illustrates is not simply the racism and the Eurocentrism of Western thought, but the way in which Western thought both shapes and is shaped by imperial power relations. The literary critic Edward W. Said subjected such values and ideas to critical scrutiny in his 1978 study *Orientalism*. For Said, European literature and culture has historically defined the Orient as a peripheral place of otherness and foreignness against

which Europe defines its place as the core or center of culture, civilization, and modernity. As he puts it:

> The Orient is not only adjacent to Europe; it is also the place of Europe's greatest and richest and oldest colonies, the source of its civilizations and languages, its cultural contestant, and one of its deepest and most recurring images of the Other. In addition, the Orient has helped to define Europe (or the West) as its contrasting image, idea, personality, experience. Yet none of this Orient is merely imaginative. The Orient is an integral part of European material civilization and culture. Orientalism expresses and represents that part culturally and even ideologically as a mode of discourse with supporting institutions, vocabulary, scholarship, imagery, doctrines, even colonial bureaucracies and colonial styles. (1978: 1–2)

Just as Hegel defined Africa as unhistorical in contrast to Europe, so Orientalism – the body of writing and scholarship produced about the Orient – defined the Orient as culturally inferior and peripheral to Europe. And it was precisely this idea that aided and abetted the justification of European colonialism in Africa, the Middle East, and South Asia.

If European writers and thinkers such as Hegel seemed to reinforce the view of Western civilization as more modern and superior to non-Western civilization, the rise of national liberation movements in Africa, South Asia, and the Caribbean during the 1950s and 1960s brought about a sea change in the way in which the relationship between the core and the periphery was defined in literary and cultural theory. As Robert J. C. Young explains, "If so-called 'so-called poststructuralism' is the product of a single historical moment, then that moment is probably not May 1968 but rather the Algerian War of Independence" (1989: 1). For many French intellectuals, including Jacques Derrida, Jean-François Lyotard,

Hélène Cixous, Louis Althusser, and Jean-Paul Sartre, the Algerian war of independence was an important reminder of how the freedom of the human subject in the core (in this case France) was secured through colonial exploitation and capitalist expansion in the rest of the world, or the periphery. In *Monolingualism of the Other*, for example, Jacques Derrida argues that his French mother tongue is not his own. As he puts it, "I only have one language; it is not mine" (1998: 1). For Derrida, this position of inhabiting a language that is not his own is a performative contradiction because the subject of the French language does the opposite of what he says in the statement that he makes (3). This performative contradiction is significant not only for understanding Derrida's biography as a Franco-Maghrebian Jew who was expelled from his lycée in French-occupied Algeria and subsequently sent to a Jewish school set up for the expelled Jewish students and staffed by the expelled Jewish teachers (see Baum 2004); it also sheds some light on the trajectory of Derrida's work as a thinker who has always negotiated with the constitutive margins of Western philosophical conceptuality (see Derrida 1998: 71–2).

At the same time, Derrida is careful to stress that his biography cannot be taken to explain his intellectual project: "A Judeo-Franco-Maghrebian genealogy does not clarify everything, far from it. But could I explain anything without it, ever?" (1998: 72).

Derrida's thought has not only sought to question the foundations of the Western philosophical tradition; it has also drawn attention to the relationship between Western systems of thought and Western representations of other cultures. In *Of Grammatology*, Derrida offers a polemical critique of Claude Lévi-Strauss's representation of the Nambikwara, an aboriginal community as a people without writing in

his study *Tristes Tropiques*. In the first section of *Of Grammatology*, Derrida emphasizes how the coherence and continuity of Western thought has been predicated on the "debasement of writing and its repression outside 'full' speech" (1976: 3). Derrida refers to this repression of writing as phonocentric, because it privileges the voice as a transparent medium through which the subject represents *him*self as a coherent subject. Yet as Derrida emphasizes, even the physical act of speech relies on a process of writing, or a system of differentiation to generate meanings. By critically inhabiting the narrow concept of writing as a transparent vehicle for speech, Derrida traces a movement of general writing that secures the production of meaning. Yet he also emphasizes how this general writing cannot be understood as a positive concept or category. Indeed, it is precisely the exclusion of this general writing from representation (56), which regulates the opposition between speech and writing, where writing is defined as a transparent vehicle for speech. As Derrida writes:

> This arche-writing, although its concept is *invoked* by the themes of "the arbitrariness of the sign" and of difference, cannot and can never be recognised as the *object of a science*. It is that very thing which cannot let its self be reduced to the form of presence. The latter orders all objectivity of the object and all relation to knowledge. (1976: 57)

Although this "concept" of arche-writing "communicates with the vulgar concept of writing" (56), it cannot be known as a positive thing within Western conceptuality; instead, it leaves a trace of its effectivity in the liminal spaces of Western discourse. As Derrida proceeds to demonstrate, the systematic effacement of arche-writing in Western philosophical notions of truth is also evident in Western ethnographic descriptions of oral-based cultures.

In his critique of Lévi-Strauss's self-reflexive, anti-ethnocentric representation of the Nambikwara in *Tristes Tropiques*, Derrida argues that Lévi-Strauss ultimately falls back on the ethnocentric trope of a "people without writing." In Derrida's account, Lévi-Strauss's representation of the Nambikwara employs the conventions of a colonial travelogue, where the anthropologist personifies an evil Western culture that contaminates a world untouched by the violence of writing and Western technology. The anthropologist, in short, constitutes "the other as a model of original and natural goodness" (Derrida 1976: 114). Against this representation of the Nambikwara, Derrida contends that Lévi-Strauss falls back on the phonocentric opposition between speech and writing: an opposition which conceals a more originary movement of writing that is instituted prior to the anthropologist's intervention. Derrida traces this unrepresentable movement of writing in a discussion of the practice of naming among the Nambikwara (112).

By unraveling the layers of violence underpinning the exchange between Lévi-Strauss and the Nambikwara, Derrida suggests that the oratory of the Nambikwara articulates the differentiation of writing before it disappears into Western anthropological representation. The refusal of the Nambikwara to speak the "proper names" of their enemy does not signal their authentic self-presence within an oral tradition that is uncontaminated by writing. Rather, this refusal draws attention to the obliteration of "the proper" in the general writing of oral-based cultures. If Western, phonocentric models of writing privilege speech as the expression of a single, self-present subject, oral-based cultures emphasize the movement of speech in performance, where meanings are mediated across time and space in a differential movement between

the speaker and the audience. What is implicit in Derrida's argument is the idea that oral-based cultures can also have a coercive, socially binding function that is analogous to the narrow, transparent system of Western writing. The ethno-anthropological work of Lévi-Strauss is unaware of this coercive aspect of oral culture, and is therefore unable to make distinctions between the situated and constitutive employment of oral-based cultures in different social and political contexts.

Significantly, Derrida's deconstruction of Western thought has had a major impact on postcolonial theory, especially the work of Gayatri Chakravorty Spivak and Homi Bhabha. In the "Translator's Preface" to *Of Grammatology*, Spivak notes a "geographical pattern" in Derrida's argument, whereby a relationship between logocentrism and ethnocentrism is "indirectly invoked" (Spivak, in Derrida 1976: lxxxii). While Spivak acknowledges that "the *East* is never seriously studied in the Derridean text" (lxxxii), she does say in a later interview with Elizabeth Grosz that there is a parallel between Derrida's deconstruction of the Western philosophical tradition and Spivak's interrogation of the legacy of the colonial education system in India, which taught students to regard the Western humanist subject as a universal standard of enlightenment to which non-European subjects should aspire (Spivak 1990: 7). In his essay "The commitment to theory," by contrast, Bhabha offers a forceful critique of Derrida's reading of Lévi-Strauss in *Of Grammatology*. For Bhabha, Derrida's theoretical presentation of the Nambikwara Indians in his critique of Lévi-Strauss's anthropology is part of a "strategy of containment where the Other text is forever the exegetical horizon of difference, never the active agent of articulation" (Bhabha 1994: 91).

Bhabha's criticism of Derrida here cannot be gainsaid. Yet Derrida's interrogation of the geographical and geopolitical determinants of Western knowledge has nonetheless enabled an important challenge to the conceptual mastery of the Western core over the non-Western periphery. In *A Critique of Postcolonial Reason* (1999), for example, Spivak cites the admonition of social scientist Carl Pletsch to dismantle the Three Worlds paradigm informing area studies and development studies in the Western academy using the critical tools provided by Kant, Hegel, and Marx. In so doing, Spivak argues that the critical tools available for challenging the imperialist determinants of Western knowledge are themselves a product of Western critical thought. Such an approach bears an important resemblance to Derrida's thought. For just as Derrida argued that the enterprise of deconstruction always in a certain way falls prey to its own work, so postcolonial critics of Western culture and thought often draw on the conceptual resources of Western thought to challenge the Eurocentric distinction between the core and the periphery.

SEE ALSO: Althusser, Louis; Bhabha, Homi; Cixous, Hélène; Derrida, Jacques; Lyotard, Jean-François; Orientalism; Postcolonial Studies and Diaspora Studies; Said, Edward; Spivak, Gayatri Chakravorty; Young, Robert

REFERENCES AND SUGGESTED READINGS

Baum, D. (2004). How to survive Jacques Derrida. *Jewish Quarterly*, 196. At: www.jewishquarterly.org/article.asp?articleid=39 (accessed August 22, 2008)

Bhabha, H. K. (1994). *The Location of Culture*. London: Routledge.

Derrida, J. (1976). *Of Grammatology* (trans. G. C. Spivak). Baltimore: Johns Hopkins University Press.

Derrida, J. (1998). *Monolingualism of the Other, Or, The Prosthesis of Origin* (trans. P. Mensah). Stanford: Stanford University Press.

Hegel, G. W. F. (1975). *Lectures on the Philosophy of World History: Introduction: Reason in History* (trans. H. B. Nisbet). Cambridge: Cambridge University Press. (Original work published 1830.)

Said, E. W. (1978). *Orientalism*. London: Routledge and Kegan Paul.

Spivak, G. C. (1990). *The Postcolonial Critic: Interviews, Strategies, Dialogues* (ed. S. Harasym). London: Routledge.

Spivak, G. C. (1999). *A Critique of Postcolonial Reason: Toward a Critique of the Vanishing Present*. Cambridge, MA: Harvard University Press.

Young, R. J. C. (1990). *White Mythologies: Writing History and the West*. London: Routledge.

D

Deconstruction

MICHAEL RYAN & DANIELLE SANDS

Deconstruction is a term coined by the philosopher Jacques Derrida to name his critique of Western philosophy. Western philosophy, according to Derrida, is founded on an architecture of values that are never examined. Those values favor presence, proximity, selfsameness, animation, naturalness, and substantiality over non-presence, otherness, technique, repetition, substitution, difference, and artifice in the determination of what counts as true and good. Invariably, Western philosophy claims that identity is prior to difference, presence to representation, nature to technique, thought to signification, speech to writing, substance to fabrication, and so on. Deconstruction consists of reading philosophical texts carefully to find moments where the conceptual scheme and value structure employed break down. Derrida usually finds that notions of identity or selfsameness that seem to be secure foundations of truthfulness are in fact products of differentiation, a process that remains outside the conceptual framework of philosophy because it cannot be assigned an identity and grasped by consciousness as a presence in the mind. Derrida develops a new kind of thinking that takes the differential constitution of identity into account.

Difference means that one thing relates to another to be what it is. It can therefore have no identity "of its own." It exists instead in a relationship with something other (hence the use of the term "alterity" or "otherness" to characterize the way identity is split in two by difference). Another term used to characterize this change in how we conceive of identity in philosophy is "mediation," which means that one concept exists through the medium of another (in the way that the idea of light is mediated by a related term such as darkness). The meaning of one term is determined by the meaning of another. Finally, space and spatialization are bound up with difference since the relationship of one thing to another means that there is a spatial interval between them. Taking these new elements of philosophy into account means thinking without the assistance of simple values founded on notions of unproblematic identity. A more complex, multivariable kind of philosophy is required. One must think differentially.

Drawing on the work of Ferdinand de Saussure, who characterized language as a system of differential relations between terms so that one term's identity depends on its relationship to all other terms in the language system, Derrida asked how philosophy might work in a similar way. Does its founding axioms, all of which assume some kind of identity, rest on a process of differential relations between terms? Derrida's name for that process, which he conceived as being both spatial (a difference between terms) and temporal (a deferment of one term by another that substitutes for it), is *différance*. To identify a positive philosophic term such as presence – the presence of an idea in the mind which is the gold standard of truthfulness – one must differentiate it from non-presence, and what this means is that difference is antecedent to and generative of presence. Presence cannot therefore serve as an axiological criterion of truthfulness. The same is true of all the founding or axiological terms of philosophy; as concepts that are part of a system of interconnected terms, they are identities made possible by difference.

Because his early work arose at the juncture in the history of French philosophy when phenomenology (the philosophy of consciousness) was giving way to structuralism (the study of sign systems), Derrida was initially concerned with the philosophic distinction between idea and sign. To know things clearly, phenomenological philosophy argues, one must assign to them a clear idea that is graspable as a presence in the conscious mind. Language is true to the degree that it approximates that presence, but presence itself is outside language. Ideational truth, according to phenomenology, is a pure mental experience extracted from the empirical or sensible world. It transcends space and exists in a kind of temporal eternity. In relation to this norm of truthfulness, signification in language is conceived as being a mere form, a conventional arrangement of terms rather than a real thing, a technique that substitutes for something present but that has no value of its own in regard to truthfulness.

This distinction between ideation and signification attracted Derrida's attention. He found that the standard criterion of truthfulness – the presence of an idea grasped by the mind or logos – is usually conceived as being untainted and untouched by the qualities and characteristics of signification such as repetition, substitution, difference, mediation, and alterity, yet, when examined, that ideal of truthfulness required something akin to repetition, mediation, substitution, and differentiation in order to exist at all.

In his early work, Derrida conducts his argument in terms of the distinction in the tradition between speech and writing. In the philosophic tradition, speech is usually valued because, as mental speech, it connotes the presence of the conscious mind or logos, while writing is devalued because it is portrayed as an empty substitute, an artificial technique, and a mere repetition that takes the place of spoken thoughts and connotes the absence of the speaker. As the sign of a sign (the written sign of the spoken sign), writing is mediated and differential, while mental speech, according to logocentric philosophy, expresses directly a living plenitude of presence in consciousness.

Derrida shows that the characteristics of writing that make it lesser and suspect – its association with mediation, for example, or its conventionality – are not simply features of writing but features of language generally. Mental speech cannot be distinguished from writing in order to be established as a criterion of truthfulness if the very qualities that disqualify writing can be found in it. Because it too is made possible by systemic conventions, each part of mental speech must refer to some systemic rule or norm in order to be "itself." Each part is made possible by a differential relationship between terms. Mental speech therefore cannot express a unique "presence" because it is made possible by differences that distinguish one term of speech from other terms that also acquire their identity from the language system. Moreover, the plenitude of presence that speech supposedly affords is made possible by sonic intervals that distinguish one sound from another, intervals that have no "presence" but that are essential to the presence of the sonic plenitude that allows speech to be identified with ideational truth. Mental speech, which is supposedly superior to writing because it is more proximate to ideational presence, turns out to be not that different from written letters on a page that require space that distinguishes one letter from the other. Speech, in effect, turns out to be a form of writing if, by writing, we mean "signification founded on differential relations."

Something similar is the case with presence itself. It supposedly transcends the spatial difference between terms while enduring over time and remaining consistent. Yet an interval of difference between terms that create discrete identities out of a continuum also proves essential to presence. It could not endure over time if it did not repeat itself. In logocentric philosophy, presence is declared aloof from repetition (in representation), but is described as requiring repetition (the repetition of past, present, and future moments over time) in order to be what it is. The only way to avoid repetition, differentiation, and mediation is to imagine a transcendental form of truth, such as Plato's, that is so abstract as to be entirely non-empirical and non-spatial and that is a realm of pure temporal eternity. It is to fall back on spiritualism, and, indeed, Derrida contends that the distinction between the soul and the body lies at the root of the metaphysical prejudices regarding truth that he critiques.

Deconstruction thus exposes a forgotten side to philosophy's founding concepts and asks us to think about the fact that to think philosophically, which is to say to think in terms of identities such as presence that supposedly transcend the spatial world of signs and exist in a kind of temporal eternity, is actively to forget that those identities are made possible by differentiations which imply spatial intervals between things. Nothing exists in a non-relational, non-differential identity. Deconstruction consists of exposing this reality and of pursuing its implications.

The argument usually takes the form of noting how philosophy posits a point of transcendence, a concept of meaning or truth that is outside the empirical world and especially outside differential relations of the kind that make signification possible. That point of transcendence is usually characterized as a unique moment of self-identity such as the pure presence of an idea in the conscious mind that is living, proximate, unmediated, and selfsame. It does not depend on anything else to be what it is. It stands outside such relations of differential interconnection between one thing and an "other." Although formulated in language, it is aloof from signification. Such transcendental signifieds, according to Derrida, can always be shown to be based on an erasure of differential relations that constitute them. Rather than being outside a structure of relations, they are made possible by such structuring relations. Ideas, for example, have identity only in as much as they are differentiated from other ideas. A differential relation to an "other" is essential to any conceptual identity. One cannot therefore rigorously distinguish ideation, conceived as a realm of self-identical presence, from signification, conceived as a realm of differential relations between terms, in the way that the philosophic tradition assumed. At no point, according to Derrida, can one step outside the field of differential relations in time and space that makes signification alien to truth-as-presence. There is, as he famously puts it, no outside to the text, if by "text" we mean the texture of differential relations that make up our thoughts about the world and indeed the world itself.

(It is important to remember that it is not signification in signs itself that Derrida claims is generative of the basic terms of philosophy, but the process of difference and mediation that signification is associated with in the Western philosophic tradition. Whenever he uses the terms "text" and "writing," he is referring to the generative process of difference. They are metaphors for *différance*. It is also important to note that deconstruction is not a critique of "binary thinking" or thinking in oppositions. Derrida does attend to oppositions, but only to the extent that they are the form that logocentric philosophy's founding values assume. The values are the target of his critique, not the oppositions qua oppositions.)

Plato proved an easy target for Derrida's critical argument. Derrida maintains that the variant and contradictory meanings of the term *pharmakon* in Plato's work, most strikingly poison and cure, constitute a "founding paradox" of Platonism. Translators have traditionally tried to resolve the undecidability of the term by settling on the single most appropriate meaning in each given context. But this project cannot succeed because each meaning requires the other in a differential dynamic. In the *Phaedrus*, Socrates recounts the story of Theuth, the Egyptian god of writing. Theuth visits King Thamus, offering him writing as a tool or remedy (*pharmakon*) to aid memory and increase wisdom. Thamus rejects the gift on the grounds that, rather than improving memory, it will encourage forgetfulness and dependence on writing. Thamus maintains that Theuth is passing off a poison (*pharmakon*) as a cure. For Plato, the association of *pharmakon* with writing reinforces phonocentrism by securing the distinction between speech and writing, and between good writing, which is faithful to speech, and bad writing, which is not. However, Derrida argues that Plato cannot avoid the ambiguity of the *pharmakon* and secure its meaning: rather, it is the very condition of oppositions such as that between speech and writing. In preceding and producing these oppositions, is irreducible to them. The significatory movement and play of the *pharmakon* enables terms to be connected as binaries, facilitating the production of difference in general and denying the *pharmakon* a stable essence. For Derrida, its ambivalence, which "resists any philosopheme" and its association with writing, destabilizes the binaries such as mythos and logos and rhetoric and dialectic on which Platonism is grounded. Derrida makes a similar argument regarding the undecidable term *khôra*. *Khôra* derives from Plato's *Timaeus* as the name of the place in which the Forms or Ideas are inscribed. It precedes the distinction between sensible and intelligible, is "unspeakable" and therefore can't be conceptualized. Derrida observes the way in which *khôra* disrupts the *Timaeus*, tracking the two concurrent yet conflicting languages with which Plato describes it. The first language uses metaphors and negations to reappropriate *khôra* and inscribe it within the Platonic system. The other rejects metaphors as, proceeding from the distinction between the physical and the ideational, they cannot define the conditions of this distinction. Therefore, *khôra* cannot be reincorporated within the system and forms an aporia or "irreducible spacing" interior and exterior to Platonism (Derrida 1992). The term "aporia" is also significant in Derrida's work and is sometimes interchangeable with *khôra*. It designates an impassable path or point, whose impassibility is, paradoxically, a condition of passage. Derrida uses the term to refer to a contradiction or "blind spot" in a metaphysical system which cannot be resolved using the logical rules of that system. Aporia and *khôra* are both elements within language which cannot be conceptualized, thematized, or ontologically reappropriated; both are referred to spatially. For Derrida, the "irreducible spacing" of *khôra* undermines Plato's claim about the purity of philosophy, demonstrating that the non-philosophical insists within philosophy and is inaccessible to its language. Like the *pharmakon*, *khôra* evades philosophy's dualisms, even the most fundamental distinction between presence and absence.

Khôra also relates to questions of the secret, the promise, gender, and naming which recur in Derrida's later work. Derrida's concept of the gift is an example of the idea of "unconditionality" which pervades his writings on hospitality (in regard especially to immigration), responsibility, and justice. Derrida's understanding of the gift is influenced by and engages with Heidegger's ideas about Being and the *es gibt*. In thinking the gift, Derrida (1992a [1991]) departs from traditional anthropological models which locate the gift within an economy, a circular model in which the giving of a gift creates a debt or the expectation of reciprocity and admits calculation and measurement into the act of gift-giving. A true gift, Derrida maintains, would need to break with this economic contract by removing the expectation of a counter-gift. Even gratitude, recognition, or stipulating the recipient would symbolically close the circle and invalidate the gift. Therefore, the gift cannot ever be made present; as soon as it is recognized, it ceases to be a gift. For Derrida, the gift is impossible, or rather "the very figure of the impossible."

Trying to escape the logic of identitarian exchange, Derrida insists upon the singularity and unconditionality which, for him, defines all true acts of forgiveness, hospitality, and responsibility. Therefore, true forgiveness would demand forgiving the unforgiveable, responsibility would be personal, non-substitutable, and non-universalizable,

and hospitality would be toward the completely unknown other, irrespective of their response. Nevertheless, it is the relationship between the unconditional and the conditional which informs Derrida's later claims about the ethical and political implications of deconstruction. Gift and economy are not simply opposed; the gift is given unconditionally yet activates the movement of the economic circle. Similarly, in "Force of law: The 'mystical foundation of authority'," a text often regarded as a turning point for deconstruction and containing the now famous claim that "deconstruction is justice," Derrida (1992) argues that deconstruction operates between the infinite openness or unconditionality of justice and the calculable and conditional strictures of law. Derrida's (2001[1997]) contention that "ethics is hospitality" requires a concept of hospitality which is divided between the unconditional (which designates complete openness to an unknown other) and the conditional (which must take law and duty into account). In discussing contemporary political issues such as immigration and international law, Derrida argues that deconstruction must ensure the interrelation of the two terms, with the limitations of the latter always challenged by their unconditional counterpart.

Although Derrida worked primarily on the continental philosophic tradition, he argued that metaphysical assumptions could be found in those most antimetaphysical of philosophers, the English analytic philosophers. He demonstrated that J. L. Austin distinguished between true speech acts and merely rehearsed ones, yet he ignored the fact that both true and rehearsed were equally dependent on conventions in order to function or to be "true." The quality that made false speech acts false – that they cited real ones – was in fact a characteristic of supposedly "real" ones. They too had to cite conventions in order to be "real" or "true."

Derrida's point was to suggest that we need to learn to think more self-consciously about concepts and about strategies of conceptualization that we inherit from the Western tradition. We use a style and a language of thinking that we assume is neutral, but it is in fact not innocent at all. When practitioners of international politics simply assume that Iran is a "rogue state" and Israel a normal one that does not even have to be named as one kind of state or another, even though the criterion that supposedly establishes a state as "rogue" (the illegal possession of nuclear weapons) applies equally to Israel and Iran, then we encounter bad thinking of the kind Derrida wanted to rid us of. What we find in the Iran/Israel example is what he called a "return of the same," a commonality across a supposed clear opposition between non-identical terms, so that "normal" and "rogue" come to seem versions of each same thing. They are different but not an opposition, and they are in fact non-opposed moments on a range of differences. If you were to summarize deconstruction as a practical method for helping us to think differently about the world, it would be to say that it encourages us to see the normal as rogue and the rogue as normal. This would apply to all the bad thinking that gets done in human culture and that allows one social group to think of itself as better than another for some criterion that is "true." Deconstruction questions such claims by noticing that they are always made possible by differentiations within a medium of sameness that renders oppositional hierarchies and moralistic oppositions more difficult to justify.

Derrida and other proponents of deconstruction argue that the implications of the metaphysical assumptions that deconstruction critiques are not merely theoretical, but also political, because the way of thinking and valuing one finds in Western meta-physics also appears in Western society and its structures and institutions. Numerous feminist thinkers, for example, notably Luce Irigaray and Hélène Cixous, use Derrida's ideas to critique patriarchy or male rule and the way of thinking – phallocentrism – that sustains it. In the text "Sorties" (in Cixous & Clément 1986[1975]), which combines deconstructive insight with a skeptical approach to Freudian and post-Freudian subjective theory, Cixous asks the seemingly simple question "Where is she?" This, Cixous argues, is answered by a complex web of associations and by "hierarchized oppositions" in different fields and domains, yet all of which designate the term "Woman" as inferior to the term "Man." According to Cixous, the "double braid" which relates the privileged term "man" to the supplement "woman" can be traced back across centuries and disciplines, naturalizing and sedimenting certain beliefs within Western culture. The connotations of the supplementary term – for example, the association of women with passivity and matter – are not accurate representations of the term "woman" but instead function to reinforce the identity and superiority of the privileged term "man," and to naturalize the hierarchy. Cixous argues that phallocentrism has a negative impact on both women and men.

The potential for the logocentrism which deconstruction identifies to generate and fortify racism has insured the interest of postcolonial thinkers such as Gayatri Chakravorty Spivak and Homi Bhabha in the processes of deconstruction. Bhabha (1994) identifies the binary oppositions which support colonial discourse, for example: white/black, West/East, colonizer/colonized, inside/outside. Whereas these discourses are predicated on the assumed stability and purity of their identities, Bhabha uses the concepts of ambivalence, mimicry, and hybridity to reveal their internal dissonance.

The power of the colonial presence is dependent on its projected identity as originary, undivided, independent, and fully self-present. However, Bhabha argues that the identity of the colonial presence is subject to the "double inscription" of *différance* and is rearticulated as "repetition and difference." This *differantial* effect is inevitably disavowed as it undermines the singularity and independence of the colonial identity. Its sovereignty is undermined by relationality, and hybridity dissolves the strict binaries of inside/outside and self/other, revealing the supplementary "other" to be constitutive of its self-identity, and not simply opposed, detached, and secondary. For Bhabha, the hybridity which destabilizes colonial presence can be appropriated and mobilized as a tool of resistance and subversion. Mimicry and mockery in the form of the parodic repetition of the professed identity of colonial power dispel the image of its superiority and singularity, thereby replacing its logocentrism with pluralities of knowledge and heterogeneous sites of power.

Deconstructive thinking was also instrumental in advancing the work of gender theorists Judith Butler and Eve Kosofsky Sedgwick. Butler noted that gender norms are differential, while Sedgwick suggested that supposedly normal heterosexuality and deviant homosexuality exist on a continuum that makes them more similar than the discourse of gender normativity suggests they in fact are.

The 1970s saw a popularization of deconstruction within university literature departments, which regarded it as a theoretical approach applicable to literary texts. The "Yale School" is a term used to describe a group of thinkers at Yale in the 1970s and '80s whose work was indebted to Derrida and deconstruction. The most famous examples were the literary critics Paul de Man, J. Hillis Miller, Geoffrey Hartman, and Harold Bloom, although Bloom's work in particular often differs greatly from Derrida's in its preoccupations. The Yale School's engagement with deconstruction tended to focus on its literary and post-structural implications rather than its philosophical inheritance. The publications generated by these thinkers include Paul de Man's celebrated text *Allegories of Reading* (1982) and the anthology *Deconstruction and Criticism* (Bloom et al. 1979), which included a contribution by Derrida. Yale was generally regarded as the US home of deconstruction until Derrida became professor of the humanities at the University of California, Irvine in 1986.

SEE ALSO: Derrida, Jacques; Husserl, Edmund; de Man, Paul; Miller, J. Hillis; Phenomenology; Postmodernism; Poststructuralism; Saussure, Ferdinand de; Structuralism; Yale School

REFERENCES AND SUGGESTED READINGS

Beardsworth, R. (1996). *Derrida and the Political*. London: Routledge.

Bhabha, Homi K. (1994). *The Location of Culture*. London: Routledge.

Bloom, H., Derrida, J., Miller, J. H., de Man, P., & Hartman, G. (1979). *Deconstruction and Criticism*. New York: Continuum.

Caputo, J. D. (1997). *The Prayers and Tears of Jacques Derrida: Religion Without Religion*. Bloomington: Indiana University Press.

Cixous, H., & Clément, C. (1986). *The Newly Born Woman* (trans. B. Wing). Minneapolis: University of Minnesota Press. (Original work published 1975.)

Critchley, S. (1992). *The Ethics of Deconstruction: Derrida and Levinas*. Oxford: Blackwell.

de Man, Paul. (1982). *Allegories of Reading: Figural Language in Rousseau, Nietzsche, Rilke, and Proust*. New Haven: Yale University Press.

Derrida, J. (1973). *"Speech and Phenomena" and Other Essays on Husserl's Theory of Signs* (trans.

D. B. Allison). Evanston: Northwestern University Press. (Original work published 1967.)

Derrida, J. (1976). *Of Grammatology* (trans. G. C. Spivak). Baltimore: Johns Hopkins University Press. (Original work published 1967.)

Derrida, J. (1978). *Writing and Difference* (trans. A. Bass). New York: Routledge. (Original work published 1967.)

Derrida, J. (1979). *Spurs: Nietzsche's Styles* (trans. B. Harlow). Chicago: Chicago University Press.

Derrida, J. (1981a). *Positions* (trans. A. Bass). Chicago; London: University of Chicago Press. (Original work published 1967.)

Derrida, J. (1981b). Plato's Pharmacy. In *Dissemination* (trans. B. Johnson). London: The Athlone Press. (Original work published 1972.)

Derrida, J. (1982). *Margins of Philosophy* (trans. A. Bass). Chicago; London: Chicago University Press.

Derrida, J. (1984). Deconstruction and the other. In R. Kearney (ed.), *Dialogues with Contemporary Continental Thinkers*. Manchester: Manchester University Press.

Derrida, J. (1987). *The Post Card: From Socrates to Freud and Beyond* (trans. A. Bass). Chicago: Chicago University Press. (Original work published 1980.)

Derrida, J. (1988). Letter to a Japanese Friend (trans. A. Benjamin & D. Wood). In R. Bernasconi & D. Wood (eds.), *Derrida and Difference*. Evanston: Northwestern University Press.

Derrida, J. (1989). *Of Spirit: Heidegger and the Question* (trans. G. Bennington & R. Bowlby). Chicago: University of Chicago Press. (Original work published 1987.)

Derrida, J. (1992a). *Given Time: I. Counterfeit Money* (trans. P. Kamuf). Chicago: University of Chicago Press. (Original work published 1991.)

Derrida, J. (1992b). How to avoid speaking: Denials (trans. K. Frieden). In H. Coward & T. Foshay (eds.), *Derrida and Negative Theology*. Albany: SUNY Press.

Derrida, J. (1992c). Force of law: The "mystical foundation of authority." In D. Cornell, M. Rosenfeld, & D. G. Carlson (eds.), *Deconstruction and the Possibility of Justice*, New York: Routledge, pp. 3–67.

Derrida, J. (1992d). Canons and Metonymies: An Interview with Jacques Derrida. In R. Rand (ed.), *Logomachia: The Contest of the Faculties*. London: University of Nebraska Press.

Derrida, J. (2001). *On Cosmopolitanism and Forgiveness* (trans. M. Dooley). London: Routledge. (Original work published 1997.)

Derrida, J. (2002). Faith and knowledge: The two sources of religion at the limits of reason alone (trans. S. Weber). In G. Anidjar (ed.), *Acts of Religion*. New York: Routledge.

Derrida, J. (2004). *Rogues: Two Essays on Reason* (trans. P.-A. Brault & M. Naas). Stanford: Stanford University Press.

Eaglestone, R. (2004). *The Holocaust and the Postmodern*. Oxford: Oxford University Press.

Hägglund, M. (2008). *Radical Atheism: Derrida and the Time of Life*. Stanford: Stanford University Press.

Janicaud, D. et al. (2000) *Phenomenology and the "Theological Turn": The French Debate*. New York: Fordham University Press.

Johnson, B. (1984). Gender Theory and the Yale School. *Genre*, 17 (1–2), 101–112.

McQuillan, M. (ed.) (2000). *Deconstruction: A Reader*. Edinburgh: Edinburgh University Press.

Powell, J. (2006). *Jacques Derrida: A Biography*. London; New York: Continuum.

Said, E. (1979). *Orientalism: Western Conceptions of the Orient*. New York: Vintage Books.

Saussure, Ferdinand de (1983). *Course in General Linguistics* (trans. R. Harris; ed. C. Bally & A. Sechehaye). La Salle, IL: Open Court.

Smith, J. K. A. (2005) *Jacques Derrida: Live Theory*. New York: Continuum.

Wolin, R. (1993). *The Heidegger Controversy*. Cambridge, MA: MIT Press.

Wyschogrod, E. (1989). Derrida, Levinas and violence. In H. Silverman (ed.), *Derrida and Deconstruction: Continental Philosophy II*. New York: Routledge.

Žižek, S. (2007). A plea for a return to *différance* (with a minor *pro domo* sua) In C. Douzinas (ed.), *Adieu Derrida*. Basingstoke: Palgrave Macmillan.

Deleuze, Gilles

EVA ALDEA

The French philosopher Gilles Deleuze (1925–95) is best known for the two volumes *Anti-Oedipus: Capitalism and Schizophrenia* (1977[1972]) and *A Thousand Plateaus* (1987[1980]), co-authored with Félix Guattari, and considered by many to be central post-1968 texts. However, Deleuze's philosophical work had started already in the 1950s. He wrote numerous monographs on philosophers (Nietzsche, Kant, Bergson, Spinoza, Foucault, Leibniz), all of which, at the same time as being rigorous considerations of philosophical concepts, are at an angle to received wisdom about these subjects. In addition, he produced a handful of books on artists and writers (Proust, Kafka, Sacher-Masoch, Bacon) as well as a two-volume work on cinema. All of his oeuvre shows a preoccupation with similar metaphysical ideas, adding up to an eclectic but consistent philosophy most coherently articulated in his two central philosophical theses *Difference and Repetition* (1994[1968]) and *The Logic of Sense* (1990[1969]).

Deleuze was born, and lived most of his life, in Paris. His secondary school years coincided with World War II, when he attended the prestigious Lycée Carnot. He went on to study philosophy at the Sorbonne in 1944–8 under Fernand Alquié and Jean Hyppolite, among others, and then taught at various lycées. Deleuze published his first monograph *Empiricism and Subjectivity*, on Hume, in 1953. In 1957 he took a position at the Sorbonne, followed by various academic positions including a professorship at the University of Lyon. In 1969 he was appointed to the University of Paris VIII at Vincennes, known for its radical philosophy department established by Michel Foucault, where he remained until his retirement in 1987. During the last years of his life he was severely debilitated by respiratory disease, and, unable to continue his work, took his own life in 1995.

From a contemporary perspective Deleuze's philosophy emerged in contrast to the French existentialist and phenomenological thinkers of the 1950s such as Jean-Paul Sartre and Maurice Merleau-Ponty, whose thought drew on Husserl, Heidegger, and Hegel. Inspired instead by the development of Saussure's linguistic ideas by structuralists such as Claude Lévi-Strauss and Jacques Lacan, Deleuze, like his contemporaries Jacques Derrida and Michel Foucault, rejected phenomenology and developed ideas and theories that came to be known as poststructuralist. However, the term "poststructuralism" implies a far more coherent school of thought than these thinkers ever represented. Therefore, it is perhaps more useful to consider how Deleuze's philosophy developed from an historical perspective. He explicitly defines himself as an heir of the "outsider" philosophical tradition of the Stoics, Spinoza, Leibniz, Bergson, and Nietzsche, against the thought of Plato, Descartes, Kant, and Hegel. Indeed, a large proportion of Deleuze's philosophical work is devoted to attempting to correct the persistently erroneous "image of thought" of this, according to Deleuze, "orthodox" Western philosophical tradition, and articulating a truer metaphysics, based on the voices of dissent that have always been present in philosophical history. Deleuze's clearest consideration of this "image of thought" is to be found in his *Difference and Repetition*.

Deleuze's use of the term "image" in identifying erroneous thought is indicative of his philosophical stance. Deleuze positions himself in opposition to any mediation of being such as the Platonic distinction between ideal forms and their copies in the world. In the place of these concepts of original ideal and copy, Deleuze suggests difference and repetition. This difference, which is not predicated on identity – that is, not a difference-*from* or not-*x*, but a self-differing difference or dx – forms the basis of Deleuze's ontology. In the absence of the hierarchy of ideal and copy, every instance of being is just another repetition of Being as difference. The central tenet of Deleuzian ontology, traced by Deleuze to medieval philosopher Duns Scotus, is "Being is univocal" (Deleuze 1994), where Being is a nontotalizing One and each being is singular at the same time as existing in the same way as every other being. This means that there is no transcendent ground or privileged thinking subject, both concepts which are part of the erroneous "image of thought."

Deleuze, however, states that these errors are explicable, since at the point when univocal Being becomes a multiplicity of beings, its pure difference appears as merely the difference *between* beings, reintroducing identity and representation. Deleuze therefore distinguishes between a pre-individual transcendental field of Being, called the virtual, and the realm of beings that exists in time and space – matter and form, but also ideas and thoughts, and subjectivity itself – called the actual. If we attempt to understand reality by considering merely the actual, says Deleuze, we are bound to be deceived. Since the actualization of the virtual leads to error, Deleuze's philosophy, or what he calls his "transcendental empiricism," centers around affirming the transcendental field of the virtual in a vast range of contexts. Such an affirmation allows for what he calls a "counter-actualization" implying not only liberation from error but also the freedom to create new thought in the unrestricted field of the virtual. Indeed, Deleuze states that the imperative to counter-actualization constitutes his only ethics.

This imperative is also exemplified in his work with Félix Guattari. While using a dizzying array of terms and approaches, Deleuze and Guattari in fact continually and coherently pit that which is determined, "rigid," "segmented," or "territorialized" against that which is undetermined, "fluid," "smooth," or "deterritorialized." They use these and other similar terms to describe a range of structures or "assemblages" – socio-logical, economical, linguistic, biological, psychological. The idea of the assemblage allows Deleuze and Guattari to describe relations between beings without any subjective agency, hierarchy, or organizing principle, but rather as presupposed only by the transcendental field of difference-in-itself. Such assemblages thus have to be described by their relative ontological "orientation": toward the virtual or toward the actual.

To Deleuze, structures in the actual tend to be territorialized, limited, and organized in rigid segments. In contrast, the virtual is entirely deterritorialized, without organization, identity, or limits. The aim of Deleuze and Guattari's project is an articulation of the possibility for any given assemblage of moving from a rigid actual orientation towards a fluid virtual one, which they see as a deterritorializing and despecifying movement toward greater freedom from determination, whether it be psychological or physical, subjective, collective, or even entirely nonhuman. However, assemblages are reterritorialized as well as deterritorialized in a continual dual dynamic that they trace between such terms as molar and molecular, macropolitical and micropolitical, sedentary and nomadic, and so on.

To Deleuze, the highest form of affirmation of the virtual lies in the very process of Being itself, its repetition, or creation of the new. While his own field, philosophy, is the creation of new thought, Deleuze also privileges art in general, and literature in particular, as paths to "counter-actualization," since they constitute the creation of new sensation. Deleuze's work on art and literature must be seen, then, not as mere criticism, but as an integral part of his philosophical project. In *Logic of Sense* (1990 [1969]) Deleuze develops a theory of language based on his metaphysical stance. It is here he appears most closely related to the poststructuralist rejection of representation and subjectivity. To Deleuze, language is another instance of the actualization of virtual Being. Difference-in-itself allows language to produce rather than re-produce sense, thus it is never a copy but always a unique being. However, when removed from this virtual, language appears a mirror of the world, reflecting precisely the rigid and territorial actual.

In response to such rigid language, Deleuze and Guattari (1986[1975]) develop the concept of minor literature, predicated on a deterritorialized use of language. This is an inherently political use of language, insofar as deterritorialization always implies an undoing of the territories necessary to politics and power. It is also necessarily collective, insofar as deterritorialization also implies an undoing of the particular territory of a single subject. Literature ceases to be an author's utterance or communication, and becomes an independent, collective, "assemblage of enunciation." In terms of literature, then, the work is an assemblage with, not an image of, the world. The work does not represent the world; instead, it interacts with and affects the world.

In his *Proust and Signs* (2000[1964]), an influential work only relatively recently translated into English, Deleuze offers a reading of Proust's *In Search of Lost Time* that demonstrates how, at its best, literature, through so called "signs of art" becomes a pure affirmation of Deleuze's metaphysical system. The process of art is revealed to be analogous to that of Being: the creation of the singular and unique through an affirmation of difference-in-itself.

Many readings of Deleuze, taking their cue primarily from his two influential works with Guattari, focus on Deleuze as a revolutionary philosopher of plurality and freedom. The multifaceted character of his work with Guattari itself seems to inspire such a reading, which Constantin Boundas in the introduction to his *Deleuze Reader* (1992) sees as a "ritornello" of deconstruction and radical pluralism. Influential works on Deleuze from this perspective include Brian Massumi (1992) and Michael Hardt (1993). Massumi interprets deterritorialization as essentially a proliferation of imaginative possibilities in the social field, and Hardt sees Deleuze's project as a fundamentally political task, a construction of a new positive and inventive society, leading toward the articulation of a "radically democratic theory." However, Hardt notes that to arrive at this political theory, Deleuze requires an extensive "ontological detour."

While these readings remain influential, the decade after Deleuze's death has seen two key works which privilege precisely this "ontological detour." Both Alain Badiou (2000[1997]) and Peter Hallward (2006) consider Deleuze's proclamation of the univocity of Being as central to his project, a project which is therefore essentially metaphysical rather than political. Badiou argues against what he sees as the commonly accepted image of Deleuzian thought as centered on the anarchic liberation of desires, and suggests that Deleuze's fundamental task revolves around a renewed concept of Being as One. To Hallward, this implies a philosophy which is explicitly apolitical, where the constant drive to affirm the virtual, univocal Being precludes the possibility of a practical engagement with the real world.

SEE ALSO: Badiou, Alain; Derrida, Jacques; Foucault, Michel; Grosz, Elizabeth; Heidegger, Martin; Lacan, Jacques

REFERENCES AND SUGGESTED READINGS

Badiou, A. (2000). *Deleuze: The Clamor of Being* (trans. L. Burchill). New York: Routledge. (Original work published 1997.)
Boundas, C. (ed.) (1992). *Deleuze Reader*. New York: Columbia University Press.

Deleuze, G. (1990). *The Logic of Sense* (trans. M. Lester & C. Stivale). New York: Columbia University Press. (Original work published 1969.)

Deleuze, G. (1994). *Difference and Repetition* (trans. P. Patton). London: Athlone Press. (Original work published 1968.)

Deleuze, G. (2000). *Proust and Signs* (trans. R. Howard). Minneapolis: University of Minnesota Press. (Original work published 1964.)

Deleuze, G., & Guattari, F. (1977). *Anti-Oedipus: Capitalism and Schizophrenia* (trans. R. Hurley, M. Seem, & H. R. Lane). London: Athlone Press. (Original work published 1972.)

Deleuze, G., & Guattari, F. (1986). *Kafka: Toward a Minor Literature* (trans. D. Polan). Minneapolis: University of Minnesota Press. (Original work published 1975.)

Deleuze, G., & Guattari, F. (1987). *A Thousand Plateaus: Capitalism and Schizophrenia* (trans. B. Massumi). London: Athlone Press. (Original work published 1980.)

Hallward, P. (2006). *Out of This World: Deleuze and the Philosophy of Creation*. London: Verso.

Hardt, M. (1993). *Gilles Deleuze: An Apprenticeship in Philosophy*. Minneapolis: University of Minnesota Press.

Massumi, B. (1992). *A User's Guide to Capitalism and Schizophrenia: Deviations from Deleuze and Guattari*. Cambridge, MA: MIT Press.

Derrida, Jacques

MICHAEL RYAN & DANIELLE SANDS

OVERVIEW

Algerian born philosopher Jacques Derrida (1930–2004), one of the most influential and controversial thinkers of the twentieth century, is best known for developing "deconstruction," a critical approach to philosophy that interrogated that philosophy's founding assumptions. Although affirmative as well as critical, Derrida's mode of engagement uses textual analysis initially to critique the Western philosophical tradition, then to displace its conceptual frame-work toward a new, more complex mode of differential thought. His influences include the philosophers Martin Heidegger, Friedrich Nietzsche, Georg Hegel, and Emanuel Levinas, as well as the writers Stéphane Mallarmé and Maurice Blanchot. Although the impact of his own work is primarily in philosophy and literary theory, Derrida's influence extends much further, to disciplines including law, religion, architecture, and psychology.

LIFE

Derrida was born to a Sephardic Jewish family in El Biar, near Algiers, during the period when Algeria was a French province. He was subject to anti-Semitism, which resulted in his expulsion from school in 1942. His identity both as a Jew and as an Algerian often rendered him an outsider, and this experience influenced his writing throughout his life. A voracious reader of literature and philosophy, Derrida moved to France aged 19 to study at the Lycée Louis-le-Grand in Paris and, eventually, at the Ecole normale supérieure, where he encountered some of the key thinkers of the day, including Louis Althusser, Jean Hyppolite, and Michel Foucault.

After finishing his studies, Derrida completed his compulsory military service teaching in Algeria before taking up his first full teaching post in 1959 and publishing his first three books in 1967: *Writing and Difference*, *"Speech and Phenomena" and Other Essays on Husserl's Theory of Signs*, and *Of Grammatology*. These publications raised his profile and are now amongst his most highly regarded texts. Derrida wrote prolifically throughout his career, traveling and lecturing extensively and holding various teaching positions both in Europe and in the United States, notably at the University of California at Irvine, where the Derrida archives are now held. He died of pancreatic cancer in 2004. His death generated a continuing surge of scholarship which aims to assess his importance, discern his legacy, and predict the futures of deconstruction. Fields and issues explored in such publications include posthumanism, animality, and theories of life; politics, political futures, and models of community and democracy; religion; and technology.

EARLY WORK AND KEY CONCEPTS

Derrida's early work is a meditation on the implications for philosophy of Ferdinand de Saussure's idea that all identity is constituted through difference. Saussure contended that all parts of language such as the word "hat" can function and have identity only by differing from other words such as "pat" or "fat." They have no identity of their own apart from this differentiation; identity is made possible by difference. Derrida generalized this notion to a broad epistemological and ontological principle called *différance*, which combines the sense of difference in space between two different things and deferment in time that inserts a delay in arriving at a presence (of a thing or an idea). He argued that the fundamental terms of Western philosophy are not, in fact, fundamental at all. They are made possible by a process of differentiation.

Derrida inherits from Heidegger the idea that truth in philosophy is defined in terms of presence, the presence of an idea or a thing to the conscious mind. Language can be said to be truthful to the degree that it refers to ideas that are presences that our mind can grasp and know. *Différance* is Derrida's name for the processes that give rise to presence, but it can never itself be "present" and can never therefore be grasped "as such" by the conscious mind. Derrida thus put in question the simple

assurance philosophy has taken for granted that words are guaranteed truthfulness by being measured against the standard of ideational presence. He proposes a new kind of differential thinking that moves beyond old assumptions about identity and the identity of presence especially to "think difference."

Différance plays on the double meaning of *différer* as both to differ and to defer. *Différance* implies that both non-identity and delay are inherent in presence and make it possible. Edmund Husserl and many other philosophers felt that the presence of an idea grasped by the mind was an assurance of truthfulness. Language was guaranteed truthfulness by referring to such presences. Signification itself was a merely technical device that was outside presence and truth.

Presence, Derrida contended, cannot act as such an assurance of truthfulness because it is itself merely an effect of processes such as substitution and repetition that are in fact the very qualities of signification that make it alien to presence in the eyes of the philosophic tradition. Any present moment refers to other present moments past and future, and the presence can only be delineated as an identity by being differentiated from other things. To get to presence, one has therefore to go through relays and delays. And another term for such relays and delays in Husserl is "signification," the way a sign substitutes for and repeats an idea, preserving presence in another form but also distancing and deferring it. Such repetition (of an idea in its sign) and substitution (of the sign for the idea) is an unavoidable part of the presence of ideas in the mind. To be present, an idea must repeat over time, and each repetition substitutes for the previous one. One cannot therefore purge the structure of signification from presence. Presence in the mind is in fact possible only as the effect of processes of substitution, repetition, and differential relation that also characterize signification. Derrida thus put in question one of Western philosophy's founding assumptions – the distinction between ideation and signification.

Derrida found that regardless of how central the process of signification conceived as a structure of repetition, substitution, and differentiation seemed to be to its founding principles and concepts, Western philosophy usually relegates signification to a secondary status in regard to the standard of truthfulness defined as a living presence in the mind or *logos*. Such logocentric philosophy makes presence primary as a criterion of truthfulness and ignores how it is constituted by differentiation of a kind generally associated in the tradition with signification.

This argument has been widely misunderstood and misrepresented by Derrida's detractors. They mistakenly portray him as arguing that language or linguistic signification make truth possible. But Derrida was not a language philosopher. By such terms as "writing," he meant the structure and process of difference, substitution, and repetition, without which no ideation could occur in the mind. That process makes presence possible, and philosophy is therefore mistaken in declaring ideation conceived as the grasping of a living presence in the mind to be primary and normative.

Derrida lays out this program of critique in his 1967 texts, *"Speech and Phenomena" and Other Essays on Husserl's Theory of Signs*, *Writing and Difference*, and *Of Grammatology*. Through analyses of specific texts, he identifies a "metaphysics of presence," which, he argues, persists throughout the history of Western philosophy. Such philosophy usually erases and suppresses the power of language and signification by declaring the best kind of language, the most "true," to be mental speech that is close to the conscious mind and is directly expressive of its meaning. Such philosophy also posits the idea of a "transcendental signified," a point where the mechanics of signification ends and something like a semantic or ideational presence exempt from signification can be grasped by the conscious mind. Such a signified supposedly exists outside of language and verifies all signification, knowledge, and meaning. Declaring that this distinction goes all the way back to the one between soul and body, Derrida observes how the concept of a transcendental signified takes the form of a privileging of speech over writing in the Western philosophical tradition. This phonocentric preference stems from the idea that writing is at two removes from thought (a sign of a sign), whereas speech refers directly to thought (a sign of an idea), and is an immediate expression of the speaker's intentions. Speech, therefore, is associated with the presence of the speaker and with full presence and unmediated meaning, while writing is associated with substitution and repetition, neither of which bears living presence. Speech is immediate and living, according to metaphysical philosophers such as Plato and Rousseau, whereas writing is associated with inanimate representation. Writing is always conceived as the sign of a sign (a scriptural representation of a phonic sign). It is itself (or has an identity) only through a relay through an other from which it differs and which defers it. It is therefore another name for *différance*. Whenever Derrida uses the word "writing," he means "the structure of the sign," whereby, in order for something to have meaning, it must refer to something else in order to be itself, as writing refers to speech or as any sign refers by definition to something else in order to be what it is.

Derrida's critical method at this point in his work consists of reversing the logocentric hierarchies of presence (speech) and non-presence (writing) and of showing that the characteristics of writing – substitution, repetition, differential relation – are in fact necessary for presence, meaning, and mental speech to exist at all. As an antidualist materialist, Derrida will argue that the ideal of an ideational presence in the mind that is supposedly aloof from signification is an "onto-theological" illusion. To posit such a presence is akin to positing a soul apart from the body.

Derrida pursues this argument in his analysis of Husserl in *Speech and Phenomena*. Husserl distinguishes between expressions (signs which mean something in themselves) and indications (signs which "stand in" for something else), and Derrida notices that Husserl's preference for expressions is linked to the privilege he accords mental speech, which reflects the speaker's living presence. Indicative signs connote exteriority, absence, difference, repetition, and substitution – all insubstantial things that imply the absence of a living presence. Yet Derrida demonstrates that the structure of indicative signification is essential to Husserl's ideal of a consciousness that can grasp truth as presence and express it in language. Communication requires both indication and expression. Husserl claims that these are separable and that the phenomenological ego is purely expressive, a stance which assumes the unmediated self-presence of the voice as distinct from the absence of the subject in writing. But in order for consciousness to exist, it must be characterized by the structure of signification whereby one moment of consciousness refers to another previous and future moment. The presence of the idea in consciousness, moreover, must bear within itself the possibility for external signification if it is to achieve representation in indicative signs. What is exterior thus cannot rigorously be excluded from the interior of consciousness. Derrida finds that language

understood as something communal and externally formed exists within, and is necessary to, the interior of the ego's individual, psychological experience. The self present ego is rendered unsustainable by its dependence on mediation and otherness. These qualities, usually associated only with writing, are here shown by Derrida to be the conditions of consciousness and of the notion of truth-as-presence associated by Husserl with it.

Of Grammatology challenges logocentrism by focusing on the structuralist Claude Lévi-Strauss, Enlightenment thinker Jean-Jacques Rousseau, and the status of the signified in Saussure's semiotics. Tracking the phonocentric distrust of writing in Lévi-Strauss's anthropology, Derrida observes the association of writing with exteriority, violence, mediation, and, ultimately, absence and death. He responds by arguing that mediation and a constitutive relation to an external "other" in a differential relation are the features of *différance* that exceed (or precede) the conceptual distinctions created by a "metaphysics of presence." Such a differential and relational structure is incompatible with the phonocentrism which Derrida locates in both Lévi-Strauss and Rousseau. In that phonocentrism, writing and all that it represents in regard to empty substitution and mere repetition are declared secondary to the living speech of the conscious mind. Speaking of the relationship between speech and writing, Rousseau refers to writing as a "supplement," a secondary addition which makes up for the absence of the living presence of the speaker. In response, Derrida invokes the undecidability between supplement as both addition and as indicator of an inherent lack that makes addition necessary "in the first place." The living presence delivered in speech always arises through mediation, the shuttling of past and future through the present moment, and the dependence on otherness in the supposedly selfsame. The features of writing – repetition, substitution, differential mediation – that make it supposedly secondary to speech are in fact necessary to speech. The supplement of writing is therefore not something added on. It has to be at work for the speech to which it is added to exist. Speech and the presence it delivers are made possible by supplementarity.

Derrida works out this argument in the terms Rousseau himself provides. In Rousseau, the supplement of writing is added on to living speech, which is characterized as more present and more natural and therefore more true, but the very possibility of such an addition suggests that speech is deficient. Writing fulfils an originary need, a lack in the ideal of nature that for Rousseau is the criterion for determining truth because it is entirely self-sufficient and requires no external supplement. Rather than being an extraneous element which perverts nature and diverts speech away from natural presence of the speaker's truth, writing is the indicator of an inherent lack (of a self-identical presence) in nature which renders the supplement necessary and natural "in the first place." For Rousseau, speech conveys a natural presence that is betrayed by written substitution. But when he does his history of the origin of languages, he describes the origin, the most natural point where a living natural presence assures the truth of speech, as a structure of substitution and signing akin to writing – visual graphic signs from one human to another that are a more original form of communication than speech. Nature, in other words, contains its own perversion; a form of writing – graphic signaling whereby a sign substitutes for and repeats an idea in the mind – is at the origin of language. The substitution that is the sign, something supposedly alien to nature, is at the origin of what Rousseau calls

natural language. Rousseau inadvertently admits that the structure of writing – substitution, repetition, differentiation – underwrites his ideal of an origin of truth in living speech and the natural presence it supposedly delivers intact without substitution. Derrida concludes that for presence, even in Rousseau's terms, to exist and to serve as a guarantor of truthfulness in thought and language, it must be supplemented by an "other relation" in a structure of differential, spatiotemporal mediation. If another name for that differential structure is "supplement" (because in such a structure, an identity is such only by being supplemented by others to which it relates and is different), then the supplement is, as Derrida puts it, at the origin. If presence requires supplementation to be at all, then supplementation is part of the make-up of presence; it cannot be rigorously excluded from it and declared to be something merely secondary and derivative, like writing. Therefore, that which writing represents and Rousseau fears – absence, mediation, alterity, difference – is intrinsic to presence.

Derrida maintains that Western thought has always structured itself in terms of oppositions, such as speech/writing and presence/difference, in which one term is declared to be axiologically prior (here speech, presence) and the other supplementary and secondary (here writing, difference). The adoption and reinforcement of such a system naturalizes this "violent hierarchy" (Derrida 1981[1967]), maintaining logocentrism and perpetuating its prejudices, including those based on gender and race that are explored in the work of Hélène Cixous and Homi Bhabha amongst others. Although not a "method," by inhabiting the workings of a text deconstruction disrupts these foundational logocentric oppositions in two stages. Derrida notices that a privileged term is associated with values such as authenticity, nature, life, presence, truth, proximity, identity, self-sameness, center, and substance. The subordinate term is usually associated with artifice, technique, mechanics, substitution, repetition, spatiality, alterity, death, distance, loss of identity, margin, and form. He first inverts the hierarchy by demonstrating the importance of the marginalized term. He demonstrates that the primary term could not exist without the secondary one and is usually an effect of the processes named by the secondary term. The secondary terms usually connote some version of *différance*. What this inversion and displacement of the usual hierarchies and oppositions implies is that there can be no primary term of the kind logocentric philosophy has imagined. Every possible primary term is itself made possible by a structure of differences. If such terms require a differentiation from secondary terms to be established in the first place, then difference, not the versions of identity those primary terms name, is at the "origin." But that means there is no "origin," no primary term, as logocentrism imagines it. At the origin is a differential structure of mediation in which no single term is primary. What is needed, Derrida argues, is a thinking that considers reality without prejudicial conceptual hierarchies and without a yearning for a transcendental signified, a primary term to secure thought and meaning. Our thinking, he argues, should become more differential and complex.

In *Of Grammatology*, Derrida claims that "*Il n'y a pas de hors-texte.*" Spivak translates this as "There is nothing outside of the text." This famous statement has been much misunderstood as meaning either that there is nothing outside of language, or that politics, history, and social context are irrelevant in textual exegesis. Rather, Derrida emphasizes the manner in which *différance* affects all experience, including politics and history, and that, through deconstructive reading,

all texts are revealed to be knit into their contexts in a field-dependent fashion. "Text" is a metaphor, like writing, for the fact that all things are differentially mediated; all things exist in time and space and therefore are shaped by non-presence as much as presence. "Text" is the name for the fact that all things are relational and differential.

PHILOSOPHICAL RECEPTION AND THE IMPORTANCE OF LITERATURE

Although some philosophers, such as Richard Rorty, Christopher Norris, and Rodolphe Gasché, have championed Derrida, his work has been opposed by proponents of analytic philosophy, including John Searle and W. V. O. Quine, who accuse Derrida of obscurantism and nihilism, largely because his texts use a new idiom that is difficult for men with their training to understand.

While the Anglo-American philosophical establishment snubbed Derrida, his work was celebrated within literature departments, which adopted his ideas about deconstruction as part of a broader turn to theory. This is exemplified by the Yale School, a varied group of literary scholars at Yale in the 1970s and '80s which included Paul de Man, J. Hillis Miller, and Geoffrey Hartmann, who adapted deconstruction for use as literary theory. This popularized Derrida's work, although critics of the movement suggested that its solely literary framework overlooked the philosophical heritage and implications of his writing.

Derrida's association with literature is not merely pragmatic or coincidental. He claimed that his interest in literature preceded that in philosophy, and he emphasized the importance of literature for the deconstructive project, as literature is the "institution which tends to overflow the institution" (Derrida 1992a: 36). Whereas philosophy has been limited by its inherent logocentrism, and therefore denies its own rhetorical strategies, literature is unhampered by the assumption of a transcendental signified, and instead acknowledges the importance of signification in generating truth. Historically, this difference has generated a philosophical suspicion of literature, as exemplified by Plato's decision to exile the poets from his ideal state. Derrida's own interest in the relationship between philosophy and literature has been widely misunderstood. Rather than collapsing the distinction between the two, as some critics claim, he explores their differences and divergent possibilities, as well as the necessary contamination between the genres, in order to reach a more questioning understanding of both philosophy and literature. Derrida's literary readings often focus on modernist or *avant-garde* writers such as Franz Kafka, James Joyce, Paul Celan, and Francis Ponge, and consider the far-reaching ways in which their formal subversion destabilizes logocentrism by showing how powerful signification is in generating our sense of reality. Much Continental philosophy, especially, depends on language while pretending it does not exist or has no importance, while literature if often aware of the power of language.

From the 1970s onwards, Derrida channels some of his interest in the possibilities of the literary into writing texts which are increasingly performative, autobiographical, and experimental in form and style. This guarantees his isolation from mainstream philosophy, but by no means indicates a cessation to his philosophical concerns; rather, Derrida uses form as a way to express and question them. Published in 1980 in France and in English translation in 1987 in the volume *The Post Card: From Socrates to Freud and Beyond*, "Envois" comprises a number of fictive postcards intended for a lover, rendering the discourse of "private" correspondence available to a much wider audience. Beginning with philosophy's logocentric presuppositions in the form of a picture postcard from the Bodleian Library in Oxford, in which the roles of Plato and Socrates are reversed, Derrida dramatizes and deconstructs the distinction between public and private, thereby exposing the "failure to arrive" which permeates the linguistic system without sparing philosophical concepts.

THE 1990S AND BEYOND: ETHICS AND POLITICS

Many of Derrida's commentators perceive a shift in focus from approximately 1990 onwards. The nature of this shift is debated, but broadly speaking it marks a change in preoccupation from theoretical conditions and frameworks to their concrete expression in particular institutions, leading to consideration of the ethical and political implications of deconstruction. The delivery of a paper entitled "Force of law: The 'mystical foundation of authority'" in 1989 (see Derrida 1992a) is a key point in this progression. Having been regarded as nihilistic or apolitical by his critics, here, in a text which explores the relationship between law, as a generalized system of calculable rules, and justice, the singular immeasurable instance which exceeds law, Derrida declares that "Deconstruction is justice."

Derrida's work is always concerned with that which has been marginalized or excluded, and, in the later work, these are embodied rather than simply theoretical, appearing as politicized figures such as the "foreigner" in *Of Hospitality* (2000). Derrida focuses on the possibilities and limits of political categories, with deconstruction operating between the calculability of law and the exorbitance of justice. His political focus peaks with the publication of *Specters of Marx* (1994[1993]), in which he declares that his inheritance from Marxism is two-fold, both in deconstruction's insistence of infinite critique or questioning, and in the idea of an affirmative horizon. This is formalized as a "democracy to come," and elsewhere, particularly in *Rogues: Two Essays on Reason* (2004), linked to its philosophical heritage as an "Enlightenment to come." "*A venir*" or "to come" is a plan on *avenir* or "future." The "to come" doesn't refer to an assured future or have determinate content, but refers to a formal, *differantial* structure which is open to a variety of possible futures.

SEE ALSO: Deconstruction; Postmodernism; Poststructuralism; Structuralism

REFERENCES AND SUGGESTED READINGS

Beardsworth, R. (1996). *Derrida and the Political*. London: Routledge.

Caputo, J. D. (1997). *The Prayers and Tears of Jacques Derrida: Religion Without Religion*. Bloomington: Indiana University Press.

Critchley, S. (1992). *The Ethics of Deconstruction: Derrida and Levinas*. Oxford: Blackwell.

Derrida, J. (1973). *"Speech and Phenomena" and Other Essays on Husserl's Theory of Signs* (trans. D. B. Allison). Evanston: Northwestern University Press. (Original work published 1967.)

Derrida, J. (1976). *Of Grammatology* (trans. G. C. Spivak). Baltimore: Johns Hopkins University Press. (Original work published 1967.)

Derrida, J. (1978). *Writing and Difference* (trans. A. Bass). London: Routledge. (Original work published 1967.)

Derrida, J. (1981). *Positions* (trans. A. Bass). Chicago: University of Chicago Press. (Original work published 1967.)

Derrida, J. (1982). Différance. In *Margins of Philosophy* (trans. A. Bass). Chicago: Chicago University Press.

Derrida, J. (1986). *Glas* (trans. J. P. Leavey, Jr. & R. Rand). Lincoln: University of Nebraska Press.

Derrida, J. (1987). *The Post Card: From Socrates to Freud and Beyond* (trans. A. Bass). Chicago:

Chicago University Press. (Original work published 1980.)

Derrida, J. (1992a). Force of Law: The "mystical foundation of authority." In D. Cornell, M. Rosenfeld, & D. G. Carlson (eds.), *Deconstruction and the Possibility of Justice*. New York: Routledge, pp. 3–67.

Derrida, J. (1992b). This strange institution called literature. An Interview with Jacques Derrida (trans. G. Bennington and R. Bowlby). In D. Attridge (ed.), *Acts of Literature*. New York: Routledge. (Original interview 1989.)

Derrida, J. (1993). Circumfession. In J. Derrida, with G. Bennington, *Jacques Derrida* (trans. G. Bennington). Chicago: Chicago University Press.

Derrida, J. (1994). *Specters of Marx: The State of the Debt, the Work of Mourning, and the New International* (trans. P. Kamuf). New York: Routledge. (Original work published 1993.)

Derrida, J. (2000). *Of Hospitality* (trans. R. Bowlby). Stanford: Stanford University Press.

Derrida, J. (2004). *Rogues: Two Essays on Reason* (trans. P.-A. Brault & M. Naas). Stanford: Stanford University Press.

Gasché, R. (1986). *The Tain of the Mirror*. Cambridge, MA: Harvard University Press.

Hägglund, M. (2008). *Radical Atheism: Derrida and the Time of Life*. Stanford: Stanford University Press.

Rorty, R. (1989). *Contingency, Irony and Solidarity*. Cambridge: Cambridge University Press.

Smith, J. K. A. (2005). *Jacques Derrida: Live Theory*. London; New York: Continuum.

Stiegler, B. (2002). Derrida and technology: Fidelity at the limits of deconstruction and the prosthesis of faith. In T. Cohen (ed.), *Jacques Derrida and the Humanities: A Critical Reader*. Cambridge: Cambridge University Press.

Disability Studies

TOM COUSER

Lennard Davis has memorably characterized the historical plight of disabled people: "For centuries, people with disabilities … have been isolated, incarcerated, observed, written about, operated on, instructed, implanted, regulated, treated, institutionalized, and controlled to a degree probably unequal to that experienced by any other minority group" (2006: xv). Although it is difficult to know how many people belong in this category (because of definitional issues), widely accepted estimates hover around 15 percent of the US population; that number will grow as life expectancy rises. The percentage is probably higher in developing countries, where poverty is a strong contributing factor. Activism among members of this minority has gained force and momentum in developed countries since the 1970s, and the roots of disability studies are as much in advocacy as in theory. A relatively new addition to "minority studies" fields like African American studies and women's studies, disability studies emerged as a by-product of the political struggle of a group of marginalized people for access and rights, and it continues to be associated with that goal. Like other minority studies, then, disability studies is closely linked to a civil rights movement, in this case the Disability Rights Movement.

Although disability studies has been driven less by high theory than by the pragmatic concerns of people living with disability, the field has been most strongly influenced by poststructuralist critiques of norms regarding the body. Thus, the insights of the French philosopher Michel Foucault into sexuality, madness, and bio-power have been of particular importance to disability studies. Erving Goffman's *Stigma* (1963) is also a foundational text, insofar as it analyzes the way in which anomalous bodies may be marked and marginalized. Fundamental to the formation and the focus of the field has been a conceptual distinction between impairment and disability, in which the latter term is defined in a counterintuitive way, as a social construct. Thus, whereas "impairment" denotes a defect, dysfunction, or other anomaly in the body itself, "disability" refers to features of the environment which disfavor, exclude, or somehow limit those with bodily impair-

ments. The *locus classicus* of this distinction is a monograph, *Fundamental Principles of Disability*, issued in 1976 by a British disability organization, the Union of the Physically Impaired Against Segregation (UPIAS). In this text disability is defined as "the disadvantage or restriction of activity caused by a contemporary social organisation which takes little or no account of people who have physical impairments and thus excludes them from participation in the mainstream of social activities." Thus, in this formulation, disability is defined as gratuitous restriction, exclusion, and/or discrimination against the impaired – that is, as oppression.

Discourse using the term impairment focuses on the intrinsic bodily limitations entailed by a somatic condition. Deploying such discourse is associated with the medical model, according to which that condition may be amenable to cure, prevention, rehabilitation, or amelioration through prosthesis. This approach is thought to interpellate the population in question as passive clients and thus to minimize or deny their agency and autonomy. In contrast, disability discourse shifts attention to how the environment – social, cultural, legal, attitudinal, and architectural – responds to the condition in question. The social model, then, seeks to examine critically and alter the context in which the individual lives, rather than the individual's body. This approach addresses collective concerns, like exclusion from education, employment, and public affairs. It focuses primarily on barrier removal.

The distinction between the medical and social models is built into the history and institutional location of disability studies. The older, medical model has been more characteristic of disability studies programs housed in schools of education, human services, public administration, allied health professions, or university centers of excellence in developmental disabilities (UCEDDs). (The majority of listed programs in disability studies today are in this category.) Such programs are mainly devoted to training people who are entering the so-called helping professions, such as medicine, education, and social work; thus, their constituency has traditionally not been people with disabilities. In contrast, the social model has been more characteristic of programs housed in colleges of liberal arts and sciences. To distinguish the latter approach (which is the main subject of this article) it is sometimes referred to as "New Disability Studies" or "Critical Disability Studies." (This distinction between programs housed in different schools has become blurred recently, and today the medical and social models may be found within colleges, disciplines, and even departments.)

New, or critical, disability studies, however, exists in two distinct, complementary strains. The first to emerge, the British school, was largely sociological in orientation and methodology. This approach was spearheaded in the 1970s by a group of disabled academics and activists, including Paul Hunt, Colin Barnes, Len Barton, Mike Oliver, Paul Abberley, and Victor Finkelstein (a displaced South African anti-apartheid activist). Significantly, disability studies in the UK did not materialize first in a traditional university but, instead, in Britain's aptly named Open University, which offered an interdisciplinary course, "The Handicapped Person in the Community," in 1975. The course proved very popular and continued to be offered for two decades, although it was significantly renamed "The Disabling Society." Eventually Kent University initiated a graduate program in disability studies; other redbrick universities, notably Sheffield and Leeds, incorporated the field into their curricula as well, usually in social science departments.

In the US, the 1977 White House Conference on Handicapped Individuals helped to jumpstart the field by bringing together key advocates. As in the UK, in the US activists, like Frank Bowe (1978), and sociologists, like Irving Zola (1982), made important early contributions to the field. But about a decade or so after the inauguration of disability studies in the UK, a separate strain emerged in the United States. Most of the leading American intellectuals in the American school of disability studies have been situated in humanities departments – English or modern languages (Michael Bérubé, Brenda Brueggemann, Lennard Davis, Tobin Siebers), women's studies (Rosemarie Garland-Thomson), philosophy (Ronald Amundson, Martha Nussbaum, Anita Silvers), law (Martha Fineman), history (Douglas Baynton, Paul Longmore, Cathy Kudlick) – or in the creative arts, such as theater, dance, performance (Petra Kuppers, Victoria Lewis), or creative writing (Georgina Kleege, Steven Kuusisto). (Of course, given its cross- or interdisciplinary nature, disability studies also lends itself to joint appointments with programs like human development and deaf studies.) Not surprisingly, given the profile of these pioneers, disability studies in the United States has tended to focus on cultural issues; it has focused on disability as a subject and source of cultural production.

If the major contribution of British disability studies has been to illuminate the many ways in which societies, even liberal democracies, have excluded and oppressed people with disabilities, that of American disability studies has been to demonstrate, and deconstruct, the way in which disability has functioned as a cultural property in Western civilization from ancient times, particularly in narrative. David T. Mitchell and Sharon L. Snyder (2000) have shown that disability functions as a kind of literary prosthesis: a crutch upon which Western narrative has relied again and again to propel plot and define character. So while disabled populations may have been socially marginalized, economically disadvantaged, and politically disenfranchised, individuals with disabilities have featured prominently in major cultural texts: Sophocles' Oedipus, Shakespeare's Richard III, Dickens's Tiny Tim, Hawthorne's Chillingworth, Melville's Ahab, Faulkner's Benjy, and Tennessee Williams's Laura, for example. Indeed, disability has been fundamental material for entire genres: Gothic fiction and the horror film, the freak show, the sentimental novel and the Hollywood weepy, and the charity telethon. For millennia, then, disability has been hidden in plain sight in Western culture, rarely recognized as such. Typically, in these texts and genres, the impairments of disabled figures serve as tropes for moral conditions or visible signs of character flaws.

That so many of the British founders of disability studies were white men with mobility impairments helps to explain two aspects of the British school. One is the tendency to think of the population in question as a single, more or less monolithic, class of oppressed people. Another is the exclusive reliance on the social model, which emphasizes issues of access. A common illustration of the distinction between impairment and disability has to do with the fact that while wheelchairs make mobility possible for people who, for a number of reasons, are unable to walk, they are of little use if the larger environment – schools, public buildings, private businesses, public transportation – is not wheelchair accessible. In environments that feature ramps and elevators, wheelchair users are not confined to, but liberated by, their wheelchairs.

Like race and gender studies, then, disability studies initially sought to characterize bodily differences as social constructs rather than facts of nature, and disability

studies scholarship borrowed heavily from those fields early on. But as the field has matured, awareness of the limitations of this approach has led to division and revision. As white men in wheelchairs, the British founders of disability studies were privileged in ways that many people with disabilities are not – and in ways that they may not have appreciated. Removal of physical barriers can make a dramatic difference for such individuals, granting them autonomy and freedom. The same is not true for people with many other sorts of impairments, especially mental illnesses, chronic illnesses, degenerative conditions, and intellectual or cognitive deficits. Nor is it necessarily true for disabled people who have another devalued characteristic, such as being female, nonwhite, gay, or lesbian.

Both strains of disability studies today are seeking to reckon more fully with the fact that the category of disabled people is not monolithic, that other differences inflect disability in significant ways. The category of disability is being analyzed not only in terms of the oppression that is common to all but also with sensitivity to matters that create distinct constituencies with different needs and agendas. Thus, rather than, or in addition to, understanding disability by analogy with race and gender, disability studies scholarship currently seeks to explore the intersections of these different aspects of the body with disability (and the variety of ways in which people are impaired).

Furthermore, as crucial as the social model has been, and as central as it continues to be, disability scholarship is now beginning to reckon with its limitations. Some scholars feel that disability has eclipsed impairment and that the field needs to acknowledge ways in which impairment confounds the social model. That is to say, some feel that the critique of the medical paradigm – necessary to shift attention to the larger issues facing disabled people collectively – has muted or silenced testimony about the body itself, about the lived experience of various conditions. The field is reckoning with the fact that although the minority model (the idea of disabled people as an oppressed group) is good for morale and political action, a civil rights approach does not adequately address the needs of those with conditions like serious mental illness and cognitive deficits. For them, removing barriers, or even offering accommodation, is less helpful than for the (literally) iconic wheelchair user.

The division in the field is captured in a recurring conflict between two key identifiers. The older (medically oriented) disability studies advocates "people first" terminology, according to which one does not refer to an autistic person (much less an autist, *pace* Oliver Sacks) but rather to a person with autism. One puts the person first as a distinct individual; his or her impairment is acknowledged only as a modifier, not as a defining term. In contrast, social model thinkers, who see disability as a civil rights issue, prefer the term "disabled people," in which "disabled" refers to the effect of social arrangements on people with a wide range of impairments. (Indeed, sometimes the term "disenabled" is used to suggest that "normal" people are not unimpaired but rather enabled by a society that readily accommodates them.) Today, disability studies scholarship seeks ways of balancing, integrating, or moving beyond these two complementary approaches, acknowledging that neither alone is satisfactory.

A notable recent critique of the field, if not a breakthrough, has come from Tom Shakespeare, a British scholar who has challenged the social model, which he sees as limited, indeed gravely flawed. In his most recent book, *Disability Rights and Wrongs* (2006), Shakespeare has criticized the social model for undermining political organization on the basis of particular impairments and for generating unhelpful suspicion of, if

not overt hostility to, medical research and development. Having relied initially on the argument that disability is analogous to race and gender in being another harmful social construction, then, disability studies scholars are now reckoning with ways in which the analogy fails. For one thing – and this is a difficult admission to make, for obvious reasons – there is some sense in which, unlike race and gender, impairment entails limitation that is not social or cultural in its basis and which social reform cannot ameliorate. As Shakespeare has observed: "The oppression which disabled people face is different from, and in many ways more complex than, sexism, racism, and homophobia" (41). This is because impairment, unlike sex, race, and sexual orientation, does affect function and capability. Thus an exclusive focus on disability fails to fully reckon with bodily limitation, which can cause degeneration, pain, early death.

> These features of impairment cause distress to many disabled people, and any adequate account of disability has to give space to the difficulties which many impairments cause. . . . Disabling barriers make impairment more difficult, but even in the absence of barriers impairment can be problematic. (2006: 41)

One irony of the social model is that, although the first wave of British scholars came from the political left and were very critical of capitalism, the removal of barriers – for which they successfully lobbied – has not dramatically changed the economic condition and employment statistics of the vast majority of people with disabilities in the North Atlantic world. As Shakespeare has observed:

> [A]n individual, market-based solution, by failing to acknowledge persistent inequalities in physical and mental capacities, cannot liberate all disabled people. . . . Need is variable, and disabled people are among those

who need more from others and from their society. . . . Creating a level playing field is not enough: redistribution is required to promote true social inclusion. (2006: 66–7)

The dire economic consequences of disability thus demand new approaches and new remedies.

Another difference between disability, on the one hand, and race and gender, on the other, also needs to be acknowledged: disability is more fluid and indeterminate than other marginalized conditions. Race, though it may be in some cases disguised, is given at birth; sex, although it may be disguised – or changed with effort and expense – is also given at birth. But anyone can become disabled at any time, and some impairments can be outgrown, cured, or effaced. So the border between the categories of nondisabled and disabled is far more porous than that between male and female, or white and nonwhite. If disability may befall anyone at any time, then disability studies may have broader appeal than most "minority studies" fields. Thus, disability studies has a claim to a large, even universal, constituency. At the same time, however, as a condition to which everyone is vulnerable (and one which is often economically disastrous), disability is also commonly feared and shunned; this may be one reason that it has been one of the last oppressions to be recognized and theorized.

Currently, disability studies is most well established in the US, Canada, the UK, Scandinavia, Australia, and New Zealand. The US has no free-standing departments of disability studies, but an increasing number of American universities do offer disability studies as a major, a minor, or a concentration – notably Berkeley, Ohio State, Temple, and Toledo. A number of universities offer master's degrees, and the University of Illinois at Chicago has a PhD program. Canada boasts a School of Disability Studies at Ryerson in Toronto, as well as programs

at Manitoba and York. The field is now well represented in organizations like the Modern Language Association, the American Comparative Literature Association, the American Historical Association, and on conference programs of many other disciplinary organizations. Since 1982, the field has had its own organization, the Society for Disability Studies (SDS), which holds an annual summer convention. The field has professional journals, as well. Called *Disability, Handicap and Society* in 1986, when it began publication in England, *Disability and Society* is the field's flagship journal. In the US, *Disability Studies Quarterly* is the official journal of the SDS. The latest addition to these is the *Journal of Literary and Cultural Disability Studies*. Based in the UK and founded by a British scholar, David Bolt, but focusing on the cultural, this journal may represent a bridge between the British and the American schools.

Perhaps Lennard Davis has best expressed the promise, or at least the ambition, of the field:

In its broadest application, disability studies aims to challenge the received in its most simple form – the body – and in its most complex form – the construction of the body. . . . Perhaps disability studies will lead to some grand unified theory of the body, pulling together the differences implied in gender, nationality, ethnicity, race, and sexual preferences. (2006: xviii)

The work is ongoing.

SEE ALSO: Foucault, Michel

REFERENCES AND SUGGESTED READINGS

Barnes, C., Oliver, M., & Barton, L. (2002). Introduction. In *Disability Studies Today*. Cambridge: Polity, pp. 1–17.

Bowe, F. (1978). *Handicapping America: Barriers to Disabled People*. New York: Harper.

Davis, L. (2006). Introduction. In *Disability Studies Reader*, 2nd edn. New York: Routledge, pp. xv–xviii.

Fineman, M. A. (2004). *The Autonomy Myth: A Theory of Dependence*. New York: New Press.

Goffman, E. (1963). *Stigma: Notes on the Management of Spoiled Identity*. Englewood Cliffs, NJ: Prentice Hall.

Mitchell, D. T., & Snyder, S. L. (2000). *Narrative Prosthesis: Disability and the Dependencies of Discourse*. Ann Arbor: University of Michigan Press.

Nussbaum, M. C. (2006). *Frontiers of Justice: Disability, Nationality, Species Membership*. Cambridge, MA: Harvard University Press.

Shakespeare, T. (2006). *Disability Rights and Wrongs*. London: Routledge.

Siebers, T. A. (2008). *Disability Theory*. Ann Arbor: University of Michigan Press.

UPIAS (1976). *Fundamental Principles of Disability*. London: Union of the Physically Impaired Against Segregation.

Zola, I. (1982). *Missing Pieces: A Chronicle of Living with a Disability*. Philadelphia: Temple University Press.

E

Eagleton, Terry

GAVIN GRINDON

Terry Eagleton is a British literary critic working in the Marxist tradition. His writing has covered a very broad range of topics, including literary theory, Marxism, nineteenth-century literature, and Irish culture. He was a fellow at both Cambridge and Oxford before moving to Manchester University in 2004. Eagleton was born in 1943 and studied at Trinity College, Cambridge. While there, he was a student of another renowned British Marxist, Raymond Williams. Eagleton belongs to the same New Left tradition of English literary Marxist studies, although bringing to it the theoretical concerns of Continental thinkers such as Jacques Lacan and Louis Althusser.

Though Eagleton's writing is very broad, taking in close literary criticism, theoretical writing, and works for a more general audience, it has maintained distinct themes, particularly the relationship between literature and ideology. Committed to making complex Marxist ideas part of an accessible popular tradition of thought, Eagleton often presents common themes across all these genres of his writing. As a result, the arguments presented between these works often work over the same themes at different levels of complexity. His written style is often equally playful and polemical, and he has been involved in disputes with Williams, of whom he published a critique after studying under him, as well as more recently with Martin Amis and Richard Dawkins. He has also written a novel, *Saints and Scholars*; a play about Oscar Wilde; the script of a Derek Jarman film on Wittgenstein; and an autobiography, *The Gatekeeper*.

His most well-known text is *Literary Theory: An Introduction* (1983), which offers a highly critical introduction to the sphere of literary criticism, as well as – in the first two chapters – a history of the formation of the discipline of English literature. Written as an accessible (but controversial) introductory text, it helped introduce and legitimate literary theory to undergraduate teaching and was influential in opening up critical and theoretical perspectives in the teaching of the discipline of English literature. After surveying most of the dominant theoretical models for approaching literature, from new criticism and new historicism to poststructuralism and psychoanalysis, Eagleton provides a conclusion which employs the Marxist method. He argues that there is no discrete field of study of "English literature" or "literary theory," and that "literature" is simply those texts valued for ideological reasons by the dominant class in a society at a particular moment. Literary theory, though itself a disparate and contradictory academic field which emerges as secondary to literature, opens up the possibility for a social and political criticism of that ideology.

Looking back at Eagleton's earlier writing can help one understand how he arrived at this radical position. His earliest criticism began critically to interpret eighteenth- and nineteenth-century British literature from a Marxian viewpoint, in texts such as *Myths of Power* (1975), *The Rape of Clarissa* (1982), and *Exiles and Émigrés* (1970). However, he also began to develop broader, more purely theoretical texts, which would prove the mainstay of his writing. Many of these were attempts to critique, engage with, and apply Marxist theoretical concepts to the study of culture.

Criticism and Ideology (1976a) is Eagleton's fullest elaboration of a Marxist approach to critical reading, and is a dense and difficult text. Though he rejects a crude, vulgar Marxist determination between economic base and cultural superstructure, he holds to the notion of historical materialism in the face of developing poststructural tendencies in critical academic writing. He sets out a position in which texts are understood not as simply determined by the economic base, but not as wholly autonomous, either. Instead, he sets out a series of complex levels of determination which condition literary textual production, indebted to, but critical of, both Raymond Williams's cultural materialism and Pierre Macherey and Louis Althusser's reworking of the theory of ideology. Although a text produces and is produced by ideology, it can yet critically display its relation to the ideology it produces by its own internal dissonance and self-contradiction. The task of the critic is to rupture a text's apparent unity and make clearer the relation of the text to ideology, by drawing our attention to these moments of contradiction within a text. In texts such as *The Function of Criticism* (1984) and *Walter Benjamin: or, Towards a Revolutionary Criticism* (1981), Eagleton has explored the role and place of criticism, and criticized the whole discipline of literary criticism. In broad terms, he argues that, traditionally, criticism had a role in constituting what Jürgen Habermas called the public sphere, a critical realm independent from the state and important for the functioning of a progressive democracy. But academic criticism now has lost this socially critical role as well as its sense of purpose and audience. His writing seeks to move back toward a revolutionary criticism, allied to the attempts by New Left movements to recompose the power of a critical public sphere.

At the same time, Eagleton has been a steady critic of many aspects of postmodernism, and in texts such as *The Illusions of Postmodernism* (1996), he argues against the theoretical antimaterialism of most postmodern theory while attempting also to appropriate its subversive critical impulses and concerns with the body. Against postmodernism's use of surfaces, irony, and multiplicity, Eagleton poses a positive project of a common, but pluralist culture, in his next text, *The Idea of Culture* (2000). Similarly, in *After Theory* (2003a), which was proposed as a kind of follow-up to *Literary Theory*, Eagleton returned critically to examine the popular incorporation of theory and cultural studies into the study and teaching of the humanities and questioned the fashionable claims of "radicality" and "subversion" often put forward by such critical methods in relation to the grounded political radicalism of a Marxist approach.

Eagleton is a prolific writer and has produced many texts which interrogate Marxist theory, from *Marxism and Literary Criticism* (1976b) to *Ideology: An Introduction* (1991). Equally, he has applied these methods to the study of culture in texts such as *The Idea of Culture* (2000). His most major work in this respect is undoubtedly *The Ideology of the*

Aesthetic (1990). This broad-ranging text examines multiple philosophical theories of the aesthetic from Kant onwards and unpicks their ideological underpinnings.

In the 1960s, Eagleton was associated with a radical Catholic milieu around the magazine *Slant*, to which he contributed a number of theological articles. In his most recent work, he has returned to the theme of religion and Christianity in texts such as *The Meaning of Life* (2007) and *Reason, Faith and Revolution* (2010). He has simultaneously tied this concern with the spiritual to a return to the concerns of *The Ideology of the Aesthetic*, re-examining the notions of the sublime and the tragic in texts such as *Sweet Violence* (2003b) and *Holy Terror* (2005).

SEE ALSO: Althusser, Louis; Marxism; Williams, Raymond

REFERENCES AND SUGGESTED READINGS

Alderson, D. (2004). *Terry Eagleton*. Basingstoke: Palgrave Macmillan.
Eagleton, T. (1970). *Exiles and Emigrés: Studies in Modern Literature*. London: Chatto and Windus.
Eagleton, T. (1975). *Myths of Power: A Marxist Study of the Brontës*. London: Macmillan.
Eagleton, T. (1976a). *Criticism and Ideology: A Study in Marxist Literary Theory*. London: New Left Books.
Eagleton, T. (1976b). *Marxism and Literary Criticism*. London: Routledge.
Eagleton, T. (1981). *Walter Benjamin: or, Towards a Revolutionary Criticism*. London: Verso.
Eagleton, T. (1982). *The Rape of Clarissa: Writing, Sexuality and Class Struggle in Samuel Richardson*. Oxford: Basil Blackwell.
Eagleton, T. (1983). *Literary Theory: An Introduction*. Oxford: Blackwell.
Eagleton, T. (1984). *The Function of Criticism*. London: Verso.
Eagleton, T. (1990). *The Ideology of the Aesthetic*. Oxford: Blackwell.
Eagleton, T. (1991). *Ideology: An Introduction*. London: Verso.
Eagleton, T. (1996). *The Illusions of Postmodernism*. Oxford: Blackwell.
Eagleton, T. (2000). *The Idea of Culture*. Oxford: Blackwell.
Eagleton, T. (2001). *The Gatekeeper: A Memoir*. London: Penguin.
Eagleton, T. (2003a). *After Theory*. London: Allen Lane.
Eagleton, T. (2003b). *Sweet Violence: The Idea of the Tragic*. Oxford: Blackwell.
Eagleton, T. (2005). *Holy Terror*. Oxford: Oxford University Press.
Eagleton, T. (2007). *The Meaning of Life: A Very Short Introduction*. Oxford: Oxford University Press.
Eagleton, T. (2008). *Trouble with Strangers: A Study of Ethics*. Oxford: Blackwell.
Eagleton, T. (2010). *Reason, Faith and Revolution: Reflections on the God Debate*. Yale: Yale University Press.
Smith, J. (2008). *Terry Eagleton: A Critical Introduction*. Cambridge: Polity.

Eco, Umberto

MONICA FRANCIOSO

Umberto Eco, semiotician and novelist, was born in Alessandria, Italy in 1932. Eco graduated from the University of Turin with a thesis on Thomas Aquinas's aesthetics under the supervision of the Italian philosopher Luigi Pareyson, whose theory of interpretation and formativity influenced Eco's early works. After a few years at RAI, Italian national television, where he worked in cultural and artistic production, Eco started his academic career and in 1971 he was appointed to the University of Bologna, where he has worked ever since. From his early book, *Opera aperta* (1962; *The Open Work*, 1989), Eco has shown interest in the study of signs, in the creation of a theory of semiotics and in theoretical problems of interpretation.

Opera aperta moved away from the influential aesthetics of Benedetto Croce, who had considered the work of art as the artist's expression of an intuition. This approach excluded, among other things, the analysis of the processes of conceptualization, reception, and consumption. Eco's aesthetics, on the other hand, sees the work of art more as a product of the artist's poetics to which the reader, listener, or viewer responds through an act of interpretation. Indeed, the work of art generates multicoded messages whose actualization largely depends on the receivers' activity of interpretation. The receivers therefore lose their passive role as simple recipients. In this first work Eco introduces the term "abduction" that he borrows from the philosopher Charles Peirce, a term that indicates the various hypotheses that the receiver proposes as an attempt to understand the author's message. *Opera aperta* was conceived within the milieu of artistic experimentation with which Eco worked closely: the neo-avant-garde Group 63.

Eco's next book *Apocalittici e integrati* (1964; *Apocalypse Postponed*, 1994a), investigates contemporary mass cultural phenomena and the intellectuals' reaction to these: the "apocalyptic" intellectuals consider contemporary art and mass communications as the ruin of culture as they knew it, whereas the "integrated" ones accept and embrace the changes. Eco's attitude is closer to that of the integrated intellectuals, even though he retains some degree of criticism and detachment towards it.

The collections of essays published between 1968 and 1978 work toward the creation of a systematic semiotic theory through which all cultural phenomena can be explained: *La struttura assente* [The absent structure] (1968), *Il segno* [The Sign] (1973), *Trattato di semiotica generale* (1975; *A Theory of Semiotics*, 1976) are the most significant. Many of these essays are collected in *The Role of the Reader: Explorations*

in the Semiotics of Texts (1979). His semiotic concerns overlap with his interests in the modes of interpretation of the text on which works such as *Lector in fabula* (1979), *I limiti dell'interpretazione* (1990; *The Limits of Interpretation*, 1990), *Interpretation and Overinterpretation* (1992), *Six Walks in the Fictional Woods* (1994b) focus. In these 1990s collections the ideas expressed in *Opera aperta* are further explored. Eco's concern here is to make clear that the range of interpretations that a text offers the reader is not unlimited, despite the fact that potentially there is no end to the numbers of connections that can be made from one sign to the next. This process of "unlimited semiosis," a term that Eco borrows once more from Peirce, simply leads to overinterpretation, ignoring the constraints created within the text itself by the textual and stylistic strategies of the "model" author – which does not coincide with the "empirical" or the "real" one. These strategies form the "aesthetic idiolect" specific to that text and are directed to an ideal readership, the "model" reader – different, of course, from the "empirical" or "real" reader – who knows how to decode and interpret them. Therefore, the reader's response is constrained by the *intentio operis* expressed through the "aesthetic idiolect" despite the principle of "unlimited semiotics." The limitations, though, stem also from the intellectual, cultural, and political background of the readers. Therefore the polysemy and ambiguity of a message, a text in this specific case, are limited by both internal and external context and circumstances.

For some critics, one of Eco's most original contributions to the founding of semiotics is his critique of iconism. He challenged the idea that a visual and iconic sign differs from a written sign by losing the conventional connection with the object to which it refers as a natural representation of it. For Eco, the conventionality of signs applies to icons too, which therefore do not reproduce the properties of the object but rather recall some aspects of it. This applies to any form of visual art, including cinema.

Eco's preoccupations have been translated into fiction. In 1980, he published one of the most important Italian novels of the past 30 years. *Il nome della rosa* [*The Name of the Rose*] was the first bestseller of what has been described as a new phase of Italian literature, characterized by the rejection of the straitjacket of ideology and experimentalism which had burdened Italian narrative production since the 1950s. Moreover, *Il nome della rosa* and the "reflections" attached to it, mark the beginning of the Italian debate about postmodern literature. The "reflections" clearly reinforce Eco's rejection of the distinction between high and low culture and offer an account of postmodernism. This is not an historical category but rather – Eco suggests – an ideal one, a "way of operating" which can belong to any historical period. Moreover, Eco points out that postmodernism is a reaction against modernism and the way in which it had used the past to make something new. Instead of destroying it, for its destruction would result in silence, the past must be revisited ironically, in a way which is not innocent.

Eco has also been highly active as a social commentator for magazines such as *L'espresso*, where he has a weekly and popular column: "Le bustine di minerva." Eco has been linked to one of the bestsellers of the 1990s, *Q*, by the collective group of writers Luther Blissett, since *Q* is a novel that shares Eco's narrative strategies developed in his theoretical as well as his narrative work.

SEE ALSO: Narratology and Structuralism; Semiotics

REFERENCES AND SUGGESTED READINGS

Bondanella, P. (1997). *Umberto Eco and the Open Text: Semiotics, Fiction, Popular Culture.* Cambridge: Cambridge University Press.
Caesar, M. (1999). *Umberto Eco: Philosophy, Semiotics and the Work of Fiction.* Cambridge: Polity.
Capozzi, R. (ed.) (1997). *Reading Eco: An Anthology.* Bloomington: Indiana University Press.
Eco, U. (1976). *A Theory of Semiotics.* Bloomington: Indiana University Press. (Original work published 1975.)
Eco, U. (1979). *The Role of the Reader: Explorations in the Semiotics of Texts.* Bloomington: Indiana University Press.
Eco, U. (1983). *The Name of the Rose* (trans. W. Weaver). New York: Harcourt Brace Jovanovich. (Original work published 1980.)
Eco, U. (1989). *The Open Work* (trans. A. Cancogni). Cambridge, MA: Harvard University Press. (Original work published 1962.)
Eco, U. (1990). *The Limits of Interpretation.* Bloomington: Indiana University Press. (Original work published 1990.)
Eco, U. (1992). *Interpretation and Overinterpretation.* Cambridge: Cambridge University Press.
Eco, U. (1994a). *Apocalype Postponed* (ed. R. Lumley). Bloomington: Indiana University Press. (Original work published 1964.)
Eco, U. (1994b). *Six Walks in the Fictional Woods.* Cambridge, MA: Harvard University Press.
Ross, C., & Sibley, R. (eds.) (2004). *Illuminating Eco: On the Boundaries of Illumination.* Aldershot: Ashgate.

Eco-Criticism

GREG GARRARD

Eco-criticism is the most popular term for the study of literature and culture from a perspective informed by environmental politics or scientific ecology, although some critics prefer the terms "environmental criticism" (Lawrence Buell), "ecocritique" (Tim Luke), or "ecopoetics" (Jonathan Bate). Just as feminist critics share a moral and political commitment to women's liberation in spite of their theoretical disagreements, all eco-critics are motivated by an acute sense of the threats to natural environments from human population levels, unconstrained technological development, the ecological consequences of both wealth and poverty, and ideologies considered hostile to environmentalism, such as consumerism, Christianity, and patriarchy. Although analysis of culture may seem remote from the urgency of climate change, one of the founders of the eco-critical movement in America, Cheryll Glotfelty, argues that "[i]f we're not part of the solution, we're part of the problem" (Glotfelty & Fromm 1996: xx–xxi).

Unusually for a literary critical movement, much eco-critical research and debate takes place under the auspices of a single academic organization: the Association for the Study of Literature and the Environment (ASLE), which holds conferences in North America, publishes the journal *Interdisciplinary Studies in Literature and the Environment* (*ISLE*) and supports related associations in Europe, Asia, and Australasia. While most literary theories have tended to draw upon ideas from philosophy (e.g., deconstruction), psychology (e.g., psychoanalysis), and sociology (e.g., Marxism, feminism), the interdisciplinary ambition of eco-criticism also reaches out to the biological sciences. Moreover, its political activism is reflected in an interest in pedagogy, with many eco-critics emphasizing the importance of field trips and other direct experience alongside textual and theoretical knowledge. John Elder argues that one ought to experience cutting grass without power-tools in order to enhance a reading of American poet Robert Frost's poem "Mowing": "To confine our readings and reflections to the library or classroom – as if we had neither arms to swing a scythe nor legs to step forward into the mystery of dewy, snake-braided grass –

would be an impoverishment" (Armbruster & Wallace 2001: 322).

Eco-criticism as such begins in the late 1980s with special sessions at American conferences, and the founding of ASLE in 1992, but some of its central concerns are evident in much earlier texts: *The Country and the City* (1973) by Welsh Marxist critic and novelist Raymond Williams, is an historical study of pastoral that shows how its typically nostalgic images of "nature" often serve to obscure conflicting economic interests and the importance of labor in the making of the countryside. However, alongside his awareness of the ideological function of this idea of nature, Williams shows keen concern for real ecological relationships threatened by modernization, and celebrates "[t]he song of the land, the song of rural labour, the song of delight in the many forms of life with which we share our physical world" (271). Williams is both suspicious of the delusions of nostalgia and aware that it might mark genuine loss. Another study now claimed by eco-critics is Annette Kolodny's *The Lay of the Land* (1975), which brings a perspective to pastoral shaped by considerations of gender rather than class. Colonists represented unconquered America both as a nurturing mother and as a desired virgin, Kolodny shows, so that the hard, virile work of colonization was attended with both breathless enthusiasm and remorse at the seeming idyll destroyed by that very work. A third key work, Joseph Meeker's *The Comedy of Survival* (1973), draws on ethology, the study of animal behavior, to argue that the genre of tragedy promotes environmentally damaging behavior: the tragic hero's struggles – with gods, with the law, the family, or idealized love – matter more than mere survival, and although the hero suffers death, his confrontation brings transcendence or moral victory. Against the *anthropocentrism* or human-centered arrogance of this tragic perspective, Meeker promotes the comic virtues: durability, survival, and reconciliation. Such adaptability is also the hallmark of a species that takes its allotted place in a balanced, harmonious ecosystem: "Evolution itself is a gigantic comic drama, not the bloody tragic spectacle imagined by the sentimental humanists of early Darwinism" (Glotfelty & Fromm 1996: 164). Whereas Meeker adapts a strand of biological science to provide a benchmark for a more "ecological," less anthropocentric, literature, Williams and Kolodny address a genre – pastoral – that overtly concerns nature, and assess its implications in terms of class and gender.

THE ECO-CRITICAL INSURGENCY

In addition to examining the idea of nature and critiquing anthropocentrism in literature, eco-criticism in the 1990s is marked by a suspicion of the excessive emphasis on texts and their relationships to each other in poststructuralism and New Historicism, that is, their interest in *semiosis* and *intertextuality* rather than literal *reference* to reality. Jonathan Bate's *Romantic Ecology* (1991) is expressly meant to counter Marxist readings of Romanticism and return William Wordsworth to his position as an inspirational nature poet in a period of environmental crisis. Similarly, Lawrence Buell's *The Environmental Imagination* (1995) places Wordsworth's American counterpart Henry Thoreau at the head of a "green" tradition of American nature writers. An eco-critical canon of Romantic poetry and nature writing would be backed up by a theoretical emphasis that Buell calls "critical realism" in a recent introductory text: "The majority of ecocritics ... look upon their texts of reference as refractions of physical environments and human interactions with those environments,

notwithstanding the artifactual properties of textual representation and their mediation by ideological and other sociohistorical factors" (Buell 2005: 30). Eco-critics are not naive realists; they do not confuse books and texts, or texts and things, and they know that nature cannot represent itself and is therefore perhaps uniquely susceptible to politically loaded social construction. Nevertheless, as eco-socialist philosopher Kate Soper puts it in *What is Nature?*: "it is not language that has a hole in its ozone layer" (1998: 167; also Garrard 2004: 166–8). So even as eco-critics have revalued nature writing and eco-poetry for their *mimesis*, or representation of reality, they have addressed questions of artistry, imaginative reconstruction, and intertextuality.

Since the eco-critic's concern is always in some sense to ask how a given text or genre might shape the readers' environmental perception, and perhaps their actions as well, studies have ranged increasingly widely. The early interest in Romantic poetry and nature writing has been sustained, with particular emphasis on the idea that such texts might teach modern readers, who live primarily through connections to the *technosphere* (TV, the internet, etc.), how to "dwell" with more knowledge, attention, and affection for their local environment and *biosphere* (McKibben 1992; Roorda 1998). Moving further afield, David Ingram analyzes the environmental implications of Hollywood cinema in *Green Screen* (2000), Patrick Curry's *Defending Middle-Earth* (2004) promotes the "radical nostalgia" of fantasy writer J. R. R. Tolkien's epic *The Lord of the Rings*, and *The Nature of Cities* (Bennett & Teague 1999) explores a range of urban genres and environments. Richard Kerridge pays attention to the implications of both literary and popular genres, arguing that recent environmentalist novels, for example, paradoxically "take failure for granted" and generate "narratives of resignation": "the problem is that conventional plot structures require forms of solution and closure that seem absurdly evasive when applied to ecological questions with their extremes of timescale and complexities of interdependence" (Parham 2002: 99; also Kerridge, in Coupe 2000). Eco-critics fear that existing art forms will struggle to represent adequately vast, nebulous, largely imperceptible problems like climate change and biodiversity loss.

At the same time, some eco-critics have raised concerns that the "ecological" concepts used by literary critics are misrepresented or misunderstood. The idea of the intrinsic "harmony" or "balance" of nature undisturbed by humans, as invoked by Meeker, for example, has been largely abandoned by ecologists (Botkin 1992), but remains a moral touchstone for environmentalists and eco-critics, leading Greg Garrard to distinguish between the "pastoral ecology" of popular myth and the "postmodern ecology" of the science itself (2004: 56–8). Dana Phillips's extended consideration of this problem in *The Truth of Ecology* (2003: 45) argues: "Ecology sparks debates about environmental issues, it doesn't settle them." It is not yet clear how these critiques will be assimilated within the field.

ECO-CRITICISM AND LANGUAGE

The structuralist thought derived from Swiss linguist Ferdinand de Saussure is held responsible by some eco-critics for a tenacious and anthropocentric notion of language: that it is radically distinct from animal communication, and founds a fundamental gap between nature and culture. Philosopher David Abram observes: "Language, in this view, is rather like a *code*; it is a way of *representing* actual things and events in the perceived world, but it has

no internal, nonarbitrary connections to that world, and hence is readily separable from it" (1996: 77). Abram, influenced by the French phenomenologist Maurice Merleau-Ponty (1908–61), argues for a shift from a metaphor of language as code or structure to a web or network that is itself constantly being transformed by individual, creatively speaking biological bodies. As the poet Gary Snyder puts it, "Languages were not the intellectual inventions of archaic schoolteachers, but are naturally evolved wild systems whose complexity eludes the descriptive attempts of the rational mind" (Coupe 2000: 127). If language is seen as "wild" – biophysical as well as mental, self-organizing, and creative – the chasm between nature and culture is greatly reduced, and nature itself may be seen not as mere "silent" physical matter, but as expressive in its own fashions.

Whereas Abram and Snyder see the naturalization of language in terms of a return to a premodern *animistic* worldview, in which natural entities have speaking spirits, other eco-critics find a similar conclusion sustained by biological science. Some biologists now characterize both the development of an individual organism and evolution in terms of flows of information, including the "analogue" information of the organism's senses and the "digital" information encoded in DNA. On this "biosemiotic" view, not only are sign systems not restricted to human cultures, they are coextensive with life itself. As Wendy Wheeler puts it, "life is primarily semiotic. … The organism-environment coupling is a form of conversation, and evolution itself a kind of narrative of conversational developments. … Evolution … is the play and education of life forms, which lead to higher, emergent levels of informational complexity" (2006: 126). Both the phenomenological approach (see also Westling, in Gersdorf & Mayer 2006) and the biosemiotic (see also Maran, in Gersdorf & Mayer 2006) aim to emphasize the role of the biological human body in perception, language, and knowledge, and to unseat the human subject from its position of assumed privilege as sole sign user in nature. Such humility is seen as warranted by the displacement of the human species from the pinnacle of creation achieved by Charles Darwin's (1809–82) evolutionary theory; as Christopher Manes argues: "As far as scientific inquiry can tell, evolution has no goal, or if it does we cannot discern it, and at the very least it does not seem to be us" (Glotfelty & Fromm 1996: 22).

The sense that language inevitably falls short in terms of representation of nature may be given a positive gloss. For Lawrence Buell in *Writing for an Endangered World*, "environmental unconscious" names a "foreshortening" of perception, a consistent failure fully to see or know nature, but also a "potential: ... a residual capacity ... to awake to fuller apprehension of physical environment and one's interdependence with it" (2001: 22). Kate Rigby's study of British and German Romanticism's "sacralisation" of nature, on the other hand, proposes "negative ecopoetics" as an ethical demand: when poets admit the inadequacy of their art to represent the more-than-human world, it "in some measure protects the otherness of earth from disappearing into a humanly constructed world of words" (2004: 119). Eco-criticism involves a unique moral imperative and relationship to science, and an altered canon, but its anti-anthropocentric theory of language most radically distinguishes it from other theoretical positions.

NEW DIRECTIONS

Despite the accusations of theoretical naivety sometimes aimed at them, eco-critics have always sustained interests in other reading practices, most notably feminism. Eco-feminist literary criticism sees environmental destruction as conceptually and practically interlinked with male domination of women, and "advocates the centrality of human diversity and biodiversity to our survival on this planet" (Gaard & Murphy 1998: 12; see also Westling 1996). In recent years, eco-critics in North America have gone on to place increasing emphasis on the cultural dimensions of environmental racism and justice, because social exclusion of ethnic groups and exposure to toxic environments frequently go together. There are other eco-critical hybrids with existing theories:

- Two major critical works have made extensive use of concepts derived from the German philosopher Martin Heidegger. Robert Pogue Harrison's *Forests: The Shadow of Civilization* (1992) is a survey of "the role forests have played in the cultural imagination of the West" (ix), in which each epoch – prehistorical, ancient Greek, etc. – is seen as distinguished by the way in which its language allows nature to "be," or emerge into consciousness. *The Song of the Earth* (2000) by Jonathan Bate adopts Heideggerian concepts in its analysis of canonical literature, but Heidegger's Nazism suggests that "[t]he dilemma of Green reading is that it must, yet it cannot, separate ecopoetics from ecopolitics" (266).

- Tim Luke's *Ecocritique* (1997) adapts the French philosopher Michel Foucault's concept of "governmentality" into that of "environmentality": a global system of scientific surveillance of a multitude of ecological factors, from stratospheric ozone to forest cover and ocean currents, that turns the Earth into "an ensemble of ecological systems, requiring human managerial oversight, administrative intervention, and organizational containment" (90). Environmentality disciplines citizens, Luke claims, into "green" behavior such as recycling, while leaving destructive socioeconomic relationships unaltered.

- *Ecology without Nature* (2007), by Timothy Morton, brings the deconstructive logic and difficult, playful language of French philosopher Jacques Derrida to eco-criticism. Far from challenging destructive modern ideologies, Morton argues, Romanticism and environmentalism are complicit with them: "Environmentalisms *in general* are consumerist" and environmental literature exists to "soothe the pains and stresses of industrial society" (114). Morton rejects the search for unpolluted purity of environmentalism, and the false immediacy of mimetic nature writing, and promotes "dark ecology": "The task becomes to love the disgusting, inert, and meaningless. . . . The most ethical act is to love the other precisely in their artificiality, rather than seeking to prove their naturalness and authenticity" (195).
- Running counter to the usual eco-critical emphasis on learning to dwell in a known local environment, Ursula Heise's *Sense of Place and Sense of Planet* (2008) offers a critical account of attempts to represent the whole earth. Arguing that we cannot help living in a globalized environment, Heise draws upon risk theory from sociology to illuminate how threats alter our social and individual consciousness, and advocates a "cosmopolitan" eco-criticism: "The challenge for environmentalist thinking . . . is to shift the core of its cultural imagination from a sense of place to a less territorial and more systemic sense of planet" (56).

The intersection of postcolonial and eco-critical perspectives will soon no doubt generate much research, and there is potential for interdisciplinary exploration in evolutionary psychology, the philosophy of biology and – crucially – the cultural dimensions of climate change. As environmental crisis worsens, the urgency of eco-criticism as a complement to political and scientific analysis will only increase.

SEE ALSO: Evolutionary Studies

REFERENCES AND SUGGESTED READINGS

Abram, D. (1996). *The Spell of the Sensuous: Perception and Language in a More-Than-Human World.* New York: Vintage.

Armbruster, K., & Wallace, K. R. (eds.) (2001). *Beyond Nature Writing: Expanding the Boundaries of Ecocriticism.* Charlottesville: University of Virginia Press.

Bate, J. (1991). *Romantic Ecology: Wordsworth and the Environmental Tradition.* London: Routledge.

Bate, J. (2000). *The Song of the Earth.* London: Picador.

Bennett, M., & Teague, D. W. (1999). *The Nature of Cities: Ecocriticism and Urban Environments.* Tucson: University of Arizona Press.

Botkin, D. (1992). *Discordant Harmonies: A New Ecology for the Twenty-First Century.* Oxford: Oxford University Press.

Buell, L. (1995). *The Environmental Imagination: Thoreau, Nature Writing, and the Formation of American Culture.* Princeton: Princeton University Press.

Buell, L. (2001). *Writing for an Endangered World: Literature, Culture, and Environment in the US and Beyond.* Cambridge, MA: Belknap.

Buell, L. (2005). *The Future of Environmental Criticism: Environmental Crisis and Literary Representation.* Oxford: Blackwell.

Coupe, L. (2000). *The Green Studies Reader: From Romanticism to Ecocriticism.* London: Routledge.

Curry, P. (2004). *Defending Middle-Earth: Tolkien, Myth, and Modernity.* New York: Houghton Mifflin.

Gaard, G., & Murphy, P. D. (1998). *Ecofeminist Literary Criticism: Theory Intepretation, Pedagogy*. Urbana: University of Illinois Press.

Garrard, G. (2004). *Ecocriticism*. London: Routledge.

Gersdorf, C., & Mayer, S. (2006). *Nature in Literary and Cultural Studies: Transatlantic Conversations on Ecocriticism*. Amsterdam: Rodopi.

Glotfelty, C., & Fromm, H. (eds.) (1996). *The Ecocriticism Reader: Landmarks in Literary Ecology*. Athens: University of Georgia Press.

Harrison, R. P. (1992). *Forests: The Shadow of Civilization*. Chicago: University of Chicago Press.

Heise, U. (2008). *Sense of Place and Sense of Planet: The Environmental Imagination of the Global*. Oxford: Oxford University Press.

Ingram, D. (2000). *Green Screen: Environmentalism and Hollywood Cinema*. Exeter: University of Exeter Press.

Kolodny, A. (1975). *The Lay of the Land: Metaphor as Experience and History in American Life and Letters*. Chapel Hill: University of North Carolina Press.

Luke, T. (1997). *Ecocritique: Contesting the Politics of Nature, Economy, and Culture*. London: University of Minneapolis Press.

McKibben, B. (1992). *The Age of Missing Information*. New York: Random House.

Meeker, J. (1972). *The Comedy of Survival: Studies in Literary Ecology*. New York: Scribner's.

Morton, T. (2007). *Ecology without Nature*. Cambridge, MA: Harvard University Press.

Parham, J. (2002). *The Environmental Tradition in English Literature*. Aldershot: Ashgate.

Phillips, D. (2003). *The Truth of Ecology: Nature, Culture, and Literature in America*. Oxford: Oxford University Press.

Rigby, K. (2004). *Topographies of the Sacred: The Poetics of Place in European Romanticism*. Charlottesville: University Press of Virginia.

Roorda, R. (1998). *Dramas of Solitude: Narratives of Retreat in American Nature Writing*. Albany: State University of New York Press.

Soper, K. (1998). *What is Nature?* Oxford: Blackwell.

Westling, L. H. (1996). *The Green Breast of the New World: Landscape, Gender, and American Fiction*. Athens: University of Georgia Press.

Wheeler, W. (2006). *The Whole Creature: Complexity, Biosemiotics and the Evolution of Culture*. London: Lawrence and Wishart.

Williams, R. (1973). *The Country and the City*. Oxford: Oxford University Press.

Écriture Féminine

ANNE DONADEY

L'écriture féminine is a concept coined by French feminist Hélène Cixous in her landmark manifesto "The laugh of the Medusa" in 1975. Translated into English the following year, the essay became particularly influential in US academic feminism and continues to be taught in feminist theory classes. The translators rendered *écriture féminine* as the more generic "women's writing," with the result that the French term has become common usage in Anglophone academic feminism.

Cixous exhorts women to write *l'écriture féminine*, a fluid, liberatory practice that she claims cannot be defined or theorized: "Write! Writing is for you, you are for you; your body is yours, take it" (1976[1975]: 876). Cixous enacts *l'écriture féminine* in her performative manifesto, which is loosely organized in stream of consciousness style and veers from high theory to poetry to humorous barbs at psychoanalysis. *L'écriture féminine* rejects coherently organized arguments and realist narrative techniques and embraces instead a fragmented, poetic, exploded style open to the play of the unconscious and the libido. Cixous believes that female desire is threatening to a masculinist society and has therefore been repressed as women have been taught to hate themselves and resent other women. She draws a parallel between the repression of women's bodies and desires and the repression of women's language: writing and *jouissance* are pleasurable activities, and both have been repressed for women and seen as male preserves. Like Luce Irigaray, Cixous believes that Western societies are based on the repression of women's desires and language, or, in other words, that women are the unconscious of masculinist society: "Write your self. Your body must be heard. Only then will the immense resources of the unconscious spring forth" (1976[1975]: 880). In Cixous's model, if women regain access to their desire and to language, this return of the repressed will explode the structures of phallocentric society. Against Jacques Lacan, for whom women can never have access to language, Cixous calls for women to seize language and to write (through/ with) the body in order to reconnect with their libido and with each other, find themselves anew, and effect a new revolution. Influenced by the avant-garde poetics of modernism in general and James Joyce in particular, Cixous explodes the structures of the French language in her essay, creating neologisms, using slang terms alongside poetic words, and refusing a linear organization of writing. Like Gloria Anzaldúa in *Borderlands/La Frontera*, she provides us with an example of the kind of writing she is seeking to inspire other women to write and, like Anzaldúa, she weaves back and forth between essentialism and anti-essentialism.

As influential as the concept of *écriture féminine* has been, it has also received its share of critiques on the part of other feminists such as Ann Rosalind Jones, Nina Baym, and Toril Moi. For critics, Cixous's (and Irigaray's) belief that female desire is inherently different from male desire steers too close to biological essentialism; Cixous's theory relies too much on a masculinist psychoanalytic framework; her focus on women's nonlinear thinking and sexuality reproduces masculinist stereotypes about women's lack of rationality; the male/female binary opposition on which her argument rests elides differences among women; and, besides its feminist themes, the *écriture féminine* that she promotes seems hard to differentiate from high modernist aesthetics. As such, and

because *l'écriture féminine* may not be a very effective concept materially and politically, Cixous's call for *l'écriture féminine* appears to be more relevant to middle- and upper-class, educated white women than to other women. This is especially true given that she uses Freud's racist and colonialist metaphor of women as the dark continent of Africa somewhat uncritically. In contrast, however, other scholars, such as Ruth Salvaggio, have noted affinities between Cixous's *écriture féminine* and African American lesbian feminist poet and theorist Audre Lorde's view that poetry is not a luxury but a central need as well as Lorde's redefinition of the erotic as power.

Some of the critiques of Cixous's essentialism may rely on something of a misreading. Following Jacques Derrida's insights, Cixous deconstructs the concept of the body. When she says that women must write the body, she rejects the idea that the act of writing is an intellectual pursuit divorced from the concreteness of the body. In her deconstructive redefinition, the body includes the mind. When she says that women write "in white ink" (881), referring to the mother's milk, she is not saying that women must only write out of their bodily fluids and experiences. Her comment is made metaphorically, as a critique of the masculinist ideology that men create and women procreate, thus reclaiming the possibility for women to be mothers and writers at the same time and deconstructing patriarchal binary oppositions.

SEE ALSO: Anzaldúa, Gloria; Body, The; Cixous, Hélène; Deconstruction; Derrida, Jacques; Essentialism/Authenticity; Feminism; Irigaray, Luce; Lacan, Jacques; Modernism; Modernist Aesthetics; Psychoanalysis (to 1966); Psychoanalysis (since 1966).

REFERENCES AND SUGGESTED
READINGS

Anzaldúa, G. (2007). *Borderlands/La Frontera, The
New Mestiza*, 3rd edn. San Francisco: Aunt Lute
Books. (Original work published 1987.)
Baym, N. (1987). "The madwoman and her lan-
guages: Why I don't do feminist literary theory."
In S. Benstock (ed.), *Feminist Issues in
Literary Scholarship*.Bloomington:Indiana Uni-
versity Press, pp.45–61.
Cixous, H. (1976).The laugh of the Medusa (trans.
K. Cohen and P. Cohen). *Signs*, 1(4), 875–893.
(Original work published 1975).
Jones, A. R. (1981). Writing the body: Toward an
understanding of *l'écriture féminine*. *Feminist
Studies*, 7(2), 247–263.
Lorde, A. (1984). *Sister Outsider*. Freedom, CA:
Crossing Press.
Salvaggio, R. (1997). Skin deep: Lesbian interven-
tions in language. In D. A. Heller (ed.), *Cross-
Purposes: Lesbians, Feminists, and the Limits of
Alliance*. Bloomington: Indiana University
Press, pp. 49–63.

Essentialism/Authenticity

MELANIE WATERS

Essentialism is a metaphysical doctrine which proposes that any being, object, or concept possesses certain fixed, or "essential," properties by which it is defined and without which it would not be what it is. While broad, this definition usefully fore-grounds the vital coordinates of essentialism as they are set forth by Aristotle in *The Metaphysics*. In this paradigmatic philo-sophical treatise, which continues to func-tion as the foundation text for contemporary debates about essentialism, Aristotle situates the concept of essence at the heart of his epistemological project, arguing that it is the fundamental objective of scientific in-quiry to uncover the natural "essences" of things in order to understand why they exist and what they contribute to the universe. In clarifying his position, Aristotle makes

a keen distinction between the "essential" properties of a thing, by which it is imper-atively defined, and its "accidental" char-acteristics, which are contingent and can be acquired (or lost) by chance without altering the fundamental identity of the thing in question. Once the essence of a thing has been distinguished from its ac-cidental properties it can be positioned in a fixed relation to other orders of things within a larger, hierarchical scheme of classification. In accordance with the logic of this scheme, those things which share the same essential characteristics must necessarily belong to the same cate-gory, regardless of any other properties they may or may not possess. In this con-text, the variable or "accidental" features of a thing are rendered wholly negligible; all that matters is that which is viewed as intrinsic, definitive, and immutable. Classical essentialism, then, not only holds that the "true" essence of a thing can be meaningfully and definitively located, but also identifies that essence as natural, causa-tive, and unchanging. Taking these things into account, essentialism significantly com-plicates theoretical formulations of a concept with which it is intricately entangled, and which is necessarily central to contemporary critiques of essentialist thought: authenticity.

Notoriously difficult to define, the con-cept of authenticity is inextricable from ongoing debates about essentialism and its validity as a theoretical approach. Within classical philosophical discourses, authen-ticity is generally associated with the qual-ities of being "real" or "true in substance" (*OED*); the authentic, therefore, is precisely what it purports to be in terms of its origins or authorship. As is the case with Aristote-lian definitions of essence, these accounts of authenticity pivot on a basic understanding of truth as something objective and verifi-able. While conveniently stable, such deci-sive formulations have been unsettled by more recent lines of philosophical inquiry. For Martin Heidegger in *Being and Time* (1962[1927]), authenticity evades any easy classification, though the concept remains crucially relevant to his detailed excavation of the way in which the individual exists in the world. Proceeding from the thesis that the essence of human being lies in the ability to exist – and, more explicitly, in the ability to reflect upon or interpret this existence – Heidegger argues that there are two modes of being available to the individual: the authentic and the inauthentic. In Heidegger's view, most humans exist in a state of inauthenticity, subscribing unreflectively to prevailing conventions, ignoring the fact of mortality, and negating freedom of choice; the "inauthentic" individual thus defers decisions about his or her own life to others. The authentic life, conversely, involves existing on one's own terms, regardless of social expectations. Authentic selfhood, then, is only achieved – as far as it can be achieved – when the individual, in recognition of the possibility of his or her death, is thrown open to the possibilities of his or her own existence and is, therefore, able to make choices on an independent basis.

Heidegger's delineation of authenticity is famously seized upon by Jean-Paul Sartre as the scaffolding for his influential philosophy of existence, existentialism. Like Heidegger, Sartre contends that authentic existence entails a sustained confrontation with the fact of one's own, inevitable mortality. Similarly, and as for Heidegger, Sartre lays a primary emphasis on this mortal knowledge as an antecedent to authenticity, viewing the recognition of death as an effective prompt to authentic action. For Sartre, freedom of choice is an absolute prerequisite for authentic selfhood, but he is careful to acknowledge the potential reluctance of individuals to recognize and act upon such liberty. According to Sartre, human beings

are less inclined to exercise than to deny their freedom and are, more often than not, happy to cede responsibility for their decisions to external forms of authority. This act of self-denial is, argues Sartre, an act of inauthenticity or "bad faith."

As the bedrock of Aristotelian metaphysics, the doctrine of essentialism has had a directive role in the development of Western thought, with its conceptual, ideological, and practical implications being rigorously explored within and across the sciences, arts, and humanities. Since the 1970s, moreover, essentialism has functioned as a key point of reference in ongoing debates within feminist, postcolonial, and queer studies about the politics of identity and the dynamics of social control. After all, by making assumptions about the nature of things in order to discriminate between (or against) them, essentialism engages intimately in the processes of classification, generalization, and hierarchization – processes which necessarily give way to division, prejudice, and inequality. For anti-essentialists, then, sexism, racism, homophobia, and other forms of cultural bigotry are the inevitable outcomes of a metaphysical project which is rooted in the belief that the character, behavior, and morality of a person are determined by an "essential" set of traits that remain the same across all historical periods and cultural contexts. In analyzing the issues to which essentialism gives rise, critics tend to trace most of its limitations to the core set of related principles on which it is predicated: reductivism, objectivism, and universalism.

Essentialism's reductivist logic is radically evidenced in its assumption that people and things are reducible to their "essential" characteristics – an assumption which, in turn, provides the rationale for essentialist attempts to schematize the world in accordance with a rigid system of hierarchical classification. As Michel Foucault has reasoned, such attempts are misleading, in that they camouflage – rather than illuminate – the differences that exist between things which are regarded as possessing the same "essential" nature. In other words, essentialism promotes the polite fiction that the world can be divided, neatly and definitively, into a series of discrete, if related, categories; in doing so, however, it fails to account for any diversity and plurality within those same categories. Furthermore, the essence to which a thing is reduced is not anterior to it, but posterior. If one "listens to history," Foucault claims, "there is 'something altogether different' behind things: not a timeless and essential secret, but the secret that they have no essence or that their essence was fabricated in a piecemeal fashion from alien forms" (1977: 142). According to Foucault, then, essence is not natural but constructed; rather than preceding and determining the development of a thing, it is invented in particular cultural contexts and grafted onto people and objects at significant historical junctures. For example, as Foucault explains in the introductory volume of *The History of Sexuality* (1990[1976]), homosexuality is a socially constructed category that emerged in Europe in the late nineteenth century. Prior to this, an individual may have engaged in intimate activities with persons of the same sex but, without a name, this behavior would not have been regarded as defining; it would not, therefore, be understood as the fixed, unalterable "essence" of a subject's identity.

Just as queer theorists have questioned the extent to which sexuality is essential – and thus natural and unchanging – feminist scholars have interrogated the essentialist positioning of "man" and "woman" as stable markers that designate two discrete, static gender identities. In *The Second Sex* (1997[1949]) Simone de Beauvoir tele-

graphs the constructedness of femininity in her famous declaration that "one is not born, but rather becomes, a woman" (295). De Beauvoir here rejects the claim that women have a fixed, identifiable essence with which they are endowed from birth and instead draws a sharp distinction between sex – an immutable anatomical fact – and gender – a variable set of cultural meanings that the sexed body assumes over time. Underlining the status of gender as contextual, and not essential, de Beauvoir argues that "woman" has been strategically constructed as the negative "other" against which the masculine subject is traditionally defined. Throughout the history of Western metaphysics, de Beauvoir continues, women have existed only as objects, not as autonomous beings; thus locked in the role of man's "other," women have been unable to position themselves as subjects within the patriarchal system. For de Beauvoir, working within the strictures of existential discourse, this system gives rise to the problem of "bad faith": women who seek to conform to the prescriptive versions of femininity sanctioned by patriarchy, argues de Beauvoir, are not acting in accordance with their desires as free, independent agents but are instead deferring their liberty to external structures of authority and are, therefore, existing in a perpetual state of inauthenticity, or Sartrean "bad faith."

While many feminists, including de Beauvoir, are critical of the essentialist logic in which patriarchal representations of women are rooted, feminism – as far as it can be discussed as a coherent movement – tends to replicate this same logic in that it presupposes the existence of women as a category of persons with a common identity at whom its political work is aimed. For Judith Butler, the notion of a natural, universal womanhood is inherently limiting in that it denies the fact that "gender is not always constituted coherently or consistently in different historical contexts" and suppresses the complexity of racial, sexual, ethnic, and regional factors that interact at the site of identity: "If one 'is' a woman," Butler observes, "that is surely not all one is" (1999: 6). As well as featuring prominently within academic discussions of gender and sexuality, questions relating to essentialism and authenticity are equally central to contemporary postcolonial discourses. Working within the field of postcolonialism, the theorist Gayatri Chakravorty Spivak has questioned the outright rejection of essentialist strategies by some postmodernist and poststructuralist critics and examined the potential usefulness of essentialism as a political tool. Focalizing the ways in which essentialist methodologies have been deployed to give voice to the experiences of marginalized individuals that would otherwise be lost to history, Spivak lends speculative support to what she refers to as "a *strategic* use of positivist essentialism in a scrupulously visible political interest" (1985: 214). This "strategic essentialism" holds that there may be some instances in which it might be politically advantageous for certain groups to essentialize themselves – to understate the differences that exist between individuals within the group in order to pursue particular collective goals.

Although the emergence of poststructuralist discourses seemed, to some, to augur the demise of traditional approaches to essentialism and authenticity, these discourses have only complicated the terms of the debates that swirl around these concepts, ensuring their ongoing centrality to theories of the self, nature, difference, and the world.

SEE ALSO: de Beauvoir, Simone; Butler, Judith; Feminism; Foucault, Michel; Heidegger, Martin; Postcolonial Studies and Diaspora Studies; Postmodernism; Poststructuralism; Sartre, Jean-Paul; Spivak, Gayatri Chakravorty

REFERENCES AND SUGGESTED READINGS

Aristotle. (1991). *The Metaphysics* (trans. J. H. McMahon). New York: Prometheus Books. (Original work published *c.* 350 BC.)

de Beauvoir, S. (1997). *The Second Sex* (trans. H. M. Parshley). London: Vintage. (Original work published 1949.)

Butler, J. (1999). *Gender Trouble: Feminism and the Subversion of Identity*. London: Routledge. (Original work published 1990.)

Foucault, M. (1977). Nietzsche, genealogy, history. In D. Bouchard (ed.), *Language, Counter-Memory, Practice: Selected Essays and Interviews* (trans. D. Bouchard & S. Simon). Ithaca: Cornell University Press.

Foucault, M. (1990). *The History of Sexuality: An Introduction* (trans. R. Hurley). New York: Vintage. (Original work published 1976.)

Fuss, D. (1989). *Essentially Speaking: Feminism, Nature and Difference*. London: Routledge.

Heidegger, M. (1962). *Being and Time* (trans. J. Macquarrie & E. Robinson). New York: Harper. (Original work published 1927.)

Moi, T. (2001). *Sexual/Textual Politics: Feminist Literary Theory*. London: Routledge. (Original work published 1985.)

Sartre, J.-P. (2003). *Being and Nothingness: An Essay on Phenomenological Ontology*, 2nd edn. London: Routledge. (Original work published 1956.)

Spivak, G. C. (1985). Subaltern studies: Deconstructing historiography. In D. Landry & G. MacLean (eds.) (1996), *The Spivak Reader: Selected Works of Gayatri Chakravorty Spivak*. London: Routledge.

Ethical Criticism

ROBERT EAGLESTONE

The term "ethical criticism" does not refer to a school or critical approach, but rather to an upsurge of interest in the relationship between ethics, literature, criticism, and theory since the late 1990s, often called the "turn to ethics." However, in some ways this term is misleading, since the study of literature has always had a strong involvement with ethics since its inception and vigorous arguments have taken place as to how that involvement should be understood. The recent turn to ethics in literary studies stems from two very distinct approaches and, as such, can be divided into two very different (and sometimes opposing) camps. Both of these camps developed in relation to the growth of theory in the 1970s and '80s, and both offer different histories of that development and different ways of understanding the relationship between ethics and literature.

The 1970s and '80s – the period of the rapid growth of literary theory – were exciting but also disorienting times for the study of literature. Many new questions and approaches emerged into the field: ideas from feminism and other questions of gender relations and sexuality; ideas about race, racism, and of the postcolonial condition, ideas about migration and state power. Moreover, many of this generation of critics were explicitly political, and were reading literary texts in a Marxist or broadly leftist manner. The impact of deconstruction too, in its more French Derridean form, or in its more American form, influenced and shaped by Paul de Man, seemed to be at odds with traditional understandings of the ethical.

In response to this, some critics, for example Wayne Booth, argued that this meant that considerations of ethics had disappeared from literary criticism: "ethical criticism" had, in fact, become "a banned discipline" (1998[1988]: 3). In contrast to criticism in the 1950s and '60s, when, Booth and others argued, critics made ethical judgments about texts that said something about the ultimate value of life, or about the interrelationship between ethics and literature, theory offered ethically neutral approaches to texts, unable or unwilling to make judgments of literary (and so, they argued, moral) value. Other critics

went further and suggested that political aims behind feminism, political criticism, and postcolonialism had overtaken ethics and ethical judgments, and that much theory – especially deconstruction, and postmodernism more widely – was nihilistic and opposed to any sense of the ethical. At the same time, there was, outside of the discipline of literary studies, a renaissance of interest in ethical matters in philosophy and in adjacent disciplines which found in literature, and especially in narrative, a vital resource for developing and deepening understandings of ethics: leading examples of this are the philosophers Alasdair MacIntyre, Paul Ricoeur, and Martha Nussbaum, who all looked to literature for deep understandings of ethical traditions and for ethical guidance. In response to this, Wayne Booth and others began developing a renewed ethical criticism, working on issues of judgment and morality and often focusing on questions of narrative, in some ways as a backlash against what they saw as overly politicized and often unethical theory.

As Martha Nussbaum puts it:

[Literature] speaks *about us*, . . . As Aristotle observed, it is deep and conducive to our inquiry about how to live because it does not simply . . . record that this or that event happened; it searches for patterns of possibility – of choice and circumstance, and the interaction between choice and circumstance – that turn up in human lives with such a persistence that they must be regarded as *our* possibilities. (1990: 171)

Nussbaum, who draws deeply on Aristotle, argues that readers identify with the characters in fiction and in doing so enact their stories and it is this imaginative re-enactment which generates an understanding of other people's points of view, and often suffering, and of the moral demands placed on us. The text is an "adventure of the reader" (143), almost as if it were an educational or therapeutic role-playing exercise and it is this that makes us better and more responsive people. This sort of claim is one often made for classic realist texts, such as George Eliot's *Middlemarch*. Part of the work of the novelist – and especially the realist novelist – is the education of sympathy. This idea too underlines much work in the "medical humanities," where a sense that, for example, doctors who read widely in fiction may understand better the experience of being a sick patient, and so may become a better and more insightful doctor.

Alasdair MacIntyre claims an even more important role of narrative: he argues that narratives are vital in orienting ourselves in the world, especially ethically:

> I can only answer the question "What am I to do?" if I can answer the prior question "Of what story or stories do I find myself a part?" We enter human society, that is, with one or more imputed characters – roles into which we have been drafted – and we learn what they are in order to be able to understand how others respond to us and how our responses to them are partly to be constructed. It is through hearing stories about wicked stepmothers, lost children, good but misguided kings, wolves that suckle twin boys, youngest sons who receive no inheritance but must make their own way in the world and eldest sons who waste their inheritance on riotous living and go into exile to live with the swine, that children learn or mislearn what a child is and what a parent is, what the cast of characters may be in the drama into which they have been born and what the ways of the world are. (1985: 216)

For MacIntyre, there is no way of understanding ourselves except through our narratives – our stories – and these then shape ourselves and our society.

Despite their appeal, some critics suggested that there are a number of problems with arguments of this sort. First, while they work quite well for understanding the realist novel, other forms of literature – poetry, drama, nonrealist fiction – seem to offer very different problems and ask different questions, and are not so easily seen as "adventures of the reader." Second, this sort of reading, keen to address ethical or moral problems, often passes over the very textual nature of the artworks they read and are blind to numerous different interpretations and points of view. Third, it would be hard to show that people who had read a great deal of literature are, in some ways, morally better than others.

In contrast to this approach, there was another turn to ethics that stemmed not from a backlash against theory but from questions that developed within more theorized approaches. Some critics argued that "ethics" had not at all disappeared from criticism, and that questions of gender, of race, and of politics were specifically ethical questions: politically motivated leftist criticism clearly has an ethical agenda (the historian Hayden White remarks that the "best reasons for being a Marxist are moral ones" [1973: 284]) and feminism, gender, and race studies clearly have ethics at their core offering visions of equality and social justice. Similarly, other philosophers – notably Robert Bernasconi and Simon Critchley – have argued that deconstruction, often the focus for anger about the disappearance of ethics from literary studies, is in fact very concerned with ethical matters: a long essay by Derrida, "Violence and metaphysics," from 1963 (sometimes discussed as the first act of deconstruction) is about the ethical philosophy of Emmanuel Levinas. The very first sentence of Derrida's influential *Of Grammatology* states that his aim is to "focus attention on the ethnocentrism which, everywhere and always, had controlled the concept of writing" (1976: 3) and, later, Derrida argued that "Deconstruction is Justice."

However, three factors led to a necessary deepening and concern for ethics in this more "theorized" strand of criticism, and thus this part of the turn to ethics. The first was a sense that the Marxist project per se had failed. This was not belief that literature and social justice had no relation to one another, but rather that the Marxist intellectual framework which had generated either sufficient certain answers or, at the very least, provided a framework for intellectual inquiry, had withered away and could no longer provide ethical answers. The second factor was the need for a response to the criticisms made of deconstruction and other theoretical paradigms by both opponents, such as Nussbaum and Booth cited above, and supporters: if theory was ethical, then the manner of this needed to be clarified. Institutionally, this demand was intensified by the "Paul de Man affair," in which de Man, a prominent deconstructive critic, had been found to have written some arguably anti-Semitic articles for a collaborationist newspaper in occupied Belgium during World War II. The third factor was the quite normal development of critics' own interests: in part, this followed the interest in ethics of the later Derrida, in part it developed through an interest in trauma. However, both the second and third factors turned on a discovery by the English-speaking world of the philosophy of Emmanuel Levinas, often mediated by Derrida's work.

The work of Levinas, a French Jewish philosopher, originally from Lithuania, was centrally concerned with the question of ethics. Influenced by Edmund Husserl and Martin Heidegger, Levinas argues that "ethics is first philosophy" meaning that the concrete moment of a particular encounter with an other, another person (with what he calls the "face" of the other)

is the beginning of not only philosophy, but also personal identity as well. That is, for Levinas, we are not first people who then interact with others: it is our interaction with others that creates us as persons. Thus, the experience of ethics does not just come from but is the experience of the other. In his second major work, *Otherwise than Being*, he asks why "does the other concern me? What is Hecuba to me? Am I my brother's keeper?" Levinas's answer is:

> [These questions] have meaning only if one has already supposed the ego is concerned only with itself, is only a concern for itself. In this hypothesis, it indeed remains incomprehensible that the absolute outside-of-me, the other, would concern me. But in the "prehistory" of the ego posited for itself speaks a responsibility, the self is through and through a hostage, older than the ego, prior to principles. (1981: 117)

Levinas's work does not generate rules: instead, it stresses how our experience of ethics constantly overflows rules and our established ideas to explain how obligations arise in the first place and what this means: it is a form of what some philosophers call metaethics. This has caused some, perhaps understandable, confusion in commentators on Levinas, who think that his work is an exhortation to a moral life: it is not. Rather, it is descriptive of the grounds of possibility of such behavior in the first place. Levinas is not demanding that we become aware of the other, but is instead arguing phenomenologically that we always already are aware of the other.

Levinas, then, stresses the ideas of the origins of responsibility, singularity (that is, the concrete moment of response to the particular other), and otherness. This last idea, the idea of otherness, has been widely taken up. Often, this has led to rather banal generalities that amounted only to exhortations to "be good": but the term also points to a complex series of interactions between the world and systems of thought. It can mean both a concrete living other, a person, persons, or categories of traditions that are different from the accepted conventions or general consensus. It can also be understood to mean that which is outside, an indefinable thing outside a system which indicates that the system is not and cannot be closed. For Levinas, the term is descriptive: indeed, recognizing "otherness" does not lead to what one might normally call moral behavior. Indeed, in one of the most complex passages in his first major work, *Totality and Infinity*, Levinas argues that murder already acknowledges the other. Murder is not an act of domination which turns another person into a tool. Instead, it is to recognize them as other, as beyond one's power: the "Other is the sole being I can wish to kill" (1991[1969]: 198). One does not speak of killing a chair, or of murdering a cup of coffee. (One might speak of murdering – rather than butchering – a cow, which would raise the question, if, for Levinas or post-Levinasian thought, animals can be "other" in this ethical sense.)

Although Levinas himself has quite profound concerns about art – he distrusted ontological claims for art as something which can give knowledge of the absolute or which claimed for art a transcendent role beyond ethics and truth and he was also troubled by the ways in which representation stand might disrupt the "face-to-face" relationship so important to his thought – his work, often mediated through Derrida, has been very highly influential in discussions of the relation between ethics and literature.

One leading example of this is the work of the leading British-based critic Derek Attridge (2004), who argues that using literature for a particular purpose – to further a political cause, or to illuminate, as

evidence, a historical period – is to pass over its distinctiveness, and, while part of what "defines" literature is its impossibility of definition, we can see three key interwoven characteristics of the literary, all of which both evoke the ethical. The first, for Attridge, is its singularity: an artwork is a unique event, each one, and each author's oeuvre, a special instance of a coming together of language and circumstance, just as for Levinas each encounter is not an example of meeting an example of a person, but a unique encounter with a unique "face." Each artwork demands to be read as singular, as a particular instance, and cannot only be read as an example of some other category. The second characteristic for Attridge is alterity: an artwork, like another person, is profoundly other: there are no rules for it and to work to understand it is hard and demanding. Indeed, the "process of responding to the other person through openness to change is not dissimilar ... to the one that occurs when a writer refashions norms of thought to realize a new potential in a poem or an argument" (2004: 34). The third characteristic is inventiveness: the act of creation is both an openness to newness but also an awareness of what has gone before, which is remade. This creativity can reach us, even across time. Each singular work, each act of creation is experienced as inventive, and transforms both the previous cultural forms and ourselves as readers or performers of the literary event. He writes that to "respond to the singularity of the work I read is thus to affirm its singularity in my own singular response, open not just to the signifying potential of the words on the page but also to the specific time and place where the reading occurs, the ungeneralizable relation between this work and this reader" (81). Thus, in contrast to Nussbaum, for example, for Attridge the special ethical force of literature lies not in the world a work invents, but in the singular and inventive use of language in which that world is invented. Texts that fairground this (for example, modernist or postmodern texts) are clear examples of ethical engagement.

Although many thinkers have turned to Levinas's work, there are other responses. One early influential work to address these issues was J. Hillis Miller's *The Ethics of Reading*. Here, Miller, suggests that "without storytelling there is no theory of ethics" (1987: 2–3) "not because stories contain the thematic dramatization of ethical situations, judgments and choices" (3) but because an ethical rule (such as "do not lie") can be made to make sense only in particular situations which are themselves presented in and as narrative (when asked if I cut down the tree, what should I do? To what principle should I adhere?). This means that "ethics is not just a form of language but a running or sequential mode of language, in short a story. Ethics is a form of allegory, one form of those apparently referential stories we tell to ourselves and to those around us" (50). This leads Miller to conclude that, in making an ethical judgment, one is "unable . . . to know whether ... I am subject to a linguistic necessity or to an ontological one" (127). Again, influenced by deconstruction, the new interest in "trauma" is also one form of interest in ethics: if deconstruction and accounts like those of Miller were seen as too divorced from history and real events, an interest in the most awful and traumatic events in modernity seems to answer this. Cathy Caruth's *Unclaimed Experience* argues that because "linguistically oriented theories" like deconstruction "do not necessarily deny reference, but rather deny the possibility of modeling the principles of reference on those of natural law, or, we might say, of making reference like perception" (1996: 74), they are very suited to better approach and comprehend the events and responses to atrocity and traumatic events which "break the frame" between event, language, and representation, and so express a concern with ethics more profoundly. These two "wings" make up a sense of the ethical turn, the recent renewed interest in the relationship between literature and the question of how we should live.

SEE ALSO: Booth, Wayne; Deconstruction; Derrida, Jacques; Levinas, Emmanuel; de Man, Paul; Miller, J. Hillis; White, Hayden

REFERENCES AND SUGGESTED READINGS

Attridge, D. (2004). *The Singularity of Literature*. London: Routledge.

Booth, W. (1998). *The Company We Keep: An Ethics of Fiction*. Berkeley: University of California Press. (Original work published 1988.)

Caruth, C. (1996). *Unclaimed Experience*. Baltimore: Johns Hopkins University Press.

Davis, T. F., & Womack, K. (eds.) (2001). *Mapping the Ethical Turn*. Charlottesville: University Press of Virginia.

Derrida, J. (1976). *Of Grammatology* (trans. G. C. Spivak). Baltimore: Johns Hopkins University Press.

Eaglestone, R. (1997). *Ethical Criticism: Reading After Levinas*. Edinburgh: Edinburgh University Press.

Levinas, E. (1981). *Otherwise than Being; or, Beyond Essence* (trans. A. Lingis). The Hague: Martinus Nijhoff.

Levinas, E. (1991). *Totality and Infinity* (trans. A. Lingis). London: Kluwer. (Original work published 1969.)

MacIntyre, A. (1985). *After Virtue*, 2nd edn. London: Duckworth.

Miller, J. H. (1987). *The Ethics of Reading*. New York: Columbia University Press.

Newton, A. Z. (1995). *Narrative Ethics*. Cambridge, MA: Harvard University Press.

Nussbaum, M. (1990). *Love's Knowledge: Essays on Philosophy and Literature*. Oxford: Oxford University Press.

White, H. (1973). *Metahistory*. Baltimore: Johns Hopkins University Press.

Evolutionary Studies

JOSEPH CARROLL

Evolutionary literary scholars, commonly called "literary Darwinists," use concepts from evolutionary biology and the evolutionary human sciences to formulate principles of literary theory and interpret literary texts. They investigate interactions between "human nature" and the forms of cultural imagination, including literature and its oral antecedents. By "human nature," they mean a pan-human, genetically transmitted set of dispositions: motives, emotions, features of personality, and forms of cognition. Because the Darwinists concentrate on relations between genetically transmitted dispositions and specific cultural configurations, they often describe their work as "biocultural critique."

Typically, the literary Darwinists argue that any literary text can be analyzed at four levels: (1) as a manifestation of a universal human nature; (2) as a special instance within a specific cultural formation that organizes the elements of human nature into shared imaginative constructs (conventions, beliefs, myths, and traditions); (3) as the work of an individual author, whose identity has been shaped by some unique combination of inherited characteristics and historical circumstances; and (4) as a specific imaginative construct that reflects cultural influences but also displays original creative power.

The first monographs in this movement appeared in the mid-1990s (Carroll 1995; Storey 1996). Recent years have witnessed many new monographs, articles, edited collections, and special issues of journals. The journal *Philosophy and Literature* has been a main venue for articles adopting a biocultural perspective, but the Darwinists have also published widely in other journals. Several Darwinists from the humanities have published essays in social science journals, and some have used the empirical, quantitative methods characteristic of the sciences. Most literary Darwinists, though, have used the discursive methods traditional in the humanities. Whether empirical or discursive in method, evolutionary critique in the humanities is necessarily interdisciplinary, crossing the divide between science and the humanities. In 2009, a new annual journal, *The Evolutionary Review: Art, Science, Culture* (*TER*), was created specifically to provide a cross-disciplinary forum for biocultural critique. Aiming to demonstrate that an evolutionary perspective can encompass all things human, the first volume of *TER* (in press) contains essays and reviews on evolution, science, society, politics, technology, the environment, film, fiction, theater, visual art, music, and popular culture. *TER* contains essays by both scientists and humanists – with some humanists writing on scientific subjects, and some scientists writing on subjects in the humanities. In this respect, *TER* follows the pattern set by three collections of essays dedicated to evolutionary literary study (see Gottschall & Wilson 2005; Headlam Wells & McFadden 2006; Boyd et al. 2010).

Many of the Darwinists do not regard their approach as just one of many potentially fruitful approaches to literature. They believe that evolutionary research provides a comprehensive, empirically sound, and scientifically progressive framework for the study of literature. Accordingly, they believe that biocultural critique can and should ultimately subsume all other possible approaches to literary study. Most literary Darwinists refer approvingly to sociobiologist Edward O. Wilson's (1998) concept of "consilience": the unity of knowledge. Like Wilson, they regard evolutionary biology as the pivotal discipline uniting the physical sciences, the social sciences, and the humanities. They draw heavily on research in multiple interlocking fields of evolutionary biology and the evolutionary human sciences: physical and cultural anthropology, paleontology, cognitive archaeology, ethology, sociobiology, behavioral ecology, evolutionary psychology, primatology, comparative psychology (research comparing humans and other animals), developmental psychology, family psychology, cognitive, affective, and social neuroscience (research focusing on brain mechanisms), personality theory, behavioral genetics, linguistics, and game theory (mathematical modeling of social interactions).

In its simplest, crudest forms, evolutionary literary criticism consists only in identifying basic, common human needs – survival, sex, and status, for instance – and using those categories to describe the behavior of characters depicted in literary texts. More ambitious efforts pose for themselves an overarching interpretive challenge: to construct continuous explanatory sequences linking the highest level of causal evolutionary explanation to the most particular effects in individual works of literature. Within evolutionary biology, the highest level of causal explanation involves adaptation by means of natural selection. Starting from the premise that the human mind has evolved in an adaptive relation to its environment, literary Darwinists undertake to characterize the phenomenal qualities of a literary work (tone, style, theme, and formal organization), locate the work in a cultural context, explain that cultural context as a particular organization of the elements of human nature within a specific set of environmental conditions (including cultural traditions), identify an implied author and an implied reader, examine the responses of actual readers (for instance, other literary critics), describe the sociocultural, political, and psychological functions the work fulfills, locate those functions in relation to the evolved needs of human nature, and link the work comparatively with other artistic works, using a taxonomy of themes, formal elements, affective elements, and functions derived from a comprehensive model of human nature.

The one concept that most clearly distinguishes the literary Darwinists from other current schools of literary theory is "human nature." In the last two decades of the twentieth century, this concept was rejected by most literary theorists. Before that time, though, most creative writers and literary theorists presupposed that human nature was their subject and their central point of reference. The literary Darwinists argue that the concepts available in the evolutionary human sciences converge closely with the understanding of human nature available in common speech and articulated more fully in literary texts. When writers invoke human nature, or ordinary people say, "That's just human nature," they presuppose a shared set of ideas about the characteristics that typify human behavior. Evolutionary psychologists use the term "folk psychology" to designate these common, intuitive ideas. By using modern scientific concepts of human nature, literary Darwinists believe that they can construct interpretive critiques that are concordant with the intentional meanings of literary texts but that encompass those meanings within deeper levels of biocultural explanation.

The folk understanding of human nature includes the basic animal and social motives: self-preservation, sexual desire, jealousy, maternal love, favoring kin, belonging to a social group, and desiring prestige. It also includes basic forms of social morality: resentment against wrongs, gratitude for kindness, honesty in fulfilling contracts, disgust at cheating, and the sense of justice in its simplest forms – reciprocation and revenge. All of these substantive motives are complicated by the ideas that enter into the folk understanding of ego psychology: the primacy of self-interest and the prevalence of self-serving delusion, manipulative deceit, vanity, and hypocrisy. Folk versions of ego psychology might seem to have a cynical tinge, but they all imply failures in more positive aspects of human nature – honesty, fairness, and impulses of self-sacrifice for kin, friends, or the common good.

The model of human nature available in the evolutionary human sciences is a relatively recent construct, and indeed, as of 2009, it is still under construction. Though with antecedents extending back to Darwin's *Descent of Man* (1981[1871]), the evolutionary human sciences did not begin to develop in a systematic, collective way until late in the 1960s, with the advent of "sociobiology." Sociobiologists tended to concentrate on reproductive success not just as a long-term principle regulating natural selection but as a direct motive for individual people. In the 1990s, "evolutionary psychologists" distinguished themselves from sociobiologists by deprecating reproduction as a direct motive and emphasizing instead the "proximate mechanisms," such as sexual desire, that advanced reproductive success in ancestral environments. Melding sociobiology with cognitive science, evolutionary psychologists described the brain as a collection of "modules," that is, dedicated bits of neural machinery designed by natural selection to solve specific adaptive problems in ancestral environments. While concentrating on specific psychological mechanisms, the evolutionary psychologists lost sight of the larger systemic organization of human behavior. Instead of formulating a comprehensive model of human nature, they

merely offered open-ended and unorganized lists of specialized modules.

In the first decade of the twenty-first century, behavioral ecologists and developmental psychologists formulated the systemic idea necessary to make sense of human nature as an integrated set of adaptive mechanisms. The term for this systemic idea is "human life history." All species have a "life history," a species-typical pattern for birth, growth, reproduction, social relations (if the species is social), and death. For each species, the pattern of life history forms a reproductive cycle. In the case of humans, that cycle centers on parents, children, and the social group. Successful parental care produces children capable, when grown, of forming adult pair-bonds, becoming functioning members of a community, and caring for children of their own. "Human nature" is the set of species-typical characteristics regulated by the human reproductive cycle. This concept of human nature assimilates the sociobiological insight into the significance of reproductive success as a regulative principle, and it allocates proximal mechanisms a functional place within the human life cycle.

Human life history is similar in some ways to that of chimpanzees, but humans also have unique species characteristics deriving from their larger brains and more highly developed forms of social organization. Human offspring take longer to reach adulthood than the offspring of any other species; their brains take longer to mature and their social, technical, and intellectual skills take longer to develop. In ancestral human populations, provisioning the metabolically expensive human brain required dual parental care and a sexual division of labor, with males doing the hunting and females doing the gathering and cooking. Hunting provided important but irregular supplies of animal protein. Bearing and tending children made hunting impracticable for females, but female gathering ensured that the family group received regular provisioning despite unsuccessful days spent in hunting. Cooking made food consumption much more energy-efficient, reducing the size of the gut and releasing metabolic resources for a larger brain.

In humans as in most species, males compete for sexual access to females. Consequently, for pair-bonded dual parenting to have evolved in large, cooperative social groups containing multiple adult males, humans had to have developed cultural norms defining and limiting rights of sexual access to females. Other species have adaptations for cooperation in social groups with specialized functions and status hierarchies. Humans alone regulate conduct by appealing to cultural norms. Using cultural norms requires a capacity for symbolic thought that exceeds the cognitive capabilities of any other species. The hunter-gatherer way of life thus formed a complex of interdependent causal forces in which specifically human cognitive capabilities co-evolved with specifically human strategies for nutrition, reproduction, and social organization.

Animals of other species make tools, share information, and learn behaviors from observing each other. Because humans have exceptionally large brains, they have been able to expand these rudimentary capabilities in three ways unique to human culture: (1) they produce art; (2) they retain and develop social, mechanical, and intellectual innovations, adding new innovations to old; and (3) they extrapolate general ideas. Animals of other species produce emotionally expressive vocalizations and engage in play. Humans alone produce oral narratives and visual artifacts designed to depict objects and actions, evoke subjective sensations, give aesthetic pleasure, and delineate through symbols the salient features of their experience. Through cumulative innovation, humans have transformed techniques into technology, tribes into civilizations, discoveries into progressive sciences, and artistic novelties into aesthetic traditions. By extrapolating general ideas, they have produced theology, philosophy, history, the sciences, and theories about the arts.

The most hotly debated issue in evolutionary literary study concerns the adaptive functions of literature and other arts – whether there are any adaptive functions, and if so, what they might be. Steven Pinker (1997) suggests that aesthetic responsiveness is merely a side effect of cognitive powers that evolved to fulfill more practical functions, but Pinker also suggests that narratives can provide information for adaptively relevant problems. Geoffrey Miller (2000) argues that artistic productions serve as forms of sexual display. Brian Boyd (2009) argues that the arts are forms of cognitive "play" that enhance pattern recognition. Boyd and Ellen Dissanayake (2000) also argue that the arts provide means of creating shared social identity. Dissanayake, Joseph Carroll (2008), and Denis Dutton (2009) all argue that the arts help to organize the human mind; they give emotionally and aesthetically modulated form to the relations among the elements of human experience. The idea that the arts function as means of psychological organization subsumes the ideas that they provide adaptively relevant information, enable us to consider alternative behavioral scenarios, enhance pattern recognition, and serve as means for creating shared social identity. And of course, the arts can be used for sexual display. In that respect, the arts are like most other human products – clothing, jewelry, shelter, means of transportation, etc. The hypothesis that the arts help to organize the mind is not incompatible with the hypothesis of sexual display, but it subordinates sexual display to a more primary adaptive function.

According to the hypothesis that the arts function as media for psychological organization, the uniquely human need for art derives from the unique human powers of cognition. To all animals except humans, the world presents itself as a series of rigidly defined stimuli releasing a narrow repertory of stereotyped behaviors. For human minds, the world presents itself as a vast and potentially perplexing array of percepts, inferences, causal relations, contingent possibilities, analogies, contrasts, and hierarchical conceptual structures. High intelligence enables humans to generate plans based on mental representations of complex relationships, engage in collective enterprises requiring shared mental representations, and thus produce novel solutions to adaptive problems. Humans do not operate automatically, but neither do they operate on the basis of purely rational deliberations about means and ends. Art, like religion and ideology, is charged with emotion, and indeed, religion and ideology typically make use of the arts to convey their messages in emotionally persuasive ways. In all known societies, humans regulate their behavior in accordance with beliefs and values that are made vividly present to them in the depictions of art, including fictional narratives.

Ways of exploring and evaluating hypotheses about the adaptive function of the arts include paleoanthropological research into the evolutionary emergence of symbolic culture, cross-cultural ethological research into artistic practices among hunter-gatherers and tribal peoples, neuroscientific research into the way the brain processes artistic information, psychological research into the way art and language enter into childhood development, and social science research into the systemic social effects produced by shared participation in imaginative experience.

One leading example of biocultural critique is Jonathan Gottschall's work: he has conducted numerous quantitative studies on folk tales and fairytales across multiple cultures in different continents (2008a). In his study of Homer's epics, Gottschall (2008) integrates sociobiological theory with archaeological and anthropological research in order to reconstruct the motivating forces in Homer's cultural ecology. He also vividly evokes the Homeric ethos. Robin Headlam Wells (2005) and Marcus Nordlund (2007) both locate Shakespeare's plays within the context of Elizabethan views on human nature. Robert Storey (1996) discusses reader responses to *Hamlet* among a Nigerian tribal population, thus illuminating the pan-human features of the text and also delineating a culturally circumscribed interpretive perspective. Joseph Carroll (in press) also discusses *Hamlet*, incorporating recent research on personality and the neurobiology of depression and examining the emotional responses of playgoers and readers in various literary periods. Carroll (2004) uses biocultural methods to interpret various Victorian novels. Using quantitative methods, Carroll et al. (2009) identify ancestral political dispositions governing the organization of characters in Victorian novels. Judith Saunders (2009) locates Edith Wharton's novels in cultural environments ranging from that of the patrician elite in the American *fin de siècle* to that of decadent cosmopolites in the jazz age. Brett Cooke (2002) situates Zamyatin's dystopian novel *We* in the utopian/dystopian literary tradition and also in the sociopolitical conditions of Soviet Russia. Brian Boyd (2009) gives close attention to specific cultural beliefs and practices in Homeric Greece and also focuses minutely on the political context – Japan shortly after World War II – to which Dr Seuss responds in *Horton Hears a Who*. The essays in a collection by Hoeg &

Larsen (2009) focus on issues specific to Hispanic cultural contexts.

SEE ALSO: Authorial Intention; Cognitive Studies; Latino/a Theory; Master Narrative; Mimesis; Poststructuralism; Semiotics; Social Constructionism

REFERENCES AND SUGGESTED READINGS

Boyd, B. (2009). *On the Origin of Stories: Evolution, Cognition, and Fiction*. Cambridge, MA: Belknap.

Boyd, B., Carroll, J., & Gottschall, J. (eds.) (2010). *Evolution, Literature, and Film: A Reader*. New York: Columbia University Press.

Carroll, J. (1995). *Evolution and Literary Theory*. Columbia: University of Missouri Press.

Carroll, J. (2004). *Literary Darwinism: Evolution, Human Nature, and Literature*. New York: Routledge.

Carroll, J. (2008). An evolutionary paradigm for literary study. *Style*, 42(2–3), 103–135.

Carroll, J. (in press). Intentional meaning in *Hamlet*: An evolutionary perspective. *Style*.

Carroll, J., Gottschall, J., Johnson, J. A., & Kruger, D. J. (2009). Human nature in nineteenth-century British novels: Doing the math. *Philosophy and Literature*, 33(1), 50–72.

Cooke, B. (2002). *Human Nature in Utopia: Zamyatin's "We."* Evanston, IL: Northwestern University Press.

Darwin, C. (1981). *The Descent of Man, and Selection in Relation to Sex* (ed. J. T. Bonner & R. M. May). Princeton: Princeton University Press. (Original work published 1871.)

Dissanayake, E. (2000). *Art and Intimacy: How the Arts Began*. Seattle: University of Washington Press.

Dutton, D. (2009). *The Art Instinct: Beauty, Pleasure, and Human Evolution*. New York: Bloomsbury.

Gottschall, J. (2008a). *Literature, Science, and a New Humanities*. Basingstoke: Palgrave Macmillan.

Gottschall, J. (2008b). *The Rape of Troy: Evolution, Violence, and the World of Homer*. Cambridge: Cambridge University Press.

Gottschall, J., & Wilson, D. S. (eds.) (2005). *The Literary Animal: Evolution and the Nature of Narrative*. Evanston, IL: Northwestern University Press.

Headlam Wells, R. (2005). *Shakespeare's Humanism*. Cambridge: Cambridge University Press.

Headlam Wells, R., & McFadden, J. (eds.) (2006). *Human Nature: Fact and Fiction*. London: Continuum.

Hoeg, J., & Larsen, K. S. (eds.) (2009). *Interdisciplinary Essays on Darwinism in Hispanic Literature and Film: The Intersection of Science and the Humanities*. New York: Edwin Mellen.

Miller, G. (2000). *The Mating Mind: How Sexual Choice Shaped the Evolution of Human Nature*. New York: Doubleday.

Nordlund, M. (2007). *Shakespeare and the Nature of Love: Literature, Culture, Evolution*. Evanston, IL: Northwestern University Press.

Pinker, S. (1997). *How the Mind Works*. New York: Norton.

Saunders, J. (2009). *Reading Edith Wharton through a Darwinian Lens: Evolutionary Biological Issues in Her Fiction*. Jefferson, NC: McFarland.

Storey, R. (1996). *Mimesis and the Human Animal: On the Biogenetic Foundations of Literary Representation*. Evanston, IL: Northwestern University Press.

Wilson, E. O. (1998). *Consilience: The Unity of Knowledge*. New York: Knopf.

F

Felman, Shoshana

JANE KILBY

Shoshana Felman (b. 1942) is Woodruff Professor of Comparative Literature and French in the Department of Comparative Literature at Emory University and her influence in the field of cultural and literary studies is accredited to the generative and interdisciplinary nature of her psychoanalytic reading. Like all critics of importance, Felman's contribution is methodological in origin, and for that reason more concerned with questions of pedagogy than knowledge production per se. She received her PhD from the University of Grenoble, France, before moving to Yale University, where she taught from 1970 until 2004, holding the post of Thomas E. Donnelley Professor of French and Comparative Literature from 1986.

Embracing the radical teaching of Jacques Lacan in France during the late 1960s, Felman's early work centers on the question of reading and how psychoanalysis, or, rather more precisely, how Lacan, might allow us to read literature differently. At issue for Felman is not a question of applying psychoanalysis to literature, such that psychoanalysis is the subject or agent of interpretation and literature the object, but rather it is a matter of reading literature with psychoanalysis, and just as importantly

for Felman, of reading psychoanalysis with literature. In other words, rather than assume that literature and psychoanalysis are separate such that it makes sense to speak of the application of one to the other, Felman argues, the relationship is one of mutual implication. However, this is not to suggest harmony, since their difference serves to establish that they are both outside and inside each other. Thus, according to Felman, literature and psychoanalysis compromise each other in their very constitution. In sum, and as a consequence, "Each is thus a potential threat to the interiority of the other, since each is contained in the other as its *otherness-to-itself*, its *unconscious*" thus in "the same way that psychoanalysis points to the unconscious of literature, *literature, in its turn, is the unconscious of psychoanalysis*" (1982: 10; emphasis original).

Importantly, then, for Felman neither literature nor psychoanalysis can claim mastery and thus her readings are characterized by a dynamic exploration of what can be read beyond the text, with text referring to both the text of psychoanalysis and the literary text. For Felman, and in a manner escaping her critics, psychoanalysis is not a doctrine but a method for reading or listening to that which is in excess of what can be written or said. This method, however, does not afford the reader sovereignty with respect to the meaning of a text, for the process of reading necessarily escapes the reader. The reader is also unknowing. Thus reading is a creative, if necessarily blind, transferential practice, with the reader an effect of the text, as, equally, the text is an effect of the reading. In this respect, Felman is inspired by the work of Paul de Man, who became her colleague during her time at Yale University. Alongside Barbara Johnson, Geoffrey Hartman, J. Hillis Miller, Harold Bloom, and Jacques Derrida, Felman was a leading figure of the Yale School. She was also an exponent of deconstruction, albeit, for her, a deconstruction in dialogue with psychoanalysis; she offered important critiques of Jacques Derrida's reading of Austin, for example, in *The Scandal of the Speaking Body* (2002b). Her difference from the Yale School was also signaled by her interest in gender, sexual difference, and feminism, captured by her book *What Does a Woman Want?* (1993).

However, it is with the publication of the co-authored *Testimony* that Felman's influence reaches beyond the audience attuned to the Yale School (Felman & Laub 1992). Marking a significant shift from her reading of literary and philosophical texts, which included her canonical analysis of Henry James's *The Turn of the Screw*, *Testimony* brings Felman to the question of reading of nonliterary texts and debates as well as literary texts after and in respect of the Holocaust. Associated with the advent of Holocaust studies, Felman's more recent work is concerned with the contemporary status of history and memory, as well as law and justice, as suggested by her subsequent book *The Juridical Unconscious* (2002a). At this point in her career, Felman's writing is marked by an increasing ethical and political sensitivity to the relationship between texts and life, especially those marked by violence and trauma. Importantly, though, and taking her inspiration from the creative

genius of Paul Celan, Claude Lanzmann, and Albert Camus, among other witnesses to the Holocaust, Felman continues to read creatively with her hallmark strategy of shuttling between one text and an often unlikely counterpart (such as Molière's *Don Juan* and J. L. Austin's *How To Do Things With Words*, or, more recently, between the case of O. J. Simpson's first trial and Tolstoy's *The Kreutzer Sonata*). The effect of this strategy is frequently surprising with respect to insight, but it is always, as is Felman's lesson, a way of sustaining the life of the text in question.

SEE ALSO: Austin, J. L.; Bloom, Harold; Deconstruction; Derrida, Jacques; Lacan, Jacques; de Man, Paul; Miller, J. Hillis; Yale School

REFERENCES AND SUGGESTED READINGS

Felman, S. (ed.) (1982). *Literature and Psychoanalysis: The Question of Reading: Otherwise*. Baltimore: Johns Hopkins University Press. (Original work published 1977.)

Felman, S. (1987). *Jacques Lacan and the Adventure of Insight: Psychoanalysis in Contemporary Culture*. Cambridge, MA: Harvard University Press.

Felman, S. (1993). *What Does a Woman Want? Reading and Sexual Difference*. Baltimore: Johns Hopkins University Press.

Felman, S. (2002a). *The Juridical Unconscious: Trials and Traumas in the Twentieth Century*. London: Routledge.

Felman, S. (2002b). *The Scandal of the Speaking Body: Don Juan with J. L. Austin, or Seduction in Two Languages*. Stanford: Stanford University Press. (Original work published 1980.)

Felman, S. (2003). *Writing and Madness: Literature/Philosophy/Psychoanalysis*. Palo Alto: Stanford University Press. (Original work published 1978.)

Felman, S., & Laub, D. (1992). *Testimony: Crises of Witnessing in Literature, Psychoanalysis, and History*. London: Routledge.

Sun, E., Petetz, E., & Baer, U. (eds.) (2007). *The Claims of Literature: The Shoshana Reader.* New York: Fordham University Press.

Feminism

KATIE GARNER & REBECCA MUNFORD

Feminism describes the campaigns, activities, and texts concerned with challenging and transforming how women are treated and represented in society. It is a political movement and discourse that encompasses a diverse range of perspectives, theories, and methods. As well as analyzing patriarchal structures, feminist theory seeks to propose new ways for women to bring about social change. This drive underlies much feminist activity, from public campaigns for new political rights, to the search for a new "feminine" writing. Current Anglo-American models often conceptualize the history of Western feminism in terms of three movements, or "waves." The first wave of activity dates from the end of the eighteenth century through to the beginning of collective female political action in the form of the Suffragette and New Women's movements in Britain and the US, and the granting of partial (1918) and full (1928) franchise for women in Britain. The 1960s signal the beginnings of the "second wave," when women collectively campaigned on a broad range of issues including sexual health and contraception, pornography, domestic abuse, and gender discrimination in the workplace. This chapter of feminist theory is marked by the emergence of three different models of feminist politics: liberal feminism, which focuses on achieving full equality and opportunities within existing social structures; radical feminism, which is revolutionary rather than reformative in its conviction that creating alternative, woman-centered institutions and realities will bring about social change; and socialist feminism, which sees

"femaleness" and "femininity" as socially and historically contingent, and is concerned with the economic and cultural contexts of women's oppression. Following the decline of organized second-wave activities in the 1980s, different accounts of feminism from black and Third World women began to readdress the First World bias of the first and second waves. These differing positions, alongside developments in the fields of gender studies, postcolonial theory, queer theory, and postmodernism, inform third-wave feminism, which accordingly takes a more global and plural view of the relationship between power and subjectivity.

The history of feminism does not have a definitive origin. As early as the beginning of the fifteenth century Christine de Pizan was cataloguing the achievements of women and challenging female stereotypes in *The Book of the City of Ladies* (1983[1404–5]). However, Mary Wollstonecraft's *A Vindication of the Rights of Woman* (1992[1792]) is often regarded as heralding the beginning of modern feminism in Britain. Written in the form of a philosophical essay, Wollstonecraft's provocative call for reform foregrounded the social, political, and economic marginalization of women at a time when the question of the "rights of man" was being debated in France and the US. Key to Wollstonecraft's argument was her belief that social structures constructed female inequality as "natural" and that women do not *choose* to behave as they do, but are instead enslaved by a society that forces them to behave in certain "sentimental" ways. In particular, Wollstonecraft identified gallantry and sensibility as major social fabrications which had been developed (by men) to encourage women's subordination. The overarching problem, she argued, was women's lack of access to education, which held them in a "state of perpetual childhood" (1992[1792]: 11). She proposed that Enlightenment principles of rational thought and the ability to acquire knowledge should be extended to women, and that, in line with Enlightenment logic, it was irrational to exclude women from the social sphere and to curtail their political citizenship.

The *Vindication* had an immediate international influence. It was quickly translated into French and published in three separate editions in the US. Wollstonecraft's articulation of femininity as a condition resembling slavery also provided a springboard from which American women involved in antislavery campaigns could turn their attention to female suffrage. In the 1840s, American suffragettes Lucretia Mott and Elizabeth Cady Stanton jointly campaigned for the abolishment of slavery and the granting of suffrage. Stanton's "Declaration of Sentiments," which imitated the American Declaration of Independence (1776), extending the equal rights doctrine to include women, was issued at the Seneca Falls women's rights convention in July 1848. In 1869 Stanton founded the National Woman Suffrage Association (NWSA) with Susan B. Anthony, whose roots were also in antislavery activities. The NWSA merged with the American Woman Suffrage Association (AWSA) to form the National American Woman Suffrage Association (NAWSA) in 1890. The NAWSA played a vital role in ratifying the Nineteenth Amendment, also known as the Susan B. Anthony amendment, which granted American women full suffrage in 1920.

In Britain, in the second half of the nineteenth century, debates about women's lack of access to education expanded into a wider questioning of women's political inequality, and the terms "feminism" and "feminist" entered public usage by the 1890s. The British philosophers and political theorists John Stuart Mill and Harriet Taylor developed aspects of Wollstonecraft's liberal feminist thought, campaigning for women's suffrage and equal access to education. "The subjection of women" (1869), which Mill worked on with his wife, was published three years after he first introduced a parliamentary bill calling for the extension of enfranchisement to women. The essay argued that all women were repressed citizens. It also blamed British marriage laws – which denied women their own rights to children, land, and property – for producing and sustaining inequality between men and women. Although "The subjection" is recognized as a progressive feminist text in its call for gender equality, Mill's stance has been criticized for its refusal to question women's position in the domestic sphere.

By the latter part of the nineteenth century, underground female discontent had begun to translate into more radical, public statements and women formed a number of activist groups. Incorporating both the lobbying strategies of the National Union of Women's Suffrage Societies (NUWSS), led by Millicent Fawcett, and the direct action of the Women's Social and Political Union (WSPU), founded by Emmeline Pankhurst and her daughters, the British suffrage movement represented a demand for equality, grounded in political and legislative reform. The passing of the 1928 Representation of the People Act marked the culmination of over six decades of political and social agitation, and extended the partial suffrage that women had received ten years previously in 1918. The same decades marked a period of literary experimentation and innovation, with writers such as Virginia Woolf, H. D., Edith Wharton, Zola Neale Hurston, and Djuna Barnes subjecting the relationship between women and literature, and gender and language, to new focuses. The most influential of these was Woolf's *A Room of One's Own* (1929). Developed from two lectures that Woolf had delivered to women students at Newnham and Girton Colleges in Cambridge in

1928, and playfully crossing the boundaries between fiction and polemic, the essay tackles the question of "women and fiction" and the various ways in which this relationship might be imagined. Her underlying and much celebrated assertion is that "a woman must have money and a room of her own if she is to write fiction" (1929: 4). She is concerned, then, with the relationship between economics, education, and creativity. "Women," she argues, "have served all these centuries as looking-glasses possessing the magic and delicious power of reflecting the figure of man at twice its natural size" (1945[1929]: 5). Placing questions of representation and literary agency firmly within a broader social, economic, and historical context, Woolf highlights how woman's disenfranchisement – her exclusion from electoral and civil privilege – is not only the result of political legislation and economic inequity, but also of cultural mores. Woolf's essay, then, foregrounds why women need to undertake critical and creative activity alongside political activity. Sketching out a critical language for addressing questions about gender and sexuality, the canon and literary production, and language and subjectivity, A Room of One's Own presaged many of the debates that characterize the "second wave" of feminist activity, and remains one of the most influential texts of the twentieth century.

World War II and its aftermath separate the activities of first- and second-wave feminism. In Britain and the US, women's war work and the labors of home-front living had expanded responsibilities and freedoms, but at the war's end, government propaganda expected women to return to their prewar roles – roles which were increasingly seen as confining. Just as liberal, socialist, and radical politics coexisted in the women's movement, the 1960s onward saw the emergence of a diverse, and often discordant, body of theoretical analyses of the

social-economic, cultural, and linguistic experiences of women and the complex and various operations of patriarchal ideologies, as well as innovatory moves to transform extant structures. In 1963, Betty Friedan, one of the pioneers of the US women's movement, published The Feminine Mystique, an investigation of the cultural construction of femininity and the manacles of domesticity. This landmark study of "the problem that has no name" drew attention to the home as a prison rather than a stronghold for women and the psychological distress experienced by unwaged and bored housewives. What Friedan termed the "mystique" stood for the inconsistency between women's real experience in the home and the idealization of domesticity in marketing and the media. Focused on individual experience and autonomy, Friedan's work belongs to a tradition of liberal feminist thinking that has been criticized for privileging the experiences of white, middle-class women. Nevertheless, in foregrounding the significance of ideological processes, it does share aspects of Marxist and socialist feminist thought. Marxist feminist critics, however, are concerned with analyzing the ways in which women's subordination is related to the organization of social class – a relationship that was often sidelined or ignored in mainstream Marxist theory – as well as the ways in which capitalist relations of production (e.g., the division of labor) were gendered (see Barrett 1980).

The 1960s were also a period of direct feminist action, and formed part of the broader cultural questioning and collective challenges to authority made by civil rights, student, and antiwar movements. Drawing on previous suffragette activities, women once again began to form organized political bodies, including the liberal National Organization for Women (NOW) in 1966, of which Friedan was a co-founder. Rooted in a conviction that sexism – women's subordination to the class of men – is the cause of women's oppression, radical feminism focused on women's experiences of subjugation *as women*. A key aim was to encourage all women to become involved in political activity and to challenge the separation between the personal and the political (see Morgan 1970; Whelehan 1995). Consciousness raising (CR) – the practice of women speaking openly about their lives to one another – was viewed as an important tool for social change. From the 1960s onwards, many all-women CR groups formed to share and analyze personal experiences and issues as a starting point for collective political action. This emphasis on the individual sphere and private experience meant that early feminist agendas focused on such issues as housework, abortion, contraception, the family, and division of labor; the phrase "the personal is political" quickly became the epigram for second-wave activity.

CR groups also served as platforms for organizing large-scale public demonstrations. The most famous of these took place in September 1968, when the New York Radical Women demonstrated against the Miss America Beauty Pageant in Atlantic City. Throwing such items as bras, girdles, high heels, and fashion magazines into a "freedom trash can," the pageant protesters challenged traditional definitions of femininity and the oppressive paraphernalia of the beauty industry – giving birth, at the same time, to one of the most resilient myths of feminist history: the caricature of the militant bra-burner. In 1968, then, culture was clearly identified as a site for challenging repressive representations of gendered identity – and, specifically, for destabilizing and overcoming male authored definitions of femininity.

Of pressing concern to many Anglo-American and European theorists from the late 1960s onward were the androcentric scripts of Freudian psychoanalysis and, in particular, a representation of woman as "lacking a sexual organ" (Greer 1970). Constructions of woman as lack or absence are addressed in two seminal texts of second-wave feminist criticism, Kate Millett's *Sexual Politics* and Germaine Greer's *The Female Eunuch* (both published in Britain in 1970). Millett in particular established an influential reading of Freudian penis envy as a misogynist model which disallowed the little girl any desire of her own other than to become a man. Alternatively, the British psychoanalyst Juliet Mitchell presented a feminist revision of Freudian psychoanalysis in her study *Psychoanalysis and Feminism* (1974), which argued Freud's theories opened up new ways of thinking about the construction of sexual subjectivity for women (see also Rose 1986).

Millett's *Sexual Politics* created a long-lasting trend for identifying evidence of misogyny in texts, as Millett looked at works by male authors (including D. H. Lawrence and Henry Miller) and illustrated how each enacted a sexual power politics which forced women to occupy negative positions. Millett was not concerned with how Lawrence and Miller chose to present women; rather, she undertook to illustrate how the reader responded to the gender structures inherent in their texts. Greer's *The Female Eunuch* was in part an extension of Wollstonecraft's offensive against "pretty feminine phrases" and social frames in a modern context. Greer argued that romance novels were the "opiate of the supermenial" as they prescribed false models of experience for women (Greer 1970: 188). These texts, along with Mary Ellmann's groundbreaking *Thinking About Women* (1968), offered cutting analyses of dominant scripts of femininity, placing them in the political context of patriarchy. Their focus on the sexist ideologies underlying the male authored canon provided the foundations for what is referred to as "images of women" criticism.

The 1970s saw serious critical attention paid to women's writing and its traditions by Anglo-American academics. The focus on the sexist ideologies underlying the male authored canon integral to "images of women" criticism was followed by a female-centered approach or, in Elaine Showalter's coinage, "gynocritics," that is, an approach that was engaged with "*woman as writer* – with woman as the producer of textual meaning, with the history, themes, genres, and structures of literature by women" (Showalter 1979: 25). In the second half of the decade, three key texts appeared: Ellen Moers's *Literary Women* (1976), Elaine Showalter's *A Literature of their Own: British Women Novelists from Brontë to Lessing* (1977), and Sandra Gilbert and Susan Gubar's *The Madwoman in the Attic: The Woman Writer and the Nineteenth-Century Literary Imagination* (1979). Offering revisionist literary histories, these works were concerned with rereading women writers with established literary reputations (such as Jane Austen, the Brontës, Emily Dickinson, and Ann Radcliffe), but also with extending the female canon to recover forgotten or marginalized female writers. Moers's *Literary Women* saw women's literature as a definitive movement, "apart from, but hardly subordinate to the mainstream" (1978[1976]: 42). Showalter's *Literature of Their Own* opens with the claim that "women have had a literature of their own all along" (1977: 10). Showalter disagreed with Moers's claim that women's writings could be said to form a "movement," by stressing that as each past female writer was relatively unaware of the fact that other women wrote alongside herself, she saw herself as an individual rather than as part of a collective.

Revising Harold Bloom's concept of the male author's "anxiety of influence," Gilbert and Gubar's *Madwoman in the Attic* argues that the female author suffers from a similar and yet more distressing "anxiety of authorship": "a radical fear that she cannot create" (2000[1979]: 49). Their redeployment of Bloom's model has been criticized for appearing to confirm the idea that the feminist critic must write from within the already established structures of patriarchy (here, male dominated literary criticism). Thus, Gilbert and Gubar's text illustrates one of the most pressing problems within feminism: the question of how to critique and transform male models without remaining within their frameworks. Nineteenth-century women writers also provided the focus for the Marxist-Feminist Literature Collective, a group of women who met between 1976 and 1979, and whose critical practice was informed by a conviction that a synthesis between Marxism and psychoanalysis was necessary to "unfold the crucial interdependence of class structure and patriarchy" (1996[1978]: 330; see also Kaplan 1986).

One of the most frequent accusations leveled at second-wave feminist criticism is that it attempts to speak on behalf of all women by universalizing the experience of some. Specifically, it has been taken to task for its failure to attend to the ways in which experiences of gender intersect with and are shaped by experiences of class, race, sexuality, religion, nationality, and ethnicity, alongside other categories of identity. In trying to reclaim a past for "women," gynocritics met opposition from black feminists and women of color, as well as lesbian feminists, for whom the "new history" of women bore the familiar hallmarks of exclusivity and monolithic assumptions – the very principles feminists detested about male histories. In her groundbreaking essay, "Toward a black feminist criticism" (1977), Barbara Smith discusses the ways in which the literary world ignores or relegates the existence of black women writers and black lesbian writers and calls for a more rigorous treatment of the complex ways in which race, sexuality, class, and gender are interconnected.

The work of bell hooks has played a pioneering role in defining a position for black feminists. In *Ain't I a Woman* (1982) and *Feminist Theory* (1984), hooks exposes and redresses two key political blind spots in white feminisms: "drawing endless analogies between 'women' and 'blacks'"; and assuming that the word woman "is synonymous with white woman" (hooks 1982: 139). *Feminist Theory* opens by highlighting how Friedan's *The Feminine Mystique* constructs a white, middle-class feminism as a universal feminism that suppresses the link between race and class – and thus privileges the misery of the bored, middle-class suburban housewife while ignoring the needs and experiences of women without homes (hooks 1984). hooks argues that the practices of sexist oppression in developing countries call for a feminism that recognizes how the practices of *sati* and genital mutilation oppressed women's bodies in a more physical way than the social discrimination encountered in Britain and the US. This prompted other black feminists to propose new theoretical terms to better express their position, and to challenge the wave model for its Anglo-American bias. In *In Search of Our Mothers' Gardens* (1983), Alice Walker coined the term "womanist" to refer specifically to black feminist activities. Walker emphasized that "womanist" is not a separatist term, but encompasses both male and female concerns, as well as those of race.

An analysis of the complex dynamics of domination and subordination, exclusion and inclusion, underpins feminist postcolonial studies and US Third World feminisms. This vital line of questioning is exemplified by the work of Gayatri Chakravorty Spivak, who asks "not merely who am I? but who is the other woman? How am I naming her?" (1987: 150). Spivak relates these questions not only to literary texts, but also to the relations between First and Third World feminists, and between French and Anglo-American models. Chandra Talpade Mohanty (1991), for example, has foregrounded the ways in which some Western feminist texts enact a form of discursive colonization in their construction of "Third World women" as an ostensibly coherent and unified category. The pioneering anthology *This Bridge Called My Back* (1981), edited by Chicana feminists Cherríe Moraga and Gloria E. Anzaldúa, represented a move to expand the meanings of "feminism" and feminist solidarity. Moving across a range of genres, the contributions redefined the meanings and modes of feminist theoretical discourse. Anzaldúa's *Borderlands/La Frontera* (1987) articulates what she describes as a "new *mestiza* consciousness," a hybrid and plural consciousness that expresses the tensions between different identities.

As adumbrated by Barbara Smith, a need to articulate a lesbian feminist discourse intersected with the rise of black feminism. Adrienne Rich's "Compulsory Heterosexuality and Lesbian Existence" (1980) and Bonnie Zimmerman's "What has never been: An overview of lesbian feminist criticism" (1981) were central to defining the relevance of lesbianism for feminism. Zimmerman took issue with the gynocritics' construction of a female canon for not recognizing lesbian texts and argued that lesbian literary history is doubly repressed by both patriarchy and heterosexuality. Rich was similarly concerned with how heterosexuality is always the assumed (and preferred) sexual orientation in texts, and the ways in which the institution of "compulsory heterosexuality" structures patriarchal culture more broadly. Calling straight feminism to account for its heterosexist assumptions, Rich emphasizes the wider political and social importance of various interconnections and bonds between women (see Whelehan 1995). Rejecting the term "lesbianism," which historically belongs to the vocabulary of sexology, Rich proposes instead the terms "lesbian existence" and "lesbian continuum," which include a range of woman-identified experiences and relationships (including mother–daughter relationships, female friendships, and networks). Following a similar line, the French theorist Monique Wittig advocated an exclusive lesbian feminism and encouraged feminists to adopt a lesbian identity. Concerned with locating a lesbian subject outside of androcentric linguistic registers, she stressed the need for women to drop the label "woman" in exchange for "lesbian." For Wittig, lesbianism offers the capacity for a woman-defined identity, which can transfer the power to name the subject from the patriarchal order over to women (Wittig 1992). Works such as Jane Rule's *Lesbian Images* (1975) and Lillian Faderman's *Surpassing the Love of Men* (1981) played a vital role in developing a tradition of lesbian-feminist criticism. Judith Butler's *Gender Trouble* (1990) was also significant for lesbian feminism and is acknowledged as a founding text of queer theory. *Gender Trouble* proposes that it is only because heterosexist society defines heterosexuality as normal and authentic that it functions as the dominant trend – but this much could be inferred from the writings of Zimmerman and Rich. Where *Gender Trouble* is radical is in its debunking of the belief that heterosexuality is grounded in anatomy; rather, it argues that both gender and sexuality should be considered as impersonations rather than part of a "true" integral biologism. Butler's notion of gender as a performative effect has been hugely influential in terms of contemporary feminist understandings of subjectivity.

The importance of French thought to the history of feminist criticism cannot be overestimated. It was the French philosopher Simone de Beauvoir's *Le Deuxième Sexe* (1949), translated into English as *The Second Sex* in 1953, which began work on the demystification of "woman" and female stereotypes that became the theoretical focus of much feminism in the second half of the twentieth century. De Beauvoir separated "human females" from "women" and made the famous proclamation that "[o]ne is not born, but rather becomes, a woman" (1953[1949]: 295), which established a binary distinction between sex and gender. Her existentialist philosophy informed her argument that women do not possess an essential characteristic of "femininity"; rather, the notion of "femininity" is itself constructed through certain cultural, social, and linguistic practices. Her assertion that gender was culturally constructed produced a marked shift in feminism, away from previous essentialist arguments that viewed gender as biologically determined and toward a social constructionist understanding of gender. Although Anglo-American writers such as Millett and Greer were influenced by de Beauvoir's ideas, it was in France that her socialist feminism became synonymous with the nation's perception of feminism and its political orientation.

"New French feminisms" emerged from the politicized intellectual and activist events of 1968, and the radical women's groups that were referred to as the Mouvement de Libération des Femmes from 1970 (Marks & de Courtivron 1981). New French feminist thinkers such as Hélène Cixous, Luce Irigaray, Julia Kristeva, and Monique Wittig do not represent a theoretically coherent body of thought, nor do they represent the totality of French feminist intellectual thought. They are, however, committed to a radical critique and deconstruction of phallocentrism – which places man as the central reference point of Western thought and the phallus as a symbol of male cultural authority. Making use of Lacanian psychoanalysis and Derridean deconstruction, their work moves across the domains of psychoanalysis, linguistics, and philosophy, attacking androcentric linguistic and cultural regimes.

In spite of their divergences from its existentialist feminism, de Beauvoir's *The Second Sex* remains an important cornerstone for new French feminist thinking. Her argument that throughout history "woman" has been constructed as the "other" of man and, as such, she has been denied the right to her own subjectivity, informs Hélène Cixous's and Luce Irigaray's explorations of otherness. Cixous's landmark essay "Sorties: out and out: attacks/ways out/forays" (1986[1975]) opens with a series of binary oppositions arranged around the central opposition of "man/woman." Cixous proposes that this system of ordering and understanding the world is hierarchical in structure. In other words, it consists of two poles – and one of these poles is always more privileged; it is given more status and more power than the other. For Irigaray, woman is not only "other" to man, but also "indefinitely other in herself" (1985a[1977]). Like Cixous, she identifies "difference" as defined by and within the woman's body. In *Speculum of the Other Woman* (1985b[1974]), Irigaray interrogated the work of Western philosophers from Freud to Plato in order to demonstrate how philosophy places woman outside of the capacity for representation. Her use of the terms "speculum" and "specularization" is a deliberate play on the word's dual signification for a mirror, and an instrument for examining the female genitals. Irigaray argues that philosophers are caught up in the act of speculating, but never speculate upon the female. On a wider scale, Irigaray's

investigations into the masculinity of the dominant gaze – and its impact for considering female subjectivity – provided a springboard for subsequent work by feminist theorists in the fields of film and feminist art history.

Perhaps the most significant proposal by the French feminists was their search for a mode of feminine discourse that could disrupt or subvert phallocentric language, and bring the body back into discourse. The French-Bulgarian linguist and psychoanalyst Julia Kristeva proposes a distinction between the semiotic and the symbolic order. The semiotic is a pre-Oedipal, bodily drive characterized by rhythmic pulses and the movement of signifying practices, and associated with the maternal body. It precedes the subject's entry into the symbolic order, associated with the structure of signification (that which makes meaning possible), but erupts into and is present in the symbolic (Kristeva 1984[1974]). For Cixous, an alternative mode could be found in "*écriture féminine*," a term which translates as either "female/feminine writing," or "writing on the body." The duality of the phrase encapsulates Cixous's belief, expressed in her essay "The laugh of the Medusa," that "woman must write her self: must write about women and bring women to writing" (1976[1975]: 875). Cixous argues that every instance of female writing is a new, or even first, "utterance" and implies that women's entrance to language is always a painful struggle. This essay is both an exploration and an example of *écriture féminine*. By embracing the Lacanian concept of *jouissance* and the body as a site of subversion, Cixous practices a language which aims to break from the linearity of phallocentrism (1976[1975]). Irigaray proposed an alternative concept in "*parler femme*," or "womanspeak." Where *écriture féminine* refers to the act of writing, womanspeak is the specific discourse produced when women speak together. If men are present, womanspeak cannot be performed (Irigaray 1985a[1977]). The idea of a distinct feminine discourse is not without its problems, however, as any overtly "feminine" model is ripe for criticism as separatist or, at the very worst, nonsensical. Owing to their emphasis on developing alternative modes of expression outside of phallocentrism, French feminist writings can often appear frustratingly elusive and poetic.

What has been described as a "third wave" of feminist activity and theorizing emerged in the late 1980s and early 1990s. Moving away from second-wave feminist identity politics, third-wave feminist ideas about identity embrace notions of contradiction, multiplicity, and ambiguity, and emphasize the need for new feminist modalities in the twenty-first century. Third-wave feminism is influenced and informed by postmodern theory, as well as other anti-foundationalist discourses, such as postcolonialism and poststructuralism. Some feminists have expressed concern that theoretical moves to deconstruct the female subject pose a threat to the politics of a feminism founded on a conception of women as social subjects (see Soper 1990). Nancy Fraser and Linda Nicholson argue that, in spite of inevitable tensions, an alliance between postmodernism and feminism could be politically advantageous, especially in redressing the universalizing tendency in feminist thought which privileges heterosexist and ethnocentric claims about female identity (Fraser & Nicholson 1988). Donna Haraway's landmark essay "A cyborg manifesto" (1985; collected in Haraway 1991) offers an irreverent critique of feminist orthodoxies and essentialist categories. Combining postmodernism and politics, Haraway conceptualizes the figure of the "cyborg" as one that embraces otherness and difference. Foregrounding the idea of "oppositional consciousness," and

echoing some of the concerns articulated by Mohanty, Chela Sandoval's work on US Third World feminisms has played an influential role in the development of third-wave feminist thinking and activity. Sandoval argues that the third wave of the women's movement needs a "differential consciousness" that will provide "grounds for alliance with other decolonizing movements for emancipation" (Sandoval 1991: 5).

Insofar as thinking about and describing a "third wave" implies that second-wave feminism is over, it is sometimes conflated with "postfeminism" (or post-feminism). An ambiguous and contested term, postfeminism has two key meanings. Within an academic context, it is sometimes used to describe feminism's intersection with poststructuralist, postmodernist, and postcolonial theorizing (see Brooks 1997). However, this account is often eclipsed by the media-defined notion of postfeminism which, since the 1980s, has been used to imply that (radical) feminism is outdated and no longer a productive practice for a society which offers women varied channels of expression. The third-wave model has also come under criticism for forcing inauthentic cut-off points within the movement, and for alienating current feminists from their feminist foremothers (see Henry 2004). Nonetheless, the tendency of feminist criticism to deconstruct its own theories is especially clear to feminists themselves, and is undoubtedly a strength of the movement. Feminism is not a monolithic category; rather, feminisms are multiple, complex, and diverse.

SEE ALSO: de Beauvoir, Simone; Cixous, Hélène; *Ecriture Féminine*; Gender and Cultural Studies; Gender Theory; hooks, bell; Phallus/Phallocentrism; Postmodernism; Spivak, Gayatri Chakravorty; Woolf, Virginia

REFERENCES AND SUGGESTED READINGS

Anzaldúa, G. (1987). *Borderlands/La Frontera: The New Mestiza*. San Francisco: Aunt Lute Books.

Barrett, M. (1980). *Women's Oppression Today: Problems in Marxist Feminist Analysis*. London: Verso.

de Beauvoir, S. (1953). *The Second Sex* (trans. H. M. Parshley). London: Jonathan Cape. (Original work published 1949.)

Belsey, C., & Moore, J. (eds.) (1989). *The Feminist Reader: Essays in Gender and the Politics of Literary Criticism*. Basingstoke: Macmillan.

Brooks, A. (1997). *Postfeminisms: Feminism, Cultural Theory and Cultural Forms*. London: Routledge.

Butler, J. (1990). *Gender Trouble: Feminism and the Subversion of Identity*. New York: Routledge.

Cixous, H. (1976). The laugh of the Medusa. *Signs*, 1(4), 875–893. (Original work published 1975.)

Cixous, H. (1986). Sorties: out and out: attacks/ways out/forays. In H. Cixous & C. Clement, *The Newly Born Woman* (trans. B. Wing). Manchester: Manchester University Press, pp. 63–132. (Original work published 1975.)

Eagleton, M. (ed.) (1995). *Feminist Literary Theory: A Reader*. Oxford: Blackwell.

Ellmann, M. (1968). *Thinking About Women*. New York: Harcourt.

Faderman, L. (1981). *Surpassing the Love of Men: Romantic Friendship and Love between Women from the Renaissance to the Present*. New York: HarperCollins.

Fraser, N., & Nicholson, L. (1988). Social criticism without philosophy: An encounter between feminism and postmodernism. *Theory, Culture and Society*, 5(2–3), 373–394.

Friedan, B. (1963). *The Feminine Mystique*. New York: Norton.

Gilbert, S., & Gubar, S. (2000). *The Madwoman in the Attic: The Woman Writer and the Nineteenth-Century Literary Imagination*, 2nd edn. New Haven: Yale University Press. (Original work published 1979.)

Greer, G. (1970). *The Female Eunuch*. London: MacGibbon and Kee.

Haraway, D. (1991). *Simians, Cyborgs and Women: The Reinvention of Nature*. New York: Routledge.

Henry, A. (2004). *Not My Mother's Sister: Generational Conflict and Third-Wave Feminism*. Bloomington: Indiana University Press.

hooks, b. (1982). *Ain't I a Woman: Black Women and Feminism*. Boston: South End Press.

hooks, b. (1984). *Feminist Theory: From Margin to Center*. Boston: South End Press.

Irigaray, L. (1985a). *This Sex Which Is Not One* (trans. C. Porter). Ithaca: Cornell University Press. (Original work published 1977.)

Irigaray, L. (1985b). *Speculum of the Other Woman* (trans. G. C. Gill). Ithaca: Cornell University Press. (Original work published 1974.)

Kaplan, C. (1986). *Sea Changes: Culture and Feminism*. London: Verso.

Kristeva, J. (1984). *Revolution in Poetic Language* (trans. M. Waller). New York: Columbia University Press. (Original work published 1974.)

Marks, E., & de Courtivron, I. (eds.) (1981). *New French Feminisms: An Anthology*. Brighton: Harvester Press.

Marxist-Feminist Literature Collective (1991). Women's writing: *Jane Eyre, Shirley, Villette, Aurora Leigh*. Ideology and Consciousness. In T. Eagleton & D. Milne (eds.), *Marxist Literary Theory: A Reader*. Oxford: Blackwell, pp. 328–350. (Original writings published 1978.)

Mill, J. S. (1869). The subjection of women. In *The Collected Works of John Stuart Mill*. Vol. 21: *Essays on Equality, Law, and Education* (ed. J. M. Robson). Toronto: Toronto University Press, pp. 259–340.

Millett, K. (1970). *Sexual Politics*. New York: Doubleday.

Mitchell, J. (1974). *Psychoanalysis and Feminism*. Harmondsworth: Penguin.

Moers, E. (1978). *Literary Women*. London: Women's Press. (Original work published 1976.)

Mohanty, C. T. (1991). Under Western eyes: Feminist scholarship and colonial discourses. In C. Mohanty, A. Russo, & L. Torres (eds.), *Third World Women and the Politics of Feminism*. Bloomington: Indiana University Press, pp. 51–80.

Moi, T. (1985). *Sexual/Textual Politics*. London: Routledge.

Moraga, C., & Anzaldúa, G. E. (eds.) (1984). *This Bridge Called My Back: Writings by Radical Women of Color*, 2nd edn. New York: Kitchen Table: Women of Color Press.

Morgan, R. (1970). *Sisterhood Is Powerful: An Anthology of Writings from the Women's Liberation Movement*. New York: Vintage.

de Pizan, C. (1983). *The Book of the City of Ladies* (trans. E. J. Richards). London: Picador. (Original work published 1404–5.)

Rich, A. (1980). Compulsory heterosexuality and lesbian existence. In *Blood, Bread and Poetry: Selected Prose 1979–1985*. London: Virago, pp. 23–76.

Rose, J. (1986). *Sexuality in the Field of Vision*. London: Verso.

Rule, J. (1975). *Lesbian Images*. New York: Doubleday.

Sandoval, C. (1991). US Third World feminism: The theory and method of oppositional consciousness in the postmodern world. *Genders*, 10, 1–24.

Showalter, E. (1977). *A Literature of Their Own: British Women Novelists from Brontë to Lessing*. Princeton: Princeton University Press.

Showalter, E. (1979). Towards a feminist poetics. In M. Jacobus (ed.), *Women Writing and Writing about Women*. London: Croom Helm, pp. 22–41.

Smith, B. (1977). Toward a black feminist criticism. In E. Showalter (ed.), *The New Feminist Criticism: Essays on Women, Literature and Theory*. London: Virago, pp. 168–185.

Soper, K. (1990). *Troubled Pleasures: Writings on Politics, Gender and Hedonism*. London: Verso.

Spivak, G. C. (1987). *In Other Worlds: Essays in Cultural Politics*. London: Methuen.

Walker, A. (1983). *In Search of Our Mothers' Gardens*. London: Women's Press.

Weedon, C. (1997). *Feminist Practice and Poststructuralist Theory*, 2nd edn. Oxford: Blackwell.

Whelehan, I. (1995). *Modern Feminist Thought: From the Second Wave to Post Feminism*. New York: New York University Press.

Wittig, M. (1992). *The Straight Mind and Other Essays*. Boston: Beacon.

Wollstonecraft, M. (1992). *A Vindication of the Rights of Woman*, 2nd edn. (ed. M. Brody). London: Penguin. (Original work published 1792.)

Woolf, V. (1945). *A Room of One's Own*. London: Hogarth Press. (Original work published 1929.)

Zimmerman, B. (1981). What has never been: An overview of lesbian feminist criticism. *Feminist Studies*, 7(3), 451–475.

Fish, Stanley

ROBERT EAGLESTONE

Stanley Fish (b. 1938) is one of the founders of reader-response criticism, an approach to literature that emphasizes the reader's role in constructing literary meaning. He was educated at the University of Pennsylvania and Yale University, where he took his PhD in 1962. He taught English for many years at Johns Hopkins University, served as Dean at the University of Illinois at Chicago, and ended his teaching career at Duke University. He has also written on contemporary political issues and law. He is an outspoken opponent of the move to make literary study more socially responsible and is a fervent advocate of a neo-Humean skepticism regarding values.

Fish's early work was on medieval literature and on the poet John Skelton in particular. His second book, *Surprised by Sin* (1967), argued that the "center of reference" of *Paradise Lost* was not Adam or Satan, but, rather, the reader of the poem, and that the purpose of the work was to "educate the reader to an awareness of his position and responsibilities as a fallen man" by recreating in the "mind of the reader (which is, finally, the poem's scene) the drama of the Fall, to make him Fall again, exactly as Adam did and with Adam's troubled clarity" (1). This argument, inspired by theorists like Wolfgang Iser and Roman Ingarden, was the basis for a new school of criticism in the US, referred to as "reader response" because it focused on the effects that the literary text has on readers. Fish went on to develop what he called "affective stylistics," a way of thinking about interpretation that lent more weight to the way readers constructed meaning in texts. Affective stylistics, a decisive move away from formalism and the new critical assumption that the text was an autonomous object, is a way of thinking about texts "without the assumption that the text and reader can be distinguished from one another and that they will hold still" (1980: 1). In "Is there a text in this class?" – perhaps his most famous essay – Fish argues that the literary text in fact does not exist until it is read. A poem is just markings on a page until readers activate it and lend it meaning. Communities of readers learn competencies that enable them to ascribe meaning to particular words or images in a text. Each inhabitant of what Fish calls an "interpretive community" is an "informed reader":

> someone who (1) is a competent speaker of the language ... (2) is in full possession of "the semantic knowledge that a mature ... listener brings to his task of comprehension" including ... the knowledge ... of lexical sets, collocation probabilities, idioms professional other dialects, and so on; and (3) has literary competence. (1980: 48)

Fish also argues that critics (and other readers) are part of, and indeed shaped by, "interpretative communities," an idea that has some affinity to what Ludwig Wittgenstein calls "language games." He suggests:

> [The] reason that I can speak and presume to be understood by someone ... is that I speak to him *from within* a set of interests and concerns ... If what follows is communication or understanding, it will not be because he and I share a language, in the sense of knowing the meanings of individual words and the rules for combining them, but because a way of thinking, a form of life, shares us, and implicates us in a world of already-in-place objects, purposes, goals, procedures, values and so on ... Thus [another critic] and I could talk about whether or not a poem was a pastoral, advance and counter arguments, dispute evidence, concede points, and so forth, but we could do these things only because "poem" and "pastoral" are possible labels of identification within a universe of discourse. (303–4)

These forms of life are, in literary critical terms, "interpretive communities" and an education in literary and cultural studies is an education into the ways – the languages – of these communities. They also determine what are "acceptable" and "unacceptable" interpretations, and occasions of critical controversy are usually not about particular instances (if a poem is "pastoral" or not) but over the rules that govern interpretation per se. This same idea underlies Fish's intervention in legal and other debates over interpretation. He believes that values such as truth, justice, and the like are the products of "interpretive communities" rather than being transhistorical or universal. As he put it in "Interpreting the *Variorum*," "the choice is never between objectivity and interpretation but between an interpretation that is unacknowledged as such and an interpretation that is at least aware of itself" (1980: 167).

Fish's work in the twenty-first century has focused on academic politics and the politics of academics and academic institutions. In *Save the World on Your Own Time* (2008) Fish robustly defends universities against both the right, which attacks them for being "uneconomic," and the left, which in his view over-politicizes teaching. He argues that a university is a place for teaching and research, traditions – forms of life or communities – that have built up over time and have their own rationale: these traditions are not defensible on strictly economic grounds, nor should they be suborned to moral or political ends. Universities and their faculty should defend scholarly rigor, excellence in teaching, and the value of a liberal education, but should not, as institutions or as professionals speaking for those institutions, support political causes or ends. Instead, he advocates that academics should "do your job" (that is, teach and research the subject in which you are an expert), "don't try to do someone else's job" (that is, don't take on the role of a politician or preacher), and "don't let anyone else do your job" (that is, defend the role and aims of a university and a liberal education as a good in their own right).

SEE ALSO: Iser, Wolfgang; Phenomenology; Poststructrualism; Reader-Response Studies

REFERENCES AND SUGGESTED READINGS

Fish, S. (1967). *Surprised by Sin*. Cambridge, MA: Harvard University Press.
Fish, S. (1980). *Is There a Text in This Class?* Cambridge, MA: Harvard University Press.
Fish, S. (1989). *Doing What Comes Naturally*. Durham, NC: Duke University Press.
Fish, S. (2008). *Save the World on Your Own Time*. Oxford: Oxford University Press.

Foucault, Michel

LISA DOWNING

Michel Foucault was a French historian, philosopher, and literary critic whose analyses of the workings of power, language, and subjectivity have influenced contemporary debates on subjects as varied as sexuality, medicine, and social institutions. He is often associated, along with Jacques Derrida and Jacques Lacan, with the poststructuralist current in French thought, partly a development of, partly a reaction against, linguistic and literary structuralism. However, it is difficult to ascribe any definitive disciplinary or philosophical label to Foucault's work. Foucault was born in 1926. He studied philosophy and psychology at university, undertook clinical work at the Parisian mental asylum Saint-Anne, and contemplated training as a psychiatrist, before turning instead to critical historiography. He held academic positions in various disciplines (including literature, psychology,

and philosophy) and institutions (including posts in Sweden and Tunisia), and was appointed to a Chair in the History of Systems of Thought at the prestigious Collège de France in 1970. Foucault died in 1984 from an HIV-related illness.

To understand Foucault's concern with subjectivity, power, and institutions, it is necessary to consider the intellectual currents that surrounded and influenced his formative years. In post-World War II France, existentialist phenomenology and Marxist thought provided the dominant and – to some extent – conflicting forces in intellectual life. The former, championed by vibrant public intellectuals Jean-Paul Sartre and Simone de Beauvoir, attributed political agency and free will to individual consciousness, arguing that authentic freedom was a genuine possibility and that its achievement was a matter of responsibility for each citizen. In this regard, existentialism diverged from Marxism, as the latter dismissed the idea of individual free will as nothing more than a comforting bourgeois fiction, and held that only through collective struggle could the oppressed working classes liberate themselves from domination.

Despite an early interest in the phenomenological works of Martin Heidegger and Edmund Husserl, the bulk of Foucault's work forms part of an explicit and politicized reaction against the "philosophy of consciousness," associated primarily with Sartre's existentialist phenomenology. As for Marxism, Foucault would engage with ideas central to Marxian philosophy and politics throughout his opus, but his methodology diverged from that of Marx in a number of ways. Where Marx proposes a global philosophy, Foucault is concerned with specificity. Where Marx puts forward a system, Foucault seeks to demystify the working of systems. And – most significantly – where Marx locates power in the oppression of one group, the proletariat, who, via the raising of class consciousness, should be incited to revolution, Foucault develops a more complex and multidirectional model of power relations, rather than power.

When preparing his early work on mental illness (*The History of Madness*, 2006 [1961]), Foucault was drawn to the therapeutic discourse of *Daseinanalysis* developed by Ludwig Binswanger and Roland Kuhn. This therapy draws on Heideggerian phenomenological theories of experience, or "being in the world" to explore psychical phenomena. (So, that which occurs for a Freudian psychoanalyst at the level of phantasy or dream, occurs for the *Daseinanalyst* at the level of experience.) Works by Foucault on mental illness, sexual psychopathology, and the "dangerous individual" are also clearly influenced by *Daseinanalysis*'s rejection of the therapeutic tendency to reduce individual suffering to the generic label or category. However, Foucault's attitude to the notion of experience, central to a Heideggerian phenomenological perspective, mutates considerably at different points in his corpus. While declaring himself an exponent of George Canguilhem's "philosophy of the concept" rather than the "philosophy of experience" prized by phenomenology, Foucault's critical interest in experience nevertheless persisted. His controversial *History of Madness* sought to inscribe a history of the experience of the mad, whose voice had been silenced by the authorized discourse of psychiatry and resurged only in fragments of creative writing.

Despite the theoretical and political concerns that persist throughout Foucault's writing, the common critical perception is that his work can be neatly divided into two distinct chronological and methodological phases, namely archaeology and genealogy. The Foucauldian method of archaeology was developed in *The Birth of the Clinic*

(2003[1963]), the subtitle of which is "An Archaeology of Medical Perception"; but the works that are most usually associated with archaeology are *The Order of Things* (1970[1966]) and *The Archaeology of Knowledge* (2002[1969]). The term "archaeology" as propounded in these works designates an analysis of the conditions necessary for a given system of thought to come into being and to impose itself authoritatively. The rules underpinning any system of thought – rules that are not always transparent even to those employing them – are defined as the "historical unconscious" of that period, or its "episteme" or "archive."

The Order of Things is an attempt to uncover the tacit, submerged rules pertaining to knowledge that allowed the human sciences (sociology, criminology, anthropology, etc.) to be created in the nineteenth century, or, to put it another way, how the human being came to be both the subject and object of knowledge at a given moment in history. The book was greeted as a key text of structuralism; indeed, Foucault himself privately described this book as his "book about signs" (typical structuralist terminology), while at the same time vehemently denying that he was, or had ever been, a structuralist. Archaeology shares with structuralism the aim of evacuating personal agency from language and history, and pursuing a synchronic rather than diachronic analysis (the study of how systems work rather than the historical observation of their development). *The Order of Things* ends famously with Foucault's apocalyptic assertion that, just as the human sciences created the human as an object, so, one day, in a different "epistemic" moment, the human might be erased like a face drawn in sand at the edge of the sea. This statement has led to Foucault being identified as a precursor of postmodernism and posthumanism.

As well as writing his histories of episte-mology in the 1960s, Foucault wrote nu-merous short works and one book-length study about literature. Much of Foucault's writing about literature can be understood as a way of reconciling his interest in the "authentic," silenced voices that preoccu-pied the early writing on madness, on the one hand, and the archaeological/structur-alist concern with the impersonality of identity, or language devoid of human ref-erentiality, on the other. With the exception of the celebrated essay "What is an author?" (1977[1969]), that dismantles the "man and his works" method of criticism so prevalent in Anglo-American literary studies, and parallels Roland Barthes's announcement of the "death of the author," Foucault's writing on writing has received relatively little sustained critical attention. This may be accounted for by the fact that one cannot straightforwardly "do" a Foucauldian read-ing of a piece of literature or other cultural product in the way that one can "do" a psychoanalytic, Marxist, or phenomenolog-ical reading. Rather than putting forward a theory of literature that can be "applied," Foucault is concerned, first, with observing the evacuation from literary language of individual authorial identity, in order to give access to "the lightning-flash" in which the voices of madness or transgression can speak (for Foucault, the writing of the Mar-quis de Sade, Gérard de Nerval, Raymond Roussel), and, second, with analyzing the necessary conditions that allow literary values to be thought or discursively expressed at given moments. So, Georges Bataille's notion of transgression could not be produced in any epoch other than that of post-Nietzschean atheism. Even when writ-ing of avant-garde literature as the voice of madness, however, the voice (and experi-ence) discussed are not personalized. The full-length work on Roussel (*Death and the Labyrinth*, 1986[1963]) resembles in some

ways a Barthesian structuralist analysis, as it focuses on Roussel's use of certain repetitive syntactic and phonemic patterns that sug-gest a hollowness at the center of sounds, words, and ontological meaning. Foucault does not adopt a biographical approach to the experience of psychiatric patient Rous-sel, as this would wholly contravene the spirit of Foucault's critique of the fiction of the "author" and detract attention from the archaeological concern with seeing what rules about meaning allowed Roussel to write in the way that he did.

Foucault largely abandoned talking about archaeology at the end of the 1960s. This rejection occurred, perhaps, in tandem with the reassertion of the imperative for the French intellectual to be politically motivat-ed at a grassroots level. The students' revolts of May 1968, the ensuing general workers' strike, and the climate of unrest and oppo-sition that surrounded them, provided a political and intellectual watershed. The aftermath of the student insurrections created a strong oppositional political sen-sibility among French intellectuals of the generation. This expressed itself in an in-creasingly vociferous criticism of American neocolonialist foreign policy and institu-tionalized racism in France. It also found expression at a more local level. For Marxist thinker, Henri Lefebvre, the everyday be-came the sphere in which the political was most at stake. For Foucault too, the revolt against institutions heralded by the events of 1968 broadened the definition of politics. With this in mind, the mere identification of signs and their functions within systems may have begun to seem redundant or sterile, and a more explicit critique of the workings of institutions beckoned.

In the 1970s, Foucault began to think and write about genealogy. Genealogy seemed to offer Foucault a more politically engaged methodology than archaeology. Foucault's genealogical works are *I Pierre Rivière*

(*Moi, Pierre Rivière* ..., 1973); *Discipline and Punish* (1991[1975]); and volume 1 of *The History of Sexuality, The Will to Knowledge* (1990[1976]). The methodology of these books is heavily indebted to the German philosopher Friedrich Nietzsche. Nietzsche offered a way of thinking about history that was in direct opposition to the popular Hegelian dialectical model and the currents of thought that were inspired by it (e.g., Marxism). Nietzsche sought to uncover, via the observation of localized and relational, rather than continuous, historical operations of power, the installation of "false universals." False universals are interested ideologies that are made to pass as neutral and naturally occurring "facts." Nietzsche's concern to throw into question the nineteenth century's prevalent discourse of progress and improvement through the lauding of rationality offered Foucault a context for his attempts to put "truth" into question and to catalogue the invention of forms of knowledge and the conditions of their crystallization into institutions of authority. This objective, if not the specific methodology, underlies not only the later genealogical critiques, but in fact, much of Foucault's oeuvre.

Discipline and Punish and *The Will to Knowledge* are critical histories of, respectively, the carceral system and sexual science. The uniqueness of Foucault's perspective in treating these institutions lies in his overturning of a commonplace about the post-Enlightenment idea of knowledge as humanitarian. In *Discipline and Punish*, Foucault argues that the move from bodily torture to imprisonment should not be viewed straightforwardly as a symptom of a more tolerant and caring society. The book charts a move from the punishment of the body to the punishment of the soul, whereby prisoners are kept alive and looked after, but are scrutinized and controlled at every moment of their day until they internalize

the sense of being policed. The techniques of control developed in the carceral system extend in modern societies to all facets of life, such that citizens routinely subjected to surveillance begin to act as "docile bodies" and self-policing citizens. In *The Will to Knowledge*, Foucault challenges what he calls the "repressive hypothesis": that is, the assumption that the Victorian age was characterized by a prohibition on speaking about sex that had to be overcome by the liberating energies of psychoanalysis. Instead, as Foucault shows, in the nineteenth century, the nascent disciplines of sexology and psychology exhorted subjects to produce confessional discourse about their sexual desires and practices in an unprecedented way, and used those confessions to found systems of knowledge about typologies of the sexual subject that inscribe them in networks of disciplinary power. Rather than sex being a secret that needed unlocking, sexual science *created* sexuality as the exemplary secret of identity.

It is in these works that Foucault explicates his model of subjectivity and power relations. Subjectivity for Foucault signifies that individuals in society are both *subject to* and the *subjects of* disciplinary discourses. This means that individuals are made into self-identifying subjects as the result of their place within a set of systems of knowledge to which they are subject. To call the object of Foucault's analysis "power relations," rather than just "power," helps us to see the nature of the workings of power for Foucault. Power operates in a network or force field of influence, which is never the unique preserve of the dominator over the dominated. Rather, power operates from the bottom up, via resistance, and, in modernity, is intimately concerned with language and knowledge. An example of this is the "pervert" or "homosexual" named by nineteenth-century sexual science. While these labels may at first seem to be straightforwardly oppressive and pathologizing ways of controlling dissident subjects (and indeed may have been put to such uses by medicojuridical bodies), Foucault shows that it is by adopting the labels but twisting their meanings – using them in other contexts than the official, institutional ones – that individuals were able to construct subcultures and make allegiances. The medicolegal discourse used against its disciplinary context constituted an example of power relations mobilized by those in the apparently subordinate position. This form of linguistic resistance is called counter or reverse discourse.

While reflecting critical orthodoxy, this overview of the two principal Foucauldian methodologies – archaeology and genealogy – leaves out several important factors; first, that certain concepts and ideas interested Foucault throughout his life's work, even if they were articulated differently at various moments. A good example of this is that Foucault's early work on psychiatric and anatomical medicine, *The History of Madness* and *The Birth of the Clinic*, can be seen as sharing the central preoccupation of the late genealogical works with overturning Enlightenment commonplaces, even though Foucault had not at that stage begun to discuss genealogy as such. In *The History of Madness*, for example, he argues that the move from the confinement of the mad to the treatment of their symptoms in asylums, with the birth of psychiatry, should not be understood straightforwardly as a history of humanitarian reform. Rather, the shift in treatment charged the patient with a moral responsibility to conform better to the mores of society, but still continued to silence the voice of unreason and render invalid the experience of those labeled as mad. Another example is that of the concept of discourse, which was first introduced in *The Archaeology of Knowledge* to

illustrate the contention that utterances do not "belong" to individuals, but can only be articulated from given subject positions. Discourse was an important idea to Foucault, then, even before he had articulated the theory of disciplinary power that would give the concept its specifically Foucauldian meaning as an utterance issuing from a site of institutional knowledge.

A second problem of reducing the whole of Foucault's work to the archaeology/genealogy divide is that it risks ignoring works that adopt a slightly different methodology, such as the second and third volumes of the *History of Sexuality*, which pursue "problematizations" of ancient moral codes governing erotic life, rather than offering a genealogy of their trajectory. Volumes 2 and 3, *The Use of Pleasure* (1992[1984]) and *The Care of the Self* (1990[1984]), form the starting point for a project theorizing the limits and possibilities of personal ethics via a reflection on ancient mores: a project that was interrupted by Foucault's untimely death. "Problematization" signifies the means by which individuals confront their existence via a series of choices. The areas of experience which are problematized are culturally specific and determined, but the way in which the individual relates to them and makes creative personal choices within their limits and strictures is what is of interest to Foucault. Problematizations are inherently matters of ethics. Foucault compares the codes governing the conduct of free male Athenian citizens with regard to sexual behavior with early Christian customs. Whereas in the ancient Greek world, sex with other men and outside of marriage were facets of life which simply had to be managed responsibly and judiciously, as part of a project of "care for the self," in Christianity they were absolutely prohibited. Foucault distinguishes between moral systems in which "code" is more important than "ethics," and vice versa.

He sees Christianity as a system of morality in which "codes" predominate, insofar as individuals are called upon to obey absolutely the externally imposed rules of behavior, rather than to interpret and modify cultural guidelines in the service of a personal ethics.

A commonly voiced objection to Foucault's project in these late works, particularly by feminist scholars, is the fact that the privileged subjects whose choices and freedoms Foucault focuses on are free male citizens, not slaves or women. The possibilities for self-expression and self-stylization would have been considerably more limited for these marginal subjects. Foucault is clear, however, that the social models he is uncovering in the ancient world should *not* form a utopian template for restructuring our society. Rather, they may offer analogous and heuristic guides for questioning the limits and possibilities of projects of self-creation, given our own cultural norms and restrictions. In late interviews with the gay and mainstream US press, just prior to his death, Foucault was interested in using these ancient models as inspiration for imagining alternative relationship structures and erotic possibilities to the ones offered by mainstream hetero-patriarchy. He held up the BDSM gay subcultures of San Francisco as contemporary sites of exploration, in which people were playing with notions of power, relationality, and eroticism, and making concrete his exhortation in *The Will to Knowledge* that we need to replace the knowledge systems of sex and desire with the creative possibilities of "bodies and pleasures." Foucault's late, speculative writings and interviews about sexuality and ethics have had considerable influence on gender and sexuality studies in recent years, particularly the branch of deconstructive sexuality theory known as queer theory.

SEE ALSO: Barthes, Roland; Bataille, Georges; de Beauvoir, Simone; Deconstruction; Derrida, Jacques; Feminism; Gender and Cultural Studies; Gender Theory; Heidegger, Martin; Husserl, Edmund; Lacan, Jacques; Lefebvre, Henri; Marxism; Nietzsche, Friedrich; Phenomenology; Posthumanism; Postmodernism; Poststructuralism; Queer Theory; Sartre, Jean-Paul; Structuralism

REFERENCES AND SUGGESTED READINGS

Downing, L. (2008). *The Cambridge Introduction to Michel Foucault.* Cambridge: Cambridge University Press.

Foucault, M. (1970). *The Order of Things: An Archaeology of the Human Sciences* (trans. A. Sheridan). London: Tavistock. (Original work published 1966.)

Foucault, M. (1972). *The Archaeology of Knowledge* (trans. A. Sheridan). London: Routledge. (Original work published 1969.)

Foucault, M. (1977). What is an author? In *Language, Counter-Memory, Practice: Selected Essays and Interviews* (ed. D. F. Bouchard). Ithaca: Cornell University Press, pp. 113–138. (Original essay published 1969.)

Foucault, M. (1986). *Death and the Labyrinth: The World of Raymond Roussel* (trans. C. Ruas). New York: Doubleday. (Original work published 1963.)

Foucault, M. (1990). *Herculine Barbin: Being the Recently Discovered Memoirs of a Nineteenth-Century French Hermaphrodite* (trans. R. McDougall). Brighton: Harvester. (Original work published 1978.)

Foucault, M. (1990). *The Care of the Self, The History of Sexuality,* vol. 3 (trans. R. Hurley). Harmondsworth: Penguin. (Original work published 1984.)

Foucault, M. (1990). *The Will to Knowledge, The History of Sexuality,* vol. 1 (trans. R. Hurley). Harmondsworth: Penguin. (Original work published 1976.)

Foucault, M. (1991). *Discipline and Punish* (trans. A. Sheridan). Harmondsworth: Penguin. (Original work published 1975.)

Foucault, M. (1992). *The Use of Pleasure, The History of Sexuality*, vol. 2 (trans. R. Hurley). Harmondsworth: Penguin. (Original work published 1984.)

Foucault, M. (1997). *The Essential Works of Michel Foucault 1954–1988*. Vol. 1: *Ethics: Subjectivity and Truth* (trans. R. Hurley et al.; ed. P. Rabinow). New York: New York Press.

Foucault, M. (1998). *The Essential Works of Michel Foucault 1954–1988*. Vol. 2: *Aesthetics: Method and Epistemology* (trans. R. Hurley et al.; ed. J. Faubion). New York: New York Press.

Foucault, M. (2000). *The Essential Works of Michel Foucault 1954–1988*. Vol. 3: *Power* (trans. R. Hurley et al.; ed. J. Faubion). New York: New York Press.

Foucault, M. (2001). *Madness and Civilization: A History of Insanity in the Age of Reason* (trans. R. Howard). London: Routledge. (Original work published 1961.)

Foucault, M. (2003). *The Birth of the Clinic: An Archaeology of Medical Perception* (trans. A. M. Sheridan Smith). London: Routledge. (Original work published 1963.)

Foucault, M. (2006). *History of Madness* (trans. J. Murphy & J. Khalfa; ed. J. Khalfa). London: Routledge. (Original work published 1961.)

Gutting, G. (ed.) (1994). *The Cambridge Companion to Foucault*. Cambridge: Cambridge University Press.

Macey, D. (1993). *The Lives of Michel Foucault*. London: Hutchinson.

May, T. (2006). *The Philosophy of Foucault*. Chesham: Acumen.

Sawacki, J. (1991). *Disciplining Foucault: Feminism, Power and the Body*. London: Routledge.

G

Gates, Henry Louis

JENNIFER LEWIS

Henry Louis Gates, Jr., is a major figure in African American literary studies, a critic who has, since the 1980s, had a profound influence upon the ways in which African American literature has been studied and taught. His main interests have been the recovering, editing, and publishing of previously overlooked African American texts, and the development of what he has called indigenous literary criticism. As an editor Gates has published major anthologies that have brought African American texts to a wide audience (e.g., Gates & Appiah 1986; Gates & McKay 1997). He has also authenticated and assisted in the publication of two early novels: Harriet Wilson's *Our Nig: or, Sketches from the Life of a Free Black*, and Hannah Craft's *The Bondswoman's Narrative*. As a critic Gates has authored several major works of literary criticism, developing formal literary theories through which to read black texts (e.g. Gates 1987; 1988b).

Gates was born on September 16, 1950, in Mineral County, West Virginia. He graduated *summa cum laude* from Yale University with a degree in history and received his MA and PhD in English Literature from Clare College, Cambridge. He joined the faculty of Harvard in 1991, where he is now Alphonse Fletcher University Professor and the Director of the W. E. B. Du Bois Institute for African and African American Research.

Gates is a pivotal figure in African American literary studies not only because he has consistently sought to bring to light marginalized, forgotten texts, but also because he was one of the first African American critics who, influenced by poststructuralism, brought literary theory to bear on black texts. Before Gates and others, such as Houston Baker, Jr., began to question notions of authenticity and even blackness, African American literary criticism had tended to read black texts as having a direct and straightforward relationship with black lives and as being important primarily for the ways in which they revealed to readers the cultural forces which attempted to oppress them. Black criticism of black texts, therefore, had been more interested in what these texts appeared to say than how they said it. Aesthetic concerns – such as the structure of a text, its language, its style – were suppressed in favor of a mode of reading that treated texts as though they were transparent representations of the world and pure polemic.

The poststructuralist ideas that Gates draws upon, however, called into question this assumption that texts can straightforwardly represent the world. It rejected the idea that language is a transparent medium that allows unproblematic access to experience and suggested instead that our sense of ourselves, of our experiences and what they mean are all structured through language itself. In this way language came to be understood less as a medium through which we understand a "real" world, than the only world we "really" live in. Consequently, such concepts as selfhood, identity, and race became understood, not as essences that exist somehow outside language, but rather constructs of language that offer us the illusion of essence. This theory has been challenged by many African American intellectuals, who argue that they are simply new ways to disempower oppressed peoples' attempts to assert themselves and their rights. Some have rejected these ideas as anti-black and have accused those who use them of succumbing to a form of intellectual slavery that actively negates the critic's blackness. Gates, however, argues that to insist upon a straightforward relationship between black art and life, and to tie literary criticism to the aims of emancipatory politics is to remain trapped within a discourse that is hostile to the idea of racial equality and that was established by whites as early as the seventeenth century. This discourse, that Gates sees at work in a variety of texts from the philosophical works of David Hume to the publications of countless nineteenth-century slaveholders, takes a perceived lack of original black literature to be evidence of a lack of black equality, even humanity. Gates suggests that while black artists and critics have attempted to defy this discourse by confronting it in their work, they have, paradoxically, implicitly privileged it, creating texts that continue to be preoccupied with an agenda established by whites.

Gates argues that poststructuralist theory is useful to the black critic because it creates a kind of critical distance that enables him or her, in his words, to defamiliarize, both the European American and the African American traditions, and as a result to decipher and define them. Gates though, only advocates the use of theory as a beginning in a process that should lead to the definition of principles peculiar to the African American literary tradition. His aim, then, has been not simply to apply poststructuralist theory to black texts, but rather to invent his own "black, text-specific theories" (Gates & Appiah 1986).

Gates's own indigenous theory is most fully articulated in *The Signifying Monkey* (1988b). In this book, he uses theory to uncover the formal workings of otherwise highly informal texts, and to detect a different kind of cultural inheritance to the one outlined above. Exploring through meticulous, contextualized examination, or close reading, marginalized oral and literary African, Caribbean, and African American texts, Gates delineates a tradition in which the black artist responds to a different set of questions than those posed by racist whites. He describes a tradition in which black equality does not require confirmation, as it is simply assumed, and in which the dialogue in which it is bound up is not with hostile whites, but with other blacks.

This alternative inheritance depends upon an understanding of "blackness" not as a material object, but as a trope: a figure of speech, an effect of language. Gates rejects the idea that blackness is an essence that precedes language and exists outside of it. Instead, he draws on the work of the linguist Ferdinand de Saussure in order to propose that blackness is a sign; a concept that arbitrarily divides reality. This is central to Gates's argument, not only because it enables him to examine the different ways in which the sign blackness, in a racist society, has been attached to different referents – the absence of humanity, for example – but also because the gap that Saussure's work opens up between language and the world to which it refers is one which Gates identifies as central to the alternative literary and cultural tradition he uncovers. He argues that it is the arbitrariness of language and the fact that it exists, not through a special, concrete connection between words and the things they represent, but rather in a relatively self-contained system with its own rules, that this tradition repeatedly points to, exploits, and plays with in such a way as to undermine the kinds of easy understandings we often imagine language to allow us.

Blackness, for Gates, then, becomes a matter of what he calls an identifiable "Signifyin(g) difference" (1988b) that is found most prominently in the black vernacular tradition: the tradition of folktales, songs, poems, and novels that have taken the English language and played with it, encoding it with rituals and meanings that are private yet shared within the African American community. The word "signifyin(g)" is central to this. Meant to recall the act of speech – the parenthesized "g" reminding the reader of the orality of this tradition – Gates presents this as a central trope in the African American tradition and consequently as a central trope for the criticism that arises out of it. For while, in standard English, the word "signifying" denotes the meaning that a term conveys – the OED definition is "signification, intimation, indication" – in the African American vernacular it means participating in certain rhetorical games that, far from intimating or indicating secure and communicable meaning, foreground the instability and slipperiness of language by deliberately evoking, through puns, figurative substitutions, and other word games, the chaos of what Saussure calls associative relations within language – all of the unconnected words which are stored together in the mind and which must be suppressed in order for

meaning to be in any way achieved. Thus, whereas signification, in standard English, relies upon the exclusion of these unconscious associations in order to create coherence, Signification, in the African American vernacular, revels in the inclusion of these associations. Gates claims that this trope, which he goes on to find occurring in a range of African American texts has enabled writers to resist and subvert both language and the received concepts it communicates, creating a literature which has the potential to redress imbalances of power.

While this concept of signifyin(g) rests on a poststructuralist understanding of the nature of language and knowledge, it also demonstrates that Gates's poststructuralism has its limits. For Gates traces signifyin(g) back to the Caribbean and beyond that to Africa, holding to a kind of historical continuity that insists upon the past as readable and recoverable. Finding traces of African tropes in modern African American speech acts, Gates stresses cultural continuity in a way that conflicts, to a degree, with his other pronouncements. However, he never lays claim to an essential blackness, always describing this inheritance as learned and passed on rather than essential, or "racial." In this way signifyin(g) is presented not as an ahistorical occurrence, which reoccurs regardless of time or place, but rather as a willed act of resistance, a communal response to history and to the experience of language as power. In this way Gates suggests that African Americans have, through their specific history of transportation, alienation, and enforced immersion into a new language, developed a culture that is implicitly theoretical: a culture that knows language to be a system that constructs, rather than reflects, the world, and understands it as a structure that, while imposing meaning, also, through its barely suppressed chaos, opens up the possibility of subversion and play.

Recently Gates has, with K. Anthony Appiah, co-edited the encyclopedia *Encarta Africana*. As well as continuing his work of recovery and retrieval of marginalized African American texts, he has become increasingly interested in investigating and reporting on the lives of contemporary African Americans. He is the co-author, with Cornel West, of *The Future of the Race* (1996), which reflects on the relationship between the black elite and the larger black community, and has written and produced a number of documentaries that explore African Americans' history and their present. The publications that accompany these series include *America Beyond the Color Line* (2004). In the last few years, he has increasingly taken on the role of public intellectual, not only broadcasting on PBS but also publishing articles in such mainstream publications as the *New Yorker* and *New York Times*.

SEE ALSO: Appiah, Kwame Anthony; Baker, Houston A., Jr.; Poststructuralism; Saussure, Ferdinand de; West, Cornel

REFERENCES AND SUGGESTED READINGS

Crafts, H. (2002). *The Bondswoman's Narrative*. New York: Warner.

Gates, H. L., Jr. (1987). *Figures in Black: Words, Signs, and the "Racial" Self*. New York: Oxford University Press.

Gates, H. L., Jr. (ed.) (1988a). *The Schomburg Library of Nineteenth-Century Black Women Writers*, 30 vols. New York: Oxford University Press.

Gates, H. L., Jr. (1988b). *The Signifying Monkey: A Theory of African-American Literary Criticism*. New York: Oxford University Press.

Gates, H. L., Jr. (ed.) (1990). *Reading Black, Reading Feminist: A Critical Anthology*. New York: Meridian.

Gates, H. L., Jr. (2004). *America Beyond the Color Line: Dialogues with African Americans*. New York: Warner.

Gates, H. L., & Appiah, K. A. (eds.) (1986). *"Race," Writing, and Difference*. Chicago: University of Chicago Press.

Gates, H. L., Jr., & Appiah, K. A. (eds.) (1993–4) *Critical Perspectives Past and Present* (Amistad Literary Series), 9 vols. New York: Amistad Press.

Gates, H. L., Jr., & Appiah, K. A. (eds.) (1999) *Encarta Africana*. Redmond, WA: Microsoft Press.

Gates, H. L., Jr., & McKay, N. Y. (eds.) (1997). *The Norton Anthology of African American Literature*. New York: Norton.

Gates, H. L., Jr., & West, C. (1996). *The Future of the Race*. New York: Knopf.

Joyce, A. J. (1987). The black canon: Reconstructing black American literary criticism. *New Literary History*, 18(2), 335–344.

Wilson, H. E. (1983). *Our Nig: or, Sketches from the Life of a Free Black*. New York: Vintage.

Gender Theory

KAYE MITCHELL

GENDER

Historically, the term "gender" has been used primarily as a grammatical term, referring to the classification of nouns (in languages including Latin, French, and German) as masculine, feminine, or neuter. It is derived from the Old French term for "genre" which, in turn, derives from the Latin *genus*, meaning "birth," "family," or "nation," but also referring back to older and broader meanings such as "kind" or "type." The other use of "gender," to refer to the (human) state of being male or female, also dates back to the fourteenth century, but it's not until the twentieth century that the latter usage becomes common. In the late twentieth century, thanks largely to the influence of feminism, "gender" tends to be distinguished from "sex," with the former seen as referring to the culturally attributed characteristics associated with being a woman or a man, and the latter viewed as a matter of nature or biology, although, as

I'll go on to discuss, the sex/gender distinction continues to be a source of debate and contention both within and beyond feminism.

Despite considerable evidence of argument and speculation on the allegedly differing characteristics of the sexes through history, the active theorizing of gender as a concept and category really begins in the nineteenth century, thanks to the competing influences of psychoanalysis and sexology, so it's to those discourses that I'll turn first, before highlighting just a few of the contributions to gender theory made by feminism, masculinity studies, queer theory, and transgender studies, respectively.

SEXOLOGY AND
PSYCHOANALYSIS

The pseudo-scientific investigations of sexual behavior in the late nineteenth and early twentieth centuries, which acquired the disciplinary name of "sexology," have much to say about questions of gender and are instructive in the way that they reveal the complex imbrication of (biological) sex, gender, and sexuality, the difficulty of talking about one without invoking the others. Sexual desire, increasingly, is viewed either as one of the contributing factors to gender identity, or as a product or expression of one's gender; either way, the relationship is figured as causal and unorthodox sexual practices or desires tend, in sexology, to be associated with (or blamed on) forms of gender dysmorphia. This is evident, for example, in Richard von Krafft-Ebing's characterization of female homosexuality as "the masculine soul, heaving in the female bosom," and his assertion that "uranism may nearly always be suspected in females wearing their hair short, or who dress in the fashion of men" (Bland & Doan 1998: 46–7). Writers and clinicians such as Krafft-Ebing, Iwan Bloch, Otto Weininger, and Havelock Ellis, then, sought to taxonomize and analyze human sexual behavior, but in doing so often helped contribute to a developing discourse of gender difference.

Although Havelock Ellis is more liberal than Krafft-Ebing in his treatment of female homosexuality, suggesting that sexual inversion need not be accompanied by "aesthetic inversion," the assertion of a primary difference between the genders is to the fore in his popular 1894 publication, *Man and Woman*. Here, Ellis describes women as characterized by "a certain docility and receptiveness," possessed of an "emotional nature" and a tendency to "suggestibility," "less able than men to stand alone" and to think and act independently; such characteristics are, in Ellis's assessment of them, rooted in the physiological differences between men and women (Bland & Doan 1998: 22). Despite being quite a radical thinker in his pronouncements on sexual freedom and supposed sexual deviance (of which he was remarkably tolerant), Ellis reinforces a myth of women as inherently contradictory – "the affectability of women exposes them … to very diabolical manifestations. It is also the source of very much of what is most angelic in women" – and of men as significantly more active, and as driven primarily by libidinal impulses – "in men the sexual instinct is a restless source of energy which overflows into all sorts of channels" (Bland & Doan 1998: 23).

The outcome of such characterizations is a vision of maleness and femaleness as opposed and complementary, interdependent in their definitions. As Weininger asserts, in *Sex and Character* (1903): "The ideas 'man' and 'woman' cannot be investigated separately; their significance can be found out only be placing them side by side and contrasting them" (Bland & Doan 1998: 27). However, while much of this sexological work might appear to be quite conservative in its treatment of gender, more dissonant voices emerged under the aegis of sexology, notably that of Jean Finot, who took issue with the "reasoning of the biologists and of the psychologists" and their attempt to "derive all the qualities of woman" from "their observation of the differences of the two cells that produce life"; Finot suggested, by way of a counterargument, that "woman, morally, is only the result of the conditions imposed upon her by life. She will be sublime in goodness or odious in cruelty, according to the surrounding environment which makes her think and act" (Bland & Doan 1998: 37–8). This suggestion – that gender is shaped by environment, by forms of cultural conditioning – was to become central to much of the feminist theorizing of gender that would appear later in the twentieth century.

In the period of the late nineteenth and early twentieth century, however, the emerging science of psychoanalysis was also contributing to the popular and academic understanding of gendered personhood, and Freud's work is pre-eminent (and continues to be influential) in this respect. In his essay on the subject, Freud notes that "throughout history people have knocked their heads against the riddle of the nature of femininity" (1977: 146). Although he does little to dispel this notion of femininity as mysterious or unfathomable, Freud does imply that the distinction between the sexes has no firm basis in either biology or psychology, leaving open the suggestion that it is culture that enforces such distinctions. As he had earlier claimed in the "Three essays on the theory of sexuality," "a certain degree of anatomical hermaphroditism occurs normally," and "in every normal male or female individual, traces are found of the apparatus of the opposite sex," suggesting that both men and women possess "an originally bisexual physical disposition" which "has, in the course of evolution, become modified

into a unisexual one" (1977: 52) This idea of "anatomical hermaphroditism" was not a new one, as Glover & Kaplan (2000) confirm in their assertion that, "until at least the middle of the eighteenth century the human body was conceived as being of one flesh" (xiii) possessing both male and female sexual organs (and the "humoral" theories of the Renaissance period, for example, suggest that women possessed the same sexual organs as men, only internal rather than external to the body, due to women lacking the "heat" that was necessary to push those organs outwards). Despite acknowledging that, "when you say 'masculine,' you usually mean 'active,' and when you say 'feminine,' you usually mean 'passive,'" Freud refuses to provide any kind of evidential ground for these meanings, beyond cultural convention, and instead sets out to inquire "how she comes into being, how a woman develops out of a child with a bisexual disposition" (1977: 147–8, 149). Ultimately, this development is facilitated both by the Oedipus complex, and by adaptation to social convention, in the way that Freud represents it, yet his representation of the female as (symbolically) castrated, and traumatized by her awareness of this fact (i.e., governed by "penis envy"), led, for many years, to the rejection of Freudian psychoanalysis by feminist theorists.

FEMINISM AND MASCULINITY STUDIES

Mary Wollstonecraft, in her 1792 work *A Vindication of the Rights of Woman*, is not primarily concerned with offering definitions of gender or theorizing the sex–gender relationship. However, her examination of female education, and the ways in which women are "formed in the mould of folly," rather than being permitted to be "rational creatures," does raise questions about the extent to which gender (in this case, womanhood) is natural, and the extent to which it is molded by cultural expectations, educational practices, and so forth (1992[1792]: 154) In this way she is often seen as inaugurating a feminist investigation of the meanings and potentialities of femininity which achieves greater force and clarity through the course of the nineteenth century, and which acquires a more critical bent in the twentieth. In 1949, Simone de Beauvoir famously opens *The Second Sex* by expressing her initial reluctance "to write a book on woman" as "the subject is irritating, especially to women; and it is not new," before proceeding to ask "what is a woman?" – a question that would become central to feminist theory in the twentieth century, and that clearly distinguishes matters of (biological) sex from matters of (cultural) gender (1988[1949]: 13). According to de Beauvoir, it is necessary to ask this question precisely because the answer is not at all clear, and because "woman" in fact lacks a positive definition. This, claims de Beauvoir, is because

> Humanity is male and man defines woman not in herself but as relative to him; she is not regarded as an autonomous being . . . She is defined and differentiated with reference to man and not he with reference to her; she is the incidental, the inessential as opposed to the essential. He is the Subject, he is the Absolute – she is the Other. (1988: 16)

With the advent of second wave feminism in the late 1960s and early 1970s, feminist authors such as Germaine Greer, Kate Millett, and others, developed de Beauvoir's philosophical investigation into how one "becomes" a woman into political, polemical writings which addressed the subordination of women, and sought also to challenge the conceptions of femininity (as passivity, as weakness, as governed by biological imperatives) which kept women

in that subordinate position. As Greer asserts, at the beginning of *The Female Eunuch*:

> We know what we are, but know not what we may be, or what we might have been. The dogmatism of science expresses the status quo as the ineluctable result of law: women must learn how to question the most basic assumptions about feminine normality in order to reopen the possibilities for development which have been successively locked off by conditioning. (1991[1970]: 16–17)

De Beauvoir's suggestion that one is not "born," but rather "becomes" a woman, opens up the possibility that one might become something quite different, or that the process of "becoming" might be substantially altered by social and cultural change. "Femininity," then, takes on quite different connotations – many of them negative – in the feminist theory of the 1960s and 1970s: in Betty Friedan's *The Feminine Mystique* (1992[1963]), it is linked to the "nameless aching dissatisfaction" of middle-class women, encouraged into the public sphere through education and the temporary opportunities of the war years, only to be coerced back into more limited, domestic roles (30); in *Sexual Politics* (1977[1970]), Kate Millett opines how "expectations the culture cherishes about his gender identity encourage the young male to develop aggressive impulses, and the female to thwart her own or turn them inward," placing the emphasis firmly upon cultural conditioning as productive of gender (31); more generally, feminists since the second wave have deployed a skepticism about the traditional associations of "femininity," and have emphasized instead "the mutability and instability of gender" (Glover & Kaplan 2000: 9); feminism of the third wave could perhaps be seen as taking a more tolerant view of femininity, as something which is a source of pleasure for many women, not simply a means of their oppression.

Yet positive reconceptualizations of femininity are also evident in the work of French feminists of the 1970s such as Luce Irigaray and Hélène Cixous: while the former decried the Freudian perception of femininity as lack or absence, she looked to a definitively feminine mysticism as a means of countering the masculinist "logic of the same"; meanwhile, Cixous attacked the troubling binaries with which male/female and masculine/feminine were associated (activity/passivity, culture/nature, form/ matter, and so on), seeing power imbalances as built into such binaries which permitted woman only a position of negativity and otherness; she proceeded to develop a notion of écriture féminine which celebrated a femininity associated with the poetic and the orgasmic, with jouissance.

The tendency, in feminist theory of the late twentieth century, however, has been toward a view of gender as culturally constructed and this argument reaches its apogee in the work of Judith Butler. In Gender Trouble, Butler develops a theory of gender as performative, in which:

> Acts, gestures, and desire produce the effect of an internal core or substance . . . Such acts, gestures, enactments, generally construed, are *performative* in the sense that the essence or identity that they otherwise purport to express are *fabrications* manufactured and sustained through corporeal signs and other discursive means. That the gendered body is performative suggests that it has no ontological status apart from the various acts which constitute its reality. (1999 [1990]: 173)

It's difficult to overstate the radical nature, or the impact within the field of gender studies, of this argument. While earlier feminist theorists had viewed gender as cultural,

rather than natural (and Butler is building on the work of theorists such as de Beauvoir and Monique Wittig), Butler here redescribes what had previously been seen as the *expressions* of some innate gender identity as part of the cultural means by which, and through which, that identity is produced *as natural*; so an effect is here redescribed as a cause, and gender becomes an incessant action (or series of actions), a kind of "doing," rather than a kind of "being."

This is borne out by Butler's use of drag as an example:

> The notion of an original or primary gender identity is often parodied within the cultural practices of drag, cross-dressing, and the sexual stylization of butch/femme identities. . . . As much as drag creates a unified picture of "woman" (what its critics often oppose) it also reveals the distinctness of those aspects of gendered experience which are falsely naturalized as a unity through the regulatory fiction of heterosexual coherence. *In imitating gender, drag implicitly reveals the imitative structure of gender itself – as well as its contingency.* (1999[1990]: 174–5)

In watching a drag act, our attention is drawn to the disjunctions between the "anatomical sex" of the performer, their "gender identity," and the gender that they are performing and this, for Butler, is productive of a kind of gender "dissonance" (175). Drag, then, is not a parodic imitation of some authentic, original femininity; instead it reveals the performative nature of all gender identities, which require almost constant labor to uphold the impression of that naturalness (a point which opens up the merest possibility of gender subversion, for Butler). Butler's constructivist argument figures gender as "a free-floating artifice, with the consequence that *man* and *masculine* might just as easily signify a female body as a male one, and *woman* and *feminine* a male body as easily as a female one" (10).

Having severed gender from sex in this way, Butler proceeds to ask "what is 'sex' anyway?" and to suggest that "perhaps this construct called 'sex' is as culturally constructed as gender," a thought that she expands and elaborates in her subsequent book, *Bodies That Matter* (1993).

If it seems, however, as though the sex/gender distinction has been resolved (or, more radically, done away with), or as though the constructivist position has definitively trumped all essentialist arguments, the situation is not as straightforward as this. More recent feminist theorizing on sex and gender (e.g., by the likes of Elizabeth Grosz, Karen Barad, and Vicky Kirby) has sought to counter a perceived "linguistic turn" or "constructivist turn" within feminism (under the influence of poststructuralism), by returning to questions of corporeality and materiality, and by making use of the biological sciences to advance a more sophisticated understanding of both "nature" and the female body than had hitherto been available. One result of this is that the suggested opposition between the material and the discursive (central to much debate about the sex/gender distinction within feminism) is substantially problematized.

It must be conceded that much of this overview of gender theory, so far, has been concerned with the theorization of femininity in particular, rather than of gender in general. There are clear reasons for this, not least the historical conception of femininity as a puzzle or mystery or danger requiring attention, and of masculinity as a given, the norm, somehow uncomplicated and uncontroversial – unless tainted (and thereby rendered "effeminate") by any suggestion of homosexuality. In the 1980s, the successes of women's studies as a discipline were, however, beginning to invite complaints that questions of maleness and masculinity were being either overlooked or vilified. A

men's movement had emerged in response to (and largely as a reaction against) the women's movement, but this tended to be separatist and regressive, so there was space for a more interrogative study of masculinity to emerge both within feminism and beyond it. This new form of masculinity studies is evident in the work of feminists such as Lynne Segal (whose *Slow Motion*, initially published in 1990, is a landmark text) and R. W. Connell (whose *Masculinities* appeared in 1995). This more positive (rather than reactive) branch of masculinity studies builds on, and acknowledges its debt to, feminism, with theorists such as Carrigan et al. (2004) noting, in an essay first published in 1985, that "One of the central facts about masculinity ... is that men in general are advantaged through the subordination of women" (152). It has also been centrally concerned with, and has sought to critique, the homophobia built into traditional models of masculinity and the forms of racism which inflect power relations between men and women, thus complicating that picture of dominant men and subordinate women and seeking to "[recognize] a range of masculinities" (152).

In *Slow Motion*, Segal (1990: 89ff.) traces the emergence and consolidation of a "masculine ideal" (which Carrigan et al. refer to as "the culturally exalted form of masculinity, the hegemonic model" [2004: 154]), which stresses aggression, athleticism, and courage, and disparages both introspection and the outward expression of emotion, from the nineteenth century to the present. Segal examines the influence of institutions (such as boys' public schools), global events (like the two world wars) and iconic masculine figures (such as Ernest Hemingway and John Wayne) in the formation of this understanding of masculinity, and in doing so reveals the very unstable foundations upon which it is built. As she writes:

The closer we come to uncovering some form of exemplary masculinity, a masculinity which is solid and sure of itself, the clearer it becomes that masculinity is structured through contradiction: the more it asserts itself, the more it calls itself into question. But this is precisely what we should expect if ... masculinity is not some type of single essence, innate or acquired. As it is represented in our culture, "masculinity" is a quality of being which is always incomplete, and which is based as much on a social as on a psychic reality. It exists in the various forms of power men ideally possess: the power to assert control over women, over other men, over their own bodies, over machines and technology. (1990: 103–4)

Segal, then, encourages more diverse masculinities (in the plural) which explore men's positives roles as fathers and partners, and refuse the elements of violence and homophobia which are part and parcel of the ideal; to follow this path would, she suggests, "spell the end of masculinity as we have known it" (260).

QUEER THEORY AND TRANSGENDER STUDIES

Although primarily concerned with issues around sexuality, queer theory has also been responsible for theorizing gender "queerness," questions of gender crossing, passing, gender bending, transvestism, transgenderism, and unintelligible genders – anything, really, that might fall under the heading of a non-normative practice or presentation of gender. Annamarie Jagose has defined "queer" as describing "those gestures or analytical models which dramatize incoherencies in the allegedly stable relations between chromosomal sex, gender and sexual desire," and as focusing in particular on "mismatches between sex, gender and desire" (1996: 3).

This definition reveals the fraught relationship between gender and sexuality, such that "woman" is conventionally taken as meaning "attracted to men" (i.e., heterosexual) and that supposedly unorthodox desires or sexual practices can be seen as disrupting or problematizing perceptions of that person's gender. By contrast with the sexological models considered earlier in this essay, this disruption is something that queer theory generally seeks to celebrate, with the "mismatches" of which Jagose writes, opening up the possibility for more diverse and challenging experiences and expressions of gender.

As in its treatment of sexuality, queer theory sets itself against any suggestion of a stable or determinate identity, as far as gender is concerned, and instead looks for those instances of fluidity, indeterminacy, or apparent contradiction in one's gender presentation (as Butler's analysis of drag, cited earlier, exemplifies). Any notion of "natural" gender is, then, complicated by the existence of bodies, desires, and identities which counter the suggestions that maleness should produce masculinity, and femaleness femininity, or that both sex and gender should be unequivocally established. In *Female Masculinity* (1998), Judith Halberstam sets out to reclaim and celebrate masculinity as part of the overall experience of womanhood. She presents this as a radical project – "a seriously committed attempt to make masculinity safe for women and girls" – noting that, "despite at least two decades of sustained feminist and queer attacks on the notion of natural gender, we still believe that masculinity in girls and women is abhorrent and pathological" (268). If this project involves the reimagining of femaleness, as something which can include forms of behavior, desire, and self-presentation traditionally coded as "masculine," it also involves a reimagining of masculinity, which distances it from the discredited model of hegemonic masculinity that I mentioned earlier in this essay and which separates it from "maleness" without, then, exclusively tying it to lesbianism. As Halberstam asks at the outset:

> If masculinity is not the social and cultural and indeed political expression of maleness, then what is it? I do not claim to have any definitive answer to this question, but I do have a few proposals about why masculinity must not and cannot and should not reduce down to the male body and its effects. (1998: 1)

Halberstam's argument is centrally concerned with the "immense social power that accumulates around masculinity," which she sees as explaining why masculinity "has been reserved for people with male bodies and has been actively denied to people with female bodies" (269) As her argument moves through a consideration of androgyny, inversion, forms of lesbian "butchness," and the contemporary culture of "drag kings," Halberstam therefore works to resignify masculinity and to reduce the stigma attached to those women deemed to be "manly."

As part of her discussion of "female masculinity," Halberstam explores questions around transgenderism and transsexuality, and in the years since the publication of her book, transgender studies has achieved a disciplinary status in its own right, through the work of writers and activists such as Susan Stryker, Stephen Whittle, and Jay Prosser. Stryker claims:

> The field of transgender studies is concerned with anything that disrupts, denaturalizes, rearticulates, and makes visible the normative linkages we generally assume to exist between the biological specificity of the sexually differentiated human body, the social roles and statuses that a particular form of body is expected to occupy, the subjectively experienced relationship between a gendered sense of self and social expectations of gender-role performance, and the cultural mechanisms that work to sustain or thwart specific configurations of gendered personhood. (2006: 3)

In this way, transgender studies can be seen as building on the interrogations of gender normativity previously posited by feminism and queer theory. The sheer range of experiences that a "trans identity" can describe includes, according to Whittle, "discomfort with role expectations, being queer, occasional or more frequent cross-dressing, permanent cross-dressing and cross-gender living, through to accessing major health interventions such as hormonal therapy and surgical reassignment procedures" (2006: xi). Joseph Bristow has noted "the proliferation of sexual identities" in the twenty-first century, and arguably this has also been the case for gender (1997: 219). As relatively new identities and descriptions such as "transman" become available – often identities which disrupt attempts at categorization and containment, and celebrate indeterminacy and inbetweenness – discussions of gender have moved far beyond the taxonomical models of the sexologists and beyond any simple analysis of the characteristics of masculinity and femininity. If we have not yet moved beyond gender altogether (as certain advocates of techno-cultural theory might have hoped, in the wake of Donna Haraway's "Cyborg manifesto"), it is clear that the impetus to reflect upon and theorize gender has not yet abated, and our understanding of it continues to develop.

SEE ALSO: Butler, Judith; Feminism; Gender and Cultural Studies; Lesbian, Gay, Bisexual, and Transgender Studies; Phallus/Phallocentrism; Poststructuralism; Psychoanalysis (since 1966); Psychoanalysis (to 1966); Queer Theory

REFERENCES AND SUGGESTED READINGS

de Beauvoir, S. (1988). *The Second Sex*. London: Picador. (Original work published 1949.)

Bland, L., & Doan, L. (eds.) (1998). *Sexology Uncensored: The Documents of Sexual Science*. Cambridge: Polity.

Bristow, J. (1997). *Sexuality*. London: Routledge.

Butler, J. (1993). *Bodies that Matter*. London: Routledge.

Butler, J. (1999). *Gender Trouble*. London: Routledge. (Original work published 1990.)

Carrigan, T., Connell, B., & Lee, J. (2004). Toward a new sociology of masculinity. In P. F. Murphy (ed.), *Feminism and Masculinities*. Oxford: Oxford University Press, pp. 151–164.

Cixous, H. (1996). *The Newly Born Woman*. London: I. B. Tauris. (Original work published 1975.)

Connell, R. W. (1995). *Masculinities*. Berkeley: University of California Press.

Ellis, H. (1894). *Man and Woman*. London: W. Scott.

Freud, S. (1973). Femininity. In *New Introductory Lectures on Psychoanalysis*. Harmondsworth: Penguin, pp. 145–169.

Freud, S. (1977). Three essays on the theory of sexuality. In *On Sexuality*. Harmondsworth: Penguin, pp. 31–169.

Friedan, B. (1992). *The Feminine Mystique*. Harmondsworth: Penguin. (Original work published 1963.)

Glover, D., & Kaplan, C. (2000). *Genders*. London: Routledge.

Greer, G. (1991). *The Female Eunuch*. London: Paladin. (Original work published 1970.)

Halberstam, J. (1998). *Female Masculinity*. Durham, NC: Duke University Press.

Jagose, A. (1996). *Queer Theory: An Introduction*. New York: New York University Press.

Millett, K. (1977). *Sexual Politics*. London: Virago. (Original work published 1970.)

Segal, L. (1990). *Slow Motion*. Basingstoke: Palgrave Macmillan.

Stryker, S. (2006). (De)Subjugated Knowledges. In S. Stryker & S. Whittle (eds.), *The Transgender Studies Reader*. London: Routledge, pp. 1–17.

Whittle, S. (2006). Foreword. In S. Stryker & S. Whittle (eds.), *The Transgender Studies Reader*. London: Routledge, pp. xi–xvi.

Wollstonecraft, M. (1992). *A Vindication of the Rights of Woman*. Harmondsworth: Penguin. (Original work published 1792.)

Genre

OLIVER BELAS

From the French for "kind" or "sort," and etymologically derived from the Latin *genus*, the word "genre" has connotations of biological kind, and its use in relation to the arts begins in the late eighteenth century, not long after the establishment of Linnaean taxonomy. Theoretical and critical work on commercial or popular genres – notably detective and science fiction, but also pornography, the erotic thriller, the western, the romance – are relatively recent developments, emerging in number first in the late 1960s and early 1970s against the backdrop of New Left cultural politics. In literature, genre – for example, detective fiction in Auster (1987) – has been used as a metafictional cast within which questions of individual, collective, and authorial identity, as well as ideas of "textuality" and a textual or linguistic self, are interrogated. Notions of genre are implicated to varying degree in all literary study; the more refined and complex the study of literature becomes, the less stable are the ideas of genre and genres themselves. In literary studies today, scholarly focus has to some degree shifted away from definition: volumes in a series such as the Cambridge Companions to Literature dedicated to science fiction, crime fiction, the Gothic novel suggest, implicitly, that such genres should be thought of in the same terms as, say, modernism, Victorian, African American, or even single-author studies – as broad fields of inquiry, rather than stably defined sets of texts.

Though the idea that the term "genre" conveys, of coherent and distinct classes of texts, is simple enough, the level at which distinctions are drawn and the criteria against which they are to be decided are not fixed or certain. "Genre" can refer to broad, overarching forms (poetry, the novel, drama), their defining characteristics and transformations over time and between cultures; or to subdivisions within certain artistic forms or media – one speaks of "genre film" or "genre fiction" when speaking, for example, of *film noir*, westerns, science fiction, detective fiction. In either case, discussion of genre always raises, implicitly or explicitly, questions of the relationship between parts and wholes, or, perhaps more accurately, smaller and larger systems – the relationship of "genre novels" to "the novel," or "the novel" to "literature."

Theories of genre sometimes form part of a broader investigation of literature as a whole, as in Wellek & Warren (1963) and Frye (1990). Though both works were first published before 1966 – in 1949 and 1957, respectively – Wellek & Warren went through second and third editions in 1954 and 1963, while Frye was republished in 1971, 1990, and 2006. Their appearance in Penguin editions indicates their (relative) popularity. Both works are important points of reference for Todorov (1990); both continue to inform discussions of literary theory and criticism. For Frye, genres are more or less universal, characterized first of all by their imagined or ideal mode of presentation. Frye is thinking of genre not as the distinctions of the novel, drama, and poetry, but as the differences between works meant to be acted in front of, spoken or sung to, or read by their audiences. Genres for Frye, then, are determined by the relationship of the work to its audience. In his work on commercial or popular fictions in the late 1960s, Cawelti takes his cue from Frye, distinguishing between genres, *pace* Frye, and formulas,

understood as specific cultural embodiments of genres. Cawelti has since loosened and refined this distinction, suggesting different degrees of genre (the archetypal genres of tragedy and comedy, and the culturally or historically more limited genres of the western or romance, for example), and gesturing toward a subtler articulation of genres and formulas (see essays in Cawelti 2004). Wellek and Warren recognize tragedy and comedy as genres, but not as archetypal genres in Cawelti's sense. "Genres" in Frye and Cawelti are, for Wellek and Warren, "ultimates"; only historically limited, second-order divisions of, say, prose fiction should be called "genres," they argue. Moretti (2005), in his attempt to outline an abstract model of literary history, has argued that "the novel" does not exist in any ideal sense, but only as the system of its historically changing genres.

Genres might be conceived of "extrinsically" in terms of cultural history, or "intrinsically" in terms of poetics (see Wellek & Warren 1963); in terms of function (what they "do") or structure (what they "are") (see Todorov 1990). The stability of such distinctions as "extrinsic" and "intrinsic" critical methods, or structural and functional definitions, are not unproblematic, however, as determining what constitutes a genre involves identifying from "outside" the genre "rules," trends, characteristics, forms, and so on, that are thought to recur "inside" that genre's constitutive texts. The presumed coherence of genres is in many ways an imposition made primarily from the side of criticism broadly conceived – whether the "critic" be an author, academic, journalist, or fan. Thus, Delany's (1978) influential essay on the functional character of science fiction is as much a blueprint for both ways of writing and reading, speculation as to what science fiction *should be*, as it is a description of what the genre "is." Similarly, one might read Moretti's (1983) analysis of Doyle's Sherlock Holmes stories – in which Moretti attempts to demonstrate the necessary, dialectical relationship between structure and function – as being as much a product of his Marxist theoretical framework as of Doyle's works. Todorov (1990) argues that because no definition of literature – which is the always changing system of its genres – can be found that admits all that is literary and nothing that is not, and because neither literature nor nonliterature is a single, coherent entity, poetics must be replaced by the analysis of discourse. According to Todorov, the system of genres available in a given language originates in discourse, understood as the hardening of linguistic possibilities or choices into sociocultural rules or conventions. Similarly, at a more local level, in science fiction studies Suvin's still often cited definition of science fiction as a literature of "cognitive estrangement" – simply put, nonrealism (estrangement) with recourse to reason (cognition) – has been criticized, notably by Delany, for admitting much that is not science fiction and for excluding much that is (Suvin 1979; Delany 1994).

Analysis of literary type extends back, of course, to Aristotle (indeed, Frye remarks that since Aristotle and the several genre divisions of classical Greek inheritance, precise terms and procedures for literary study have not much developed). In the *Poetics*, Aristotle distinguishes comedy, epic poetry, and tragedy typologically and hierarchically. The purpose of poetry, he states, is to arouse feelings of fear and pity in the audience. According to Aristotle, tragedy does this best of all, and so, by definition, it is the best kind of poetry (Aristotle expands "poetry" and "poet" to refer not to works and practitioners of verse forms only, but to all works and practitioners of mimesis). By distinguishing comedy, epic poetry, and tragedy

typologically and hierarchically, and because Aristotle is concerned with what is most effective in and proper to each, the *Poetics* contains the principle that genres are and must be distinct, pure, unmixed – a critical axiom noted by Wellek and Warren and, in ironic fashion, by Derrida. Derrida (1992) argues that no text can exist without generic identification – the principle of literary identification presupposes the prior existence of models, rules, and so on – but that no genre can ever be "pure." On the one hand, genres function like laws, pre- and pro-scribing. At the same time, as a genre incorporates ever more texts it cannot ever be considered closed or replete. For Derrida, genres are fundamentally contaminated by other genres that exist in parasitical relationship with one another, and it is, therefore, a model of "participation" rather than "belonging" that Derrida proposes for thinking about genre. This model of genre is rather close to Derrida's broader conception of what he dubs the "strange institution called literature," which is constitutionally always in excess of its own apparent boundaries (Derrida 1992).

Derrida is not much interested in genre fiction, but ideas of contamination or hybridity are increasingly to be found in dedicated genre studies. Botting (1996) provocatively suggests that, because it is a synthesis of literary and paraliterary genres, the Gothic can perhaps claim to be the only genuinely literary tradition. A recent issue of *Science Fiction Studies* – containing essays on science fiction and the gendered body, Latour, Castell, Serres, and Kittler – has attempted to move theoretically inflected work on science fiction away from the dominant influences of Jameson, Haraway, and Suvin, emphasizing ideas of sociological and discursive networks or assemblages, and topological relation (Luckhurst & Partington 2006).

L. R. Williams (2005) analyzes the erotic thriller as a composite genre formed from, among other influences, pornography and *film noir*. Referring to pornography as "the forgotten genre," Williams points out that with few significant exceptions little has been done to define pornography, arguably the most controversial of genres. Definition would seem to be necessary for a genre that has been challenged on moral, aesthetic, and legal grounds, yet relatively little attention has been paid to what makes pornography pornography. The genre is often treated as monolithic, the differences between investigations and representations of "alternative" or "marginal" sexual practices and "hardcore" pornography seldom acknowledged. The tendency has been to argue "for" or "against" pornography from positions of anti-censorship or anti-sexism/exploitation, though historical, philosophical, and cultural work from L. Williams (1999), Kipnis (1996), O'Toole (1998), and Pease (2000), among others, has contributed to a more nuanced body of knowledge that is focused on the genre itself rather than its sociological implications.

Genre and its ethical significance have also been analyzed in scholarship on Holocaust literature. Eaglestone (2008) states that genre is a way of both writing and reading, the meeting point of the two processes. Fiction is shaped in large part by readers' processes of identification; with testimony, the Holocaust has produced a new genre, in part, but not exclusively, because it alters the processes by which we identify when reading. Testimony, Eaglestone argues, attempts to foreclose identification.

SEE ALSO: African American Literary Theory; Derrida, Jacques; Hybridity; Jameson, Fredric; Marxism; Modernity/Postmodernity; Moretti, Franco; Scholes, Robert; Self-Referentiality; Žižek, Slavoj

REFERENCES AND SUGGESTED READINGS

Aristotle (1982). *Poetics* (trans. J. Hutton). New York: Norton.

Auster, P. (1987). *The New York Trilogy: City of Glass, Ghosts, The Locked Room*. London: Faber and Faber.

Botting, F. (1996). *Gothic*. London: Routledge.

Cawelti, J. G. (2004). *Mystery, Violence, and Popular Culture*. Madison: University of Wisconsin Press.

Delany, S. (1978). About five thousand seven hundred and fifty words. In *The Jewel-Hinged Jaw: Notes on the Language of Science Fiction*, Elizabethtown, NY: Dragon Press, pp. 21–37.

Delany, S. (1994). Science fiction and criticism: The Diacritics interview. In *Silent Interviews: On Language, Race, Science Fiction, Sex, and Some Comics. A Collection of Written Interviews.* Middletown, CT: Wesleyan University Press, pp. 186–215.

Derrida, J. (1992a). "This strange institution called literature": An interview with Jacques Derrida. In *Acts of Literature* (ed. D. Attridge). London: Routledge, pp. 33–75.

Derrida, J. (1992b). The law of genre. In *Acts of Literature* (ed. D. Attridge). London: Routledge, pp. 221–252.

Eaglestone, R. (2008). *The Holocaust and the Postmodern*. Oxford: Oxford University Press.

Frye, N. (1990). *Anatomy of Criticism: Four Essays*. London: Penguin. (Original work published 1957.)

Kipnis, L. (1996). *Bound and Gagged: Pornography and the Politics of Fantasy in America*. New York: Grove.

Luckhurst, R., & Partington, G. (eds.) (2006). *Science Fiction Studies*, 33. (1).

Moretti, F. (1983). Clues. In *Signs Taken for Wonders: On the Sociology of Literary Forms*. London: Verso, pp. 130–156.

Moretti, F. (2005). *Graphs, Maps, Trees: Abstract Models for a Literary History*. London: Verso.

O'Toole, L. (1998). *Pornocopia: Porn, Sex, Technology and Desire*. London: Serpent's Tail.

Pease, A. (2000). *Modernism, Mass Culture, and the Aesthetics of Obscenity*. Cambridge: Cambridge University Press.

Suvin, D. (1979). *Metamorphoses of Science Fiction: On the Poetics and History of a Literary Genre*. New Haven: Yale University Press.

Todorov, T. (1990). *Genres in Discourse* (trans. C. Porter). New York: Cambridge University Press. (Original work published 1978.)

Wellek, R., & Warren, A. (1963). *Theory of Literature*, 3rd edn. Harmondsworth: Penguin.

Williams, L. (1999). *Hard Core: Power, Pleasure, and the "Frenzy of the Visible,"* expanded edn. Berkeley: University of California Press.

Williams, L. R. (2005). *The Erotic Thriller in Contemporary Cinema*. Bloomington: Indiana University Press.

Greenblatt, Stephen

MARK ROBSON

Stephen Greenblatt (b. 1943) has pursued a form of cultural criticism that is known either as new historicism or – in his own preferred term – as cultural poetics, in a series of influential texts mainly devoted to Shakespeare and early modern English literature. Beginning from an interest in literary texts, Greenblatt's historicist practice brings these texts into relation with other aspects of a broadly conceived notion of culture, and as a consequence Greenblatt's writings touch on art, architecture, politics, and religion alongside more traditional literary concerns.

Greenblatt acknowledges a wide range of influences on his work, and it is the eclectic nature of those influences that has given his criticism its distinctive character. Inflected by an early interest in Marxist aesthetics, Greenblatt's cultural poetics owes much to the cultural materialism of Raymond Williams, particularly in his insistence that the "great" works of art are always part of a wider network of forms of cultural production. It is in this sense that he thinks of a poetics of culture, in which the narrow literary definition of poetics is extended to other forms of "making" (from the Greek *poiesis*). As objects made, circulated, and consumed through particular practices, literary works connect to other forms of

practice and behavior, including ritual, values, and belief. Greenblatt approaches these connections through an anthropological mode of "thick description" taken from the work of Clifford Geertz. Other influences include Michel de Certeau and Michel Foucault, but at heart Greenblatt's project is in the tradition of cultural critique established by German Romantic thinkers such as Herder. In adopting a sense of the "life-world," Greenblatt attempts to locate literature and art in a specific time and place, and to attend to the singularity of a given work of art. This concern for singularity also means that, even in a text such as *Practicing New Historicism* (2000, co-authored with Catherine Gallagher), Greenblatt is wary of establishing anything that might be thought of as a theoretical system. Asserting the necessity of thinking about singularity through practice rather than theory, Greenblatt often makes counterintuitive and startling juxtapositions, between a Shakespeare play and contemporary witchcraft texts, for example. Part of the purpose of such strategies is to unsettle expectations and inherited modes of understanding a given text or the period in which it originates, but it also relates criticism as a practice to the other forms of practice that this criticism takes as its object.

One consequence of the nonsystematic nature of his practice is that Greenblatt's work has generated very few identifiable concepts. Perhaps his most influential ideas to date have been "self-fashioning," "the circulation of social energy" and the coupling of resonance and wonder. Developed in his first major work, *Renaissance Self-Fashioning* (1980), the title concept reflects a sense that selves are constructed rather than given, and that identity is a matter not only of characteristics that are recognizable to others but also of a characteristic mode of address to the world that is at least in part willed. This emphasis on the negotiation of identity derives from Greenblatt's sense of culture as dynamic. The early modern period, he suggests, represents a cultural moment in which there are not only new possibilities for shaping identity – due to the influence of the Reformation, an emergent merchant class, and of increased social and geographical mobility, for instance – but at the same time there is powerful resistance, generating both new and reinforced limits on behavior. Self-fashioning becomes a dialectical process of negotiating these new possibilities and the forces arrayed against them. Reading the biographies of writers alongside their texts, Greenblatt seeks to reveal their connections to broader groups of people as well as patterns of behavior and social organization.

The circulation of social energy is the organizing idea for the second major book, *Shakespearean Negotiations* (1988), and is focused on the movement of objects and artifacts within a culture. By invoking social energy, Greenblatt relates objects, and their power to have an impact on those who encounter them, to the rhetorical principle of *energia*. Objects – including art-objects – are capable of arousing strong emotional or even physical responses such as fear, pleasure, anger, and so on, just as words can produce striking images in the mind. These effects are utilized in the theater, as objects, rituals, and practices travel between the stage and the world its audiences inhabit. These exchanges between theater and world both draw on and add to the objects' energy. This thinking about objects underpins his interest in resonance and wonder. Wonder, he suggests, is the response that an object provokes, whereas resonance is that quality which makes us want to understand the processes through which an object was produced, circulated, and consumed, and the changes in its use and status that occur as it travels. Where wonder may isolate the object as possessing a special nature, attention to resonance reconnects it to the life-world.

Much of Greenblatt's success has stemmed from his style. A gifted writer, his texts are studded with memorable narrative moments that often take the form of anecdotes. The lack of system that many commentators have identified in Greenblatt's work is reflected by this emphasis on a non-systematic form of writing. Most of his books are collections of essays rather than traditional monographs, and the essay form – like the anecdote – tries to avoid adding up to a closed system. Greenblatt's primary influence comes through the extension of a multidisciplinary historicism to literary studies.

SEE ALSO: Foucault, Michel; New Historicism

REFERENCES AND SUGGESTED READINGS

Colebrook, C. (1997). *New Literary Histories: New Historicism and Contemporary Criticism*. Manchester: Manchester University Press.

Gallagher, C., & Greenblatt, S. (2000). *Practicing New Historicism*. Chicago: University of Chicago Press.

Greenblatt, S. (1980). *Renaissance Self-Fashioning: From More to Shakespeare*. Chicago: University of Chicago Press.

Greenblatt, S. (1988). *Shakespearean Negotiations: The Circulation of Social Energy in Renaissance England*. Oxford: Clarendon.

Payne, M. (ed.) (2005). *The Greenblatt Reader*. Oxford: Blackwell.

Robson, M. (2008). *Stephen Greenblatt*. London: Routledge.

Veeser, H. A. (ed.) (1989). *The New Historicism*. London: Routledge.

Grosz, Elizabeth

GABRIEL NOAH BRAHM, JR.

Elizabeth A. Grosz (b. 1952) is a renowned Australian materialist feminist philosopher of "difference" and "becoming," working in the tradition of postmodern (late twentieth-century antinomian) French feminism and poststructuralism (post-Marxist, Nietzschean-inspired variations on Saussurean linguistics). Among male writers associated with the latter tendency, Gilles Deleuze increasingly occupied a privileged place in the texts of this otherwise woman-centered thinker, as her thought developed under his influence in surprising ways throughout the 1990s and 2000s. She is a noted queer theorist who controversially critiques the value of the term "queer."

Whereas her earliest published works (juvenilia dating from the mid- to late 1970s and first two books, appearing side by side in 1989–90) all derived from an overriding interest in Jacques Lacan's linguistics-centered rewriting of Sigmund Freud, on the one hand, and an affinity for some noted feminists associated with Lacan's school (Julia Kristeva and Luce Irigaray in particular), on the other; subsequent work would de-emphasize language per se, in favor of an even more literally "materialist" interest in biology, nature, and a blurring of the line between ethnology (the study of human cultures) and ethology (the study of animals). The latter deconstruction of the nature/culture binary is accomplished in part through a daring rereading of the nineteenth-century English scientist, Charles Darwin, whom Grosz appropriates for feminist purposes, along philosophical lines (having to do with becoming and sexual difference) pioneered by Deleuze and Irigaray. Art, for example, is not something uniquely human, let alone ethereal, expressive of civilization's "highest spiritual capacities"; nor does it obey the "law of the signifier" in a social symbolic order that excludes the real. Rather, the creative–aesthetic impulse is rooted in the real of Darwinian sexual selection, the immediate outgrowth of embodied exuberance – therefore something we share with all superabundant life forms, (other) animals, if not also plants (and possibly computers).

Best known for her pathbreaking work on time, space, and the body, Grosz understands the very fundamentals of our existence as first and foremost inherently gendered. She criticizes previous attempts at conceptualization of these bedrock coordinates – even by such radical male thinkers as Henri Bergson, Freud, Lacan, Maurice Merleau-Ponty, Michel Foucault, Deleuze, and Jacques Derrida – for their failure to appreciate adequately the full importance of the inescapable fact (universal, transcultural, and transhistorical) of sexual difference. Drawing attention to certain corporeal experiences unique to women – such as menstruation, pregnancy, childbirth, lactation, menopause – she explores ways of fundamentally rethinking our most basic categories of thought beyond patriarchy's limiting horizons.

She does not confine herself to studying sexual difference in isolation from other salient contrasts, however – insisting that a variety of subordinated alterities (racial and economic, for example) should also provide keys to unlock the unpredictable self-overcomings that might lead us into a qualitatively different future. There are no guarantees, however. Capitalism, homophobia, and racism are also among her major political concerns. Though she frankly does not anticipate an end to either male domination or these other pervasive injustices in our lifetime (or possibly ever), she nonetheless remains committed to vigorously contesting and subverting these overarching evils – even if such struggles are endless and, as she says, possibly "not resolvable" (Ausch et al. 2000). Her faith in a radicalized Darwin – instructing us yet again to beware the folly of teleology and essentialism – allows her to take the long view of politics, along with everything else, since "evolution is a fundamentally open-ended system that pushes toward a future with no real direction, no promise of any particular result, no guarantee of progress or improvement, but with every indication of inherent proliferation and transformation" (Grosz 2008: 38). In spite of global capitalism's retrenchments, her politics remain planetary if not cosmic in scale and duration.

Instead of seeing philosophy as a meta-language elevated above life for the expression of static truths outside time and space, she bravely values thought – like Deleuze – for its creativity and nomadic waywardness, rather than its reassurances. Philosophy at its best does not somberly hold itself apart and pretend to govern practice a priori, but instead collaborates playfully with lived experience, in a series of experiments that anticipate, and potentially help bring about, altered states and new intensities. The former "Platonic" dream of the (wrong kind of) philosopher is impossible anyway, since becoming and not being is what matters.

"Mattering," for Grosz, is literally material and never simply about what (already) counts (for the other). Indeed, her early interest in Lacan wanes as she comes to agree with Deleuze that "psychoanalysis is fundamentally boring" since it seeks and finds "Oedipus everywhere" (Ausch et al. 2000). Her own practice, on the other hand, is anything but redundant or sedentary. Continually on the move and discovering new topics to explore in novel ways, her texts spread out tendrils like rhizomes, freely traversing conventional disciplinary boundaries in order to range over, under, around, and through a dazzling array of subjects – from pornography to the preconditions for art-making of any kind, from commodity fetishism to lesbian fetishism – in fields as ostensibly far apart as architecture, anthropology, art history and evolutionary biology, as well as linguistics, political economy, psychoanalysis, and philosophy. She thereby invites her reader to wander off the beaten path, abandon the metaphysical comforts of traditional distinctions, and give up

ideological safety and security for the scary thrills that come with risking rigorous scrutiny of all of our taken-for-granted assumptions about what it means to be and do – for humans, animals, "freaks," viruses, computer viruses, carbon- and silicon-based "life," the work of art, the earth itself, etc.

Like similar figures of her generation – for example, the American philosopher and queer theorist, Judith Butler, to whom she is sometimes compared, and the Slovenian celebrity thinker, Slavoj Žižek – Grosz is at once fearlessly eclectic and iconoclastic, in some ways (her peripatetic choice of subject matter, her refusal to compromise with the resurgent liberal humanism of the 1980s and 1990s), and yet remarkably consistent and faithful to origins in another way: she continues to show us startling things both in and by means of engagement with "la pensée de soixante-huit" – work generated out of literary and cultural theory's fecund period of the 1960s–70s – while holding unswervingly to its rebellious, anarchic spirit. She has not shown interest in any neoconservative "return of the subject."

Rather, she resolutely presses ahead in the abandonment of the centered subject. Unlike her peers, Butler and Žižek, she rejects the German idealist philosopher G. W. F. Hegel and the "politics of recognition" associated with his master–slave dialectic, in favor of a "politics of imperceptibility." Perhaps this is why so far she remains less iconic, with less of a cult following, than Butler, and less visible to the mainstream media, popular press, and internet, than Žižek. Her work, however, is as challenging and rewarding as that of either – although her prose is more conventionally transparent and relatively uncluttered with jargon. In place of Butler's emphasis on gender as "performance," which as Grosz points out presumes the role of the other as audience, she prefers the notion of "acts," which need no other. She likewise finds "queer" a reactive category, which defines itself in relation to the straight norm. And to Žižek's old-school revolutionary communist (some have said Stalinist) insistence on the singular "event" that decisively ushers in a new order, decisively liberated from the hypocrisy and misery of the capitalist present, she juxtaposes a less dramatic and showy – but no less radical – more open-ended quest for thousands of incommensurable high points or plateaus. "It's kind of depressing," she says in an interview, "that I'm not ever going to lie in the sun and relax and forget about patriarchy. It's true, though, I'm not" (Ausch et al. 2000).

Grosz was born in Sydney, Australia. She earned both her BA and PhD in philosophy from the Department of General Philosophy, University of Sydney, where she also taught from 1978 to 1991. In 1992 she moved to Monash University, in Melbourne, to assume the role of Director of the newly formed Institute of Critical and Cultural Studies. She has been a visiting professor at the University of California, Santa Cruz; the University of California, Davis; and the University of California, Irvine; Johns Hopkins University; the University of Richmond; and George Washington University. In 2002 she joined the Department of Women's and Gender Studies at Rutgers University. In 2007 she delivered the twenty-seventh Wellek Library Lectures in Critical Theory at the University of California, Irvine.

SEE ALSO: Deleuze, Gilles; Feminism; Irigaray, Luce; Kristeva, Julia; Lacan, Jacques; Postmodernism; Poststructuralism; Queer Theory; Semiotics; Žižek, Slavoj

REFERENCES AND SUGGESTED READINGS

Ausch, R., Doane, R., & Perez, L. (2000). Interview with Elizabeth Grosz. In Found Object 9. At: http://web.gc.cuny.edu/csctw/found_object/text/grosz.htm (accessed April 23, 2010).

Copeland, J. (2005). The creative urge: Elizabeth Grosz [interview]. ABC Radio International. At: www.abc.net.au/rn/arts/sunmorn/stories/s1381964.htm (accessed April 23, 2010).

Grosz, E. (1989). Sexual Subversions: Three French Feminists. Sydney: Allen and Unwin.

Grosz, E. (1990). Jacques Lacan: A Feminist Introduction. London: Routledge.

Grosz, E. (1994). Volatile Bodies: Toward a Corporeal Feminism. Bloomington: Indiana University Press.

Grosz, E. (1995). Space, Time and Perversion: Essays on the Politics of Bodies. New York: Routledge.

Grosz. E. (ed.) (1999) Becomings: Explorations in Time, Memory and Futures. Ithaca: Cornell University Press.

Grosz, E. (2001). Architecture from the Outside: Essays on Virtual and Real Space. Cambridge, MA: MIT Press.

Grosz, E. (2004). The Nick of Time: Politics, Evolution and the Untimely. Durham, NC: Duke University Press.

Grosz. E. (2005). Time Travels: Feminism, Nature, Power. Durham, NC: Duke University Press.

Grosz, E. (2008a). Chaos, Territory, Art: Deleuze and the Framing of the Earth. New York: Columbia University Press.

Grosz, E. (2008b). Darwin and feminism. In S. Alaimo & S. Hekman (eds.), Material Feminisms. Bloomington: Indiana University Press.

Grosz, E., & Pateman, C. (eds.) (1986). Feminist Challenges: Social and Political Theory. Boston: Northeastern University Press.

Grosz, E., & Probyn, E. (eds.) (1995). Sexy Bodies: The Strange Carnalities of Feminism. New York: Routledge.

Grosz, E., Threadgold, T., Kress, G., & Halliday, M. A. K. (eds.) (1986). Language, Semiotics, Ideology. Sydney: Sydney Association for Studies in Society and Culture.

Grosz, E., & Threadgold, T., Kelly, D., & Cholodenko, A. (eds.) (1987). Futur*Fall: Excursions into Postmodernity. Sydney: Power Institute of Fine Art Publications.

Grosz, E., Caine, B., & Lepervanche, M. de (eds.) (1988). Crossing Boundaries: Feminisms and the Critique of Knowledges. Boston: Allen and Unwin.

H

Habermas, Jürgen

MIN WILD

Jürgen Habermas is a central figure in the philosophy of communication and of the legacy of the Enlightenment; he is the major living proponent of critical theory as originally practiced by the Institute for Social Research at the University of Frankfurt am Main. Germany's most eminent and controversial living philosopher, his prolific, neo-Marxist works have consistently argued for the possibility of social change through rational discussion and intersubjective engagement, where humans as active agents can find common ground. His work stands as a substantial and persuasive alternative to poststructuralism because it grounds humans as effective subjects, having the ability to reach logical agreements. His view of the Enlightenment is largely positive, in that it represented a period of unprecedented social criticism and potentially fruitful change.

Habermas was born in Düsseldorf in 1929 and has lived most of his life in Germany. Too young to have fought in World War II, his interdisciplinary work in the fields of philosophy, sociology, history, linguistics, and literature has always sought ways to oppose totalitarianism. He is known as a "second generation" thinker of the Frankfurt School, and his work in critical theory is shaped in dialogue with the German philosopher Theodor Adorno (1903–69); it stands in most stark opposition to the work of Martin Heidegger (1889–1976). For the major part of his career he has worked at the Johann Wolfgang Goethe University at Frankfurt am Main, but from 1971 to 1983 he was the Director of the Max Planck Institute in Starnberg, after which he returned to Frankfurt as the Director of the Institute for Social Research. Now retired, he continues to write extensively; his attention has shifted to finding ways in which secularism and religion might coexist positively through mutual dialogue.

Of major importance to literary and cultural theory is his earliest work, *The Structural Transformation of the Public Sphere: An Inquiry into a Category of Bourgeois Society* (1989[1962]). Scholars of the seventeenth and eighteenth centuries have found in it a rich way to theorize material culture and social change in their period. Habermas argued that, beginning in Britain in the latter half of the seventeenth century, a "bourgeois public sphere" arose. This special category is separate from the public sphere of political domination and administration, and is of a "private" character in that it has no official place: it is thus of great interest to feminist scholars. It arises out of the private sphere of ordinary people's home-based discussion and small-scale

The Encyclopedia of Literary and Cultural Theory   General editor: Michael Ryan
© 2011 Blackwell Publishing Ltd

economic exchange, and is fired by the increasing accessibility of the printed word to ordinary people, centered in the new coffeehouses and places of public meeting. This period of vast expansion of print culture, when restrictions on publishing lapsed, saw the sustained rise of the exchange of critical debates in periodicals, newspapers, and pamphlets; rational argument and radical thought produced a new realm of political influence, later to emerge as the new concept of "public opinion." Other European countries followed suit, most notably France, where such public criticism led to revolution. Habermas argues that this bourgeois public sphere withered in the later nineteenth century, when entrenched capitalist and establishment interests combined to turn the press into a mere mouthpiece of commerce and the political public sphere. Importantly, however, in this book Habermas sees political criticism and debate arising out of seventeenth- and eighteenth-century *literary* criticism.

Continuing to work on social theory and the establishment of a rational society through the 1960s and 1970s, Habermas published his major philosophical work *The Theory of Communicative Action* in 1981. In 1985 came his *Philosophical Discourse of Modernity*, in which he engaged closely with the philosophy underlying modern literary theory, especially poststructuralism. Here Habermas discusses ways in which humans can come to terms with living in modernity, in an age which can no longer ground itself with models from the classical past, or through commonly held religious certainties. The work stands in opposition to the philosophical descendants of the German philosopher Friedrich Nietzsche (1844–1900), who tend to dominate in critical theory, and who, questioning the possibility of stable meaning in language, reject the autonomy and coher-

ence of the human subject. While Habermas finds much to admire in Nietzsche's thinking, he considers that, in their attention to Heidegger, a wrong turning had been taken by French poststructuralists, especially Jacques Derrida (1930–2004). Vital to Habermas's thought is the continuing significance of the Enlightenment; questioning Adorno's distrust of the role of reason and rationality in human affairs, he contends that the problem of Enlightenment thought was that it was not allowed to go far enough. While one should recognize, as the poststructuralists do, the decentered, fractured nature of humans' interior lives, and the ever-present deceptions of language, Habermas insists here and throughout his work that we can use reason as the foundation for noncoercive mutual understanding and intersubjectivity, and thus for recognition of and dialogue with others. In this, Habermas can most fruitfully be read alongside two other twentieth-century champions of mutual understanding: the Russian Mikhail Bakhtin (1895–1975) and the German Hans-Georg Gadamer (1900–2002). Habermas's *Inclusion of the Other* (1992) attests to this, as well as much of his other 1990s writings on reason, truth, and human nature.

Habermas's latest work on the possibility of meaningful interaction between the secular and the religious is marked by the publication of *The Dialectics of Secularization* (2006), a book of debates with Joseph Ratzinger, now Pope Benedict XVI. Most recent is his *Between Naturalism and Religion* (2008); here he returns to the question of rational communication and understanding, this time as a basis for combating hostile religious orthodoxy.

SEE ALSO: Adorno, Theodor; Critical Theory/ Frankfurt School; Derrida, Jacques; Gadamer, Hans-Georg; Heidegger, Martin; Marxism; Poststructuralism

REFERENCES AND SUGGESTED READINGS

Dews, P. (1999). *Habermas: A Critical Reader*. Oxford: Blackwell.

Habermas, J. (1984–7). *The Theory of Communicative Action* (trans. T. McCarthy). Cambridge: Polity. (Original work published 1981.)

Habermas, J. (1986). *Autonomy and Solidarity: Interviews* (ed. P. Dews). London: Verso.

Habermas, J. (1987). *The Philosophical Discourse of Modernity: Twelve Lectures* (trans. F. G. Lawrence). Cambridge, MA: MIT Press. (Original work published 1985.)

Habermas, J. (1989). *The Structural Transformation of the Public Sphere: An Inquiry into a Category of Bourgeois Society* (trans. T. Burger). Cambridge, MA: MIT Press. (Original work published 1962.)

Habermas, J. (1998). *The Inclusion of the Other: Studies in Political Theory* (ed. C. Cronin & P. de Greiff). Cambridge, MA: MIT Press. (Original work published 1992.)

Habermas, J. (2008). *Between Naturalism and Religion: Philosophical Essays*. Cambridge: Polity. (Original work published 2005.)

Held, D. (1980). *Introduction to Critical Theory: Horkheimer to Habermas*. London: Hutchinson.

McCarthy, T. (1978). *The Critical Theory of Jürgen Habermas*. Cambridge, MA: MIT Press.

Outhwaite, W. (1994). *Habermas: A Critical Introduction*. Cambridge: Polity.

Ratzinger, J., & Habermas, J. (2006). *The Dialectics of Secularization: On Reason and Religion* (trans. B. McNeil). San Francisco: Ignatius. (Original work published 2005.)

Hybridity

NICOLE M. GYULAY

An important term in postcolonial studies, hybridity is the intermixing of cultures that has occurred as a result of colonialism. Its full meaning in contemporary discourse is grounded in the theories of major postcolonial theorist Homi K. Bhabha, who conceives of hybridity as a "third space" in which cultural identity is negotiated in a way that subverts the power relations between colonizer and colonized.

Hybridity originally referred to cross-breeding of plant or animal species in order to create a third, or "hybrid" species. In the nineteenth century, the term "hybrid" was used in a derogatory fashion to refer to people of mixed racial backgrounds, the implication being that interracial subjects were "impure" and thus inferior to their unmixed counterparts. Before "hybridity" took on the more positive connotations it has today, the term "creolization" was often used to describe the intermixing of cultures. "Creole" originally described the descendants of Caribbean colonists who were born and raised in the New World, but has been more widely used to describe the "new" languages formed by the mixing of native, African, and European languages within Caribbean colonial territories. Poet and historian Edward Kamau Braithwaite argues that Caribbean society can only be understood with reference to the enduring influence of creolization.

The first to use the term "hybrid" in a more positive formulation was Soviet cultural theorist Mikhail Bakhtin, who argued that a single speaker could speak with a hybrid voice containing more than one language, culture, or belief system. For Bakhtin, this linguistic hybridity contributes to the aesthetic and political efficacy of the novel form, by creating the opportunity for competing voices to undermine singular, authoritative discourses.

Following on from this, Bhabha's notion of hybridity completely rejects the idea that culture is ever fixed or "pure." Instead, cultural identities are constantly shifting, incorporating a multiplicity of influences. Cultures do not exist in a vacuum, but are rather constantly interacting with one another, in an ongoing historical process. Therefore, there was never a moment in time when culture was not undergoing hybridization. Although it may appear that there are clear differences between cultures, for Bhabha these differences were in fact created by resistance to the process of hybridization. Cultural meaning is created in a "third space" that exists on the borderlands between perceived oppositional identities. Bhabha calls what exists in this space the "liminal."

This conception of hybridity is important to postcolonial studies because it undermines the discursive basis for colonial authority. Colonial discourse depends upon its ability to set up clear oppositional differences between self and other, black and white, ruler and ruled. British colonial rulers in India, for example, relied on the notion that "pure" British culture was not only different from, but also superior to, Indian culture. Hybridity, however, denies that these are absolute differences and makes illegitimate any claims to cultural superiority. The very similarities between colonizer and colonized implode the notion of hierarchical difference. Furthermore, hybridity as a postcolonial discourse works to deconstruct the very notion of splitting the world into opposites – or binary differences – thus allowing space for more productive discussions about cultural meaning in a globalized world.

Hybridity can be seen in the work of postcolonial authors such as Salman Rushdie, V. S. Naipaul, and J. M. Coetzee, among many others. Rushdie's work is probably the most cited as an example of hybridity in literature because of its obvious mixing of different literary and cultural traditions. For example, Rushdie's second novel, *Midnight's Children* (1981), alludes to *The Arabian Nights* when the main character Saleem says that he must work "faster than Scheherazade" (4), and also in the fact that there are 1,001 children of midnight. At the same time, Rushdie invokes Laurence Sterne's *Tristram Shandy* (1767) in the form of his narrative, in which Saleem begins his story before his own birth, and in

the importance placed on Saleem's nose throughout the novel.

Hybridity can also be seen within Rushdie's individual characters. His extremely controversial third novel, *The Satanic Verses* (1988), portrays migrant character Saladin Chamcha as one who struggles to strike a balance between English and Indian influences on his identity. As an Indian living in England, Chamcha attempts to assimilate himself into English culture. At the same time, his Indian background continues to be a strong part of his identity, despite his own attempts to deny it. As a result, Chamcha can never be wholly English or wholly Indian, but instead inhabits the third, hybrid, liminal space to which Bhabha refers, in which competing cultures come together to create something new and completely different. Bhabha describes this notion fully in his essay titled "How Newness Enters the World," published in *The Location of Culture* (1994).

Hybridity has been adopted by many postcolonial theorists, including Edward Said, as a useful concept, but others, such as Aijaz Ahmad, reject it. Ahmad argues that the idea of hybridity as a shared condition within the postcolonial world is an example of how postcolonial theory can have a tendency to homogenize the widely different cultures it addresses.

Robert Young defends hybridity from this criticism, arguing that it provides a framework for discussion without denying the existence of difference, given that the one thing all postcolonial cultures have in common is their experience of colonialism. He does, however, express his reservations about using a term which was originally used as part of racist discourse about mixed-race colonial subjects. He suggests that the term be used sparingly, with an awareness of its history and an emphasis on hybridity as a form of political resistance, rather than unconscious cultural homogenization.

SEE ALSO: Bhabha, Homi; Colonialism/ Imperialism; Mimicry; Postcolonial Studies and Diaspora Studies; Said, Edward

REFERENCES AND SUGGESTED READINGS

Ahmad, A. (1992). *In Theory: Classes, Nations, Literatures*. London: Verso.

Braithwaite, E. K. (1971). *The Development of Creole Society in Jamaica, 1770–1820*. Oxford: Oxford University Press.

Bakhtin, M. (1981). *The Dialogic Imagination: Four Essays* (trans. C. Emerson & M. Holquist; ed. M. Holquist). Austin: University of Texas Press.

Bhabha, H. K. (1994). *The Location of Culture*. London: Routledge.

Huddart, D. (2006). *Homi K. Bhabha*. London: Routledge.

Rushdie, S. (1981). *Midnight's Children*. London: Jonathan Cape.

Rushdie, S. (1988). *The Satanic Verses*. London: Viking.

Sanga, J. C. (2001). *Salman Rushdie's Postcolonial Metaphors*. Westport, CT: Greenwood.

Young, R. J. C. (1995). *Colonial Desire: Hybridity in Theory, Culture and Race*. London: Routledge.

I

Ideology

MICHAEL RYAN

"Ideology" is a word that was first used to name a "science of ideas" in the late eighteenth century. In the nineteenth century, the word began to be used in its modern sense to name a systematic body of ideas or doctrines. One therefore today speaks of "liberal ideology" or "conservative ideology" or of "the ideology of racism." The modern use of the word often has a mildly derogatory sense. It names a doctrine that is overly prescriptive and not supported by rational argumentation.

In literary and cultural studies, the word is used primarily in its Marxist sense to name a way of thinking that supports the rule of one economic or social class over another. This use of the word derives from Karl Marx's famous characterization of ideology as "ruling ideas" in *The German Ideology*:

> The ideas of the ruling class are in every epoch the ruling ideas, i.e. the class which is the ruling material force of society, is at the same time its ruling intellectual force. The class that has the means of material production at its disposal, has control at the same time over the means of mental production, so that thereby, generally speaking, the ideas of those who lack the means of mental production are subject to it. The ruling ideas are nothing more than the ideal expression of the dominant material relationships, the dominant material relationships grasped as ideas; hence of the relationships which make the one class the ruling one, therefore, the ideas of its dominance. (Marx & Engels 1970[1845]: 64)

Several important ideas regarding ideology are contained in this passage: ownership of economic power means that one has some control over the production of ideas in a society; the dominant ideas of a society express the economic situation of that society, especially the power relations of that society's economy; and finally, the ideas in dominance exert force against those in a subordinate position in that society. Such ideas, according to Marx, present themselves as "eternal." They thus appear to be incontestable or beyond question. They therefore provide authority to social institutions that are human inventions but that, as a result of ideology, seem unchangeable because "eternal."

As an example, Marx offers the Middle Ages, when the aristocracy ruled economic life. Serfs and peasants did all the agricultural labor, and their product was largely given to a leisure class of people who called themselves "noble" and claimed their blood or genetic inheritance made them superior to serfs. They cultivated a martial lifestyle that allowed them to exercise violence against the peasant class and to keep them

The Encyclopedia of Literary and Cultural Theory   General editor: Michael Ryan
© 2011 Blackwell Publishing Ltd

in a position of subordination. The rule of the aristocracy was supported by ideas and ideals such as honor and loyalty. Loyalty or "fealty" meant that lower "lords" owed service to a regional lord who could call on them for military assistance when needed to promote or defend their shared economic interest and social power. "Honor" mandated that such commitments be respected. Ideas such as "nobility" gave expression to the real material dominance in society of that class of people, and those ideas in turn made the rule of the aristocracy seem eternal and mandated by nature. The legend of Arthur in England, for example, portrays the king and his fellow knights as superior figures who are endowed by some magical force in nature with the right to rule. It was more difficult to challenge the actual rule of leisure-class aristocrats and to contest their monopoly of the society's economic product or wealth if ideas of the kind promoted by the Arthur legend were common in the culture. Ideology is thus an expression of social power as well as a way of defending social power by soft, nonviolent means. Ideology provides those in power with a set of attitudes, such as justified arrogance, that allow them to behave toward those lower in the social hierarchy with condescension and contempt. And ideology instills in those in a subordinate social position attitudes of justified deference that makes them more likely to assume a subordinate or submissive position in relation to their "superiors."

The coming into being of a merchant class in sixteenth- and seventeenth-century England prepared the way for the invention of capitalism in the eighteenth century. The merchants and early capitalists used new ideas such as "liberty" and "equality" to express their economic interests. They wished to be able to trade freely, and the restrictions of the old feudal economy stood in their way. Liberty, a relatively new idea,

allowed them to argue that all members of a society, not just aristocrats, should be free to do what they want, especially economically, without having restrictions put on them by aristocratic monarchies. The idea of equality undercut the aristocratic ideology that claimed blood made some more deserving to rule society. The new idea of rights allowed merchants and capitalists to lay claim to access to political power in the form of representative governmental bodies such as the English Parliament. As the new dominant economic group, the merchants and capitalists expressed their power in new ideas that in turn made their position of dominance seem legitimate, natural, and eternal.

In the United States in recent years, a revived version of this pro-capitalist ideology has become dominant at the same time that a new economic situation has come about that favored the interests of a postindustrial class of primarily finance-based entrepreneurs and investors. This new class of finance capitalists promoted the ideal of "freedom," by which they meant their right to do whatever they wished to increase returns on investment even if that destroyed communities through disinvestment from old industries or undermined nations by seeking cheap labor overseas. "Freedom" expressed their interest in unrestricted economic activity regardless of social or national consequences and effects, and it was an ideological weapon in arguing against the power of governments to restrain and regulate such activities in order to protect the community those governments represented. Using the ideal of freedom, the new class of finance capitalists argued successfully against the restraints that had been placed on economic activity after the Great Depression of the 1930s. The result was a renewal of unrestrained economic and especially financial activity that resulted in the great recession of 2009.

"Ideology" has one additional meaning in literary and cultural theory. Those who are in a subordinate economic position and who have to work for others in order to survive must believe that the economic system is fair and just. For their own psychological survival and well-being, they must see themselves as striving individuals rather than as exploited dupes. To use a contemporary film metaphor, they must remain asleep in the matrix. Ideology in this acceptation is the sense of individual identity that capitalism fosters. People may be part of a homogeneous class of workers and consumers whose activities are guided and regulated by work routines and leisure consumption overseen by advertising and marketing, but for the economic system to operate successfully, they must perceive themselves as "free" individuals. This imaginary sense of identity fuels capitalism and prevents those subordinated in it from perceiving the true state of affairs in which they are trapped.

SEE ALSO: Althusser, Louis; Eagleton, Terry; Marx, Karl; Marxism

REFERENCES AND SUGGESTED READINGS

Althusser, L. (1971). *Lenin and Philosophy and Other Essays*. London: New Left Books.
Marx, K., & Engels, F. (1970). *The German Ideology* (ed. C. J. Arthur). London: Lawrence and Wishart. (Original work published 1845.)

Intertextuality

MARY ORR

"Intertextuality" names a text's relations to other texts in the larger "mosaic" of cultural practices and their expression. An "intertext" is therefore a focalizing point within this network or system, while a text's "intertextual" potential and status are derived from its relations with other texts past, present, and future. Unlike the term "reference," to which it is closely allied, "intertextuality" has no verb form and hence has unlimited powers of designation, but not specification to a particular kind of textual activity (Orr 2003). However, unlike critical terms such as "allusion," "intertextuality" has a specific provenance and date. In her work on the Russian critic and theorist Mikhail Bakhtin, Julia Kristeva described and named the concept of "intertextualité" in a series of essays between 1966 and 1968 published in French in 1969 (as *Semeiotikè: recherches pour une sémanalyse*). While *Semeiotikè* has been translated into English only in part (by L. Roudiez in 1980 and others in Moi 1986), Kristeva's term needed no translation into cognate European tongues sharing Greek and Latin heritages. Its instant and spontaneous success lay in its applicability, to multifarious cultural forms and practices, on the one hand, and, on the other hand, to the cultural sea change post-1968 in notions about language and power, namely that these were decentered and in process rather than being given or fixed. Kristeva's complex and careful redefinitions of Bakhtin's work on "dialogism," "carnival," and "polyphony" as "intertextuality" were thus rapidly re-spun in a plethora of theoretical and applied work on language, cultural practices, and power structures now understood as "the linguistic turn." Roland Barthes, Jacques Derrida, Philippe Sollers, and Michel Foucault all variously inflected and reshaped Kristeva's "intertextuality" by focusing on its core idea, the notion that there is nothing outside of language, and hence of the text.

Since the first wave of its dissemination in French theory and usage as a critical term for the multiple relations between texts

(Riffaterre 1978; Jenny 1982), intertextuality also struck chords with emergent, increasingly politicized voices which had been excluded from dominant intellectual mainstreams. The malleability of "intertextuality" to describe multiple power relations between the text and its worlds thus immediately attracted feminist, gay, and subaltern practitioners and cultural critics for its power to unsettle grand, colonial narratives, and to name cultural blank and nonwhite spaces. Intertextuality as an interplay of coequal texts meant that the marginal spaces in a dominant culture do not exist. The generative potentiality of intertextuality can therefore be seen in the explosion of postcolonial forms of cultural expression in the 1980s, together with the circulation of these "texts" in academe (particularly in the US). Yet the seemingly unstoppable expansions and possibilities of intertextuality were offset by retractions of its use within the heartlands of cultural production and criticism of the 1990s. Eminently catchall to name general relations within networks of texts, the term "intertextuality" dealt with, but could not overtly delineate, specific forms, qualities, or operations of textual cross-reference. It had therefore only limited cultural leverage, as Genette's work of reclassification from the 1970s exemplifies (his "architext," "palimpsest," and "paratext"). His redefinitions of Kristeva's term aside, intertextuality thus everywhere elides meta- and microtextual activity, where definitions and reworking of genres, rhetorical figures, and tropes, for example, do not.

But the retraction of intertextuality was also due to cultural forces of much greater magnitude at work in the 1980s onwards, in particular the development and accessibility of electronic media and their resources. These overtly challenged its core concept, "text," although intertextuality always presumed to encompass non-print "texts," and

forms. Pressures from these new media to decenter the hegemony of print text were in fact replicated by two rival critical theory movements of the 1980s and 1990s. The one offered alternative umbrella terms to intertextuality such as the highly successful notion of "deconstruction" within high theory, or in sociology and linguistics the concept of "interdiscursivity" (Angenot 1983), which recast the impact of oral discourses and popular cultural forms. The other sought sharper terminological precision for intertextuality by redefining its intrinsic principles, taxonomies, and major variants in edited theoretical and applied critical readers (Lachmann 1982; Broich & Pfister 1985; Worton & Still 1990; Plett 1991). Most striking about these was, first, that national European literatures, cultures, and canons were back in force to provide key examples of intertextuality at work. Second, the theories of intertextuality as disseminated in the English language (in parallel with the vocabulary of the internet) were only part of "critical theory" more broadly, mainly undertaken in English departments and through English translations. While not an edited volume, Allen (2000) is indicative. It also marks an important point of no return in critical readers on intertextuality, seeking to clarify and popularize it. Henceforth, the term cannot be regarded as a singular noun, or a concept for a network of texts in all languages. Ordinary users also largely ignore its semiotic thrusts by employing it as an imperfect synonym variously for "allusion," "parody," or "contact point."

In the new millennium, responses to the developments of intertextuality develop these strands of its theoretical displacement. Moves to stricter definition have sought to capture various geographies of intertextual endeavor. For example, Samoyault (2001) focuses on the mnemonic activities of intertextuality in French literature, which reflect upon the space of intertextuality in French cultural memory more generally, whereas Bauman (2004) has pointed up the cross-cultural forces of intertextuality, in particular its folkloric, anthropological, and popular dimensions. Orr (2003) was the first to engage overtly with the specific geographical and historical *contexts* which gave rise not just to a neologism, but Kristeva's invention of the term within Barthes's seminar and the *Tel Quel* circle. As a French- and Russian-speaking Bulgarian émigrée, Kristeva was its privileged non-French and female outsider voice. Juvan (2008) has taken up Orr's cue for others to explore central and eastern European ramifications of Kristeva's term. By returning intertextuality to its Bakhtinian lineages, he qualifies its "citationality." For Juvan, the reader and the text are very far from dead. Intertextuality thus remains a viable term, not only for poetics in countries enriched by being multiethnic, such as his native Slovenia, but also for those seeking to understand wider transnational cultural impacts upon their national literatures.

For others, however, intertextuality has always been one phenomenon among several in the longer history of comparable and contrastive terms. "Influence," "imitation," and "quotation" (as older forms of "contact point," "parody," "allusion") have always been, and remain, motors of the establishment, adaptation, and transformation of cultural forms and practices, with specific vocabularies to match (Orr 2003). In discussing the forms and functions of intertextuality, Broich & Pfister (1985) had already pinpointed its contemporary rivals, including intellectual movements such as "interdisciplinarity," which encapsulate multiple discourses, or networks and mosaics with greater multimedia potential, such as the internet. The fact of new technologies has pressed hardest on the limits of print media, so that "intertextuality" as a term for cross-

and intergeneric cultural operations is now already superseded by its more precise cousin, "intermediality." This describes how cultural productions are facilitated by their (re)interpretation and adaptation in a variety of media including text, performance, the plastic, and the virtual arts (Wagner 1996; Chapple & Kattenbelt 2006; Wolf & Bernhart 2006). In an online journal aptly named *Intermédialités*, which pluralizes the concept from the outset, Kajewsky (2006) elucidates the differences between "intermediality," "intertextuality," and "remediation." Her work is indicative of other studies where literary texts (and intertextuality) are set alongside nonprint media of all kinds, so that "intermediality" emerges as the more effective term for cultural interrelationships in the digital age as a culminating moment for both oral and print text traditions. As against the era of mass media of the fourth estate (the press, TV, radio as inflections of the three feudal estates of the realm, the clergy, the nobility, and the commoners, respectively), however, the fifth estate of information and communication technologies is seen by intellectual historians of postmodernity as a force for action against global corporations. Through strategic electronic networking and the formation of special interest websites, bloggers can enter in unprecedented ways into bottom-up, one-to-global engagements that target initiatives for cultural change and for the accountability of faceless megalopolises (Dutton 2009).

In its 40-year history, intertextuality thus offers a term that perhaps best pinpoints a moment of last resort to name relations between texts, where "text" had not yet taken on its now ubiquitous sense of "text-messaging." In the France of May 1968, Kristeva's intertextuality served the purposes of overturning previous hierarchies of high-cultural understanding by translating and adapting Bakhtinian dialogism and the carnivalesque into an intellectual movement claiming a more democratic face for categories of texts. "Intertextuality," like "intermediality" after it, is only the latest name for "adaptation" and "translation" of ideas and expression, to make sense of contemporary culture. Like the multiform species of nature, culture in all its forms, including the virtual, has constantly adapted to changing climates and conditions for its ongoing existence. As in the past, the protean possibilities for cultural production will continue to depend upon the acts of human engagement and recording. Whether in transient oral and bodily performances (speech, poetry, folk tales, drama, dance), or in material forms that outlive the instance of expression (writing, painting, sculpture, tapestry, architecture, the internet), particular movements will form, develop, and change shape thanks to temporal and spatial possibilities, including contact with neighboring or rival cultural practices and their new media. The practices of renewal, parody, and resistance to censorship that maintain and subvert cultural work cannot be sustained without the newcomer (in time), outsider (in space), or the highly skilled adaptations of the insider to disturb preset orders of things. Intertextuality still has work to do, to recuperate texts forgotten or invisible in the global cultural matrix. If this work depends on digitization of the world's libraries and archives, the remit of intertextuality is guaranteed for at least the next 40 years, but it will probably be known by a different name.

SEE ALSO: Narratology and Structuralism; Structuralism

REFERENCES AND SUGGESTED READINGS

Allen, G. (2000). *Intertextuality*. London: Routledge.

Angenot. M. (1983). Intertextualité, interdiscursivité, discours social. *Texte*, 2, 101–112.

Btauman, R. (2004). *A World in Other's Words: Cross-Cultural Perspectives on Intertextuality*. Malden, MA: Blackwell.

Broich, U., & Pfister, M. (eds.) (1985). *Intertextualität: Formen, Funktionen, anglistische Fallstudien*. Tübingen: Niemeyer.

Chapple, F., & Kattenbelt, C. (eds.) (2006). *Intermediality in Theatre and Performance*. New York: Rodopi.

Dutton, R. (2009). Democracy on the line: The fifth estate? *Oxford Today*, 21, 12–15.

Genette, G. (1992). *The Architext: An Introduction* (trans. J. E. Lewin). Berkeley: University of California Press. (Original work published 1979.)

Genette, G. (1997). *Palimpsests: Literature in the Second Degree* (trans. C. Newman & C. Doubinsky). Lincoln: University of Nebraska Press. (Original work published 1982.)

Genette, G. (1997). *Thresholds of Interpretation* (trans J. E. Lewin). Cambridge: Cambridge University Press. (Original work published 1987.)

Jenny, L. (1982). The strategy of forms (trans. R. Carter). In T. Todorov (ed.), *French Literary Theory Today: A Reader*. Cambridge: Cambridge University Press, pp. 34–64. (Original work published 1976.)

Juvan, M. (2008). *History and Poetics of Intertextuality* (trans. T. Pogačar). West Lafayette, IN: Purdue University Press.

Kajewsky, O. J. (2006). Intermediality, intertextuality and remediation: A literary perspective on intermediality. *Intermédialités: histoire et théorie des arts, des lettres et des techniques*, 6, 43–64.

Kristeva, J. (1969). *Semeiotikè: Recherches pour une sémanalyse*. Paris: Points.

Lachmann, R. (ed.) (1982). *Dialogizität; Theorie und Geschichte der Literatur und der schönen Künste*. Munich: Wilhelm Fink.

Moi, T. (ed.) (1986). *The Kristeva Reader*. Oxford: Blackwell.

Orr, M. (2003). *Intertextuality: Debates and Contexts*. Cambridge: Polity.

Plett, H. E. (ed.) (1991). *Intertextuality*. Berlin: Walter de Gruyter.

Riffaterre, M. (1978). *Semiotics of Poetry*. Bloomington: Indiana University Press.

Samoyault, T. (2001). *Intertextualité: Mémoire de la littérature*. Paris: Hachette.

Wagner, P. (1996). *Icons – Texts – Iconotexts: Essays on Ekphrasis and Intermediality*. Berlin: Walter de Gruyter.

Wolf, W., & Bernhart, W. (eds.) (2006). *Framing Borders in Literature and Other Media*. Amsterdam: Rodopi.

Worton, M., & Still, J. (eds.) (1990). *Intertextuality: Theories and Practices*. London: Routledge.

Irigaray, Luce

REBECCA MUNFORD

Luce Irigaray (b. 1932) is a Belgian-born feminist philosopher and practicing psychoanalyst whose work ranges over the disciplines of philosophy, psychoanalysis, linguistics, social theory, and law. Irigaray has famously eschewed questions about her personal life in order to prevent biographical references from "disrupting" people when they read her work (Amsberg & Steenhuis 1983). This means that biographical information about Irigaray is both limited and difficult to verify. Common accounts convey that she was educated at the University of Louvain and, after teaching for several years in Brussels, moved to France and attended the University of Paris, where she received a Master's in psychology and a diploma in psychopathology. In the 1960s she taught at the University of Vincennes and was a member of L'École Freudienne de Paris, where she trained with the French psychoanalyst Jacques Lacan. From 1964 she worked at the Centre National de Recherche Scientifique, where she later became Director of Research in Philosophy. More recently, Irigaray has been a visiting professor in the School of Modern Languages at the University of Nottingham and the Department of Philosophy at the University of Liverpool.

A persistent thread in Irigaray's work is the relationship between female subjectivity and language, and the marginalization of the feminine in language. One of her most pressing claims is that the logic of Western philosophical thought suppresses sexual difference and excludes women. Her thinking offers a radical challenge to the assumptions underpinning philosophical discourse which, she argues, lays down the law to all the others, because it constitutes the discourse of discourses (1985b[1977]). Challenging Sigmund Freud's thesis that the basis of Western culture lies in an act of patricide, Irigaray (1991a[1981]) argues that the symbolic and social order are founded on an act of matricide. The symbolic murder of the mother silences and marginalizes all women, who are associated with nature and the material body. Irigaray is not just concerned with theorizing language as a site of exclusion and marginalization; her work is also committed to exploring the possibility of an alternative discourse that gives expression to the feminine.

Irigaray's first published work arose from her research in psycholinguistics, the subject of her first doctorate. *Le Langage des dements* [*The Language of Dementia*] (1973) analyses patterns of linguistic disturbance and disintegration in senile dementia. It argues that senile dementia patients are no longer able to use the structures of language creatively to speak as active subjects of enunciation in response to other speakers. Rather, they have a passive relation to language that involves reusing previous enunciations. Although Irigaray was not intentionally exploring differences in the forms of linguistic disintegration experienced by women and men, she found their speech to be impaired in different ways. It is in this respect that her radical theorization of women's language, and investigation into expressions of sex in language, can be seen as emerging from her early work in psycholinguistics.

Irigaray's first major contribution to feminist theory was *Speculum of the Other Woman* (1985[1974]). The publication of this text, Irigaray's second doctorate, led to her being expelled from L'École

Freudienne de Paris and relieved from her teaching position at Vincennes. In her own words, she was "put into quarantine" for her political commitments (see Whitford 1991a; Irigaray 1993b[1990]). That Irigaray's radical challenge to psycho-analytical orthodoxies should be suppressed in this way is all too pertinent. In this highly influential and controversial work, she fore-grounds and critiques the phallocentrism of Western philosophical and psychoanalytical discourses. Here, she exposes and contests Freudian and, implicitly, Lacanian psycho-analysis for assuming that female sexual identity is grounded in either deficiency or lack. Reading backwards from Freud to Plato, she demonstrates how Western thought is based on a logic of sameness and visibility that privileges masculine identity and places woman outside the capacity for representation. She argues that "woman" is envisaged as man's "specularized Other" – as "a lack, an absence, outside the system of representa-tions and autorepresentations . . . a *hole* in men's signifying economy" (1985a: 50). Irigaray's use of the term "speculum" plays on the word's dual signification as a curved mirror and an instrument for examining the female genitals. Like Lacan, Irigaray is con-cerned with the ways in which subjectivity is constructed in language. For her, however, the symbolic (the order of language which constructs our sense of reality and of iden-tity) is masculine language and thought. Anything that falls outside this order cannot be articulated. The intimate and curved mirror of the speculum, which is designed to see inside the body's cavities, highlights the limitations of the Lacanian mirror and promises the possibility of more plentiful reflections on/of female sexual identity.

In *Speculum of the Other Woman*, Irigaray rereads the history of Western philosophy and foregrounds its assumptions and aporia through a mixture of citation and analysis.

In so doing, she deploys a mimetic strategy that is similar to the deconstructive practice of the French philosopher Jacques Derrida. In the first section of the book, entitled "The blindspot of an old dream of symmetry," Irigaray cites extracts from Freud's lecture "On femininity," in which he describes femininity as a "riddle." Her analysis of Freud's argument about the anatomical distinctions between the sexes and the acquisition of gender identity exposes a slippage between visibility and ownership in his description of the little girl's realiza-tion that she is "lacking" a penis. Irigaray argues that Freud's logic fails when he assumes that "*nothing to be seen is equivalent to having nothing*" (Irigaray 1985a: 47–8). The middle section of the book, "Speculum," offers rereadings of several Western philosophers, including Plato, Aristotle, Plotinus, Kant, Hegel, and Der-rida, in relation to "woman." The third section of the book, "Plato's *Hystera*," is a reading of Plato's myth of the cave (and the womb). The structure of the book thus reverses the chronology of these male thin-kers and, in so doing, reflects the upside down image reflected in a speculum (see Moi 1985). *Speculum of the Other Woman* also addresses another recurrent theme in Irigaray's work: the mother–daughter rela-tionship and its impoverished representa-tion in Western culture. Irigaray advocates that reimagining this relationship is vital if women are to create new identities outside male signifying systems.

This Sex Which Is Not One (1985b[1977]) develops some of the arguments, explora-tions, and strategies in *Speculum of the Other Woman*. Here Irigaray discusses mimesis, a strategy that is used in several of her works to challenge traditional structures of discourse and power. She outlines how the unfaithful miming of conventional images of femininity not only reveals that they are constructed and artificial, but also that "if women are such good mimics, it is because they are not simply reabsorbed in this function. *They also remain elsewhere*" (Irigaray 1985b: 76). The idea of multiplicity and difference is a central theme in this work as Irigaray counters the phallocentrism of Freud's accounts of female sexuality by refusing its "logic of sameness." The title of the book playfully references Freudian psychoanalytic understandings of female sexuality and, especially, Freud's view of the little girl child's "castrated" body. On one level it refers to understandings of female sexuality as a negative (as *not* centered on the unitary image of the penis). However, it also brings to the fore an alternative understanding of female sexuality as *more than one* (as made up of various elements). In this interpretation, woman's sex is not *just* one: it is multiple, plural, and heterogeneous. Destabilizing the predominance of the penis as the visual marker of sexual identity in Freudian and Lacanian models, Irigaray emphasizes tactility and an understanding of female sexuality as distributed across multiple erogenous zones (because "*woman has sex organs more or less everywhere*" [1985a: 28]). She uses the motif of "two lips" (with its genital and conversational resonances) to signify the plurality of woman's pleasure and the possibilities of speaking difference rather than sameness. Irigaray is not only concerned with exposing the unitary and exclusive logic of sameness which, she argues, characterizes a particular tradition of thinking, but with exploring (and enacting) an alternative syntax that celebrates sexual difference in language and expresses the feminine in positive terms. This demand for a "feminine syntax" is linked to her conceptualization of "*parler femme*," as a language by, about, and between women.

Another central strand in Irigaray's work is her dialogue with the history of philosophy and its canon of male thinkers. In *An Ethics of Sexual Difference* (1993a[1984]),

for example, Irigaray "mimes" the philosophical discourses of Plato, Descartes, Merleau-Ponty, Spinoza, and Levinas to examine their constructions of the feminine. *The Marine Lover of Friedrich Nietzsche* (1991b[1980]), *Elemental Passions* (1992 [1982]) and *The Forgetting of Air in Martin Heidegger* (1999[1983]) all engage in "amorous dialogues" with male philosophers. These texts use an elemental vocabulary to explore, amongst other things, questions of love, desire, and the repression of the maternal (see Whitford 1991b). The question of sexual difference and the concept of otherness remain consistent preoccupations in Irigaray's work in the 1980s and 1990s, and inform her thinking on subjects such as the divine, civil law, and environmentalism. Some of her more recent work has focused on exploring the possibility of a relationship between two sexed subjects. *Je, Tu, Nous* (1993b[1990]), for example, is a collection of interviews and essays concerned with how "I" and "you" become "we" – a question that is considered in relation to such diverse topics as AIDs, abortion, and the mother–daughter relationship.

While Irigaray is well known for her theorization of women's marginalization from the symbolic order, she is a philosopher who is committed to social and political change. She has been actively involved with the women's movements in France and Italy. In the 1990s, she worked with the Commission for Equal Opportunities for the region of Emilia-Romagna in Italy to advise on promoting training in citizenship. A working collaboration with this Commission underpins her *Democracy Begins Between Two* (2000[1994]), a collection of essays addressing gender and civil identities. *Between East and West* (2002[1999]) examines the yogic tradition in Eastern philosophy as part of a meditation on breathing and sexual difference. Irigaray's most recent work is similarly concerned with questions about human life and experience in contemporary global contexts.

Since 2003, Irigaray has held an annual seminar for graduate researchers undertaking doctoral theses on her work. The dynamic and collaborative model of teaching represented by the seminars underpins her collection, *Luce Irigaray: Teaching* (2008), edited with Mary Green. This collection of 20 essays, including three by Irigaray herself, explores contemporary issues in education centered around five key themes in her work. *Conversations* (2008) is a collection of 10 interviews in which Irigaray meditates on a range of topics, including the Virgin Mary, charges of "essentialism" leveled at her work, architecture, and yoga, and thus represents the variety, creativity, and influence of her contribution to continental philosophy and feminist theory.

SEE ALSO: Derrida, Jacques; Feminism; Freud, Sigmund

REFERENCES AND SUGGESTED READINGS

Amsberg, K., & Steenhuis, A. (1983). Interview with Luce Irigaray. *Hecate*, 9(1/2), 192–202.

Burke, C., Schor, N., & Whitford, M. (eds.) (1994). *Engaging With Irigaray: Feminist Philosophy and Modern European Thought*. New York: Columbia University Press.

Irigaray, L. (1985a). *Speculum of the Other Woman* (trans. G. C. Gill). Ithaca: Cornell University Press. (Original work published 1974.)

Irigaray, L. (1985b). *This Sex Which Is Not One* (trans. C. Porter). Ithaca: Cornell University Press. (Original work published 1977.)

Irigaray, L. (1991a). The bodily encounter with the mother (trans. D. Macey). In. M. Whitford (ed.), *The Irigaray Reader*. Oxford: Blackwell, pp. 34–46. (Original work published 1981.)

Irigaray, L. (1991b). *The Marine Lover of Friedrich Nietzsche* (trans. G. C. Gill). New York: Ciolumbia University Press. (Original work published 1980.)

Irigaray, L. (1992). *Elemental Passions* (trans. J. Collie & J. Still). London: Athlone. (Original work published 1982.)

Irigaray, L. (1993a). *An Ethics of Sexual Difference* (trans. C. Burke & G. C. Gill). London: Athlone. (Original work published 1984.)

Irigaray, L. (1993b). *Je, Tu, Nous: Toward a Culture of Difference* (trans. A. Martin). New York: Routledge. (Original work published 1990.)

Irigaray, L. (1999). *The Forgetting of Air in Martin Heidegger* (trans. M. B. Mader). London: Athone. (Original work published 1983.)

Irigaray, L. (2000). *Democracy Begins Between Two* (trans. K. Anderson). London: Athlone. (Original work published 1994.)

Irigaray, L. (2002). *Between East and West: From Singularity to Community* (trans. S. Pluhácek). New York: Columbia University Press. (Original work published 1999.)

Irigaray, L. (2008). *Conversations*. London: Continuum.

Irigaray, L., & Green, M. (eds.) (2008). *Luce Irigaray: Teaching*. London: Continuum.

Moi, T. (1985). *Sexual/Textual Politics*. London: Routledge.

Stone, A. (2006). *Luce Irigaray and the Philosophy of Sexual Difference*. Cambridge: Cambridge University Press.

Whitford, M. (ed.) (1991a). *The Irigaray Reader*. Oxford: Blackwell.

Whitford, M. (1991b). *Luce Irigaray: Philosophy in the Feminine*. Oxford: Blackwell.

Iser, Wolfgang

JOHN PAUL RIQUELME

Wolfgang Iser (1926–2007), German literary theorist and critic, became influential in the English-speaking world in the 1970s when reader-response criticism emerged as an alternative to New Criticism. He later wrote extensively about creativity and about literature from a philosophical anthropological perspective. As William St Clair (2007) has noted, aspects of Iser's views about the reading process have become so thoroughly absorbed into literary critical thinking attentive to the audience that their origin is often forgotten. In 1981, Stanley Fish pointed out that Iser's *The Implied Reader* and *The Act of Reading*, both available in paperback, were widely studied in graduate courses on literary theory in the 1980s and were the bestselling titles in literary theory from Johns Hopkins University Press, an influential publisher in that field.

Although Iser's focus on the reader was welcomed, especially in North America, as an alternative to the formalist emphasis on the text, on the Continent it provided a way to think about literature that was not oriented toward the author or politics. Like some other English and European literary intellectuals who lived through World War II, Iser eschewed politics and history as determining frames for understanding literature and literature's place in culture. That choice was in itself a political act, since it put him at odds with Marxist literary theory, which was important throughout Europe in the postwar era. He argued that literature provides evidence and an arena for the exercise of human plasticity, a self-transforming capacity within us that we experience when we read literary works. The concern with creative transformation is a main thread connecting his work about the reader to his later speculative writing about the fictive and the imaginary and on to his late interest in the concept of "emergence."

Following the war, during which he had been conscripted, while still in his teens, into the German army, Iser studied literature and philosophy at Leipzig, Tübingen, and Heidelberg, where he earned his doctorate in English literature in 1950. After teaching at various universities in the UK and the Federal Republic of Germany, in 1967 he became one of the founders, along with Hans Robert Jauss, of the program in literary theory (*Literaturwissenschaft*) at the newly established University of Konstanz in Germany near the Swiss border. Iser focused on the reading experience as an act of the mind engaging with the text (*Wirkungstheorie*), while Jauss focused on the reception of literary texts (*Rezeptionstheorie*) – that is, the history of readers' judgments about them. The program soon became well known internationally as the Konstanz School for its innovative approach to literature, which it treated as communication from theoretical perspectives and through institutional groupings. There was no segregation of national literatures into separate departments. Iser taught at Konstanz until 1991. In 1978 he also became a professor of English at the University of California, Irvine, where he taught until 2005.

Iser's work was affected by the hermeneutics of Hans-Georg Gadamer, with whom he studied, but his influential writings concerning the reading process draw significantly on the interpretation by the Polish philosopher, Roman Ingarden, of Edmund Husserl's phenomenology. Iser's investigation of reading does not concern subjective reactions, because phenomenology focuses on mental acts as processes that occur generally, not on the level of personal responses. Iser does not subscribe to the notion of the person assumed by ego psychology, prevalent in North America; nor does he accept Freudian descriptions of the mind. In addition to phenomenology, he draws on diverse lines of thought: art psychology (Rudolph Arnheim, E. H. Gombrich, Anton Ehrenzweig), systems theory (Niklas Luhmann), theories of interpretation (Paul Ricoeur, Clifford Geertz, Franz Rosenzweig), the theory of play (Roger Caillois), and emergence theory in the biological sciences (Francisco Varela), among many others. He draws as well on the work of his older contemporary, the German philosopher Hans Blumenberg, with whom he was closely associated as a founding member of the German research group, Poetik und Hermeneutik, constituted in 1963.

Equally important for placing Iser intellectually are the influences and attitudes that he rejected, often silently, including not only Marxist cultural theory but also the work of Martin Heidegger. Like many German intellectuals of his generation, he resisted Heidegger's influence by ignoring it because of Heidegger's membership in the Nazi Party. Iser read Heidegger only late in his career. This swerve distinguishes him from French theorists, such as Derrida and Lacan, who engaged more directly with Heidegger's writings. Iser's work, however, was, like theirs, poststructuralist in character. He absorbed the concepts and vocabulary of structural linguistics and structuralist work in the human sciences, such as Jean Piaget's psychological investigations. But he used structuralist concepts to describe transformational processes that are structur*ings*, not unchanging, synchronic structures. The emphasis on the reader rather than the author is typical of poststructuralism, as in the writings of Roland Barthes. Iser's emphases on the coexistence of opposites and the emergence of a third element from interacting binaries are also poststructuralist. Non-Marxist (rather than overtly anti-Marxist), unHeideggerian, skeptical about the essentialist tendencies of psychoanalysis and structuralism (but drawing selectively on both), informed about diverse strands of intellectual inquiry, Iser created a distinctive body of writings concerning response, creativity, and interpretation that regularly takes literature as its object and evidence.

Iser's career can be broadly divided into three stages marked by his move to Konstanz and his appointment at Irvine. Having published a book on Henry Fielding (never translated into English) and one on Walter Pater early in his career, by the time he became involved at Konstanz (in 1967), Iser was publishing the theoretical and interpretive essays that brought him to prominence outside Germany. His inaugural lecture at Konstanz in 1969, "Indeterminacy and the reader's response in prose fiction," was soon presented at a meeting of the English Institute in the US, directed by Paul de Man and published in *Aspects of Narrative*, edited by J. Hillis Miller. Iser's claim that "indeterminacy is the fundamental precondition for reader participation" provides the kernel for his books that appeared in English in the 1970s. The chapters of *The Implied Reader* (1974[1972]) range widely across prose narrative in English from Bunyan to Scott and Thackeray to modernist fiction. The chapters on Joyce were particularly influential, suggesting that Iser's theory of reading, with its emphasis on gaps that the reader fills, is well suited for interpreting modernist narrative, which is more dissonant, fragmented, and experimental than realistic writing. The title phrase responds to the term, "the implied author," from Wayne Booth's *The Rhetoric of Fiction*. The last chapter of the book in its English version, "The reading process: A phenomenological approach," is not in the German original. It reprints instead an essay that appeared first in the widely read journal *New Literary History*, with which Iser was associated during the entire period of his teaching in the US. More theoretically focused than the other chapters, this essay moves beyond the indeterminacy essay toward the theoretical model of *The Act of Reading* (1978[1976]). There, and in the essay on the reading process, he distinguishes his approach from the literary phenomenology of Georges Poulet, who understood reading as the author taking over the reader's consciousness. Iser's vision of reading involves instead an active interaction between reader and text that produces the virtual aesthetic object, which is not a wholly subjective creation. Instead, aspects of the text guide what the reader does, but the channeling is not narrowly restrictive because the reader's varying activity is triggered by different kinds of textual gaps. By reacting to those gaps, or areas of indeterminacy (not fully determinate in the text), the reader brings the aesthetic object into being in a sequential process of ongoing adjustments.

Iser's thinking of the middle period takes him to wider frames of reference to develop "literary anthropology" as a way to understand literature's place in culture. *Prospecting* (1989) reprints uncollected essays, including the one on indeterminacy, along with new treatments of representation, not as mimesis but as performance, and of literature as play. This line of theorizing culminates in *The Fictive and the Imaginary* (1993[1991]), a challenging, speculative work about creativity that presents literature as a *staging* of human malleability in which we discover ourselves as "in-between." Iser presents art as a form of "play," an anthropological imperative that differs from its counterpart, "work." Literature, as verbal play, depends on negativity to trigger responses in which we recognize not what we already think we are but something surprising. Fictions actualize and enable human plasticity in response to the limitations that we face, especially our mortality. Iser regularly evokes the protean, the kaleidoscopic, traveling viewpoints, and our ineluctable mortality, so evident in the work of Beckett, who has a central place in the book. Iser's critical studies of *Tristram Shandy* and of Shakespeare during this part of his career develop the relevance to understanding literature of the staging of subjectivity and of roles.

Iser went on to publish books surveying theories of interpretation and presenting literary theory in ways that are accessible to students and that treat the material, and the writers chosen, distinctively. Some of the choices reflect his collaborative work with Israeli colleagues. He was co-director (1988–91) of a German-Israeli project on interpretation and member of the steering committee (1990–6) of the Franz Rosenzweig Research Center at the Hebrew University in Jerusalem. In *How to Do Theory* (2006), where he considers psychoanalysis, Iser treats Jacques Lacan briefly but devotes considerable attention to his contemporary, Anton Ehrenzweig, who fled Austria from the Nazis in 1938. In his synoptic commentary on theories of interpretation in *The Range of Interpretation* (2000), Iser devotes a chapter to Franz Rosenzweig, the German Jewish theologian and philosopher who was Heidegger's contemporary, but mentions Heidegger only in passing. He also considers at length Francisco Varela on biological emergence, as part of his long-term concern with how the new comes into being. In these late works, Iser's theoretical and literary interests continue to intermingle, with appendices focusing on a range of writers – Spenser, Keats, Carlyle, Pater, and T. S. Eliot – as the objects necessary for his speculative thinking to find its specific cultural focus.

SEE ALSO: Authorial Intention; Barthes, Roland; Booth, Wayne; Cultural Anthropology; Derrida, Jacques; Fish, Stanley; Heidegger, Martin; Implied Author/Reader; Hermeneutics; Husserl, Edmund; Ingarden, Roman; Lacan, Jacques; Marxism; Miller, J. Hillis; Narrative Theory; Pater, Walter; Phenomenology; Poulet, Georges; Reader- Response Studies; Structuralism; Poststructuralism

REFERENCES AND SUGGESTED READINGS

Armstrong, P. (2005). *Play and the Politics of Reading: The Social Uses of Modernist Form.* Ithaca: Cornell University Press.

Cohen, R. (ed.) (2000). On the writings of Wolfgang Iser. *New Literary History*, 31(1).

Freund, E. (1987). *The Return of the Reader: Reader-Response Criticism.* London: Methuen.

Hamilton, Cr. A., & Schneider, R. (2002). From Iser to Turner and beyond: Reception theory meets cognitive criticism. *Style*, 36, 640–658.

Holub, R. C. (1984). *Reception Theory: A Critical Introduction.* London: Methuen.

Iser, W. (1960). *Walter Pater: The Aesthetic Moment.* Cambridge: Cambridge University Press.

Iser, W. (1970). Indeterminacy and the reader's response in prose fiction. In J. Hillis Miller (ed.), *Aspects of Narrative*. New York: Columbia University Press, pp. 1–45.

Iser, W. (1972). The reading process: A phenomenological approach. *New Literary History*, 3, 279–299.

Iser, W. (1974). *The Implied Reader: Patterns of Communication In Prose Fiction from Bunyan to Beckett.* Baltimore: Johns Hopkins University Press. (Original work published 1972.)

Iser, W. (1978). *The Act of Reading: A Theory of Aesthetic Response.* Baltimore: Johns Hopkins University Press. (Original work published 1976.)

Iser, W. (1988a). *Laurence Sterne: Tristram Shandy* (trans. D. H. Wilson). Cambridge: Cambridge University Press.

Iser, W. (1988b). *Staging Politics: The Lasting Impact of Shakespeare's Histories* (trans. D. H. Wilson). New York: Columbia University Press.

Iser, W. (1989). *Prospecting: From Reader Response to Literary Anthropology.* Baltimore: Johns Hopkins University Press.

Iser, W. (1993). *The Fictive and the Imaginary: Charting Literary Anthropology.* Baltimore: Johns Hopkins University Press. (Original work published 1991.)

Iser, W. (2000). *The Range of Interpretation.* New York: Columbia University Press.

Iser, W. (2006). *How to Do Theory.* Oxford: Blackwell.

Shaffer, E., & Brady, A. (2004). The Act of Reading and After: The Reception of Wolfgang Iser in Britain. *Comparative Critical Studies*, 1, 1–168. (Includes a curriculum vitae and publications list.)

St Clair, W. (2007). Professor Wolfgang Iser: Radical literary theorist. At: www.independent.co.uk/news/obituaries/professor-wolfgang-iser-435322.html (accessed April 27, 2010).

Yeghiayan, E. (n.d.). Works by Wolfgang Iser: A bibliography. At: www.lib.uci.edu/about/publications/wellek/iser/ (accessed April 27, 2010).

J

Jameson, Fredric

ADAM ROBERTS

Fredric Jameson (b. 1934) is an American literary and cultural critic, and is currently William A. Lane Professor in Literature and Romance Studies at Duke University. His body of publications is notably, even prodigiously, diverse; however, his wider influence has mostly been felt in two areas. One is as one of America's most prominent Marxist thinkers; the other is as one of the defining voices in 1980s and 1990s debates about "postmodernism."

Jameson's earliest works, while not without value in themselves, are in retrospect way stations on the road to his mature approach. His first book *Sartre: The Origins of a Style* (1961) was developed from his PhD thesis and explores the role that literary style, and literary form more generally, play in the ideological and social dimension of the text. *Marxism and Form* (1971) is in part a record of Jameson's extensive readings into traditions of European Marxist philosophy, something that by the 1970s had come to shape Jameson's own theoretical perspective. *The Prison-House of Language* (1972) enabled Jameson to interrogate the tenets of structuralism just as the then-emergent debates around poststructuralism and deconstruction (which, of course, also engaged or critiqued structuralist thought)

came to prominence. The emphasis on form and formalism, combined with a reading of literature, and more widely culture as a whole, in the context of a Marxist understanding of "history," is at the heart of Jameson's work.

All these intellectual traditions informed his first major contribution to critical thought: *The Political Unconscious* (1981). This combined Marxist, formalist, and psychoanalytic criticism with a nascent sense of the reaction against the rigidities of structuralism that was also shaping the 1980s developments in deconstruction. *The Political Unconscious* is a reading of the development of particular sorts of prose fiction, tracing the way romance and fantastic prose paradigms shifted under the logic of emergent modernism, through novels by Balzac, Gissing, and Conrad. Jameson argues that the form and style of these important texts articulate the stresses of capitalist modernity; that literature functions in effect symptomatically as expressions of larger social, political, and ideological stresses. As a Marxist he does not believe art can be separated out into an ideologically neutral "aesthetic" zone; but, more than this, he holds that a critic needs to do more than simply relate the *content* of (for instance) novels to the political realities of life; he or she needs to explore the ways in which the forms, styles, and cultural coding

The Encyclopedia of Literary and Cultural Theory   General editor: Michael Ryan
© 2011 Blackwell Publishing Ltd

of texts themselves articulate their ideological ground.

Despite the book's title, and although some critics have sometimes taken it this way, *The Political Unconscious* is not a naive welding together of Marx and Freud; nor is it an attempt to psychoanalyze politics. What particularly interests Jameson about Freud's notion of the unconscious is its mechanism of repression; for on a larger scale he finds cultural repressions, blind spots, and traumatic symptoms everywhere in art. Indeed, one of its strengths is its exploration of the extent to which individuality, the personal subjectivity with which we are all familiar, and which forms the topic of so much fiction, functions precisely in terms of its alienation from collective social praxis.

The key to this is history. For Jameson, criticism is blind if not informed with a proper historical sense. Ian Buchanan puts it well: "always historicize!" (the slogan with which *The Political Unconscious* opens) "means something rather more than simply reading texts in their historical context," despite the fact that "this is very often how it is understood" (2007: 55). Jameson's project is not the subject-centered restoration of a historical "context" to any given literary work, but rather, in Buchanan's words, "an object-centred view of history," in which it is history itself that is placed center-stage, the Other that inevitably defines all textual practice.

Interests in science fiction and utopian writing run right through Jameson's career. His essay on the logic of utopian representation, "Of islands and trenches" (collected in *The Ideologies of Theory* [1988]), has been particularly influential, with its argument that utopian texts incorporate a foundational severing from the rest of the world – a trench dug or an island location – which in turn means that "utopia" as a mode is determined by its

separation from conventional political interaction. Some of Jameson's most insightful essays have covered writers such as Philip K. Dick and Ursula Le Guin; many of the best are collected in *Archaeologies of the Future* (2005).

Jameson argues that "the dialectic is not a thing of the past, but rather a speculative account of some thinking of the future which has not yet been realised ... a way of grasping situations and events that does not yet exist as a collective habit because the concrete form of social life to which it corresponds has not yet come into being" (1998: 359). Jameson thus suggests that one mission of Marxist criticism is "to explain and to popularise the Marxist intellectual tradition," to secure "the legitimation of the discourses of socialism in such a way that they do become realistic and serious alternatives for people" (1988: xxvi).

Jameson's cultural critique is an interrogation of what he calls "late capitalism," borrowing the term from Marxist philosopher Enrst Mandel. Marx argued that the conflict inherent in capitalism would inevitably bring about its destruction; and the persistence, and indeed global dominance, of capitalism, might be thought to contradict this view. Mandel refined Marx's analysis into a three-part narrative: first, market capitalism, which dominated the West in the 1800s and early 1900s evolved at the end of the nineteenth century, into, second, monopoly capitalism, which was characterized by the quasi-imperial domination by capital of international markets. The third phase, late capitalism, is taken by Mandel (and Jameson) as beginning after World War II, and witnesses the complete interpenetration of global culture by the logic of capitalism: multinational companies, mass consumption, and the commodification of culture – the features of what is now often called "globalization."

Jameson's particular kind of Marxist analysis is less concerned with "surface" diagnosis of the ills of society (although he does, of course, engage with these), and more interested in the dialectical method, and the force with which a properly Marxist analysis can unearth otherwise buried features of culture.

This is the case in *Postmodernism, or, The Cultural Logic of Late Capitalism* (1991), which describes "the prodigious expansion of culture throughout the social realm," such that "everything in our social life – from economic value and state power to practices and to the very structure of the psyche itself can be said to have become 'cultural' in some original and as yet untheorized sense" (48).

It is this that Jameson calls "postmodernism"; and the various and often enormously influential concepts that he identifies as characteristic of this cultural logic – the flattening of "affect" or emotional resonance; the dominance of irony; the replacement of grounded "parody" by a flat, depthless, promiscuous "pastiche"; the interpenetration of "high" and "popular" culture, and especially erasure of historical perspective – are actually precisely attempts to theorize this logic. Jameson also ascribes to contemporary postmodern culture a "skepticism towards metanarratives"; which is to say, a sense that in contemporary culture the grand stories that used to structure existence (humanism, scientific progress, and so on; "metanarrative" means roughly "stories about stories") have crumbled away, and moreover that we now, generally speaking, no longer believe any such single overarching narrative.

Postmodernism is also characterized by the disorientations of contemporary urban space (most famously, an account of the postmodern architectural logic of the Bonaventura Hotel in Los Angeles). Jameson sees postmodern culture as neither "immoral, frivolous or reprehensible because of its lack of high seriousness, nor as good in the McLuhanist, celebratory sense of the emergence of some wonderful new utopia" (Stephanson 1986–7: 70).

SEE ALSO: Ideology; Marxism; Postmodernism

REFERENCES AND SUGGESTED READINGS

Buchanan, I. (2007). *Fredric Jameson: Live Theory*. London: Continuum.

Jameson, F. (1961). *Sartre: The Origins of a Style*. New Haven: Yale University Press.

Jameson, F. (1971). *Marxism and Form: Twentieth Century Dialectical Theories of Literature*. Princeton: Princeton University Press.

Jameson, F. (1972). *The Prison-House of Language: A Critical Account of Structuralism and Russian Formalism*. Princeton: Princeton University Press.

Jameson, F. (1981). *The Political Unconscious: Narrative as a Socially Symbolic Act*. Ithaca: Cornell University Press.

Jameson, F. (1988). *The Ideologies of Theory: Essays 1971–1986*. Vol. 1: *Situations of Theory*. Minneapolis: University of Minnesota Press.

Jameson, F. (1991). *Postmodernism, or, The Cultural Logic of Late Capitalism*. Durham, NC: Duke University Press.

Jameson, F. (1992). *The Geopolitical Aesthetic: Cinema and Space in the World System*. Bloomington: Indiana University Press.

Jameson, F. (1998). Persistencies of the dialectic: Three sites. *Science and Society*, 62(3), 358–372.

Jameson, F. (2005). *Archaeologies of the Future: The Desire Called Utopia and Other Science Fictions*. London: Verso.

Sedgwick, E. K. (2004). *Touching Feeling: Affect, Pedagogy, Performativity*. Durham, NC: Duke University Press.

Simons, J. (2004). *Contemporary Critical Theorists from Lacan to Said*. Edinburgh: Edinburgh University Press.

Stephanson, A. (1986–7). Interview with Fredric Jameson. *Flash Art*, 131(Dec./Jan.), 69–73.

Johnson, Barbara

ALLISON WEINER

Barbara Johnson (1947–2009) was an American literary critic known for her exemplary deconstructive readings that engage textually and politically with feminism, psychoanalysis, legal theory, and race. Her astute translation of Jacques Derrida's *Dissemination* allowed English audiences access to some of the French philosopher's most significant essays. She was Professor of English and Comparative Literature and the Frederic Wertham Professor of Law and Psychiatry in Society at Harvard University, having previously taught at Yale University.

Johnson received her undergraduate degree from Oberlin College in 1969, and then pursued a doctorate in French at Yale, where she encountered the theory and practice of deconstruction, particularly under the mentorship of Paul de Man. She received her PhD in 1977, though the work of deconstruction that she began at Yale would continue to occupy her intellectual projects in the decades to come.

Johnson's first book, *The Critical Difference* (1980), offers a series of judicious and meticulous readings of European and American texts which radically alter our understanding of the traditional logic of binary oppositions. Instead, she writes, "the differences *between* entities (prose and poetry, man and woman, literature and theory, guilt and innocence) are shown to be based on a repression of differences *within* entities, ways in which an entity differs from itself" (x–xi). In her widely taught essay, "Melville's fist: The execution of *Billy Budd*," Johnson performatively shows how "gaps in cognition" work not to erase meaning from action, but to complicate our understanding of it. Discrepancies between the characters of Billy Budd and John Claggart, knowing and doing, and

intention and meaning are shown not to ensure strict binaries between opposites, but function as differences that subtly take shape within each concept, such that no word or deed can ever really hit its intended target, as Billy Budd would seem to suggest otherwise. Ultimately we must recognize that we are left not with a choice of "between" or "within," but with the way in which a relation of the two marks the spaces of multiplicity. Johnson thus complicates traditional understandings of justice and politics, but in turning away from the "limits" of interpretation, she opens the possibility for each.

A World of Difference (1987) goes yet one step further, asking if the idea of difference may be taken "out of the realm of linguistic universality or deconstructive allegory and into contexts in which difference is very much at issue in the 'real world'" (2). That Johnson retains quotation marks around the phrase "real world," however, shows that the very possibility of going *beyond* the text has to do with the way in which worldly institutions are as much structured by fallacies and fictions as the language and texts which shape them. But questions about different kinds of difference must be asked nonetheless. She writes: "It was when I realized that my discussion of such differences was taking place entirely within the sameness of the white male Euro-American literary, philosophical, psychoanalytical, and critical canon that I began to ask myself what differences I was really talking about" (2). Thinking from within and between the margins of the textual and the political, Johnson moves deftly from discussions of gender in the Yale School, to figurations of sexuality in Zora Neale Hurston, to the relationship of rhetoric, motherhood, and the lyric, constantly reworking traditional logic to address possibilities of otherness.

Johnson's concern about the "referential validity" of deconstruction at work in the world coincided with de Man's death and the contentious aftermath of the discovery of his early journalism. Johnson responds by showing that the ethical potential of deconstruction is not to dwell on the difficult referentiality of language, but to try to understand its implications for thinking through injustice and political oppression when legal and governmental institutions are similarly marked by a repression of differences at work within. Deconstruction, for Johnson, is not about the impossibility of participating in the world, but about participating differently. The two essays which comprise *The Wake of Deconstruction* (1994), "Double mourning and the public sphere" and "Women and allegory," continue to address these very concerns. The former considers the way in which deconstruction's deferral of meaning brings forth not a denial of interpretation, but an "affirmation" of meaning, an increase in its very possibilities. It is this "struggle" that we are left with in the "wake" of deconstruction, and it is our task to meet it exigently.

The *Feminist Difference* (1998) and *Mother Tongues* (2003) take up this struggle in readings of psychoanalysis, gender, race, and sexuality. In her last work, *Persons and Things* (2008), Johnson is concerned not so much with the post-Enlightenment task of separating a "person" from a "thing," but with thinking through differentiations of a "non-person" from a "thing," and crucially, how "persons" might ultimately treat other entities as "persons." From Shakespeare to Barbie dolls and Kant to artificial intelligence, Johnson considers definitions of slavery, abortion, and corporations in order to understand how it is we might recognize the difference, and personhood, of others.

SEE ALSO: Deconstruction; Derrida, Jacques; Feminist Theory; de Man, Paul; Psychoanalysis (since 1966)

REFERENCES AND SUGGESTED READINGS

Derrida, J. (1981). *Dissemination* (trans. and ed. B. Johnson). Chicago: University of Chicago Press. (Original work published 1972.)

Johnson, B. (1979). *Défigurations du langage poétique: La seconde revolution Baudelairienne*. Paris: Flammarion.

Johnson, B. (1980). *The Critical Difference: Essays in the Contemporary Rhetoric of Reading*. Baltimore: Johns Hopkins University Press.

Johnson, B. (1987). *A World of Difference*. Baltimore: Johns Hopkins University Press.

Johnson, B. (1990). Writing. In F. Lentricchia & T. McLaughlin (eds.), *Critical Terms for Literary Study*. Chicago: University of Chicago Press.

Johnson, B. (1994). *The Wake of Deconstruction*. Oxford: Blackwell.

Johnson, B. (1998). *The Feminist Difference: Literature, Psychoanalysis, Race and Gender*. Cambridge, MA: Harvard University Press.

Johnson, B. (2003). *Mother Tongues: Sexuality, Trials, Motherhood, Translation*. Cambridge, MA: Harvard University Press.

Johnson, B. (2008). *Persons and Things*. Cambridge, MA: Harvard University Press.

Johnson, B. (in press). *Moses and Multiculturalism*. Cambridge, MA: Harvard University Press.

K

Kermode, Frank

ROBERT EAGLESTONE

Frank Kermode was an English literary critic. Born in 1919 on the Isle of Man, he taught at Reading, Newcastle, Manchester, Bristol, University College London and Cambridge, where he was King Edward VII Professor of English. Knighted in 1991, he died in 2010.

While Kermode practiced a distinct form of literary criticism, philosophically and theoretically informed, it is hard to pin this down to a school or single set of ideas. On the one hand, Kermode was a crucial institutional influence in introducing "literary theory" to Britain and to the Anglophone world, through a now famous seminar series he ran in London and as editor of the Modern Masters series which introduced many key theoretical figures in accessible ways: on the other, he was critical of the "excesses" of much French theory. Again, while Kermode's work is critical of highly politicized readings of literature, it is not formalist or overly scholastic. Moreover, Kermode's criticism covers the whole span of English literature, from work on *Beowulf* and its translations, an early study of Wallace Stevens (whose poetry and thought remained a touchtone for Kermode) to books on and an edition of Shakespeare, to work on contemporary fiction.

However, perhaps what characterizes Kermode's work most of all, and makes it "theoretical" in the largest sense, is a sense of the difficulty involved in reading and understanding literature. Kermode's work does not evade the problems of hermeneutics, that is, the problems raised by the very nature of interpretation. Instead, it explores them not, usually, in the abstract – as some theorists do – but in relation to a very wide selection of literary and nonliterary works (with Robert Alter, for example, he helped pioneer approaching the Christian Bible as a literary text). Influenced by work in theological and philosophical studies of interpretation, Kermode suggests that our readings of texts are much more complex affairs than we usually allow. For example, he argues that in encountering a literary text, we are immediately distracted from literal interpretations by the "inherent proclivity of the mind for metaphor; the pressure exerted by context . . . ; and the pressure of authoritative institutions of interpretation" (Alter 1992: 88). That is to say that our senses of metaphor and ways of finding similarities, which are often quite random in relation to the texts we read but are inextricably part of our interpretative process, influence how we understand texts. How we see "the relation of any given moment in a text to the texts that immediately and proximately surround it"

The Encyclopedia of Literary and Cultural Theory   General editor: Michael Ryan
© 2011 Blackwell Publishing Ltd

(Alter 1992: 88) also shapes how we understand both that text and the larger text of which is is it a part. And, finally, because interpreters "usually belong to an institution, such as a guild" (or, one might add, a university, newspaper, or website) they are led, sometimes consciously, sometimes unconsciously, into following received (and authoritative) interpretations of texts. These factors, which are implicit in any act of interpretation, shape how we come to understand literary texts.

Because of this, too, Kermode's work is concerned by the relationship between fictions (in the widest sense, including poetry) and reality. He argued that our understanding of the past, and of the world, are intertwined with the same forces that shape our interpretation of fictions. For Kermode, our making sense of reality is both shaped by and shapes our interpretations of fictions: yet our interpretation of fictions is itself a shaping force. He wrote: "World and book ... are hopelessly plural, endlessly disappointing; we stand alone before them, aware of their arbitrariness and impenetrability, knowing that they may be narratives only because of our impudent intervention, and susceptible of interpretation only because of our hermetic tricks" (145).

Kermode's concern with interpretation coincided with his interest in literary value and the canon. While well aware of the nonliterary forces that make texts "canonical," Kermode was also clear that there is such a thing as literary value, even if it is impossible to define.

These ideas come together in perhaps his most famous book, *The Sense of an Ending: Studies in the Theory of Fiction*, which aims to outline a general theory of fictions, with a central interest in the issue of closure, the way in which fictions end. Beginning by examining fictions and beliefs about eschatology (the end of the world), he suggests that these are our own fears of death writ large, and that – just as we make up stories about the apocalypse – so we use fiction to make sense of our own lives and deaths. We need "fictive concords with origins and ends, such as give meaning to lives and to poems" (1966: 7). With this idea in mind, he goes on to distinguish between "chronos," the mere passing of time, and "kairos," moments of time that make up decision and are existentially significant. The book then turns to modernism, and argues that it represents a new version of fictionalized apocalyptic time.

Frank Kermode wrote that it is "not expected of critics as it is of poets that they should help us to make sense of our lives; they are bound only to the attempt the lesser feat of making sense of the ways in which we try to make sense of our lives" (1966: 3). Although this sounds typically self-abnegating – criticism as the handmaid of literature – on reflection, it can be seen another way: making sense of how we make sense is, after all, the task of reason.

Although Kermode founded no school or theoretical movement, his careful reading and judgment, and his role as a teacher, have been highly influential on a leading generation of British critics. His work is clearly an influence on Jacqueline Rose, and more recently this influence can be seen in critics like Mark Currie.

SEE ALSO: Narratology and Structuralism; Rose, Jacqueline

REFERENCES AND SUGGESTED READINGS

Alter, R. (1992). *The World of Biblical Literature.* London: HarperCollins.
Currie, M. (2007). *About Time: Narrative, Fiction and the Philosophy of Time.* Edinburgh: Edinburgh University Press.

Kermode, F. (1966). *The Sense of an Ending: Studies in the Theory of Fiction*. Oxford: Oxford University Press.

Kermode, F. (1979). *The Genesis of Secrecy: On the Interpretation of Narrative*. Cambridge, MA: Harvard University Press.

Kristeva, Julia

SHAHIDHA BARI

One of few women working in modern Continental philosophy, Julia Kristeva is a significant contributor to poststructuralist, psychoanalytical, and feminist thought. Born in Bulgaria in 1941, Kristeva completed her doctoral thesis in Paris and established a career as an eminent writer, theorist, and literary critic in France and abroad. Her doctoral thesis was published as *The Revolution in Poetic Language* in 1974 and secured her a chair in linguistics at Paris Diderot University. She is married to the French novelist and critic Philippe Sollers, and was a contributor to *Tel Quel*, a journal for avant-garde literary-philosophical thought, published by Editions du Seuil in Paris between 1960 and 1982. Fellow contributors included Roland Barthes and Michel Foucault. Kristeva's early work for the journal indicate her particular interests in semiotics, language, and linguistics, and demonstrate the strong psychoanalytical influences that later prompted her to train as an analyst. She was made a Chevalière de la légion d'honneur in 1997.

Kristeva's writing is notable for yielding terms that have since been absorbed into the collective vocabulary of critical theory, such as "abjection." Her work is characterized by an ability to adopt and revise psychoanalytical terms in the service of structural and linguistic analysis. This analysis has extended from literature and language to issues of racial and sexual difference. Kristeva's early work sought to restore the body and psychic life to structuralist theories of language.

Revising Lacanian terms of analysis, Kristeva posited an idea of "semiotic" experience prior to Lacan's "symbolic" order of language, referring to the extralinguistic bodily desires and psychic drives which emerge in language through indicators like rhythm, tone, metaphor, and figure. For Kristeva, as for Lacan, collective social life is conducted through the symbolic order of language, which is rigid, strictly coherent, and authoritative. Kristeva notes that while language asserts the law of the father and is thereby coded as masculine, the semiotic is resolutely feminine and associated with maternal attachment. Infant induction into the symbolic realm of language is dependent on the suppression of the semiotic and entails a rejection of the mother. In her later work, Kristeva explores how the linguistically coherent subject is constituted by the "abjection" of this original maternal relationship, theorizing that the subsequent sexual discrimination and oppression of women both derives from and repeats this original abjection.

Kristeva observes that structuralist theories of language operate in a realm of signs without bodies, and she seeks to rectify this by positing an embodied subject that is prior to language and capable of infiltrating it. The preverbal semiotic is an attempt to reconnect the body and its drives with language, thereby disrupting the symbolic system of orderly referential signs. If symbolic language gives coherent expression to consciousness, the semiotic might, by contrast, betray the unconscious, through more unruly or illogical expression. Here, Kristeva fuses Lacanian terms with Freudian drives. The semiotic offers the articulation of unconscious processes and unspoken desires, threatening to throw the orderly logic of the symbolic into disarray. Importantly, the body that is coextensive with language is capable of penetrating the illusion of authority that the symbolic maintains, and so retains the possibility of expressing radical dissent. In recalling the corporeality of speech, Kristeva observes how symbolic identifications are derived from the body. In *Powers of Horror* (1982) and *Black Sun* (1989) she explores the particular implications for the female body and its maternal identifications.

Maternity and infancy are topics to which Kristeva returns and which reveal her psychoanalytical debt to Melanie Klein. Infant echolalia she cites as an example of a semiotic, preverbal expression of demands and drives that are subsequently repressed with the development of formal language. Kristeva draws a parallel between the language acquisition of children and the prosodic forms of poetry, since both present language forms that are infused by psychic drives and bodily desires. For Kristeva, both the preverbal child and the poet offer semiotic expressions that derail symbolic order, engaging in imaginative and radical practices that contest the coherent authority of language. Poetry is particularly capable of semiotic signification, insofar as the creative manipulations of tone, pitch, cadence, rhythm, and metaphor express the unconscious. Poetry that is capable of subtle ambiguities, obscurities, and illogicality emblematizes the radically disruptive and transformative possibilities of the semiotic which challenges the rule-governed and syntaxed realm of symbolic language. Kristeva recognizes literature as a privileged place for the elaboration and disruption of meaning, and avant-garde art as a site of radical critique. Kristeva aligns semiotic expression to anti-authoritarianism, pitching a creative femininity against the rigid masculinity of the symbolic. She notes that in language the desirous semiotic is not separable from the orderly symbolic, and so discourse is neither purely masculine nor feminine but combined in complex identifications.

In her examination of female identification in particular, Kristeva interrogates the limited symbolic understanding of women and their sexual identities, observing how the discourse of maternity in the West elides women with their biological function. In *Powers of Horror*, Kristeva focuses on the complex mother–infant relationship, modifying the program of infant development delineated by Lacan where the mother–child mirror stage of ego identification ends with the child's severance from the mother and a lasting experience of lack. Breaking with Lacan, Kristeva depicts a pre-mirror stage and considers the implications of the infant's rejection from the mother's perspective. This "abjection," which refers to the negative reaction by which a subject severs themselves from an object with which they were in contact, is critical in the formation of infant identity. It entails an affective repulsion registered bodily; Kristeva offers as a memorable likeness the example of the skin of milk that is distasteful to contact with lips. Where Lacan specifies that the child's entry into language constitutes an accession to the law of the father, Kristeva notes that this moment is prefaced by the rejection of the mother. This abject mother, positioned as the inverse of the ideal father, is subject to a violently felt severance. Pregnancy itself, in which mother and child are bound and then severed, prefigures this abjection and preempts the symbolic interruption of a pre-Oedipal unity. Although, the mother's breast continues to exercise temporary maternal regulation, the pre-Oedipal child is en route to language and the law of the father which necessarily entails the supplanting of the mother. Kristeva observes that the primary identification engendered by a child's fantasy of a father initiates an ongoing symbolic logic of identity that requires the suppression of the semiotic order of body and drives, and the abjection of the maternal body.

The child struggling in its transition from dependence on a maternal body to independence finds the mother endangering the boundaries it seeks to delineate. The maternal separation they initiate leads either to hatred or withdrawal, and the maternal function never recovers from this abjection.

Although the maternal function leaves women abject, Kristeva notes that it also endows them with the radical potential of the semiotic body. The reproductive mother is the guarantor of social order in her generative capacity, and also presents its challenge as an affective and psychic body beyond the constraints of symbolic inscription. Although the child's original maternal-semiotic identification is supplanted by its entrance into a paternal-symbolic order of language, it is the maternal body which generates and continues to challenge that symbolic order. In *Black Sun* Kristeva connects female depression with the subjection of female sexuality which is reduced to maternity and permitted only a minimal position in the discourse of a limited symbolic order. The development from mother–child identification to father identification enjoins the child to accede to the laws of the father, which includes normative heterosexuality, and female sexuality is reduced to an especially limited register. Observing how the experience of maternal abjection limits and prescribes female identity to what is normative to sociocultural contexts and often contrary to desire, Kristeva explores whether female sexuality might be represented differently. In the limited register of a symbolic order, women are marginalized and unrepresented, but Kristeva notes that this marginality might itself offer resources for new imaginative identifications.

Kristeva discovers a creatively radical semiotic promise in marginalized female identity, but feminist thinkers rebuke her analysis since it connects femininity to transgression. They accuse her of reinscribing biological specifications of femininity in her analysis of maternity. While Kristeva sees the semiotic and symbolic orders of language as promisingly dialectical, to others her analysis is limitedly dualist. Kristeva herself is critical of feminism that pursues imitative phallic power, arguing instead for representations of difference that might transform the logic of the symbolic. Her feminism seeks to question the existing terms of analysis and to devise new terms that might bring to language the desire and drives of a semiotic body. Reflexively, she considers how women's contribution to the humanities in the twentieth century might itself pose a challenge to their identification in a symbolic order in which they are secondary. Her conception of a political imagination enabled by its excluded femininity indicates her optimism for critical work that takes place in a linguistic order that might also be capable of proliferating heterogeneity.

Kristeva's conception of heterogeneity broadens in her work on national and racial difference. In *Strangers to Ourselves* (1994) she observes that both woman and foreigner are compelled to identify within the linguistic terms of the culture in which they exist, but neither can overcome the estrangement of their inalienable difference. Kristeva registers this twofold estrangement (gender and nationality) personally as a Bulgarian-born academic, French and female, owning to another mother tongue in the masculine order of a "master" discipline. She suggests that hostility to otherness derives from a refusal to recognize one's own strangeness, and is symptomatic of a compulsive commitment to a coherent symbolic order that is resistant to difference. Accepting the strange other enjoins one to recognize and integrate the strangeness one might find in oneself, just as an acknowledgment of this individual otherness might exercise a capacity to relate to different others. The "foreigner" who neither wishes for nor is capable of integration offers a new form of individualism, asserting an exilic logic beyond the limits of symbolic identification: belonging to nothing and to no law, they circumvent the law and posit themselves as a new law. In this regard, the stranger's radical stance reflects the native's own desire to circumvent the limit of law. For Kristeva, this heterogeneity is the principle of a universal republic whose diversity defends against any absolute monarchic principle. The incorporation of the stranger follows the example of the Freudian unconscious which betrays to the subject its own barely discernable strangeness. The subject that can incorporate the foreigner recognizes their own foreignness and together they form a paradoxical community of foreigners reconciled to their otherness. For Kristeva, the otherness of the stranger is unraveled in one's own estranged psyche. Psychoanalysis that ventures into the strangeness of one's self cultivates an ethics of respect for the irreconcilable. Femininity and foreignness are connected in Kristeva's conception of a heterogeneous production of difference which develops new versions of womanhood and nationality.

For Kristeva, dissidence is the function of the intellectual in political life. In her early essay "A new type of intellectual: The dissident" (1986[1977]) she identifies three types: first, the rebel who attacks political power; second, the psychoanalyst, capable of transforming the dialectic of law and desire into a productive discursive contest; and last, the writer who experiments with the limits of identity and whose creative language might overturn, puncture, and proliferate ideas of normativity. Kristeva unites those rebellious, psychoanalytical, and writerly functions in her own work, adopting a critical approach to conceptions of sexual, racial, national, and linguistic identity. Language remains, for Kristeva, the means of articulating the diversity of identifications that are otherwise unnamed, unrepresented, or denied.

SEE ALSO: Barthes, Roland; Foucault, Michel; Freud, Sigmund; Klein, Melanie; Lacan, Jacques

REFERENCES AND SUGGESTED READINGS

Kristeva, J. (1982). *Powers of Horror* (trans. L. Roudiez). New York: Columbia University Press.

Kristeva, J. (1984). *Revolution in Poetic Language* (trans. M. Waller). New York: Columbia University Press. (Original work published 1974.)

Kristeva, J. (1986). A new type of intellectual: The dissident. In T. Moi (ed.), *The Kristeva Reader*. New York: Columbia University Press. (Original work published 1977.)

Kristeva, J. (1989). *Black Sun* (trans. L. Roudiez). New York: Columbia University Press.

Kristeva, J. (1994). *Strangers to Ourselves* (trans. L. Roudiez). New York: Columbia University Press.

Lacan, J. (1977). *Ecrits: A Selection* (trans. A. Sheridan). London: Routledge.

L

Laclau, Ernesto and Mouffe, Chantal

ANDREW CLARK

In 1985 the publication of *Hegemony and Socialist Strategy: Towards a Radical Democratic Politics* turned socialist theory into a new direction. Its authors, Ernesto Laclau (b. 1935 in Buenos Aires, Argentina) and Chantal Mouffe (b. 1943 in Charleroi, Belgium), open their book by referring to the "crossroads" of the contemporary Left: "Left-wing thought today stands at a cross-roads" (2001[1985]: 1). At stake in their work is thus a rethinking of the nature of leftist political theory – which in their eyes requires a deconstruction, rather than a dismissal, of the Marxist tradition.

This deconstruction functions in *Hegemony and Socialist Strategy* by reworking the concept of "hegemony" as it is found in the history of Marxism, and finds its highest point in the work of the Italian Marxist Antonio Gramsci. For Laclau and Mouffe, the concept of hegemony has the potential to both (1) explain the increased dissemination or dispersion of what they call "subject positions" (i.e., forms of power relations between people) in advanced capitalist society; and (2) provide a more coherent theoretical framework for socialist action, intervention, and decision, given the complexity of this dispersion. The

main problem with Marxism that they identify is that its theory functions within an "essentialist" paradigm: that is, where the *identity* of the "proletariat" and the "bourgeoisie" as natural enemies is a *pre-given* state of affairs. What has a tendency to take place within Marxist thinking is thus the reduction of all other antagonisms within society to this economic base: where it is thought that if the relations of production are transformed, then some communist utopia will develop. However, for Laclau and Mouffe, this optimism of Marxist thinking reduces the complexity of the antagonisms that function within society. For them, not only is the idea of a "pregiven identity" of the working and capitalist classes a theoretical and practical falsity, but it is also wrong to reduce essentially "political" antagonisms to the order of the economic base. They therefore call themselves "post-Marxist" in their affirmation of the primacy of the political over and above the idea of the economic base (thereby freeing themselves from the base/superstructure distinction in Marxist theory).

In contrast to an optimistic approach, Laclau and Mouffe are not pessimists, but instead rework the concept of hegemony around the paradox of affirming the negative and tragic concept of "antagonism." For them, antagonism is intrinsic to the idea of the political: which is not to say that "this or that" antagonism cannot be resolved, but rather that, regardless of whether or not "this or that" antagonism *is* resolved, there will always be another, or at least the *possibility* of another, antagonism. And where there is the possibility of antagonism, there is the possibility of subordination and oppression. What the concept of hegemony therefore refers to are the *multiple sites of antagonism* that are at work within society. For example, in today's world there are various types of movements that form an antagonism, including antisexist, antiracist, environmentalist, human rights, animal rights, and so on. For Laclau and Mouffe, the socialist movement, which is no longer about the overturning of the bourgeoisie by the proletariat but rather about the *eradication of poverty*, is henceforth one movement among others in a democratic regime. Socialism should not come into conflict with democracy for it involves *deepening the democratic impetus*. Consequently, they propose the idea of a "radical democracy," that is, a democracy that on the one hand affirms *political* liberalism and pluralism, but on the other hand questions the *economic* liberalism characteristic of capitalist structures. As such, they say that "socialism is *one* of the components of radical democracy, not vice versa" (2001 [1985]: 178). That is, it aids us in the critique of the capitalist economy, and it aids us with its imagery of a world without poverty; but it can no longer bring about the ideal "commune," for there are too many antagonisms that have the potential to form sites of oppression that lie outside the economy.

What Laclau and Mouffe above called "left-wing thought" can, today, be left-wing "proper" only if it accounts for the *plurality* of antagonisms that are at work within society. However, insofar as it is impossible to account for the *totality* of these antagonisms, intrinsic to the concept of hegemony is thus the idea of this impossible totality. With such arguments, Laclau and Mouffe draw upon the work of French poststructuralist philosophers in order to support their reading of the Marxist tradition – including Jacques Lacan, Michel Foucault, and Jacques Derrida. From these thinkers they gain a critique of the traditional philosophical conception of the "autonomous human subject" that lies at the heart of many politico-economic theories. For Laclau and Mouffe, a critique of the traditional "subject" of action provides the foundation for a radical democratic, and hence truly left-wing, political theory. And in the case of Marxism in particular, it helps them to eradicate the essentialism at the heart of the pregiven identities of "proletariat" and "bourgeoisie."

In 2001 Laclau and Mouffe published an updated second edition of *Hegemony and Socialist Strategy* which included a preface. Much had taken place between the mid-1980s and the turn of the millennium, but there were in particular two notable events. First, the fall of communism, which involved a subsequent right-wing capitalist triumphalism; and second, the growth of a pragmatist third-way politics of the center, which involved an optimistic (and hence complacent in relation to the capitalist triumphalism that surrounded it) eradication of the political ideologies of the Left and the Right as such. These events, among many others, show that the poignancy and critical potential of Laclau and Mouffe's work, of rethinking the Left, is as important today and tomorrow as it was in 1985.

SEE ALSO: Derrida, Jacques; Foucault, Michel; Gramsci, Antonio; Lacan, Jacques; Marxism

REFERENCE AND SUGGESTED READING

Laclau, E., & Mouffe, C. (2001). *Hegemony and Socialist Strategy: Towards a Radical Democratic Politics*, 2nd edn. London: Verso. (Original work published 1985.)

Lacoue-Labarthe, Philippe

IAN JAMES

The philosophical writing of Philippe Lacoue-Labarthe (1940–2007) engages with many of the key preoccupations of late twentieth-century French thought: the relation of literature to philosophy and the uncertain status of philosophical subjectivity; questions of representation and mimesis in relation to art, the political, and history; the identity of meaning and of the individual self. Consisting largely of meticulous commentaries on philosophers, artists, and poets, Lacoue-Labarthe's writing situates itself clearly within a tradition which emerges in the wake of the speculative idealism of the German Enlightenment (principally Kant and Hegel) and the artistic legacy of Romanticism. In particular his writing has focused on the question of the subject within post-Enlightenment thought and aesthetics and the relation of philosophical conceptions of subjectivity to political forms, and to determinate historical and political events (e.g., the place of Nazism and the extermination camps in relation to wider European culture and history).

Lacoue-Labarthe's early political affiliations can be situated on the nonconformist French Left: he was associated with the libertarian socialist group Socialisme et Babarie and had strong sympathies with Guy Debord's Situationist International. His philosophical work can be placed within the project of an overcoming of metaphysics that informed much French philosophy from the 1960s onward which developed the legacies of Nietzsche and Heidegger. More specifically, Lacoue-Labarthe's early work of the 1970s pursued this Nietzschean/Heideggerian overcoming of metaphysics in collaboration with his close friend and colleague Jean-Luc Nancy and under the strong influence of Derridean deconstruction. The French literary-philosophical essayist, novelist and critic Maurice Blanchot also exerted a decisive influence on the development of Lacoue-Labarthe's thinking.

Lacoue-Labarthe's writing of the 1970s is dominated by the question of the relation of literature to philosophy, a question which is closely intertwined with his analysis of the status and fate of the subject and its attempt, within philosophical reasoning, to ground itself as an autonomous, rational, and self-present ground for thought and knowledge. In this context Lacoue-Labarthe argues that philosophy inevitably fails in its attempt to reserve for itself a form of language which would transcend the ambiguities and slippages of textuality, or the figural and rhetorical dimension of language which is foregrounded by literature. The fate of the philosophical subject in the rhetorical and figural texture of philosophical language is carefully explored by Lacoue-Labarthe in a range of texts (some co-authored with Nancy) on Lacan, Kant, Nietzsche, and German Romanticism. Building on the philosophies of both Nietzsche and Heidegger he develops a thinking whereby, not only the language of philosophy, but also the shared horizons of historical becoming and worldly existence can be shown, at a fundamental level, to be bound up with a logic of myth, fiction, or fable. Within this wider logic of textuality, fiction, or fable, the thinking subject, both of philosophy and of lived experience, is seen always to withdraw or unground itself in the very moment of its attempted presentation or self-grounding.

At the beginning of the 1980s Lacoue-Labarthe, at the instigation of Derrida, and in collaboration with Nancy, founded the Centre for Philosophical Research on the Political. The work of the center lasted for four years during which time its founders sought to explore the political dimension of thinking opened up by Derrida's philosophy. In particular, they sought to interrogate the dimension of the political as distinct from the activity of politics. Here, the political was conceived as that fundamental order of essence which would be prior to politics per se but which would underpin its possible modes of articulation or becoming. The political would articulate that primary order of meaning which can be shown to be co-originary with the fable or fictioning of the world that structures historical becoming, and that philosophy itself figures. In this sense, for Lacoue-Labarthe, the political, the philosophical, the aesthetic, and the historical can all be related to each other at a fundamental level.

Lacoue-Labarthe's key text on Heidegger, *Heidegger, Art and Politics* (1990 [1987]) can be seen as a development of his early work with the center. In it he explores Heidegger's relation to Nazism in the 1930s and engages in a close reading of the infamous Rectoral Address of 1933. Seen by some as a misguided attempt to excuse Heidegger's Nazism, Lacoue-Labarthe's book explicitly affirms the culpability of the German thinker's self-association with the Hitler regime. It also seeks to engage with the way in which an unthought legacy of the subject within Heideggerian philosophy underpins its thinking in relation to history and comes to motivate the political decision made by Heidegger himself. This unthought legacy of the subject which attaches Heideggerian philosophy to Nazism is a legacy of the subject which can be shown to be at work within the wider field of European, thought, culture, and history. Lacoue-

Labarthe's aim, here, is less to excuse the inexcusable in Heidegger than it is to relate his culpability to a wider field of cultural, philosophical, and political fictioning which belongs to the European tradition more generally.

Lacoue-Labarthe's later work, while continuing a sustained engagement with Heidegger, is increasingly preoccupied with poetry, and with various art forms: with, for example, figures such as Hölderlin, Wagner, Mallarmé, Baudelaire, and Pasolini. To date critical reception of his work has focused on his collaboration with Nancy and his thinking around the political, but also on his pursuit of the question of the (philosophical) subject. The specific return that Lacoue-Labarthe makes to the question of representation, fictioning, and fable, and in particular, his recovery of the problem of imitation and mimesis in the post-Enlightenment German tradition, is likely to provoke and inform much future scholarship and debate.

SEE ALSO: Blanchot, Maurice; Debord, Guy; Deconstruction; Derrida, Jacques; Nancy, Jean-Luc

REFERENCES AND SUGGESTED READINGS

Lacoue-Labarthe, P., with Nancy, J.-L. (1988). *The Literary Absolute: The Theory of Literature in German Romanticism* (trans. P. Barnard & C. Lester). Albany: SUNY Press. (Original work published 1978.)

Lacoue-Labarthe, P. (1990). *Heidegger, Art, and Politics: The Fiction of the Political* (trans. C. Turner). Oxford: Blackwell. (Original work published 1987.)

Lacoue-Labarthe, P. (1992). *The Title of the Letter* (trans. F. Raffoul & D. Pettigrew). Albany: SUNY Press. (Original work published 1973.)

Lacoue-Labarthe, P. (1993). *The Subject of Philosophy* (trans. T. Trezise et al.). Minneapolis:

University of Minnesota Press. (Original work published 1979.)

Lacoue-Labarthe, P. (1994). *Musica Ficta: Figures of Wagner* (trans. F. McCarren). Stanford: Stanford University Press. (Original work published 1991.)

Lacoue-Labarthe, P., with Nancy, J.-L. (1997). *Retreating the Political* (ed. S. Sparks). London: Routledge.

Lacoue-Labarthe, P. (1998). *Typography: Mimesis, Philosophy, Politics* (trans. C. Fynsk). Cambridge, MA: Harvard University Press. (Original work published 1986.)

Lacoue-Labarthe, P. (1999). *Poetry as Experience* (trans. A. Tarnowski). Stanford: Stanford University Press. (Original work published 1986.)

Lacoue-Labarthe, P. (2002). *Poétique de l'histoire*. Paris: Galilée.

Martis, J. (2005). *Philippe Lacoue-Labarthe: Representation and the Loss of the Subject*. New York: Fordham.

Latino/a Theory

FREDERICK ALDAMA

Latino/a theory covers a massive range of disciplinary pursuits and explorations. Given that we are and have been active shapers of all facets of our North American reality, such scholarly impulses seek to make visible the culture, history, and presence of Latino/as in the US. This essay will map the territory that makes up contemporary or "postclassical" theories of Latino/a cultural production that build on and extend classical Latino/a studies theory.

Briefly, I consider Latino/a pioneers of the arts and scholarship to be those working in and around the time of the late 1960s and early 1970s to make up the classical Latino/a theory. Corky Gonzalez's *raza* epic poem, "I am Joaquín" (1967), Abelardo Delgado's *Chicano Manifesto* (1970), and Chicano poet Alurista's *Floricanto en Aztlán* (published with the first Chicano press Quinton Sol in 1971) embody the early spirit of this

epoch: to build a bridge between aesthetic acts, scholarship, and political activism. In the Southwest, for instance, such first-wave cultural activism sought to reclaim territorial rights and thus establish in the Southwest a Chicano nation informed by mestizo/a (Amerindian Aztec/Mayan and Spanish) culture.

In many ways, it was the appearance in 1981 of the lesbian feminist-charged, woman-of-color-voiced poems, short stories, and essays collected in *This Bridge Called My Back* (Anzaldúa & Moraga 1983) that opened the door to the postclassical Latino/a theory that we see today. Lesbian Latina artists and scholars such as Cherríe Moraga and Gloria Anzaldúa, among many others, looked less romantically at the Chicano/a community and responded more complexly to earlier *raza*-identified binaries such as white versus brown, male versus female, and queer versus straight. All forms of experience and identity were to be embraced. As Anzaldúa would write later in her poetic essay "El día de la chicana," "To rage and look upon you with contempt is to rage and be contemptuous of ourselves. We can no longer blame you, nor disown the white parts, the male parts, the pathological parts, the queer parts, the vulnerable parts. Here we are weaponless with open arms, with only our magic. Let's try it our way, the mestiza way, the Chicana way, the woman way" (1993: 82–3).

Anzaldúa's 1987 publication of *Borderlands/La Frontera* – a hybrid mix of poetry, prose, and metaphysical inquiry – became the apotheosis of this move away from fixed notions of Chicano/a identity and experience. While *Borderlands/La Frontera* experimented with genre, it was not to be confused with a contemporary, Anglo-identified, postmodernist disaffection. For Anzaldúa, playing with language and form was ultimately to unfix heterosexist histories and metaphysics, and then to anchor once again Chicano/a being within a more radically inclusive, hybrid ontology. For Anzaldúa, then, to deform language and destabilize generic expectation was to intervene in and to radically transform heterosexist and racist master narratives. Her textualizing of a borderland ontology (straight/queer, male/female, brown/white, Spanish/Amerindian) emphasized inclusivity, fluidity, transformation, and transfiguration, radically sidestepping the earlier biological and cultural essentialism of the *raza* nationalist socioaesthetics.

The 1990s and the first decade of the twenty-first century saw the development of postclassical Latino/a theory. Nothing is off limits to these postclassical Latino/a theorists. Here are some highlights.

THEORIES OF LATINO/A CULTURE-MAKING AND UNMAKING

Many Latino/a scholars today choose to set their sights on the cultural production by and about Latino/as. While the publication of Saldívar & Calderón's *Criticism in the Borderlands* (1991) marked an important milestone in the analysis of Latino/a cultural phenomena, it remained focused largely on literature. Latino/a scholars today such as Aldama & Quiñonez (2002), Brown (2002), Marez (2004), and Nericcio (2007) decode a wider range of popular cultural representations as sites of Latino/a political (symbolic and real) resistance and intervention into dominant, patriarchal (white and brown), capitalist (neocolonialist) "norms."

Several such scholars focus on how certain Latino/a authors and artists dislodge and strike back at long traditions of negative representations of Latino/as as, one way or another, destructive denizens of the underworld. Monica Brown (2002) excavates the literature written by and about Chicano and Latino/a gangs to excavate sites of political

and social acts of resistance. She moves from analyses of Puerto Ricans such as Edwin Torres and Piri Thomas to Chicanas such as Xyta Maya Murray and Mona Ruiz, theorizing this array of gang autobiography, narrative fiction, and drama as making "real" and human those subjects otherwise depicted as one-dimensional and marginal within a racist United States. For Brown, gangster narratives do more than send a shiver down the spine. They shake up those power structures, she argues, "that have been held in place by the mechanisms of a monolithic 'national culture' invested in maintaining the status quo" (2002: xxvii).

Curtis Marez (2004) analyzes a number of texts, from Leslie Marmon Silko's *Almanac of the Dead* to popular *narcocorridos* and Robert Rodriguez's *El Mariachi*, to show how drug wars and cross-border traffic justify and extend the nation-state's oppressive juridical and militaristic powers within and outside the US. However, Marez is also interested in showing how a certain number of Latino/a authors and directors, Robert Rodriguez for instance, offer cultural forms of resistance "to capital and the state" (2004: x). Of the latter, Marez declares, "Whether in the form of crime, violent rebellion, labor radicalism, or oppositional cultural production, marginalized groups have directly and indirectly opposed the expansion of state and capitalist power that drug traffic supports" (x).

William Nericcio (2007) explores more generally the negative stereotypes of Latino/as in mainstream culture: from the Frito Bandito commercials, Speedy Gonzalez cartoons, to postcards sold of the death and destruction along the US/Mexico border during the early twentieth century, exotically packaged Maria dolls, and Duro Decal appliqués of pastoral señoritas and snoring, sombrero-toting Mexicans. Rather than catalog each and every representational instance and type, Nericcio digs into and chips away at the very psychological marrow that holds up and feeds a US cultural mainstream. For Nericcio, this hallucination isn't a thing of the past, nor is it benign. Woven around Americans brown and white, it sets in motion cognitive scripts that straightjacket the way Latino/as – Te[x]t-Mexicans – can exist and act in the world.

THE ARTS

Other scholars turn their sights to other cultural phenomena such as the arts. Habell-Pallán (2005) analyzes the performance art (and poetry) of Luis Alfaro, Marga Gomez, and Marisela Norte, as well as the revisionary rock 'n' roll of El Vez and Latina feminist punk. Pérez (2007) analyzes painting, printmaking, sculpture, performance, photography, film and video, comics, sound recording, interactive CD-Rom, altars, and other installation forms that articulate a hybrid spirituality that challenge racism, bigotry, patriarchy, and homophobia. Latorre (2008) extends this effort, focusing her analytical lens on the aesthetic, historical, and political ingredients that inform Latina mural art in the twentieth and twenty-first centuries, building a "visual vocabulary" specifically attuned to Latina mural art as it is created in time (history) and place (geographic region and community). Responsive to the art and artist, Latorre not only demonstrates how Latina artists created murals that spoke to the specifics of the Chicana/o experience in the US, but also how they used techniques and allusions that reached beyond. To show such an interface with non-Chicana/o artists, Latorre details the work of famous Mexican muralists such as Diego Rivera, José Clemente Orozco, and David Alfaro Siqueiros who were commissioned to create murals in the US. Not only do we see several of the use of indigenous

leitmotifs picked up by Chicana/o artists working in the late 1960s and 1970s, but we see a like tension in both: the mestiza as erotic and the indigenous people as exotic frozen in some bygone era versus a representation that contests such a reductive, racist and sexist worldview.

Such postclassical Latina scholars of the arts extend and deepen the criticism already begun in the 1980s with Latina feminists such as Maria Herrera-Sobek, Tey Diana Rebolledo, Lucha Corpi, Gloria Anzaldúa, and Cherríe Moraga: to critique a male-dominated Chicano movement (el movimiento) and its implicit and explicit sexism that sidelined Latina creators of culture generally. Indeed, as Latorre explains, many Latina artists created murals that recalibrated viewer's engagement with otherwise macho-oriented pre-Columbian symbols and icons: male Aztec god-warriors, codex, pyramids, snakes, eagles, and the like. While Latina artists recognized the importance of the impulse to use such iconography in el movimiento's symbolic reclamation of lost territory (northern Mexico) and a silenced history, they considered the depiction of women as either virgin, whore, or betrayer demeaning and destructive.

QUEER THEORY

While again many of the seeds were sown in the 1980s, the 2000s saw a watershed in gay and lesbian Latino/a studies theory. With feminist foundations solidified in the work of Norma Alarcón, Yvonne Yarbro-Bejarano, Angie Chabram-Dernersesian, María Herrera-Sobek, Norma Cantú, Sonia Saldívar-Hull, Emma Pérez, and Tey Diana Rebolledo, the new century saw the publication of Mary Pat Brady's *Extinct Lands, Temporal Geographies* (2002), Catrióna Rueda Esquebel's *With Her Machete in Her Hand* (2006), Frederick Luis Aldama's

Dancing with Ghosts (2004) and *Brown on Brown* (2005), Ricky T. Rodriguez's *Next of Kin* (2009), Lawrence La Fountain-Stokes's *Queer Ricans* (2009), and Sandra K. Soto's *Reading Chican@ Like a Queer* (2010), to name but a few. Such scholarly works variously explore cultural expressions of gay and lesbian Latino/as in the US, developing theories of the influence of internal and external migrations and particularized histories (Puerto Rican Island versus Nuyorican mainland, Mexican versus Chicano/a or Hispano/a, for instance) as well as cultural responses to discrimination within communities and the mainstream in terms of class, gender, and sexuality. While Pérez suggests that neither desire nor love could ever stand outside of national and racial frameworks, this form of approach alleviates the burden of sexual transgression and broken loyalties that Chicanas have shouldered for 500 years.

MUSIC

Scholars such as Arturo J. Aldama, Ana Patricia Rodríguez, Pancho McFarland, and Josh Kun, among others, have begun to theorize Latino/a music. Kun (2005) examines the punk-thrash rock band Tijuana No! and how they use technology and capitalist modes of production – they were signed by BMG International and run their videos on MTV – to disseminate an anti-imperialist, revolutionary (pro-Zapatista) messages. And McFarland (2008) focuses on how Chicano youth have adopted and adapted rap music and hip-hop culture to express their views on gender and violence. He focuses on two kinds of Chicano rap artists: the regressive ones who reproduce the misogyny and violence in the US mainstream media and the progressive ones who seek to reach Chicano/a youth with empowering and liberating messages.

LATINO/A THEORIES AT THE CROSSROADS

Given our shared cultural and genealogical histories with Central and South America and the Hispanophone Caribbean, several postclassical Latino/a scholars have actively sought to expand the critical purview beyond the US/Mexico border.

Saldívar (1997) begins to build bridges between Chicano/a borderland scholarship, Latin American postcolonial culturalism (Nestor García-Canclíni and Angel Rama), and Afro-British diaspora scholarship (Paul Gilroy, Kobena Mercer, and Stuart Hall). Saldívar's work begins much Latino/a theory that seeks to identify a what is identified as "borderland theory" or transhemispheric studies – the cultural products that result from a hybrid cultural, historical, genealogical past and present for Latino/as who share with other postcolonial communities worldwide an exile-like status within a US homeland.

Indeed, we see this very impulse in Castillo & Tabuenca Córdoba (2002), who carve out a space for Mexican and Chicana women authors writing on or about the US/Mexico border. In their edited collection, Benito & Manzanas (2002) draw a line in the sand around "border writing" that remaps a US literary topography that's less Euro-Anglocentric and more Iberian/Caribbean/Latin American-focused. Kevane (2003) focuses on 11 Latino/a writers as "creators of Latino culture," adding that this representative sample aims also to complicate one's ideas of Latino/as as a group as "each piece of fiction offers a different tradition or approach to gender, religion, immigration, or exile" (13).

The hemispheric reach is especially foregrounded in the essays that make up Habell-Pallán & Romero's *Latino/a Popular Culture* (2002), which explores a wide variety of Latino/a cultural phenomena that make up a so-called "transnational imaginary" (7) that functions as "counter-sites" that can help (or hinder) the struggle for social transformation within otherwise restrictive paradigms of nation. And we see this same impulse bear fruit in Pérez-Torres (2006). Here Pérez-Torres explores how our shared past of racial mixings can make for a theory of *mestizaje* as a way to enrich our understanding of history, culture, and politics; its embrace can lead to the coming into an empowering multiracial identity as Latino/as.

We also see this transnational reach in Hiraldo (2003), Díaz (2002), Rosman (2003), and Saldaña-Portillo (2003). Saldaña-Portillo considers, for instance, the writing of Rigoberta Menchú and Subcomandante Marcos as revealing a revolutionary imagination not determined by a premodern (local) to modern (global) teleology with a grand payoff at the end –"'universal' model of full humanity" (260) – but rather as an articulation of "an alternative modernity" (256) that is both nativist and universalist, premodern and modern, local and global.

PEDAGOGY

Latino/a theory also extends into teaching. For instance, Lunsford & Ouzgane (2004) present several methods for using "borderland theory" in the classroom. Accordingly, concepts like "hybridity," "third space resistance," "new mestiza consciousness," "radical *mestizaje*" can liberate students and teachers from regulatory systems such as rules of grammar, Western canonical reading assignments, and more generally society's discursive structures that contain and control racialized subjects. Part of this impulse includes the making of anthologies for teaching. For instance, Christie & Gonzalez (2006) focus exclusively on innovative literature written in English published since 1985 as a way to "broaden the book's range to include Latino/a authors who have been underrepresented in anthologies and other collections, namely women and other less well-known writers from a wide range of ethnic and cultural backgrounds" (xiv). And Olivas (2008) brings together short stories by and about Latino/as living in Los Angeles.

LITERATURE

Refocusing the lens on aesthetic concerns after a period of identifying Latino/a literature as *counter*history, established by Saldívar (1990), several scholars of Latino/a cultural production focus on literature, both in the recovering of Latino/a novels, short stories, and comic books and in their analysis. Aranda (2003) recovers late nineteenth-century Mexican American literature (Amparo Ruiz de Burton, for instance) as it informs and is informed by late nineteenth-century Anglo-American literature (Hawthorne, for instance). And Rodriguez (2005) uncovers a rich tradition of detective fiction in Chicana/o literature. Contreras (2008) explores an uncritical and critical primitivism in US/Mexico borderland fiction in her analysis of Chicano/a literature alongside D. H. Lawrence, Malcolm Cowley, and Cormac McCarthy. And, in the work of Aldama (2003; 2005; 2009), there is a move to give Latino/a literature its due: to pay attention to form, content, and context in ways that deepen knowledge of how Latino/a literature is made, transformed, and consumed both on its own terms and within larger world literary systems of influences and interrelations. One way or another, in Aldama's work there is a focus on how a given Latino/a author uses his or her imagination and "will to style" to reorganize the building blocks of reality to engage and even challenge readers cognitively and move them emotively in new and interesting ways.

Latino/a theory continues to grow in many other disciplines and fields of knowledge-making – all with the drive to understand better the particular and shared histories of Latino/as as well as how Latino/as have come to transform the world in our activities and the cultural phenomena that we spin out of ourselves.

SEE ALSO: Feminism; Postcolonial Studies and Diaspora Studies; Queer Theory

REFERENCES AND SUGGESTED READINGS

Aldama, A. J., & Quiñonez, N. (2002). *Decolonial Voices: Chicana and Chicano Cultural Studies in the Twenty-First Century.* Bloomington: Indiana University Press.

Aldama, F. L. (2003). *Postethnic Narrative Criticism: Magicorealism in Ana Castillo, Hanif Kureishi, Julie Dash, Oscar "Zeta" Acosta, and Salman Rushdie.* Austin: University of Texas Press.

Aldama, F. L. (2004). *Dancing with Ghosts: A Critical Biography of Arturo Islas.* Berkeley: University of California Press.

Aldama, F. L. (2005). *Brown on Brown: Chicano/a Representations of Gender, Sexuality, and Ethnicity.* Austin: University of Texas Press.

Aldama, F. L. (2009). *A User's Guide to Postcolonial and Borderland Fiction.* Austin: University of Texas Press.

Alurista (1971). *Floricanto en Aztlán.* Los Angeles: Chicano Cultural Center, University of California.

Anzaldúa, G. (1987). *Borderlands: The New Mestiza/La Frontera.* San Francisco: Spinsters/Aunt Lute.

Anzaldúa, G. (1993). El día de la chicana. In T. D. Rebolledo & E. S. Rivero (eds.), *Infinite Divisions: An Anthology of Chicana Literature.* Tucson: University of Arizona Press, p. 82.

Anzaldúa, G., & Moraga, C. (eds.) (1983). *This Bridge Called My Back: Writings by Radical Women of Color.* New York: Women of Color.

Aranda, J., Jr. (2003). *When We Arrived: A New Literary History of Mexican America.* Tucson: University of Arizona Press.

Benito, J., & Manzanas, A. M. (2002). *Literature and Ethnicity in the Cultural Borderlands.* Amsterdam: Rodopi.

Brady, M. P. (2002). *Extinct Lands, Temporal Geographies: Chicana Literature and the Urgency of Space.* Durham, NC: Duke University Press.

Brown, M. (2002). *Gang Nation: Delinquent Citizens in Puerto Rican, Chicano, and Chicana Narratives.* Minneapolis: University of Minnesota Press.

Castillo, D. S., & Tabuenca Córdoba, M. S. (2002). *Border Women: Writing from La Frontera.* Minneapolis: University of Minnesota Press.

Christie, J. S., & Gonzalez, J. B. (eds.) (2006). *Latino Boom: An Anthology of US Latino Literature.* New York: Pearson/Longman.

Contreras, S. (2008). *Blood Lines: Myth, Indigenism and Chicana/o Literature.* Austin: University of Texas Press.

Delgado, A. (2008). Chicano manifesto. In D. Gilb (ed.), *Hecho en Tejas: An Anthology of Texas-Mexican Literature.* Albuquerque: University of New Mexico Press, pp. 175–178. (Original work published 1970.)

Díaz, R. I. (2002). *Unhomely Rooms: Foreign Tongues and Spanish American Literature.* Lewisburg, PA: Bucknell University Press.

Esquebel, C. R. (2006). *With Her Machete in Her Hand: Reading Chicana Lesbians.* Austin: University of Texas Press.

Gonzalez, R. (1967). *I am Joaquín.* Santa Barbara, CA: La Causa.

Habell-Pallán, M. (2005). *Loca Motion: The Travels of Chicana and Latina Popular Culture.* New York: New York University Press.

Habell-Pallán, M., & Romero, M. (2002). *Latino/a Popular Culture.* New York: New York University Press.

Hiraldo, C. (2003). *Segregated Miscegenation: On the Treatment of Racial Hybridity in the US and Latin America.* New York: Routledge.

Kevane, B. (2003). *Latino Literature in America.* Westport, CT: Greenwood.

Kun, J. (2005). *Audiotopia: Music, Race, and America.* Berkeley: University of California Press.

La Fountain-Stokes, L. (2009). *Queer Ricans: Cultures and Sexualities in the Diaspora.* Minneapolis: University of Minnesota Press.

Latorre, G. (2008). *Walls of Empowerment: Chicana/o Indigenist Murals of California*. Austin: University of Texas Press.

Lunsford, A. A., & Ouzgane, L. (eds.) (2004). *Crossing Borderlands: Composition and Postcolonial Studies*. Pittsburgh: University of Pittsburgh Press.

Marez, C. (2004). *Drug Wars: The Political Economy of Narcotics*. Minneapolis: University of Minnesota Press.

McFarland, P. (2008). *Chicano Rap: Gender and Violence in the Postindustrial Barrio*. Austin: University of Texas Press.

Nericcio, W. (2007). *Te[x]t-Mex: Seductive Hallucinations of "Mexican" in America*. Austin: University of Texas Press.

Olivas, D. (2008). *Latinos in Lotusland: An Anthology of Contemporary Southern California Literature*. Tempe, AZ: Bilingual Press/Editorial Bilingüe.

Pérez, L. (2007). *Chicana Art: The Politics of Spiritual and Aesthetic Altarities*. Durham, NC: Duke University Press.

Pérez-Torres, R. (2006). *Mestizaje: Critical Uses of Race in Chicano Culture*. Minneapolis: University of Minnesota Press.

Rodriguez, R. (2005). *Brown Gumshoes: Detective Fiction and the Search for Chicana/o Identity*. Austin: University of Texas Press.

Rodriguez, R. T. (2009). *Next of Kin: The Family in Chicano/a Cultural Politics*. Durham, NC: Duke University Press.

Rosman, S. N. (2003). *Being in Common: Nation, Subject, and Community in Latin American Literature and Culture*. Lewisburg, PA: Bucknell University Press.

Saldaña-Portillo, M. J. (2003). *The Revolutionary Imagination in the Americas and the Age of Development*. Durham, NC: Duke University Press.

Saldívar, J. (1997). *Border Matters: Remapping American Cultural Studies*. Berkeley: University of California Press.

Saldívar, J., & Calderón, H. (1991). *Criticism in the Borderlands: Studies in Chicano Literature, Culture, and Ideology*. Durham, NC: Duke University Press.

Saldívar, R. (1990). *Chicano Narrative: The Dialectics of Difference*. Madison: University of Wisconsin Press.

Soto, S. K. (2010). *Reading Chican@ Like a Queer*. Austin: University of Texas Press.

Lesbian, Gay, Bisexual, and Transgender Studies

MATTHEW HELMERS

Lesbian, gay, bisexual, and transgender studies are interlinked fields of critical theory that address a very wide range of issues around these minorities. In order to understand the development of this field and the activism it accompanies, it is necessary to understand the history of its development.

In 1969, police raided the known gay bar Stonewall Inn in Greenwich, New York. This raid was not out of the ordinary; police frequently targeted known gay establishments, but that morning, in front of Stonewall, the small group of gays and drag queens fought back against the police. This action turned into further minor riots, and gave rise to secondary protests against newspapers that printed homophobic articles about the raid on Stonewall Inn. These riots and protests became a symbol for the gay rights movement. The Stonewall riots acted as a catalyst: gay activists took to the streets, arguing for equal rights and equal protection under the law. Politically, gay rights activists followed other civil rights movements and embraced an identity politics model, arguing for minority rights based on the inherent and therefore valid nature of the collective gay identity. Organizations like the Gay Activist Alliance and the Gay Liberation Front continued the battle. By the 1980s, in response to US and UK government inactivity around the AIDS issue, Larry Kramer and other activists founded the Gay Men's Health Crisis organization and, later, the organization ACT UP. A potent symbol of ACT UP, and one of their most recognizable slogans, is the pink triangle with the words SILENCE = DEATH printed in bold letters underneath. Six activists created this poster prior to the formation of ACT UP and then gave the logo and slogan to the organization in order to aid the fight against government silence regarding HIV/AIDS. But in a broader sense, this poster crystallizes the efforts of all activists, whether they advocate rights for gays, lesbians, bisexuals, or transgender people. Activists realize that silence is both the literal and the figurative death of these people; and it is the past decades of silence around LGBT issues that proved so destructive to LGBT people and their lives.

Understanding this legacy of activism helps us to follow the literary critical field of LGBT studies. It was the experience and traditions of activism that opened space to allow discussions and examinations of LGBT cultures, to look into the lives of LGBT people and understand the various factors that shape and inform their existence. After the general and protracted silence surrounding these issues, LGBT studies asks questions such questions as "Is there an LGBT literature?" "What authors are/ were lesbian, gay, bisexual, or transgender?" "What does it mean to live as an LGBT person in the past or in the present?" "How far are the categories of lesbian, gay, bisexual, or transgender 'real,' or are these categories just historical or political or medical inventions?"

These core questions anchor LGBT studies, and while many LGBT critics answer them in a manner pertinent to all four fields that make up LGBT studies (lesbian, gay, bisexual, transgender), more commonly each field establishes its own academic and literary demesne, one that engages with, but is still distinct from, the other fields. Because of this specialization, each of the four aspects of LGBT studies will be explored individually, before assessing their common ground to analyze both their similarities and their numerous differences.

LESBIAN STUDIES

One of the first differences that sets lesbian studies apart from the other fields of LGBT studies is the extent to which it problematizes exactly this activist history. While those in lesbian studies generally regard early activism as important and foundational to LGBT endeavors, they also often point out that, generally, the history of activism is a history of gay male activism, which often overlooks some of the important feminist work on gender and sexuality already in motion before Stonewall. Because of this emphasis, there is a tendency to associate gay studies with gay male activism and Stonewall, and lesbian studies with feminism. More accurately, lesbian studies reinvigorates the importance of feminist studies within all of LGBT criticism, while acknowledging the legacy and centrality of Stonewall-inspired activism.

This said, the interaction between feminism and lesbian studies is problematic. In the late 1970s, the feminist critic Sheila Jeffreys pioneered the concept of the political lesbian (Jeffreys 2003). This idea, nominally part of lesbian feminism, suggested that all females should embrace the concept of lesbianism. Importantly, Jeffreys was not claiming that all females needed to engage in compulsory same-sex eroticism, but rather that through the figure of the lesbian, females should endeavor to minimize their interactions with men, limit the types of sexual acts they engage in with men, and thereby avoid the oppressive influence of the patriarchy. This concept helped to found the lesbian feminism movement, while other concepts like the woman-identified woman established lesbian feminism's commitment to placing relations between women at the forefront of the feminist agenda. As a movement, lesbian feminism broke away from both the Gay Liberation Front and the Women's

Liberation Movement in order to critique both groups' silence around the concept of lesbianism. However, in embracing ideas of the woman-identified woman and the political lesbian, lesbian feminism (perhaps overly) broadened the concept and identity of lesbian. If, as Jeffries and others suggested, all women embrace lesbian identity as a political model to subvert patriarchy, then this masks the roles of women engaging in same-sex eroticism as part of their everyday lives, for whom lesbianism is not a political stance, but, rather, a lived experience.

Part of the problem with this rebuttal to Jeffreys's concept, and a tension throughout all LGBT studies, is the extent to which anyone can actually be LGBT. Popular culture typically frames this debate around the idea of nature versus nurture: are people inherently LGBT, or are they taught to be LGBT? In LGBT studies during the 1970s and '80s, this debate occurred under the terms of "essentialism" versus "constructivism." On one side of the debate, essentialists search for ultimate "truth" affirming that LGBT people each have a common, unchangeable factor that makes them either lesbian, gay, bisexual, or transgender. For essentialists, the truth of LGBT people can be (among other things) their biological truth (their genes, their brain, their hormones); their psychological truth (their drives, their desires); their evolutionary truth (their instincts, their (non) reproductive impulse); or their subjective truth (their soul, their subjectivity, their identity, their existence). On the other hand, constructivists examine the ways in which these truths are produced, rather than essential. A constructivist would look at the ways in which historical, cultural, and political factors establish the legitimacy of biology, psychology, or evolution as discourses that tell the truth. Furthermore, a constructivist would examine the cultural factors that construct ideas like subjectivity and identity, rather than assuming subjectivity and

identity to be essential parts of being human. Thus, broadly speaking, thinkers who attempt to demonstrate the inherent, biological, and/or psychological existence of LGBT people can be grouped as essentialists, while those who attempt to demonstrate the culturally and historically variable, politically determined, and/or socially constructed definition for LGBT people can be grouped as constructivists.

But while the activist and popular debate around nature versus nurture and the LGBT community still gains a large amount of media attention, the parallel academic debate on essentialism versus constructivism has been mostly over since the early 1990s. In place of this debate, LGBT critics attempt either to create a coherent definition for their central term (lesbian, gay, bisexual, or transgender) or, conversely, to destabilize the solidified categories of lesbian, gay, bisexual, and transgender. These two actions of creation and destabilization are not positioned against one another, but, rather, present two complementary actions within each field of study.

Thus, asking "What is a lesbian?" is to ask an essentialist question, searching for a solidification of the identity of a lesbian; and to ask "What does culture say a lesbian is?" is to ask a constructivist question, searching for the historical, political, and/or cultural ideas that make the concept of lesbianism possible. However, after the works of Michel Foucault (1978) and Judith Butler (1990), most LGBT critics affirm that essentialist questions are always constructivist questions, meaning that in order to ask the question "What is a lesbian?" a person first has to have an understanding of the concept of lesbianism, or at least know the word lesbian, and therefore be participant in a culture that recognizes that people have something called an identity, and that this identity can be lesbian. Because of this intervention, most contemporary LGBT critics seek to understand the construction of LGBT people, rather that attempting to affirm an inherent or essential existence for LGBT people. Importantly, constructivists do not believe that concepts like lesbian, gay, bisexual, or transgender are false or fake; rather, they affirm that these concepts were constructed, and now affect, structure, and determine our lives in a profound way. For a constructivist critic, living life identified as a lesbian is not an illusion; it is a real experience that affects the everyday existence of that person, but that does not necessarily negate the fact that the identity of lesbian arises from years of political, medical, and historical discourses about *what* a lesbian *is*.

Thus, part of lesbian studies (and another part shared between all LGBT studies) is collecting and elucidating these textual historical accounts of lesbianism that inform the everyday experience of lesbians. In this way, we can say that Sheila Jeffreys, with her concept of political lesbianism, presents one aspect of lesbian culture, but also that Terry Castle (2003), in his edited collection *The Literature of Lesbianism*, presents another view on the construction of lesbianism. Neither of these critics is "more correct" in their description of lesbianism, as both present a specific vantage point on the possibilities for living as a lesbian. To put it simply, lesbian studies influenced by feminism and LGBT activism seeks to give voice to lesbian experience, while also understanding the cultural, political, and historical forces that go into constructing lesbianism as a coherent identity.

GAY STUDIES

Similarly, gay studies attempts to understand its central term, gay, both as a stable identity category and as problematic construction. Like lesbian studies, gay studies collects and anthologizes works by gay authors, and/or works with gay themes and characters; however, in gay studies, this incitement to canonize can be traced back to the 1860s, when sexologists began to advocate for the rights of people with non-normative sexualities. Sexology is the term given to the work of a diverse group of scientists who studied and classified people based on their sexuality. Sexologists coined the term homosexuality, among numerous others, and while some sexologists sought to cure or eradicate homosexuality, others advocated for it to be accepted and tolerated. In 1865, a German sexologist named Karl Ulrichs published *Bylaws for the Urning Union*. "Urning" was Ulrichs's term for the homosexual, and in the bylaws for the proposed Urning Union (a sort of hypothetical gay activist organization), Ulrichs affirmed that Urnings must create "an Urning literature" (Woods 1998): Ulrichs was speaking of the need for Urnings to represent themselves through literature in order to end the silence surrounding their alternate sexuality. Gay studies still produces, collects, and discovers homosexual figures and authors, generating numerous anthologies (e.g., Abelove et al. 1993; Woods 1998; Fone 2001). One of the central problems, however, in assembling a gay canon is the question of gay literature. Is literature gay because a gay author wrote it? or because it has gay characters or gay themes? Is there a specific gay form? These questions are continually debated in gay studies, but mostly return to the central question of "What is gay?" Perhaps circuitously, one of the ways in which gay studies answers this question is through the assembling of gay literature. In this process of canonization, gay studies is able to generate a solidified gay culture, one that speaks for and represents a lived gay experience, and thereby answers the questions on gay literature, authorship, and form through example rather than through axiom. While these anthologies also challenge this unified idea of gay experience (usually in the prefaces written by the editors), the act of establishing a gay canon does the same thing Ulrichs advocated in 1865: it gives voice to the previously silenced gays.

But another prominent gay critic, Michel Foucault, in his landmark examination *The History of Sexuality* (1978), critiques the idea that gays need to be heard because they previously have been silenced. Foucault, arguing against what he calls "The Repressive Hypothesis," challenges the idea that the Victorian era was sexually repressed and that only the contemporary explosion of open discussions about homosexuality have allowed us as a culture to become more tolerant and accepting of LGBT lifestyles. Through historical research, Foucault demonstrates that the Victorians were obsessed with discussing sexuality (in fact, Foucault is key in revitalizing examinations of sexologists like Karl Ulrichs). In doing so, Foucault affirms that the contemporary fascination with discussing, representing, and theorizing sexuality is in actuality an effect of certain conservative discourses. Thus, collecting and producing anthologies of gay literature is, according to Foucault, not a libratory move but instead solidifies and rigidifies the prisons of identity that entrap homosexuals. Rather than opening up the possibilities for existence, Foucault argues that the incitement to discourse cements what a homosexual must *be*.

Foucault (1978) also critiques gay critics who trace homosexuality and homosexual practices back to the Ancient Greeks by announcing that sexology invented homosexuality in 1870. This affirmation does not mean that same-sex erotic desire did not exist before 1870, but rather that the concept of homosexuality depends upon certain models of biology, desire, identity, and the body that did not come together until 1870.

Some critics have found fault with Foucault, for example French philosopher Jean

Baudrillard published an essay entitled *Forget Foucault* (1987) taking issue with almost all of Foucault's work, while David Halperin (1995) critiques the way gay studies incorporates and deploys Foucault's works. Similarly, John Boswell (1980) rejected Foucault's constructivism, affirming that even without the label "homosexual," homosexuality existed throughout history. This is still a contentious debate within gay studies, and again returns us to the central question: what is a gay?

Whether answered through anthology, historical examination, theoretical speculation, or any other of the diverse methods within gay studies, gay critics argue for a specific interpretation of what it means, and what it is, to be gay. Importantly, from this debate, and coming back to the activist legacy, prominent critic Jeffrey Weeks enjoins all gay critics to understand their research as a process of speaking *for* a certain community (see Sandfort et al. 2000). To summarize: gay critics assemble, protect, question, and challenge the concept of gayness both as a cultural structure and as a lived experience in order to give voice to gay people by speaking for gay people.

But to say that gay critics and lesbian critics focus solely on the concepts of gayness or lesbianism is to omit one of the most important factors of both endeavors. For, as Eve Sedgwick (1990) points out, lesbian and gay studies, while representing the minority of those with homosexual desires, also examine the universal ideas of sexuality applicable to all people. Thus, gay studies examines both homosexual male desire *and* heterosexual male desire, and the possibilities for male desire in general, while lesbian studies similarly examines both hetero- and homosexual female desire. Furthermore, as Sedgwick affirms, cultural structures like homophobia do not just oppress homosexuals, but also govern the ways in which heterosexuals live their lives by barring certain modes of expression, existence, and desire for everyone, not just for those who wish to engage in same-sex eroticism.

This opening up of gay and lesbian studies into the realms of all male and female experience causes some boundary issues with other critical schools. For example, feminism already includes the study of female sexuality, so where does feminism end and lesbian studies begin? The traditional answer is that feminists place gender/sex issues at the center of their studies, while lesbian critics place sexuality at the center, but even this answer erases the complex interrelation between gender, sex, and sexuality. A more nuanced response to this question is that all these critical fields of sexuality have a good deal of cross-over, and it is often impossible to distinguish feminist projects from lesbian or even gay projects. This does not mean that these fields of study are "really" just one field of sexuality studies, but rather that through overlap, confusion, dispute, and resolution, these three fields arrive at enriched understandings of sexuality, sex and gender.

BISEXUAL STUDIES

According to the field of bisexual studies, these understandings of sexuality are still necessarily (and problematically) binary. Bisexual studies typically examines the extent to which gay studies and lesbian studies, even in the opening up of discussions about sexuality, restore the concept of sexuality to rigid considerations of being either straight or gay. Against this rigidity, bisexual studies posits a fluid model of sexuality, one that challenges popular notions of monogamy, coupling, and binarism. For example, Marjorie Garber (1995) characterizes bisexual studies as deconstructing and reconstructing the assumptions implicit in gay and lesbian studies, presenting theories of

sexuality that are not straight/gay, inside/outside, partnered/plural. In this way, bisexual studies challenges the attempts of certain gay and lesbian critics and writers to make sexuality conform to a binary. In the anthology *RePresenting Bisexualities*, Maria Pramaggiore similarly explains bisexuality as fence-sitting: a refusal to enter into binary identity, sexuality, and eroticism by acknowledging the possibility of fluid desire (Hall & Pramaggiore 1996). The various articles in such anthologies affirm that bisexuality is an unrepresentable, unstable, indefinable sexuality. Yet Hall and Pramaggiore simultaneously motion toward the stability necessary for bisexual identities to exist. Some people *are* bisexual; they occupy a coherent identity space labeled as bisexual. As Clare Hemmings (1995) affirms in the introduction to her article "Locating bisexual identities," some people "come-out" as bisexual, while others practice bisexuality without ascribing to the identity category.

Bisexual studies, then, presents and critiques an identity that refutes binarism and opens up the possibilities for desire and desiring, while still engaging in identity politics and representation. Because of this dual action of bisexual studies, anthologies like *Bi Any Other Name* (Hutchings & Kaahumanu 1991) collect and preserve representations of a stable bisexual identity while simultaneously presenting bisexuality as a fluid form of desire, critiquing the efforts of gay and lesbian studies. Bisexual studies uses identity politics to open up new understandings of desire and identity while still representing and making visible previously ignored or underrepresented people.

TRANSGENDER STUDIES

In a similar manner, the field of transgender studies attempts both to narrate the lives of transgendered individuals, while also questioning the reliance upon specific models of sex and gender within LGB studies. In a special issue of *GLQ*, Susan Stryker (1998) discusses the ways in which the debate between material and performative issues surrounding gender and sex anchors much of transgender studies. Basically, one of the predominant models of gender and sexuality in contemporary LGBT critical practice is that gender, sex, and sexuality are what the constructivist Judith Butler (1990) calls "performative," meaning that these identities are constructed through repeated acts of stylization. This does not mean that our genders, sexes, or sexualities are freely chosen, and that people can move seamlessly and fluidly between any sex or sexuality, but rather that everyday people (re)perform the aspects of our sexes and sexualities and therefore confirm and produce these sexes and sexualities. To use an example, most people would say "She is a woman; therefore, she wears make-up," but performativity claims "She wears make-up; therefore, she is a woman." In her introduction, Stryker highlights times when performativity occurs in disjunction to a material reality of the body, for example: "He has male genitals, but wears make-up and a dress"; or even, "The baby's sex chromosomes are XXY; do we classify it as a boy or a girl?" These issues, and the ways in which these issues reflect back upon the LGB debates over sexuality and sex, constitute the majority of the field of transgender studies. In this way, one of the things that transgender studies adds to the debates of LGB studies is the extent to which these sexualities are always tied up with sex/gender. For example, imagine a person who is born with XX chromosomes, who is assigned a female sex at birth, who lives her life as a man, and who then sleeps with men: is s/he gay? lesbian? bisexual? What if s/he has sex reassignment surgery? Does this change his/her sexuality?

In this hypothetical case, we also see the schisms between the ideas of transvestism, transgender, and transsexuality. Traditionally, transvestism refers to those who wear clothing properly belonging to the other gender; transgender individuals live their lives as the opposite gender while materially remaining their 'original' sex; and transsexual individuals undergo sex reassignment surgery to alter their material body, becoming the opposite sex. However, the term "transgender" has come to signify the possibilities of existence outside gender and/or the transitory nature of both gender and sex. Transgender can thus omit traditional gender binaries and represent individuals who do not neatly fit into either male or female sexes. In this broader interpretation, transgender becomes roughly synonymous with the term "gender-queer." And while some feminists and queer theorists have spoken out against what they view as transgender studies' emphasis on reinforcing normal ideas of gender and sex, the debates coming out of transgender studies focus on the possibilities for identity representation that are no longer rigidly sexed or gendered. As Patricia Elliot and Katrina Roen (1998) suggest, transgender studies must include spaces for political and social action, and also question the representation and promulgation of a sex/gender system. Like bisexual studies, transgender studies seeks to open up spaces of fluidity, but at the same time it recognizes and reinforces the importance of creating a tentative collective identity for those living transgendered lives.

LGBT STUDIES

This tension between opening up possibilities while simultaneously creating coherent identities underlies all four fields of LGBT studies. Additionally, all four fields establish a canon of literature, while questioning the tendency of that canon to construct essential identities. All four fields engage in identity politics, and therefore affirm stable identities, but they also destabilize the foundations for their specific identities by questioning the various forces that influence and construct these identities. All four fields are profoundly influenced by feminism and activism and they all occur in the legacy of the constructivism versus essentialism debate. And all four fields attempt to give a voice to people for whom silence can mean death.

A final note about silence surrounding LGBT people concerns the extent to which LGBT studies is still, after almost 40 years of critical practice, regarded as nonacademic or irrelevant by many universities. In the beginning, LGBT studies had extreme difficulty just entering into the academic world. Universities were reluctant to fund LGBT research endeavors or to establish LGBT posts within their departments. The introduction of queer theory into academia in the 1990s only worsened this bias, as most universities accepted queer theory instead of LGBT, causing many LGBT critics to criticize queer theory as a sanitized version of LGBT studies. Even now, with decades of academic history and a vibrant research and activist community, LGBT studies struggles with continual challenges to its legitimacy as an academic discipline.

SEE ALSO: Butler, Judith; Foucault, Michel; Queer Theory; Sedgwick, Eve Kosofsky

REFERENCES AND SUGGESTED READINGS

Abelove, H., Barale, M. A., & Halperin, D. A. (eds.) (1993). *The Lesbian and Gay Studies Reader*. New York: Routledge.

Baudrillard, J. (1987). *Forget Foucault* (trans. P. Beitchman, L. Hildreth, & M. Polizzotti). New York: Semiotext(e).

Boswell, J. (1980). *Christianity, Social Tolerance and Homosexuality: Gay People in Western Europe from the Beginning of the Christian Era to the Fourteenth Century*. Chicago: University of Chicago Press.

Butler, J. (1990). *Gender Trouble: Feminism and the Subversion of Identity*. New York: Routledge.

Castle, T. (ed.) (2003). *The Literature of Lesbianism: A Historical Anthology from Ariosto to Stonewall*. New York: Columbia University Press.

Elliot, P., & Roen, K. (1998). Transgenderism and the question of embodiment: Promising queer politics? *GLQ: A Journal of Lesbian and Gay Studies*, 4(2), 231–261.

Fone, B. R. S. (ed.) (2001). *The Columbia Anthology of Gay Liteature: Readings from Western Antiquity to the Present Day*. New York: Columbia University Press.

Foucault, M. (1978). *The History of Sexuality. Volume 1: An Introduction* (trans R. Hurley). New York: Vintage Books.

Garber, M. (1995). *Vice Versa: Bisexuality and the Eroticism of Everyday Life*. New York: Simon and Schuster.

Hall, D. E., & Pramaggiore, M. (eds.) (1996). *RePresenting Bisexualities: Subjects and Cultures of Fluid Desire*. New York: New York University Press.

Halperin, D. (1995). *Saint Foucault: Towards a Gay Hagiography*. Oxford: Oxford University Press.

Hemmings, C. (1995). Locating bisexual identities: Discourses of bisexuality and contemporary feminist theory. In D. Bell & G. Valentine (eds.), *Mapping Desire: Geographies of Sexualities*. New York: Routledge.

Hutchings, L., & Kaahumanu (eds.) (1991). *Bi Any Other Name: Bisexual People Speak Out*. Boston: Alyson.

Jeffreys, S. (2003). *Unpacking Queer Politics: A Lesbian Feminist Perspective*. Cambridge: Polity Press.

Sandfort, T., Schuyf, J., Duyvendak, J. W., & Weeks, J. (eds.) (2000). *Lesbian and Gay Studies: An Introductory, Interdisciplinary Approach*. London: Sage.

Sedgwick, E. K. (1990). *Epistemology of the Closet*. Berkeley: University of California Press.

Stryker, S. (1998). The transgender issue: An introduction. *GLQ: A Journal of Lesbian and Gay Studies*, 4(2), 145–158.

Woods, G. (ed.) (1998). *A History of Gay Literature: The Male Tradition*. New Haven: Yale University Press.

Levinas, Emmanuel

NEMONIE CRAVEN RODERICK

The Lithuanian-born French philosopher and Jewish scholar Emmanuel Levinas (1906–95) has come to be regarded as a central figure in the history of twentieth-century French philosophy, particularly in the areas of phenomenology and ethics, although his influence is now to be found in literary and film theory – despite the suspicions about "the aesthetic element" he raises in his essay "Reality and its shadow" (1989[1948]) and elsewhere – and in other diverse fields. His description of human subjectivity and its formation in an encounter with "the Other" of ethics has been attractive to those seeking to decenter human experience, in order to complicate an understanding of subjectivity as, in Levinas's words, "home" or as "conquest and jealous defense" (1981). Levinas's thinking of "alterity" is pitched against what he describes as ontology's totalizing grip on philosophy. "The Other" is a common translation of Levinas's *l'Autre* or *Autrui*, although his own use of terms and capitalization is inconsistent, as part of a refusal to "thematize" his work. This refusal of thematization is made manifest, structurally, in the metonymic chains through which Levinas seeks to rehabilitate philosophical terms such as "truth" (1981). An important interlocutor was Jacques Derrida, whose essay "Violence and metaphysics" (1978[1964]), constituted a major response to Levinas's *Totality and Infinity* (1969[1961]) – one that in many ways shaped Levinas's later work.

A major concern in Levinas's work post-1945 is the attempted rehabilitation of metaphysics as the thinking of an "exteriority" – elsewhere called "transcendence," "alterity," "the infinite" – which is unthematizable, and yet which orientates responsibility.

Levinas seeks also to rehabilitate a form of humanism – which Heidegger, a figure central to Levinas's intellectual formation, rejected. Levinas describes a "humanism of the other man" in response to the realization that humanism "has not been sufficiently human" (1981: 128). Dominique Janicaud (2000) positions Levinas's work as part of the "theological turn" in French phenomenology, yet (leaving Levinas's Talmudic readings and other writings about the idea of God aside) this is perhaps to overlook the extent to which the "religious being" Levinas describes is, independently of any theology, a description of being "otherwise" than the "political being" laid bare in the preface to *Totality and Infinity*, where politics is at first defined as the art of foreseeing and of winning war by any means. Describing the evolution of his thinking in an autobiographical text, "Signature" Levinas stated that it was "dominated by the presentiment and the memory of the Nazi horror" (1990: 291).

Sartre acknowledged that he was introduced to phenomenology by Levinas – through Levinas's translation, with Gabrielle Pfeiffer, of Husserl's *Cartesian Meditations* in 1931, and his *The Theory of Intuition in Husserl's Phenomenology* (1930), the first book on Husserl to be published in French. Yet, the years 1940–5 marked a rupture in Levinas's life, which was to profoundly affect his work and its place in any history. Levinas was drafted into the French army, and served as an interpreter of Russian (his mother tongue) and German. He was subsequently taken prisoner of war, and held in forced labor for five years. During this time he composed a fragment, entitled "il y a" – "there is," of *Existence and Existents* (*De l'Existence à l'existant*, 1978[1947]). His parents and two brothers, murdered in Levinas's hometown of Kaunas, Lithuania, are among "those closest" mentioned in the dedication of *Otherwise Than Being; or, Beyond Essence* (1981[1974]).

Despite his pivotal role in the history of phenomenology, Levinas's description of the encounter with the Other occupies an ambiguous position within the realm of the senses. *Totality and Infinity* focuses on "the face" as the point of an epiphany of alterity, which is nonetheless absolutely transcendent and therefore removed from the sensible. *Otherwise Than Being*, however, foregrounds the experiences of proximity, hostage, and psychism (a diachrony of Same and Other in sensibility), emphasizing "sensibility" through a description of ethical experience that is often visceral.

Levinas's description of intersubjectivity explicitly and implicitly positions itself against conceptualizations of human self-sufficiency and striving, such as Heidegger's. Indeed, any potential foreclosure of the narrative of human life is something Levinas writes against, despite his conceptualization of heteronomy, which bears comparison with the psychoanalysis he nonetheless openly disapproved of. His work is often concerned with the relationship between the individual and the state – particularly, as Howard Caygill (2002) has pointed out, France, and then Israel – as an ideal and as a political entity. One of the key concerns of Levinas's thought is justice, and his work frequently describes an experience of injustice. Levinas's work has been subject to various feminist criticisms since its initial reception by Simone de Beauvoir. His account of the erotic relation in *Totality and Infinity* has often been interpreted as conservative, yet his emphasis on sexual difference is of interest to feminist thinkers seeking to refocus attention on this area of research.

SEE ALSO: de Beauvoir, Simone; Deconstruction; Derrida, Jacques; Ethical Criticism

REFERENCES AND SUGGESTED READINGS

Caygill, H. (2002). *Levinas and the Political*. London: Routledge.

Critchley, S. (1992). *The Ethics of Deconstruction: Derrida and Levinas*. Oxford: Blackwell.

Derrida, J. (1978). Violence and metaphysics. In *Writing and Difference* (trans. A. Bass). London: Routledge & Kegan Paul. (Original work published 1964.)

Eaglestone, R (1997). *Ethical Criticism: Reading After Levinas*. Edinburgh: Edinburgh University Press.

Eaglestone, R. (2004). *The Holocaust and the Postmodern*. Oxford: Blackwell.

Janicaud, D., et al. (2000). *Phenomenology and the "Theological Turn": The French Debate*. New York: Fordham University Press.

Levinas, E. (1969). *Totality and Infinity: An Essay on Exteriority* (trans. A. Lingis). Pittsburgh: Duquesne University Press. (Original work published 1961.)

Levinas, E. (1978). *Existence and Existents* (trans. A. Lingis). The Hague: Martinus Nijhoff. (Original work published 1947.)

Levinas, E. (1981). *Otherwise Than Being; or, Beyond Essence* (trans. A. Lingis). Pittsburgh: Duquesne University Press. (Original work published 1974.)

Levinas, E. (1989). Reality and its shadow (trans. A. Lingis). In S. Hand (ed.), *The Levinas Reader*. Oxford: Blackwell, pp. 129–143. (Original work published 1948.)

Levinas, E. (1990). Signature. In *Difficult Freedom* (trans. S. Hand). Baltimore: Johns Hopkins University Press, pp. 289–295.

Lyotard, Jean-François

SIMON MALPAS

Jean-François Lyotard (1925–98) was a French political philosopher, art critic, and cultural theorist who became best known in the English-speaking world for having been one of the key thinkers to define and advocate postmodernism.

After graduating with an *agrégation* in philosophy in 1950, Lyotard worked as a schoolteacher in France and also in Algeria, which was at the time a French colony. As a young and radical Marxist, he became involved in Algeria's struggle for independence from France and was an active member of the Trotskyite political groups Socialisme ou barbarie (Socialism or Barbarism) and, later, Pouvoir Ouvrier (Worker's Power) which he co-founded in 1963. After his return home from Algeria, Lyotard became a university professor, and worked at a range of institutions in France, including Paris-VIII (Vincennes, Saint-Denis), Nanterre, and the Sorbonne, and in the United States, including Yale, Emory, and California, Irvine. Besides his work as a teacher and academic, Lyotard also acted as curator of a number of important art exhibitions, including, most notably, the influential *Les Immatériaux* for the Centre Pompidou in Paris in 1985, which was one of the first exhibitions to engage explicitly with the idea of postmodernism in art. He also wrote more than 25 books, whose subjects included the history of philosophy, political theory, art theory and criticism, technology, theology, psychoanalysis, and literature. Lyotard died in Paris on April 21, 1998.

Lyotard's first major publication was *Phenomenology* (1991[1954]), an introduction to and investigation of the philosophical movement of that name which developed form the work of the German philosopher Edmund Husserl (1859–1938) and sought to produce a systematic analysis of the forms by which consciousness perceives and experiences the world. Although the main focus of this book, which went into 10 editions between 1954 and 1986 and is still in print today, is largely on the technical introduction to a mode of philosophy, the final pages move on to investigate the potential that phenomenological thinking might have for political action in a manner that anticipates a great deal of Lyotard's

later arguments. Although only translated into English in 1991 once Lyotard's work on postmodernism had become well known, *Phenomenology* illustrates clearly his practice of generating modes of political engagement from detailed explorations of philosophical systems and theories.

Lyotard's next publications, many emerging from his experiences of the political struggle in Algeria and the student uprisings in Paris during May 1968, mark a turn away from the traditional party politics of the communist left as they launch a series of critiques of the ideas of his former Marxist comrades as well as the broader culture of modern Europe. In his texts of the late 1960s and early 1970s, Lyotard focuses on the capacity of discursive, figural, and political systems to carry the seeds of their own disruption, and much of the work celebrates the energy produced by the disintegration of particular conceptual systems. The arguments developed in these works culminate in the publication of what is viewed by many critics as Lyotard's most radical text, *Libidinal Economy* (1993 [1974]), which violently brings together the ideas of the political philosopher Karl Marx (1818–83) and the originator of psychoanalysis Sigmund Freud (1856–1939) to explore ways in which theories that attempt to provide universal or all-encompassing accounts of the world necessarily fail to grasp the complexities of particular situations and can serve to undermine the potential for resistance or transformation. The book diagnoses the violent and destructive powers of capitalism, but refuses to endorse the sorts of systematic critiques generated by Marxism and, instead, finds a potential for resistance in the exacerbation of that violence as the system turns against itself. Lyotard later referred to this as his "evil book" (1988[1983]: 13), acknowledging that in it he comes close to abandoning any possibility of theoretical critique in favor of a violent denunciation of all forms of identity, system, and program.

This analysis of the problems of identity and system, and the refusal of any position outside capitalism from which it can be critiqued, is modified and extended in his best-known book *The Postmodern Condition* (1984[1979]). In this, Lyotard explores "the condition of knowledge in the most highly developed societies" (xxiii) by analyzing the ways in which such societies ascribe value to scientific and technological research. He concludes that, in contrast to traditional ideas that the accumulation and distribution of knowledge (research and teaching) are valuable in their own rights, in the contemporary world knowledge is treated solely as a commodity: its value comes to be based entirely on its capacity to generate money. This commercialization of knowledge, according to Lyotard, marks a moment of transformation from a modern world in which the systematic pursuit of knowledge is perceived as a value in itself (which he calls the grand narrative of speculation) or as a means of freeing humanity from superstition and unnecessary suffering (the grand narrative of emancipation). In contrast to these, he describes postmodern knowledge as fragmented, diffuse, and incapable of grounding its legitimacy in any greater historical, scientific, moral, or political narrative. And this, he argues, leads to the definition of the postmodern as a condition of "incredulity toward metanarratives" (xxiv): a situation where larger collective goals and aspirations ("metanarratives") have been replaced by short-term, individualistic commercial imperatives of minimizing costs to maximize profits. "In matters of social justice and scientific truth alike, the legitimation of ... power is based on its optimising the system's performance – efficiency." he claims, and the criteria for success are simple: "be operational ... or disappear" (xxiv).

This operational criterion, Lyotard argues, is used not only for calculating the value of scientific research, but also underpins all social and cultural interactions in the postmodern world: the postmodern condition is one where capitalism has spread to every aspect of identity and experience, and the bonds of rationality and emancipation that used to hold communities together are in the process of being destroyed.

While *The Postmodern Condition* is concerned to explore the grounds that give rise to the contemporary commercialization of knowledge and identity, it provides few useful arguments about how this might be challenged or resisted. In his later postmodern work, however, Lyotard is keen to develop just such a critique. To achieve this, he turns to the philosophy of the German Enlightenment thinker Immanuel Kant (1724–1804), and particularly his theory of the sublime, to find ways to challenge both the modern structures that pretend to present universal positions and the operational imperative of postmodern capitalism. The dominant forms of representation in a given culture present the world in ways that are immediately recognizable for its citizens, and constitute their sense of reality through a mode that Lyotard calls "realism": realism is "the art of making reality, of knowing reality and knowing how to make reality" (1997[1993]: 91). Such realism, however, also excludes and silences anything that cannot be presented according to its rules: it has the capacity to make particular ideas, impulses, feelings, things, and even people "unpresentable." According to Lyotard, the sublime presents "the existence of something unpresentable" (1984[1979]: 78); the feeling of awe and terror associated with the sublime occurs, he argues, at moments where the dominant realism is shattered by some alternative form of presentation. In other words, Lyotard's postmodern sublime indicates that there are things that are impossible to present in established languages, voices that have been silenced, or ideas that cannot be formulated. Postmodern art, he asserts, "invokes the unpresentable in presentation itself ... not to take pleasure in them, but to better produce the feeling that there is something unpresentable" (1992[1988]: 15).

The political potential of this postmodern sublime is explored in one of Lyotard's most important books, *The Differend* (1988 [1983]). Here, he develops the idea of realism to argue that experience is constructed through a range of competing genres of discourse that organize knowledge and identity in relation to particular ends. He examines the ways in which these genres permit certain types of phrasing but prohibit others, thereby erecting value systems that always have the potential to exclude or silence particular groups or interests. What he calls a "differend" occurs when a genre of discourse prevents the possibility of testifying to an idea or experience: the structure of the language or political system in which something occurs is such that speaking about it becomes impossible. The role of the postmodern thinker or artist, Lyotard argues, is to expose those moments where ideas or people are silenced and to develop alternative genres where they can appear: "What is at stake in literature, in philosophy, in politics perhaps, is to bear witness to differends by finding idioms for them" (13). This is not a process of discovering a particular style of postmodern sublimity that avoids all realisms and recognizes the existence every differend; rather, Lyotard asserts that because each differend is unique, a new idiom will be required for each sublime moment and must be generated by that moment rather than anticipated in advance. In other words, for Lyotard, there can be no "postmodernist system" whose rules can be laid out for all time. Rather, the sublime resistance to totalities and systems must be recreated at every moment and unique in each case.

Lyotard's later writings continued to work through these problems, focusing on the potentialities of postmodern theory and philosophy, the impact of different modes of art on culture, and the problems that contemporary capitalism and technological development present to ideas of identity and community.

SEE ALSO: Derrida, Jacques; Postmodernism

REFERENCES AND SUGGESTED READINGS

Lyotard, J.-F. (1984). *The Postmodern Condition: A Report on Knowledge* (trans. G. Bennington & B. Massumi). Manchester: Manchester University Press. (Original work published 1979.)

Lyotard, J.-F. (1988). *The Differend: Phrases in Dispute* (trans. G. Van Den Abeele). Manchester: Manchester University Press. (Original work published 1983.)

Lyotard, J.-F. (1991). *Phenomenology* (trans. B. Bleakley). Albany: SUNY Press. (Original work published 1954.)

Lyotard, J.-F. (1992). *The Postmodern Explained: Correspondence 1982–1985* [*Le Postmoderne expliqué aux enfants*] (trans. D. Barry, B. Maher, J. Pefanis, V. Spate, & M. Thomas). Minneapolis: University of Minnesota Press. (Original work published 1988.)

Lyotard, J.-F. (1993). *Libidinal Economy* (trans. I. Hamilton Grant). London: Athlone. (Original work published 1974.)

Lyotard, J.-F. (1997). *Postmodern Fables* (trans. G. Van Den Abeele). Minneapolis: University of Minnesota Press. (Original work published 1993.)

Readings, B. (1991). *Introducing Lyotard: Art and Politics*. London: Routledge.

Sim, S. (1996). *Jean-François Lyotard*. Hemel Hempstead: Prentice Hall/Harvester Wheatsheaf.

M

de Man, Paul

MARTIN MCQUILLAN

Paul de Man (1919–83) was a Belgian literary critic and theorist most commonly identified with the Yale School of deconstruction and the posthumous revelation of his wartime journalism in occupied Belgium. However, de Man's life and work is considerably more diverse and complex than these associations would suggest.

De Man studied engineering, chemistry, and, later, social sciences in Brussels in the years before World War II and the German occupation. His uncle, Hendrik de Man, was a socialist minister in the prewar Belgian government. At this time Paul de Man was a member of the editorial board of the left-wing student literary journal *Les Cahiers du Libre Examen*. During the occupation, de Man's university closed and his uncle, having initially helped to negotiate the surrender of the Belgian army and a non-violent transition to German military rule, went into political exile in Switzerland. During the early years of the war Paul de Man wrote literary and cultural reviews for *Le Soir* and other Belgian newspapers. While the vast majority of these reviews are noncontentious, even banal, a small number demonstrate an attitude of accommodation with the Nazi occupation. One text in particular, "The Jews in con-temporary literature," published as part of an anti-Semitic special issue of *Le Soir* has marked de Man's posthumous reputation. This early writing is collected in the volume *Wartime Journalism, 1934–1943* (Hamacher et al. 1988).

Shortly after the publication of this article, de Man left *Le Soir* to work at Agence Dechenne, covertly employing and publishing members of the Resistance. When he was eventually removed from his editorial position, because of fears over Nazi censorship, he took his young family to live with his father near Antwerp, where he worked on a translation of Melville's *Moby Dick*. After the war, he traveled to the US, initially as part of an art-publishing venture. The business soon folded, but de Man stayed on in the States. He taught French at Bard College before studying for a doctorate at Harvard. His thesis was entitled "The Post-Romantic Predicament." The first half, on Yeats, is reproduced in the posthumous volume *The Rhetoric of Romanticism* (1984); the second half, on Mallarmé, is reproduced in *The Romantic Predicament* (McQuillan, forthcoming). De Man held the post of lecturer and was a member of the Society of Junior Fellows at Harvard from 1954 to 1957, contemporaneous with Stanley Cavell and Noam Chomsky. A selection of published critical material from this time, including significant essays on Heidegger, appears in a

The Encyclopedia of Literary and Cultural Theory   General editor: Michael Ryan
© 2011 Blackwell Publishing Ltd

collection edited by Lindsay Waters (1989). De Man remarried in the States and went on to hold academic posts at Cornell and John Hopkins, as well as the University of Zurich.

In 1970 he moved to Yale, where he became the Sterling Professor of French and Comparative Literature. It was here that he produced his most significant critical and theoretical writing, including *Blindness and Insight* (1983[1971]) and *Allegories of Reading* (1979). De Man was an accomplished essayist and the divergent interests of his later work are collected in a number of subsequent volumes: *The Rhetoric of Romanticism* (1984), *The Resistance to Theory* (1986), *Romanticism and Contemporary Criticism* (1993), and *Aesthetic Ideology* (1996).

De Man died of cancer in December 1983 and was greatly mourned by colleagues at Yale and the generations of extraordinary graduate students he had trained. In 1988 his wartime journalism came to light as a Belgian PhD student, Ortwin de Graef, carried out research into his early writing. The media controversy that followed has considerably muddled the general understanding of de Man whereby short texts of juvenilia are said either to explain or to overturn important mature volumes of literary theory. De Man's singular errors are at the same time neither excusable nor comparable to significant collaborationist and "Nazi scholars" such as Martin Heidegger and Carl Schmidt. Rather, his later more fully elaborated rhetorical reading or "deconstruction" might go some way to offering a critique of totalitarianism.

His mature "deconstructive" work can be considered as falling into three parts. First, his hypothesis on critical blindness and insight – namely, that any critical text is unaware of its own ignorance concerning the key tropes that it interrogates. It would be a necessary illusion of any critical text that it be able to produce a definitive reading of any given literary or philosophical work. However, de Man suggests that in the movement between the literary text and its critical reading, any such mastery is undone and the key terms of the reading are rendered unreadable in any straightforward sense. Second, this understanding of the self-displacement of textuality gives rise to de Man's more considered disarticulation of language in *Allegories of Reading* (1979). In the second half of this book, through an extensive account of tropes in Rousseau, de Man suggests that what we normally consider to be the aberrant or eccentric uses of figural language in poetry and literature are in fact the general conditions of all language and communication. He develops an understanding of different orders of textual allegory, in which a text is said to be always referring to something other than itself just as it seeks to maintain the illusion of its univocal or closed nature, subsequently demonstrating first the impossibility of the closure and, secondly, the unsustainability of its "deconstruction." He takes this term from his Yale colleague Jacques Derrida. However, he uses it sparingly elsewhere and while, like Derrida, much of his later work might be considered the result of his earlier reading of Heidegger, his critical project around "the linguistics of literariness" is quite distinct from that of Derrida's deconstruction of logocentrism.

Much of de Man's critical work after *Allegories of Reading* involves a continued attempt to think through the problems of figural language in relation to romantic and postromantic literature. The final and third phase of his work is represented by the essays collected under the title *Aesthetic Ideology* (1996) in which de Man gives his attention to ideology as a linguistic problem in eighteenth-century philosophy, notably in Kant and Hegel. It is here that he develops his understanding of the materiality of the letter." In a late interview he suggested that he was working on a study of Marx and Kierkegaard as thinkers of ideology and readers of Hegel. This work was not completed.

De Man's writing covers readings of, amongst others, Rousseau, Keats, Shelley, Wordsworth, Yeats, Proust, Mallarmé, Nietzsche, Benjamin, Holderlin, and Rilke, as well as his contemporaries in literary theory. In turn, his work has been the subject of productive readings by Jacques Derrida, J. Hillis Miller, and Rodolphe Gasché.

SEE ALSO: Deconstruction; Derrida, Jacques; Heidegger, Martin; Miller, J. Hillis; Yale School

REFERENCES AND SUGGESTED READINGS

de Graef, O. (1993). *Serenity in Crisis: A Preface to Paul de Man, 1939–1960*. Lincoln: University of Nebraska Press.

de Graef, O. (1995). *Titanic Light: Paul de Man's Post-Romanticism* Lincoln: University of Nebraska Press.

de Man, P. (1979). *Allegories of Reading: Figural Language in Rousseau, Nietzsche, Rilke, and Proust*. New Haven: Yale University Press.

de Man, P. (1983). *Blindness and Insight: Essay in the Rhetoric of Contemporary Criticism*, 2nd edn. Minneapolis: University of Minnesota Press. (Original work published 1971.)

de Man, P. (1984). *The Rhetoric of Romanticism*. New York: Columbia University Press. (Essays originally written 1956–83.)

de Man, P. (1986). *The Resistance to Theory*. Minneapolis: University of Minnesota Press.

de Man, P. (1988) *Wartime Journalism, 1939–1943* (ed. W. Hamacher, N. Hertz, & T. Keenan). Lincoln: University of Nebraska Press.

de Man, P. (1993). *Romanticism and Contemporary Criticism: The Gauss Seminar and Other Papers* (ed. E. Burt, K. Newmark, & A. Warminski). Baltimore: Johns Hopkins University Press.

de Man, P. (1996). *Aesthetic Ideology* (ed. A. Warminski). Minneapolis: University of Minnesota Press.

McQuillan, M. (ed.) (forthcoming). *Paul de Man, The Romantic Predicament*. Edinburgh: Edinburgh University Press.

Waters, L. (ed.) (1989). *Paul de Man: Critical Writings, 1953–1978*. Minneapolis: University of Minnesota Press.

Marxism

GAVIN GRINDON & MICHAEL RYAN

Marxism is the intellectual and political movement founded by Karl Marx (1818–83). The socialist and communist movements, which seek to bring about economic equality and a fairer distribution of wealth, antedated Marx, but he gave them a sense of intellectual coherence in his major works (some co-authored with Friedrich Engels) – *The Communist Manifesto*, *The German Ideology*, and *Capital*. Marx also provided the basis for a "Marxist" literary and cultural theory in his theory of ideology, in which he famously proclaimed that the ruling ideas of any society are the ideas of the ruling class. Later theorists would also draw on his reworking of Hegel's dialectical method of analysis to describe the complex ways culture both reflects reality and prefigures new versions of social life.

Marxism is both a method of analysis and a body of ideas about how culture and society operate. Marxists believe that capitalism, the economic form invented in England in the eighteenth century and still practiced worldwide, is inherently unfair. Workers, who have no way to survive except by selling their labor to others who possess wealth enough to buy it, are systematically exploited under capitalism. They manufacture things or perform services, and those things and services are worth more on the market than the money workers are paid.

This "surplus value" allows the owners of enterprises to profit – often considerably – from the labor of others. Capitalism is a way of mobilizing people together to work on tasks and projects that can be sold for others' benefit. Although it is a way of addressing human needs, it also allows those with economic power to take advantage of others for their own greater gain. One critique made of capitalism is that it invariably produces unequal results; indeed, if it is to function, it must produce economic inequality in the form of lower wages for workers in relation to higher profit for owners. Control over the economic market and the workplace, for example, allows one man like Bill Gates to walk away with $35 billion, while the workers who do the work that produces that wealth earn significantly less.

According to Marx, humans are defined by their active labor in the natural world around them. They are also social creatures whose beings are defined by interaction with others. Capitalism perverts these two qualities of human life by converting the products of human laboring activity to use for private gain and by making one social group subordinate to another in a hierarchy that can never be modified given the rules of operation of the capitalist system. Workers put value into things through labor. Those products of labor ("commodities") have use value for others, and they also have exchange value on the economic marketplace. The surplus value in the commodities, the increment in value over cost injected into commodities in the manufacturing process that gives rise to profit and financial wealth, is, according to Marx, the result exclusively of insufficiently remunerated labor. Workers thus live in penury, while owners enjoy a lavish leisure lifestyle. Marx felt that this situation was untenable and that capitalism would eventually give rise to a countermovement on the part of workers (what

he called the "proletariat") that would bring about socialism.

He based this claim on the method of dialectic he borrowed from German philosopher Georg Hegel. For Marx, social life operates according to dialectical principles. The dialectic is a relational principle that describes social life as a necessary interaction between parts. Thus, capital cannot exist without workers; it only makes sense when workers are available to allow capital to exploit them in order to produce more capital or wealth. Capital thus presupposes wage labor both logically and in reality. And the same is true of wage labor. Absent capital, wage labor makes no sense. The two sides of capitalism exist in a dynamic exchange, therefore, and cannot exist without the other. Together they make up the complex totality of capitalism.

The dialectic is also a historical principle that describes how things develop and change. Feudalism was an economic form whose internal dynamics propelled it toward further evolution. As economic production developed, a surplus became available for trade, and trade in turn made possible cities and a new class of merchants. Those merchants' interests were opposed to the interests of the landed feudal nobility, and the conflict between the two groups eventually brought feudalism to an end. A new economic form developed out of it, and that was capitalism. Marx argued that a similar evolution would occur in capitalism. Eventually, its internal contradiction between a laboring class that earned little and an owning class that benefited inordinately from others' labor would break it apart. The proletariat would assert its own interests and bring about an end to a system that was based entirely on the interests of capitalists.

Several terms from dialectics become central to Marxism. One is "contradiction." According to dialectical theory, all societies are characterized by dynamic conflicts between social groups or economic classes. These contradictions tend toward resolution and propel the society toward change and further evolution. Hence, in this understanding of things, as capital forces labor to accept ever lower wages, the contradiction between the two groups will become exacerbated. Another term is "totality." According to dialectical theory, one cannot understand any one element of a society without taking the whole into account. The whole of a society is implied in any one of its parts. That is the case because all parts of a social system are dialectically related one with the other. One cannot therefore isolate one part of a society from the surrounding parts. Any one part presupposes all the others.

Another important term is "negation." The dialectic is also a doctrine of knowledge. Indeed, Hegel first elaborated the theory in terms of how the mind knows the world. The mind begins with simple sense perception. But simple sense perceptions immediately evoke the idea of universal ideas because individual determinate things are the opposite of universal and indeterminate ones. If one thinks of this in terms of traditional dialectics, it would go something like this: Socrates is a human. All humans are mortal. Therefore, Socrates must be mortal. Notice how one begins with a simple determinate thing: Socrates is human. One then moves to a general or universal principle: all humans are mortal. And the two side by side generate a logical and necessary conclusion: Socrates must be mortal. Necessity is essential to this process, and this explains why dialectical thinkers see things evolving by necessity in the world. To return to the issue of knowledge, when one knows something specific and determinate, one immediately, as in the example of Socrates, evokes a more general term because specific concrete things evoke the idea of their opposite – a general idea. Any single determination of sensory knowledge ("I see the screen") evokes the general idea of "all screens" or "all computers." Each example summons its genre, its class, or its type if it is to be named accurately. The general type, however, is the negation of the first empirical or sensory example, as the example in turn is the negation of the general type or class. Each is the opposite of the other. Negation is the propulsion mechanism of the dialectic; it means that conflict and change and inevitably logical evolution are what characterize society, not stasis and equilibrium. Labor is the negation of capital because it consists of work rather than ownership of the means of production, and that negation can never be resolved into a non-conflictual stasis.

A final important term is "mediation." Labor mediates capital, as capital mediates labor in the social dynamic that includes the two. To understand one, you have to understand the other. Neither can be isolated from the other.

Marx provided the first terms for a Marxist understanding of literature and culture in his theory of ideology. According to this theory, the ideas that dominate discussion in a society are the "ruling ideas of the ruling class." One might expect literature, which deals with ideas, to embody this principle, though not always. Shakespeare was a toady for the nobility, and he justifies their rule over society in his plays. But Virginia Woolf was an opponent of wars conducted by unintelligent men for foolish ends. Moreover, Marxists apply the dialectic to culture and see contradictions there between interests, groups, and ideas. Contradictions are also evident in the way ideas produce results at odds with the interests that fostered them in the first place. Capitalism survives by foregrounding the value of "freedom" as a way of fending off the use of government to change the economic system for the common good. But that means capitalists cannot restrain cultural freedom and must tolerate a high level of criticism of their practices.

The success of Bolshevism, a kind of authoritarian state communism, in Russia allowed Russian thinkers like Leon Trotsky to set the tone for early Marxist investigations of literature and culture. Burdened by the conviction that literature must somehow contribute to socialist revolution, these thinkers tended to criticize cultural tendencies that seemed to have other ends in mind (such as studying literature as an autonomous cultural form entirely independently of social context, as in formalism, or experimenting with literary form in a way that abandoned previous assumptions about realist representation, as in modernism). Early Marxist literary critics such as Georg Lukács favored realism over modernism. They argued that realist writers more accurately represented the totality of a society and therefore showed its truth more clearly, even if, like Balzac, they were political conservatives. Such literature, it was believed, was more likely to help bring about a socialist revolution.

With the decline of Russian communism across the late twentieth century, and the various directions taken by Marxist or communist organizations around the world, the political allegiances of Marxists have become highly diffuse and complex, with some looking to small parties of the Left, indigenous guerrilla struggles, or the progress of extra-parliamentary social movements in the West or elsewhere. Despite what could be great differences, in each case Marxist cultural critiques always held that its analyses were tied to a commitment to radical social change. The Marxist concepts of ideology and alienation, and issues of agency and the relationship between culture and history, remained central concerns of Marxist cultural thought in the late twen-

tieth century. Marxist critics all still insisted that to understand culture one had to place it in its historical context using Marxist theory, but they increasingly began to reexamine the workings and key terms of that theory.

Contemporary Marxist approaches to culture have almost universally been marked by the Western Marxism of the Frankfurt School, even if that meant taking a position against it, and it had little relation to the "official" Marxism of the Communist Party. Jürgen Habermas and Herbert Marcuse, who were both affiliated with the Frankfurt School, had begun to produce work in the 1960s which grew in influence into the 1970s; also in the 1960s, many Marxists in France and the UK were newly discovering and engaging with the work of Antonio Gramsci, Theodor Adorno, and Walter Benjamin. Similarly, in the late 1960s the work of the Russian Marxist Mikhail Bakhtin and his circle from the 1930s was first introduced to academics in France, the UK, and the US, where Bakhtin's notions of dialogism, heterogeneity, and carnival had an immediate influence. They shared with these earlier Western Marxists a concern with approaching culture in terms of alienation, hegemony, and ideology, and questions of culture's role in democratic participation and social change.

As the 1960s progressed, Western societies tended to develop from a basis in industrial production to postindustrial economies producing services (including mass media) rather than material objects and becoming what is often termed a "consumer society." This shift meant culture became increasingly central to the economy, and the Western Marxist emphases on culture, alienation, and the city appeared ever more relevant. Moreover, 1968 saw radical social movements explode across the globe, with a general strike in France and serious urban unrest in the US. Students played an important part in the protests and activism of these movements – Marxist theorists at the time were often close to these movements and many later theorists would look back on 1968 as an inspirational turning point (Henri Lefebvre's *The Explosion* [1969] provides a good account of the events in France). It was an exciting time to be a radical, and this turbulent historical context was a central influence on the cultural concerns of Marxist critics.

WESTERN MARXIST LEGACIES

The academic and philosophical version of Marxism called "Western Marxism," which had developed in the 1930s with Adorno, Benjamin, and Max Horkheimer, was a central point of influence and critique for Marxists in this period. The second wave of Frankfurt School Marxists were still current in the late 1960s, and the work of Marcuse and Habermas was particularly influential. Writing in a period of prosperity and growing social movements, these philosophers tended to be less negative toward popular culture and the possibility of change than the early Frankfurt School Marxists had been. Their texts contain hopeful theories of liberation, action, community, communication, and "The Great Refusal," which are quite distant from the despair and pessimism of Benjamin and Adorno. Marcuse's major works had already been published by 1966; his *One Dimensional Man* and *Repressive Tolerance* were especially influential on activists and academics in the 1960s and 1970s. In 1978 he published *The Aesthetic Dimension*, which attempted to critique Marxist approaches to art and aesthetics by arguing that the whole content and value of an artwork was not historically determined. Habermas, meanwhile, had published as his first book the highly influential *The Structural Transformation of the Public*

Sphere (1992[1962]), and went on to explore the relationship between civil society and social power structures in the 1970s and '80s in texts such as *Legitimation Crisis* and *The Theory of Communicative Action*.

Other Marxists in this period, though they did not study with the Frankfurt School, were often deeply indebted to its use of the dialectical critique drawn from Hegelian philosophy, and applied it to a wide range of phenomena. Theorists such as Guy Debord and Henri Lefebvre were looking toward the increasing orientation of Western society around the urban space of the city, the consumption of commodities (the "consumer society"), and the role of the mass media. Lefebvre developed Western Marxism's critique of alienation and reification (his early introductory text on *Dialectical Materialism* was deeply influential in France) in terms of urban space and the organization of everyday life under capitalism. In the three volumes of *The Critique of Everyday Life*, he opened up "everyday life" as a new object of critical inquiry. He demonstrated how culture, leisure practices, and social interaction and experience were shaped and determined by capitalism. Meanwhile, in works such as *The Right to the City* and *The Production of Space*, he demonstrated how space itself is not a natural occurrence, but is socially produced, and that, furthermore, capitalism produces particular formations of social space, and conditions how we experience it. He also charted the historical changes in such space, focusing, for example, on how the modern "city" space produced by capital was extending to a more general urbanization of society. In English, his accounts of this social construction of space have been enthusiastically received by critical geographers.

The Situationist International was formed to develop practices to resist the commodification of everyday life that Lefebvre perceived. Its most famous theorist, Guy Debord, would provide his own critique, *The Society of the Spectacle*, which argued that where alienation was once a matter of being turning into having, having had now turned into mere appearing. Life appeared now only as an accumulation of spectacles, and real human experience was replaced by its mere representation. Debord's theory has been very influential in the analysis of media, visual, and cultural studies. Raoul Vaniegem provided this daunting critique with a positive counter-point, *The Revolution of Everyday Life*, which proposed techniques such as the re-fusal of social roles and argued that this dire situation could yet be subverted. It proved most influential amongst Marxists and acti-vists outside the academy. Both Lefebvre and the Situationists were, like the first generation of Western Marxists, influenced by surrealism, and together developed the peculiar claim that the revolution should resemble a festival. The Situationists' ideas in this direction, which were concerned with rethinking the role that culture could play in social change, have been deeply influential on radical strands of art, cultural criticism, and activism up to the present day, both inside and outside the academy. These debates on the role of culture were also prompted by movements within culture. The rise of "neo-avant-garde" pop and conceptual art prompted a rethinking of the trajectory of modernity in Peter Bürger's *Theory of the Avant-Garde*.

THE NEW LEFT AND AFTER

This international reinvigoration of Marxist thought, which broke with the Communist Party and rode on the wave of social activ-ism that exploded in 1968, was given the name the "New Left." While in the US this tended to denote a more activist and less theoretical turn toward countercultural, civil rights, and antiwar social movements, in the UK the New Left was the name of a more theoretical, intellectual break with official forms of Marxism, exemplified in the writing of the journal *New Left Review* after 1960, with Perry Anderson as its editor. In the late 1960s in the UK, the New Left drew on the work of earlier British Marxists who addressed culture, such as E. P. Thompson and Richard Hoggart, whose work had often combined Marxist criticism with existing but more reactionary culturalist traditions of British literary criticism, by focusing on and valuing ordi-nary working-class culture positively along-side "high" cultural production. Against culturalism's narratives of cultural decline, this tradition began to develop the notion that the antithesis of mass culture was not the narrow cultural canon of the intelligent-sia, but the common culture of the working class. This perspective would be developed most fully by Raymond Williams in works which built on his earlier publication of *Culture and Society* and *The Long Revolu-tion*. Williams also insisted on seeing culture in its social context, in his famous claim that "culture is ordinary" – not a collection of cultural objects, but "a whole way of life," which included social institutions and social relationships. He would develop sev-eral key concepts in the 1960s and '70s which attempted to explain how culture and society are related. Most famously, Williams used the term "cultural materi-alism" to negotiate a position between a crude Marxist determinism where culture was merely the ideological superstructure produced by the economic base, and a con-servative idealism where culture is solely the product of creative consciousness. He pro-posed that culture is a "structure of feeling," again attempting to mediate between the delicate treatment of social experience and the determinate realities of social relations. In *Marxism and Literature* (1977), he reworked and complicated the often crude Marxist account of culture, such that the economic base determined the cultural superstructure, by arguing that in any particular period, such relations of determination are uneven and mobile. Alongside the dominant social and cultural forms of any particular period, emergent and residual forms may contest and support them.

Perry Anderson, who edited *New Left Review* for most of its existence, was another key figure in the British New Left. As the 1970s progressed, he produced critical texts such as *Considerations on Western Marxism* as well as playing a crucial role as an editor in influencing the direction of discussion amongst English-speaking academic Marxists, introducing them to new work such as that of Louis Althusser (see below). These developments among the Left were not uncontroversial. E. P. Thompson, an English Marxist of an earlier generation, attacked these turns in Marxism in *The Poverty of Theory* (1978), prompting a response by Anderson, *Arguments Within English Marxism* (1980).

RETHINKING DISCIPLINES

British cultural Marxism often had a literary orientation, but, as with the example of Williams in literature, in art history there were precedents of Marxist scholarship before 1966, for example in the work of Arnold Hauser or Meyer Schapiro. However, such perspectives became much more widespread and accepted in all disciplines within the academy during this later period.

In the study of literature, Terry Eagleton, a student of Williams, contributed centrally to this rethinking when he published *Literary Theory* (1983), which presented an account of the study of English literature – and of the different theoretical approaches to it – as the products of the values of different class interests, and which has be-

come a required text for many undergraduate courses. He has gone on to produce other important Marxist engagements with culture, such as *The Ideology of the Aesthetic*, drawing on continental philosophy, the work of Althusser, and British cultural Marxism. In literary studies in the US, Frederick Jameson's *The Political Unconscious: Narrative as a Socially Symbolic Act* and *The Prison House of Language* explored culture and language from a perspective indebted to Althusser, while in art history T. J. Clark made similarly influential innovations in his critical social art-historical readings of nineteenth- and twentieth-century art in texts such as *The Image of the People* and *The Absolute Bourgeois*. Elsewhere, David Harvey's *Social Justice and the City* and *The Limits to Capital* wrought similar changes in geography, and Stanley Aronowitz made notable Marxist interventions in the field of sociology and cultural studies. Beyond these influential figures, during the 1970s and '80s a number of other studies appeared across the humanities which brought politics and social context to bear on the study of culture. These theoretical revisions within academic disciplines, which bring in matters of history, politics, and society, have played an important part in the contextual broadening and crossing of academic disciplines to incorporate popular and visual culture among other areas. For example Stuart Hall, a figure central to the development of the discipline of cultural studies, produced work informed by Marxist theory. As Marxism was increasingly employed as a methodological tool for interpreting culture in the academy, it also influenced other approaches and was partially adopted or combined with them in various ways. We can find examples of this in aspects of New Historicism and poststructuralism as well as cultural studies. Some critics would contend that these uses of Marxist ideas tended to drop the critique of relations of class and power in culture alongside a commitment to radical social change, while others combined Marxist approaches to culture with other political concerns oriented around race, gender, and sexuality. In each case the Marxist element of such a critical practice was not simply to present a text against an abstract "context," but to show texts as implicated within and constitutive of the movements of social power relations.

ALTHUSSER AND STRUCTURALIST MARXISM

In this period, many Marxists also began to engage with new ideas emerging in French and continental philosophy. The most influential example of such work was that of Louis Althusser. Distinct from the Western-Marxist styled work of Lefebvre and Debord, and from culturalist English Marxism, Althusser brought Marxist approaches together with those of structuralism, and was to elicit a huge influence over Marxist thought in the 1970s and '80s. In his most famous works, *For Marx* and *Reading Capital*, he proposed a return to Marx's works which offered a new interpretation. Rather than focusing on the "humanist" issues of the subject's alienation with which Western Marxism had been concerned, Althusser advanced an antihumanist, structuralist Marxism. To this end, he argued that there was an "epistemological break" in Marx's work between his youthful work (which was concerned with alienation and humanity's species-being) and his later writing (concerned with a critical analysis of capitalist society). Althusser's account of ideology was structuralist in that ideology was not a matter of a subject separated from reality by a spectacle or false consciousness that could be rent asunder, but was a more complex situation, of the imaginary set of relationships of individuals to their real conditions of existence. In this situation, ideology constitutes the subject's very identity *as* a subject. Confronting ideology meant uncovering the ways in which we are caught and inscribed as subjects within ideological practices and social apparatuses. Althusser's approach to culture was set out clearly in his essay "Ideology and Ideological State Apparatuses," in which he identified such apparatus in the form of the media, the family, and the education system. His approach was to be influential for a generation of English- and French-speaking Marxists. In *For a Theory of Literary Production* (1966), his student, Pierre Macherey, argued that all texts contain their real material conditions of production inscribed within them in the form of absences the text cannot integrate into its ideological resolution. Texts should therefore be read symptomatically. In later work with Etienne Balibar ("On Literature as an Ideological Form"), Macherey argued that the idea of literature should be abandoned because it, like aesthetics, fostered ideological domination.

POSTSTRUCTURAL MARXISM

Many Marxist theorists also attempted to explain and engage with culture and society by making use of poststructuralist ideas, or by posing the possibility of a postmodern Marxism. Often, this theoretical move was aligned to an attempt to make sense of social changes in the West: both the decline of traditional working-class movements and the growth of a multiplicity of movements oriented around issues and identities such as race, gender, sexuality, animal rights, climate change, nuclear proliferation, etc.

In France, some of Althusser's students have gone on to become increasingly prominent figures in Marxist thought by doing exactly this. The most prominent of these are Etienne Balibar and Jacques Rancière. Balibar has written on issues of nation, race, and globalization in the 1990s, in texts such as *Masses, Classes, Ideas* and *We, the People of Europe? Reflections on Transnational Citizenship*. In the same period, Rancière's translated texts, *The Politics of Aesthetics* and *The Future of the Image*, have become recently influential on the field of visual culture. Elsewhere, the many and varied publications of Slovenian critic Slavoj Žižek have marked a critical return to the structuralist approaches of Jacques Lacan and Althusser, addressing subjects such as multiculturalism, Lenin, film, and violence in texts such as *The Parallax View, The Sublime Object of Ideology*, and *The Ticklish Subject*. Žižek's eclectic and playful writing courts controversy and has been attacked by a number of critics.

In 1985, Ernesto Laclau and Chantal Mouffe published their controversial book *Hegemony and Socialist Strategy*, which came to be associated with the general term "post-Marxist," which some have also used to describe the French theorists above. In their attempt to rethink Marxism, Laclau and Mouffe also took issue with how culture is historically determined. Close to Althusser's ideas, they returned to the Gramscian concept of "hegemony" and argued that, instead of class as a material relation which produces ideology, class is itself a concept a product of hegemony, as but one identity in a web of hegemonic positions incorporating sexual, race, and gender positions. They proposed multiplying democratic spaces for these new social movements as the best tactic for radicals now. They were criticized both by more classical Marxists for this attack on their ideas, and by others who saw their strategy as a move away from revolutionary commitment and into a liberal "identity" politics. This academic tendency to combine Marxism and poststructualism has been influential on other radical currents in the academy in the 1990s and 2000s, such as the growing body of writing on post-anarchist theories of culture and society, which bring anarchist and poststructuralist thought together. In this same period in the academy, the critical methodologies of Marxism were challenged from without, by feminists and postcolonialists, as well as by an emerging queer theoretical tendency. Nonetheless, these writers were also indebted to the critical scholarly path which had been opened by Marxist scholars before them, and engaged positively with their ideas as well.

The most cited and influential combination of Marxism and poststructuralist thought is that of Michael Hardt and Antonio Negri's *Empire*, published in 2000 amidst the swell of the global justice movement of the 1990s which had shut down a World Trade Organization meeting in Seattle the year before. Their approach brought a raft of interest in autonomist Marxism, a current which had developed writing on economics and philosophy since the 1970s, but which only began really to influence thinking on culture after 2000. Autonomist Marxist perspectives break with the dialectical traditions of Marxism, and are concerned not with the critique of ideology or hegemony but with the self-organization of the working class. Developing in Italy, France, and the US in the 1970s, theorists such as Negri and Mario Tronti developed concepts of "class composition" and "the refusal of work," positing not a Western Marxist society of the spectacle or a society of passive consumers, but a subsumption of society to the factory, a "social factory" in which all social activity becomes a form of work that reproduces profit for capitalism. However, reversing most Marxist thought, they argue that refusal and resistance are primary, and that this kind of capitalist restructuring of society is always a reaction to, and reflection of, gains made by working-class movements. Developing the notion of the social factory, more recent autonomist theorists in this line, such as Paolo Virno and Maurizio Lazzarato, have proposed that the creative industries and artwork are exemplary forms of a new category of "immaterial labor" which is central to contemporary capitalism (see, for example, Virno 2003). These perspectives have recently become more influential in writing on art and cultural studies, thanks to readers such as that edited by Virno and Hardt (1996).

Empire and its sequel, *Multitude*, attempted to synthesize this current with the radical poststructuralism of Michel Foucault and Gilles Deleuze. They were the most commercially visible of a wave of new approaches to Marxist and radical theory informed by the global justice movement, just as many theorists of the 1960s and '70s had been inspired by the movements of the 1960s. Rather than a model of hegemony or late capital, Hardt and Negri propose that capital is (metaphorically) an empire, which attempts to subsume the world to its reproduction. Leading this development is the new category of immaterial labor, found in the move to service industries, flexible and deregulated work, and immaterial goods. But this situation produces a new figure, the multitude, which takes the place of the working class as agent of revolution. It is composed of these workers, whose very flexibility and movement within the system provides new possibilities to undo it. Their analysis has been incredibly popular, particularly in analyses of mass culture and political art practices. However, it has not been uncontroversial. Contesting similar theories – for example John Holloway's *Change the World Without Taking Power* (2002) – vied with criticisms by other Marxists, such as those collected in Gopal Balakrishnan's *Debating Empire*.

Diffuse hybrid Marxian or Marxist-informed perspectives have also begun to emerge in the academy from within the global justice movement, in literature, cultural studies, and art history, in collections such as David Graeber and Stevphen Shukaitis's *Constituent Imagination* and Gregory Sholette and Blake Stimson's *Collectivism After Modernism*. Colored by the recent wave of anticapitalist social movements, they have often variously attempted to bring the now mostly academic Marxist traditions of cultural analysis discussed above into conversation with the anarchist, autonomist, and Situationist ideas which predominate in contemporary social movements. Meanwhile, there has been a related growth in academics relating anarchist theory and history to the themes that Marxism has traditionally engaged, in works such as Allan Antliff's *Anarchy and Art* (2007), and Josh MacPee and Erik Reuland's edited collection, *Realizing the Impossible* (2007).

SEE ALSO: Adorno, Theodor; Alienation; Althusser, Louis; Bakhtin, M. M.; Base/Superstructure; Benjamin, Walter; Commodity; Commodity/Commodification and Cultural Studies; Critical Theory/Frankfurt School; Eagleton, Terry; Gramsci, Antonio; Habermas, Jürgen; Hall, Stuart; Ideology; Jameson, Fredric; Lefebvre, Henri; Lukács, Georg; Marcuse, Herbert; Marx, Karl; Negri, Antonio and Hardt, Michael; Rancière, Jacques; Reification; Situationist International, The; Williams, Raymond; Žižek, Slavoj

REFERENCES AND SUGGESTED READINGS

Alderson, D. (2004). *Terry Eagleton*. London: Macmillan.

Anderson, P. (1980). *Arguments Within English Marxism*. London: Verso.

Antliff, A. (2007). *Anarchy and Art: From the Paris Commune to the Fall of the Berlin Wall*. Vancouver: Arsenal Press.

Blackledge, P. (2004). *Perry Anderson: Marxism and the New Left*. London: Merlin.

Day, R. (2005). *Gramsci Is Dead*. London: Pluto.

Debord, G. (1968). *The Society of the Spectacle*. London: Rebel Press.

Eagleton, T. (1983). *Literary Theory*. Oxford: Blackwell.

Elden, S. (2006). *Understanding Henri Lefebvre: Theory and the Possible*. London: Continuum.

Eliot, G. (2006). *Althusser: The Detour of Theory*, Boston: Brill.

Gopal B. (ed.) (2003). *Debating Empire*. London: Verso.

Habermas, J. (1992). *The Structural Transformation of the Public Sphere* (trans. T. Burger). Cambridge: Polity. (Original work published 1962.)

Hardt, M., & Negri, A. (2000). *Empire*. Cambridge, MA: Harvard University Press.

Hardt, M., & Negri, A. (2004). *Multitude: War and Democracy in the Age of Empire*. New York: Penguin.

Hemingway, A. (ed.) (2006). *Marxism and the History of Art*. London: Pluto.

Holloway, J. (2002). *Change the World Without Taking Power: The Meaning of Revolution Today*. London: Verso.

Lefebvre, H. (1969). *The Explosion: Marxism and the French Revolution* [*L'Irruption de Nanterre au sommet*] (trans. A. Ehrenfeld). London: Monthly Review Press.

MacPee, J., & Reuland, E. (2007). *Realizing the Impossible: Art Against Authority*. Oakland, CA: AK Press.

Plant, S. (1992). *The Most Radical Gesture: The Situationist International in a Postmodern Age*. London: Routledge.

Regan, S. (1998). *The Eagleton Reader*. London: Blackwell.

Sim, S. (2000). *Post-Marxism: An Intellectual History*. London: Routledge.

Smith, A. (1998). *Laclau and Mouffe: The Radical Democratic Imaginary*. London: Routledge.

Thoburn, N. (2003). *Deleuze, Marx and Politics*. London: Routledge.

Thompson, E. P. (1978). *The Poverty of Theory: And Other Essays*. London: Merlin Press.

Virno, P. (2003). *A Grammar of the Multitude* [*Grammatica della moltitudine*] (trans. I. Bertoletti, J. Cascaito, & A. Casson). Cambridge, MA: Semiotext(e).

Virno, P., & Hardt, M. (ed.) (1996). *Radical Thought in Italy: A Potential Politics*. Minneapolis: University of Minnestoa Press.

Williams, R. (1977). *Marxism and Literature*. Oxford: Oxford University Press.

Master Narrative

DEIRDRE RUSSELL

Master narrative, metanarrative, metadiscourse, and grand narrative, as expounded by the French philosopher Jean-François Lyotard (1924–98), are broadly synonymous terms which refer to totalizing social theories or philosophies of history which, appealing to notions of transcendental and universal truth, purport to offer a comprehensive account of knowledge and experience. "Meta" means beyond or about, and therefore here refers to all-encompassing narratives which explain other, smaller narratives. Lyotard's account of metanarratives and their demise is a founding element of postmodernism. (Within narratology, "metanarrative" is also used in a distinct sense, as coined by the literary theorist Gérard Genette, to refer to stories within stories.)

MODERNITY'S GRAND NARRATIVES

Lyotard developed his critique of metanarratives in *The Postmodern Condition* (1984 [1979]; the English translation includes an additional appendix entitled "Answering the question: What is postmodernism?"). Although this short book, commissioned by the Council of Universities of Quebec, is concerned specifically with late twentieth-century scientific knowledge, its reflections on the different forms that knowledge takes, how it is legitimated and shared, and how these have changed since World War II have proved hugely influential in a range of fields, and the text is considered a founding work of the postmodernist movement.

The Postmodern Condition is concerned with how the status of knowledge has changed in the postindustrial age of computerized societies. The central problem Lyotard seeks to assess is that of "legitimation": how knowledge claims authority and purpose. To explore this problem, he uses the concept of "language games," borrowed from the Austrian philosopher Ludwig Wittgenstein. He identifies two competing forms of knowledge: scientific and narrative. The latter – expressed in myths, legends, and popular tales, for example – is the dominant form in traditional societies. The narrative language game organizes knowledge in a way that constitutes the social bond, cementing a society's institutions and activities. Narrative knowledge requires no legitimation beyond adherence to its own rules and internal consistency. Modern Western scientific knowledge, in contrast, requires argumentation and proof; it makes claims of universality and authority, and "truth" is a greater issue. Science spurns narrative knowledge as primitive, ignorant, ideological, and prejudiced in favor of abstract, logical, denotative methods.

However, Lyotard claims, scientific knowledge *does* have recourse to narrative in establishing legitimacy and purpose. In order to stake a valid place in society, it appeals to metanarratives. Lyotard identifies two principal metanarratives which have legitimated science: the "emancipatory" narrative of progress and the advancing liberation of humanity (associated with the Enlightenment) and the "speculative" narrative of the reach towards the totality and unity of all knowledge (derived from the German Hegelian philosophical tradition). These, according

to Lyotard, are the two great metanarratives of modernity.

Metanarratives have a rhetorical, moral force, regulating society according to their proclaimed truths. They are *narratives* in the sense that they organize history as the revelation of meaning. These teleological (goal-oriented) narratives are *meta*narratives in that they organize, account for, and reveal the meanings of all other narratives, from stories of scientific discovery to individuals' development, while these smaller narratives emulate and substantiate the grand narratives. It is through their universal explanatory scope that they hold a society together. Master narratives give credence to the status quo of institutions and activities: they orient decision-making, prescribe behaviour, order social life, give it a sense of purpose, determine rules and conventions and what counts as valid practice, establish what is true and just, and provide means of interpreting and valuing human action and experience. They are static, universal, absolute, and totalizing.

For Lyotard, metanarratives are a definitive feature of modernity; their reach toward totality relates to the distinguishing features of modernity – order, stability, reason, progress, and so forth – which are maintained precisely through their master narratives. A discourse is "modern" when it appeals to one of these metanarratives for legitimation. Lyotard cites "the dialectics of the Spirit, the hermeneutics of meaning, the emancipation of the rational or working subject or the creation of wealth" (1984 [1979]: xxiii) as versions of the grand narratives of modernity. The notions of progress and liberty associated with such projects can be identified, for example, in Marxism: a classic master narrative which offers a comprehensive theory based on the eventual emancipation of the working class. Lyotard critiques the totalizing nature of grand narratives of the modern age, rejecting the possibility of grasping the nature of history and society as a whole. His antipathy towards metanarratives corresponds to his and other postmodern thinkers' distrust of universal philosophies as repressive of difference, diversity, and rebellion, ignoring or suppressing all which does not fit their model.

POSTMODERNITY'S LITTLE NARRATIVES

The most important and influential element of Lyotard's account is what he identifies as a shift in twentieth-century postindustrial societies involving a decline of grand narratives' power, credibility, and capacity to forge consensus. Technological progress – in areas of computer science and cybernetics among others – have changed the nature of knowledge itself and the ways it is acquired, used, and shared. Knowledge is no longer perceived as an end in itself; it is no longer primarily concerned with "truth," but produced according to its uses.

Lyotard famously describes this new, postmodern era as defined by "incredulity towards metanarratives" (1984[1979]: xxiv). People no longer believe that a total philosophy or single theory (such as Marxism) is capable of uniting, ordering, and explaining all experience and knowledge as a coherent whole. The universalistic, humanistic narratives of secure knowledge have thus lost their authority; notions that scientific knowledge and reason will solve social ills and provide the basis for creating a better world have been discredited.

Instead, according to Lyotard, grand narratives are replaced by a plethora of smaller, finite narratives. These multiple and incompatible little stories or theories function in local, limited contexts: they account for or reveal the meanings of certain specific phenomena, but do not claim universal truth,

applicability, or legitimacy. In the absence of the legitimation of metanarratives, legitimation resides once again in first-order narratives: each discourse has its own self-referential and nontransferable principles. Thus, the legitimation of knowledge in the postmodern age derives from how well it performs, how effective it is in achievements, not in its relations to abstract principles.

With the bankruptcy of metanarratives, Lyotard argues, like other postmodern thinkers, postmodern culture is characterized by fragmentation, pluralism, and diversity: all of a society's micronarratives cannot be brought together to create one coherent, unified explanation. The premises of totality and universality on which metanarratives are based have been abandoned; the small-scale, modest systems of knowledge and values are aware of their own limited nature and validity. Consensus should be sought only locally and contingently. The social bond is now formed by interweaving discourses, practices, and people without a single, continuous, unifying narrative.

Thus, amid the inability to explain society and history as a whole, pluralism and contingency replace modernity's aims of universality, stability, and truth. Lyotard favors the multiplicity of small stories over what he sees as the totalitarianism of metanarratives. All dominant ideologies, as master narratives, exclude minorities and threaten the heterogeneous reality of society, whereas the cohabitation of a diverse range of locally legitimated narratives allows for difference and the diversity of human experience.

CRITICISM AND INFLUENCE

Although the focus of *The Postmodern Condition* is science, the book has had little impact in this field (it contains, in any case, little actual scientific content). It has been hugely influential, however, in a range of other domains, particularly amongst literary and cultural analysts concerned with the distinguishing features of postmodernity. Metanarratives and little narratives are founding concepts of postmodern thought, echoing broader descriptions of the transformations from modernity to postmodernity, including the increased emphasis on difference and diversity of identities, the rise of micropolitics, and the emphasis on ambivalence and contingency over the certainty of notions of progress and truth inherited from the Enlightenment.

The Postmodern Condition can be interpreted as a veiled attack on the German philosopher Jürgen Habermas and his defense of the "unfinished project" of modernity. He has critiqued Lyotard's position (and other poststructuralist and postmodernist French philosophers) on the grounds that the suspicion of universality entails an abandonment of liberal politics' goals of social progress. Related concerns are raised by American Marxist critic Fredric Jameson in his preface to *The Postmodern Condition*, and by the American philosopher Richard Rorty in "Habermas and Lyotard on postmodernity" (1985). Similarly, critics have been wary of the assumption that all grand narratives are dogmatic and that all are essentially the same: even if some are oppressive and some have failed, this might not necessarily mean that they should all be discarded.

These concerns chime with wider critiques of postmodernism as relativist and politically ambivalent. On the one hand, for example, feminists and postcolonial critics share the postmodernist desire to challenge the repressive powers of culturally dominant grand narratives (such as patriarchy, Western imperialism, and capitalism), and the emphasis on difference and "little narratives" is welcomed by those seeking

to have marginalized voices and stories heard. Postcolonial scholars, for instance, might critique Western metanarratives which defend colonial projects – underpinned by tenets of universalism, civilization, and progress – and rehabilitate suppressed local and national histories. On the other hand, resistance to emancipatory metanarratives can be seen to limit strategies which posit universal struggles. That is, feminism, for example, might itself be viewed as a metanarrative. Lyotard's thesis, with its emphasis on heterogeneity and resistance to totalities, disarms forms of social criticism employing general categories of identity such as class, gender, and ethnicity. (Several critics have also pointed out that Lyotard's own description of postmodernity is a kind of metanarrative: a totalizing account of the postmodern condition as the decline of modernity's grand narratives.)

Notions of grand and little narratives have nonetheless been taken up in myriad ways by postmodern literary and cultural analysts, where the term "master narrative" has been applied to a broad range of strategies which preserve the status quo regarding power relations, exclusion, and difference. Postmodern social and literary criticism (of which the Canadian scholar Linda Hutcheon's *A Poetics of Postmodernism* [1988] is a prime example) might be concerned with identifying and describing particular grand narratives, or with examining how individuals and texts appeal to, confirm, modify, undermine, or subvert dominant master narratives. The term "master narrative" is also used in literary analysis to refer simply to plots which recur so often and so pervasively that they appear to be universal: quests and revenge stories are prominent examples. Interest in metanarratives can also be seen to relate to a broader shift in interest, across the humanities, from the literary forms and functions of narrative (in narratology, for example) to the cultural and ideological dimensions of narrative. In postmodern art itself, the prominence on parody, irony, intertextuality, and self-reflexivity can be interpreted as strategies for undermining metanarratives; the postmodern aesthetic emphasis on discontinuity, ambiguity, lack of closure, and so forth can all be seen as expressions of Lyotard's proclamations that fragmentation, incoherence, and provisionality are definitive qualities of postmodernity's web of little narratives, and are to be embraced rather than lamented.

SEE ALSO: Habermas, Jürgen; Jameson, Fredric; Lyotard, Jean-François; Narrative Theory; Postmodernism; Rorty, Richard.

REFERENCES AND SUGGESTED READINGS

Conner, S. (1997). *Postmodernist Culture: An Introduction to Theories of the Contemporary*, 2nd edn. Oxford: Blackwell.
Hutcheon, L. (1988). *A Poetics of Postmodernism: History, Theory, Fiction.* New York: Routledge.
Lyotard, J.-F. (1984). *The Postmodern Condition: A Report on Knowledge* (trans. G. Bennington & B. Massumi; foreword by F. Jameson). Minneapolis: University of Minnesota Press.
Readings, B. (1991). *Introducing Lyotard: Art and Politics.* London: Routledge.
Rorty, R. (1985). Habermas and Lyotard on postmodernity. In R. J. Bernstein (ed.), *Habermas and Modernity.* Cambridge: Polity, pp. 161–175.

McClintock, Anne

ANNA L. H. GETHING

Anne McClintock (b. 1954) has published widely on imperialism, nationalism, and postcolonialism; race, gender, and sexuality; cultural theory, including feminist, psycho-analytic, and queer theory; and popular and visual culture. Her work is interdisciplinary and transnational, covering the literatures and cultures of Victorian and contemporary Britain, South Africa, Ireland, twentieth-century and contemporary United States, as well as world literature. McClintock has been the recipient of numerous awards, including two prestigious MacArthur-SSRC fellowships and many creative writing fellowships. She lectures worldwide; her work has been widely anthologized, and translated into Spanish, Portuguese, French, Taiwanese, Mandarin, and Swedish. McClintock is currently Simone de Beauvoir Professor of English and Women's and Gender Studies at the University of Wisconsin, Madison. She was born in Harare, Zimbabwe, moving as a child to South Africa where she was later involved in the anti-apartheid movement. She began her university studies at the University of Cape Town, completing a BA in English in 1977, before traveling to the UK to study for an MPhil in Linguistics at the University of Cambridge. In 1989 she gained a PhD in English Literature from Columbia University, where she became an associate professor of gender and cultural studies, teaching in the Department of English and the Institute of African Studies. She then held a visiting professorship at New York University.

McClintock is best known for her book *Imperial Leather: Race, Gender and Sexuality in the Colonial Contest* (1995), which has been widely translated and taught internationally. It is a sweeping study, described by McClintock as "a sustained quarrel with the project of imperialism, the cult of domesticity and the invention of industrial progress" (4). Spanning the century between Victorian Britain and twentieth-century struggles for power in South Africa, the book draws on a diverse range of cultural forms: drawings and cartoons, photographs, advertisements, oral history, novels, poetry, and diaries inform an engaging analysis of imperial and anti-imperial narratives. At its centre is McClintock's premise that "no social category should remain invisible with respect to an analysis of empire" (9). Race, gender, and class are, she argues, "articulated categories" – social categories that do not exist in isolation but, rather, emerge in relation to each other. In turn, these social categories exist in crucial but often concealed relations with imperialism. By employing a number of theoretical discourses – feminism, postcolonialism, Marxism, psychoanalysis among them – McClintock exposes and interrogates complex and overlapping categories of power and identity, namely the intimate relations between imperial power and resistance, money and sexuality, race and gender.

Two key concepts introduced in *Imperial Leather* are what McClintock calls "commodity racism" and the Victorian "cult of domesticity." In the last decades of the nineteenth century there occurred, she suggests, a significant shift from scientific racism (evident in, for example, travel writing and anthropological and medical journals) to commodity racism, which converted the narrative of imperial progress into mass-produced consumer spectacle. Finding form in the Victorian developments of photography and advertising, as well as in the burgeoning museum movement, commodity racism enabled imperial power to be marketed on an unprecedented scale. Advertisements for household items such as soap and polish featured images of imperial racism and projected them directly into the Victorian middle-class home. These images directly related the ordering and cleaning of the home with the control and civilization of colonized people. In this way, the domestic commodity became both symbol and agent of imperialism, and the cult of domesticity, McClintock argues, became

central to the consolidation of British national identity.

Imperial Leather also presents "panoptical time" and "anachronistic space" as primary tropes of imperialism. Panoptical time represents the late nineteenth-century preoccupation – epitomized by Darwin's *On the Origin of Species* (1859) – with determining a unified world history, with capturing the image of global history and evolutionary progress in a single spectacle. McClintock gives the family Tree of Man as an exemplary figure of this. Crucially, however, such visual narratives of historical progress were marked by their absence of women. Instead, women were relegated to the realm of nature and to what McClintock calls the late Victorian invention of anachronistic space. Anachronistic space presents geographical difference (space) as historical difference (time). In colonial terms, imperial progress across the space of empire was perceived as a journey backwards in time to an archaic past and, in turn, the colonizers' return journey emulated the evolution of historical progress – onwards and upwards through civilization toward the pinnacle of European Enlightenment. Anachronistic space, then, existed as an undesirable and regressive state: "prehistoric, atavistic and irrational, inherently out of place in the historical time of modernity" (40), and into this anachronistic space were placed abject groups such as unruly women, the colonized and the industrial working class.

McClintock has also written short biographies of Simone de Beauvoir and Olive Schreiner, as well as a monograph on madness, sexuality, and colonialism (2001). She has co-edited *Dangerous Liaisons* (1997), as well as journal issues on sex work, and race and queer theory. Her creative non-fiction book on sex work, *Skin Hunger: A Chronicle of Sex, Desire and Money*, is forthcoming from Jonathan Cape; *The Sex Work Reader* is forthcoming from Vintage; and a collection of essays on sexuality, *Screwing the System*, is forthcoming from Routledge. Current projects include a book on post-9/11 US imperialism, torture, and photography, called *Paranoid Empire: Specters from Guantanamo and Abu Ghraib*, and a novel entitled *The Honest Adulterer*.

SEE ALSO: Feminism; Marxism; Postcolonial Studies and Diaspora Studies; Psychoanalysis (since 1966)

REFERENCES AND SUGGESTED READINGS

McClintock, A. (1995). *Imperial Leather: Race, Gender and Sexuality in the Colonial Contest.* New York: Routledge.

McClintock, A. (2001). *Double Crossings: Madness, Sexuality and Imperialism.* Vancouver: Ronsdale.

McClintock, A. (in press). Sex work and globalization. In G. Pratt & V. Rosner (eds.), *The Global and the Intimate.* New York: Columbia University Press.

McClintock, A., Shohat, E., & Mufti, A. (eds.) (1997). *Dangerous Liaisons: Gender, Nation and Postcolonial Perspectives.* Minneapolis: University of Minnesota Press.

McClintock, A., Harper, P., Munos, J. E., & Rosen, T. (eds.) (1997). Queer Transexions of Race, Nation, and Gender. Special issue of *Social Text* 15(52/53).

Miller, J. Hillis

ROBERT EAGLESTONE

J. Hillis Miller (b. 1928) is an American critic, specializing in Victorian and modern literature, as well as in American and European literature of the past two centuries. He was closely aligned, first, to phenomenological criticism or "criticism of consciousness," and then, after 1968, to deconstruction. He was a key member of the Yale School.

Miller received his BA in English from Oberlin College in 1948 and his PhD from Harvard in 1952, for a dissertation entitled "The symbolic imagery of Charles Dickens." It made use of Kenneth Burke's idea that a literary work is a form of "symbolic action" in which its author attempts to work out indirectly some personal problem or impasse. After a year teaching at Williams College, he taught for 19 years at Johns Hopkins University, then 14 years at Yale, after which, in 1986, he moved to the University of California at Irvine, where he is UCI Distinguished Research Professor of Comparative Literature and English Emeritus. He was President of the Modern Language Association of America in 1986.

Miller has always been interested in literary theory and its uses: nevertheless, his primary focus has always been on what he saw from the beginning as the strangeness of literary language. Literary theory, in Miller's view, is useful not so much as an end in itself as in the way it facilitates accounting for the strangeness of literature and transmitting that strangeness to others in teaching and writing. He has also argued that works of literary theory must be read with the same attention to detail and expectation of idiosyncrasy that should preside over the reading of literary works themselves.

Charles Dickens: The World of His Novels (1958), Miller's first book, mixes new critical close reading of major Dickens novels with "phenomenological" or "Geneva School" ideas about the way literary works transmit the consciousness of the author to the consciousness of the reader by way of the words. He encountered the latter ideas through the work of Georges Poulet. Reading Poulet and other Geneva School critics was a turning point in Miller's thinking about how to write about literature.

The Disappearance of God (1963), Miller's second book, was written during his period at Johns Hopkins University, and was a major intervention in the understanding of five Victorian writers: Thomas De Quincey, Robert Browning, Emily Brontë, Matthew Arnold, and Gerard Manley Hopkins. It was followed in 1965 by *Poets of Reality*, with chapters on six twentieth-century poets: Joseph Conrad, W. B. Yeats, T. S. Eliot, Dylan Thomas, Wallace Stevens, and William Carlos Williams. The chapters in these two books use Pouletian techniques of reading to weave together comment on thematic citations from everywhere in a given author's writings. This is done in order to assemble a dialectical representation of the abiding structure of that author's consciousness. The idea is that you can follow the structure of a given consciousness by way of careful attention to key citations, from some starting assumption to some identifiable endpoint.

A second turning point in Miller's work was instigated by his encounter with Jacques Derrida's *De la Grammatologie* in its short first version in the journal *Critique* in 1966–7, by subsequently reading Derrida's early books, by an encounter with Derrida himself at the famous Hopkins Symposium on "The languages of criticism and the sciences of man" in October 1966, and by attending Derrida's seminars at Hopkins and then at Yale and Irvine in subsequent years. The reorientation of Miller's work back to a concern with the complexities of literary language and with the integrity of individual works, along with a dispensing of the presumption of a presiding authorial consciousness, can be discerned in his next three books, *Thomas Hardy: Distance and Desire* (1970); *Fiction and Repetition: Seven English Novels* (1982); *The Linguistic Moment* (1985). This reorientation coincided with Miller's move to Yale in 1972, where he became a close colleague of the critics Harold Bloom, Geoffrey Hartman, and Paul de Man. Along with Jacques Der-

rida, who moved to Yale from Johns Hopkins for annual seminars as a visiting professor at the same time Miller joined the Yale faculty, these five critics and theorists became known collectively as the Yale School. In 1979, they published a joint volume, sometimes seen as a manifesto, *Deconstruction and Criticism*.

In spite of Miller's evident focus on readings of literary works, his more purely theoretical essays have been widely read and anthologized. One of his most famous and paradigmatic articles, written during his time at Yale, is "The critic as host" (1977). Given in response to an attack on deconstruction by the critic M. H. Abrams, Miller asks what "happens when a critical essay extracts a 'passage' and cites it? . . . Is a citation an alien parasite within the body of its host, the main text, or it is the other way around, the interpretative text the parasite which surrounds and strangles the citation, which is its host" (439). Miller analyzes the logic of "parasite" and "host," pointing out that "guest" has the same origin as "host," and that the order of "parasite" and "host" is complex and often reversible. He argues that deconstruction recognizes the "great complexity and equivocal richness of apparently obvious or univocal language" (443). In fact, he argues, "there is no conceptual expression without figure [meaning, figurative language], and no intertwining of concept and figure without an implied story, narrative or myth. . . . Deconstruction is an investigation of what is implied by this inherence of figure, concept, and narrative in one another" (443). He goes on to argue that, because of this intertwining, there can be no simple reading of a text, indeed that texts are "'unreadable,' if by 'readable' one means open to a single, definitive, univocal interpretation . . . . Neither the 'obvious' reading nor the 'deconstructionist' reading is 'univocal'": the text, an obvious reading, and a deconstructive reading are all interwoven; each is "itself both host and parasite" (447).

In another celebrated essay – along the same deconstructive lines, but with a different target: his address as president of the MLA – Miller focused on critics who turned to history and historical and ideological readings in order to be "ethically and politically responsible" (1986: 283). While he said that he was sympathetic to this, he suggested that this sort of reading sometimes suspends the "obligation to read, carefully, patiently, with nothing taken for granted beforehand" (283). A text is not explained by its relation to history, the "material base" and its context: Miller directly addresses those critics who think it is, arguing:

> Your commitment to history, to society, to an exploration of the material base of literature, of its economic conditions, its institutions, the realities of class and gender distinctions that underlie literature ... will inevitably fall into the hands of those with antithetical positions to yours as long as you hold to an unexamined ideology of the material base, that is, to a notion that is metaphysical through and through, as much a part of western metaphysics as the idealism you would contest. "Deconstruction" is the current name for the multiple and heterogeneous strategies of overturning and displacement that will liberate your own enterprise from what disables it. (290–1)

Miller expanded the argument of this address in his influential book *The Ethics of Reading* (1986). Here he argues that "there is a necessary ethical moment in that act of reading as such, a moment neither cognitive, nor political, nor social, nor interpersonal, but properly and independently ethical" (1). This is not because stories are didactic or contain morals, but because while we often think of ethics as a series of commandments ("do not lie"), these can only be made sense of in narra-

tives. Miller's position has been criticized as "thin" and lacking in social content: "[E]thics becomes just the name for a certain, albeit highly sophisticated practice of reading, one that obeys the deconstructionist imperative to take nothing on trust and attend always to the letter of the text" (Norris 1988: 165). However, Miller's argument does not deny social content in literary texts, but sees it as part of the text's own formation.

In a later work, *Versions of Pygmalion* (1990), Miller outlines four "laws" for deconstructive interpretation. He argues, first, that the "relation of literature to history is a problem, not a solution" (33); second, that the scholar-critic must read "guided by the expectation of surprise, that is, the presupposition that what you actually find when you read is likely to be fundamentally different from what you expected. ... Good reading is also guided by the presupposition of a possible heterogeneity in the text" (33). The third rule is that context and text have a relationship in language, not in materiality: "the relations of literature to history and society is part of rhetoric" (34). Finally, Miller argues that reading is transformative, that a work of literature "intervenes in history when it is read" (34).

An example of Miller's work lies in Nathaniel Hawthorne's short story, "The minister's black veil" (see Miller 1991). In this story, the minister dons a veil: it has been interpreted as a sexual symbol. However, Miller argues that it is, in fact, "unreadable" – that is, it is impossible to work out what the veil means on the basis of the evidence given in the text. In turn, this instability means that the whole process of interpretation in general is cast into question: reading "would then be a perpetual wandering or displacement that can never be checked against anything except another sign" (97). The veil is an allegory for allegory itself.

One thread that can be followed on a long course through Miller's writing is narrative theory. As he says in the preface to *Ariadne's Thread* (1992), he sat down early in the morning on January 4, 1976, in his house in Bethany, Connecticut, to write what he expected to be a short introduction to a new book he was finishing, *Fiction and Repetition*. He wanted that introduction to be a brief account of the seven different uses that might be made, in interpreting novels, of line imagery: in writing about narrative sequence, about character, about interpersonal relations, about topography in fiction, in taking account of the way so many names for figures of speech are line images (hyperbole, parable, etc.), and in discussing illustrations for novels or the image/text relation generally. The text got longer and longer, and a new preface had to be written for *Fiction and Repetition*. That small early morning insight, if it was such, led ultimately to a whole series of books on lines and the interruption of lines in novels: *Ariadne's Thread: Story Lines* (1992a); *Illustration* (1992b); *Topographies* (1994), and *Reading Narrative* (1998). The inordinate expansion of that small germ of an idea was caused not just because the working out of the narrative theory for each of the seven topics took many words, but because that working out, in each case, demanded exemplification through close reading of novels and stories in order to show how lines actually work in literary works. This long series of new readings was carried out in faithfulness to that demand for a detailed accounting for particular literary works that has remained Miller's central vocation.

When Miller moved to Irvine in 1986, he had as visiting professor colleagues Wolfgang Iser and Jean-François Lyotard. Derrida followed Miller to Irvine to give five weeks of seminars annually. In a series of books written after his move to Irvine and then since his semi-retirement to Maine in 2001, Miller's work has continued to offer both readings of major authors and explorations of reading's social uses. He has written about literary issues stemming from speech-act theory in *Speech Acts in Literature* (2001b) and in *Literature as Conduct* (2005). The latter is a book on Henry James's representations of moments of decision as they are registered in fictive speech acts in his novels. Miller has investigated the effects of new digital media, for example in *The Medium is the Maker* (2009b). His *For Derrida* (2009a) gathers all the essays on specific aspects of Derrida's work that he has written for conferences and journals since Derrida's death in 2004. This book exemplifies Miller's conviction that a philosopher-theorist-critic like Derrida cannot be encapsulated in a few putatively totalizing formulas taken out of context, like "There is nothing outside the text." Derrida must rather be read patiently, carefully, *in extenso*, with the expectation that his work may be heterogeneous. One way to do this is to follow the destiny of a given salient Derridean word, such as "*destinerrance*" as it wanders through Derrida's writing, appearing and reappearing here and there in quite different contexts.

Miller latest book, as yet unpublished, is *The Conflagration of Community: Fiction Before and After Auschwitz*, which explores what happened to communities in the twentieth century along with the related question of whether fiction can testify validly to the Holocaust. A number of literary works are then read in the light of the questions chosen, in this case novels by Franz Kafka, Thomas Keneally, Ian McEwan, Art Spiegelman (if you can call *Maus* a novel), André Kertész, and Toni Morrison. This book, like other recent work by Miller, tests out the hypothesis that older literary works can be read now, anachronistically, as foreshadowing later events of which the author cannot have been aware. Kafka's work anticipates the Holocaust; Wallace Stevens's short poem of 1942, "The man on the dump," prefigures our present situation in which the whole earth is becoming a garbage dump.

Miller has influenced several generations of critics. He describes his vocation as the responsibility to account for literary works by teaching them or by writing essays about them that are attentive to their linguistic complexities, to what might be called their "rhetoric."

SEE ALSO: Bloom, Harold; Deconstruction; Derrida, Jacques; Ethical Criticism; de Man, Paul; Yale School

REFERENCES AND SUGGESTED READINGS

Bloom, H., Derrida, J., Miller, J. H., de Man, P., & Hartman, G. (1979). *Deconstruction and Criticism*. New York: Continuum.
Miller, J. H. (1958). *Charles Dickens: The World of His Novels*. Cambridge, MA: Harvard University Press.
Miller, J. H. (1963). *The Disappearance of God: Five Nineteenth-Century Writers*. Cambridge, MA: Harvard University Press.
Miller, J. H. (1965). *Poets of Reality: Six Twentieth-Century Writers*. Cambridge, MA: Harvard University Press.
Miller, J. H. (1970). *Thomas Hardy: Distance and Desire*. Cambridge, MA: Harvard University Press.
Miller, J. H. (1977). The critic as host. *Critical Inquiry*, 3(3), 439–447.
Miller, J. H. (1982). *Fiction and Repetition: Seven English Novels*. Cambridge, MA: Harvard University Press.
Miller, J. H. (1985). *The Linguistic Moment: From Wordsworth to Stevens*. Princeton: Princeton University Press.
Miller, J. H. (1986). *The Ethics of Reading: Kant, de Man, Eliot, Trollope, James, and Benjamin*. New York: Columbia University Press.
Miller, J. H. (1987). Presidential Address 1986: The triumph of theory, the resistance to reading and the question of the material base. *PMLA*, 102(3), 281–291.
Miller, J. H. (1990). *Versions of Pygmalion*. Cambridge, MA: Harvard University Press.
Miller, J. H. (1991). *Hawthorne and History: Defacing It*. Cambridge, MA: Harvard University Press.
Miller, J. H. (1992a). *Ariadne's Thread: Story Lines*. New Haven: Yale University Press.
Miller, J. H. (1992b). *Illustration*. Cambridge, MA: Harvard University Press.
Miller, J. H. (1994). *Topographies*. Stanford: Stanford University Press.
Miller, J. H. (1998). *Reading Narrative*. Norman: Oklahoma University Press.
Miller, J. H. (2001a). *Others*. Princeton: Princeton University Press.
Miller, J. H. (2001b). *Speech Acts in Literature*. Stanford: Stanford University Press.
Miller, J. H. (2002). *On Literature*. London: Routledge.
Miller, J. H. (2005). *Literature as Conduct: Speech Acts in Henry James*. New York: Fordham University Press.
Miller, J. H. (2009a). *For Derrida*. New York: Fordham University Press.
Miller, J. H. (2009b). *The Medium is the Maker: Browning, Freud, Derrida and the New Telepathic Ecotechnologies*. Brighton: Sussex Academic.
Miller, J. H., & Asensi, M. (1999). *Black Holes*. Stanford: Stanford University Press.
Norris, C. (1988). *Deconstruction and the Interests of Theory*. London: Pinter.

Mimicry

STEPHEN MORTON

Mimicry in its conventional sense is the action, practice, or art of copying or closely imitating, or reproducing through mime (*OED*). In this definition, mimicry is closely related to mimesis or the practice of representation in literature, performance, and the visual arts. Yet in contrast to mimesis, which often seeks to reproduce an image of the object that is being copied, mimicry can have a humorous and even subversive potential that deliberately sets out to challenge the meaning of the object that is being copied or represented. This is not to say

that the act or practice of imitation is restricted to literature and the visual
arts, however, since the imitation of
other human beings is also one of the formative processes through which children
learn to speak, act, and perform as socialized
human subjects. Furthermore, in biology,
the practice of mimicry denotes the close
external resemblance of an animal or plant
to another, or to an inanimate object
(*OED*), in some instances as a tactic of
self-defense.

The French psychoanalyst Jacques
Lacan has provided a significant account
of mimicry, which has influenced some of
the most well-known theories of mimicry,
especially that of the postcolonial theorist
Homi K. Bhabha, the feminist philosopher
Luce Irigaray, and the social theorist
Judith Butler. In his Seminar XI, published in English as *The Four Fundamental
Concepts of Psychoanalysis* (1998[1973]),
Lacan invoked the concept of mimicry
to formulate his theory of the gaze. In
his definition, the gaze is synonymous
with the object of looking or the scopic
drive. For Lacan, the gaze refers to the gaze
of another who looks at a subject and the
subject who gazes at the other person in
the act of gazing at them. As he puts it:
"You never look at me from the place from
which I see you" (103). Lacan develops
this idea in a chapter from his Seminar XI
titled "The line and light," in which he
argues that "the facts of mimicry" provide
the subject with a "phenomenal domain"
that "enables us to view the subject in
absolute overview" (98). He does not elaborate on what he means by the "facts of
mimicry" in this chapter; instead, he confines himself to the question of how important "the function of adaptation" is in
mimicry (98). To address this question,
Lacan begins by invoking an example from
biological science, in which "an animal-
cule" adapts to the colour of the natural

environment in order to defend itself
against the light. As he puts it:

> In an environment in which, because of
> what is immediately around, the colour green
> predominates, as at the bottom of a pool
> containing green plants, an animalcule – there
> are numerous ones that might serve as exam-
> ples – becomes green for as long as the light
> may do it harm. It becomes green, therefore,
> in order to reflect the light *qua* green, thus
> protecting itself, by adaptation, from its
> effects. (98)

For Lacan, however, mimicry is
something "quite different" (99) from adaptation. Citing the example of a small
crustacean that imitates the particular phase
of a quasi-plant animal known as brio-
zoaires, which resembles the shape of a stain,
Lacan asserts that this crustacean demonstrates the "origin of mimicry" because "[i]t
becomes a stain, it becomes a picture, it is
inscribed in the function of the picture"
(99). In so doing, Lacan draws a parallel
between the function of mimicry in the
natural world and the function of mimicry
or imitation in the visual arts. Furthermore,
drawing on Roger Callois's theory of mimicry in *The Mask of Medusa*, Lacan argues
that mimicry "reveals something in so far as
it is distinct from what might be called an
itself that is behind" and that "the effect of
mimicry is camouflage, in the strictly technical sense." In other words, "It is not a
question of harmonizing with the background but, of becoming mottled – exactly
like the technique of camouflage practiced
in human warfare" (99).

Lacan's account of mimicry as a form of
camouflage is particularly crucial to the
postcolonial theorist Homi K. Bhabha,
who applies this idea to colonial discourse.
In Bhabha's argument, "colonial mimicry
is the desire for a reformed, recognizable Other, that is almost the same, but not quite"
(1994: 86). Mimicry for Bhabha is

"constructed around an ambivalence," and, as a consequence, colonial discourse is "stricken by an ambivalence" whereby the colonized subject threatens to destabilize the authority of colonial discourse (86). Invoking Charles Grant's "Observations on the state of society among the Asiatic subjects of Great Britain" (1792) and Thomas Macaulay's "Minute on Indian Education" (1835), Bhabha asserts that these texts exemplify the radical instability of colonial mimicry in their attempt to produce a "reformed" colonial subject through institutions of European learning and colonial power. To elucidate this instability of mimicry, Bhabha refers to Lacan's theory as a form of camouflage: "[M]imicry is like camouflage, not a harmonisation of repression of difference, but a form of resemblance, that differs from or defends presence by displaying it in part, metonymically" (90). A metonym denotes a particular kind of rhetorical figure in which a particular object is evoked by its parts. In Bhabha's explanation of Lacan, mimicry operates as a form of metonymy because the subject of mimicry mimics a particular aspect of the subject being imitated, such as the cultural habits, speech, non-verbal physical gestures, or costume of that subject. For Bhabha, the place of the subject of mimicry is beyond representation, and in that precise sense the subject may not seem to exist as a positive presence. In this sense, Bhabha seems to follow Lacan's rather elliptical observation that mimicry "reveals something in so far as it is distinct from what might be called an itself that is behind" (Lacan 1998: 99). Significantly, Bhabha's account of mimicry also resonates with the increasingly politicized, *bhadralok* class in early twentieth-century colonial Bengal. Members of this young, upper-middle-class elite group were trained in the British colonial education system in India and imitated the cultural manners of

the British, while, at the same time, they plotted against the British Empire through the establishment of seditious newspapers and secret societies. Such a subversive form of mimicry could be understood as an example of what Bhabha elsewhere refers to as "sly civility." in that it imitates the cultural signs and practices associated with British colonial civility, while secretly plotting its demise.

Bhabha's theory of mimicry bears a conceptual resemblance to the French feminist philosophy of Luce Irigaray. In *This Sex Which is Not One* (1985[1977]), Irigaray argues that in the masculine logic of gendered representation there is only one role available to "the feminine" – "that of mimicry" (76). In Irigaray's argument, the critical task for the feminine subject defined by the masculine logic of European thought and representation is to strategically assume the "feminine role" of mimic deliberately so as to "convert a form of subordination into affirmation, and thus to begin to thwart it" (76). As she goes on to explain:

> To play with mimesis is thus, for a woman, to try to recover the place of her exploitation by discourse, without allowing herself to be simply reduced to it. It means to resubmit herself – inasmuch as she is on the side of the "perceptible," of "matter" – to "ideas," in particular to ideas about herself, that are elaborated in/by a masculine logic, but so as to make "visible," by an effect of playful repetition, what was supposed to remain invisible: the cover-up of a possible operation of the feminine in language. It also means "to unveil" the fact that, if women are such good mimics, it is because they are not simply absorbed in this function. (76)

If mimicry for Irigaray offers a mode of subverting the masculine order of mimesis, for social theorist Judith Butler, mimicry can in some circumstances offer a rhetorical strategy for subverting predominant heteronormative gender roles. Butler describes how "the parodic repetition of gender exposes ... the illusion of gender identity as an intractable depth and inner substance" (1990: 146). In Butler's argument, gender is "an 'act' ... that is open to splittings, self-parody, self-criticism, and those hyperbolic exhibitions of 'the natural' that, in their very exaggeration, reveal its fundamentally phantasmatic status" (147). Here, mimicry, or the radical restaging of gender as an act, may seem to destabilize the discursive construction of sex as a natural, biological fact. Such a destabilization is particularly exemplified for Butler in "the cultural practices of drag, cross-dressing, and the sexual stylization of butch/femme identities." As she puts it, "*In imitating gender, drag implicitly reveals the imitative structure of gender itself – as well as its contingency*" (137; emphasis original).

Another example of mimicry that both combines and develops Bhabha's account of mimicry with that of Irigaray can be found in Ranjana Khanna's analysis of Algerian women's role in the Algerian war. Khanna examines a key sequence in Gillo Pontecorvo's 1966 film *The Battle of Algiers* in which three Algerian women remove their veils in front of a mirror and assume the guise of European women in order to pass through a military checkpoint, infiltrate the French colonial city, and carry out a bomb attack. In her account of this sequence, Khanna describes how the Algerian women perform a version of Western femininity that denies a sense of their historical being and agency: "In the process of transformation we get very little sense of what these women are. They seem to be no more than the images that have been created ... in the imagination of the French by ... Pontecorvo" (2008: 122). Instead of reflecting an image of the Algerian women imitating a European image of femininity, Khanna argues that the representation of

Algerian women breaks down at the precise moment that they unveil themselves on the cinematic screen and in front of a mirror: "The mirror scene in *The Battle of Algiers*, where women, like actresses, dress and rehearse as they prepare to act, reflects the drama of revolution and of filmmaking, forming a space ... where representation breaks down because it turns in on itself" (123).

What Khanna's analysis of *The Battle of Algiers* reveals is one of the limitations with mimesis, both as a representational and as a political strategy. For in restaging the appearance of European women, the political identity, desire, and interests of the Algerian women in this sequence are subordinated to the cause of the Algerian national struggle, a struggle that may not lead to the emancipation of Algerian women. Alan Sinfield makes a similar criticism of mimicry in his essay titled "Diaspora and hybridity" (1996). In Sinfield's account, "Bhabha and Butler are proposing that the subtle imperfection in subaltern imitation of colonial discourse, or in the drag artist's mimicking of gender norms, plays back the dominant manner in a way that discloses the precariousness of its authority." Yet Sinfield is sceptical of the subversive potential that both Butler and Bhabha seem to assign to mimicry/imitation:

> I fear that imperialists cope all too conveniently with the subaltern mimic – simply, he or she cannot be the genuine article because of an intrinsic inferiority; and gay pastiche and its excesses may be easily pigeonholed as illustrating all too well that lesbians and gay men can only play at true manliness and womanliness. To say this is not to deny resistance; only to doubt how far it may be advanced by cultural hybridity" (282–3)

Mimicry may offer a space for agency or resistance for socially marginalized, "subaltern" groups to contest the authority of a dominant class or group. Yet, as Judith Butler suggests, this space is always contingent and provisional.

SEE ALSO: Bhabha, Homi; Butler, Judith; Irigaray, Luce; Lacan, Jacques; Postcolonial Studies and Diaspora Studies

REFERENCES AND SUGGESTED READINGS

Bhabha, H. (1994). *The Location of Culture*. London: Routledge.
Butler, J. (1990). *Gender Trouble: Feminism and the Subversion of Identity*. London: Routledge.
Irigaray, L. (1985). *This Sex Which Is Not One* (trans. C. Porter). Ithaca: Cornell University Press. (Original work published 1977.)
Khanna, R. (2008). *Algeria Cuts: Women and Representation, 1830 to the Present*. Stanford: Stanford University Press.
Lacan, J. (1998). *Seminar XI: The Four Fundamental Concepts of Psychoanalysis*. (ed. J.-A. Miller; trans. A. Sheridan). New York: Norton. (Original work published 1973.)
Sinfield, A. (1996). Diaspora and hybridity: Queer identities and the ethnicity model. *Textual Practice*, 10(2), 271–293.
Young, R. J. C. (1995). *Colonial Desire: Hybridity in Theory, Culture, and Race*. London: Routledge.

Mitchell, W. J. T.

JONATHAN HENSHER

W. J. T. Mitchell (b. 1942) is a scholar and theorist of media, visual art, and literature and is Gaylord Donnelly Distinguished Service Professor of English and Art History at the University of Chicago. He is also editor of *Critical Enquiry*. His extremely wide-ranging output examines the relations between text and image across the frontiers of era and genre, from illuminated manuscripts to *Jurassic Park*. Firmly poststructuralist in his approach, Mitchell consistently seeks to question the definitions and boundaries of the verbal and the visual, rather than formulating any monolithic theory of textuality and visuality.

Having begun his career as a scholar of English literature and romanticism, Mitchell's work on the illustrated poems of William Blake led him to engage more generally with issues of the relation between verbal and visual representation. In *Iconology* (1986), certainly his most programmatic work, Mitchell examines the work of four theorists of verbal–visual relations: semiotician Nelson Goodman, art historian Ernst Gombrich, and the eighteenth-century aesthetic and political theorists Gotthold Lessing and Edmund Burke. He then analyzes the role of visual images and technologies in the writings of political philosopher Karl Marx. By historicizing the field of discourse on the verbal–visual divide in this way, he problematizes such engrained categories as the distinctions between conventional and natural signs, time and space, and beauty and power that are routinely left unquestioned in our dealings with images.

Rather than proposing an "iconology" in the sense of a "science of images," then, Mitchell seeks to elucidate the political stakes invested in approaches to the visual. Specifically, he points to an undeclared "iconophobia" that pervades a vast range of critical thought, from structuralist semiotic attempts to subsume images within a "language" of the visible, through the implicitly gendered accounts of the passive, voiceless, feminized image (as opposed to the sublime, masculine power of poetic language) found in Enlightenment theories of representation, to postmodern critiques by theorists such as Jean Baudrillard of the proliferation of "simulacra" in today's multimedia world. Mitchell argues, however, that an uncritical celebration of the power of images is equally undesirable, and that the iconoclasm of Marx's rhetorical use of the camera obscura and its inverted images as a metaphor for the fetishizing transformations of ideological projection cannot be ignored in an ultra-commodified, visually saturated age. The "liberal pluralism" that he advocates in approaches to visual culture thus involves a tempering of the reflex to condemn the monetary, political and psychological influence wielded by images with a recognition of their potential to serve the real aesthetic and social interests of their users.

These ideas are developed further in subsequent books (1994, 2005), where discussion extends beyond the notion of "the image" as a theoretical entity to its material manifestations in "pictures," from paintings to computer-generated special effects. In particular, echoing philosopher Richard Rorty's description of the "linguistic turn" in postwar philosophy, Mitchell identifies what he terms a "pictorial turn" in the human sciences and the wider cultural sphere, whereby the unprecedented volume and breadth of visual production has led to uncertainty in intellectual circles as to how to incorporate images within critical practices. There is, he argues, a resulting need for "iconological awareness," an acknowledgement in critical approaches that representation is inevitably heterogeneous (he employs the term "imagetext" to designate this overlap between the visual and the verbal), that the notion of spectatorship must be seen as different from, but just as complex as, that of reading, and that any explanation of visual experience based purely on textual models may well be insufficient. To this end, Mitchell pays particular attention to what he terms "metapictures," those images, such as French surrealist René Magritte's *Ceci n'est pas une pipe*, which bring the observer face to face with the fundamental workings of

representation that usually pass unnoticed. By fostering a critical awareness of the powers and limitations of visual representation, Mitchell seeks to counter iconophobic reactions from conservative and progressive quarters alike and, drawing on the writings of the founder of psychoanalysis Sigmund Freud and the structuralist anthropologist Claude Lévi-Strauss, modify the status of images from that of "idols" or "fetishes," both of which are objects invested with excessive power and value, to that of "totems," forms around which our collective identity is established, and with which we may engage in a productive, social dialogue.

SEE ALSO: Marxism; Postmodernism; Poststructuralism; Semiotics; Structuralism

REFERENCES AND SUGGESTED READINGS

Mitchell, W. J. T. (1978). *Blake's Composite Art*. Princeton: Princeton University Press.
Mitchell, W. J. T. (1986). *Iconology: Image, Text, Ideology*. Chicago: University of Chicago Press.
Mitchell, W. J. T. (1994). *Picture Theory: Essays on Verbal and Visual Representation*. Chicago: University of Chicago Press.
Mitchell, W. J. T. (1998). *The Last Dinosaur Book: The Life and Times of a Cultural Icon*. Chicago: University of Chicago Press.
Mitchell, W. J. T. (2005). *What Do Pictures Want? The Lives and Loves of Images*. Chicago: University of Chicago Press.

Modernity/Postmodernity

SIMON MALPAS

The terms "modernity" and "postmodernity" are used by critics to designate the ways in which particular historical periods identify themselves and their relations with the past and future. Rather than focusing solely on simple historical chronology, modernity and postmodernity are used to refer to and encompass analyses of the dominant philosophical, social, artistic, and political practices and beliefs of each period; in short, the worldviews generated by them. The two terms almost always occur together, with critics tending to present arguments in favor of one over the other. Despite the comparatively wide use of the two terms, there is little overall consensus about the precise dates of the periods they cover or the defining social, cultural, and intellectual features of either category. Different definitions of and arguments about modernity and postmodernity produced by competing theories and thinkers, however, frequently reveal important things about the political and philosophical premises of the particular critical stance each one has adopted.

It is important to note from the outset that although postmodernity and postmodernism are often used by critics as either interchangeable or closely related terms (often with the former as the "condition" in which the latter "style" becomes dominant), the relation between modernity and modernism tends to be somewhat more complicated. While modernism is generally deployed to refer to the group of literary and artistic movements that developed in Europe and North America in the late nineteenth and early twentieth centuries, modernity is often defined on the basis of a considerably longer historical period, dating back at least to the end of the eighteenth century and, for some theorists, substantially longer than that.

In contrast to this distinction between modernity and modernism, critics such as the American Marxist theorist Fredric Jameson insist that postmodernism "is not just another word for the description of a particular style. It is also ... a periodising concept whose function is to correlate the emergence of new formal features in culture with the emergence of a new type of social life and a new economic order" (1983: 113). In other words, while critics tend to be fairly confident in reading, for instance, Thomas Pynchon's novel *Gravity's Rainbow* (1973), with its playful and fragmentary experimentation with genres, mixture of esoteric and popular cultural references, and complex meandering plot, as an example of postmodernism that is representative of the wider cultural transformations of economics and communication technologies that a theorist such as French political philosopher Jean-François Lyotard (1984) identifies with social and political postmodernity, the same sort of immediate relation is much more problematic for modernism and modernity. For this reason, this entry will only deal very briefly with the term "modernism," and those wishing to know more should refer to that entry (in volume I).

An early and fairly straightforward use of the terms "modernity" and "postmodernity" can be found in Arnold Toynbee's book *A Study of History* (1954). Toynbee defines them as the final two moments in a series of historical epochs, occurring at the end of a long and steady progress during which humanity moves from the "Dark Ages" (675–1075), through the "Middle Ages" (1075–1475) to the "Modern Age" (1475–1875) and finally into a "post-Modern Age" (1875–). The Modern Age, according to Toynbee, is thus the period that sees the rise of "humanism": it is an epoch which understands the world in terms of the idea that the foundations of knowledge and action are located in the free will of human beings themselves rather than some divine or supernatural agency, and that humans are thus inherently valuable and dignified in and of themselves. He presents the Modern Age as a period of progressive emancipation from the superstition and mysticism of the Dark and Middle Ages as Enlightenment philosophy and science work to produce a rational basis for human experience and interaction. Toynbee claims that, following this period, a post-Modern Age begins in the final quarter of the nineteenth century and is a time of almost continual strife that has persisted ever since: "A post-Modern Age of Western history," he argues, sees "the rhythm of a Modern Western war-and-peace broken . . . by the portent of one general war following hard on the heels of another" (235). If the Modern Age marks the height of human progress and development, then the post-Modern Age is a period of decline in which war rages almost incessantly and the humanist projects of the Enlightenment are abandoned for the nationalist conflicts that marred much of the first half of the twentieth century. Since Toynbee first produced his definitions in 1954, a wide range of critics have adopted the terms and developed their own analyses of the cultural, political, philosophical, and historical stakes of modernity and postmodernity. Although there has been significant debate about where to locate the origins of modernity, Toynbee's identification of postmodernity as a predominantly twentieth-century phenomenon is one that most more recent accounts generally tend to support.

An alternative, but equally accessible, definition of modernity is produced by the American cultural critic Marshall Berman (1982). Modernity, he asserts, is the period of the new: the moment at which science, economics, technology, and politics develop to a stage where people's experience of their world becomes one of being caught up in a continual process of economic change and cultural transformation. It marks, according to Berman, a "maelstrom of perpetual disintegration and renewal":

To be modern is to find ourselves in an environment that promises us adventure, power, joy, growth, transformation of ourselves and the world – and, at the same time, that threatens to destroy everything we have, everything we know, everything we are . . . it pours us into a maelstrom of perpetual disintegration and renewal, of struggle and contradiction, of ambiguity and anguish. To be modern is to be part of a universe in which, as Marx said, "all that is solid melts into air." (1982: 15)

Modernity is an epoch in which change and transformation have become the central facets of experience. According to Berman, they are the social and cultural expressions of the rise of modern capitalist economics which began in the eighteenth century and put innovation and competition at the heart of political life. Nothing in life is exempt from modern upheaval as the economic, political, and philosophical discourses that govern social interaction are subject to continual revolutions, which in turn transform completely the everyday lives of individuals and communities. Berman identifies changes in knowledge, politics, the environment, communication technologies, bureaucracy, and the markets that perpetually dissolve any sense of stability or tradition that might bind people together. He argues that modern literature and culture can be read critically as engagements with this experience of modernization, and that a writer such as the German poet and polymath Johann Wolfgang von Goethe, in his two-part play *Faust* (1808, 1831), captures the processes of industrialization as "the whole movement of the work enacts the larger movement of Western society" (Berman 1982: 39). For Berman, though, the function of modern art is not simply to produce a reflection of modern life. Rather, the artistic work acts to champion or challenge (or even to do both simultaneously) the social and psychological processes of modernization, and so his readings of both the French poet Charles Baudelaire (1821–67) and the Russian novelist Fyodor Dostoyevsky (1821–81) explore their capacity to examine the "interfusion of [modernity's] material and spiritual forces, the intimate unity of the modern self and the modern environment" (Berman 1982: 132) in a manner that is at once celebratory and critical.

What Berman's account of modernity focuses on is what he identifies as the experience of constant, inescapable, and sudden changes that shape human life under capitalism. His definition of the experience of modernity as a continual confrontation with the new is one that is shared quite widely by critics. Despite this shared emphasis on modern innovation, however, while Berman's analysis of modernity identifies capitalism as the dominant driving force of this change and locates its origins in the eighteenth century, there are many other descriptions of the founding forces and moments of modernity that present alternative rationales and beginnings. Some critics identify the modern with other developments at the end of the eighteenth century such as American independence, which saw the birth of the contemporary world's chief superpower, the French Revolution with its invocations of new ideas of social equality and human rights, and the revolutions in philosophy, science, and the arts that accompanied these events (this approach is developed in, for example, Habermas 1987[1985]). Others discover the beginnings of modernity much earlier by locating its roots in the development of Christian theology, and especially the work of key theologians such as St Augustine, who lived and wrote during the fourth century (see, for example, Lyotard 2000[1998]).

Some critics, focusing much more explicitly on the global effects of exploration, conflict, and oppression, identify modernity with the period of European expansion that began in the later Middle Ages and became the colonial conquest and imperialism that drove nineteenth-century industrialization (for a particularly influential example of this approach, see Said 1985). For others, what is important is the transformation of ideas of image and representation, and the key period for this type of account is the Renaissance, which began in Italy during the fourteenth century and quickly spread throughout Europe to include such ideas as the realignment of the cosmos in Copernicus' discovery that the earth moves around the sun, the invention of perspective in art, and the self-reflexive account of modern subjectivity in the philosophy of René Descartes (these ideas of reflection and representation are central to Jean Baudrillard's 1983 book *Simulations*, to cite just one example). Finally, and in a manner that places modernity far closer to artistic modernism, a number of critics argue that it reaches its apotheosis in the industrialized slaughter of the battlefields of World War I and the innovations in psychoanalytic theory and avant-garde artistic representation that developed at that time (Randall Stevenson (1992) presents a particularly coherent case for this idea).

Each of these versions of modernity develops a different point of focus, ranging from global political change to theological arguments about personal identity, and thus produces a quite distinct worldview. What all of the above accounts have in common, though, is the identification of modernity as the story of a period guided by humankind's striving for continual progress. Jameson identifies this "story" structure as crucial when he argues that "Modernity is not a concept but rather a narrative category" (2002: 94). What he means by this is that all of the versions of modernity mentioned above function to generate specific points of focus for a modern narrative that describes and gives meaning to the historical transformations produced by modernization: each account identifies the meaning of those changes according to the categories central to the work of a particular set of disciplines, philosophies, or political outlooks, and tells its story of change on that basis. In a similar manner, in his influential book *The Postmodern Condition* (1984[1979]), Lyotard identifies modernity as the age of the "grand narrative." What he means by this term is that modern discourse works by producing a form of narrative organization that draws together into one great story all the smaller narratives that make up a people's experience of the world and thus provides them with a shared sense of history, present culture, and future orientation. In a grand narrative, Lyotard argues, all the different areas of knowledge that circulate in a culture are brought together to achieve a goal that is projected forward into the future as being the answer to the problems facing society: "[A]ll of the discourses of learning about every possible referent are taken up not from the point of view of their immediate truth-value, but in terms of the value they acquire by virtue of occupying a certain place in the itinerary of Spirit or Life" (35). Organized by a modern grand narrative, all the social institutions such as law, art, education, and technology combine to strive for a common goal for all humanity such as absolute knowledge or universal emancipation that is projected as the utopian end of that culture's journey through history. In this sense, according to both Jameson and Lyotard, modernity produces itself as a narrative construct: modern thought seeks ways to link together systematically the events and ideas of the past in order to produce an account of the meaning of the present and a vision of a future utopia that can form the basis of a culture's aspirations and projects.

Perhaps the most influential defender of such an account of modernity is the German philosopher and social theorist Jürgen Habermas, whose *The Philosophical Discourse of Modernity* (1987[1985]) sets out to defend the integrity of such grand narrative projects in the face of what he sees as the self-undermining critiques of postmodern theorists. Like the critics just mentioned, Habermas sees modernity as tied to the process of transformation: "[I]t is the epoch that lives for the future, that opens itself up to the novelty of the future" (5). He argues in an important earlier essay (1996[1981]) that this future-orientated modernity emerges as a philosophical discourse at the end of the eighteenth century in the work of the German Enlightenment philosopher Immanuel Kant, whose critique of traditional metaphysics transformed the ways in which arguments about the world could be framed. Here Habermas describes philosophical modernity as being characterized by the

> separation of substantive reason, formerly expressed in religious or metaphysical world-views, into three moments, now capable of being connected only formally with one another. . . . In so far as the world-views have disintegrated and their traditional problems have been separated off under the perspectives of truth, normative rightness and authenticity or beauty, and can now be treated as questions of knowledge, justice or taste respectively, there arises in the modern period a differentiation of the value sphere of science and knowledge, of morality and of art. (45)

What Habermas means by this is that with the onset of modernity, the foundations of knowledge change. He reads Kant's work as having successfully undermined the indemonstrable or mythological premises of earlier religious and metaphysical worldviews to produce a modern philosophy in which natural scientific claims, moral and ethical values, and questions of beauty and artistic value are open to verification within their own disciplines (scientists rather than priests should determine the truth of physical laws, for example), and the connections between them are susceptible to formal philosophical and political argument rather than fixed in some principles that lay beyond human understanding. For Habermas, this new mode of philosophical discourse alters entirely the ways in which knowledge, morality, and aesthetics function as ways of engaging with the world, and reorientates philosophy in relation to a society that is in a state of continual development and alteration.

Despite their differences in focus, their alternative chronologies. and their diverse political outlooks, these accounts of modernity all agree on the idea that it is an epoch in which revolution, transformation, and the new become central aspects of experience. If that is the case, and there are few critics who reject this idea, questions arise about how the idea of postmodernity can be defined. What sense does it make to think of a period as "more new than new" or "after the now"? This problem is central to many of the attempts to define and characterize postmodernity: for the most rigorous and influential theorists of the postmodern, the relation between modernity and postmodernity is not one of simple succession but is, instead, much more a question of a change of quality or focus, a disruption of progress, and a destabilization of the narrative structures of philosophy, history, and politics. As Lyotard puts it, albeit somewhat bleakly: "[T]he project of modernity has not been forsaken or forgotten, but destroyed, 'liquidated'" (1992: 18). Each of the three most influential characterizations of postmodernity, by Jameson, Baudrillard, and Lyotard, focus on the transformation and intensification of a particular aspect of

modernity, and explore the ways in which this disrupts the progressive narrative.

Jameson's *Postmodernism, or the Cultural Logic of Late-Capitalism* (1991) depicts postmodernism as the culture produced by an intensification of the range and scope of contemporary capitalism: "[E]very position on postmodernism in culture ... is also at one and the same time, and *necessarily*, an implicitly or explicitly political stance on the nature of multinational capitalism today" (3). In other words, according to Jameson, the styles and artistic forms of postmodernism are the cultural superstructure produced by the economic forces unleashed in capitalist postmodernity. He sees the intensification of capitalism as a move beyond the commodity-based forms of modernity that traditional Marxism was able to criticize to an even more encompassing form in which ideas and images have themselves become commodities:

> What has happened is that aesthetic production today has become integrated into commodity production generally: the frantic economic urgency of producing fresh waves of ever more novel-seeming goods (from clothing to airplanes), at ever greater rates of turnover, now assigns an increasingly essential structural function and position to aesthetic innovation and experimentation. (4–5)

In postmodernity, the "economic urgency" of innovations and fashions makes consumption a matter not just of useful products but also of images and lifestyle choices. This produces what Jameson calls a "new depthlessness" (6) in which commodities are reduced to interchangeable images and fashionable accessories purchased in a desperate attempt to remain up to date. Objects that might once have been experienced in terms of their use values are commodified to such an extent that exchange value, in fact the infinite exchangeability of all commodities, has come to account for the entirety of experience.

According to Jameson, the depthlessness of postmodernity produces in the consumer a mode of experience akin to schizophrenia in which the world "comes before the subject with heightened intensity, bearing a mysterious charge of affect, here described in the negative terms of anxiety and loss of reality, but which one could just as well imagine in the positive terms of euphoria, a high, an intoxicatory or hallucinogenic intensity" (27–8). What concerns Jameson is the lack of space for critique and reflection in the immediacy of this postmodernity. In a culture of schizophrenic depthlessness, traditional forms of critique are no longer possible, he argues, and "our most urgent task" becomes "tirelessly to denounce the economic forms that have come for the moment to rein supreme and unchallenged" (1992: 212) Consequently, the task of postmodernism in art and literature is to rediscover a political edge:

> the new political art . . . will have to hold to the truth of postmodernism, that is to say, to its fundamental object – the world of multinational capital – at the same time at which it achieves a breakthrough to some as yet unimaginable new mode of representing this last, in which we may again begin to grasp our positioning as individual and collective subjects and regain a capacity to act and struggle which is at present neutralised by our spatial as well as our social confusion. (1991: 54)

Postmodernist art must seek out new modes of representation in order to come to terms with the transformation of experience in the culture of postmodernity.

Like Jameson, Baudrillard's account of postmodernism also focuses on a loss of depth, perspective, and reality, and one of the key areas where he identifies this loss is in the mass media. According to Baudrillard, the ubiquity of contemporary media presents a "*dizzying whirl of reality*" that in turn generates a simulated world in which "we live, sheltered by signs, in the denial of the real" (1998: 34). In *Simulations*, the book often cited as his most influential account of postmodernity, Baudrillard argues that postmodernity marks a change in the very nature of appearance:

> Three orders of appearance, parallel to the mutations of the law of value, have followed one another since the Renaissance:
>
> - *Counterfeit* is the dominant scheme of the "classical" period, from the Renaissance to the industrial revolution;
> - *Production* is the dominant scheme of the industrial era;
> - *Simulation* is the reigning scheme of the current phase that is controlled by the code.
>
> The first order of simulacrum is based on the natural law of value, that of the second order on the commercial law of value, that of the third order on the structural law of value. (83)

Baudrillard account of the image ties it to the move from modernity to postmodernity. In the first order, appearance counterfeits reality as the image represents it in its absence: the portrait represents its subject and is judged on its likeness. In the second order, the value associated with an image changes: what becomes important is its ability to be bought and sold, produced, reproduced, and circulated. This is the order of mass production, and, as Baudrillard argues, once images are produced on this scale, "The relation between them is no longer that of an original to its counterfeit . . . but equivalence, indifference" (97). In the third order, questions of originality and reality drop out altogether as images become placeholders in a structural system in which all values have become equivalent and exchangeable: representation is an infinite code to which no one has the key. Images and simulations become more immediate, more apparently real, more seductive, and more desirable as they produce the reality in which people exist: contemporary culture is not the producer of simulations, but the product of them. On this basis, Baudrillard argues that the real is now "produced from miniaturised units, from matrices, memory banks and command models. … It is a hyperreal: the product of an irradiating synthesis of combinatory models in a hyperspace without atmosphere" (3). Postmodernity marks the loss of the reality that was the object of modern knowledge.

Jameson's and Baudrillard's are two among many analyses of postmodernity. Although there are significant differences between different theorists, the general ideas presented here of immediacy, depthlessness, and a loss of reality in the simulations of the contemporary media are commonly found at the centre of any account of postmodernity.

SEE ALSO. Baudrillard, Jean; Habermas, Jürgen; Jameson, Fredric; Lyotard, Jean-François; Master Narrative; Modernism; Postmodernism

REFERENCES AND SUGGESTED READINGS

Baudrillard, J. (1983). Simulations (trans. P. Foss, P. Patton, & P. Beitchman). New York: Semiotext(e).
Baudrillard, J. (1998). The Consumer Society: Myths and Structures. London: Sage.
Berman, M. (1982). All That Is Solid Melts Into Air: The Experience of Modernity. London: Verso.
Habermas, J. (1987). The Philosophical Discourse of Modernity: Twelve Lectures (trans. F. Lawrence). Cambridge: Polity. (Original work published 1985.).
Habermas, J. (1996). Modernity: An unfinished project. In M. P. d'Entrèves & S. Benhabib (eds.), Habermas and the Unfinished Project of Modernity. Cambridge: Polity, pp. 38–55. (Original work published 1981.)
Jameson, F. (1983). Postmodernism and consumer society. In H. Foster (ed.), Postmodern Culture. London: Pluto, pp. 111–125.
Jameson, F. (1991). Postmodernism, or, the Cultural Logic of Late Capitalism. London: Verso.
Jameson, F. (2002). A Singular Modernity: Essay on the Ontology of the Present. London: Verso.
Lyotard, J.-F. (1984). The Postmodern Condition: A Report on Knowledge (trans. G. Bennington & B. Massumi). Manchester: Manchester University Press. (Original work published 1979.)
Lyotard, J.-F. (1992). The Postmodern Explained (trans. D. Barry, B. Maher, J. Pefanis, V. Spate, & M. Thomas). Minneapolis: University of Minnesota Press.
Lyotard, J.-F. (2000). The Confession of Augustine (trans. R. Beardsworth). Stanford: Stanford University Press. (Original work published 1998.)
Pynchon, T. (1973). Gravity's Rainbow. London: Jonathan Cape.
Said, Edward (1985). Orientalism, Harmondsworth: Penguin.
Stevenson, R. (1992). Modernist Fiction: An Introduction. Hemel Hempstead: Harvester Wheatsheaf
Toynbee, A. (1954). A Study of History, vol IX. Oxford: Oxford University Press.

Moretti, Franco

ANTHONY FOTHERGILL

Franco Moretti is a literary comparativist and theoretician whose roots in Marxist theory lend his work a sociological and historical orientation, while his innovatory methodology is increasingly global in its data-based range of application and claims. "Global formalism" may best describe it.

Born in Italy in 1950, Moretti studied comparative literature at the University of Rome. He taught at the Universities of

Salerno and Verona, publishing his first major critical works, *Signs Taken for Wonders* (1983) and *The Way of the World* (1987). Earlier publications included an anthology on T. S. Eliot and a study of English left-wing intellectuals of the 1930s. He became a professor of English and comparative literature at Columbia University, New York, before moving, in 2000, to Stanford University, where he became the founding Director of the Stanford Center for the Study of the Novel. In 2006 he was named to the American Academy of Arts and Science.

For many years Moretti has been closely associated with *New Left Review* (*NLR*). Not only is this indicative of his Marxist intellectual heritage and his commitment to a reading of literature within a broad historical, geographical, and social framework – he cites Galvano della Volpe and the early Georg Lukács as important influences – but it is also significant because much of his recent writing has originated as essays in *NLR*, which in turn has generated lively discussion (see Prendergast 2001; Arac 2002; Kristal 2002). His essays evolved through this dialogue (as almost a new form of scholarly production) into the project *Graphs, Maps and Trees* (2005).

Although, at heart, Moretti is a comparativist, he is critical of what he now sees as an outmoded form of comparative criticism restricting itself to close textual analysis of a few canonical Western works. His aim has been to develop a methodology for describing the historical and spatial evolution of genres (particularly the novel) and locating the transformation of their literary forms and narrative devices. Paradoxical for many, but not for Moretti, this is a marriage between a commitment to a certain kind of formalism and a broad world-historical view embedded in his early Marxist reading, with an indebtedness to Immanuel Wallerstein's theory of the late

capitalist "world-system" and latterly from evolutionary science (Darwin). He also cites Max Weber and Karl Popper as offering theoretical models for scientific postulation, explanation, and experimental "falsifiability." With Weber, he emphasizes not new raw material but new ways of conceptualizing problems about it; from Popper, he takes the idea that theories require "a leap, a wager, a hypothesis which can be tested and refuted" (Moretti 2000: 55) – a spirit that his iconoclasm clearly embraces.

Moretti's discussion of *Weltliteratur* (world literature) has been compared in ambition to that of Erich Auerbach and Edward Said, but evident in his recent critical practice is his enthusiasm for presenting a cultural geography as the data-based quantitative analysis of facts from which he seeks to establish a model for a general description of cultural production. Characteristically, he draws on the use of abstract diagrams to elaborate data and arguments. The origin of this methodological thrust was Moretti's growing disquiet with the fact that of the many thousands of novels published in France, England and Germany from the late 1700s to the late 1800s "only some 200–300 were considered by literary critics. That is about one percent." (Moretti 2005: 4) The emphasis on "close reading" makes it physically impossible to read anything but a tiny proportion of cultural output. This distortion elevates these works above those other now long-forgotten novels which we dismissively label "mass culture," and so blinds us to the realities of cultural production. Moretti wants to abandon the "academic" canon in favor of the "social" canon of actually circulating books. His position also carries powerful implications for new forms of literary research. He calls for "distant reading," a more generalized historical and geographical mapping of literary works; that is, not an individual critic reading thousands of novels (impossible), but a process of data-collection by whole teams of researchers who feed into the modeled maps or graphs "information" which gets centrally "read." As Moretti admits, its usefulness depends on the quality of the questions then being asked of this data. It is "formalism without the close reading" (Arac 2002: 41).

This break with established disciplinary areas is already found in *Signs* (1983). Whether discussing Shakespearean tragedy, Frankenstein or Dracula, Balzac or Conan Doyle, Moretti places literary forms and conventions within the broadly conceived social/political moment of the work's production. With the "world-system" in his mind, his *Modern Epic* (1996) describes a new super-genre embracing the modern monumental works of Goethe's *Faust*, Wagner's *Ring*, Joyce's *Ulysses*, Eliot's *The Wasteland*, and García Márquez's *One Hundred Years of Solitude*.

Most excitement, but also criticism, has been raised by Moretti's *Graphs* (2005). The "world system" of imperialistic globalization works with a theory of expanding literary influence from the "centre" (Western Europe and America) to the "periphery" (South America, Asia, Africa). Moretti's early arguments proposing such an evolution of literary forms, whereby the originating central models got locally refashioned at the periphery, has come in for much debate (see Prendergast 2001; Kristal 2002). The "map" of the circulation of books (in translation) within Europe was a major chapter in Moretti's *Atlas* (1998). Now he has gone global. Some argue this is itself a cultural imperialist ideology, particularly with its undebated assumption of the hegemony of the English language as the world language. Moretti would argue that he is describing, not endorsing, the cultural evolution of literary globalization. It is characteristic of his procedures, though, that he is happy to acknowledge weaknesses or provocative overstatements in his arguments, and thus recognizes now the importance of the "semi-periphery," for example. Critics have argued that it is unclear whether his scientific or economic models are to be seen as metaphorical analogues to literary evolution or actual strictly comparable sets. If the latter, then the few hundred years of the novel's evolution can hardly be compared to Darwinian evolutionary time, thus making the model an empty piece of rhetorical flourish, not the "science" it claims to be. His alleged cavalier handling of statistics in *Atlas* has also been criticized. But Moretti is generous in dismissing the critique: "in absolute terms our [statistical] findings have no definitive value" (Moretti 1998: 151)

SEE ALSO: Canons; Core and Periphery; Cultural Geography; Formalism; Globalization; Lukács, Georg; Marxism; Mass Culture

REFERENCES AND SUGGESTED READINGS

Arac, J. (2002). Anglo-globalism? *New Left Review*, 16, 35–45.
Kristal, E. (2002). "Considering coldly …": A response to Franco Moretti. *New Left Review*, 15, 61–74.
Caesar, M. (2007). Franco Moretti and the world literature debate. *Italian Studies*, 62(1), 125–135.
Lindberg-Wada, G. (ed.) (2006). *Studying Transcultural Literary History*. Berlin: Walter de Gruyter.
Lukács, G. (1978). *The Theory of the Novel* (trans. A. Bostock). London: Lawrence and Wishart. (Original work published 1920.)
Moretti, F. (1983). *Signs Taken for Wonders: On the Sociology of Literary Forms* (trans. S. Fischer, D. Forgacs, & D. Miller). London: Verso.

Moretti, F. (1987). *The Way of the World: The* Bildungsroman *in European Culture* (trans. A. J. Sbragia). London: Verso.

Moretti, F. (1996). *Modern Epic. The World-System from Goethe to García Márquez* (trans. Q. Hoare). London: Verso.

Moretti, F. (1998). *Atlas of the European Novel: 1800–1900.* London: Verso.

Moretti, F. (2000). Conjectures on world literature. *New Left Review,* 1, 54–68.

Moretti, F. (2005). *Graphs, Maps, Trees: Abstract Models for Literary History.* London: Verso.

Moretti, F. (2006). The end of the beginning: A reply to Christopher Prendergast. *New Left Review,* 41, 71–86.

Moretti, F. (ed.) (2006). *The Novel.* Vol. 1: *History, Geography and Culture*; Vol 2: *Forms and Themes.* Princeton: Princeton University Press.

Karl Popper, K. (2002). *The Logic of Scientific Discovery* (London: Routledge). (Original work published 1935.)

Prendergast, C. (2001). Negotiating world literature. *New Left Review,* 8, 100–121.

N

Nancy, Jean-Luc

IAN JAMES

Jean-Luc Nancy's philosophy emerges in the wake of the twentieth-century French reception of Nietzschean and Heideggerian thought most commonly associated with thinkers such as, among others, Maurice Blanchot, Georges Bataille, Jacques Derrida, and Gilles Deleuze. His early work of the 1970s includes important readings of key modern philosophers such as Descartes, Hegel, and Kant, and also develops critiques of German Romanticism, Lacanian psychoanalysis, and philosophical subjectivity. His more mature work of the 1980s, 1990s, and early twenty-first century offers a radical reformulation of Heideggerian ontology in the context of which he publishes a number of important works which engage with a range of major philosophical questions: community, the nature of the political, freedom, embodiment, and shared worldly existence. Since the mid-1990s his work has increasingly focused on questions relating to aesthetics, to the inner structure of monotheism, and to the legacy of Christianity within Western thought and culture.

Nancy's early work of the 1970s was heavily marked by his collaborations with Philippe Lacoue-Labarthe and by the influence of Derridean deconstruction. Both Nancy and Lacoue-Labarthe had been politically committed in the 1960s (the former in the context of Christian socialism and involvement with the CFDT union, one of the five major French confederations of trade unions, the latter with the Socialisme et Barbarie movement). This association with the French nonconformist Left inflects much of Nancy's thinking in relation to politics and to the political, in particular his collaboration with Lacoue-Labarthe in the early 1980s in the Centre for Philosophical Research on the Political and his later thinking about community and globalization.

Nancy's most significant contribution to contemporary French philosophy is undoubtedly his reworking of existential phenomenology into an ontology of finite sense which affirms the fragmentary multiplicity, or more precisely, the nontotalizable singular plurality of shared worldly existence. In this context Nancy is explicitly deconstructing and reformulating Heidegger's early and late thinking of being. In a less explicit manner he also builds upon, and in crucial ways transforms, Merleau-Ponty's late ontology of flesh. For Nancy, sense needs to be viewed as a fundamental order of meaning which underpins and makes possible our apprehension of the world in the first instance; sense is the sense of existence which is or makes sense, which without sense would not exist. The fundamental ontological and existential status of sense in Nancy's thinking places it in excess of abstract conceptuality, of language, or of any relation of signifier to signified. Sense is that which bodily existence has always already engaged in order to experience an intelligible spatial or worldly environment. Most importantly, for Nancy, sense is that shared horizon against which the experience of a meaningful world is experienced in common with others. Nancy's ontology of sense is one in which the relation to others is always primordial. At the same time the horizon of sense and meaning which makes worldly existence possible is always shared in a fragmented multiplicity of bodies, or in Nancy's terms, it exists only in a singular-plural bodily spacing of sense. Nancy's thinking about community, embodiment, aesthetics and politics can all be related to his philosophy of sense as it develops throughout the 1980s and 1990s.

Nancy's philosophical career can be separated into a number of distinct phases. Throughout the 1970s his work mostly takes the form of close readings or commentaries of specific philosophical figures, on, for example, Hegel, Kant, and Descartes. This tendency toward commentary is displaced in his writing of the 1980s and early '90s in favor of more ambitious and wide-ranging works. From the mid-1990s onward Nancy's work has focused more on questions relating to art and aesthetics, and has increasingly centered around a project which has come to be known as the "Deconstruction of Christianity." During this period Nancy has published books which treat the question of art and artistic presentation in more general terms. He has also published works on Christian painting. What has come to characterize both his later writing about art and his thinking about the deconstruction of Christianity is a shift away from the Heideggerian language of finitude and finite existence toward a language of infinity and the infinitude of bodily sense experience.

Initial responses to Nancy's philosophy in the 1980s and '90s tended to focus on the political dimension of his work and, in particular, on his thinking about community. This initial phase could be more broadly related to widespread interest in the political dimension of deconstructive or poststructuralist thought more generally. More recently there has been a burgeoning of interest in Nancy's thinking about art and aesthetics. Nancy's philosophy of sense has opened the way for a contemporary and future reconsideration of the referential function of literature and art, as well as for a rethinking of the status of the artistic image, particularly in relation to the visual arts and to film.

The deconstruction of Christianity is the major ongoing work of Nancy's later philosophy and engages a broad range of question relating to the fate of Western cultural values at the beginning of the twenty-first century. His thesis that Christianity, and monotheism more generally, carries within it the logic of its own self-overcoming destabilizes, at a very profound level, received notions of the theological and the secular, of theism and atheism. This project will continue to stimulate philosophical and theological research in the future and represents an important contribution to European philosophy at the beginning of the twenty-first century.

SEE ALSO: Bataille, Georges; Blanchot, Maurice; Deleuze, Gilles; Derrida, Jacques; Lacoue-Labarthe, Philippe

REFERENCES AND SUGGESTED READINGS

Hutchens, B. C. (2005). *Jean-Luc Nancy and the Future of Philosophy*. Chesham: Acumen.

Jamesl, I. (2006). *The Fragmentary Demand: An Introduction to the Philosophy of Jean-Luc Nancy*. Stanford: Stanford University Press.

Nancy, J.-L. (1991). *The Inoperative Community*. Minneapolis: University of Minnesota Press. (Original work published 1983.)

Nancy, J.-L. (1992). *Corpus*. Paris: Métailié.

Nancy, J.-L. (1993). *The Experience of Freedom* (trans. B. McDonald). Stanford: Stanford University Press. (Original work published 1988.)

Nancy, J.-L. (1996). *The Muses* (trans. P. Kamuf). Stanford: Stanford University Press. (Original work published 1994.)

Nancy, J.-L. (1998). *The Sense of the World* (trans. J. S. Librett). Minneapolis: University of Minnesota Press. (Original work published 1993.)

Nancy, J.-L. (2000). *Being Singular Plural* (trans. A. E. O'Byrne & R. D. Richardson). Stanford: Stanford University Press. (Original work published 1996.)

Nancy, J.-L. (2003). *A Finite Thinking* (trans. S. Sparks). Stanford: Stanford University Press. (Original work published 1990.)

Nancy, J.-L. (2008). *Dis-Enclosure: The Deconstruction of Christianity* (trans. B. Bergo, G. Malenfant, & M. B. Smith). New York: Fordham University Press. (Original work published 2005.)

Narratology and Structuralism

PAUL WAKE

Narratology is a formalist-structuralist attempt to theorize and define the nature of narrative. The term itself was introduced in 1969 by Bulgarian-born naturalized French literary critic Tzvetan Todorov, whose description of "narratologie" as "la science du récit [the science of narrative]" (1969: 10) is a clear indication of the "scientific" aspirations evinced by narratology in its early manifestations.

In common with the structuralist theory from which it emerged, narratology, despite its early focus on the literary text, finds application across the range of the social sciences, the humanities, philosophy, and, arguably, beyond. This wide-ranging application is well remarked by French literary critic and theorist Roland Barthes, who famously described narrative as "international, transhistorical, transcultural: it is simply there, like life itself" (1977: 78), while the insight offered by Gerald Prince, an Egyptian-born American critic whose work is central to the development of narratology, that narrative "does not simply record events; it constitutes and interprets them" (2000b: 129) indicates the crucial insights that narratology might offer for our understanding of both ourselves and our world.

As might be expected, narratology, which has become thoroughly international in scope, has attracted a good deal of critical attention since its emergence as an autonomous discipline in the mid-1960s, attention that has called into question the possibility of its supposed insularity as an area of study and which has led to a proliferation of positions competing for attention. As American literary critic David Herman puts it, "*narratology* has in fact ramified into *narratologies*; structuralist theorizing about stories has evolved into a plurality of models for narrative analysis" (1999: 1). Recognizing this plurality, this entry will be structured according to three apparently distinct, but in fact always already merged, "phases" of narratology; in this tripartite structure, "structuralism," a crucial antecedent to narratology proper, precedes, to use the now-established terminology, "classical" and "postclassical" narratology.

STRUCTURALISM

As Barthes makes clear in his "Introduction to the structural analysis of narratives" (1977 [1966]), the opening essay in a special issue of the French-language journal *Communications*, "Recherches sémiologiques: L'Analyse structurale du récit" ["Semiological research: Structural analysis of narrative"], structuralism takes linguistic studies as its "founding model" (82). Specifically, there is an appeal to the work of Swiss linguist Ferdinand de Saussure, whose lectures at the University of Geneva, delivered in 1906–11, were published posthumously as *Course in General Linguistics* in 1916. Central to Saussure's *Course* was the separation of "*langue*" (the rules or code of language) from "*parole*" (the specific manifestations of that code). Following Saussure, structuralist critics privileged *langue* over *parole*, seeking to identify in their analyses the underlying codes by which narratives might be apprehended. Barthes makes this impulse clear when he defines "structuralism's constant aim" as the attempt "to master the infinity of utterances [*paroles*] by describing the 'language' [*langue*] of which they are the products and from which they can be generated" (80). With this emphasis, structuralist theories of narrative concentrated on the fundamental elements governing the construction of predominantly literary texts and demonstrated a concomitant lack of interest in the specifics of the individual stories, their writers and readers, and the contexts within which both writers and readers operate in the generation of text and meaning.

The result of this search for narrative's underlying "code" was an "action-" or "event-"centered analysis that finds perhaps its most celebrated example in the work of Russian scholar Vladimir Propp, whose *Morphology of the Folktale* (1968 [1928]) considers 100 Russian folktales. Focusing on structure rather than story content or social significance, Propp's analyses allow him to identify a set of 31 "functions," minimal units of plot that he defines as "act[s] of a character, defined from the point of view of its significance to the course of the action" (21), such as "the hero leaves home" or "the villain is defeated." Similarly, Propp outlines a seven-fold *dramatis personae* defining character in terms of "roles" corresponding to the functions (such as "hero," "villain," and "helper"), thereby subordinating character to plot. Propp concludes that these functions provide a core set of components common to every folktale and that while no single folktale features every one, all tales can be summarized in terms of those that they contain, which, he notes, always appear in the same order.

Propp's work was largely neglected until the late 1960s when, following the translation of *Morphology of the Folktale* into English, it would have a massive impact on structuralist study. In particular Propp's influence can be seen in the work of French structural anthropologist Claude Lévi-Strauss, Lithuanian semiotician Algirdas Julien Greimas, and French linguist Claude Bremond. Perhaps, following the work of Propp, the most significant application of structuralist theory to the analysis of literary narrative came with Todorov's *Grammaire du Décaméron* [The Grammar of Décaméron] (1969) which, despite the reference to Boccaccio's tales in its title, is an attempt to discuss the structures of narrative in general. Setting out the position that language acts as a master code for all signifying systems, Todorov outlines a narrative grammar based on what he termed the "syntactic" (the links between units of narrative) rather than the "semantic" (the content of narrative) or the "verbal" (the sentences which make up the text).

As should be clear, the structuralist analysis of narrative led to a privileging of the code of literature as a whole at the expense of the study of the manifestations of that code within individual texts. Barthes, whose "Introduction to the structural analysis of narratives" marked him as one of the founders of structuralist-informed narratology, would challenge the prioritizing of code as a means by which narratives might be apprehended in his groundbreaking *S/Z* (1990[1970]), a book which has been described as the opening statement of poststructuralism. Through a painstaking analysis of "Sarrasine," a nineteenth-century short story by French writer Honoré de Balzac, according to what he identifies as the five "codes" of narrative, Barthes demonstrates the ways in which the structural analysis of texts might challenge rather than affirm the structures of meaning to which they appeal. Thus his reading of Balzac's text lays bare the narrative strategies by which it attempts to apprehend, and make intelligible, the gender of a castrato protagonist whose very name, "Sarrasine," reveals in its feminization of a male referent an ambiguity that the text's structural principles are unable to contain. The attendant "blanks and looseness" in the structural analysis are "footprints," as Barthes puts it, "marking the escape of the text; for if the text is subject to some form, this form is not unitary, architectonic, finite" (20). Thus the act of what Barthes calls "structuration" comes to be the imposition rather than the discovery of structure in the narrative text.

CLASSICAL NARRATOLOGY

Classical narratology, what readers today might recognize as narratology proper, shares a number of characteristics, and a good number of its key proponents, with structuralism. In fact, it is perhaps best regarded as a subdomain of, rather than as a break from, structuralism. However, while classical narratology retains a central interest in the structuring of narratives and shares with structuralism a desire for a precise terminology with which to discuss and analyze the texts that it takes as its objects, there is a move away from the search for the code underlying narrative in general (a move from, for example, the attempt to formulate a "grammar" of plots as evinced in Propp's work) toward an attempt to generate a terminology and a methodology with which to facilitate the study of individual literary texts. This development can be readily seen in the handling of "plot" in the work of classical narratologists in which plot typologies, increasingly regarded as reductive and political in nature (Jameson 2002[1981]), are supplanted by readings of the internal relations between plot elements. Accordingly, American literary critic Seymour Chatman discusses the events of story in terms of a hierarchy that distinguishes between what he terms "kernels" (those events that are essential) and "satellites" (minor plot events that could be deleted without disturbing the logic of the plot) (1978: 53–6), while Prince usefully advances the discussion of plot with the introduction of the "disnarrated" (1988) – those elements in a narrative that refer to events that do not take place. In this way, by pursuing an analysis of the internal functioning of fictional narrative, classical narratology demonstrates what Israeli narratologist Shlomith Rimmon-Kenan describes as a "double orientation" that allows it to "present a description of the system governing all fictional narratives" and, at the same time, "to indicate a way in which individual narratives can be studied as unique realizations of the general system" (2002[1983]: 4). Having noted this dual orientation, it should be stressed that classical narratology follows structuralism in emphasizing (narrative) langue, the description of the "system" governing narratives, over (narrative) parole, the individual text, a fact that the following discussion, which pays little mind to specific literary texts, demonstrates.

Of the numerous works of narratology published in the 1980s, French literary critic Gérard Genette's *Narrative Discourse* (1980) has arguably been (and indeed remains) the most influential. Systematizing earlier work and developing a new and extensive terminology, Genette's insights were rapidly taken up and developed in the work of, among others: Chatman (1978), Dutch cultural theorist and critic Mieke Bal (1997[1980]), Prince (1982), and Rimmon-Kenan (2002[1983]). While Genette's title promises that his focus will be on "discourse" and "method," and might therefore be more concerned with narrative's codes than with its particular manifestations, his methodology affords the possibility of studying the code of narrative alongside its manifestation within the individual text – in his case this is Marcel Proust's seven-volume *A la Recherche du temps perdu* [Remembrance of Things Past] (1913–27). Genette develops a threefold model of narrative in which "narrative" (the discourse/narrative text) is placed in relation to "story" (the succession of events that are recounted) and "narrating" (the event that consists of someone recounting something). Genette's narratology is concerned with the relation of these three "narratives." Placing minimal emphasis on "story," the narrative "events" that so clearly concerned structuralist studies of narrative, his project is to set out a methodology by which it might be possible to undertake "a study of the relationships between narrative and story, between narrative and narrating, and (to the extent that they are inscribed in narrative discourse) between story and narrating" (1980[1972]: 29). With the object of his study thus identified, Genette's narratology functions according to three basic classes of determinations: tense (dealing with time), mood (the forms of narrative representation), and voice (which deals with the ways in which

the act of narrating itself appears within narratives).

As Russian literary historian, critic, and philosopher Mikhail Bakhtin has remarked, "literature's primary mode of representation *is* temporal" (1981: 146), and it is unsurprising that "tense" has proved to be one of the most interesting and productive aspects of narrative theory. Genette begins his discussion of the temporal aspect of narratives with a consideration of "order," noting the discrepancies, what he terms "anachronies," between the ordering of the events that make up the story (story time) and their appearance in the narrative (narrative time: Chatman's "discourse time"), going on to describe these anachronies in terms of analepses (flashbacks) and prolepses (flashforwards/anticipation). Narrative "speed" is discussed under the heading of "duration," and concerns the amount of space or text allotted to the events of story; thus Genette offers a scale that takes "ellipses" (omission, literally infinite speed) as one extreme and "pause" (text in which no time elapses) on the other. Between these two extremes are "summary" (narrative time is shorter than story time), "scene" (where narrative time approximates story time), and "stretch" (where narrative time exceeds story time). Finally, Genette's analysis considers "frequency," distinguishing between "singulative" (a single event is recounted once), "repeating" (a single event is recounted more than once), and "iterative" (a recurring event is recounted once) narrative.

"Mood" concerns the point of view of a narrative vis-à-vis the material it presents and is assessed according to notions of "distance" and "perspective" and operates on a scale between what Genette terms the "mimetic," in which the presence of information is maximized (effectively "showing" the action), and the "diegetic," in which information is reduced and the presence of the informer is increasingly evident (the action is "told"). "Voice," which is related to mood, is concerned with the manner in which information in a text is conveyed takes as its central concern issues of "distance" and "perspective" – notions which enable the discussion of the relation of the narrator to the events recounted. The distinction between mood and voice roughly follows Genette's oft-quoted distinction between "who sees" (mood: the "focalizer") and "who speaks" (voice). For Genette, "seeing," can be "nonfocalized" (omniscient narration where all perspectives are accessible to the narrator), "internal" (from the "fixed" perspective of a single character, or "variable" coming from multiple characters within the narrative), or "external" (which allows itself a knowledge only of the external actions of its characters). These categories, in particular that of "external focalization," are challenged and reworked by Bal (1997 [1980]).

While mood and voice consider the narrator, theories of narrative communication also account for the presence of the addressee of this narrator: the "narratee." Distinguished from the "real reader," just as the narrator is distinguished from the "real author," the narratee is a textual construct who appears at the same narrative level as the narrator. Narratees (whether readers or listeners, single or multiple) may be overt, fully developed characters, or covert "nonnarratees" who do not appear at all. Their role in the story may be central or minimal and they might be the intended recipients of the narrator's story or entirely unintended and undesired. The possibility of asking such questions suggests that the transaction between narrator and narratee forms a narrative in its own right (see Prince 1980).

Running across Genette's discussion of mood and voice is the extremely useful concept of narrative "levels." Usually con-

ceived in spatial terms (higher/lower: inside/outside), the notion that narratives are not monologic (i.e. that they *are* multiple and often self-referential structures) allows for a multiplication of perspectives existing alongside one another within the same text. This notion that narrative operates on numerous levels is usefully discussed in terms of what Bakhtin calls "dialogism," the interaction evident in multivoiced narratives, and in terms of metafiction and metanarratives (narratives that comment on narratives).

POSTCLASSICAL NARRATOLOGY

For all its successes, narratology in its classical form is limited by what Prince has called an "exacerbated textocentrism" (1991: 545). As Genette remarks, reflecting on his earlier work, "I am well aware that a narrative text can be viewed from other angles" (1988[1983]: 8). With this in mind, it is possible to return to Prince's *Dictionary* which, if it reveals the predominant focus of narratology as it developed in the late 1970s and early 1980s, also makes manifest a number of the "movement's" blind spots and weaknesses. Thus it reveals a certain insularity that becomes obvious in the absence of references to theorists whose work might be regarded as outside the field proper, with no mention made of writers and thinkers whose work has been usefully deployed in the development and theorizing of narrative; psychologists such as Sigmund Freud, Carl Gustav Jung, and Jacques Lacan, and theorists and philosophers such as Gilles Deleuze, Jacques Derrida, Michel Foucault, Fredric Jameson, and Georg Lukács. Similarly, the focus on the literary text is to the exclusion of other media such as film, painting, video, music, and dance. It is the increased engagement with theories and subjects that fall "outside" its classical remit that introduces narratology's current, postclassical, phase.

Postclassical narratology, which Herman describes in terms of "re-emergence," "re-contextualizing," and "rethinking" (1999: 3), and which British critic Martin McQuillan, in his useful *The Narrative Reader* (2000), places under the heading "Diaspora," is by its very nature, resistant to summary or definition. It demonstrates a nature that is both porous in its integration of other theoretical approaches and promiscuous in its ready application to a wide array of fields beyond the literary text. Thus conceived, postclassical narratology finds application in, and draws on, cognitive science (Manfred Jahn; Herman), deconstruction (Paul de Man; Barbara Johnson; J. Hillis Miller), digital media and technology (Marie-Laure Ryan), ethics (James Phelan), feminism (Marianne Hirsch; Susan S. Lanser), film (David Bordwell), history and historiography (Hayden White), identity (Monika Fludernik), ideology, linguistics, postcolonial studies, postmodernism (Jean François Lyotard), psychoanalysis (Elizabeth Bronfen; Peter Brooks), phenomenology (Paul Ricoeur), reader theory (Wolfgang Iser), and rhetoric. With such an inclusive program, it becomes clear that postclassical narratology is far from the unified field that it was in its classical phase.

A truly interdisciplinary endeavor, postclassical narratology is unified, if such a thing is possible or indeed desirable, by an increasing movement from study of text to the study of text in context. In other words, it moves from its ahistorical-textocentric structuralist origins toward a more relativistic and political understanding of narrative. This can be seen in the proliferation of "types" of narratology, be they feminist, postcolonial, phenomenological, ethical, or otherwise. While the insights of classical narratology remain useful and in use, this context-centered

analysis emphasizes the application of theory over formalist description and taxonomies. As German literary critic Ansgar Nünning puts it, "putting the analytic toolbox to interpretative use" is one of the main goals of postclassical narratology (2003: 244).

SEE ALSO: Bakhtin, Mikhail; Bal, Mieke; Barthes, Roland; Genette, Gérard; Greimas, A. J.; Lévi-Strauss, Claude; Master Narrative; Propp, Vladimir; Saussure, Ferdinand de; Structuralism

REFERENCES AND SUGGESTED READINGS

Bakhtin, M. M. (1981). *The Dialogic Imagination: Four Essays by M. M. Bakhtin* (ed. M. Holquist; trans. C. Emerson & M. Holquist). Austin: University of Texas Press.

Bal, M. (1997). *Narratology: Introduction to the Theory of Narrative.* Toronto: University of Toronto Press. (Original work published 1980.)

Barthes, R. (1977). Introduction to the structural analysis of narratives. In R. Barthes, *Image, Music, Text* (trans. S. Heath). New York: Hill and Wang, pp. 79–124. (Original work published 1966.)

Barthes, R. (1990). *S/Z* (trans. R. Miller). Oxford: Blackwell. (Original work published 1970.)

Bordwell, D. (1985). *Narration in the Fiction Film.* Madison: University of Wisconsin Press.

Brooks, P. (1984). *Reading for the Plot: Design and Intention in Narrative.* Oxford: Clarendon.

Chatman, S. (1978). *Story and Discourse: Narrative Structure in Fiction and Film.* Ithaca: Cornell University Press.

Fludernik, M. (1996). *Towards a "Natural" Narratology.* London: Routledge.

Genette, G. (1980). *Narrative Discourse: An Essay in Method* (trans. J. E. Lewin). Ithaca: Cornell University Press. (Original work published 1972.)

Genette, G. (1988). *Narrative Discourse Revisited* (trans. J. E. Lewin). Ithaca: Cornell University Press. (Original work published 1983.)

Herman, D. (2002). *Story Logic: Problems and Possibilities of Narrative*. Lincoln: University of Nebraska Press.

Herman, D. (ed.) (1999). *Narratologies: New Perspectives on Narrative Analysis*. Columbus: Ohio State University Press.

Hirsch, M. (1989). *The Mother/Daughter Plot: Narrative, Psychoanalysis, Feminism*. Bloomington: Indiana University Press.

Jameson, F. (2002). *The Political Unconscious: Narrative as a Socially Symbolic Act*. London: Routledge. (Original work published 1981.)

Lanser, S. S. (1992). *Fictions of Authority: Women Writers and Narrative Voice*. Ithaca: Cornell University Press.

Lévi-Strauss, C. (1963). *Structural Anthropology* (trans. C. Jacobson & B. G. Schoepf). New York: Basic Books.

McQuillan, M. (2000). *The Narrative Reader*. London: Routledge.

Nünning, A. (2003). Narratology or narratologies? Taking stock of recent developments, critique and modest proposals for future usages of the term. In T. Kindt & H.-H. Müller (eds.), *What is Narratology? Questions and Answers Regarding the Status of a Theory*. Berlin: Walter de Gruyter, pp. 239–277.

Phelan, J. (2005). *Living to Tell About It: A Rhetoric and Ethics of Character Narration*. Ithaca: Cornell University Press.

Phelan, J., & Rabinowitz, P. J. (eds.) (2005) *A Companion to Narrative Theory*. Oxford: Blackwell.

Prince, G. (1980). Introduction to the study of the narratee. In J. P. Tompkins (ed.), *Reader-Response Criticism*. Baltimore: Johns Hopkins University Press, pp. 7–25.

Prince, G. (1982). *Narratology: The Form and Functioning of Narrative*. Berlin: Mouton.

Prince, G. (1988). The disnarrated. *Style*, 12, 1–8.

Prince, G. (1991). Narratology, narrative, and meaning (trans. A. Noble). *Poetics Today*, 13 (3), 543–551.

Prince, G. (1995). Narratology. In R. Selden (ed.), *The Cambridge History of Literary Criticism*. Vol. 8: *From Formalism to Poststructuralism*. Cambridge: Cambridge University Press, pp. 110–130.

Prince, G. (2000a). *A Dictionary of Narratology*, 2nd edn. Lincoln: University of Nebraska Press.

Prince, G. (2000b). Remarks on narratology (past, present, future) In M. McQuillan (ed.), *The Narrative Reader*. London: Routledge, p. 129.

Propp, V. (1968). *Morphology of the Folktale* (trans. L. Scott). Austin: University of Texas Press. (Original work published 1928.)

Rimmon-Kenan, S. (2002). *Narrative Fiction: Contemporary Poetics*, 2nd edn. London: Routledge. (Original work published 1983.)

Ryan, M.-L. (ed.) (2004). *Narrative Across Media: The Languages of Storytelling*. Lincoln: University of Nebraska Press.

Saussure, F. d. (1983). *Course in General Linguistics* (trans. R. Harris). La Salle: Open Court. (Original work published 1916.)

Todorov, T. (1969). *Grammaire du Décaméron* [The Grammar of Décaméron]. The Hague: Mouton.

Todorov, T. (1987). *Literature and Its Theorists: A Personal View of Twentieth-Century Criticism* (trans. C. Porter). Ithaca: Cornell University Press.

Negri, Antonio and Hardt, Michael

BEN TROTT

Antonio Negri (b. 1933) is an Italian political philosopher best known today for the *Empire*, *Multitude*, and *Commonwealth* trilogy, authored with the American literary theorist and philosopher Michael Hardt (b. 1960). Negri was born in Padua, northern Italy. At the age of 25, he completed his doctoral dissertation on German historicism in the field of "state doctrine" or "state theory" – broadly speaking, the philosophy of law – at the University of Padua where he became a professor shortly after.

Early on in his life, he was active in the lay Roman Catholic association, Catholic Youth Action. Later, he joined the Italian Socialist Party (PSI) and was elected a city councilor in 1960. He remained secretary of the PSI in Padua until 1964, leaving following their formation of a center–left coalition government along with Christian Democracy (DC).

During his period of involvement with the PSI, Negri began to play a leading role as both an intellectual in the emerging current of Italian Marxism known as *Operaismo* ("workerism"), and, in the late 1960s and '70s, as a political militant in the student and worker movement of *Autonomia*. *Operaismo* became known for its emphasis on working-class struggle as the primary dynamic behind the movement from one period of capitalist development to another (see Wright 2002).

In the early 1960s, Negri was an editor of the *operaist* journals, *Quaderni Rossi* ("Red Notebooks") and *Classe Operaia* ("Working Class"). He made a substantial contribution toward the tradition's theorization of the "mass worker" (*operaio-massa*) of Fordism-Keynesianism (e.g., Negri 1988[1968]), and later the "socialized worker" (*operaio sociale*) of post-Fordism (e.g., Negri 2005 [1989]). Here, drawing on the work of fellow *operaisti* such as Mario Tronti, he argued production no longer took place solely within the confines of the factory wall, but throughout the whole of society.

In 1978, Negri held a series of seminars in Paris where he formulated a distinctive reading of Marx's *Grundrisse*, translated into Italian only a few years earlier. These seminars, published as *Marx Beyond Marx* (1984), attempted an interpretation of one of Marx's works most laden with Hegelian terminology in order to argue for a more thorough break with it. Negri also seized on one passage in the book in particular, the so-called "Fragment on machines," to argue that Marx had foreseen a stage of capitalist development actually realized in post-Fordism, where the technological application of science allows for the "subsumption" of the whole of society by capital and for the valorization of the "general intellect": socialized knowledge and creativity. The result, Negri argued, drawing on Marx's own surprisingly non-Marxian argument

in the "Fragment," is that labor-time at this point ceases to function as a quantitative measure of value. This is a line of argument Negri, Hardt, and fellow *operaisti* have since developed in other works, including their theorization of "immaterial" and "affective" forms of post-Fordist production.

In 1979, Negri was arrested along with dozens of other academics and intellectuals associated with *Autonomia*. He originally faced charges of kidnapping, murder, subversive association, and armed insurrection – although these were modified a number of times (for more, see Murphy 2005). While in prison, Negri wrote a number of important works, most notably *The Savage Anomaly* (1991) which reapproached the political philosophy of Baruch Spinoza by locating it in the "anomalous" seventeenth-century context of the Dutch modern state (and its emerging, corresponding form of bourgeois political economy). He also began work on an unorthodox rereading of the Old Testament Book of Job, recently published in English as *The Labor of Job*.

In 1983, Negri was released from prison, having been elected to the Chamber of Deputies of the Italian Parliament and granted immunity from prosecution. To avoid return to prison, after this was revoked, he fled into exile in Paris where his cooperation began with Michael Hardt. While in prison, Negri had received support from French poststructuralist theorists Gilles Deleuze and Félix Guattari, whose work had begun to influence that of the *operaisti* – and vice versa. In France, Negri's intellectual production continued. With Guattari, he coauthored *Communists Like Us* (1990), and he cofounded the journal *Futur Antérieur*. He also wrote a major work, *Insurgencies* (1999), reading the modern revolutionary tradition – from America and France to Russia – through his development of the concept of "constituent power."

By this point, Negri had been convicted of various crimes (none of them violent) and sentenced to 30 years in prison in absentia. This was later reduced to 13 years. In 1997, after 14 years in exile, Negri returned to Italy, where he was rearrested and imprisoned for the remainder of his sentence. While in prison, he and Hardt finished work on *Empire* (2000). The book, which became a bestseller, drew on both *operaist*, poststructuralist, postcolonial, and other theoretical frameworks in order to depict a transforming global order. "Empire" is the name they gave to an emerging decentered, networked system of rule that blurred the distinction between "First," "Second," and "Third" worlds. It was said to involve the shifting of sovereignty from the level of nation states to the global, where "biopolitical" forms of power (a term borrowed and developed from Michel Foucault) are exercised by a constellation of forces that include not only national governments but also international organizations, transnational corporations, nongovernmental organizations, media groups, and others.

Drawing on Negri's earlier work on Spinoza, as well as the theorizations of the concept by fellow *operaisti*, Hardt and Negri have attempted to develop a notion of "the multitude" as a social subject with revolutionary potential in the age of Empire (see also Hardt & Virno 2009). It has involved an effort to reject the distinction between "the one" and "the many"; or rather, the idea that the many have to become a unity in order to be capable of political decision or political action. The conditions for the emergence of the multitude – which is said to be a class concept appropriate for post-Fordism – are argued to be provided by the heterogeneity of productive social subjects and the circuits of communication and collaboration in which they are embedded today. The form of political organization that would enable the multitude to constitute itself as a (heterogeneous) subject capable of action and decision is left as an open question.

Three years after the publication of *Empire*, Negri was finally fully released from prison (he had spent several years in a condition of semi-liberty). He was granted a passport and has since been able to travel the world, speaking at conferences and events. His work, especially that carried out with Michael Hardt, has been enormously influential of the counter-globalization movement.

SEE ALSO: Alienation; Commodity; Marx, Karl; Marxism

REFERENCES AND SUGGESTED READINGS

Guattari, F., & Negri, A. (1990). *Communists Like Us: New Spaces of Liberty, New Lines of Alliance*. New York: Semiotext(e).

Hardt, M., & Negri, A. (2000). *Empire*. Cambridge, MA: Harvard University Press.

Hardt, M., & Virno, P. (2009). Multitude. In I. Ness et al. (eds.), *International Encyclopedia of Revolution and Protest: 1500–Present*, vol. 5. Chichester: Wiley-Blackwell, pp. 2369–2372.

Murphy, T. S. (2005). Editor's introduction: Books for burning. In A. Negri, *Books for Burning: Between Civil War and Democracy in 1970s Italy*. London: Verso, pp. ix–xxxi.

Murphy, T. S., & Mustapha, A.-K. (eds.) (2005, 2007). *The Philosophy of Antonio Negri*. 2 vols. London: Pluto.

Negri, A. (1984). *Marx Beyond Marx* (ed. J. Fleming; trans. H. Cleaver, M. Ryan, & M. Viano). South Hadley, MA: Bergin and Garvey.

Negri, A. (1988). Keynes and the capitalist theory of the state post-1929. In *Revolution Retrieved: Selected Writings on Marx, Keynes, Capitalist Crisis and New Social Subjects 1967–83*. London: Red Notes, pp. 5–42. (Original work published 1968.)

Negri, A. (1991). *The Savage Anomaly: The Power of Spinoza's Metaphysics and Politics* (trans. M. Hardt). Minneapolis: University of Minnesota Press.

Negri, A. (1999). *Insurgencies: Constituent Power and the Modern State* (trans. M. Boscagli). Minneapolis: University of Minnesota Press.

Negri, A. (2005). From the mass worker to the socialized worker – and beyond. In *The Politics of Subversion: A Manifesto for the Twenty-First Century* (trans. J. Newell). Cambridge: Polity, pp. 75–101. (Original work published 1989.)

Wright, S. (2002). *Storming Heaven: Class Composition and Struggle in Italian Autonomist Marxism*. London: Pluto.

New Aestheticism

JOHN J. JOUGHIN

The "new aestheticism" is a literary critical and theoretical movement which is made up of a number of important contemporary thinkers who argue that focusing on the specifically aesthetic impact of a work of art or literature has the potential to open radically different ways of thinking about identity, politics, and culture.

During the development of literary theory in the 1980s and 1990s many cultural theorists often failed to engage with the work of art in itself and with the specific aesthetic experience the artwork gives. As such, the rise of literary theory arguably coincided with the rise of an "anti-aestheticism," opposed to the aesthetic. In contrast, the "new" aestheticism argues that what has frequently been lost in theoretical criticism is the sense of art's specificity as an object of analysis – or, more accurately, its specificity as an aesthetic phenomenon. That is to say, in the rush to analyze an artwork in its cultural and political context, theoretical approaches such as cultural materialism and new historicism suggest that the contexts in which an artwork exists, whether this is history, ideology, or theories of subjectivity, determine that work's aesthetic impact. The aesthetic impact has thus been explicated in other terms and by other criteria, and its singular, unique moment of impact passed over. Theoretical criticism, then, is in continual danger of throwing out the aesthetic baby with the bathwater. Moreover, "politically committed" criticism, which often argues that "art" is seen as a "privileged realm" outside politics, is unable to explain why some artworks last while others disappear over time, except by reference to other (non-artistic) forces.

In summarizing this predicament, Joughin & Malpas (2003) argue not for a simple return to the aesthetic, but for a critical renegotiation which avoids the pitfalls of an old-style aestheticism ("art for art's sake") while also resisting the anti-aestheticism of recent cultural theory. In this, "new aestheticism" is often thought of as "post-theoretical"; that is, after theory – both historically a phase after the huge growth in literary theory in the 1980s and 1990s, and conceptually in the sense that as "theory" now enters a more reflective phase it is willing to concede that the transformative potential of artworks accommodates new forms of social interaction and cognition. As a result, a number of influential literary theorists such as Isobel Armstrong (2000), Thomas Docherty (2006), and Derek Attridge (2004) have taken what might be termed an aesthetic turn, or at least announced a willingness to explore the theoretical implications of literature's distinctiveness or singularity.

This aesthetic turn in critical thought needs to be located within its fuller intellectual and social context. And in this respect the re-emergence of an interest in the aesthetic as a qualitatively distinctive domain is interwoven with thinking about the complexities of philosophical and political modernity. As a consequence, for many critics, the emergence of a new aestheticism locates perhaps its seminal influence among a number of important contemporary philosophers, including Jay Bernstein (1992; 2006), Andrew Bowie

(1990; 1997), and Howard Caygill (1989), who have been at the forefront of negotiating a return to the question of the aesthetic. These thinkers could be said to form a constellation of approaches to art that take seriously its ability to interrogate existing ideas about knowledge and ethics, and thus indicate its potential for opening a range of new ways of thinking about culture. Bowie (1997), in particular, has argued that literary theory will need to look again to its philosophical beginnings in aesthetics. In this respect, the rise of literature is actually entwined with a more complex intellectual legacy: one that raises crucial questions concerning the what literature can tell us, and which locates its origins in changes in modern thought concerning conceptions of truth.

Certainly, one of the major shortcomings of the older, "art for arts sake" aestheticism lay in its tendency to impose a fixed or essentialist meaning to literature (often in the name of political neutrality); literature was said to present us with the "truth" of the human condition, for example. This "common-sense" view of literature actually hides its own theoretical agenda and presumes a practice of reading which is founded on what philosophers would characterize as a *correspondence model* of truth. In other words, literature's relationship to the world is conceived in terms of a naive mimeticism which posits the truth of an anterior or ideal reality, of which literature is correspondingly a "true" re-presentation. A literary text simply imitates the world.

Recent developments in literary theory have revealed just how restrictive these claims actually are. Historicist and materialist approaches to literature demonstrate that the "meaning" of a text is historically determined and is dependent on its cultural context. In turn, a poststructuralist critique of metaphysics has produced a healthy climate of hermeneutic suspicion, both in

disclosing the complicity between truth, reason, and domination, and in revealing language itself to be "perpetually in process" and productive of a potential plurality of meanings. Yet, in taking an exclusively linguistic and culturalist turn, recent criticism also runs the risk of excluding from its consideration the distinctively qualitative aspects of literary meaning. While poststructuralism usefully focuses on the reader's role in the constitution of meaning and allows for the possibility that texts are open to a number of interpretations, it tends to neglect the truth potential of the particular transformation wrought by the aesthetic experience itself – in contrast, new aestheticists are concerned with asking precisely *how* this revelation is to be construed.

Understood in relation to more conventional truth claims, the distinctive articulation of truth in works of art – in being truer than empirical or mimetic "truth" – underpins what Bowie (1997) terms a "disclosive" literary distinction, which he characterizes in the following terms: "[R]ather than truth being the revelation of a pre-existing reality, it [art's truth status] is in fact a creative process of 'disclosure'." Artworks, in this view, reveal aspects of the world which would not emerge if there were no such disclosure: "truth 'happens' – it does not imitate or represent" (33). Such moments could conceivably be construed purely in formal or "linguistic terms," in relation to overturning conventional expectations or in breaking with existing rules.

Yet the revelatory potential of aesthetic disclosure suggests that it also needs to be understood as a more participatory and consensual event, in the course of which, as Bowie puts it, in defamiliarizing habitual perceptions: 'something comes to be seen as something in a new way" (301). This comes close to the non-propositional sense of truth and its relation to literature that Heidegger (1993[1950]) elaborates on in his essay "On the origin of the work of art" where the philosopher is careful to preserve a place for the originary power of artworks. For Heidegger, art is truth setting itself to work, so that the actuality of the artwork and its happening are connected to a new beginning – an eventful world-opening "thrust" which is bound up with the artwork's historicity.

Crucially, the relationship between the "happening" of aesthetic disclosure and the interplay by which we understand it to "be" a distinctively *literary* happening could be said to throw a new light on the question of hermeneutics or interpretation. Disclosure enables us to retain a sense of the creative and evaluative dimension which informs judgment (aesthetic or otherwise), without then merely lapsing back into the restrictions which obtain to the more traditionalist truth claims of essentialism or empiricism. In developing a Heideggerian sense of the disclosive capacity of the aesthetic (without wanting to restrict "disclosure" to uncovering "some kind of already present essence"), Bowie persuasively locates "seeing as" as a constitutive "event" like experience which effectively "'discloses' the world in new ways . . . rather than copying or representing what is known to be already there" (1997: 5).

In the course of breaking its ties with tradition, it is precisely because literature is forced back on its "own" resources that, in its singular "exceeding moment," it provides new means of expression and accommodates the creative potential for new forms of social cognition, not least around the related question of subjectivity. In its modern form, this independent truth potential of art to "give the law to itself" is often discussed in terms of the notion of "aesthetic autonomy." Yet this sense of the qualitative newness of a "modern" aesthetic distinction or, indeed, of the "aestheticization" of modernity itself, also

needs some further qualification. The question of aesthetic autonomy only arises as a question, when, in the course of its progressive secularization, culture effects its own act of self-legitimation. Which is to say that, in understanding itself to be distinctively "modern," and in the course of dislodging a God-centered universe, secular art is witness to a form of secular disenchantment. As such, art's transformative potential is clearly closely linked to an utopian impulse: the felt need to overcome the limitations of the present. Yet this also places art in an ambivalent location, as, in relativizing the question of authority and theocracy, it is then often in danger of failing to deliver us from the consequence of doing so. On the one hand, the aesthetic could be said to encourage an affirmative stance, engendering a sense of autonomy and freedom: a liberation from the religious constraints which preceded it. On the other hand, the post-theological world can be a solitary place: one which locates the finiteness of the human condition and amplifies our sense of its contingency and inherent "meaninglessness." As Bowie observes, either response to modernity – liberatory or nihilistic – inevitably attaches an enormous significance to a secular aesthetic: "either as an image of what the world could look like if we were to realise our freedom, or as the only means of creating an illusion which would enable us to face an otherwise meaningless existence" (1990: 3).

In the course of its emergence during the eighteenth century the appearance of a separate aesthetic domain proceeds to provide a compensatory site for the evaluation of our experience of those sensuous particulars, which are now also increasingly denied to us, in our newly "alienated" modern condition. In 1735 Baumgarten invented the term "aesthetics" (derived from the Greek word *aeskesis*) to denote a form of sensory knowledge which is not reducible to abstract concepts. Tied to actuality, the emergence of the aesthetic allows for the creation of "possible worlds," beyond but also within the regulated sphere of its "new" bourgeois confinement. This proto-political potential of the aesthetic to un-leash "unrealized possibilities" for "human emancipation" is of particular importance to Marxist theorists of the Frankfurt School of Critical Theory, such as Max Horkheimer and Theodor Adorno (2002 [1947]) and is linked in complex fashion to a critique of the more dominative aspects of enlightened modernity. In its qualitative independence, autonomous art resists subsumption within the instru-mentalist logic of capital production and offers an enclave for the articulation of alternative values. In this form, aesthetics is not a rejection of reason; indeed, as Bowie observes: "it becomes the location in which what has been repressed by a limited conception of reason can be articu-lated" (1990: 4).

Coinciding, as it does, with the emer-gence of what Jürgen Habermas (1992 [1962]) would term the public sphere, the groundbreaking utopian potential of art to "move beyond the world of what there is to a world of as yet unrealised possibility" (Bowie 1997: 14), has theoretical as well as practical implications. In the context of an enlightened modernity, aesthetic dis-course provides new concepts and tools of analysis with which to challenge existing conceptual frameworks. In this respect, just as the modern division between distinct spheres of "knowledge" itself becomes increasingly restrictive and specialized, the "intellectual" pursuits of art and literature also begin to have potentially far-reaching effects. Yet crucially, of course, the relega-tory shift of art to the relative exclusivity of an autonomous realm, also, in the same process, proceeds to produce a considerable practical dilemma for those

who seek to articulate an oppositional critique to an "enlightened" modernity. Something of this cognitive ambiguity is already initially realized in Kant's *Critique of Judgement* (1991[1790]) which, as Jay Bernstein (1992) reminds us, in hindsight can be construed as a radical attempt to undo the "categorical divisions between knowledge, morality and aesthetics" – the failure of which nevertheless subsequently opens a space for thinking through the transformative potential of aesthetics within modernity. In this respect, Bernstein observes: "The central concepts of Kant's aesthetics – aesthetic reflective judgement, genius, *sensus communis*, the sublime – are themselves critical interrogations of standard epistemological and moral vocabulary" (8).

Yet the failure to reconcile art and pol-itics remains a notorious trouble spot for those who would critique of modernity by taking recourse to the "phenomena of art and aesthetics" (7) and the legacy of the Kantian project inevitably continues to symptomatize this. On the one hand, aesthetic autonomy insures art's signifi-cance as a potentially transgressive or "critical" location. Yet, on the other, art's "untheorizable excess" also promotes sus-picion, insofar as the distinctiveness of art's newly autonomous "self-regulating" truth claim is perceived to present an alternative to those restrictive "truth-only" correspon-dent notions of rationality which continue to govern many mainstream philosophies of art. In turn, this provides a formative dilemma for early variants of literary crit-icism, and it could be said that the cate-gorical separation of "artistic truth" from other kinds of philosophical truth in mo-dernity has also necessarily proceeded to haunt the convergence of a secularized literature and its criticism ever since. Bernstein formulates the dilemma concise-ly as a form of aesthetic alienation:

If art is taken as lying outside of truth and reason then if art speaks in its own voice it does not speak truthfully or rationally; while if one defends art from within the confines of the language of truth-only cognition one belies the claim that art is more truthful than that truth-only cognition. (2)

In a nutshell, then, the problem, as the philosopher David Wood incisively puts it, is that "poetic discourse may be able to say what philosophy can know it cannot" (1990: 2). In this sense of course, the very notion of "aesthetic theory" remains something of a contradiction in terms, so that, as Schlegel remarks: "What is called philosophy of art usually lacks one of two things: either the philosophy or the art" (1991: 98).

It is in confronting this situation that, as Bernstein argues, more recent "post-aestheticist" philosophies of art (for example, Adorno 1997[1970]), actually take art's critical potential seriously by "employ[ing] art to challenge truth-only cognition," while also facing the dilemma that "philosophy cannot say what is true without abandoning itself to that which it would criticise" (Bernstein 1992: 4, 9). As such the discordance between art and truth continues to rage.

It would be possible to extend the significance of the implications of Bernstein's thesis on the critical potential of art in terms of its related impact on recent trends within cultural criticism and literary theory. Key paradigm shifts in contemporary criticism are clearly themselves indirectly reliant on the transformative cognitive potential of the aesthetic. Consider, for example, the "disclosive" aspects of new historicism's more general recontextualization of anecdotal material, drawn from a variety of non-literary contexts and freshly deployed in "illuminating" re-readings of canonical texts. These and other interpretative procedures produce precisely the type of unsettling interpretative ambiguities which

Russian formalists, at least, would have still recognized as "literary." As Bowie argues, the disclosive power of the aesthetic has implicitly enabled cultural critics to open up "a world which was hidden by existing forms of articulation," yet crucially, in its attempt to break with the prescriptive "truth-only" formality of traditional "Eng. lit.," this reconciliatory impulse still necessarily "hibernates" only within the confines of the very metaphysical hierarchy it would seek to overcome (1997: 36). Viewed in this light, the newer formations of cultural criticism in literary studies could be viewed as "post-aestheticist" in Bernstein's sense of the term; that is to say, not merely in the weaker sense of having broken with a reductive notion of aesthetic value or in "being" postmodern anti-aestheticisms, but also in the potentially stronger sense that cultural criticism continues to deploy the cognitive import of the truth potential of the aesthetic against its own implication in disciplinary division, but has not itself always faced up to the divisive implications of its own interpretative procedures. Here, as elsewhere, it is apparent that the "fate" of art in modernity is that, inasmuch as it remains "critical," then, as Bernstein argues, it necessarily continues to "suffer" its alienation.

SEE ALSO: Adorno, Theodor; Ethical Criticism; Critical Theory/Frankfurt School; Habermas, Jürgen; Heidegger, Martin; New Historicism

REFERENCES AND SUGGESTED READINGS

Adorno, T. W. (1997). *Aesthetic Theory* (trans. R. Hullot-Kentor). Minneapolis: University of Minnesota Press. (Original work published 1970.)
Armstrong, I. (2000). *The Radical Aesthetic*. Oxford: Blackwell.

Attridge, D. (2004). *The Singularity of Literature*. London: Routledge.

Bernstein, J. M. (1992). *The Fate of Art: Aesthetic Alienation from Kant to Derrida and Adorno*. Cambridge: Polity.

Bernstein, J. M. (2006). *Against Voluptuous Bodies: Late Modernism and the Meaning of Painting*. Stanford: Stanford University Press.

Bowie, A. (1990). *Aesthetics and Subjectivity: From Kant to Nietzsche*. Manchester: Manchester University Press.

Bowie, A. (1997). *From Romanticism to Critical Theory: The Philosophy of German Literary Theory*. London: Routledge.

Caygill, H. (1989) *The Art of Judgement*. Oxford: Blackwell.

Docherty, T. (2006). *Aesthetic Democracy*. Stanford: Stanford University Press.

Eagleton, T. (1990). *The Ideology of the Aesthetic*. Oxford: Blackwell.

Habermas, J. (1992). *The Structural Transformation of the Public Sphere: An Inquiry into a Category of Bourgeois Society* (trans. T. Burger with F. Lawrence). Cambridge: Polity. (Original work published 1962.)

Heidegger, M. (1993). The origin of the work of art. In D. F. Krell (ed.), *Martin Heidegger: Basic Writings*. London: Routledge, pp. 139–212. (Original work published 1950.)

Horkheimer, M., & Adorno, T. W. (2002). *The Dialectic of Enlightenment* (ed. G. S. Noerr;trans. E. Jephcott). Stanford: Stanford University Press. (Original work published 1947.)

Joughin, J. J., & Malpas, S. (eds.) (2003). *The New Aestheticism*. Manchester: Manchester University Press.

Kant, I. (1991) *The Critique of Judgement* (trans. J. C. Meredith). Oxford: Clarendon Press. (Original work published 1790.)

Schlegel. F. W. J. (1991) *Philosophical Fragments* (trans. P. Firchow). Minneapolis: University of Minnesota Press.

Wood, D. (ed.) (1990) *Philosophers' Poets*. London: Routledge.

New Critical Theory

ROSS WILSON

New critical theory describes the type of criticism employed by contemporary thinkers working in and with the legacy of the influential "Frankfurt School" of philosophers and critics. Critical theory, in this sense, is perhaps unusual in having an institutional base – namely, the Institute for Social Research at the University of Frankfurt. The institutional continuity of critical theory, broken only by World War II and the exile from Europe of most of the members of the "Frankfurt School," does not necessarily indicate a straight path from the institute's establishment to its contemporary form. Writing in 2004, the current head of the institute, Axel Honneth, remarked that a gulf has opened up between contemporary thinkers in the tradition of critical theory and their predecessors, especially Theodor Adorno, Max Horkheimer, and Herbert Marcuse:

> With the turn of the new century, Critical Theory appears to have become an intellectual artefact. This superficial dividing point alone seems to increase the intellectual gap separating us from the theoretical beginnings of the Frankfurt School. Just as the names of authors who were for its founders vividly present suddenly sound from afar, so too the theoretical challenges from which the members of the school had won their insights threaten to fall into oblivion. (336)

Honneth is not suggesting that earlier critical theory is obsolete simply because of its age. Rather, changes in historical circumstances mean that the concerns of earlier critical theorists can come to seem dated in a nontrivial sense. In the age of the internet, the iPod, and interactive TV, the student of literature and culture might find quaint the references to Donald Duck and Mickey Rooney in Horkheimer and Adorno's critiques of the "culture industry." Honneth follows other later critical theorists in arguing that what is needed now is a "new" critical theory that maintains the fundamental aims of the old and discards what has become – and what always was – irrelevant in it.

Adorno and Horkheimer themselves addressed the problem of establishing the new and jettisoning the old in one of the most influential books of twentieth-century cultural theory, *Dialectic of Enlightenment* (1947). Horkheimer and Adorno's attitude to the new can appear contradictory. On the one hand, they hold that "the newest ideologies are a mere reprise of the oldest" (2002: 42). This suspicion of whatever declares itself a departure from the old was central to their critique of "the culture industry." On the other hand, such a suspicion seems itself to be disavowed because it petrifies wariness of whatever declares itself "new" into a ban on the possibility of the new altogether (8). This dilemma affects critical theory itself. The first generation of critical theorists did not hold that "all the great thoughts have been thought, all possible discoveries can be construed in advance" (8) and certainly not by them. If critical theory is to be relevant, it must be flexible in the face of changing societies and cultures. This does not mean, however, that critical theory is faced with societies and cultures that have changed radically. If, as the philosopher Raymond Geuss (1981) has described it, critical theory is "a reflective theory which gives agents a kind of knowledge inherently productive of enlightenment and emancipation" and if at "[t]he very heart of the critical theory of society is its criticism of ideology" (2–3), then the continued relevance of forms of critical theory suggests that enlightenment and emancipation have not yet been achieved and that ideology continues to prevail.

Rather than simply offering a list of thinkers associated with critical theory since the death of Adorno in 1969, this entry sets out some of the developments of critical theory's approach to aesthetics and culture proposed by the most prominent second-generation critical theorist, Jürgen Habermas, and by an influential interpreter of Adorno's aesthetic theory, Rüdiger Bubner, before examining developments of critical theory that differ from those discernible in figures such as Habermas and Bubner.

Before turning to one aspect of Habermas's departure from earlier critical theory which is especially significant for contemporary literary and cultural studies, it is necessary to review the intellectual background to first-generation critical theory, particularly the philosophical project of Immanuel Kant. This is because the interpretation of Kant has been important – and contested – in later developments of critical theory. The main works of Kant's philosophical maturity are called "critiques": *Critique of Pure Reason* (first edition, 1781; revised second edition, 1787); *Critique of Practical Reason* (1786); and *Critique of the Power of Judgement* (1790). While Kant's conception of a "critique" was essential for first-generation critical theorists, they found troubling his division of philosophy into three areas: knowledge, ethics, and aesthetic (and teleological) judgment. A central concern of the first generation of critical theorists was to question the tendency in modern reason to divide itself up in such a way. By contrast, Habermas views the distinctions between knowledge and ethics and aesthetics as one of the achievements of modern reason:

> The formation of expert cultures, within which carefully articulated spheres of validity help the claims to propositional truth, normative rightness, and authenticity, attain their own logic …; and this development competes with the naturalistic assimilation of validity claims to power claims and the destruction of our critical capacities. (1987 [1985]: 112–13)

Habermas states that it is only when truth, justice, and taste are separated from one another that they each develop, in his terms, "their own proper logics" (113). He implies that thinking about aesthetic judgment separate from truth and justice guards its specificity. He also claims that the tendencies resulting from developments within modern reason compete. He admits that modern reason has fragmented into self-perpetuating systems, closed off from apparently external considerations, but at the same time "expert cultures" have developed, enabling precise articulation of questions peculiar to truth, justice, and taste. That these tendencies – fragmentation and expertise – compete (*konkurriert*) indicates that, for Habermas, they are distinct.

This emphasis on the ultimate distinctness of different tendencies in modern reason is fundamental to a characteristic move made by subsequent generations of critical theorists, that is, the insistence that there is a "rational impulse" or "indestructible core of rational responsiveness on the part of subjects" (Honneth 2004: 356–7). Such a move has been questioned. Espen Hammer, for example, has suggested that Habermas's view of the competition between different aspects of modern reason slips back behind Adorno's insistence that such tendencies are intricately intertwined and that "reason itself is distorted" (2006: 151)

Similar questions can be put to Rüdiger Bubner's assessment of Adorno's aesthetic theory. Bubner departs from – both by beginning and disagreeing with – Adorno's *Aesthetic Theory* (published posthumously in 1970). Where Habermas would want to preserve the distinctions between knowledge, justice, and taste, Adorno, Bubner noted, had wanted to draw those distinctions into question:

> Adorno's thought ... finds its definitive expression in the title *Aesthetic Theory*. This posthumously published work has proven to be his true philosophical testament. As is well known, the title is equivocal. "Aesthetic theory" does not only mean that theoretical aesthetics is one subdivision of an extensive, theoretical edifice. More important, it means that the text's main concern is the process by which theory itself becomes aesthetic – the convergence of knowledge and art. (1997: 148)

According to Bubner, Adorno's title expresses the central claim of his work, which is that "theory must give way to aesthetics" (148) However, rather than achieving this transposition, Adorno's work in fact relies instead, for Bubner, on a series of non-aesthetic standpoints from which to judge artworks. What matters above all for Adorno on Bubner's account is the attempt to "distinguish between reactionary and progressive art" (160). Progressive art would be that which has some sort of critical relation to existing reality. "Philosophy thus adds what is not already contained in innocent artworks," according to Bubner, "indeed what can never be contained in them: the interpretation of their meaning as *the negation of existing reality*" (161). Rather than theory becoming aesthetic, aesthetic experience is sacrificed in Adorno's account by being made to serve pre-established theoretical positions. Bubner contends instead that "*[a]esthetic experience must be made the basis for aesthetic theory* and not the other way around" (168).

Bubner, then, draws attention to the widely acknowledged equivocation of the title, *Aesthetic Theory*, taking it as emblematic of Adorno's thought. Adorno might have responded to the conclusions that Bubner draws by suggesting that it was not really his aim to make theory "become" aesthetic (or vice versa). Adorno's concern might instead have been to investigate what is at stake in the historical separation of art from truth and justice without reuniting them by means of the strenuous flexing of theoretical muscle.

What Habermas and Bubner, among others, have attempted is to salvage more from the Western Enlightenment tradition than first-generation critical theorists such as Adorno would seem to allow. Habermas wishes to preserve the tripartite division of human experience evinced by Kant's three critiques. Bubner wishes to keep aesthetic judgment separate, as Kant apparently thought it was, from knowledge. We might identify in these moves one kind of Kantianism at work in some proponents of versions of new critical theory. We might also discern a different strand of new critical theory that relies instead on a contrary interpretation of the Kantian background to some of critical theory's pivotal concerns. There is a significant trajectory of new critical theory which sees Adorno, in particular, as not simply attempting to overcome aspects of Kant's critical project but, rather, as inheriting those aspects of the modern intellectual tradition as philosophical difficulties – or "aporia" – and which, as such, are specifically expressive of the actual situation of modern reason.

This kind of interpretation and concomitant development of critical theory has taken a number of forms. J. M. Bernstein's work, for one significant instance, has offered an influential reading of Adorno that clearly diverges from that offered by second-generation critical theorists. Moreover, in recent work, Bernstein has attempted to extend Adorno's aesthetic theory into an area that it largely neglected – that is, modernist visual art.

Bernstein's approach to the problem inherited and then bequeathed by Adorno is at odds with the kind of reading put forward, for instance, by Bubner. Bernstein states: "It is the entwinement of art and truth, the experience of art as somehow cognitive and of truth as sensuous and

particular, and not the substitution of one for the other within a stable metaphysical hierarchy, that constitutes the challenge" (1993: 2). The difference from Bubner is twofold. First, Bernstein does not recognize an experience of art that is purely aesthetic in the sense that it is free from elements that have come to be categorized as "extra-aesthetic." It is part of the experience of art, Bernstein claims, that it is cognitive and ethical, as well as aesthetic. Second, the challenge facing aesthetics is neither to make theory aesthetic nor aesthetic experience theoretical but, rather, to question the distinctions upon which such a model would rest in the first place. Bernstein wishes to develop Adorno's claim that it is art itself that questions the set of philosophical divisions according to which it is supposedly comprehended (199). Furthermore, to question "the definitional duality of concept and intuition, and hence the opposition of rationality to particularity, requires that we reconceive what these moments are" (200). Like Hammer's criticism of Habermas's contention that different tendencies of modern reason are in straightforward competition with one another, Bernstein implicitly suggests against interpreters like Bubner that aesthetics and theory cannot even initially be separated for Adorno.

Bernstein has recently further articulated a number of these arguments in connection with an account of late modernist visual art. This emphasis on the continued relevance of modernism needs to be set in the context of Bernstein's resistance to the criticisms of Adorno's critique of twentieth-century mass entertainment made by postmodernist enthusiasts for a putatively democratized popular culture. Bernstein takes the standpoint of enthusiasm for "popular culture" to rely on a fairly simple acceptance of an in fact false reconciliation between high and low cultures (1991: 20–7). Connected with this rejection of postmodernist alternatives to Adorno's advocacy of modernism is Bernstein's attempt to wrest some significant art historical territory from postmodernism. He argues (2006) that perhaps one of the most emblematic figures for artistic postmodernism, the American artist Cindy Sherman, is more properly understood as a modernist in the sense that Bernstein develops out of Adorno's work. Following Horkheimer and Adorno's concern in *Dialectic of Enlightenment* with the way in which modern reason progressively expels from experience the perception of "living beings like ourselves *as living*" (Bernstein 2006: 257), Bernstein finds in Sherman's work from the 1980s an important riposte to accounts of human rationality that have no place for the recognition of objects as living:

> Nothing within these accounts gives a hint that their objects could be living beings subject to not mere breaking apart or destruction, but tearing and flaying, violation and invasion, that unlike mere things where what is outside and what inside remains spatial and contingent, the outside of a living being is the outside of an inside, a skin or flesh protecting and mediating a (heated, palpitating, viscous, stringy, dense) inside with what is external to it. (257–8)

What Sherman's disturbing, often grotesque works elaborate, for Bernstein, is a concern to testify to the (damaged, denuded) life that first generation critical theorists saw as being systematically expelled from consideration by conventional versions of modern rationality.

It is not surprising that a number of essays appearing in a book entitled *The New Aestheticism* (Joughin and Malpas 2003) should take up important strands of Adorno's aesthetic and cultural theory. However, we should not rush to the conclusion that such developments in new critical theory

offer us a lush, aestheti*cist* Adorno. After Adorno's claim that "to write poetry after Auschwitz is barbaric. And that corrodes even the knowledge of why it has become impossible to write poetry today" (1967: 34), poetry seems to have been condemned. A number of responses to this verdict of Adorno's take the form less of ripostes as of considerations regarding how poetry might be able to take up and live with, so to speak, such a verdict. The poet and writer Hans Magnus Enzensberger tentatively offered the poetry of Nelly Sachs as a possible response to Adorno's comment (Kiedaisch 1995: 73–6). The novelist Peter Härtling extended Adorno's dictum to ask whether it was possible to write poetry about Vietnam, a question that might be asked today about poetic response to any of the world's current armed conflicts (102–6). One recent interpretation of Adorno's comment on poetry after Auschwitz, which appears in chapter entitled "Cultural criticism and sociey," has looked not forward to see what prospects still remain for poetry, but back, in order to place Adorno's remarks in the context of his theory of poetry generally. The philosopher and cultural historian Howard Caygill argues that Adorno's statement that poetry after Auschwitz is impossible must be taken in the context of his general sense that "[i]n industrial society, the lyrical idea, when confronted by opposing reality, . . . becomes 'more and more something that flashes out abruptly, something in which what is possible transcends its own impossibility'" (2006: 76). What Caygill means here is that, in accordance with Adorno's sense that art stands in opposition to existing reality, lyric poetry cannot be reduced to its conditions of possibility. Such a reduction would offer the kind of historicist reading of literature that Adorno's work offers the chance of resisting. "Adorno insists in all his readings that lyric poetry is by definition impossible; it always exceeds its conditions of possibility" (81).

The editors of the volume in which Caygill's essay appears, *Adorno and Literature*, justly claim that sustained consideration of Adorno's work in connection with literature has up to now been lacking (Cunningham & Mapp 2006: 1) While the attempt to separate out and delete what is old in critical theory has been important to figures such as Habermas, Honneth, and Bubner, the return to critical theorists such as Adorno, Horkheimer, and Marcuse in order to recover what has sometimes been neglected or castigated in their work is currently emerging as another important strand of new critical theory.

SEE ALSO: Adorno, Theodor; Frankfurt School; Habermas, Jürgen

REFERENCES AND SUGGESTED READINGS

Adorno, M. (1967). *Prisms* (trans. S. & S. Weber). Cambridge, MA: MIT Press. (Original work published 1955.).

Bernstein, J. M. (1991). Introduction. In T. Adorno, *The Culture Industry: Selected Essays on Mass Culture* (ed. J. M. Bernstein). London: Routledge.

Bernstein, J. M. (1993). *The Fate of Art: Aesthetic Alienation from Kant to Derrida and Adorno.* Cambridge: Polity.

Bernstein, J. M. (2006). *Against Voluptuous Bodies: Late Modernism and the Meaning of Painting.* Stanford: Stanford University Press.

Bubner, R. (1997). The central idea of Adorno's philosophy (trans. C. Gendel Ryan). In T. Huhn & L. Zuidervaart (eds.), *The Semblance of Subjectivity: Essays in Adorno's Aesthetic Theory.* Cambridge, MA: MIT Press.

Caygill, H. (2006). Lyric poetry before Auschwitz. In D. Cunningham & N. Mapp (eds.), *Adorno and Literature.* London: Continuum, pp. 69–83.

Cunningham, D., & Mapp, N. (eds.) (2006). *Adorno and Literature.* London: Continuum.

Geuss, R. (1981). *The Idea of a Critical Theory: Habermas and the Frankfurt School.* Cambridge: Cambridge University Press.

Habermas, J. (1987). The entwinement of myth and enlightenment: Horkheimer and Adorno. In *The Philosophical Discourse of Modernity: Twelve Lectures* (trans. F. G. Lawrence). Cambridge: Polity, pp. 106–130. (Original work published 1985.).

Hammer, E. (2006). *Adorno and the Political.* Oxford: Routledge.

Honneth, A. (2004). A social pathology of reason: On the intellectual legacy of critical theory (trans. J. Hebbeler). In F. Rush (ed.), *The Cambridge Companion to Critical Theory.* Cambridge: Cambridge University Press, pp. 336–360.

Horkheimer, M., & Adorno, T. (2002). *Dialectic of Enlightenment: Philosophical Fragments* (ed. G. S. Noerr; trans. E. Jephcott). Stanford: Stanford University Press. (Original work published 1947.)

Joughin, J. J., & Malpas, S. (eds.) (2003). *The New Aestheticism.* Manchester: Manchester University Press.

Kiedaisch, P. (ed.) (1995). *Lyrik nach Auschwitz? Adorno und die Dichter* [Poetry after Auschwitz? Adorno and the Poets]. Stuttgart: Reclam.

Rush, F. (ed.) (2004). *The Cambridge Companion to Critical Theory.* Cambridge: Cambridge University Press.

New Historicism

MARK ROBSON

It is no exaggeration to say that new historicism has become the dominant mode of literary criticism in the Anglophone world since its emergence in the 1980s. Associated in particular with criticism of the early modern and romantic periods and the nineteenth century, some of the central tenets of the new historicist enterprise have seeped into criticism that would not necessarily identify itself directly with the movement. Inevitably, the force of its newness has dissipated into a retrenchment of older forms of historicism. While this mode of criticism in the forms in which it initially emerged does seem to be waning – and there have been several announcements of its "death" – its impact continues to be felt throughout Anglophone literary studies, and is also to be seen in disciplines such as art history and history.

New historicism emerged as a distinct form of study in the early 1980s, although its roots may be seen in work from the 1970s by scholars such as Stephen Orgel or J. W. Lever. The term itself is often attributed to Stephen Greenblatt, who used it in the introduction to a collection of essays in 1982 (although he has frequently expressed a preference for the term "cultural poetics" to describe his own work). It is Greenblatt's own text, *Renaissance Self-Fashioning* (1980), that is frequently taken to be the first major contribution to the new historicist enterprise, and his work remains inseparable from any attempt to define new historicism. Greenblatt's work in this period was explicitly related to that of other scholars, particularly those at the University of California, Berkeley, who formed the core of the editorial collective for the journal *Representations*. This grouping included not only literary scholars such as Catherine Gallagher and Joel Fineman but also art historians, including Svetlana Alpers. In fact, one of the most notable features of the new historicism was its avowedly interdisciplinary intent. Literature was seen to be part of a field that encompassed a diverse range of cultural products and practices, and the literary object was thus seen to circulate in a series of contexts that were in need of reconstruction. This attention to contextual material leads new historicist critics beyond traditional senses of literary history – in which texts are seen to be related primarily to other texts considered to be literature – toward a recognition of relations between the literary and the nonliterary. This leads not only to a revision of the topics or objects deemed appropriate for literary

studies, it also prompts a revision of critical methodology.

It is in this broad sense of context that historicism addresses itself most obviously to history. The invocation of historical materials and nonliterary documents in understanding literature is not in itself particularly new, however. Where the new historicists seek to make a distinctive intervention is in the dialectical sense that history does not provide a "backdrop" for literature, neither does it provide a stock of stable answers for the questions that literature raises. History is given only a partial and qualified explanatory privilege. A spatial model of surface/depth or foreground/background is rejected by new historicism in favor of an economy in which objects, ideas, and practices circulate. Literary texts do not passively reflect a background, then, nor are they inert products of an ideological formation governing a specific society at a particular moment. Instead, literary texts are related to the cultures within which they circulate to the extent that they absorb the structures of value and meaning present throughout that culture. But this absorption is not necessarily entirely uncritical, thus there is a sense of texts as interventions in rather than mere reflections of the processes by which societies accord values. The history that critics such as Gallagher and Greenblatt evoke is discontinuous, fragmentary, and unstable, always seen to be in a process of change that is neither progressive nor declining since it is not fundamentally linear. Literature is inseparable from these processes. In fact, literary and other artistic objects become especially interesting to new historicists when they open up the accepted narratives of history to forms of resistance, that is, when they reveal ideas, actions, and stories that do not "fit" neatly into the established categories through which a period is usually understood. In this respect, history – even the history of the

English Renaissance – is not finished, and the events of earlier periods cannot easily be separated from processes seen to be still at work within modern culture. In the early years of the new historicism at least, there is frequently an acknowledgment of the situatedness of the critic, and thus this form of historicism makes clear its embeddedness in its own cultural moment as well as examining the processes by which modern culture was and continues to be shaped.

In light of this approach to a fragmented and discontinuous history, literary texts are consequently seen to be similarly discontinuous. Rather than attempting to reveal the underlying formal unities of texts in a manner usually associated with the new criticism of the middle decades of the twentieth century, new historicism concerns itself with the ways in which texts refuse to cohere. Equally, the new critical orthodoxy that suggested that biography, authorial intention, and contextual information were of little importance in the reading of a text – since the text was seen to be sufficient to itself, and closed off formally from the world beyond it – is rejected in favor of a conception of the text as permeable, always open to a life-world in which it is produced, consumed, traded, and read. The most obvious sign of the significance of biography would be in the wide usage of Greenblatt's term "self-fashioning" and in his own authorship of a biography of Shakespeare, *Will in the World* (2004).

The central link between these complementary senses of literature and history is best expressed in a resonant and much quoted phrase from Louis Montrose (1986), who proposes that the new historicism is best understood as resting on two central principles, "The historicity of texts, and the textuality of history." The chiasmatic form in which this is expressed is itself a clear indication of the inextricability of these axiomatic assumptions. Literary texts are embedded in history, suffused with it, and traversed by its forces and energies, but at the same time, history is itself a textual construction. In other words, there is no unmediated access to historical events, and the texts that historians use to construct their histories – thinking of text in the widest sense – are always in need of interpretation. History is always a question of representation, and any representation has a formal dimension. In this recognition new historicist practice aligns itself with that of historians such as Hayden White. Crucially, this emphasis on textuality as well as historicity means that while the brand of formalism advocated by the new criticism is rejected, formal analysis itself remains central to the new historicist enterprise. Representations always have a formal or generic mode as well as a content, and this form can be meaningful in itself.

In spite of certain clearly identifiable methodological features, the status of new historicism as theory has always been problematic. Its main practitioners – most obviously Gallagher and Greenblatt in their co-authored book *Practicing New Historicism* (2000) – have repeatedly asserted the need to see it as a form of practice rather than as theory. Consequently, while it clearly depends upon certain key assumptions, these have rarely been elaborated in an explicit manner, and Greenblatt in particular has always resisted calls to establish any theoretical framework that would stand independent of the analysis of a particular cultural object. Despite this reluctance, it is possible to draw out some key areas of consistency in new historicist practice and to examine their critical foundations.

One of the main thrusts of the description of new historicism established by Gallagher and Greenblatt in *Practicing New Historicism* is most easily understood if it is related to the work of the German Romantic thinker Johann Gottfried von Herder. It is in

Herder that they find a clear expression of the principle that language and literature are always the product of a specific time and place. Further, Herder proposes that the character of a national literature is related to the nature of the language in which it is written. Both are seen to be conditioned by the geographical specificity of that nation, as if language grows organically, nourished by a particular kind of soil, and literature in its turn emerges organically from that language. This suggests that every cultural product – since it is nourished by the same conditions – is related to every other product in a given culture, and thus any text becomes part of a network of relations. While it is possible to relate these "internal" objects straightforwardly to each other, the connections between different cultures and different periods can be established only on the basis of analogy, not identity. Thus the tragedies of Sophocles and of Shakespeare may appear to fulfill a similar function within their respective cultures, but the differences in language, literature, and what Herder calls "climate" means that there can be only a likeness between them, not an equality. The tragedy written in ancient Greece shares formal features with the tragedy written in early modern England, but the place of tragedy within these two cultures is not the same in each case, and thus even the word "tragedy" does not mean precisely the same thing. What the new historicists take from a thinker such as Herder is a sense that it is the differences between the two forms that are more significant that the similarities. This leads to a refusal of overarching conceptual explanations. For Herder, a theory of tragedy that could be applied to both periods and cultures would erase these differences rather than making them apparent, and the task of the critic becomes one of establishing the singular nature of the differences through a "local" reading of their particular contexts.

New historicism similarly eschews the transplantable theory or portable method.

Inevitably, this should raise the suspicion, however, that there is a tension here between the insistence on the singularity of a given relation between text and context and this transhistorical romantic understanding of the relation of literature, culture, and history. In fact, most historicists focus on a single period of literary history, and many are even more specific in limiting their field – claiming to be specialists not in poetry or the novel but in British modernist poetry of the 1930s written by women, for example. But the characteristics of the historicizing practice within which this poetry is read are generated independently of those qualifications of their specialism, and most historicist critics draw on a free-floating "New Historicist methodology" (if there is such a thing) that is thought to be equally applicable to every literary period or genre.

New historicism stems from a deliberate impurity of critical origins and principles. In their attention to notions of culture, new historicist critics tend to combine insights from a variety of thinkers and disciplines in developing an eclectic methodology. While a figure such as Herder inspires some key concerns and principles, there is also a range of more contemporary thinkers to whom frequent reference is made. Chief among those influences have been Raymond Williams, Michel Foucault, and Clifford Geertz. What has allowed for the articulation of these thinkers together is a shared concern with the relation between discourse and a broad conception of culture. Thus the cultural materialism of Williams and his insistence on politicized etymologies may be combined with Foucault's genealogical approach to history and Geertz's descriptive and narrative anthropology. For each of these thinkers, the textual or linguistic and the historical or sociopolitical are bound together without one overdetermining the other. The manifest differences between these thinkers are largely left unexplored by new historicists, since only limited aspects of the work are incorporated into their practice, and there is no sense of needing to relate the more systematic elements of these thinkers or their works.

Primary among the influences on the development of new historicism is the work of Raymond Williams, and it is in light of this influence that new historicism is frequently linked with cultural materialism. Greenblatt explicitly names Williams, whom he encountered while a student at Cambridge, as an inspiration. Williams's insistence on a form of materialist criticism that focuses on both the production and reception of texts and is centered on a refusal to elevate literature and art to any kind of special status runs throughout these historicist practices. The notion that "culture is ordinary," as Williams puts it, works to undo the privilege given to literature in other forms of criticism. Similarly, there is an affinity between Herder's notion of the specificity of languages and literatures and the insistence in Williams's later work – especially in a text such as *Keywords* – on tracing the development of certain concepts through their particular manifestations and uses in different periods, national cultures, and intellectual and institutional contexts.

Foucault's genealogical approach to intellectual history and especially to the histories of objects and practices underpins much of both the thinking that informs new historicism and the form in which that thought is expressed. One of the key aspects of Foucault's influence lies in his insistence in *The History of Sexuality* (1979) that power is not best thought of in terms of domination and force. On the contrary, for Foucault, power is distributed such that it is everywhere and comes from everywhere, and is exercised in largely unconscious ways through the forms of social organization that maintain order without direct action. At the heart of this understanding of power is a sense that knowledge and the practices licensed by that knowledge are themselves bound up with power. The status accorded to literature or to literary authors is thus determined by the institutional role allotted to literature in a given culture at a specific time rather than by any transhistorical idea of literary value. But this instituted value is itself related to the wider system of values belonging to that culture, and to the modes according to which those values are regulated and perpetuated. Linked to Foucault's ideas concerning technologies, discipline, and discourse, new historicism takes this sense of literature's implication in systems of value to find in literary texts the mechanisms by which values are regulated, reinforced, or (occasionally) transformed. The influence of Foucault is particularly marked in the tendency for new historicist critics to use the apparently marginal cultural product as a limit-case in which a culture reveals its boundaries through its policing of those boundaries. Because it is always possible to assert a relation between the marginal and the central within the economic understanding of a cultural moment, this has led to a characteristic yoking together of the canonical text with the noncanonical, nonliterary, and counter-historical object.

To this mixture of elements from materialist criticism and poststructuralism, we might usefully add the work of the anthropologist Clifford Geertz. It is from Geertz that the new historicists draw one of the most characteristic aspects of their style, what Geertz calls "thick description," following the philosopher Gilbert Ryle. Thick description demands a recognition that all ethnography involves interpretation, and that it is this interpretation that in fact constitutes ethnographic work, rather than being something that is added once the data has been gathered. Geertz sees the anthropologist's work as fundamentally concerned with disentangling the structures of signification in a given culture through attention to symbolic action. All actions are embedded within a narrative that is to some extent meaningful, since these actions are carried out either for a conscious purpose (someone does something in order to achieve a specific end) or else according to a ritual or habit that has itself been learned as an approved form of conduct. These actions are therefore always meaningful, and this meaning is never private. Ethnography is at heart concerned with the processes according to which meaning is generated and the conceptual worlds within which their subjects live. Geertz's approach to culture is essentially semiotic, and the work of the anthropologist is always to produce a reading of those signs that is inescapably second or third hand. Anthropologists must always be attentive, therefore, to their own motivations and procedures in making the actions of others meaningful in their own narratives.

These varied influences – and there are, of course, others favored by particular critics or in particular texts – have led to an alignment between new historicism and a broader critical emphasis on identity politics, especially in the emergent cultural studies that also attained institutional recognition at the same time as new historicism. It is easy to see the attraction of the experiences of the marginalized for those wishing to open up traditional historical narratives to alternative voices and images; at the same time, it is clear where a practice which emphasizes the importance of the noncanonical text and the neglected document or object holds an appeal for those who wish to expand the range of materials available to the cultural critic. New historicist criticism has thus frequently drawn

upon work in feminist, colonial, and postcolonial, working-class, queer, and other forms of criticism, in literary studies and beyond it. It is also indebted to the radical history movement represented by E. P. Thompson and especially British radical feminist historians of the 1970s and 1980s, all of whom questioned the categories used to decide what was or was not historically significant. Harold Bloom's description of new historicism as part of a "School of Resentment" registers the sense in which its historical concerns are seemingly always allied to a progressive agenda in the present. There are several critics – such as David Scott Kastan or Brian Vickers – who have seen this as a weakness in the historical dimension of new historicism, suggesting that it risks distorting the concerns of the past in favor of a present intervention. Others such as Terence Hawkes have argued for a more explicit presentism because the new historicism didn't seem interested enough in the present moment. The lack of explicit theoretical self-definition, of course, is part of the reason why such divergent readings of new historicism remain possible.

One of the key elements in the success of the new historicism has been its style. Because it emphasized its status as a practice, it also developed a house-style, particularly centered on the journal *Representations*. The key feature was a preference for the essay rather than the book-length study, and even the books produced by these critics often feel like collections of essays. The essay is particularly apt for new historicism because it is necessarily partial, offering only a glimpse of a larger narrative that it can therefore call into question without engaging in its totality. The essay encourages its readers to make connections and to establish for themselves how it relates that which lies beyond it, especially the grand narratives of history. Its very incompleteness is part of its utility as a form. This is mirrored within the essay by another recurrent feature, the use of anecdotes. Like the essay, the anecdote appears to be both sufficient to itself and yet to gesture to its incompleteness, always invoking a larger whole into which it needs to be inserted. Anecdotes are memorable, often personal narratives that open up something beyond them, and they are capable of uncovering the neglected, the strange, or the unfamiliar that lies within a more familiar narrative. That which has been traditionally written off as "just anecdotal," that is, as too unrepresentative to be of genuine historical significance, might offer precisely the glimpse of the suppressed or marginal element in a culture that allows its boundaries to reveal themselves. Anecdotes are counter-historical in every sense. That they also allow for a strong sense of the personality of the critics who employ them to be established, and that they make the essays in which they appear more memorable than conventional academic prose, rendered them invaluable in the new historicist enterprise's early efforts to define and establish itself (see Fineman 1991 and the response from Gallagher & Greenblatt 2000).

For a form of criticism that did not make strong political statements, the new historicism received a great deal of critical attention regarding its own politics. The refusal to align itself with existing political divisions within the academy led to criticism from both sides. For some, it represented a prolongation of a certain Marxist tendency (marked in part by the affiliation with Raymond Williams; see Pechter 1995) while for others it was never Marxist enough in comparison with, say, the cultural materialism with which it was so closely aligned (see Porter 1990). Criticized by some critics for deflecting attention from the aesthetic qualities of literary works, its practitioners have also been seen to have remained fixated

on high-cultural works. Thus Greenblatt, for example, whatever his interests in non-canonical and nonliterary materials may have been, still largely employs them to reflect on Shakespeare, and this has led critics to suggest that while new historicism is superficially interested in "ordinary" culture, it actually maintains a strict hierarchy of cultural products, and its practice is often at odds with its proclamations of intent. In the case of Greenblatt, in particular, this means that he rarely gives attention to any early modern playwright other than Shakespeare (barring a couple of essay on Marlowe and one on Jonson), even though this drama would seem to be the most obvious context for Shakespeare's theatrical work.

While it is clear that the high-water mark of new historicism has passed, and that even its most notable practitioners have ceased to produce work of the kind that characterized that early stage, it would be misleading to suggest that new historicism has disappeared from the critical scene. In fact, so successful has it been that its relative invisibility is a mark of that success, since so many of its characteristics have been effectively absorbed into what passes for "normal" (that is, largely untheoretical) practice. The emergence of critical modes such as presentism and the new materialism, the entirely unremarkable insistence of questions about gendered, ethnic, and other identities in every form of critical activity on any literary period, and the frequency with which literary studies seek to justify themselves by reference to history, are all signs of the pervasive normalization of new historicist concerns. To some extent, this represents a falling away from new historicist practice itself, since this form of sedimentation has stabilized a critical field that the new historicist project was intended to unsettle. Equally, the avoidance of theoretical statements within new historicism has not only licensed a retreat from explicitly theoretical discourse within literary criticism more generally, it has in fact disguised a genuine lack of theoretical thinking in much of that work. So rather than expressing a choice not to articulate such thought, it marks the absence of theoretical thinking. This would certainly not be a reasonable claim regarding the early work that defined the new historicism, but there has been little progression in its theoretical dimensions for many years, and there seems little prospect of its generating any new directions in critical thought.

SEE ALSO: Anglo-American New Criticism; Foucault, Michel; Geertz, Clifford; Greenblatt, Stephen; Marxism; White, Hayden; Williams, Raymond

REFERENCES AND SUGGESTED READINGS

Brannigan, J. (1998). *New Historicism and Cultural Materialism*. Basingstoke: Macmillan.
Colebrook, C. (1997). *New Literary Histories: New Historicism and Contemporary Criticism*. Manchester: Manchester University Press.
Fineman, J. (1991). *The Subjectivity Effect in Western Literary Tradition: Essays toward the Release of Shakespeare's Will*. Cambridge, MA: MIT Press.
Foucault, M. (1979). *The History of Sexuality*. London: Allen Lane.
Gallagher, C., & Greenblatt, S. (2000). *Practicing New Historicism*. Chicago: University of Chicago Press.
Greenblatt, S. (1980). *Renaissance Self-Fashioning: From More to Shakespeare*. Chicago: University of Chicago Press.
Greenblatt, S. (1990). *Learning to Curse: Essays in Early Modern Culture*. London: Routledge.
Greenblatt, S. (2004). *Will in the World*. London: Jonathan Cape.
Greenblatt, S. (2005). *The Greenblatt Reader* (ed. M. Payne). Oxford: Blackwell.
Hamilton, P. (1996). *Historicism*. London: Routledge.
Montrose, L. A. (1986). Renaissance literary studies and the subject of history. *English Literary Renaissance*, 16, 5–12.

Pechter, E. (1995). *What Was Shakespeare? Renaissance Plays and Changing Critical Practice*. Ithaca: Cornell University Press.
Porter, C. (1990). Are we being historical yet? In D. Carroll (ed.), *The States of Theory: History, Art, and Critical Discourse*. Stanford: Stanford University Press, pp. 27–62.
Robson, M. (2008). *Stephen Greenblatt*. London: Routledge.
Ryan, K. (ed.) (1996). *New Historicism and Cultural Materialism: A Reader*. London: Arnold.
Veeser, H. A. (ed.) (1989). *The New Historicism*. London: Routledge.
Veeser, H. A. (ed.) (1994). *The New Historicism Reader*. London: Routledge.
Wilson, R., & Dutton, R. (eds.) (1992). *New Historicism and Renaissance Drama*. Hemel Hempstead: Harvester Wheatsheaf.

Nomadism

EVA ALDEA

Nomadism is a concept used by Gilles Deleuze and Felix Guattari in a vast range of contexts, including mathematics, physics, cloths manufacture, metallurgy, music, and art, in their *A Thousand Plateaus* (1987 [1980]), with a contentious legacy in cultural and socioeconomic studies.

Deleuze and Guattari initially contrast nomadic distribution with sedentary distribution in spatial terms. While a sedentary distribution sees the division of a fixed amount of space to a number of people (or animals or any other elements), nomadic distribution implies people distributing themselves in an open or unlimited space. The two types of distribution result in two types of space: striated space, where boundaries indicate the division of space, and smooth space, where, instead, there are constantly changing groupings of people across unbounded space. Such smooth or nomadic space is characterized by constant metamorphosis and flux, as the population continues to redistribute itself freely across it. Compare a village in which people and livestock are divided into enclosed spaces, to a nomad tribe and its flock of animals, continually moving across the land in search for pasture, covering more or less space in an amorphous formation.

However, the idea of nomadism is not, to Deleuze and Guattari, merely an anthropological concept, but rather one of the many terms they use throughout their work regarding social, economic, psychological, and other structures. Nomadism is inherently linked with some of Deleuze and Guattari's key concepts. The "rhizome" is, in effect, a nomadic organization, a network of fluctuating contingent connections, the elements of which form a "multiplicity," a non-totalizing grouping of elements – that is, a group without any organizing principle.

In terms of sociopolitical organization Deleuze and Guattari posit that throughout history there has always been an opposition between the state, in whatever form, which is always sedentary and striated, and its "outside," which they term the "War Machine." This idea is developed in their influential "Treatise on nomadology" – Plateau 12 in *A Thousand Plateaus*. The War Machine, although a concept derived from the Mongol hordes, does not designate warfare as such. Rather, it is the impulse to transformation that always exists in human society, which forces the fixed order of the state to change. At the same time, however, the state is always expressing the opposite impulse to sedentary and fixed living. The state and the War Machine thus work, in the context of social history, as opposing poles of territorialization and reterritorialization, an ongoing relative movement that Deleuze and Guattari find in all the structures they consider.

Deleuze and Guattari apply the idea of nomadism widely: they contrast the striated space of woven fabric with the smooth entanglement of the fibers in felt. They refer to the music of composer Pierre Boulez, who distinguished between music with a countable, standard rhythm, and music consisting of continuous developments without breaks. They mention the sea as the ultimate smooth space, which nonetheless can be striated by navigational lines. In mathematics, they consider nonmetric multiplicities, such as temperature, which cannot be divided without changing in nature, as expressions of nomadic distribution. Here they refer to Bergson's duration, Riemannian space, and Mandelbrot's fractals.

Nomadism in art describes a relationship between lines and surfaces that does not describe a fixed figure, but allows for various connections according to point of view, whether the art is figurative or abstract. Nomadic literature is not necessarily that which traces nomadic movement as such, but one that traverses and transforms boundaries, following trajectories that allow for new connections across such limits.

Nomadism has, perhaps unsurprisingly, been taken up mainly in the fields of sociological and cultural studies. It has been seen as a concept useful in negotiating ethnic and gender identities, by allowing for a nomadic rather than fixed subjectivity. It has also been used to describe the potential of various minority populations, subcultures, and gangs, and such phenomena as the internet and globalization. Michael Hardt and Antonio Negri's *Empire* (2000) is perhaps the best-known consideration of Deleuze and Guattari's thought in terms of world politics and economy. Nomadism informs their concept of multitude as the possibility of the breakdown of the massive class divisions that modern globalization has created.

On the other hand, nomadism has been criticized as an overly intellectual idea that ignores the realities of actual nomadic peoples, and the difference between various ways of nomadic life. The most vehement critic to this effect has been Christopher Miller (1998), but many feminist and post-colonial critics have also rejected Deleuze and Guattari's various terms, including nomadism, as simply stereotyping non-male, nonwhite ways of life.

Ronald Bogue (2007) defends nomadism, however, stating that while there are actual similarities in the way, say, Arctic hunters and Bedouin herders move across the land along contingent trajectories, one has to divest the idea of a nomadism from any narrow anthropological application and see it as the articulation of a tendency useful in many contexts. Bogue suggests nomadism as a model for a truly "global poetics," which would not only consider the connections between various aesthetic practices around the world, but entail an interaction between them in a rhizomatic, centerless fashion.

SEE ALSO: Deleuze, Gilles

REFERENCES AND SUGGESTED READINGS

Bogue, R. (2007). *Deleuze's Way: Essays in Transverse Ethics and Aesthetics*. Aldershot: Ashgate.

Deleuze, G. (1994). *Difference and Repetition*. (trans. P. Patton). London: Athlone Press. (Original work published 1968.)

Deleuze, G., & Guattari, F. (1987). *A Thousand Plateaus: Capitalism and Schizophrenia*. (trans. B. Massumi). London: Athlone Press. (Original work published 1980.)

Hardt, M., & Negri, A. (2000). *Empire*. Cambridge, MA: Harvard University Press.

Miller, C. L. (1998). *Nationalists and Nomads: Essays on Francophone African Literature and Culture*. Chicago: University of Chicago Press.

O

Orientalism

SHAHIDHA BARI & ROBERT EAGLESTONE

"Orientalism," a term which originally meant the depiction of Eastern or Middle Eastern culture by artists and writers in the West, or the academic discipline in the West that studied the East, was given a new burst of life and meaning by Edward Said's groundbreaking book *Orientalism*, published in 1978.

The book criticizes Eurocentric universalism, and laid the foundations for postcolonial theory. Said argues that if Europeans takes for granted their superiority, and designate all else inferior, then Europe requires what is not European in order to distinguish, by contrast, its own civilized identity. Said presents one of the earliest critical histories of "the other," tracing the cultural distortions of the East effected by the domination of European colonial rule. He proposes that European scholarship, in particular, disfigured the East and cultivated in its place a widely accepted idea of the "Orient." Denigrating its inhabitants and diminishing its cultural productions, the Occident admonishes an "Orient" in order to commend its own positive European identity. Designated weak, mystified, feminine, and other, the Orient is not only allotted the values discarded by the West for itself, but also becomes the site of

a projected identity that the West is unwilling to recognize as its own. The Orient presents to Europe the rejected image of itself, even as it confirms, by contrast, Europe's self-designation as strong, rational, masculine, and self. For Said, these reductive essentializations of Oriental and Occidental identities are ideological acts of distortion by a dominant group that creates difference as a means of positive self-affirmation. The Orient, as it is figured by the West, is subject to its invention and a representation that deforms the complex truth of what it might be in actuality. The East that is the source of European civilization and language is thereby rendered the cultural contestant of the West, mined as its imaginative resource as well as material.

The disciplinary field of Orientalism becomes, under Said's examination, a pejorative term referring to the Western study of the East, in which it is rendered an unreal place of romance, inhabited by exotic beings and formed of fantastic landscapes. Said identifies this mystification of the Orient as symptomatic of the complicity of enlightenment and colonialism in Orientalist scholarship. Yet he indicates how the "civilizing" narrative of the West is itself undercut by narratives of imperial oppression and representational violence. Said's recognition that the study of the Orient is a study of the legitimation of European

The Encyclopedia of Literary and Cultural Theory   General editor: Michael Ryan
© 2011 Blackwell Publishing Ltd

colonial power to itself through the representation of an other reflects Foucault's thesis of the discursive formation of the subject at the intersection of knowledge and power. For Said, like Foucault, there can be no Archimedean point of analysis that could be independent of the described context, and the Orientalist scholar betrays the way in which the organization of knowledge is always ideological and the subject formed by the exercise of power. Said recognizes how the figuration of the Oriental other is an act of self-making on the part of the Occidental self, and his own analysis seeks both to expose how this facilitates the justification of the colonial power to itself, and to signal the East as yet uncharted territory, more complex and diverse than any account of it produced by the West.

SEE ALSO: Bhabha, Homi; Foucault, Michel; Postcolonial Studies and Diaspora Studies; Said, Edward

REFERENCES AND SUGGESTED READINGS

Said, E. (2003). *Orientalism*. London: Penguin. (Original work published 1978.)
Said, E. (1993). *Culture and Imperialism*. New York: Random House.

P

Performativity

OLIVER BELAS

A widely used term in postmodern and "deconstructive" literary and cultural theory, "performativity" is a particularly important concept in the work of Jean-François Lyotard (1984[1979]), Judith Butler (1990[1988]; 1999[1990]), and Homi Bhabha (1994), whose theories of, respectively, gender, postcolonialism, and the postmodern have been highly influential, though not uncontested (see Connor 1997: 23–43; Nussbaum 1999; Hallward 2001). The "performative utterance" of speech act theory is another significant permutation of performativity, and while the likes of Butler and Bhabha are most obviously influenced by so-called "continental philosophy," they are certainly aware of the earlier interventions of J. L. Austin (1971; 1971[1963]), John Searle (1971 [1965]), and others (see Strawson 1971 [1964]). Indeed, the idea that language is active and constitutive (that is, it makes rather than "passively" describes), that through language things are *enacted*, is common to both "deconstructive" and speech act performativities.

At its simplest, a performative speech act, as first formulated by Austin (1971[1963]; 1975), is one in which the sentence uttered performs, or enacts, what is being said. It is contrasted with the, supposedly, plainly descriptive constative utterance; the difference between the two types of utterance is the difference between "I promise" (performative) and the report, "he said 'I promise'" (constative). The performative/constative distinction is not unproblematic, not least because apparently constative utterances might be construed as, at base, acts of uttering, or stating (Austin 1971[1963]: 20).

From the simple example "I promise," one can already infer that certain conditions must be satisfied for an utterance to be performative: promising cannot take place without the above or similar form of words being uttered; but, equally, promising will not have taken place unless these words are uttered by someone with the authority to make the promise in the first place (in promising, is the speaker committing someone else to a future act, and, if so, are they authorized to do so?). Performativity, therefore, occurs only within the context of convention and ritual, and Austin suggests that nonconventional or nonpropositional sentences can be performative, depending on their translatability to more explicit forms. (For example, "Done!" might, performatively, mark the completion of one's work; that is, it translates to something like, "With this pen-stroke, I complete my task!") In the case of nonpropositional utterances, Austin points out that intonation and gesture can affect performative force – the expostula-tion "Dog!" or, indeed, any nonlexical cry, can, uttered with urgency and accompanied by the appropriate gestures, operate as a warning of immanent danger. Thus, al-though Martha Nussbaum (1999) argues that the applicability of speech act theory to Butler's gender theory is limited at best, it should be noted that the body is invoked in both performative acts of speech and enact-ments of gender (see Butler 1999[1990]: xxv).

Austin's basic formulation has been re-fined by others. Peter Strawson (1971 [1964]) develops Austin's analysis away from the emphasis on certain classes of sentences, or the translatability of nonstan-dard or nonexplicit sentences to the form of standard or explicit performatives, and in the direction of communicative processes. Performative utterances may be essentially conventional (or standard) in form or not, but what typifies them is audience-directed intention: speakers wish their intentions to be correctly construed by their audience. Searle (1971[1965]) posits a set of necessary and sufficient conditions according to which illocutionary acts are performed, and from which the *constitutive* rules of performative speech acts can be identified. Constitutive rule are those without which the thing governed by the rules would not exist, as in organized sports. They are dis-tinguished from regulative rules, which police separately existing entities. The con-travention of certain rules carries certain penalties – that is, contravention is accounted for within the rules. But without such penalties, or faced with disruptions for which there are no contingencies, games dissolve.

It is, by now, common to view sexual difference as "neutral" biological "fact," es-sential; and gender as the socialization and naturalization of these differences. Butler's theory of gender performativity aims to make a further step, positing gender as "an 'act,' broadly construed, which con-structs the social fiction of its own psycho-logical interiority" (1990[1988]: 279). It is often taken for granted, Butler argues, that gender is a "natural" expression of the "essence" of sex (see also 1999[1990]). But, she goes on, there is no necessary link between sex and gender, and neither is there a sexual "essence" for gender to express. For Butler, sex cannot be under-stood as separate from or prior to gender, because the ways in which we understand sex are themselves gendered.

There is a tension in Butler (1999[1990]) between an implied lack of individual agen-cy altogether (we cannot escape the gender-ing processes to which we are subjected), and the possibility of asserting agency (allowed by her politics of subversion). On the one hand, normative, binary gender identities – received ideas of masculinity/femininity – precede us; we recognize, ac-cept, and accede to these received notions. Generally, the argument goes, we come to accept the apparent "necessity and nat-uralness" of "our" gender (1990[1988]: 273), which is, in fact, an expression of nothing natural, but is constituted and affirmed only by being performed. On the other hand, gender, as well as being perfor-mative, can also be intentional (272–3) – one may not be able to "free" oneself from gender altogether, but one can choose the style of one's performance; and, in doing so, one can subvert gender norms.

Butler's theory of gender performativity has been illuminating for theater studies. Consider, for example, the opening of Caryl Churchill's *Cloud Nine* (1985), in which the knowing use of formulaic verse coupled with the presentation of cross-gendered and cross-raced characters is used to per-form the condition of being trapped be-tween who and what one *has* to be (racially, sexually, and so on) and what one desires, and "knows" oneself, to be. However, Butler has remained cautious of close identifications of performativity and theatrical performance: while the theatrical irony of "cross-gendering" in theater might not discomfit because it is explained away as "unreal," "*only* an act," the sight of a transvestite walking the streets can be discomfiting precisely because, claims Butler (1990 [1988]: 422–3), in this space the transvestite *enacts* a gender no more nor less "real" or "true" than the gender norms it contravenes.

Despite its popularity and influence, Butler's work has not gone without criticism. Nussbaum (1999) accepts Butler's theory of performativity as a general description, with a very limited reach, of gender constitution. However, she argues, Butler fails to engage deeply with the traditions and problems of any academic discipline (philosophy, literature, sociology, psychoanalysis), and doesn't provide readers with either a framework for understanding, or mechanisms for making, moral or political decisions.

In Bhabha's theory of postmodernism and postcolonialism (1994), performativity is an important concept (rather than a theory in itself). Here, individual agency is said to emerge in the temporal break – or what he calls the "time lag" – between the "pedagogic" and the "performative." Simply put, pedagogy *tells* us who and what we are; it denotes the narrative processes by which identity – understood as fixed, "sedimented," given – is constituted. Pedagogy is disrupted by peformativity, the non- or extra-discursive processes by which we *enact* who and what we are. In the dialectic between pedagogy and performativity, agency emerges.

In Bhabha's performativity, identity in its pedagogic sense is absent or foreclosed; performativity is the perturbation of the grounds on which normative identity stands, a perturbation achieved by the rewriting (deforming, ironizing) of familiar pedagogic narrative. In these terms, Bhabha's is a theory in which *agency* and *subjectivity* must be understood as distinct from, and preferable to, normative (or pedagogic) identity. Bhabha's performativity involves the displacement of identity by agency subjectivity, which, similar to Butler, is posited as always in process, always shifting.

Bhabha explores the pedagogic–performative relationship by considering the construction of nationhood and "the people." Pedagogy is characterized by appeals to idealized or fictionalized pasts and traditions and their continuance. On the one hand, "the people" are invoked in nationalist narratives and rhetoric in order to ground and make authoritative those narratives: "We in Britain/the United States/France etc. are and always have been ... ." On the other hand, as well as "pedagogic objects," "the people" are also "performative subjects" (1994: 151), who enact their heterogeneity – their radical distance from any nationalist pedagogy, and their *difference* from one another. Such *difference*, Bhabha argues, is not equivalent to the binary logic of a cultural us/them and its spatial correlate insider/outsider. Rather, national culture *is* "internal" difference, and cultural difference is "a question of [the] otherness of the people-as-one" (150).

"Hybridity," another key concept in Bhabha, is closely linked to performativity; it denotes performatively constituted agencies which have no pedagogic narrative or identity (for, in Bhabha, such agencies are *identical* with nothing). Hybridity is thus contingent upon performativity: from what Bhabha calls the "disjunctive temporality" of the performative – and in the babel of voices one encounters the urban gathering sites of national and racial diasporas – properly hybrid agencies emerge, "outside" and separate from the intentions of any speaking "subjects." "Hybridity" refers not to a patchwork of pedagogic identities or narratives; Bhabha is keen to distance himself from pluralist and multiculturalist perspectives. Rather, it is the repetitive emergence of the absolutely new, the mechanism of which is performativity.

In his important discussion of the postmodern, Lyotard offers a rather different configuration of "performativity" from those discussed above. Here, it is one of the guiding logics of the postmodern epoch. First, performativity is a mode, closely tied to power, by which techno-scientific research and knowledge are legitimated. This performativity is a logic of efficiency, its goal "the best possible input/output equation" (maximum output for minimum input) (1984[1979]: 46). Because this efficiency equation affects research funding (both state and private), greater performativity increases one's – or one's group's – capacity to produce proofs, which makes it easier to be "right"; and the more "right," in this pragmatic sense, a group is, the more the world starts to look the way that group thinks or wants it to look. Thus, in the postmodern epoch, there is "an equation between wealth, efficiency, and truth" (45)

A similar model is also to be found in education, in which "knowledge" and its transmission are no longer linked to humanist ideals, but aim at passing on the information necessary for maintaining a functional, skills-based society. (There are, broadly, two levels here: the "higher," specialist skills necessary to make states competitive on the world stage; and the competencies required for "internal" social cohesion – the need for doctors, teachers, and so on.) Such a logic of performativity is indicative of a shift toward an information, or data, society: data banks, writes Lyotard, "are 'nature' for postmodern man" (51).

SEE ALSO: Bhabha, Homi; Butler, Judith; Deconstruction; Derrida, Jacques; Feminism; Gender Theory; Lyotard, Jean-François; Postcolonial Studies and Diaspora Studies; Queer Theory

REFERENCES AND SUGGESTED READINGS

Austin, J. L. (1975). *How To Do Things With Words*, 2nd edn (ed. J. O. Urmson & M. Sbisa). Oxford: Clarendon.
Austin, J. L. (1971). Performative-constative. In J. R. Searle (ed.), *The Philosophy of Language*. Oxford: Oxford University Press, pp. 13–22. (Original work published 1963.)
Bhabha, H. K. (1994). *The Location of Culture*. London: Routledge.
Butler, J. (1990). Performative acts and gender constitution: An Essay in phenomenology and feminist theory. In S. E. Case (ed.), *Performing Feminisms: Feminist Critical Theory and Theatre*. Baltimore: Johns Hopkins University Press, pp. 270–282. (Original work published 1988.)
Butler, J. (1999). *Gender Trouble: Feminism and the Subversion of Identity*. London: Routledge. (Original work published 1990.)
Churchill, C. (1985). *Cloud Nine*. In *Plays. One*. New York: Routledge, pp. 243–320.
Connor, S. (1997). *Postmodernist Culture: An Introduction to Theories of the Contemporary*, 2nd edn. Oxford: Blackwell.
Hallward, P. (2001). *Absolutely Postcolonial: Writing Between the Singular and the Specific*. Manchester: Manchester University Press.
Lyotard, J.-F. (1984). *The Postmodern Condition: A Report on Knowledge* (trans. G. Bennington & B. Massumi). Manchester: Manchester University Press. (Original work published 1979.)
Nussbaum, M. (1999). The professor of parody. *The New Republic*, 22(February), 37–45.
Searle, J. R. (1971). What is a speech act? In J. R. Searle (ed.), *The Philosophy of Language*, Oxford: Oxford University Press, pp. 38–53. (Original work published 1965.)
Strawson, P. F. (1971). Intention and convention in speech acts. In J. R. Searle (ed.), *Philosophy of language*, Oxford: Oxford University Press, pp. 23–38. (Original work published 1964.)

Phallus/Phallocentrism

ABIGAIL RINE

In psychoanalytic theory, the phallus serves as the supreme symbol of masculine power and, concurrently, of feminine lack. "Phallocentrism" is a term used primarily by feminist theorists to denote the pervasive privileging of the masculine within the current system of signification.

The term was first coined by Ernest Jones, a British psychoanalyst, in reference to the primacy of the phallus in Sigmund Freud's theories. Freud (1965[1933]) posits a phallic phase in childhood development, during which sexual difference is first encountered. In this phase, the distinction between the sexes is figured primarily through the genitalia, specifically the penis, which Freud conflates with the phallus as a symbol of power. Depicting the clitoris as a penis equivalent, Freud conceives the origins of female sexuality in terms of the masculine phallus. It is during the phallic stage that a child realizes the mother does not, in fact, have a penis and appears to be castrated. In the boy child, this apparent castration incites the Oedipal crisis, while, in the girl, it generates castration anxiety, provoking a rejection of the mother and a turn toward the father as the source of phallic power. Renouncing her clitoral phallus as inferior, the girl child exhibits Freud's controversial concept of penis envy, wherein she recognizes her lack and seeks to gain access to the phallus by having a baby/substitute penis. Though a disciple of Freud, Jones critiqued his mentor's theorization of female sexuality within a resolutely male model of development. Along with fellow Freud followers Melanie Klein and Karl Abraham, he opposed, in particular, Freud's claim that a girl child is unaware of her vagina in infancy. Abandoning the primacy of the phallic phase in female development, Jones and Klein attempted to theorize a more egalitarian, though biologically based, construction of femininity.

Throughout the work of Freud and Jones, the phallus maintains a direct correlation to the penis, and it is not until Jacques Lacan's rereading of Freud that this link is questioned. In his theorization of the human psyche, Lacan (2006[1966]) conceives identity and consciousness as conceptualized through language and employs the phallus as a central signifier that is not reducible to the penis. For Lacan, the phallus functions as a sign of power and the primary signifier of difference that distinguishes between the sexes in terms of lack. Though Lacan uses the term phallus in a variety of capacities throughout his work, ultimately the phallus symbolizes the cultural mechanisms that enable and are sustained by language. Furthermore, is it the phallus as a signifier that anchors the system of representation and upholds the categories of masculine and feminine.

Unlike the theories of Freud, Lacan's Oedipal crisis culminates with entry into the symbolic, the external realm of language and culture, where the child learns to perceive the world in terms of sameness and difference. In contrast to Freud's actual father, Lacan's father is a symbolic one, endowed with the full authority of the phallus, and it is this symbolic father that intercedes between the mother and child, creating a split between the conscious and unconscious in the emerging subject. The function of the symbolic father, what Lacan terms the "name of the father," is to curb desire by imposing restrictions and enforcing the rational structure of language. Together, the phallus and the name of the father give stability to the symbolic, enabling signification and socialization.

The primacy of the phallus in Lacan's model of the psyche highlights a sociolingual structure that is fundamentally male-centered. According to Lacan, only boys can fully enter the symbolic and attain subjectivity, because the power of the phallus is associated with the male body. Girls, perceiving their lack, conform to the linguistic and social prescriptions of femininity, which is constituted as the passive negative of masculinity. Lacan refers to the conflation of the penis and phallus as *méconnaissance* (misrecognition) and suggests that the seemingly stable masculine identities constructed around the phallus are illusory. Although Lacanian theory undermines male authority by portraying phallic identity as ultimately bogus, it leaves little recourse for women, who access phallic power only through heterosexual relations. Some feminist theorists have used Lacanian psychoanalysis as a starting point for locating and critiquing male privilege, while others have been highly critical of Lacan's thought *as* phallocentric.

Judith Butler (1993) is one theorist who employs Lacan while simultaneously exposing his bias. Butler concurs with Lacan's dissociation of the penis from the phallus and reaffirms the phallus's status as symbolic. She does, however, critique Lacan on the grounds that he privileges the phallus over other corporeal signifiers and ulti-mately fails completely to distinguish it from male genitalia. Despite his attempts to detach the phallus from the penis, she argues, Lacan offers the phallus as the metaphorical culmination of the penis. Taking Lacan's reasoning further, Butler concludes that the phallus, as a signifier with no intrinsic link to the penis, can be displaced and form symbolic relationships with other body parts, male and female.

Despite its masculine center, Lacan's thought has proved instrumental in the formulation of phallocentrism as a concept. In the wake of Lacanian psychoanalysis, the term has expanded from denoting a simple privileging of the masculine to reflect, as theorist Elizabeth Grosz (1989) describes, a system of representation that upholds a single model of male subjectivity, around which all others are defined. As such, critiques of phallocentrism have become an integral element of feminist revision, particularly within French feminist theory.

Jacques Derrida, in his critique of phallocentrism, combines the concepts of phallus and *logos* to form the neologism "phallogocentrism." Derrida's analysis of Western thought exposes a central assumption of absolute truth and a belief in *logos*, or reason, as the key to unlocking this truth. Derrida relates this notion of a single origin or meaning of the universe to the phallus and describes phallogocentric thought as a series of interconnected binary oppositions that privilege one (masculine) term over another (feminine) term. Derrida criticizes Lacan's vision of a single, masculine libido as a phallocentric erasure of difference. He takes issue, likewise, with certain philosophical concepts, such as Heidegger's *Dasein*, that purport to be non-gendered, but are always already masculine. Derrida often broaches the subject of gender indirectly, through his deconstruction of other philosophers, and his two primary meditations on phallocentric discourse are *Spurs: Nietzsche's Styles* (1979[1978]), a reading of Friedrich Nietzsche, and "Geschlect: Sexual difference, ontological difference" (1983), a reading of Martin Heidegger. In "Geschlect," Derrida conceives of a sexuality that precedes the binary construction of man/woman by positing ontology, or being, as sexually indeterminate, but not asexual. *Spurs* is Derrida's primary attempt to deconstruct the relationship between man/woman by using the term "woman" as a trope for non-truth or *undecidability*. In addition to exposing masculine bias in Western philosophy, Derrida highlights second-wave feminism's collaboration with phallogocentrism, accusing feminists of aiding the male-centered system by aspiring to gain power within it, rather than attempting to alter the system itself. Such feminists, Derrida argues, betray women by striving to become men and attain phallic power.

Despite his critiques of phallogocentrism, some feminist theorists have found Derrida's deconstruction of masculine privilege to be inadequate. Gayatri Spivak (1997) asserts that his use of the term "woman" as a deconstructive trope reiterates rather than undermines the marginalization of the feminine. Likewise, while Derrida's occasional technique of writing in a feminine voice ostensibly exceeds phallic discourse, this method, rather than asserting woman's subjectivity, creates what Spivak calls double displacement. Derrida's analysis of phallogocentrism affirms that women are already displaced within the sociolingual order, and his movement into a feminine space locates "woman" as an empty subject position that men can occupy. Thus, women are displaced twice over. Spivak concludes that although Derrida's attempt to dislodge masculine privilege fails, Derridean deconstruction remains a vital tool for feminist theorists in undermining phallocentrism. She urges theorists to reread and revise Derrida, just as he revised his philosophical predecessors.

French feminist philosopher Hélène Cixous employs Derrida's technique of deconstruction in her own account of phallocentrism. Cixous (1986[1975]) echoes Derrida's analysis of phallocentrism as a series of dual, hierarchical oppositions, pointing out that "woman" is always associated with passivity, functioning as the paralyzed other that orients the active, masculine self. Cixous asserts an urgent need for writers and theorists to undermine the amalgamation of logocentrism and phallocentrism, a system that sustains itself through the subordination of the feminine. Though phallocentrism primarily and visibly impedes female subjectivity, Cixous suggests that both sexes are harmed by a violently male-centered ideology. Using the metaphor of a machine, Cixous describes phallocentrism as an enemy to both men and women, though in disparate ways. Within the "phallocratic" apparatus, women are subordinated and defined by lack, while men are "given the grotesque and unenviable fate of being reduced to a single idol with clay balls" (1976[1975]: 884). Cixous affirms the presence of both sexes within each individual, a presence that is suppressed by the rigid bifurcation of masculinity and femininity. As a means of resisting phallocentric discourse, Cixous offers the notion of *écriture féminine*, a mode of expression that gives voice to the silenced feminine.

Like Cixous, Luce Irigaray's philosophy calls for a reinterpretation of sexual difference, one unbound by phallocentric hierarchies. Irigaray's first published works, *Speculum of the Other Woman* (1985[1974]) and *This Sex Which is Not One* (1985[1977]) serve as incisive and extensive critiques of phallocentric bias throughout Western thought. Her subsequent works have focused on establishing a new mode of exchange between the sexes, a relation that fosters difference without hierarchy or appropriation. While working with the tradition of psychoanalysis, Irigaray critiques the phallocentrism of Freud and Lacan, asserting that their theories rely on a traditional hierarchy of the senses that privilege visibility. The less-visible female genitalia are perceived as lack or absence compared to the prominent penis. Irigaray, advocating the cultivation of a feminine imaginary, mimics the idealization of the penis as phallus by presenting a metaphorical reinterpretation of the vaginal lips. The labia, in their plurality, present a distinct symbol of subjectivity, one that is fluid and open and exceeds phallic oneness. Irigaray overturns the sense hierarchy in her description of the vaginal lips continually touching, affirming their presence through senses other than sight. Irigaray's use of feminine symbolism challenges phallocentrism by revealing the undercurrent of masculine bias within language and by conceiving alternative modes of representation and expression.

SEE ALSO: Butler, Judith; Cixous, Hélène; Core and Periphery; Deconstruction; Derrida, Jacques; Écriture féminine; Feminism; Gender Theory; Grosz, Elizabeth; Irigaray, Luce; Psychoanalysis (since 1966); Subject Position; Spivak, Gayatri Chakravorty.

REFERENCES AND SUGGESTED READINGS

Butler, J. (1993). The lesbian phallus and the morphological imaginary. In Bodies That Matter: On the Discursive Limits of "Sex." New York: Routledge, pp. 57–91.
Cixous, H. (1976). The laugh of the medusa (trans. K. Cohen and P. Cohen). Signs, 1(4), 875–893. (Original work published 1975.)
Cixous, H. (1986). Sorties. In H. Cixous and C. Clément, The Newly Born Woman (trans. B. Wing). Minneapolis: University of Minnesota Press. (Original work published 1975.)
Derrida, J. (1979). Spurs: Nietzsche's Styles (trans. B. Harlow). Chicago: University of Chicago Press. (Original work published 1978.)
Derrida, J. (1983). Geschlecht: Sexual difference, ontological difference. Research in Phenomenology, 13, 65–83.
Freud, S. (1965). Femininity. In New Introductory Lectures on Psycho-Analysis (ed. J. Strachey). New York: Norton, pp. 139–167. (Original work published 1933.)
Grosz, E. (1989). Sexual Subversions: Three French Feminists. Sydney: Allen and Unwin.
Grosz, E. (1990). Jacques Lacan: A Feminist Introduction. New York: Routledge.
Irigaray, L. (1985). Speculum of the Other Woman (trans. G. C. Gill). Ithaca: Cornell University Press. (Original work published 1974.)
Irigaray, L. (1985). This Sex Which Is Not One (trans. C. Porter). Ithaca: Cornell University Press. (Original work published 1977.)
Lacan, J. (2006). Écrits (trans. B. Fink). New York: Norton. (Original work published 1966.)
Minsky, R. (1996). Psychoanalysis and Gender: An Introductory Reader. London: Routledge.
Spivak, G. C. (1997). Displacement and the discourse of woman. In N. Holland (ed.), Feminist Interpretations of Jacques Derrida. University Park: Pennsylvania State University Press, pp. 43–71.

Postcolonial Studies and Diaspora Studies

MARIAN AGUIAR, MRINALINI GREEDHARRY, & KHACHIG TÖLÖLYAN

Postcolonial studies takes an approach to the study of culture and society that pays particular attention to the practices, products, and consequences of European imperialism. In one sense, postcolonial studies begins with the period of decolonization of European empires that followed World War II. This is true not only in the sense that postcolonial studies would not be possible without the political reality of the drive to decolonize, but in the sense that the theory that we have now depends upon the body of critique, including speeches, novels, journalism, and pamphlets, that attended that political reality. In the British context, then, the era of decolonization begins roughly with the partition of India and Pakistan in 1947, followed by the independence of Ghana in 1957, and it continues into the late 1960s and early '70s when most of the former British and French colonies in Africa became formally independent nations and European empires were finally dissolved. In the French context, decolonization begins during the gradual withdrawal from French Indo-China in 1949–54 and from Tunisia in 1956 and is confirmed by Algeria winning its independence in 1962.

Before and during these years intellectuals and writers in various European centers critiqued the idea of imperialism from political, economic, and ethical perspectives, including for example, J. A. Hobson, V. I. Lenin, and Jean-Paul Sartre. The burgeoning class of intellectuals living and writing between the colonies and the metropole, including, for example, Frantz Fanon, Aimé Cesaire, Mohandas Gandhi, Albert Memmi, and C. L. R. James, were also developing their own critiques of colonization and racism. Before formal independence was declared in India, Jamaica, or Algeria, these critics were already drawing attention to the cultural, psychic, and structural problems caused by colonialism and racism. Early critics addressed the immediate concerns of the educated colonized class: How can we achieve decolonization? Should it be through peaceful, legal, or violent means? What will it mean to be a decolonized citizen in the modern world? Is the choice between modernity and tradition, or something else? Critics such as Fanon and James still offer some of the most insightful perspectives on what it means to live between cultures, to try to negotiate cultural meanings, and to create new cultural meanings.

Many of these early critics of colonialism are not accorded the status of "critic" in the present constellation of postcolonial studies, but their work nevertheless forms an important part of its intellectual and political context. Some of them are considerably more influential than others. It is notable, for example, that even though India was one of the central territories of the British Empire, and contemporary postcolonial studies is heavily slanted toward discussions of the Indian context, Fanon, the black Martinican psychiatrist who wrote about French colonialism in Algeria, is the one of those whose writings have received the most attention. Writings by figures in India's independence movement, such as Gandhi, are much less influential on contemporary postcolonial scholarship.

Postcolonial studies begins again, for the first time as an academic phenomenon, in 1978 with the publication of the groundbreaking book *Orientalism*, written by the literary critic Edward Said. Said details the ways in which the British, French, and Germans gathered and produced information about the Middle East and links the will to collect and organize knowledge with political influence and control. He argues, for example, that the British spent much more time cataloguing, classifying, and notating everything they encountered, whereas the French, who had less political influence, and certainly less political control, were more interested in the figurative Orient. Accordingly, the Orient figures in French culture and literature as more of a magical dream or fantasy than a scientific or anthropological subject. Said concludes that Orientalism has gradually ceased to be the domain of the British and French, and in the contemporary moment has become the domain of the Americans. Moreover, he suggests that under American influence, Orientalism has become more of a "scientific" discourse. It now belongs to the social sciences (part of international relations or Middle East studies) rather than the humanities.

Said's work is important not only because it produced a discursive history of the Orient as an object of Western knowledge, but also because it produced a critique of the very idea of studying the Orient, as well as the oriental "experts" themselves. Said's critique meant that writers, classicists, anthropologists, linguists, and literary critics were no longer innocent researchers merely gathering facts, but implicated in overtly political processes such as colonial conquest and rule. It also meant that the West studying the East was itself an organizing principle of Western culture that demanded scrutiny.

Much of the most recent wave of postcolonial studies is still involved in working out the implications of Said's critique and, although subsequent scholarship has ultimately challenged much of his theoretical framework, it is heavily indebted to his work. Once the originality of his arguments had been absorbed, reproduced, and digested, however, certain problems began to emerge. First, *Orientalism* seemed to leave too little space for discursive resistance. If it was true that the texts written by Western scholars, writers, and statesmen produced a strong and politically effective discursive regime of truth – what we know as the Orient – it could not be a completely invincible regime. There had to be some possibility of contesting the discourse, of rewriting it, or of outright rebellion against it.

In the early 1980s, various scholars, using poststructuralist theories, began to examine how discursive regimes of colonial authority were always already fragmented, as well as how that fragmentation was represented in history and literature. In the case of British India, the meeting between the Indians and the British complicated attempts at representation, cultural authority, and colonial control. Homi Bhabha points, for example, to the fracturing of Christianity as a discourse of brotherly love in India, partly as a result of its clear links with formal political control in the form of colonial policy. Gayatri Spivak explores those things that are not represented, and perhaps cannot even be represented according to the logic of Western philosophy and literature.

A group of historians of India, including, among others, Ranajit Guha and Partha Chatterjee, known collectively as the Subaltern Studies Group, approached the question of anticolonial resistance from yet another direction. Examination of the history of resistance in India and of previous attempts to write the history of India with concepts and assumptions derived from the

Western discipline of history led this group to question the very nature of nationalism and colonialism. Guha reminds readers that the Western history of a nation-state is premised upon the idea that, with the dominance of the bourgeoisie, it is possible to treat the power relations of the nation-state as identical with those of the civil society. However, as Guha and his colleagues discovered, before independence in India there was powerful peasant resistance that seemed to operate separately from, and without reference to, the bourgeois movement. He explains the import of this:

> [I]t has been possible therefore for historical scholarship fed on this theorem for centuries and made it into the stuff of academic common sense to represent power in its most generalized form as Civil Society = Nation = State. ... We take it upon ourselves to redefine how these three terms relate to each other in such a domain. Our attempt to face up to that task leads directly ... to the question: "What is colonialism and what is a colonial state?" (1997: xi)

The most recent stage of postcolonial studies may be described in similar terms, then, as the examination of such basic organizing ideas of postcolonial theories as colonialism, colonial state, and resistance.

Postcolonial studies has had an influence far beyond literature studies, where Said's work began, particularly in disciplines such as history and anthropology. In all cases, though, postcolonial studies may be roughly understood as comprising three strands: colonial discourse analysis, metadiscursive analysis, and materialist analysis. Though particular disciplines may exhibit preferences for analysis more heavily weighted in favor of one or the other of these strands, all three necessarily depend on and intersect with each other. Certainly the proto-postcolonial theory practiced by the early anticolonial writers and activists – the men and women who helped lead their countries to independence – drew on all methods of analyzing the colonial order of things. Fanon, for example, was as interested in the political realities of colonial rule as he was in the discursive construction of Algerians as mental patients in medical textbooks and the racializing logic of Western philosophy.

Feminist approaches are likewise deeply embedded in postcolonial studies, and are not best understood as a separate strand of approaches to postcolonial theory. It has been the struggle of women of color, both activists and academicians, to insist that issues of race and colonialism matter to them as much, sometimes more, than gender when they attempt to define themselves or their critical objectives. To group these postcolonial scholars and their studies together on the basis of the author's gender or the topics discussed, rather than of the scholar's postcolonial approach, would seem to do violence to his or her attempt to theorize other kinds of subjects.

In the context of postcolonial studies, discourse analysis takes its cues almost exclusively from Michel Foucault's and Said's attempts to combine Foucauldian and Gramscian theory. Said's book initiated a wave of discourse studies that we may divide into two groups: first, studies that focus on literary and other representations of the colonized and the colonizer; second, studies that focus on the practices of the institutions that constituted colonial authority, such as colonial hospitals, schools, missions, and prisons.

The first group of scholars is largely and often exclusively concerned with issues of representation. That is, they study how the colonizer and the colonized are represented in literature, newspapers, photographs, films, and any other media that can be "read" for structure and narrative. A representative work in this field is David Spurr's *The Rhetoric of Empire* (1993), in which he identifies 11 persistent colonial tropes that appear in travel writing, journalism, and public administration documents from French, British, and American colonies. Studies like this have been invaluable in delineating the broad and subtle contours of racism and colonialism. Representations appear to function as independent products of a wide range of authors, but studied from the point of view of colonial discourse analysis reveal a limited range of ways of speaking about and on the topic of the colonial subject, and, as Spurr, among others, notes, continue to affect the ways in which we speak about and represent the Third World and the immigrants who live in the First World today.

Discourse analysis is valuable in part because it breaks up any suggestion that such representations can be divided between low and high culture. Travel writing and popular journalism may, according to the common-sense view, be unavoidably tainted by stereotypes and prejudiced representations, but Said's work demonstrates that such misrepresentations persist at the highest level of culture, in university scholarship and classical texts. Much of colonial discourse analysis has attended, for example, to the question of the representation of people of color in the British literary canon, from Shakespeare to the Brontës, and from George Eliot to E. M. Forster.

Feminist critics working in this area have been especially interested in representations of women. However, feminist scholars have been equally active in studying women as producers and reproducers of colonial discourse themselves. A significant body of scholarship examines women writers, explorers, and painters who contributed to the othering of colonized peoples while trying to negotiate the othering that they themselves were subjected to as women. Said has been faulted for failing to note women's contribution to the production of discourse as well. Reina Lewis (1996) has examined the complex ways in which European women both affirmed and contested the tropes described by Said.

The second thread of colonial discourse analysis has focused largely on the institutions and practices that, together with the representations discussed above, formed the colonial order of things. Following Foucault, studies of colonial schools, hospitals, and child-rearing practices have demonstrated how colonialism was carried out and constructed by the most everyday actions and practice of Europeans and their colonized populations. A representative example of such studies is Gauri Viswanathan's study of the development of English language and literature curriculum and practices in British India (1989). She draws attention to the fact that teaching British literature to Indians was not simply a question of a broader education in (classic) literature, but of establishing a cultural ideal that the colonial subjects could learn and emulate. For the colonial administration "the English literary text functioned as a surrogate Englishman in his highest and most perfect state: [The Indians] daily converse with the best and wisest Englishmen through the medium of their works" (437). Another notable example is Ann Stoler's *Race and the Education of Desire* (1995), in which she traces the ways in which practices of domestic arrangements, child-rearing, and child education in the colonies intersected with discussions of class and citizenship in the metropole.

Such studies vary widely in the degree to which they treat such institutions as bearers and disseminators of colonial ideology or as constituting elements of the colonial order of things. Viswanathan's study, for example, suggests that educational practices and policy were explicitly used to further and refine colonial governance. Stoler's study, by contrast, argues that bourgeois identities were still under construction even in the metropole and borrowed from, as much as they contributed to, the construction of colonial identities. That is to say, constructing bourgeois identities in the metropole depended on child-management and sexual relations in the colonies, as much as colonial subjects were being educated in the colonial order of things by European notions of good citizenship and civil society.

The differences between the strands are best understood through their treatment of the same research object. A useful running example is the stereotype, precisely because all varieties of postcolonial scholar have addressed the problem of the stereotype. In some sense, the stereotype is a staple object of colonial discourse analysis because scholars investigate the repeated appearance and deployment of certain tropes. In this limited sense, *Orientalism* is an extended discussion of a group of stereotypical representations of some people who inhabit the Middle East, especially the Arab Muslim. Nevertheless, Said's analysis is not confined to cataloguing the stereotypes he finds; indeed, he is not principally concerned with the representations themselves, but in trying to understand how those stereotypes been transformed into a respected intellectual tradition of scholarship about the Middle East. The colonial discourse analyst may be interested in demonstrating how stereotypes appear in the most unlikely places, how they intensify in certain times and places, or how they work as part of a specific articulation of colonial governance.

Metadiscursive critique is perhaps the most difficult strand of postcolonial theory to define or characterize as a methodology. The kind of postcolonial critique offered by critics such as those who make up the Subaltern Studies Group, Spivak, and Bhabha does not always provide a method that can be easily repeated by other scholars. Instead, their work issues a series of demanding questions about the relationship between power, knowledge, representation, and subjectivity set in motion by the European colonization of the non-European world. This strand is best understood by examining the work of Bhabha, Spivak, and the Subaltern Studies Group in turn.

Bhabha's work builds upon the field already defined by Said's critical writings. Though he also writes with an emphasis on questions of representation, disciplinary power, and cultural authority, he treats colonial authority as far more contestable than Said's earliest texts seem to allow. For Bhabha, influenced heavily by Jacques Derrida and Jacques Lacan, any discourse, even one as apparently successful as colonialism or nationalism, cannot succeed in securing its authority totally. Accordingly, he examines tropes in order to detect where they undermine themselves, how they become undone by the circumstances in which they are deployed, and how they are even used by the colonized to different ends.

In particular, Bhabha is interested in questions of translation: how can one understand another culture? How can one maintain cultural authority in a situation where one does not have cultural understanding? How are cultural authority and authenticity constructed out of social actions and interactions? He is interested in these questions because they also pertain to the contemporary moment – the discourses around immigrants, multiculturalism, and diversity that we use today. In effect, he suggests that everything one might need to understand the world today is already available in a careful examination of the colonial scene.

Bhabha's main concern is not how the colonized, or formerly colonized, might represent themselves, since, in accordance with the logic of undecidability he detects in the colonizers' discourse, he does not believe that it is possible for the colonized to

secure total and stable meanings for their resistance either. This makes his critics very uncomfortable, since it seems to suggest that the colonized cannot take definitive, directed action against the colonizers. Though Bhabha produces heady and stylish analysis of the colonial scene and the postcolonial present, his work does indeed have the effect of destabilizing meanings (of the notion of colonizer, colonized, resistance, authority) without offering readers or critics any other solutions. In other words, the deconstructive tendency in Bhabha often appears to be the end rather than the means.

While Spivak shares Bhabha's interest in deconstruction and the instability of cultural meanings – indeed, she is a noted translator of Derrida into English – she combines this method with her own rigorously articulated versions of both Marxism and feminism. For Spivak, deconstruction is a useful tool not only because it destabilizes meanings as such, but because it highlights the unrepresentability of certain tropes and subjects (agents) in Western discourses. In particular, deconstruction allows Spivak to point to the unrepresentability of women of color as subjects in a range of discursive fields from Western philosophy and literary criticism to historical archives and feminism. So, for example, in "Three women's texts and a critique of imperialism" (1985), she begins with the observation that, when reading nineteenth-century novels by English writers, women or men, it should not be possible to do so "without remembering that imperialism, understood as England's social mission, was a crucial part of the cultural representation of England to the English" (798). And yet, as she demonstrates, feminist scholars of nineteenth-century literature continue to laud such heroines as Charlotte Brontë's *Jane Eyre* without remembering imperialism. Imperialism is the seemingly "invisible" structure that shapes the action of Jane Eyre; it is the base of the male protagonist's wealth, the objection (in the form of a deranged, colonial wife) to a marriage between Eyre and her master and to the possibility of Eyre's escape from the situation (as a member of the Christian mission to British India). Spivak foregrounds these things to demonstrate how even a proto-feminist text can work to naturalize an imperial ideology.

Spivak has become somewhat notorious for her insistence that the woman of color is not simply conveniently pushed aside in such discourses, but that it is not possible to represent her in the terms given by those discourses. In discussing the difficulties involved in retrieving subaltern women's voices from the historical archives, Spivak insists that to accept the subaltern woman's absence from these archives is not to accept her non-existence as a real person, or as an agent, but to recognize the full extent of the constraints placed upon understanding the woman of color as a subject.

Fortunately, Spivak has devoted considerable attention to how this problem can be solved. One possibility, almost as notorious as her assertion about unrepresentability, is what she describes as "strategic essentialism." That is, although, like Bhabha, she recognizes the impossibility of secure meanings, she acknowledges the political and performative value of behaving and acting as though stable meanings of "woman," "black," or "homosexual" are possible. In this strictly limited and political sense, she upholds the pragmatic value of an identity-based politics.

The work of both Bhabha and Spivak dovetails in some places with the third group of metadiscursive critics: the Subaltern Studies Group. As indicated above, members of this group read and rewrite the history of the nation we know today as India. For them, such questions of agency, political identity, and representation are crucial, as they try to piece together what

happened in different population groups in India as the agitation for independence increased. The effect of subaltern studies has been to question the terms of the discipline of history altogether, by examining how, in the particular case of India, Western conceptualizations of nation, dominance, colonizer, and class break down or behave in unexpected ways. Marxism has had a strong influence on historians of India, and a critique of universalist history mainly associated with Marxism is part of the subaltern studies project. Two particular focuses of critique include, first, Marx's failure adequately to theorize the importance of India as a British colony and, second, the insistence on class as a social phenomenon understood in a strictly Marxist sense. Representative examples of such work include Chatterjee's *The Nation and its Fragments* (1993), Guha's *Dominance Without Hegemony* (1997), and Dipesh Chakrabarty's *Provincializing Europe* (2000).

Postcolonial studies begins from the reality of colonialism as an economic and political formation, formalized in military conquest and law. The discourse analysts extended this definition to include apparently "innocent" and even progressive forms of social practice and representation including the study of literature, health practices, and public administration. The metadiscursive critique goes further into the grounds of Western knowledge itself, and argues that the whole framework is underpinned by a racializing logic that stems from the age of colonialism. Critics such as Bhabha, Spivak, and Guha challenge scholars not simply to examine the history and literature of the colonial age, but to read their disciplinary assumptions and foundational concepts as products of the colonial order of things. This should be read as an extension of *Orientalism*, since, although Said does not address the question in these terms, he introduced the problematic of Western academic knowledge as a product and instrument of colonialism. The logical conclusion of this, as Chakrabarty has argued, is the importance of finally "provincializing" Europe. As he notes, the fact that the "West" we have been examining, scrutinizing, and deconstructing is clearly fictive "does not lessen its appeal or power. The project of provincializing 'Europe' has to include ... the recognition that Europe's acquisition of the adjective 'modern' for itself is a piece of global history of which an integral part is the story of European imperialism" (2000: 21).

One of Bhabha's best-known analyses, which serves here as a good example, is a discussion of the colonial stereotype, in a chapter entitled "The other question: Stereotype, discrimination and the discourse of colonialism" (1994: 66–84). Here, Bhabha does not discuss any particular stereotype. Instead, he examines the function of stereotypes as a form of knowledge in the colonies where the colonizers are always already uncertain about what they do and don't know. If stereotypes simply stood in some distorted relationship to reality, as many scholars have interpreted them, then it would be easy to provide accurate information. We should simply need to educate ourselves about the "truth" in order to rid ourselves of stereotypes. Thus, many critics have examined the gap between the stereotype and the reality it attempts to represent. Bhabha argues, however, that the stereotype is not an index of reality in any sense, but, rather, a tool for managing the fact that knowledge is so uncertain and ambivalent.

Bhabha links stereotypes, in this sense, to fetishes as Freud describes them. In classical psychoanalytic theory, Freud argues that when a little boy discovers that his father has a penis and his mother does not, he must face a difficult psychological problem. He must accept that he and his mother are different, and give up his identification with her, or he will persist in the notion that he and his mother are not really so different (and thus will become a homosexual adult). The third possibility is that the boy will become a fetishist – that is, he will invest some object with the value of the penis that he knows his mother doesn't and can't really have. When this object is present, the fetishist is able to have so-called normal heterosexual relations. In this way the boy recognizes that women are different from men, but he also preserves the possibility that they are *not* in the form of the fetish. Bhabha transfers this mechanism to the colonial society, where he argues that stereotypes allow colonizers (and the colonized, for they too have their stereotypes) simultaneously to assert that the natives are unquestionably different from them, and to admit in a limited sense that the natives are exactly the same as they are.

Bhabha's theory of the stereotype is ingenious because it solves a number of methodological problems. First, it explains why stereotypes persist as a form of knowledge despite their inaccuracy. Since the stereotype is not really about reality, or accuracy, it persists long after "true" knowledge has been obtained. Second, it explains why a range of apparently contradictory (or at least inconsistent) stereotypes can all exist at the same time. Depending on which aspect of the colonial population the colonizer is trying to manage, the stereotype can be so-called "positive" (the faithful, devoted Indian *Ayah*, or nursemaid, for example) or "negative" (the deceitful, evasive *Paki*, for example). What is of interest, then, is not how the stereotype compares with reality, or even how it is understood by the colonized/colonizers, but how it functions as a particular means of managing ambivalence.

It would be more conventional to place the materialist strand before the colonial discourse analysis and metadiscursive critiques in an overview of postcolonial studies, since many of the original critics of colonialism were materialist critics, and to some degree postcolonial studies is considered to have moved beyond solely material explanations and theories of colonialism. However, postcolonial studies may be on the swing back toward a more materialist critique, not least because, in the form of work by scholars such as Aijaz Ahmad, Neil Lazarus, and Benita Parry, this approach has been invaluable in keeping postcolonial studies alert and vigilant about its own inescapable complicity with the colonial order of things.

Materialist critique is often taken as a synonym for Marxist critique, but the term should not be understood as restricted to self-professed Marxist critics. This strand of postcolonial studies also includes feminists and anticolonial critics who may write without reference to classical Marxist theory, but who always write in clear reference to the material structures of colonial rule, whether political, legal, or patriarchal. For example, it includes many historians who, although somewhat neglected in the history of postcolonial studies, do a great deal of the most careful theoretical and material scholarship available. A representative example is Bernard Cohn's *Colonialism and its Forms of Knowledge*, a study that provides an account of colonialism grounded in an analysis of clothes, antiquarian objects, and dictionaries.

A large part of feminist postcolonial criticism belongs to the category of materialist critique insofar as it draws attention to the materially different position of women living under colonialism. Colonialism is a system that intersects powerfully with patriarchy, in ways that are sometimes unexpected. In British India, for example, the colonizers sought to appear as protectors of the colonized women with legislation about child brides, dowries, and *sati*, which contravened their supposed policy of non-interference with the culture and religion of the colonized population. Indian women were, without doubt, more damaged by cultural traditions than some critics have cared to remember, but they were themselves alert to the choice implied in such legislation – choose the modern, British way or be trapped in the old, Indian way. Feminist postcolonial critics have been particularly alert in addressing the ways the legal, political, and economic structures of colonialism played into the hands of both British and Indian patriarchies. A representative study is Kumari Jayawardena's *The White Woman's Other Burden* (1995), a historical study of the part played by Indian and British women reformers in India's independence movement.

Materialist critique is no less interested in ethical and epistemological questions than it is in other strands of postcolonial studies. The difference, however, may be that colonial discourse analysis and metadiscursive critique both suspend critique of postcolonial theory itself, whereas materialist critique, particularly Marxist, is attentive to everything that surrounds the publication and dissemination of postcolonial scholarship. Thus, Ahmad, a Marxist critic, although vigorous and vigilant in his criticism of Marxism itself, examines the phenomenon of postcolonial theory and studies in the context of the historical and economic moment. For him, between the moments of "Third Worldism" and postcolonial theory, the literatures of Asia and Africa continue to be undervalued and understudied. Indeed, it is notable that postcolonial scholarship is constituted largely by analyses of canonical authors such as E. M. Forster, Rudyard Kipling, and Joseph Conrad rather than Indian, African, or other indigenous writers.

Mrinalini Sinha's study of a long-standing stereotypical character in the history of British–Indian relations known as the *babu* is an example of how materialist critique can illuminate our understanding of colonialism. The *babu* is a version of Thomas Babington Macaulay's class of interpreters, an Indian man of some education and conversant with English manners and prejudices, but with an inescapably Indian quality that is not repressed or erased by his knowledge of English ways. The *babu* is not a cultural insider, though he might like to be. The "hybrid" character is a common stereotype in other colonial societies, but in the Indian context his particular qualities include effeminacy, over-education, and pedantry. Sinha demonstrates how such an exaggerated notion of Indian masculinity was a product of a variety of structures and practices, including legal reform in British India (e.g., the Ibert Bill, 1883–4, and the Age of Consent Law, 1891), variations in colonial administrative policy and strategy, and native resistance organizations.

Sinha's analysis involves the creation of a detailed history of one particular stereotypical formation. It is by presenting the stereotype in a dense, historical context that she can "complicate either notions of modern Western masculinity or traditional Indian conceptions of masculinity as discrete or mutually exclusive categories by a recognition of their mutual implication in imperial politics" (1995: 8). Like the work of subaltern studies scholars, Sinha's study is as much a history as it is an intervention in historical method. Previous scholarship had treated the stereotype of the effeminate Indian man in some of the ways we have already discussed – as an index of reality, a product of colonial discourse, the colonizer's discursive means of dominating the colonized – but Sinha finds that the stereotype of the *babu* can't exist with the corresponding stereotype of the colonial "manly Englishman." In this case, material analysis of the colonial stereotype reveals that it is only half the stereotype, that the colonizer's character is also shaped and governed through his stereotypes about himself.

Said's application of Foucault's methods have colored the colonial discourse analyses that we have today. Later studies have found parallels of the colonial order described in *Orientalism* across fields as diverse as medicine, political philosophy, and art. However, the finding that colonial discourses are at work in such a wide range of disciplines can lead to a situation where everything is "read" for, and found to have, deeper meanings and connections with colonial or racist ideas. Said's original problem and conclusions become flattened by the fact that it is found everywhere. What was a specific history of the Western practice of researching and writing about "the Arab" and Arabic culture becomes a kind of conspiracy theory that everything said, written, and reproduced in the West is really about controlling the East.

Following Foucault, Said investigates what seems obvious to us and examines how it has been produced as obvious. For example, just as in *Discipline and Punish* (1991[1975] Foucault asks why confinement emerges as the obvious means of punishing the criminal, so Said's study is also animated by a question about something that seems "obvious." He asks why it seems normal that the West studies the East. His answer is that it is normalized by juxtaposition with several factors including, military intelligence gathering as an aspect of conquest, cultural knowledge as a prerequisite of good government and systematization of knowledge as a basic practice of Western science.

Studies that examine the "invisible" links between colonialism and, for example, medicine, painting, or architecture are both highly valuable and necessary, and yet, we must be scrupulously careful not to assume in advance that we know the precise nature or configuration of those links. The discourse analysis method is thought to be a method for examining how knowledge constitutes power (or how power produces knowledge), but more accurately it should function as a radical questioning of the different possible relations between certain forms of power and the various forms of knowledge they give rise to. Rather than assuming that we know how Western forms of knowledge are bound up with the West's colonial history, and looking for examples, we need to look at things that seem normal to us and work backwards in order to understand *how* colonial discourses might have produced this normality.

Though colonial discourse analysis has received its far share of criticism, metadiscursive critique is the most controversial and debated work in postcolonial studies. In part, this reflects the general response to poststructuralist and postmodernist theory in the humanities, from scholars who are sympathetic to its ends as well as those who are not. The linguistic turn has proved just as controversial in its postcolonial form as metadiscursive critique, as it has elsewhere. Subaltern studies scholars write in a recognizable, academic style, but both Bhabha and Spivak are notorious for their dense and sometimes impenetrable texts. Writing in this way does not seem to allow those without access to academic language and institutional power to use such scholarship for contemporary postcolonial struggles.

The point of such language is located in the critiques that each writer offers. For Spivak, as noted above, the unrepresentability of the woman of color is a central concern. If the clear and scientific style expected of academics seems easy to read, then it seems so only because it silently erases what would complicate its patriarchal and racializing narrative and structure. Spivak argues that if her texts seem difficult to understand, or difficult to enter into as a reader, then this is a reflection of the difficulties of locating or positioning herself, or indeed any other woman of color, into

Western philosophy. The text is not meant to be easy, because the "easiness" of the text is itself a symptom of its colonialist ambitions.

In a similar vein, Bhabha's text proves taxing to the reader who wants to understand clearly who did what, when, and to whom. His slippery use of pronouns, agents, and even terms such as "colonizer" or "colonized" (he prefers the term colonial) make it difficult to specify who is the agent in his analyses. Indeed, as some critics have observed, this slipperiness seems to suggest that it is the scholar him- or herself who is the primary agent in all the action described. For Bhabha, the point is that this underlines the irrationality at the heart of the history of colonialism. Rather than trying to tether his analyses to the logic and scientific explanation demanded by Western protocols, he insists, sometimes to the point of apparent incoherence, on the illogical and ambivalent components of colonial histories and discourses.

While one may feel discomfited by such experiments – and it is their intended effect that we should be shocked out of the disciplinary complacency we all develop as we "master" our respective subject – they have a legitimate value. The epistemological considerations that metadiscursive critique forces us to examine should not be deferred until we have, but it is important not to forget that deconstructing texts and concepts is only one modality among others for doing postcolonial critique.

This, finally, brings us to the question of materialist critique that has already proved to be a useful method of keeping postcolonial scholars alert to their own practices. To take just one example, we understand texts thoroughly only when we examine the conditions in which those texts are produced. For Ahmad, postcolonial theory is itself suspect, since it conceals the material circumstances that make certain kinds of Third

World critics and perspectives acceptable and continue to marginalize others. When scholars begin to speak prolifically about concepts such as colonialism or postcolonialism we should be very interested in examining when, how, and why these terms begin to flood the discussion (often, as Ahmad points out, without significant connection to the meaning of the original term).

A second important consideration is that, by examining the intersections of several materialities, as feminist critics have shown, we can understand how aspects of capitalism, racism, colonialism, and patriarchy all combine, collude, and produce realities for subjects that almost always go unmentioned as subjects – women of color. However much discourse analysis and metadiscursive critique attend to the colonial logic that underwrites Western knowledge, if either method does not actively engage with the materially different experience that women have in and of the world, it risks reproducing the patriarchal order of things.

The caveat is that materialist critique cannot and does not work alone. Commentators on postcolonial scholarship have considered the merits of materialist versus discursive critique at length, without reaching any definitive conclusions. Clearly, then, the choice is not between methods, but is a useful synthesis of them. Though Spivak's work was discussed above within the context of metadiscursive critique, it could also be considered a kind of materialist intervention, since it attempts to locate the body of the woman of color – literally and figuratively – in the history and writing of Western knowledge. More concretely, as indicated above, historians have done much of the most interesting and valuable work in the field in the past two decades, and yet their contributions remain relatively neglected when compared with more overtly theoretical work. Work by scholars such as Frederick Cooper, Ann Stoler, Jean and John Comaroff, and Uday Mehta have been building new theoretical paradigms for our understanding of colonialism and postcolonialism out of histories very much grounded in the material.

One of the most pressing questions for practitioners of postcolonial theory is what kind of future it has in a world where it is presumed that European imperialism, at least the formal variety cultivated in the nineteenth and early twentieth centuries, no longer exists. In particular, critics from inside and outside postcolonial studies have wondered if the political, economic, and cultural specificities of globalization have overtaken the need for postcolonial analyses. In their study of the contemporary political scene, Michael Hardt and Antonio Negri (2000) certainly suggest that postcolonial theory has reached the end of its natural life in terms of the response it can make to current political and cultural crises. The level of self-reflection in postcolonial studies, from all three strands of postcolonial theory described, has also tended to work as a kind of braking mechanism so that it has seemed at times that postcolonial studies as a whole were grinding to a halt.

Nevertheless, postcolonial theory is still finding life in new disciplines, such as, for example, critical management studies, where the interdisciplinary encounter may yet prove to be important for developments inside postcolonial theory. Critics of postcolonial studies, as well as postcolonial critics themselves, have long argued that postcolonial theories should be used to intervene more in those areas of life that currently structure Western society. Critical organization and management scholars, especially those interested in questions of organizational culture, have recently proposed that a postcolonial approach might just be the means "to defamiliarize organizational practices and discourses" (Prasad 2003: 32). In such a context, an encounter between postcolonial theory and organization studies seems desirable from both sides. In this interdisciplinary encounter, postcolonial studies is certainly understood to be useful in research on globalization. Critical management studies, in turn, may help postcolonial studies to orient itself more strongly toward the specificities and complexities of the globalized world. Such encounters are important not merely in terms of expanding the reach of postcolonial studies – an ambition that should sit uneasily with its ethos – but in continuing the process of knitting the three strands of postcolonial theory together.

Notwithstanding this, one of the nascent tasks of postcolonial studies is to place current discussions about globalization into a broader perspective. Placing the British model of colonialism that has dominated the field into historical and cultural perspective beside other models of colonialism would help us to assess whether globalization is a "new" phenomenon, what kinds of asymmetric relations of power it engenders, and what kinds of resistance it requires. Within Latin American studies, for example, a related but independent discourse has evolved about the complexities of postcolonial cultures that might be more germane than a purely Anglo-postcolonial model. More comparative approaches to analyses of colonialism, postcolonialism, and neocolonialism will undoubtedly open new avenues for postcolonial theory.

A related area of concern is diaspora studies, which grew out of the realization in the 1980s that immigration had given rise to new populations of ethnic and oftentimes postcolonial "others" within and adjacent to dominant native ethnic groups such as the English and the French. These postcolonial and diasporic juxtapositions afford occasions for intercultural conflict (such as the debates over whether or not traditional religious women's garb is "appropriate" in "modern" societies such as France that make a national ideal of excluding religious ideas and symbols from public life) as well as providing a rich new terrain for cultural expression, with the work of a writer such as Salman Rushdie and a filmmaker such as Gurinder Chada (*Bhaji on the Beach*) being paradigmatic.

Contemporary diasporas are largely postcolonial phenomena. Though the three classical or traditional diasporas – Jewish, Armenian, and Greek – are premodern in their origins, most diasporas were created by empire and capitalism. The first African "slave" diaspora was created by the transatlantic Portuguese, British, French, Dutch, and Spanish empires, and the preconditions for the emergence of most of the other largest diasporas – Indian and South Asian, Chinese, Filipino, Korean, North African – were fashioned by the emergence and eventual decline of the European empires and their unacknowledged American counterpart. In the aftermath of World War II, when labor was needed for the reconstruction of Europe, Afro-Caribbeans began to emigrate to the UK in the late 1940s, followed by South Asian citizens of the British Commonwealth, while North Africans went to France and Turks to Germany. Immigration reform in the US in 1965, and almost simultaneously in Canada and Australia, led to further substantial Latin American and Asian emigrations. As people, money, and ideas crossed the borders of nation-states ever more easily, transnational phenomena became more important and, after 1990, full globalization emerged as the context within which diasporas and related transnational communities developed both as phenomena and as topics of multidisciplinary study. Diaspora studies is the product of these changes.

Two political scientists studied diasporas early on as potentially influential minorities:

John Armstrong (1976) and Gabi Sheffer (1986), but it was only when the diasporic social and cultural formation became a field of study for anthropologists, sociologists, and postcolonial literary critics that the field developed. The emergence of *Diaspora: A Journal of Transnational Studies* in 1991 marks the beginning of multidisciplinary consolidation. The canon of early texts that appear in most contemporary syllabi of diaspora studies include works by the literary critic Khachig Tölölyan (1991; 1996), by the political scientist William Safran (1991), by the historian of anthropology James Clifford (1994), by a founder of cultural studies, Stuart Hall (1993), by the postcolonialist Gayatri Gopinath (1995), and by the sociologist Steven Vertovec (1997). Paul Gilroy's *The Black Atlantic* (1993) and Robin Cohen's *Global Diasporas* (2008[1997]) are the two most commonly taught books. These are often accompanied by some classic articles on transnationalism, most commonly the work of the anthropologist Nina Glick-Schiller and the sociologist Peggy Levitt, both of whom are Caribbeanists, and by important work on globalization, most frequently that of Arjun Appadurai (1990). While even in these texts the definition of diaspora remains contested, certain features recur in all definitions: diasporas are sociocultural formations produced when migrants and ethnics dispersed to many countries resist full assimilation in host societies, retain or produce identity-shaping differences in culture and behavior, and insist on remaining connected to kin across borders (transnationally), whether in other host societies or in the homeland.

A major work of diaspora studies, R. Radhakrishnan's *Diasporic Mediations*, seeks to transform the idea of diaspora. Scholars frequently understand diaspora as the fraught experience of the immigrant moving away from the homeland; Radhakrishnan uses this concept to highlight the dynamic theoretical possibilities of being between. This "in-betweenness" allows for what he calls mediation, or negotiation between theoretical and political approaches that have often been cast as antagonistic. His work undermines, for example, the binary opposition between poststructuralist and "worldly" concerns. Such a method of working with the contradictions of seemingly opposing interests – as opposed to resolving in favor of one or the other – creates what Radhakrishnan calls a "history of the present." In the final and most well-known essay of the book, Radhakrishnan uses this method of critical analysis to re-examine Indian Americans' immigrant experience.

As various disciplines of the social sciences and humanities have become involved in the construction of diaspora studies, a two-tier system has emerged. Many articles and books are written by and for specialists, as, for example, on migration (Cohen & Vertovec 1999), or cultural production (Chow 1993), which become indispensable within a discipline; they also draw from, and contribute to, the supradisciplinary discourse of diaspora studies, which is no longer identified with a single discipline and to which all can contribute, as indicated in the list of canonical work, above. The concepts shaping that discourse are not only diasporas, transnationalism, and globalization, but also postcolonialism, creolization, cosmopolitanism, hybridity, etc. Cultural practices such as the gendered and racialized remaking of collective identity through music, films, and the novel, social phenomena such as accelerated mobility, economic phenomena such as the role of the remittances migrants send to their homelands, and political topics such as the role of organized diasporas in lobbying for homeland development all draw a great deal of attention. The postcolonial moment, in which a neoliberal form of global capitalism is a dominant force, provides conditions for the continuing vigor of diasporas and diaspora studies.

SEE ALSO: Critical Discourse Analysis; Cultural Studies; Feminism; Marxism; Postmodernism; Poststructuralism

REFERENCES AND SUGGESTED READINGS

Ahmad, A. (1992). In *Theory: Classes, Nations, Literatures*. London: Verso.

Appadurai, A. (1990). Disjuncture and difference in the global cultural economy. *Theory, Culture and Society*, 7, 295–310.

Armstrong, J. (1976). Mobilized and proletarian diasporas. *American Political Science Review*, 70(2), 393–408.

Ashcroft, B., with Griffiths, G., & Tiffin, H. (1989). *The Empire Writes Back: Theory and Practice in Post-Colonial Literatures*. London: Routledge.

Bartolovich, C., & Lazarus, N. (2002). *Marxism, Modernity and Postcolonial Studies*. Cambridge: Cambridge University Press.

Bhabha, H. (1994). *The Location of Culture*. London: Routledge.

Césaire, A. (1995). *Discourse on Colonialism*. New York: Monthly Review Press.

Chakrabarty, D. (2000). *Provincializing Europe*. Princeton: Princeton University Press.

Chatterjee, P. (1993). *The Nation and its Fragments: Colonial and Postcolonial Histories*. Princeton: Princeton University Press.

Chow, R. (1993). *Writing Diaspora: Tactics of Intervention in Contemporary Cultural Studies*. Bloomington: Indiana University Press.

Clifford, J. (1994). Diasporas. *Cultural Anthropology*, 9(3), 302–338.

Cohen, R. (2008). *Global Diasporas*, 2nd edn. London: Routledge. (Original work published 1997.)

Cohen, R., & Vertovec, S. (eds.) (1999). *Migration, Diasporas and Transnationalism*. Aldershot: Edward Elgar.

Cohn, B. S. (1996). *Colonialism and its Forms of Knowledge: The British in India*. Princeton: Princeton University Press.

Fanon, F. (1967). *Black Skin, White Masks*. New York: Grove Press. (Original work published 1952.)

Fanon, F. (1968). *The Wretched of the Earth*. New York: Grove Press. (Original work published 1961.)

Foucault, M. (1991). *Discipline and Punish* (trans. A. Sheridan). Harmondsworth: Penguin, 1991. (Original work published 1975.)

Gopinath, G. (1995). Bhangra music and the engendering of the Indian diaspora. *Diaspora*, 4(3), 303–323.

Guha, R. (1997). *Dominance Without Hegemony: History and Power in Colonial India*. Cambridge, MA: Harvard University Press.

Guha, R., & Spivak, G. C. (1988). *Selected Subaltern Studies*. Oxford: Oxford University Press.

Hall, S. (1993). Cultural identity and diaspora. In P. Williams & L. Chrisman (eds.), *Colonial Discourse and Postcolonial Theory: A Reader*. Hemel Hempstead: Harvester Wheatsheaf.

Hardt, M., & Negri, A. (2000). *Empire*. Cambridge, MA: Harvard University Press.

JanMohamed, A. R. (1988). *Manichean Aesthetics: The Politics of Literature in Colonial Africa*, 2nd edn. Amherst: University of Massachusetts Press.

Jayawardena, K. (1995). *The White Woman's Other Burden: Western Women and South Asia During British Rule*. London: Routledge.

Lazarus, N. (1999). *Nationalism and Cultural Practice in the Postcolonial World*. Cambridge: Cambridge University Press.

Lewis, R. (1996). *Gendering Orientalism: Race, Femininity and Representation*. London: Routledge.

Loomba, A., Kaul, S., Bunzl, M., Burton A., & Esty, J. (eds.) (2005). *Postcolonial Studies and Beyond*. Durham, NC: Duke University Press.

Mohanty, C. T. (2003). *Feminism Without Borders: Decolonizing Theory, Practicing Solidarity*. Durham, NC: Duke University Press.

Mrinalini, S. (1995). *Colonial Masculinity: The "Manly Englishman" and the "Effeminate Bengali" in the Late Nineteenth Century*. Manchester: Manchester University Press.

Nandy, A. (1983). *The Intimate Enemy: Loss and Recovery of Self Under Colonialism*. Delhi: Oxford University Press.

Parry, B. (2004). *Postcolonial Studies: A Materialist Critique*. London: Routledge.

Paul Gilroy, P. (1993). *The Black Atlantic: Modernity and Double Consciousness*. Cambridge, MA: Harvard University Press.

Prasad, A. (2003). *Postcolonial Theory and Organizational Analysis: A Critical Engagement*. Basingstoke: Palgrave Macmillan.

Radhakrishnan, R. (1996). *Diasporic Mediations: Between Home and Location*. Minneapolis: University of Minnesota Press.

Safran, W. (1991). Diasporas in modern societies: Myths of homeland and return. *Diaspora*, 1(1), 83–99.

Said, E. (1979). *Orientalism*. London: Vintage. (Original work published 1978.)

Said, E. (1994). *Culture and Imperialism*. London: Vintage.

Sheffer, G. (ed.) (1986). *Modern Diasporas in International Politics*. New York: St Martin's Press.

Spivak, G. C. (1985). Three women's texts and a critique of imperialism. In R. R. Warhol & D. P. Herndl (eds.), *Feminisms*. Basingstoke: Macmillan, pp. 896–912.

Spivak, G. C. (1987). *In Other Worlds: Essays in Cultural Politics*. London: Routledge.

Spivak, G. C. (1999). *A Critique of Postcolonial Reason. Toward a History of the Vanishing Present*. Cambridge, MA: Harvard University Press.

Spurr, D. (1993). *The Rhetoric of Empire: Colonial Discourse in Journalism, Travel Writing, and Imperial Administration*. Durham, NC: Duke University Press.

Stoler, A. L. (1995). *Race and the Education of Desire: Foucault's History of Sexuality and the Colonial Order of Things*. Durham, NC: Duke University Press.

Tölölyan, K. (1991). The nation-state and its others: In lieu of a preface. *Diaspora*, 1(1), 3–7.

Tölölyan, K. (1996). Rethinking diaspora(s): Stateless power in the transnational moment. *Diaspora*, 5(1), 3–36.

Vertovec, S. (1997). Three meanings of "diaspora" exemplified among South Asian religions. *Diaspora*, 6(3), 277–299.

Viswanathan, G. (1989). *Masks of Conquest: Literary Study and British Rule in India*. Oxford: Oxford University Press.

Young, R. (2001). *Postcolonialism: An Historical Introduction*. Oxford: Blackwell.

Poststructuralism

CLAIRE COLEBROOK

Poststructuralism is a mode of theory in which the necessary dependence of thinking on systems of difference – such as language – is deemed to preclude any capacity to grasp a single foundation of determining origin. Unlike postmodernism, with which it is often aligned, confused, or contrasted, poststructuralism can be given two quite specific senses: chronological and logical.

Chronologically, the term refers to a number of writers, usually but not exclusively French, whose work occurs after the dominance of structuralism as an intellectual movement. Structuralism was associated with the Swiss linguist Ferdinand de Saussure's claim that a language is produced from differences without positive terms, and with the French anthropologist Claude Lévi-Strauss's argument that cultures depend upon founding differences (through myths) that vary in detail from culture to culture but are universal in their form – with the opposition between nature and culture itself always being coded or structured through certain myths and terms. There were other structuralist thinkers in other domains, such as literary criticism, Marxism, and psychoanalysis, but either these thinkers were indebted to Saussure and Lévi-Strauss or they pushed structuralism to the point at which it became poststructuralism. (The semiotician, or theorist of signs, Roland Barthes, used Marxist, structuralist, and poststructuralist motifs in his thought.) As we will see with the three critiques of structuralism undertaken by poststructuralism's key figures, poststructuralism is a radicalization of structuralism rather than its denial. First, poststructuralists argued against structuralism's closure (or the idea that one could isolate systems and study them as objects); second, they also rejected structuralism's "synchrony," or its freezing of relations and systems in time, rather than recognizing the dynamism and instability of systems; finally, structuralism tended to focus on a single determining system (such as language, culture, myth, or norms) whereas poststructuralists acknowledged a "textuality" or "difference" that could neither be identified with a single system, nor reduced to explicit and readable social structures.

The "post" of poststructuralism is therefore chronological (after structuralism) and logical (as an extension or realization of structuralism) at the same time. Saussure's claim that a language is a system of differences without positive terms leads to a new mode of reading and defining; at the level of definitions words are meaningful not because they establish a link to some direct sense, but because they are distinguished from other terms. This works at the level of language's material aspects, where an alphabet has so many characters and a language has so many sounds, and language's ideal aspects: one of the familiar demonstrations of structuralism was to show that some languages have certain distinctions that others do not. The Germans have two words for experience, *Erlebnis* and *Erfahrung*, while the French use the same verb – *aimer* – for liking and loving, suggesting that the structure of the language is also a structure of understanding. In his anthropology Claude Lévi-Strauss also employed a differential methodology which, like Saussure's linguistics, placed less emphasis on diachrony and genesis (or the emergence and passage of systems through time) and more on synchrony and structure (or the relations among terms, that were similar from one culture to another). For Saussure, one studies a language by examining its differences and relations and not the lineage of its terms (etymology); for Lévi-Strauss, myths are elucidated not by looking at distinct terms, figures, or characters, but by differential relations. Each myth would mark a distinction between pure and impure, good and evil, autochthonous and exogenous. In literary or narrative terms, this means that one would consider the relations between figures – heroes and villains, desired objects and averted disasters,

natural orders and catastrophic intrusions – rather than, say, the history of a single type. One would compare structures of good and evil across myths and narratives, rather than write about the meaning or history of a single figure. In poetry, one would not refer a text either to its author's intention, or to a referent outside the text, or to the reader's experience, but to relations of terms. The American Marxist Fredric Jameson, despite his poststructuralist variation of this commitment, nevertheless insisted that one should begin analysis of narrative, including contemporary novels, as structurations of social oppositions: so the relationship between Heathcliff and Edgar Linton in *Wuthering Heights* is both a binary between good and evil and also a way of thinking through the opposition between capitalism and landed aristocracy (Jameson 1981). William Blake's poem "The sick rose" would not be interpreted historically (as a poem about Christian and rationalist contempt for the body) or contextually (as a reference to the author's life or milieu), or semantically (as a meditation on corruption). Instead, each term of the poem creates an opposition or relation, a closed structure with no reference to an outside world other than that constituted by the poem (Riffaterre 1978).

The most important maneuver that marked poststructuralism from structuralism was the renewal of the problem of genesis, which was not used to negate structuralist insights so much as to complicate and enrich them. Poststructuralists accepted that no term in a system could have sense or identity without reference to the system as a whole; this applied to language – where a word has sense as part of a structure of differences – as much as to popular culture (where markers of style, wealth, and taste are always relative to each other). The differential nature of a system, or the fact that no identity can be determined without its relation to a system of identities, opened up two problems for traditional questions of genesis. How would it be possible to account for the genesis of structures if we are always already within a structure? If our understanding, our culture, our language, our logic, and even our sense of self are all given through the way in which our specific sociohistorical milieu structures reality through signs (including non-linguistic signs such as myths, conventions, and coded gestures), then how can we account for the emergence of structure as such? We could never be in some neutral structure-free position from which to analyze structures. The first problem of genesis and structure is therefore the limit of structure. Structuralism had seemed to offer a scientific way for thinking about traditionally nonscientific systems (such as literature, myth, fashion, gender, and norms); one could look at seemingly natural identities – such as the relation between men and women – and regard these as effects of social systems. There would be nothing intrinsically feminine about clearly trivial markers such as the color pink, skirts, lipstick, and handbags, which would only have sense in a world differentiating men from women through clothes and colors; there would also be nothing intrinsically feminine about emotions, irrationality, nurturing, or passivity. Such identities, including one's self-identity, would be effected through differential and socially coded relations. One would not be born female and, as a consequence, dress and act in a certain manner; in the beginning would be the social relations through which bodies act, dress, and speak. Only after that mode of social performance would one then assume that one was (or had been) "naturally" female. The self does not pre-exist its structural determination.

This would seem to allow for a scientific analysis of social relations. Such was implied by Louis Althusser's Marxism. Ideology, Althusser argued, was not some illusion or false belief that distorted our natural understanding and self-identity. On the contrary, ideology is a constitutive structure that grants each term – each body and event – an identity; it is not the case that capitalism exploits individuals, and then requires ideology to deceive those same individuals regarding their true interests. Ideology produces individuals through what Althusser refers to as "interpellation," which hails individuals as subjects. The self is created through being addressed. This can occur through advertising, which addresses you directly as one who wants certain things because of who you are: "How can you be sure your children will be cared for after your death?" "How can you regain that youthful glow that made him fall in love with you all those years ago?" "We can show you how to achieve your maximum potential and uncover the truly inventive, enterprising, and successful you." It also occurs more obliquely through art, where readers are addressed as fellow humans with assumed empathies and desires, and more explicitly through the legal order. Althusser's cited example was of an individual being addressed by a policeman. If I turn around (or run) when a policemen calls out "Hey you!" then I am placing myself as an individual within a system of guilt and law. Pornography, romance novels, news broadcasts, greetings cards, and department store displays all address "us," creating us as individuals. But interpellation occurs less obviously in all those aspects of a culture that presuppose a viewing or receiving point of view. If I am driving along a highway and I pass a billboard displaying a young woman in a push-up bra, a car with a red iridescent exterior, a two-story bricked home in a garden, or a happy silver-haired couple walking along a sunset beach, then I am being variously situated as a desiring heterosexual man (or desiring identifying woman), an aspiring homeowner, or a hopeful near retiree. To analyze such images, I need only look at the way in which individuals are produced as subjects who desire commodities. Ideology, for Althusser, and many of the poststructuralists who followed him, was therefore a constitutive structure: images, language, and culture were not simply added on to economic reality but were structurally determining of the sociopolitical whole.

For Althusser, this enabled a scientific form of Marxism. There could be no social or political position outside ideology (no privileged point of view of the subjected working class), but there could be a scientific analysis of the economic and ideological structures as a whole. In a similar manner, Claude Lévi-Strauss had insisted that his anthropology, which would examine structures and not their meaning or value, would be free of metaphysics and would place the anthropologist in the position of a mere "bricoleur," or purveyor of parts. Structuralism could claim to be a science because it had freed itself from commitment to a privileged origin or originary meaning. Althusser insisted that his Marxism did not presuppose a subject whose fulfillment would provide the norm and end of history; history was "without a subject," and the subject could be demonstrated to be an effect of structures.

Poststructuralism accepted the constitutive power of structures, but also refused any possibility of a scientific detachment that would enable a break or distance from structure. In many ways, the different criticisms of structuralism's refusal of genesis mark out the different poststructuralist projects. We can say that poststructuralism was unified by the political and logical problem of genesis, but varied in its mode of response. Politically, the problem of structure and genesis came to the fore in the May 1968 student uprisings that occurred in Paris and

that were matched by similar radicalizations of the university system across the globe. If one accepts the premises of traditional Marxism then it is working-class people – because they work directly with material labor – who possess a privileged point of view; only they can become aware of the crucial role of production in the creation of the social whole. When the student uprisings began in May 1968, the French Communist Party failed to support the potentially revolutionary events because it deemed the students to be an intellectual class, incapable of grasping the true nature of human concrete labor and its basis for all economic relations. If, however, one accepts Althusser's claim that ideology and culture are not merely effects of the economy but are crucial to the structure of relations that makes economic exploitation possible – by producing individuals who understand themselves to be free "workers" – then one can begin to see intellectual or cultural disruption as at least as important as material revolt.

Poststructuralism could also be said to open a new mode of politics. One can no longer begin from a polity – a group of individuals – for it is precisely the production of individuals, and their understanding or image of their own political being, that is an effect of structuration. This has a series of consequences and critical implications that can, without too much violence, be explained through five key gestures, each one of which we might associate with a major poststructuralist thinker. First, there can no longer be a truth attained by stepping outside structure; such an external position would be illusory and would merely continue what Jacques Derrida (1978) referred to as the metaphysics of presence, or the ideal of grasping truth itself, before and beyond all relations. Second, despite the inability to gain a position of unified coherence that would be distinct from the relations and instabilities of structures, there is nevertheless a lived or imagined unity, a mythic subject, posited as the illusory foundation of structures. Jacques Lacan (2002) was at once a structuralist committed to the idea that, insofar as we speak, we are always already located within systems to which we are subjected (the symbolic order); but he also maintained that we live our relation to the symbolic in an imaginary register, primarily because we misrecognize ourselves as unified beings, as egos with a self-identity and wholeness akin to the organic unity of our bodies. Third, this acceptance of a form of poststructuralist psychoanalysis – that we cannot live our structuration – gave a new force to feminist criticism, for it would no longer be assumed that there were real prelinguistic sexed individuals who were then subjected to the illusions of gender ideology. On the contrary, in the beginning are the forces and relations of bodies *from which* we imagine that there must have been some originally sexed foundation. For Judith Butler (1990), this meant that one could no longer maintain the distinction between a sexed biological reality and a gendered or constructed ideology; for the very idea of an underlying sexual reality is an effect of the ways in which we speak, act, and relate to each other. For Luce Irigaray (1985), matters were more complex still, and poststructuralism entailed an even more audacious mode of feminist critique. One would not just say, as Judith Butler and other poststructuralist feminists would do, that there can be no pure material "outside" the gender system, for "we" are always already installed within gender. The very idea of a mute and passive reality that requires the structuring or differentiation of a symbolic system was itself highly sexed. The "imaginary" of the autonomous individual who represents an otherwise silent material world to himself must repress what for Irigaray is the inaugurating

sexual relation. In the beginning is neither a mind that constructs its world, nor a matter to be represented, but a relation between two subjects whose relation to each other is not symmetrical. By understanding the world as a blank slate upon which the subject imposes its order, we imagine only one sex (the masculine) rather than a relation, and relations – for Irigaray and poststructuralism in general – are far more difficult to conceptualize precisely because they cannot be imagined as self-sufficient and stable unities.

Fourth, if stable terms are the effect of relations, and if there is no single substance that would provide the foundation for relations – if we cannot think of relations as relations *of matter* because matter is itself an effect of forces – then this leaves theory with a great task. Is it possible to liberate thought from the imaginary of foundations, individuals, and origins? Derrida suggested that any attempt to think outside the metaphysics of presence – such as a pure materialism, or even a structuralism that affirmed systems of difference – would necessarily install one more foundation, such as matter or system. He referred to the task of thinking the limit of metaphysics as a necessary impossibility: we cannot simply remain within systems, for, insofar as we use concepts and make truth claims, we are already intimating that which lies beyond the closure of any single context or system; yet any thought of that beyond is impossible without being contaminated by some determining system. By contrast, Gilles Deleuze (1994) accepted that difference was *the* concept for philosophers to create anew *and* that a proper thought of difference – one liberated from any ultimate or "transcendent" being – would have direct political consequences. Deleuze, together with Félix Guattari (1977), wrote a genealogy of late twentieth-century capitalism in order to find a space for thinking beyond the structuralist and psychoanalytic predicament of the subject: how is it that a being was formed – "man" – who imagined himself to be the foundation of all language and systems and yet who also imagined that he could not think or live outside these systems of his own making? How did "we" come to form ourselves as self-subjecting beings who willingly enslave ourselves to capitalism and its impoverished images of familial desire? For Deleuze and Guattari, the answer to this problem lies in the *essence* of capitalism. Capitalism as a social form is possible, not because it imposes a system of exchange on an otherwise coherent and self-sufficient life, but because life is nothing other than relations among powers. Capitalism in the narrow sense – the relations of individuals mediated by a system of money that quantifies labor and production – is only possible because of a deeper, original, and irreducible force of life that is an entering into relation of forces. If we can refer to something like matter, it is not as some stable ground but as that which is formed through forces and encounters. Capitalism is both a release from earlier social forms that had subjected relations to an external power (such as a despot or monarch) and also an intensification of subjection by subsuming *all* relations beneath the axiom of capital; even pleasure, leisure, and resistance are now commodities, for we purchase pornography, buy holidays and entertainment, and spend money on "green," "feminist," "fairtrade," or "ethical" products and magazines.

Fifth, and finally, this raises the important question regarding theory and the future. One could accept that there is no position outside differential structures and systems, no life in itself that might offer itself as a foundation or lever for resistance. If this were so, then one would need to consider theory, philosophy, and criticism as acts of immanent creation. Michel Foucault (1972) argued that Western thought had always taken the form of an ethic of knowledge, aiming to ground what one ought to do on some criteria other than action itself. He criticized twentieth-century intellectual movements, such as structuralism and phenomenology, for recognizing that thought is always finite because it is determined by inhuman systems, and yet producing "man" as the being who knows himself through these forces of finitude. "Life" (as the logic of the biological sciences), "labor" (as the rationale that explains capital), and "language" (as disclosed by theories of grammar) are the three concepts used by Foucault to explain "man's" understanding of himself as an effect of determining systems. Foucault suggested that it was language, in the nineteenth century, that had been varied and had demonstrated a force that was beyond that of man as a living functional being. (Poetry, after all, does not serve the logic of life and production.) It was not by stepping outside structures and systems that one could create new modes of thought, but by disturbing systems from within. Although his work differed from that of Foucault, Derrida was also critical of any attempt to exit systems of determination and think "life" beyond metaphysics. Derrida (1978) criticized Foucault's project of genealogy whereby one might think the different ways in which reason had precluded any thought of that which is outside recognition; *any history*, Derrida insisted, would have to deploy the very forces of recognition (such as concepts and identities) that are integral to reason and mastery. If Foucault thought the adequate response to our always-located position within structures was a mode of experimentation, Derrida (1994) suggested that such disturbances or solicitations of system could nevertheless operate with concepts of justice, democracy,

and the future, even if no adequate fulfillment of such concepts could ever arrive.

One might say, then, that the most important implication of poststructuralism
was the impossibility of thinking "life itself"
or any ground or foundation outside
structuration. And yet, many writers of
the twenty-first century have taken poststructuralism in the direction of an exit
from determined systems and have done
so in the name of immanence. It is possible
to argue that this constitutes a *post*-post-
structuralism: there has been a "return" to
life, affect, and matter that sets itself apart
from the idea that we only know and live the
world through systems. Michael Hardt and
Antonio Negri (2009), despite their quotation of writers like Deleuze and Foucault,
insist that it is possible for "living labor" or
the multitude of material bodies to liberate
themselves from transcendent systems and
constitute relations from, and for, themselves. Giorgio Agamben (1998) has also
criticized what he saw to be Derrida's
deconstruction's focus on "text" or systems
of relations, and has suggested that what
needs to be thought, *practically*, is the emergence of relations from life. Many writers,
considering themselves to have been influenced by Deleuze and Guattari, have turned
to a politics of "affect," arguing that bodies –
not languages or structures – are the locus of
political relations (Massumi 2002; De
Landa 2002). On the one hand this seems
to mark a "realist" turn away from a seeming
idealism that was a possible effect of poststructuralism: if structuralism argues that
the world is ordered through systems such
as language, then poststructuralism suggests
that there can be no world in itself, prior to
systems, because the world is always already
differential. On the other hand, one could
argue that such a reading of poststructuralism is mistaken, for poststructuralism challenges the notion that there is "a" mind or

"a" system of ideas that precedes the world;
the world is nothing other than relations of
forces, with words such as "real," "ideal," or
"material" being effects of the systems that
stabilize the world into some knowable order. Such words cannot explain order.

It is possible to take any of the major
poststructuralist thinkers – Foucault,
Deleuze, Lacan, Derrida, Deleuze, Irigaray,
Lyotard – and read them as bearing a close,
almost indiscernible, relation to structuralism. They would have done nothing more
than accept the claim that thought always
takes place from within systems, and would
have gone on to look at the different ways in
which such systems might be disturbed
from within. But it is also possible to read
this same series of thinkers as operating with
the question of how thought might open
itself up to the "outside." This "outside"
would not be the exterior – would not be
"matter," "reality," "life," or any of the other
terms that have always described the proper
locus to which thought ought to be directed.
The "outside" is, rather, the process or event
that produces the border between inside and
outside. Derrida referred to this, variously,
as "text," "writing," "difference," and trace:
a process known after the event, in its effects,
that creates the relations from which knowledge proceeds but which itself cannot be
known. It was this question that Jean-
François Lyotard (1991) used to describe
the postmodern. For Lyotard, postmodernism was not, as it is often understood to be,
an acceptance that there is no truth, no
reality and nothing but differential systems;
rather, the postmodern was a different experience of time and historical periods.
There can be no narrative of all narratives
(no "metanarrative" such as Marxism, enlightenment, humanism, or even evolutionary progressivism) or, as Paul de Man argued (1971), any theory of narrative is itself
a narrative, producing a before and after, a

subject of knowledge and a final state of discovery. But knowing that we can no longer be modern, that we can no longer imagine ourselves to be masters of our own systems, is no act of final enlightenment so much as an ongoing declaration of guerilla warfare on any position of finality, confidence, authority, and certainty. What we are left with is not the human being as a linguistic animal who fashions his own world, but a confrontation with the inhuman, with forces, differences, relations, grammars, systems, and programs that produce and destroy us beyond our ken.

Such issues have more than academic import. One of the key dates of poststructuralism (marking not only a point after structuralism but also after the disenchantment with organized philosophical systems such as structuralism, Marxism, phenomenology, and psychoanalysis) was May 1968, the student uprisings that were not prompted by grand narratives – such as Marxist predictions of a properly communist revolution – but by local resistance. If it is the case, as structuralism had argued, that distinct terms are the effects of systems of relations, then there can be no position – no scientific point of view – that is not itself an effect of structure. This inability to establish a ground or point of view might at once appear to be a cause of despair or even an "end" of all theory. At the same time, this structural determination of all terms that precludes scientific observation opens up a far more general problem of the contamination of any identity with non-identity. In the absence of a governing identity or given norm, one can begin to theorize.

SEE ALSO: Althusser, Louis; Butler, Judith; Deleuze, Gilles; Derrida, Jacques; Foucault, Michel; Irigaray, Luce; Jameson, Fredric; Lyotard, Jean-François; Marxism; Negri, Antonio and Hardt, Michael; Saussure, Ferdinand de

REFERENCES AND SUGGESTED READINGS

Agamben, G. (1998). *Homo Sacer: Sovereign Power and Bare Life* (trans. D. Heller-Roazen). Stanford: Stanford University Press.

Althusser, L. (1971). *Lenin and Philosophy and Other Essays* (trans. B. Brewster). New York: Monthly Review Press.

Butler, J. (1990). *Gender Trouble: Feminism and the Subversion of Identity*. New York: Routledge.

Colebrook, C. (2002). *Gilles Deleuze*. London: Routledge.

Colebrook, C. (2005). *Philosophy and Poststructuralist Theory: From Kant to Deleuze*. Edinburgh: Edinburgh University Press.

Deleuze, G. (1994). *Difference and Repetition* (trans. Paul Patton). London: Athlone.

Deleuze, G., & Guattari, F. (1977). *Anti-Oedipus: Capitalism and Schizophrenia* (trans. R. Hurley, M. Seem, & H. R. Lane). New York: Viking Press. (Original work published 1972.)

Derrida, J. (1978). *Writing and Difference* (trans. Alan Bass) Chicago: University of Chicago Press. (Original work published 1967.)

Derrida, J. (1994). *Specters of Marx: The State of the Debt, the Work of Mourning, and the New international* (trans. P. Kamuf). New York: Routledge. (Original work published 1993.)

Foucault, M. (1970). *The Order of Things: An Archaeology of the Human Sciences* (trans. A. Sheridan). London: Tavistock. (Original work published 1966.)

Foucault, M. (1972). *The Archaeology of Knowledge* (trans. A. Sheridan). London: Tavistock. (Original work published 1969.)

Grosz, E. (1989). *Sexual Subversions: Three French Feminists*. Sydney: Allen and Unwin.

Grosz, E. (1990). *Jacques Lacan: A Feminist Introduction*. London: Routledge.

Hardt, M., & Negri, A. (2009). *Commonwealth*. Cambridge, MA: Harvard University Press.

Irigaray, L. (1985). *This Sex Which Is Not One* (trans. C. Porter). Ithaca: Cornell University Press. (Original work published 1977.)

Jameson, F. (1981). *The Political Unconscious: Narrative as a Socially Symbolic Act*. Ithaca: Cornell University Press.

Lacan, J. (2006). *Écrits* (trans. B. Fink). New York: Norton. (Original work published 1966.)

De Landa, M. (2002). *Intensive Science and Virtual Philosophy*. London: Continuum.

Lévi-Strauss, C. (1963). *Structural Anthropology* (trans. C. Jacobson & B. G. Schoepf). New York: Basic Books. (Original work published 1958.)

Lucy, N. (1997). *Postmodern Literary Theory: An Introduction*. Oxford: Blackwell.

Lyotard, J.-F. (1991). *The Inhuman: Reflections on Time* (trans. G. Bennington & R. Bowlby). Stanford: Stanford University Press. (Original work published 1988.)

de Man, P. (1971). *Blindness and Insight: Essays in the Rhetoric of Contemporary Criticism*. New York: Oxford University Press.

Massumi, B. (2002). *Parables for the Virtual: Movement, Affect, Sensation*. Durham, NC: Duke University Press.

Mills, S. (2003). *Michel Foucault*. London: Routledge.

Riffaterre, M. (1978). *Semiotics of Poetry*. Bloomington: Indiana University Press.

Royle, N. (2003). *Jacques Derrida*. London: Routledge.

Saussure, F. de. (2006). *Writings in General Linguistics* (trans. C. Sanders & M. Pires). Oxford: Oxford University Press.

Sturrock, J. (ed.) (1979). *Structuralism and Since: From Levi Strauss to Derrida*. Oxford: Oxford University Press.

Williams, J. (2005). *Understanding Poststructuralism*. Chesham: Acumen.

Presentism

MARK ROBSON

Presentism as a practice has emerged from literary critical forms of historicism. Where historicism primarily stresses the connections between a literary text and the moment and context of its original production, presentism instead emphasizes the moment of reading, production, or performance in a broad sense. Skeptical about the claims for the precedence of an original version of a text, or an original moment determinative of its meaning in a decisive fashion, presentism refuses to privilege one instantiation of a text over another, instead emphasizing its pertinence at the moment in which the critic writes. While there may be the appearance of antagonism here, historicism and presentism are best thought of as rival forms of contextual criticism, and there is no simple opposition between them.

The context for the emergence of presentism itself is the dominance of new historicism and cultural materialism within early modern studies in English literary criticism, especially Shakespeare studies. Both new historicism and cultural materialism place emphasis on the political and social conditions of the moment of production. Literary texts are related to the broader modes of organization that characterize a society and thus artworks absorb the values of that culture in the same way that other objects do. There is thus no special status accorded to art objects or to the practices by which they are produced or consumed. Nonetheless, there are also possibilities for art to resist the orthodox cultural values that they absorb, and for that resistance to be readable in the work itself. Cultural materialism, in particular, also wants to make clear the ways in which literary and other artworks are used in the present for political ends.

The clearest elaboration of presentism is that given by Terence Hawkes (2002). Explicitly seeking to distance himself from forms of historicism that seek to recreate, recover, or restore the conditions of production for Shakespeare's texts, Hawkes suggests that even to claim to have identified the facts about an earlier period is misleading. To that extent, any identification of context must always be provisional, unstable, and irreducibly subjective. Facts, like texts, do not speak for themselves, suggests Hawkes, since they are always identified or selected by a critic for a particular purpose and placed within a specific narrative. This means that there is no possibility of direct access to those facts, since they have always been gathered for a purpose that serves to mediate those facts. As such, a text or a fact is always in need of interpretation and has always already been placed within an interpretation. There is no suggestion that such mediation could ever be avoided or that the need for interpretation might be diminished. For Hawkes, presentism is simply a way of being explicit about what that interpretation is, what purposes a text is being read for, and consequently what position the critic speaks from.

Hawkes's readings of Shakespeare are thus as likely to talk about devolution in the UK in the late 1990s as they are to discuss questions of national identity and sovereignty in the 1590s. The position adopted here has clear affinities with a historical materialist position in which any possibility of forgetting the course of history after the moment of a text's production is ruled out as at best naive and at worst politically suspect. The idea of seeing history "as it really was" – as the nineteenth-century German historian Leopold von Ranke, considered to be one of the founders of the modern school of history, famously suggested – is rejected in favor of a recognition of how history has been constructed for present purposes.

What emerges from this is a sense of literary texts, including drama, as ultimately performative. That is, their meaning and effect cannot be located within a moment conceived of as somehow finished or completed. Instead, presentism stresses the extent to which such texts continue to perform and to be performed, beyond reference to a world within which they were produced.

What this leads to is a sense of audience that is always necessarily in the present of any given performative moment.

Yet in the end, this presentist project appears to be a reformation and reinvigoration of cultural materialism rather than a "new" critical mode as such. Its emergence parallels and resists the retreat of new historicism into older forms of historicism; its emphasis on a form of historical understanding akin to that found in historical materialism counters a "new materialism" that eschews theoretical investigations of the situatedness of the critic while proclaiming a disinterested objectivity that manifests itself in a concern for the objects rather than the subjects of history. Presentism is thus fundamentally reactive and corrective, while also seeking to intervene in debates outside the confines of the academy. Its primary performative force remains rooted in literary critical dialogue. In these respects, its aims are close to those of the new aestheticism, which similarly seeks to make apparent the political stakes of the aesthetic in both past and present rather than seeing the aesthetic as a realm of timeless, universal values. It is too early to tell whether presentism will – or should – retain any critical urgency beyond the current critical context, that is, beyond the present.

SEE ALSO: New Historicism; White, Hayden

REFERENCES AND SUGGESTED READINGS

Dollimore, J., & Sinfield, A. (eds.) (1994). *Political Shakespeare: Essays in Cultural Materialism*, 2nd edn. Manchester: Manchester University Press.
Fernie, E. (2005). Shakespeare and the prospect of presentism. *Shakespeare Survey*, 58, 169–184.
Grady, H., & Hawkes, T. (eds.) (2007). *Shakespeare and Presentism*. London: Routledge.
Hawkes, T. (2002). *Shakespeare in the Present*. London: Routledge.

Joughin, J. J., & Malpas, S. (eds.) (2003). *The New Aestheticism*. Manchester: Manchester University Press.

Pechter, E. (2003). What's wrong with literature? *Textual Practice*, 17, 505–526.

Psychoanalysis (since 1966)

GERALD MOORE

Sigmund Freud (1856–1939) developed psychoanalysis around a predominantly biological model of the drives of the human organism, and his desire to see it recognized as a medical science saw him steer clear of philosophical discourse. Psychoanalysis also made its mark primarily as a science of "family romance," the Oedipus complex of incestuous desire, and as such, arguably, had little to do with the public sphere of politics. A number of events occurring in and around the 1960s meant that this theoretical framework began to change. Critics internal and external to the psychoanalytic movement began to cast aspersions on both the scientific bases of psychoanalysis and on what Michel Foucault has called the "Victorian," or conventional and conservative, nature of Freudian sexual morality. Assailed, on the one hand, by the emergent fields of the cognitive and social sciences and, on the other, by attempts to wed it to the sexual, political, and philosophical revolutions of the age, the orthodox Freudianism of the International Psychoanalytical Association (IPA) became increasingly sidelined, riven by internal politics. Having survived the onslaughts of both Nazism and fascism, with their respective accusations of its being a "Jewish" and a "bourgeois" science, psychoanalysis has, ironically, gone on to suffer from the scientific and social sexual awakenings it helped to bring about.

What the analyst Erich Fromm described in 1971 as "the crisis of psychoanalysis" has been compounded by the growing impression that the would-be science of the unconscious is itself "Oedipal," more dependent on charismatic father figures like Freud, Carl Jung, and Jacques Lacan than on any independently verifiable scientific ground or body of evidence. Doubts over the legitimacy of Freud's scientific method reflect both clinical concerns over the therapeutic success of the famous "talking cure" and evidence that he may have falsified the case reports from which the treatment was developed. As a result, particularly in the United States, this has led to the development of alternative psychological approaches, including cognitive behavioral therapy (CBT), which aspire to ground the treatment of mental illnesses in an understanding of the brain (rather than the unconscious or psyche) as a physico-chemical system with scientifically ascertainable malfunctions. The added factor of increasingly popular pharmaceutical options has led to calls, exemplified by Dufresne (2003) and Mayer et al. (2005), for psychoanalysis to be forcibly consigned to the past.

At the other end of the spectrum, more closely associated with literary and hermeneutical approaches to the unconscious, psychoanalytical theorists have sought to make a virtue of necessity. Emphasizing that the unconscious is not an entity that can be scientifically measured, but more an incoherent text whose depth exceeds rigid diagnoses, they argue that psychoanalysis's perceived structural weakness is precisely what makes it preferable. For example, prominent analysts like the Lacanian Elisabeth Roudinesco (2002) have criticized the current vogue for treating symptoms unilaterally as signs of depression, which serves reductively to group a whole range of symptoms under a vague and totalizing catch-all notion of illness. Often attributed, on the one hand, to the growing costs of health provision, which has deprioritized expensive psychoanalysis, and, on the other, to the increasing role of pharmaceutical corporations in the funding of scientific research, these new therapies, psychoanalysts argue, fail to treat the singularity of individual patients' problems. Such concerns have ensured that psychoanalysis retains some support. On account of the prominent role of theoretical psychoanalysis in popular "French theory," whose representatives have proffered a number of generally friendly criticisms of Freud and his legacy, psychoanalysis has even undergone something of a theoretical revival in US departments of comparative literature. As a clinical practice, however, it is, with some exceptions, now in seemingly irreversible decline.

In the US and Northern Europe, the path of this decline was already established by the mid-1960s, with Freudian psychoanalysis rapidly falling out of favor amidst the proliferation of alternative methodologies. Foremost amongst these, the cognitive and behavioral psychology pioneered by Albert Ellis and A. T. Beck were defined by their commitment to empirically verifiable scientific analysis and experimentation, which would avoid the risk of becoming wedded to founding figures of paternal authority. Rejecting the psychoanalytic treatment of the "talking cure," which they saw as overly reliant on the purely *intellectual* dissolution of symptoms through the analysis of patients' (analysands') speech, proponents of CBT use empirical and statistical observation as a basis for encouraging patients to exert more active control over their emotional responses. Distancing themselves from the seemingly all-powerful agency of the unconscious in Freud and, later, Lacan, they also prefer the less mysterious, less intimidating concept of a "subconscious" to define the stratum of nonconscious activity that we do not experience clearly.

Similar emphases on the limits of analysis meant that even those who stayed closer to the basic ideas of Freud ended up diverging irreparably. The Viennese-born Chicagoan analyst, Heinz Kohut, sought to reorientate Freudianism to account for the apparently increasing prevalence of narcissism, the pathological attachment to (material) objects he saw as symptomatic of the low self-esteem brought on by a post-Fordist, consumerist society. Kohut's theory of self-psychology emphasized people's ability rationally to train and develop their own "sense of self." He went on to call for the dissolution of traditional psychoanalysis, before being expelled from the IPA in the 1970s.

While America moved away from psychoanalysis, in France, by contrast, and most notably in and around the events of May 1968, a cooptation of the unconscious by radical Marxism and philosophy led to an unprecedented wave of activity and creativity on the borders of the psychoanalytic movement. Under the influence of Jacques Lacan, as well as theorists like Jacques Derrida, Félix Guattari, and Julia Kristeva, the evolution of psychoanalysis became bound up with those of structuralism and, subsequently, poststructuralism. The vast scope of these broad intellectual movements affirmed room and even the need for both scientific and literary, or hermeneutical, approaches to the study of the unconscious.

JACQUES LACAN, ÉCRITS, AND 1966

The stakes of a changing society, the internal politics of charisma, and the scientific bases of analysis all come together in the exemplary case of Jacques Lacan, the Parisian psychiatrist whose self-declared "return to Freud" became a constant thorn in the side of the psychoanalytic establishment. Between the late 1940s and 1970s, armed with the latest structuralist theories of language, Lacan embarked upon a revolutionary shifting of emphasis away from biology and biological drives toward the idea of an essentially *social* unconscious, created through networks of signification and linguistic exchange. This move away from the private sphere of the (Oedipal) family toward an understanding of the unconscious as a product of language saw psychoanalysis become more of a social science in the process. The effect was to open up a gap between orthodox psychoanalytic theory and a discourse of the unconscious increasingly at odds with its orthodox clinical practice.

Lacan secured his reputation on the basis of intermittent conference papers and a yearly seminar series, held in Paris from 1951, publishing almost nothing until the collection of articles and papers brought together in *Écrits* in 1966. By this time, however, he had already created several ruptures within the international psychoanalytic community, particularly over questions of psychoanalytic practice and the training of new analysts. The result was his enforced departure from the IPA, the global governing body set up by Freud, and his foundation in 1963 of a new institution, the École Freudienne de Paris. If Lacan was decisive, it is thus not so much because of his impact on the analytic community. Except in France and, later, in South America, where its technical complexity enabled his work to escape heavy state censorship, this community quickly disowned and largely ignored him. Lacan was decisive, rather, because his theoretical (as opposed to practical) analysis transformed the rest of the human and social sciences, including philosophy.

Heavily influenced by the structuralist anthropology of Claude Lévi-Strauss, who analyzed the myths of archaic societies as the symptoms of a social or "symbolic"

unconscious (1987[1950]), Lacan diverged from Freud's vision of the unconscious as a repository of incompatible sexual urges internal to the individual. Following Lévi-Strauss's idea that society is organized around unconscious structures of symbolic exchange, Lacan argued that both subjectivity (the ego) and the unconscious are produced through language, with which we are determined not by intrinsic properties of consciousness, but by the way our speech is returned to us from what he calls the big Other (*Autre*) of the unconscious symbolic order. Freud's talking cure succeeds because the unconscious is structured in the same way as language, with its symptoms therefore resolvable in language. This concept of symbolic exchange was also central to the most hotly disputed element of Lacan's analytic practice, namely his insistence on variable-length sessions with the patient, often lasting as little as five minutes, which was the ultimate cause of Lacan's expulsion from the IPA. In direct opposition to US self-psychologists and what would later become CBT, Lacan argued that the task of psychoanalysis should be to disabuse the individual of the notion that identity is in any way prior to our interactions with others. Bringing an unexpected end to sessions would theoretically achieve this by "punctuating" the patient's speech, reminding them that the unconscious is outside and in excess of individual control.

By the time *Écrits* appeared in print, Lacan's teachings had already evolved, placing more emphasis on what he called the "Real," the crucial point at which structures are undone by an excess of the very logic that makes them possible. Often seen as a shift from structuralism to *post*structuralism – though not by Lacan himself –the move coincides with the founding of the École Freudienne de Paris, announced at the opening of the 1963–4 seminar, later published as the opening chapter to *Seminar XI: The Four Fundamental Concepts of Psychoanalysis* (1978). Posing himself the guiding question of whether psychoanalysis is a science or more a form of religious revelation, Lacan undertakes a discussion of the discipline's precarious position between scientific factual description and religion's speculations into the unknown. Where others spoke increasingly of the "subconscious," Lacan now went even further in the opposite direction, emphasizing the impossibility of attaining the "real" object of unconscious desire, "*objet petit a.*"

If the 1966 publication of *Écrits* thus marked the highpoint of structuralist psychoanalysis, it also thus marked the onset of its decline against a resurgence of the discipline of philosophy, which it had once threatened to supersede. A 1965 conference on structuralism in Baltimore, Ohio, announced the emergence of a new generation of theorists, including Jacques Derrida, who would both criticize and also extend Lacan's recasting of psychoanalysis as effectively a philosophy of the subject. That they did so, for the first time, without necessarily practicing as analysts, further signaled the increasing detachment of theoretical psychoanalysis from the analysis of clinical pathologies. Poststructuralism was to confirm the shift of psychoanalysis toward what Paul Ricœur (1970[1965]) called "cultural hermeneutics," a way of interpreting society as a whole and not just its individual members.

May 1968 became a notable illustration of this, and of the potential for psychoanalysis to be political. The protesting students looked first to Lacan for leadership, but his role as celebrity doyen was short-lived. The themes of Lacan's later seminars overlapped to some extent with the questions raised by the events of 1968, most notably the 1972–3 seminar on female sexuality (Seminar XX). For the most part, however, his increasing devotion to the obscure mathematical field of topology, in which he saw the potential for expressing the "impossible" Real diagrammatically, saw Lacan lose ground against those more willing to tap into the public mood of sexual and political liberation.

ANTI-PSYCHIATRY, ANTI-OEDIPUS, AND SEXUAL LIBERATION

A philosopher by training but a practicing (Lacanian) analyst at the experimental clinic of La Borde, Félix Guattari was one of the earliest practitioners of institutional and group therapy. He suggested that the institution of one-on-one clinical sessions between the patient and analyst creates the impression that pathology is intrinsically individual, the result of biology rather than society. By abstracting from the social nature of the unconscious, he argued, traditional psychoanalysis deprives patients of the possibility of creating social solutions to their problems, new social bonds that could facilitate their escape from socially and institutionally caused repression. His theories resonate with those of Michel Foucault, who notes in the first volume of the *History of Sexuality* (1992[1977]) how the standard format of analysis prescriptively reproduces the power structures of the Catholic confessional.

There were a number of similarities in Guattari and Foucault to the British "anti-psychiatric" movement of David Cooper and R. D. Laing, who criticized the ethical norms at work in the naming and diagnosis of "madness." Cooper in particular argued that the supposedly irrational and incoherent language of the "mad" constitutes a legitimate attempt to communicate experiences that are themselves irrational and incoherent, falling outside our ability to express them in conventional terms.

These attacks on psychoanalysis's sup-posed neutrality become one of the domi-nant themes of the late 1960s and early '70s. Insights into the power relations of psycho-analysis and the social history of madness would also furnish the basis of Guattari's collaboration with the philosopher Gilles Deleuze. Published in 1972 (and translated in 1984), their *Anti-Oedipus: Capitalism and Schizophrenia* polemically argued that psy-choanalysis was grounded in an Oedipus complex whose main effect was to reduce the unconscious to a private and passive theatre of dreams. For Deleuze and Guat-tari, Lacan's formulation of desire as lack, the longing for an object ("*a*") that can never be attained, serves to conceal desire's capacity to produce and change reality. It limits desire to the production of dreams and confines it to the sphere of the family. They go on to argue that capi-talism, rather than desire, is the cause of lack in subjects. Advertising and the constant production of purportedly new and better products means that satisfaction is, at best, fleeting. Psychoanalytic attempts to natu-ralize, or ontologize, this manufactured lack serve only to legitimate it.

Driven by the idea that "the real is not impossible," Deleuze and Guattari call for psychoanalysis to be superseded by "schizoanalysis," a practice of creative ex-perimentation with new and unconvention-al forms of social (and sexual) relations, unhindered by prescriptively Oedipal con-figurations of desire. Record sales and a dramatic philosophical impact made *Anti-Oedipus* the most successful in a long line of attempts to synthesize Marxism with psy-choanalysis, including Herbert Marcuse's *Eros and Civilisation* (1955) and tentative works by the Marxist structuralist Louis Althusser.

Another social movement to benefit from the revolutionary stirrings of the 1960s was feminism. Many feminists had typically seen psychoanalysis as a bastion of patriarchal culture, to be rejected on account of its characterization of women in terms of *Penisneid* (penis envy). Others, such as the London-based New Zealander Juliet Mitchell (1974), also saw it as a vital tool for understanding male-dominated society. A one-time Lacanian, the Belgian analyst Luce Irigaray is similarly ambiva-lent, both vociferously criticizing her mentor's refusal to recognize female sexual difference, while also affirming the need to psychoanalyze the unconscious of Western philosophy from which descends the pa-triarchal tendency to denigrate women. In works including *This Sex Which Is Not One* (1985[1977]) and *To Speak Is Never Neu-tral* (1985[2002]), Irigaray's highly literary feminist critique of Freud and Lacan leads into discussions of the female body, moth-erhood, and the bisexuality of female de-sire. In this respect, she comes quite close to another practicing analyst, novelist, and literary critic, the Paris-based Bulgarian Julia Kristeva. Kristeva (1982[1980]) develops the concept of the "abject" to refer to the unsettling effect of the flows and excreta of the human body. She shows how woman has often been deemed syn-onymous with the abject in literature and argues that attempts to "purify" the abject negate the crucial role women play in giving life to children, prior to their im-mersion in the language by which women and the body are later suppressed. These critiques of the sexual and Oedipal politics of psychoanalysis have helped to pave the way for gender studies' and queer theoret-ical critiques of Freud and Lacan's hetero-normativity, such as Butler (1990) and Bersani (1995).

Particularly relevant to the literary study of psychoanalysis is its deconstruction by Jacques Derrida. Derrida (1987[1983]) deploys the idea of "phallogocentrism" to suggest that Lacan encounters the same problem that undermines much of modern Western philosophy, namely its attempt to impose reason, laws, and identity on that which refuses them. Paying particular attention to the ability of (Lacanian) psychoanalysis to yield authoritative interpretations of literary texts, Derrida suggests that psychoanalytic readings work only because they presuppose their own validity. The discovery of psychoanalytic "Truth" is achieved through the imposition of a restrictive psychoanalytic frame of reference on texts that would otherwise escape the assignation of a fixed meaning. Lacan reconstructs the literary text so that everywhere he looks he finds confirmation of his own ideas, but in so doing he suppresses the openness to interpretation by which literature is defined.

Derrida's claims have since given rise to significant debate on the exact relationship between deconstruction, literature, and psychoanalysis, with Slavoj Žižek (2000) providing a recent defense and clarification of the Lacanian position. The criticism has not stopped – particularly Lacanian – psychoanalysis from becoming a valued methodology of comparative literary studies and other related fields, including gender studies and queer theory, on the one hand, and trauma and Holocaust studies, on the other. With regard to the latter, works like Cathy Caruth's *Unclaimed Experience* (1996) have drawn on the idea of experiences too traumatic to be fully integrated into consciousness, too intense to be coherently remembered and conveyed in speech, to explain the fractured, disjointed structure of testimony.

Yet it is the aforementioned Žižek who is at the forefront of the recent resurgence in the fortunes of academic Lacanianism. Debuting in English in the early 1990s, with a number of works on how to read Lacan through film (and vice versa), Žižek's writings have grown increasingly political, promoting a politicized Lacan as the positively totalitarian alternative to what he sees as the politically correct, "weak thought" of Deleuze, Derrida, and cognitive behavioral psychology.

THE END OF PSYCHOANALYSIS?

The fate of clinical psychoanalysis seems less certain, however. In France, which (alongside Argentina) is its last remaining stronghold, a very public debate on the future of psychoanalysis has been triggered by concerns over the regulation of the country's 8,000–14,000 practicing psychiatrists, psychotherapists, and psychoanalysts. The debate has centered around the publication of the *Livre noir de la psychanalyse* [The Black Book of Psychoanalysis], a volume of some 1,000 pages containing 80 articles by 30 authors across the disciplines, united by a desire to redress the information gap that has allowed the survival of an allegedly outdated therapeutical technique. Faced with an exhaustive array of criticisms, ranging from the failure of psychoanalysis to treat depression, to the flaws in its science, its cynical manipulation of patients to fit diagnoses and the stigmatization of parents deemed to have "failed" their children, the analytic community responded with a book edited by Jacques-Alain Miller, Žižek's mentor and the son-in-law of Lacan. The *L'Anti-livre noir de la psychanalyse* (2006) rails against the dangers of cognitive and behavioral therapy and reasserts the legitimacy of the "unscientific" talking cure. It argues that CBT achieves results not by eliminating the problem or cause of suffering, but simply by eliminating the symptoms that express it.

The same has been said of prescription medicines, whose controversial role in the treatment of depression has recently been brought back into focus by clinical trials showing antidepressants like Prozac to be only marginally more effective than sugar pill placebos (see, e.g., Leader 2008). Such findings reinforce psychoanalysts' case for the importance of a more flexible, human therapeutical dimension – a treatment seeking to eliminate the sources of trauma, whose very unconsciousness makes them impossible to measure scientifically.

Caught between psychiatry and non-medical intervention, between chemical prescription and the "talking cure" of therapeutically discussing one's problems, psychoanalysis continues to struggle with questions over the legitimacy of its therapeutic role and institutional status within the medical, scientific, and academic establishment. Yet, according to Žižek, this combination of being both unfashionable and impossible is precisely what makes it so important. His *In Defence of Lost Causes* (2008) opens with the description of psychoanalysis, alongside Marxism, as one of the two great "lost causes" of contemporary debate, their respective attempts at an overarching theory of everything having given way to a proliferation of less ambitious minor sciences. The age of psychoanalysis may be over and the fragile position it has come to occupy at the intersection of the arts and natural and social sciences may well be wrong and even "crazy," Žižek acknowledges. But the attempt to occupy a position of overarching truth is still better than the alternative of not even trying, of contenting oneself with a multiplicity of surface level explanations that dull the symptoms without treating their cause.

SEE ALSO: Butler, Judith; Deleuze, Gilles; Derrida, Jacques; Feminism; Foucault, Michel; Freud, Sigmund; Kristeva, Julia; Lacan, Jacques; Žižek, Slavoj

REFERENCES AND SUGGESTED READINGS

Althusser, L. (1997). *Writings on Psychoanalysis: Freud and Lacan* (trans. J. Mehlman; ed. O. Corpet & F. Matheron). New York: Columbia University Press.

Beck. A. T. (1976). *Cognitive Therapy and Emotional Disorders*. New York: International Universities Press.

Bersani, L. (1995). *Homos*. Cambridge, MA: Harvard University Press.

Butler, J. (1990) *Gender Trouble: Feminism and the Subversion of Identity*. New York: Routledge.

Caruth, C. (1996). *Unclaimed Experience: Trauma, Narrative and History*. Baltimore: Johns Hopkins University Press.

Cooper, D. (1979). *The Language of Madness*. London: Allen Lane.

Deleuze, G., & Guattari, F. (1984). *Anti-Oedipus: Capitalism and Schizophrenia* (trans. R. Hurley, M. Seem, & H. R. Lane) London: Continuum. (Original work published 1972.)

Derrida, J. (1987). *The Post Card: From Socrates to Freud and Beyond* (trans. A. Bass) Chicago: University of Chicago Press. (Original work published 1983.)

Dufresne, T. (2003). *Killing Freud: Twentieth-Century Culture and the Death of Psychoanalysis*. London, New York: Continuum.

Foucault, M. (1992). *History of Sexuality*. Vol. 1: *The Will to Knowledge* (trans. R. Hurley). London: Penguin. (Original work published 1977.)

Fromm, E. (1971). *The Crisis of Psychoanalysis*. London: Jonathan Cape.

Irigaray, L. (1985). *This Sex Which Is Not One* (trans. C. Porter & C. Burke) Ithaca: Cornell University Press. (Original work published 1977.)

Irigaray, L. (2002). *To Speak Is Never Neutral* (trans. G. Schwab). London: Continuum. (Original work published 1985.)

Kohut, Heinz (1978). The future of psychoanalysis. In P. H. Ornstein (ed.), *The Search for the Self: Selected Writings of Heinz Kohut, 1950–1978*, vol. 2 New York: International Universities Press.

Kristeva, J. (1982). *Powers of Horror: An Essay on Abjection* (trans. L. S. Roudiez). New York: Columbia University Press. (Original work published 1980.)

Lacan, J. (1978). *Seminar XI: The Four Fundamental Concepts of Psychoanalysis, 1963–4* (trans. A. Sheridan; ed. J.-A. Miller). New York: Norton.

Lacan, J. (1998). *Seminar XX: On Feminine Sexuality. The Limits of Love and Knowledge: Encore 1972–3* (trans. B. Fink; ed. J.-A. Miller). New York: Norton.

Lacan, J. (2006). *Écrits: The First Complete Edition in English* (trans. B. Fink, H. Fink, & R. Grigg). New York, London: Norton. (Original work published 1966.)

Leader, D. (2008). The creation of the prozac myth. *Guardian* (February 27).

Lévi-Strauss, C. (1987). *Introduction to the Work of Marcel Mauss* (trans. F. Baker). London: Routledge and Kegan Paul. (Original work published 1950.)

Marcuse, H. (1955). *Eros and Civilisation*. Boston, MA: Beacon Press.

Mayer, C., et al. (2005). *Le Livre noir de la psychanalyse: Vivre, penser et aller mieux sans Freud*. Paris: Les Arènes.

Miller, J.-A. (ed.) (2006). *L'Anti-Livre noir de la psychanalyse*. Paris: Éditions du Seuil.

Mitchell, J. (1974). *Feminism and Psychoanalysis*. London: Allen Lane.

Ricœur, P. (1970). *Freud and Philosophy: An Essay in Interpretation* (trans. D. Savage). New Haven: Yale University Press. (Original work published 1965.)

Roudinesco, E. (2002). *Why Psychoanalysis?* (trans R. Bowlby). New York: Columbia University Press.

Žižek, S. (2000). *Enjoy Your Symptom! Jacques Lacan in Hollywood and Out*. New York: Routledge.

Žižek, S. (2008). *In Defence of Lost Causes*. London, New York: Verso.

Q

Queer Theory

MATTHEW HELMERS

What is queer theory? This question is precisely one that queer theory itself continually asks. Queer theory, over the 20 years of its existence, has attempted to answer this question in numerous ways: historically, by discovering or writing the history of queerness; theoretically, by examining the possibilities for a text-based methodological approach called "queering"; and even practically, by instantiating university departments and degree programs under the title "Queer Theory." Yet for all this work, queer theory remains a nebulous and unwieldy category of critical practice which has continued to polarize critics in a fashion similar to the debates over the use of the term "queer" itself.

It is possible to separate the question "What is queer theory?" from a related question "What is queer?" This separation seems to be counterintuitive, as theoretically queer theory and the instantiation of theories on queerness indicate the same thing; but queer theory signifies more than the practice of queer readings, or reading queerly, or queer itself. Queer theory, as opposed to queer, designates the existence of an institutionalized program of theoretical reading practices aimed at producing, critiquing, and queering primary and sec-

ondary texts. The question of queer, then, forms a central part of queer theory, but does not get us any closer to understanding the institutionalized and standardized form of a type of theory called queer theory. Therefore, for the time being, the emergence of "queer theory" can be examined as separate from the emergence of the *object* of queer theory: queerness.

The now (relatively standard) narrative surrounding queer theory states that queer theory officially entered the academy in February of 1990 with Teresa de Lauretis's coining of the term as the title for a University of California, Santa Cruz conference (and later for a 1991 guest-edited edition of the academic journal *Differences*). De Lauretis's inspiration for uniting the previously (and, to some, currently) derogatory term "queer" with the potentially elitist term "theory" is often attributed to a similar use of the term "queer" in the creation of the Queer Nation activist group that same year. This use relies upon the then emergent positive reclamation of derogatory terms like "queer," "faggot," and "dyke" in the late 1980s and early 1990s, and the deployment of these terms in several high-profile activist campaigns. Queer theory thus arises out of a political climate of radical identity politics, in which dykes, faggots, and queers began to challenge and rethink the possibilities for social classification, existent LGBT (lesbian, gay, bisexual/pansexual, and transgender) and ACT UP political action, AIDS activism, and (for queer theory) the role of concepts like sexuality, identity, gender, and sex within the university.

Other histories of queer theory, like the one Barry (1995) describes, trace queer theory's origins through second- and third-wave feminist practices, especially as a derivative of lesbian criticism. These critics see the origin of queer theory's commitment to problematizing gender and sex as methodologically derived from feminist interventions in the 1960s, '70s, and '80s, and downplays the importance of AIDS activism in the instantiation of queer theory as a critical practice. Furthermore, they affirm that lesbian criticism directly affects the trajectory of queer efforts, an assertion that contradicts a critique of queer theory as predominantly a practice of white, middle-class, gay males.

Still others like David Halperin, Lauren Berlant, and Michael Warner emphasize the emergence of queer theory from gay studies programs while questioning queer theory's commitment to politics, sexuality, and activism (Berlant & Warner 1995; Halperin 2003). These theorists are quick to point out that the rethinking of concepts like gender, sex, sexuality, and identity was already well established in the critical fields of gay studies, gender studies, women's studies, and institutions like UC Santa Cruz's History of Consciousness department. They tend to view queer theory as overtheorized and therefore lacking in practical application (i.e., activist politics). They also see queer theory as mischaracterizing previous feminist and gay studies programs as inherently *under* theorized, and thereby portraying gay studies and feminism as "backward" or "underdeveloped" critical schools. This marginalization of gay studies and women's studies by queer theorists causes some critics to conclude that queer

theory is actually a conservative body of practice that seeks to eliminate confrontational political and social activism from LGBT people and women by rendering central ideas like sexuality, sex, and gender amorphous, and therefore insubstantial and unthreatening. Their reasoning states that "queer" presents pacified and friendly versions of activist concepts, which explains the relatively quick acceptance of queer theory into the traditionally "conservative" university body.

Indeed, one of the problems with queer as a theoretical practice is its amorphous nature. As opposed to certain versions of other critical practices like gay studies, postcolonial studies, or women's studies, everything seems to fall under the auspices of "queer theory." For example, in gay studies, there is no injunction to "gay" heteronormative texts (though there *is* an emphasis on creating and reclaiming a canon of gay literature); contrarily, queer theory is able to "queer" any text, and thus simultaneously render the text as a text *appropriate* to queer examination. This action mirrors closely the deconstructive practice of affirming that any text *already* deconstructs itself, rather than certain versions of feminist that produce a specifically feminist *reading* of a text. Queer readings thus typically demonstrate that the potential to be queer was in the text all along; yet, paradoxically, it is in the specific practice of queering the text that the text's queer potential is realized.

Rather than reading this amorphous nature of queer theory as an inherent problem in the methodology, it is possible to look at how this claim to universal relevance enhances the efficacy of queer theory. By refusing to be relegated to a specific historical tradition, or a contemporary body of texts, queer theory simultaneously universalizes the presence and prevalence of queer. In this case, the universalization of queer theory indicates that the marginalized and marginal is already present within any text; and while many postcolonial theorists share this assumption, queer readings tend to emphasize the presence of the sexual or sexed subject over the colonized or racially othered subject. Queer theory then is able to affirm that "queer" is not something invented in the 1990s, but rather a trans-historical characteristic of numerous national and historical bodies of literature.

Simultaneously, some queer theorists build upon this universalization of method in order to universalize the object of examination. These queer theorists, instead of examining the queer desire of a minority group, examine how *all* desire within a given text is queer (including the desire of groups traditionally considered "normal," i.e., heterosexual white males). These theorists demonstrate that the ideal of "normal" forms of desire, sex, and gender is equally and inherently unachievable by *all* subjects, not just subjects traditionally considered perverse. For these critics, all subjects are queer because the demands of normalcy are impossible to meet. Therefore, queer theory *must* be a universalized and amorphous practice because the idea of queer affects all subjects, not simply marginalized subjects. This universalization in method and related universalization of critiqued object, enables queer theorists to attain purchase in numerous (if not all) academic fields, including literature, film studies, sociology, legal studies, science studies, anthropology, and so on. In each of these fields of study, queer theorists attempt to read the given text through a demonstration of the potential queerness already present within any text.

But what specifically does a queer reading look like? Eve Sedgwick's (1990) queer analysis of Henry James's "The beast in the jungle" is a paradigmatic example of a queer reading. "The beast in the jungle" centers on the life of protagonist John Marcher as he

waits for "something" to happen to him, and yet this "something" for which he waits appears to never come to pass. Sedgwick's reading of this tale attempts to delineate what this "something that never happens" could be, while at the same time analyzing the character of John Marcher himself. Through a close reading of the primary text, Sedgwick points out several moments in the tale in which John Marcher's desire is simply not active. According to Sedgwick, the character fails to desire anything other than the event in his future (and perhaps not even that), and as such, fails to desire his close female friend May Bartram. A gay reading of this text might try to explain John's lack of desire for May Bartram as due to his suppressed homosexual tendency, and thereby explain that the "thing" for which John Marcher waits is his eventual ability to "come out of the closet" as a gay man. Gay critics might also cite Henry James's continual and highly emotional correspondence with numerous hetero- and homosexual men, as well as his own self-professed celibacy toward women, in order to highlight the purportedly latent homosexual themes of the tale. They might therefore read John Marcher as an emblem of Henry James himself, yearning to "come out of the closet" as a gay man, yet never able to do so. However, Sedgwick adopts a queer approach to Marcher's future "thing," examining not what it *does* indicate (i.e., his homosexuality) but rather what it *could* indicate. Sedgwick refutes an interpretation of Marcher as a gay man, and instead shows that Marcher is a character who does not know his desire, and therefore can be neither homosexual *nor* heterosexual. According to Sedgwick, Marcher is in a closet, but it is a closet that negates *all* desire and not just a latent homosexual desire. Sedgwick weaves this interpretation of John Marcher's closet through the various events of the story, showing how Marcher becomes less of a subject as the narrative progresses (he loses agency, refuses engagement with other characters, and is hopelessly self-ignorant). Sedgwick concludes that Marcher's subjectivity erodes because he refuses to address either the societal compulsions toward heterosexuality or the societal compulsion toward homosexuality. Essentially, because John Marcher chooses to abstain from desire and sexuality all together, he is denied subjectivity. Through this conclusion, Sedgwick elucidates both the importance of sexuality to constructions of subjectivity *and* the societal compulsions that enforce and regulate sexuality. In producing a queer reading, Sedgwick demonstrates the structures that govern all modes of sexuality, while at the same time opening up the possibilities for new interpretations of sexuality, as opposed to simply "outing" John Marcher as a homosexual man. Queer theory, and queer readings, are therefore concerned with ideas of sexuality, sex, gender, and identity, but in a way that establishes the possibilities for these categories, rather than simply reproducing their previous uses to new and more radical effects.

For brevity, Sedgwick's analysis has stood as an example for all queer theoretical practice, but precisely this action of taking a singular instantiation of queer theory and forcing it to metonymically stand for all of queer theory is something that Lauren Berlant and Michael Warner critique in their 1995 *PMLA* article. They affirm that because queer theory came about without any clear definition, and was so quickly taken up by so many critics and universities, queer critics scrambled to answer the question "what is queer theory?" by exemplifying certain existent queer analyses. The critics thus answered the question "what is queer theory?" by replying "queer theory is Sedgwick's interpretation of 'The beast in the jungle'" or "queer theory is *Gender*

Trouble." In this way, nascent queer theory was able to meet the demands of a university system based around a set of "reading practices" and "established texts" and thereby gain credibility and acceptance with alacrity. Yet Berlant and Warner affirm that no singular project of queer theory can stand for all queer theory practices; again, queer theory is too nebulous to solidify.

Similarly, understanding all of queer theory through typifying certain authors and articles leads to other problems in defining queer theory; namely, the definition of queer theory changes depending on which author one considers to be the "most queer." For example, Eve Sedgwick, working on a feminist interpretation of Gothic paranoia in *Between Men* (1985) arrived at an iteration of the cultural taboo against homosexuality dubbed homosexual panic, yet *Between Men* is considered to be one of the founding texts of queer theory. However, if Sedgwick's work is classified without the label of queer theory, it appropriately falls under the fields of gender theory, feminism, and perhaps psychoanalytic theory and gay studies. Judith Butler, another "founder" of queer theory, emerges from the fields of Continental dialectic philosophy, feminism, rhetoric, and deconstructionism, in order to write *Gender Trouble* (1990), a now seminal text of queer theory, which nonetheless indicates in its subtitle that it specifically concerns "feminism and the subversion of identity" rather than any specifically "queer" idea. Lee Edelman, an important and influential queer theorist, subtitles his book *Homographesis* (1994) "Gay literary and cultural theory" and derives his analysis from Lacanian psychoanalysis and poststructuralism, while his subsequent book *No Future* (2004) with the term "queer theory" specifically in the subtitle, blends poststructuralism and Lacanian psychoanalysis with film theory. The list could go on, but here taking any of these authors' works and making them exemplary of "queer theory" simultaneously aligns queer theory with the other reading practices of that specific author. Thus, depending on who is exemplified, queer theory becomes characterized as *also* gay studies, or poststructuralism, or rhetoric, or participant in any other numerous critical practices. This is not to say that queer theory does not partake of, draw upon, and/or move away from these other schools of critical theory, but rather, that the specific composition of queer theory practices usually depends upon which authors and critics one counts as "queer." As a counter-example, primers and guides on queer theory tend to place Teresa de Lauretis at the margins of the origin narrative, usually noting only her coining of the term. This marginalization can perhaps be attributed to de Lauretis's own move away from "queer theory" in her work *The Practice of Love* (1994) in which she asserts that by 1994 queer theory had already lost its political and radical efficacy at the hands of the mass-market publishing industry. And yet, de Lauretis, in both her earlier and contemporary works, continues to be hugely influential in numerous queer theory projects. So why do some critics emphasize Sedgwick and Butler instead of de Lauretis?

Perhaps these critics wish to align queer theory strategically with specific modes of thought and thus foreground the thinkers who most exemplify this practice while minoritizing those who stand against this specific iteration of queer theory. Indeed, many of the texts considered "seminal" or "canonical" to queer theory were written before queer theory even existed, and were appropriated into the tradition only *ex post facto*. Through their inclusion in the queer canon, these texts are "queered" themselves, or made to signify (exemplify) a certain mode of queerness, even as their participation in other schools of thought are down-

played or erased. This strategy would certainly make "queer" an easy concept to assimilate into a university, as queer theory is defined as assimilative: appropriating texts already accepted by the universities and arranging them in new ways. This version of queer theory unites the disparate schools of critical practice under a new guiding methodology, affirming that gay studies, women's studies, postcolonial theory et al., were *really* just an earlier form of queer theory.

Sedgwick cautions against this structuring of queer theory as a "paranoid reading practice" in her later work *Touching Feeling* (2003), affirming that the subsuming of multiple schools of thought under a singular guiding narrative goes against the very idea of queerness. Halperin (2003) and other critics echo this critique in their affirmations that, rather than opening up possibilities, queer closes down opportunities for analysis by proclaiming that everything is already queer. These critics suggest that if everything is already queer, then queer by definition is the status quo, rather than a new or radical critical movement. These ideas are also present in the above-mentioned reading of "The beast in the jungle" as John Marcher's queerness is based on his inability to assent to a sexuality, and yet Sedgwick simultaneously claims that the dominant culture decrees that subjects *should be* ignorant of their sexuality, what she calls "erotic self-ignorance." Thus, John Marcher's queer potential is also the upholding of existent cultural norms on sexuality. These pessimistic constructions of queer theory conclude that queer theory's superseding of existent traditions reflects a conservative appropriation of the radical discourse of queer in order to quell actual effective radical projects.

Against this pessimistic view of queer theory as the status quo is an optimistic view of queer theory as oriented toward an open future. Jagose (1996) affirms, in summarizing the future-oriented claims of Butler and Halperin, that queer theory can regain its potential for radical efficacy by embracing an unknown and unknowable future. As opposed to projects which close down queer theory as *already* obsolete and *always* conservative, this version of the project of queer theory moves beyond the questions of a dying institutional past, and instead asks about the future. Importantly, Jagose argues that queer theory's orientation is not toward a predictable or knowable future, but rather toward the very possibility of a future as different from the present. Queer theory therefore counsels us to look to the future without attempting to *divine* the future, and thereby opens up the possibilities of the present.

However, both even these pessimistic and optimistic renditions of queer theory commit the error of reducing queer theory to a singular *thing*: either the upholding of the conservative status quo or the promise of the radical future. Thus, just as some critics take up a singular author in order to say what queer theory is, so too do other critics look to specific appropriations of queer theory into the university in order to affirm the liabilities of queer theory in general, or to the unknowable construction of the future in order to affirm the benefits of queer theory practices. Perhaps this problem derives from the central question itself, the one many queer theorists started with "what is queer theory"? In attempting to write a history, or describe a set of practices, or outline its institutional adoption, many critics already assume that queer theory is a "what" that "is," meaning that queer theory is a singular, measurable, understandable set of practices that occur and exist in academic culture.

But if the validity of *all* the above characterizations of queer theory are accepted, affirming that queer theory is *both* its pessimistic and optimistic instantiations, that queer theory *is* Butler, Sedgwick, Halperin, Edelman, de Lauretis, and thousands of others, and that above all queer theory enables all these contradictory currents of thought to be valid, then it is possible to conclude that queer theory as a practice seeks to instantiate *all* possibilities, or at least open up the possibility of the ability for all of those possibilities to exist. Therefore, queer theory cannot simply be a study of sexuality, for some queer theorists do not examine sexuality at all. Queer theory cannot simply be the instantiation of a new conceptualization of gender, because some queer theorists affirm that gender at present is already queer. Queer theory cannot be purely theoretical, for some queer theorists take as their objects material practices and material culture. Yet queer theory cannot be antitheoretical any more than it can be purely theory. So what more can be said about queer theory? Queer theory is (and is not) the possibility of divergent, contradictory, dominant, and radical constructions, conceptualizations and (mis)understandings of gender, sex, sexuality, and subjectivity. Queer theory is typified in certain authors, and yet exceeds these authors. Queer theory is a specific set of university practices, and yet defies the structure of the university and its own instantiation therein. Queer theory is a history of queer theory, and ahistorical. Queer theory opens up *and* closes down possibilities, whether they be radical possibilities, liberal possibilities, conservative possibilities, activist possibilities, or other possibilities. A queer reading shows (and hides) that things are not as they appear in the text: that there is more (and less) possibility in the queered work than other critical practices suggest.

Perhaps to the greatest extent, queer theory exists in the tension that arises from affirming the simultaneous existence of two (or more) mutually exclusive things.

To return to the above example of "The beast in the jungle" queer theorists ask "What if John Marcher both has, and does not have, desire *at the same time*?" or "What if desire is both something you can and cannot possess?" Queer theorists ask, "What allows me to ask the question 'Does desire exist?'" Queer theory then is not always about making sense out of a text. Sometimes it is about allowing the illogical, the impossible, or the unutterable, to exist while also affirming the conservative, the repressive, and the speakable. Thus, all of the queer theorists, from the pessimists to the optimists, characterize a piece of the infinite possibilities denoted by the idea of queer theory in practice, yet none contains it in totality.

As a final note, the boundary between the term "queer" and the practice of queer theory that this entry has endeavored to maintain quickly blurs in light of the recognition of queer theory as a practice of possibilities; for if it is accepted that queer theory endeavors to embrace the possible, then the original distinction of queer theory as a set of university practices is lost, as queer theory must indicate these practices *and* move past them into other possibilities, even the possibility that queer theory is no different from queer itself. In fact, the debate around the term "queer" crystallizes a lot of the debates around queer theory. For example, the term "queer" was originally shocking and offensive, and therefore deployed with great efficacy by activists in the late 1980s; however, continual high-profile and common usage of "queer" has rendered the term relatively banal according to most academics. Most critics cite this general neutralizing of the "shocking" power of the word queer as a vivid allegory of the loss of the radical "shocking" potential of queer theory itself. These critics encourage a reinvigoration of the offensiveness of the term "queer" within academic circles in order to revitalize the early potential to "shock" present within the first instantiations of queer theory. But this would also render "queer" as a singular meaning: the injunction to shock the populace into action. Yet queer in its transition to banality also encapsulates the quality of queer to be *both* of a mutually exclusive set: banal *and* shocking. This conflation of contrary meaning occurs again in the word "queer," as queer itself designates both a methodological practice in the verb "to queer," and an object of examination in the noun "queer" and/or functioning adjectivally as in "a queer text." Thus, "queer" as a term always means the possibility of more than it directly signifies. To queer a text is not simply to render the text queer through the application of a queer theory reading practice, but to simultaneously establish the qualities of that reading practice through a mobilization of the noun "queer," as in, producing a *queer* reading. In this way, every article and book, whether explicitly interrogating the concept of queer or just drawing upon queer practice to produce a queer reading, questions, refines, and proposes a specific idea of queer *theory* that is simultaneously *methodological* and *definitional*. Queer itself also embraces and transcends its use as just a noun, or just a verb, and indicates that which it is, and that which it *can be*. Therefore, if every examination, deployment, and critique of the word "queer" consists of, or points to, all the meanings and nonmeanings of queer theory, then this entry simultaneously describes, *and consists of,* queer theory in practice.

SEE ALSO: Butler, Judith; Gender and Cultural Studies; Gender Theory; Lesbian, Gay, Bisexual, and Transgender Studies; Phallus/Phallocentrism; Sedgwick, Eve Kosofsky

REFERENCES AND SUGGESTED READINGS

Barry, P. (1995). *Beginning Theory: An Introduction to Literary Theory*. Manchester: Manchester University Press.

Berlant, L., & Warner, M. (1995). What does queer theory teach us about x? *PMLA*, 110(3), 343–349.

Butler, J. (1990). *Gender Trouble: Feminism and the Subversion of Identity*. New York: Routledge.

Butler, J. (1993). *Bodies that Matter: On the Discursive Limits of "Sex."* London: Routledge.

Edelman, L. (1994). *Homographesis: Essays in Gay Literary and Cultural Theory*. New York: Routledge.

Edelman, L. (2004). *No Future: Queer Theory and the Death Drive*. Durham, NC: Duke University Press.

Hall, D. E. (2003). *Queer Theories*. Basingstoke: Palgrave Macmillan.

Halperin, D. M. (2003). The normalization of queer theory. *Journal of Homosexuality*, 45(2), 339–343.

Jagose, A. (1996). *Queer Theory: An Introduction*. New York: New York University Press.

de Lauretis, T. (1994). *The Practice of Love: Lesbian Sexuality and Perverse Desire*. Bloomington: Indiana University Press.

Sedgwick, E. K. (1985). *Between Men: English Literature and Male Homosocial Desire*. New York: Columbia University Press.

Sedgwick, E. K. (1990). *Epistemology of the Closet*. Berkeley: University of California Press.

Sedgwick, E. K. (2003). *Touching Feeling: Affect, Pedagogy, Performativity*. Durham, NC: Duke University Press.

Sullivan, N. (2003). *A Critical Introduction to Queer Theory*. Edinburgh: Edinburgh University Press.

R

Rancière, Jacques

ALEX MURRAY

Since the late 1990s, Jacques Rancière (b. 1940) has risen to prominence in the Anglophone world for his exploration of art and politics. Rancière's career began as co-author of the volume *Lire le Capital* (later translated as *Reading "Capital"*) with Louis Althusser and Étienne Balibar (1968). He soon parted ways with Althusser, whose "scientific" or structural model of Marxism he found limiting. The notion of a social science that circulates in the Marxist tradition takes as its premise certain assumptions about what is "good" or "beneficial" for the subjugated working classes. It also attempts to explain the failures of class revolt by creating totalizing structural theories. Yet these theoretical positions often remain aloof from the ground of history, eschewing the "experience" of those it speaks for by claiming it remains tainted by its exposure to hegemonic forms of ideology. It was in teaching in the largely Althussserian philosophy department and University of Paris VIII that Rancière realized the dogmatic nature of "scholarly" teaching.

Rancière's approach initially was to undertake a massive work of social history, *The Nights of Labor* (1989[1981]), in which he explored the writing of those young men who produced a series of journals in the 1830s in France that documented their own ambivalence to their work. For Rancière, it was necessary to deconstruct the idea of the worker that valorized work and ignored the subjective experience of work itself. In many ways it was a genealogy of an alternative worker's movement that had emerged at the same time as Marxism, yet whose possibilities had never been realized. For these men, it was not poverty that they were railing against, but the ignominy of being forced to beg for work that was maintaining their subordination and taking away their dignity.

From this very specific critique of scientific Marxism's fetishization of work, Rancière would create a broader form of historiography in *The Names of History* (1994[1992]). Rancière's concern was with the ways in which history works as a linguistic procedure, its "poetics of knowledge" that attempts to create a founding narrative that allows the historical actors to speak by making them visible. The visible, in effect, silences them, entombs them in narrative. Here, the letters of the poor, the village scribes, etc. are presented to us as objects, described in their material and narrative forms in order to be incorporated into the narrative of the historian. History is then haunted by its own poetics, which provides its legitimacy, yet can endanger its claims to scientific validity. It uses forms of mimesis to cover over both: "[H]istory can become a science *by remaining history* only through the poetic detour that gives speech a regime of truth" (89; emphasis original). For Rancière history must then be explored as a series of rhetorical tropes, its structures and style, its representability, more important than its claims to historical veracity.

In *The Philosopher and His Poor* (2003 [1983]), Rancière continued this attempt to think through the politics of representation and an attempt to speak for those whose voice is denied from history. He is struck by the paradoxical necessity of philosophers to utilize the figures of workers (the poor) to demonstrate certain arguments of political economy and philosophy, yet simultaneously he always willfully misrepresents both the conditions under which these workers are organized and their experience of the social. His work on education, *The Ignorant Schoolmaster* (1991[1987]) suggested in an analogous fashion that the principle of education had always been about enforcing division and hierarchy by attempting to naturalize its own ideology. The schoolmaster is ignorant because he is no more "intelligent" than his students, but has instead submitted to the forms of control and capture that underpin the structure of knowledge.

These moments of critiquing the representation of both experience and knowledge open out to Rancière's broader idea of politics. For Rancière, politics, as it is largely practiced, is a function of what he terms "the police," which undertakes a division of the sensible, dividing the community into social groups and positions. The object of a politics of emancipation then is about the breaking apart, the division of the sensible, forcing politics into the relational and implementing the idea of politics as equality. Democracy is about the "deregulation" of the locations and rules of speech and representation. This challenge to the separation and division of political life is to be found in works such as *Disagreements* (1999 [1995]) and *On the Shores of Politics* (1995 [1992]).

From around 1990 onward, Rancière's focus turned to art and cinema with the publication of *Short Voyages to the Land of the People* (2003[1990]). It was followed by *The Politics of Aesthetics* (2004[2000]), in which he outlines three different regimes: the ethical, the representative, and the aesthetic. The ethical establishes a distribution of images and plays a largely educative role; the representative regime removes itself from the ethical/social and posits an autonomous domain of art; the aesthetic calls into question any norm and transforms "the distribution of the sensible," which Rancière defined as "the system of self-evident facts of sense perception that simultaneously discloses the existence of something in common and the delimitations that define the respective parts and positions within it" (12). So the distribution here is about what is excluded and included in the ways in which the senses apprehend, which creates limitations and restrictions on human activity. For Rancière, artistic practices are ways of doing and making which are part of the broader distribution yet which can also intervene in it and challenge these limited ideas of the sensible. If art can provide a "redistribution" of the sensible, then it has an inherent "political" function in that it rejects and refuses the distribution of the state and the limited forms of identity it produces.

SEE ALSO: Althusser, Louis; Marxism

REFERENCES AND SUGGESTED READING

Rancière, J. (1989). *The Nights of Labor: the Worker's Dream in Nineteenth-Century France* (trans. J. Drury; intro. D. Reid). Philadelphia: Temple

University Press. (Original work published 1981.)

Rancière, J. (1991). *The Ignorant Schoolmaster: Five Lessons in Intellectual Emancipation* (trans. K. Ross). Stanford: Stanford University Press. (Original work published 1987.)

Rancière, J. (1994). *The Names of History: On the Poetics of Knowledge* (trans. H. Melehy; foreword by H. White). Minnesota: University of Minnesota Press. (Original work published 1981.)

Rancière, J. (1995). *On the Shores of Politics* (trans. L. Heron). London: Verso. (Original work published 1992.)

Rancière, J. (1999). *Disagreement: Politics and Philosophy* (trans. J. Rose). (Original work published 1995.)

Rancière, J. (2003). *Short Voyages to the Land of the People* (trans. J. Swenson). Stanford: Stanford University Press. (Original work published 1990.)

Rancière, J. (2003). *The Philosopher and His Poor* (trans. J. Drury, C. Oster, & A. Parker). Durham, NC: Duke University Press. (Original work published 1983.)

Rancière, J. (2004). *The Politics of Aesthetics: The Distribution of the Sensible* (trans. G. Rockhill). London: Continuum. (Original work published 2000.)

Rancière, J. (2007). *The Future of the Image* (trans G. Elliott). London: Verso. (Original work published 2003.)

Rancière, J. (2009). *The Emancipated Spectator* (trans G. Elliott). London: Verso. (Original work published 2008.)

Reader-Response Studies

JOE HUGHES

At its most general, reader-response studies begins with the assertion that the study of literature cannot afford to overlook the role of the reader. From this point of view, it has a long history. Plato's concerns regarding poetry in the *Republic*, Aristotle's *Poetics*, rhetoric's cultivation of the arts of pleasure, persuasion, and education, the eighteenth-century discourse on beauty and the sublime: all fall within this category. If contemporary reader-response studies distinguishes itself from this tradition, it is because it explicitly problematizes the two poles involved in the act of reading: the text and the reader. It does so from the vantage point of new, critical philosophies of the subject (primarily phenomenology, but also psychology and psychoanalysis) and of language (structuralism and linguistics). Modern reader-response theory could thus be said to begin with Husserlian phenomenology, persist through the "linguistic turn," and finally become dispersed in poststructuralist, Marxist, and new historicist theories.

Early reader-response criticism is largely an extension of the philosophical work of Edmund Husserl, called phenomenology. In his *Cartesian Meditations* (1929), Husserl characterized phenomenology as a "criticism of consciousness." Of course this "criticism" wasn't a study of literary texts; it was a study of "transcendental self-experience," by which Husserl meant that it studied the nature, the acts, and the structures of a "transcendental" or constituting consciousness. Husserl's aims were ambitious. "*The task of a criticism of transcendental self-experience*" was nothing less than "*the task of lying open the infinite field of transcendental experience*" (29–31; emphasis original). Husserl himself, however, only studied relatively small and isolated regions of this infinite field.

One notable omission in Husserl's extensive writings was any account of aesthetics in general and of the act of reading in particular (an interesting, if short, exception can be found in his introduction to *Analyses Concerning Passive and Active Syntheses* [2001]). Roman Ingarden, a Polish phenomenologist, sought to remedy this lack in his monumental work *The Literary Work of Art* (1973[1933]). Ingarden's concerns here were primarily philosophical. What interested him about the literary work was the way in which it opened up a previously neglected dimension of Husserlian thought. Husserl tended to focus on particularly well-determined objects in his criticism of consciousness: his two most frequent examples were the concrete objects of perception ("objectivities of intuition") and stable mathematical truths ("ideal objectivities"). For Ingarden, however, the literary work presented a kind of object which participated in none of the epistemological stability of these other two kinds of object. Unlike concrete objects and mathematical truths, literary works are shot through with "spots of indeterminacy." Not only are they indeterminate, they are also irreducible to their material being and, because they are created and capable of being altered (rather than discovered or "remembered"), they lack the ideality of mathematical or platonic truths. Ingarden therefore undertook an impressive study of the nature of this odd, literary object, whose existence rested somewhere between materiality and ideality. He dissected it into four "strata" ranging from phonetic components, to concepts, to the complexities of plot and characterization, and described the way in which readers create an ideal, literary object by traversing these strata in the act of reading.

Wolfgang Iser, a founding member of what was called the "Constance School" of reader-response criticism, greatly expanded on the work of Roman Ingarden. For Ingarden, the literary work of art was indeed an indeterminate object, but it was also a unifiable object. It could be "concretized" in such a way as to bring determinacy to the work. Competent readers would eventually approximate a *correct* reading as a limit. In the *Act of Reading* (1978[1976]), Iser rejects this possibility. Despite his originality, Iser argues, Ingarden remained tied to a classical aesthetics which privileged and sought out the organic unity of the text. In contrast, Iser argues that the indeterminacy of the text is irreducible. He

thus shifts our attention from a hoped-for unity to the "disjunctions" which make the indeterminacy of the text unavoidable. Iser describes two kinds of indeterminacy: "blanks" (or "gaps") and "negations." Blanks and negations disrupt the normal flow of reading and prompt the reader to make connections, fill in the gaps, or resolve the contradictions. Crucially, the imaginative filling of gaps does not bring us closer to an ideal unity of the work. Rather it opens up further gaps, and asks for more work. The structure of indeterminacy changes with each subsequent reading. The process is essentially open, and this causes Iser radically to redefine the literary work of art.

For Iser, both the text and the reader have concrete roles in the constitution of the work. In its most basic function, the reader's imagination is a continuous temporal synthesis. The reader constantly creates expectations about what will happen next and falls back on memories of what has already happened. Reading always takes place in a temporal horizon in which the reader makes connections between what has happened, what could happen, and what is happening at the moment. These connections, of course, are not arbitrary. They are directed by the text. The text itself thus takes the form of a set of directions or "schemata." It prescribes rules for the production of meaning. The text for Iser is a set of rules; the reader is a power of synthesis. The *work*, therefore, is neither. The work is the "virtual" space in which the reader's imagination brings about "passive syntheses" governed by textual schemata. It is a "virtuality," an "impersonal" field, or a space of play between text and reader in which the two meet up, interact, and mutually create the work as an effect.

While Iser took precautions to guard against such a criticism, his work does seem open to the very obvious complaint that it ignores the role of history in our interpretations of texts. It often seems as though the act of reading, for Iser, is the act of a solitary imagination taking its orders from the text alone – as though the confrontation between reader and text took place in an historical and ideological vacuum. The second major figure of the Constance School, Hans Robert Jauss, might be said to have gone just as far in the opposite direction. He too focuses on the role of readers in the constitution of the literary work, but, almost exclusively, he emphasized the effect that historically and sometimes politically determined conventions of reading have on our interpretations of a given text. These conventions, which can be generic, stylistic, and even thematic, form what Jauss calls a "horizon of expectations." He argues that it is the shifting nature of this horizon that should be the proper object of literary history.

In his 1969 essay "Literary history as a challenge to literary theory," Jauss offers as a brief example the comparative success of two novels, both of which "treated a trivial subject, infidelity in a bourgeois and provincial milieu": Flaubert's *Madame Bovary* and Feydeau's *Fanny*. In terms of popularity, these two texts suffered inverse fates. Immediately following publication, Flaubert was hardly read at all, whereas Feydeau saw widespread popularity. Today, however, *Madame Bovary* is considered one of the most important novels in the history of the genre, whereas almost nobody reads *Fanny* anymore. Jauss argues that the reasons for this reversal are to be found in the evolution of a trans-subjective horizon of expectations. In this particular instance, it was Flaubert's formal innovations that disrupted the expectations of his readers. While Feydeau had made use of the popular and "inviting tone of the confessional novel," Flaubert had employed his off-putting, machine-like, impersonal narration.

Jean Starobinski, Marcel Raymond, Albert Béguin, Jean-Pierre Richard, and Georges Poulet, among others, make up the second major school of reader-response theory, the "Geneva School." (The Parisian Maurice Blanchot is occasionally included in this group as well). These critics shared a common concern to continue the Husserlian project of a criticism of consciousness – a description of the field of transcendental experience – but unlike members of the Constance School they tended to distance themselves sharply from Husserlian concepts and methodologies, and in some cases even rejected outright the designation "Husserlian." Consequently, the different ways in which the criticism of consciousness was carried out varied greatly between these writers. Sometimes, as with Poulet, they claimed unmediated access to the consciousness of the author: in reading, the author's thoughts become my thoughts. More frequently, and less controversially, they simply focused on thematic representations of consciousness in literature; passages like Rousseau's descriptions of waking consciousness in the *Reveries* were constant points of reference. Occasionally, they would draw on various authors' own first-person reports of literary experience as recorded in their letters and journals (this is a favorite technique of Blanchot, for example). What varies even more than the methodologies of these writers, however, is their respective understandings of the very notion of consciousness – and this is what gives the Geneva Schools its richness (this is also why René Wellek once said of Poulet that he is more of a philosopher than a *literary* critic). Sometimes, consciousness was treated as a timeless transcendent point which abstracted from all content but which still underwrote all thought as its condition; sometimes, it was eminently historical. For Blanchot, it was an impersonal space of possibility in which mobile connections were established between words and sentences, while for Richard it was indistinguishable from the body and its sensations.

Poulet was one of the more prominent members of the Geneva School. In his famous essay "Phenomenology of reading," Poulet suggested that the unread text was no different from any other material object. It sits there in its brute materiality and means nothing until someone picks it up. If a book is different from other objects, however, it is because the moment we pick it up and begin reading, the book as object disappears and we become immersed in another world of words, images, and ideas. Poulet goes even further, however. What really fascinates him is that once we enter this world of images and ideas we cannot say that the ideas we think are ours. They come from the author and, what's more, as one traverses the entire set of images and ideas offered up by the text, one occasionally experiences a very distinct unity underlying them all. It is this unity, the author's "*cogito*," which Poulet is always in search of.

Poulet has often been criticized for two things: for his calm faith in the transparency of language (that is, he seems to believe that it allows one to move unproblematically from text to the author's consciousness), and for maintaining an essentialist notion of consciousness in which the ego is eternally self-sufficient and in full possession of itself. Both these criticisms are particularly evident in the career of the American critic J. Hillis Miller. Today Miller is known primarily for his influential role in introducing us to deconstruction, but in the early part of his career he was deeply influenced by Poulet, publishing several brilliant articles on him and recasting his own dissertation into *Charles Dickens: The World of his Novels* (1958), a book which draws heavily on the theoretical positions of Poulet. One of Miller's last articles on Poulet, however,

represents a turning point. In an essay, "Geneva or Paris" (1991), the thought of Poulet is set against that of a series of Parisians: Jacques Derrida, Roland Barthes, Michel Foucault, and Gilles Deleuze, amongst others. Miller calls into question a number of important theoretical presuppositions – Poulet's dependence on representation, his naive position toward language, and, above all, "the fundamental quality of *presence*" – and finds that all of these points have been "interrogated by Derrida and found wanting." Miller's point is that, after Derrida, the subject can no longer be conceived as a consciousness always present to itself. Rather, it is always outside itself, behind and ahead of itself, contaminated by the temporal synthesis which constitutes it. What is most interesting about Miller's essay, however, is his conclusion that one need not choose between Poulet and Derrida. The difference between deconstruction and the criticism of consciousness is a difference of degree. In fact, Poulet's position on consciousness is considerably more complex than his critics make it out to be. His work, in both its programmatic and practical dimensions, is indeed a continuous pursuit after a transcendental consciousness, but Poulet is remarkably open about the nature of such a consciousness. In some texts –"Phenomenology of reading" – it does indeed sound as though consciousness is an eternal and solipsistic ego, but in others – most notably "The dream of Descartes" in *Studies in Human Time* and his study of Baudelaire in *Exploding Poetry* – consciousness is treated as a continuous temporal synthesis which constantly derails the possibility of immediate self-sufficiency or self-transparency. Consciousness in these texts is always deferred. What is remarkable about Poulet's work is this refusal absolutely to characterize consciousness.

The appearance of reader-response criticism in England and the United States differs from the continental versions of the Constance and Geneva Schools in two important ways. First, in its early days, it was developed in relation to new developments in psychology, not the radicalization of Husserlian phenomenology. I. A. Richards, for example drew on the work of various psychologists from William James to the founder of behaviorism J. B. Watson. In his attempt to explain both literary value (what makes a work "good" or bad") and the validity of interpretations, Richards generalized the neurophysiologist C. S. Sherrington's theory of impulses. Simplifying a little, for Richards, the good poem is the one that allows the reader to hold together the greatest variety of impulses. The bad poem is the one that emphasizes only one, sometimes stereotypical, impulse. Later in the century, Norman Holland transformed Freudian psychology into a literary theory, arguing that the meaning of a text is produced in the reader's unconscious compensations for the ways in which that text challenges their sense of identity or their "identity theme." More recently Holland has turned toward cognitive science, exploring the ways in which certain brain processes might explain our attitudes toward literary texts.

The second way in which reader-response criticism differed in England and America was that the critical orthodoxy it attempted to overturn was not a canonical historicism as in France and Germany, but the opposite: new criticism's rejection of historical and biographical approaches in favor of the formal unity of the text. Richards's impressive blend of psychology, linguistics, and ethics would have seemed to have gotten a reader-based theory of literature off to a good start. But it was his minute attention to the text in his justly famous readings of canonical poetry that inspired the new critics. These new critics, in their pursuit of the poem itself, didn't simply downplay psychological approaches: they banished them altogether. Nowhere is this more clear than in what Stanley Fish (1980) has described as William K. Wimsatt and Monroe C. Beardsley's now infamous "ex cathedra," the "affective fallacy," which promulgated the notion that a criticism which began by studying the effects of a text would quickly find itself adrift in a sea of uncritical relativism and impressionism (see Wimsatt & Beardsley 1954).

Fish has positioned his "affective stylistics" as a theoretical antidote to a dogmatic formalism. Fish admits that attention to the emotional whims of readers does indeed end in impressionism and relativism. But he makes two important points in addition to this. First, he argues that the reader's contribution is not at all limited to whimsical connotations grounded in personal experience. This is because the reader doesn't come after the text. For Fish, the reader creates the text in the first place. Interpretation is not a second order activity which one undertakes after an objective and independent description of a poem. Interpretation is always unavoidably there from the start, at the level of our very perception of the poem. His second point is that this in no way implies that interpretation is arbitrary, relative, or impressionistic. The relative stability of interpretations, the fact that we can agree and disagree about an interpretation, and the fact that we can say one interpretation is better than another are all accounted for by Fish's concept of the "interpretative community." These trans-subjective communities determine which "interpretative strategies" are legitimate and which are not. Further, they change over time. Thus it would be considerably more difficult to publish an essay today demonstrating the degree to which Conrad explores the universal problems of human nature than it would have been 50 years ago. Now we make his texts speak of transatlantic exchanges and problems of national identity.

There have been several important criticisms of reader-based theory, both practical and theoretical. The American critic Jane Tompkins (1988) has pointed out that while most reader-response critics claimed to break radically with the new critical assumptions, in practice they still held strongly to two of the most central of those assumptions: that the text is the center and ground of all critical activity and that the role of the critic is simply to explicate the text. Most of the theoretical criticisms address the nature of the subject employed by various critics and even whether the category of the subject is even necessary. Marxist critics, for example, have argued that reader-response criticism overlooks the role ideology plays both in the production of meaning and in our most general relations to texts. For example, for Iser language acts on the reader directing his or her response, and Iser expertly details these various relations. What seems missing in his account for many Marxist critics is any strong sense of the degree to which language and the subject position are ideologically determined or even produced. Language simply appears as a set of pregiven rules, and the subject as an innocent space of negativity which these rules organize. Of course, one could equally reply that to invoke the social and ideological constitution of the subject is to invoke a problem to which no one has yet given a satisfactory answer. There is no doubt, however, that the question of the nature of the subject which has inspired reader-response criticism from the beginning will also will determine its future.

SEE ALSO: Fish, Stanley; Husserl, Edmund; Ingarden, Roman; Iser, Wolfgang; Miller, J. Hillis; Phenomenology; Poulet, Georges; Richards, I. A.

REFERENCES AND SUGGESTED READING

Blanchot, M. (2003). *The Book to Come* (trans. C. Mandell). Stanford: Stanford University Press.

de Man, P. (1983). The dead-end of formalist criticism. In *Blindness and Insight: Essays in the Rhetoric of Contemporary Criticism.* Minneapolis: University of Minnesota Press.

Fish, S. (1980). *Is There a Text in This Class? The Authority of Interpretive Communities.* Cambridge, MA: Harvard University Press.

Holland, N. (1975). *Five Readers Reading.* New Haven: Yale University Press.

Holland, N. (2009). *Literature and the Brain.* Gainesville, FL: PsyArt Foundation.

Husserl, E. (2001). *Analyses Concerning Passive and Active Syntheses: Lectures on Transcendental Logic* (trans. A. Steinbock). Dordrecht: Kluwer Academic Publishers. (Original lectures delivered 1920–5.)

Husserl, E. (1977). *Cartesian Meditations: An Introduction to Phenomenology* (trans. Dorion Cairns). The Hague: Martinus Nijhoff. (Original work published 1929.)

Ingarden, R. (1973). *The Literary Work of Art* (trans. G. G. Grabowicz). Evanston, IL: Northwestern University Press. (Original work published 1933.)

Iser, W. (1978). *The Act of Reading: A Theory of Aesthetic Response.* Baltimore: Johns Hopkins University Press. (Original work published 1976.)

Jauss, H. R. (1982). *Toward an Aesthetic of Reception* (trans. T. Bahti). Minneapolis: University of Minnesota Press.

Lawall, S. (1968). *The Critics of Consciousness: The Existential Structures of Reading.* Cambridge, MA: Harvard University Press.

Magliola, R. (1977). *Phenomenology and Literature: An Introduction.* West Lafayette, IN: Purdue University Press.

Miller, J. H. (1958). *Charles Dickens: The World of His Novels.* Cambridge, MA: Harvard University Press.

Miller, J. H. (1991). Geneva or Paris: Georges Poulet's "criticism of identification." In *Theory Now and Then.* London: Harvester/Wheatsheaf, pp. 27–61.

Poulet, G. (1969). The phenomenology of reading. *New Literary History,* 1(1), 53–68.

Poulet, G. (1984). *Exploding Poetry: Baudelaire/Rimbaud* (trans. Françoise Meltzer). Chicago:

University of Chicago Press. (Original work published 1980.)

Poulet, G. (1956). *Studies in Human Time* (trans. E. Coleman). New York: Harper. (Original work published 1949.)

Richards, I. A. (2001). *Principles of Literary Criticism* (ed. J. Constable). London: Routledge. (Original work published 1924.)

Richard, J.-P. (1954). *Littérature et sensation*. Paris: Éditions du Seuil.

Starobinski, J. (1989). *The Living Eye* (trans. A. Goldhammer). Cambridge, MA: Harvard University Press.

Tompkins, J. (1988) The reader in history: The changing shape of literary response. In *Reader-Response Criticism: From Formalism to Post-Structuralism*. Baltimore: Johns Hopkins University Press.

Wimsatt, W. K, & Beardsley, M. C. (1954). *The Verbal Icon: Studies in the Meaning of Poetry*. Lexington: University of Kentucky Press.

Religious Studies and the Return of the Religious

ARTHUR BRADLEY

In the context of contemporary literary and cultural theory, the return of the religious (which also goes under the name of the religious or theological turn) has manifested itself in a number of different ways. First, and most visibly, a significant number of leading contemporary philosophers commonly identified as atheist or, at least, secularist in orientation (Jacques Derrida, Michel Foucault, Jean-François Lyotard, Julia Kristeva, Luce Irigaray, Jean-Luc Nancy, Gianni Vattimo, Alain Badiou, Giorgio Agamben, Slavoj Žižek, Charles Taylor) began to explore religious texts, themes or problems in their work over the course of the past 20 years. Second, the return of the religious has also taken the form of a revisionist reading of the religious dimensions of continental philosophy itself which both offers reinterpretations of canonical thinkers such as Walter

Benjamin, Franz Rosenzweig, Carl Schmitt, Martin Heidegger, Maurice Merleau-Ponty, Jacques Lacan, and Emmanuel Levinas and reappraises hitherto marginalized or more secondary figures like Eric Petersen, Henri de Lubac, Jacob Taubes, and Michel de Certeau. Finally, the religious turn has also prompted a thoroughgoing re-evaluation of a Judeo-Christian tradition that had too easily been written off as metaphysical or ontotheological together with a contemporary reassessment of theological concepts such as messianic time, justice, givenness, confession, forgiveness, the universal, apophatic or negative theology, and, most recently, political theology. If the return of the religious in contemporary theory takes many different forms, though, a common theme running through all work in the field is a self-conscious reflection on its own inherent assumptions. What exactly is "the religious"? How does its "return" manifest itself? Why has it come back now – if, indeed, it ever went away in the first place?

It may well seem surprising to readers educated in a Western secular culture that sees religious faith as synonymous with superstition, uncritical obedience, or even pathology, but the return of the religious actually has a long and distinguished pedigree: Pascal, Descartes, Kant, Schelling, Hegel, Nietzsche, Freud, Bergson, and Heidegger are just some of the canonical thinkers of modernity who have written extensively on, and been fascinated by, the question of religion. To be sure, Heidegger always saw phenomenology as methodologically atheist – in the sense that it sought to articulate the ontological structures that underlie any ontic belief or disbelief – but he began to articulate his project of fundamental ontology through a reading of Paul's Letters to the Thessalonians in his 1922 lectures, *The Phenomenology of Religious Life* (2004). For Heidegger, the factical life of the early Christian Church – where the

Second Coming of Christ was not simply a future event to be awaited but something that structured life ontologically – is arguably the basis for his famous account of human existence as Being-towards-Death in *Being and Time* (1927). If Heidegger's own phenomenology was already in dialogue with religion from the start, this encounter becomes increasingly visible in the work of successors like Emmanuel Levinas: Levinas's phenomenology of the face-to-face relation to the other (*Autrui*) comes increasingly close to a theology (albeit one that is utterly remote from any determined tradition) when, for example, he insists that the face of the other contains the trace of god or *illeity*. Perhaps the most explicit recent attempt to articulate a theological phenomenology is Jean-Luc Marion's *God Without Being* (1991 [1982]), which seeks to pick up where the later Heidegger left off by attempting to rescue the God of faith and revelation from (idolatrous) philosophical or ontotheological concepts of essence and existence. In Dominique Janicaud's (1991) somewhat polemical view, it even became possible to speak of a "theological turn" (*tournant theologique*) in modern French phenomenology by the beginning of the 1990s: Levinas, Marion, Michel Henry, and other thinkers were charged with attempting to smuggle religion into phenomenology via the back door (Janicaud 1991).

For Jacques Derrida, whose philosophy of deconstruction emerged out of the French phenomenological tradition, the religious becomes a major theme from his essay "Of an apocalyptic tone recently adopted in philosophy" (1992[1980]) to his last major work *Rogues* (2004). It thus becomes possible to detect a religious "turn" in deconstruction to rival that of its phenomenological predecessors as Derrida increasingly focuses on quasi-theological,

questions and traditions like givenness, sacrifice, the apophatic, and, perhaps most importantly, the messianic. At the same time, however, his essay "Faith and knowledge: The two sources of 'religion' at the limits of reason alone" (1998[1992]) also offers a self-conscious reflection upon the philosophical and sociological phenomenon of the return of the religious in late modernity: rising Christian and Islamic fundamentalism, extremism, terrorism, and so on. To put a complex argument very simply, Derrida argues that the "return of the religious" describes something that is neither essentially "religious" nor even a "return" so much as the inevitable outworking of a logic that precedes both religion and secularism alike (1998[1992]: 42). If Enlightenment thought presupposes an opposition between faith and knowledge – religion and reason, the sacred and the secular – Derrida contends that this opposition is undermined by their common origin and condition: an immemorial faith, promise or openness to the other (28–9). Perhaps most importantly, Derrida goes on to argue that religion and reason's shared point of origin means that they are locked in a mutually defining but destructive ('auto-immune') relationship where each requires its apparent other in order to secure its own self-identity (44). In Derrida's account, the "return of the religious" – and in particular religious fundamentalism – cannot but occur as both the expression of, and the violent reaction against, this logic of mutual contamination (45–7).

If Heidegger, Levinas, and Derrida still remain the single most influential figures in the canon of contemporary continental philosophy of religion, the religious or theological turn has only intensified in their wake. To start with, Julia Kristeva, Luce Irigaray, and a number of other key feminist philosophers have begun to explore religious questions or themes. Kristeva, for example, begins to draw an important parallel between the fractured subject of both Christianity and psychoanalysis from *Au Commencement était l'amour* (1985) onwards. For the political philosopher Giorgio Agamben (2005[2000]), Pauline messianic time provides the means of criticizing the sovereign order which reaches its apotheosis in the normalization of the state of exception and the politicization of bare life in the name of a singular people or community "to come." Just as Derrida reverse-engineers secular modernity in order to reveal the immemorial faith that makes it possible, so Nancy performs the same gesture from the perspective of the Judeo-Christian tradition itself: Nancy's *Déconstruction du christianisme* [Deconstruction of Christianity] (2005) describes Christianity as a process of auto-critique or self-deconstruction that has its logical conclusion in secular modernity. Perhaps analogously, Gianni Vattimo [1999] contends that postmodernity itself is the product of the Judeo-Christian tradition insofar as the kenotic or self-emptying trajectory of that tradition reaches its apotheosis in the liberal secular pluralism that is unable to decide upon the competing epistemic claims of science and religion. In recent years, the return of the religious in postmodernity has also given rise to very divergent theological positions such as John D. Caputo's deconstructive "weak theology" or the neo-Augustinianism of John Milbank's radical orthodoxy.

Finally, and perhaps most surprisingly, the return of the religious has also manifested itself in the work of a group of thinkers who are hostile not simply to religion or theology in general but to the post-Heideggerian ethico-phenomenological tradition into which it has been received up till now: Badiou, Žižek, and their numerous disciples. It is not that Badiou and company embrace the religious turn – quite the

contrary – but that their critique of the prevailing conditions of contemporary thought has felt obliged at least partly to take the form of a counter-reading of the Judeo-Christian tradition. For Badiou, a new reading of St Paul's letters enables him to rehearse the theory of the event originally set out mathematically in *Being and Event* 2005[1988]): Paul's subjective fidelity to the event of Christ's resurrection paves the way not for another Levinasian affirmation of absolute alterity, but for a new universal truth that collapses the pre-existing difference between Judaic Law and Greek Logos. Just as Badiou counters Levinas's messianic alterity with a messianic universality, so Žižek seeks to resist Derrida's messianic futurity by celebrating the revolutionary urgency of Pauline messianism. If Žižek (2003) is disdainful of what he sees as the vacuous piety of Derrida's appeals to an empty, infinitely deferred messianic arrival, his critique takes the form of a renewed insistence upon the unconditional urgency of the messianic moment: what defines Pauline messianism is that the expected messiah has already arrived – we are already redeemed – even if the full implications of that redemption have not yet unfolded. In recent years, Agamben's, Badiou's, and Žižek's readings of Paul – together with important re-readings from figures like Carl Schmitt, Walter Benjamin, Eric Petersen, and Jacob Taubes – have prompted a renewed interest in the relationship between the theological and the political and a reopening of the ancient question (first posed by Marcus Terentius Varro and alluded to in Augustine's *City of God*) of what a "political theology" [*theologia politikē*] might look like; see de Vries and Sullivan 2006).

Why, to conclude, has contemporary continental philosophy (re-)turned to the religious? It is hardly surprising that this question has provoked considerable debate amongst philosophers and theologians alike. To begin with, it is important to clarify that the turn to religion should in no way be confused with a return to a precritical or dogmatic religious belief: Heidegger, Derrida, Badiou, and the vast majority of the philosophers discussed here remain either methodological or substantive atheists, while the remainder are (at least insofar as their philosophy is concerned) scarcely orthodox adherents to any theological tradition. For many theologians, in fact, philosophy's theological turn belongs to an Enlightenment tradition of secularizing or instrumentalizing Judeo-Christian revelation that stretches at least as far back as Kant: what clearly concerns figures like Heidegger, Derrida, and Badiou is not the determined theological *content* of Judeo-Christian tradition so much as a generalized ontological, phenomenological, temporal, ethical, or political *structure* that can be gleaned within it. If theology criticizes the return of the religious in contemporary thought for not going far enough, though, a number of philosophers – most notably Janicaud – have continued to question why it ever happened in the first place. On the one hand, for example, the theological turn has been roundly attacked as a tragic or culpable surrender to a precritical, mystical dogma: Quentin Meillassoux has contended that phenomenology's critique of the Absolute from the perspective of the subject–object correlation leads it to preside over a disturbing "becoming-religious of thought" (2008: 46). On the other hand, though, the return to the religious has also been more positively depicted as the outworking of a persistent theological remainder *within* the philosophical: Hent de Vries (1999: 435) follows Derrida in depicting the becoming-religious of thought as the symptom of an originary and inextricable contamination of religion and philosophy. Perhaps it is also worth adding in conclu-

sion that – whatever its implications turn out to be – philosophy's religious turn does not yet seem to apply to all religions equally. In many ways, the return of the religious remains a predominantly Judeo-Christian project (Islam is, with one or two exceptions, a surprising and revealing blindspot in much of the work) and it is to be hoped that this imbalance will be redressed in the future.

SEE ALSO: Agamben, Giorgio; Badiou, Alain; Deconstruction; Derrida, Jacques; Heidegger, Martin; Kristeva, Julia; Levinas, Emmanuel; Phenomenology; Psychoanalysis (since 1966); Žižek, Slavoj

REFERENCES AND SUGGESTED READINGS

Agamben, G. (2005). *The Time That Remains: A Commentary on the Letter to the Romans* (trans. P. Dailey). Stanford: Stanford University Press. (Original work published 2000.)

Badiou, A. (2003). *Saint Paul: The Foundation of Universalism* (trans. R. Brassier). Stanford: Stanford University Press.

Badiou, A. (2005). *Being and Event* (trans O. Feltham). London: Continuum. (Original work published 1988.)

De Vries, H. (1999). *Philosophy and the Turn to Religion*. Baltimore: Johns Hopkins University Press.

De Vries, H., & Sullivan L. E. (eds.) (2006). *Political Theologies: Public Religions in a Post-Secular World*. New York: Fordham University Press.

Derrida, J. (1992). Of an apocalyptic tone newly adopted in philosophy. In H. Coward & T. Foshay (eds.), *Derrida and Negative Theology*. New York: SUNY Press. (Original essay written 1980.)

Derrida, J. (1998). Faith and knowledge: The two sources of "religion" at the limits of reason alone (trans. S. Weber). In J. Derrida & G. Vattimo (eds.), *Religion*. Stanford: Stanford University Press. (Original work published 1992.)

Derrida, J. (2004). *Rogues: Two Essays on Reason* (trans. P.-A. Brault & M. Naas). Stanford: Stanford University Press.

818 RONELL, AVITAL

Heidegger, M. (1962). *Being and Time* (trans. J. Macquarrie and E. Robinson). New York: Harper. (Original work published 1927.)

Heidegger, M. (2004). *The Phenomenology of Religious Life* (trans. M. Fritsch & J. A. Gosetti-Ferencei). Bloomington: Indiana University Press.

Janicaud, D. (1991). *Le Tournant théologique de la phénoménologie française* [The Theological Turn of French Phenomenology]. Paris: L'Eclat.

Kristeva, J. (1985). *Au Commencement était l'amour: Psychoanalyse et foi* [In the Beginning was Love: Psychoanalysis and Faith]. Paris: Hachette.

Levinas, E. (1991). *Otherwise Than Being or Beyond Essence* (trans. A. Lingis). Dordrecht: Kluwer.

Marion, J.-L. (1991). *God Without Being: Hors-Texte* (trans. T. A. Carlson). Chicago: Chicago University Press. (Original work published 1982.)

Meillassoux, Q. (2008). *After Finitude: An Essay on the Necessity of Contingency* (trans. R. Brassier). London: Continuum.

Nancy, J.-L. (2005). *La Déclosion: Déconstruction du christianisme 1*. Paris: Galilée.

Vattimo, G. (1999). *Belief* (trans. L. d'Isanto & D. Webb). Stanford: Stanford University Press.

Ward, G. (2000). *Theology and Contemporary Critical Theory*. Basingstoke: Macmillan.

Žižek, S. (2003). *The Puppet and the Dwarf: The Perverse Core of Christianity*. Cambridge, MA: MIT Press.

Ronell, Avital

SIMON MORGAN WORTHAM

Avital Ronell was born in Prague in 1952. Her parents were Israeli diplomats of German-Jewish descent who settled in New York having first returned to Israel, where Ronell spent her early childhood. She studied with Jacob Taubes at the Hermeneutic Institute of Berlin, earned her doctoral degree at Princeton in the late 1970s, and subsequently worked in Paris with Hélène Cixous and Jacques Derrida. She was professor of comparative literature and theory at the University of California, Berkeley, before returning to New York to take up a chair in German and comparative literature at New York University, where for several years she taught a seminar alongside Derrida, whose texts she has helped to translate. Alongside her position at NYU, Ronell also holds the Jacques Derrida Chair at the European Graduate School in Switzerland. Ronell's critical encounters with Goethe, Nietzsche, Benjamin, Heidegger, Derrida, and Freud – and also Kathy Acker and George Bush – have lead to compelling texts on such disparate subjects as AIDS, crack, stupidity, trauma, haunting, pornography, war, and technology. Once a performance artist, she is also credited as having established addiction studies in the US.

The Telephone Book (1989) is perhaps Ronell's best-known early work. It is a book *on* the telephone. *On*, not in the sense of being *about* its subject matter, that is to say approaching its topic from a stably detached position of theoretical investigation and scholarly reflection. More radically, this is a text that takes place by way of, on condition of the telephone itself, as something like a medium of thinking. Not only does the book in its material appearance look as if it could be a telephone book (and indeed it is indexed like one), but it reads and addresses lofty figures in the European tradition (Goethe, Kafka, Heidegger, among others) according to a fictive structure that also includes prank calls, collect calls, chatter and small talk, not to mention the always theatrical act of calling up the dead in séances. (Ronell's *Dictations: On Haunted Writing* [1993b] dwells precisely on the call of the other as an indispensable condition of writing, which is therefore always summoned and inhabited by a certain spectrality.) In *The Telephone Book*, not only is pop culture (notably, the culture of a certain parodic reproducibility of one form in another) cross-wired with the high tones of philosophy and literature, but soberly disinterested scholarship gets jammed by a switchboard lit up through engaging fictive play. The unconventional layout, design, and typography which helped make the book a collector's item promotes a sense of distortion and disconnection in which the author, figured as an addressee not so much of individual callers as of an entire static-ridden (and thus phantasmic) network, participates in a fundamentally inventive kind of text in which literature and philosophy very much remain "on the line," although in nearly inaudible/newly audible ways, after the advent of the telephonic era. In the process, challenging questions of the most serious kind are raised about today's technologies and machines, about schizoid psychology, telepathy, consumer culture, the ethics, politics, and phenomenology of the other, and so forth – questions that, we end up feeling, can't be addressed *except* on the telephone.

In *Crack Wars: Literature, Addiction, Mania* (1993a), meanwhile, Ronell is less interested in the idea of drugs as a literary motif, and much more concerned with the question of whether addiction might provide something like the medium and structure of the literary text and of philosophical thought; in other words, whether literature and philosophy are themselves best understood by way of a certain narcoanalysis. Bringing "theory" down to the level and language of the street, she substitutes for the supposed dignity and heroism of intellectual and literary endeavor a powerful stimulant for rethinking received philosophical concepts: in other words, for blowing our minds. Here, again, psychoanalytic, political, and cultural critique are brought together in a heady cocktail. Ronell's trademark is to induce an excessively proximous, yet far from harmonious, confrontation with the "object" of inquiry. Neither exactly inside nor outside the subject matter, the reader – like the writer – is left no comfort zone for detached contemplation, but nor can they reconcile themselves to their "topic," come to terms with or gain posses-

sion of it. One might say, indeed, that Ronell is a "topical" writer principally in the sense that she brings or applies us to the always divisible surface of the very skin of things, neither quite inside nor outside them. Drugs, like the telephone, profoundly mediate their own investigation, without by any means restoring a self-reflexive or self-identical presence to that which they apparently name. And to inhabit this "topical" zone is perhaps what most characterizes the meticulous and irreverent acts of reading that Ronell everywhere undertakes.

In *Stupidity* (2001), Ronell refuses to endorse the age-old distinction between what is "'stupid," on the one hand, and a host of assumed opposites on the other. Instead, knowledge, learning, intelligence, and understanding are all pitched as, in part, the products of a certain stupidity; whereas the interruption of what we might call good sense and rationality by an unscholarly kind of stupidity (both forcefully unrefined and yet deeply unsure of itself) is much more – and much less – than stupid. Here, stupidity is not so stupid as to reveal itself in the form of an "object" of knowledge. Instead, stupidity provides the conditions to rethink knowledge itself from a "viewpoint" that exceeds or falls short of the perspective of any simple intentionality, and which never amounts to or produces what Derrida would call the "masterable-possible."

In short, the ethico-political commitment of Ronell's work can be aligned with an acute attentiveness to the material textures of language and thought, caught between disparate media, cultures, and technologies, and a deliberately ungainly straddling of the high–low divide, in which the magisterial accomplishments of a scholar are deeply disturbed by the summons of the other – ghost, addict, idiot, caller – in the interruptive, uncertain, and inappropriable interests of another future and another responsibility.

SEE ALSO: Derrida, Jacques;
Postmodernism; Poststructuralism; Specters

REFERENCES AND SUGGESTED
READINGS

Ronell, A. (2001). *Stupidity*. Chicago: University of
Illinois Press.
Ronell, A. (1998). *Finitude's Score: Essays for the End
of the Millennium*. Lincoln: University of
Nebraska Press.
Ronell, A. (1993). *Crack Wars: Literature, Addiction,
Mania*. Lincoln: University of Nebraska Press.
Ronell, A. (1993). *Dictations: On Haunted Writing*.
Lincoln: University of Nebraska Press.
Ronell, A. (1989). *Telephone Book: Technology,
Schizophrenia, Electric Speech*. Lincoln: University of Nebraska Press.

Rose, Jacqueline

SHAHIDHA BARI

Jacqueline Rose (b. 1949) is a British academic working in the fields of psychoanalysis, feminism and visual culture. A lecturer in English at Queen Mary College, University of London since 1993, her critical work is characterized by its interdisciplinary approach and political commitment. Rose's first published work, *The Case of Peter Pan, or, the Impossibility of Children's Fiction* (1984), explored the production and dissemination of children's literature, deploying a psychoanalytical approach to identify the determinedly ideological ends of such works. Rose's *Sexuality in the Field of Vision*, which explored the intersection of feminism, psychoanalysis, semiotics, and film criticism, supplied an important contribution to a developing field of cultural studies. The essays in the book probe the production of normative gender and sexual identities across a variety of texts, including Freud's case notes on Dora, and T. S Eliot's essay on *Hamlet*. In her readings, Rose identifies the key fantasies operating in Western culture which enforce fundamental differences in

gender identity and sexuality. For Rose, the issue of sexual difference remains a primary law of subject formation, and psychoanalysis diagnoses the problems of identification that arise from such laws. Since psychoanalysis supplies terms for understanding how identity is constituted and explains the mechanisms by which ideological processes are transformed into human actions, and psychoanalysis is able to recognize the political nature of identification.

In particular, psychoanalysis provides an account of the experience of femininity, where the conception of the unconscious indicates the complexity of a gender identity formed by practices rather than a simple internalization of norms. Rose reads Freud's own impasse in diagnosing the case of Dora, for instance, as the failure of a normative concept of femininity that implicitly recognizes the fragmented and aberrant nature of sexuality itself. Rose's analysis extends from the reading of death and sexuality in *Hamlet* to an investigation into the twin axes of identification and fantasy made visible in the technologies of film. For Rose, the psychoanalytical account of sexuality rejects any essential biological or natural content, and presents instead an economy of demand and desire. Although Rose deploys psychoanalysis in the service of feminism, deriving from it an account of the ideological imposition of female identity, she also recognizes that if feminism calls for plural conceptions of sexual identity, then psychoanalysis reveals the psychic violence with which feminist identity politics must contend.

Rose's 1991 monograph on Sylvia Plath was notable for the hostile disclaimers it provoked from Plath's estate on behalf of Ted Hughes. While Rose argued for writing as a space for exploring the ambiguities of psychic drives and desires, Hughes objected to what he perceived as an assault on Plath's sexual identity. Rose employs the heroicized

Plath produced by previous feminist criticism as a starting point to explore the distinction between fantasy and reality, distinguishing between the author's poetic explorations and their lived experience. Combining close readings of poems with psychoanalytical conceptions of fantasy, Rose considers the relation of sexuality to writing, identifying in language the possibility of disturbing the cohesive identity and secure sexuality that is designated normative.

In later work, Rose sought to track the effects of the unconscious in contemporary politics, most particularly in regard to the conflicts of Israel/Palestine and South Africa. In *States of Fantasy* (1998), Rose explores how the psychoanalytical conception of fantasy informs collective identification, recognizing literature as a particular site for securing fantasy as selfhood. Reading Amos Oz's *In the Land of Israel*, Rose identifies Oz as a critic of the occupation, a writer who diagnoses the absolutist fantasy of Israel, but whose writing also betrays the psychic and political tensions of his own identifications. Rose makes a case for a politicized literature and literary criticism that is not measured in the transformations that it effects, but which reveals instead how beings transform and obstruct themselves. For Rose, the task for literary studies is to read carefully, articulating the varying relationships of affirmation, recognition, and antagonism between peoples and cultures.

A critic of the Israeli occupation of Palestinian territories, Rose writes frequently on Middle Eastern politics. Her psychoanalytical reading of the literature of Zionism argues that the modern Israeli conception of nationhood springs both from this literature and the historical injuries of a collective Jewish political identity. In *The Question of Zion* (2005), she presents close readings of the literary and historical texts of Zionism, reappraising a Zionism that she identifies as emerging from the legitimate desires of persecuted people for a homeland. Rose analyses the psychic and political forces which inform Zionism and questions the passionate allegiance it commands, while considering the possibility for national identifications that extend beyond idealization or radical dissent. Dedicated to the Palestinian critic Edward Said, *The Question of Zion* deploys literary criticism for political analysis. In *The Last Resistance* (2007), Rose examines the role of literature in the formation of cultural memory and nationhood. Focusing on the question of Israel and Palestine, she also examines post-apartheid South Africa, and American nationalism post-9/11, offering criticism as a means of exploring psychic and subjective transformations.

Rose is a regular contributor to the *London Review of Books*. In 2004, she collaborated with Channel 4 to produce the documentary *Dangerous Liaisons: Israel and the US*. Her first novel, *Albertine*, was published in 2001. She is the sister of philosopher Gillian Rose and a Fellow of the British Academy.

SEE ALSO: Freud, Sigmund; Said, Edward

REFERENCES AND SUGGESTED READINGS

Rose, J. (1984). *The Case of Peter Pan, or, the Impossibility of Children's Fiction*. Philadelphia: University of Pennsylvania Press.

Rose, J. (1986). *Sexuality in the Field of Vision*. London: Verso.

Rose, J. (1991). *The Haunting of Sylvia Plath*. London: Virago.

Rose, J. (1998). *States of Fantasy: The Clarendon Lectures in English*. Oxford: Clarendon Press.

Rose, J. (2005). *The Question of Zion*. Princeton: Princeton University Press.

Rose, J. (2007). *The Last Resistance*. London: Verso.

S

Said, Edward

SHAHIDHA BARI

Born in Jerusalem in 1935, the literary critic, campaigner, and postcolonial scholar, Edward Said, spent his early childhood in Jerusalem and Cairo, before studying in the United States at Princeton and Harvard universities. In 1963, he took up a professorship in comparative literature at Columbia University. From his father, a Protestant Palestinian with US citizenship, and his mother, who had been born in Nazareth, Said inherited a lasting attachment to the Middle East and he remained a committed campaigner for Palestinian rights throughout his life. For Said, the childhood experiences of displacement and deracination cultivated an adult sensitivity to cultural and political acts of exclusion and awakened in him the possibility of a resistant, exilic form of identity. These experiences informed Said's thinking and surface repeatedly in his work, most visibly in *Out of Place*, his memoir of an Arab childhood and an American education, which was awarded the New Yorker Book Award for Non-Fiction in 1999. This biographical outing offered variations on the themes of exile and marginalization that run through Said's many works. A foundational thinker for postcolonial studies, Said became an internationally recognizable public intellectual.

A prolific essayist, his work ranged across the fields of literature, politics, and music. His literary criticism considered the works of canonical writers such as Swift, Austen, and Conrad, as well as contemporary writers such as Soueif and Naipaul, while his musical criticism included meditations on Wagner, Verdi, and Gould. Said's writing reflects the broad span of his influences, which extend to the early Marxist criticism of Antonio Gramsci and Theodor Adorno, and the later poststructuralist theory of Michel Foucault. In 1999 he co-founded the West-Eastern Divan Orchestra with Israeli musician Daniel Barenboim. He was president of the Modern Languages Association, and a fellow of the American Academy of Arts and Sciences. Said's damning critique of the Western disfiguration of the "Orient," his insistence on understanding aesthetic works in social and political contexts, and his conception of contrapuntal reading made a lasting contribution to modern literary theory. He died in 2003.

In his early work, *Beginnings* (1985), Said interrogates the idea of "origins" that claim to be divine, mythic, and privileged, and poses instead the idea of "beginnings" that are secular, human, and continually recalibrated. Said takes the example of literary beginnings in order to theorize the idea of many beginnings, capable of contesting a single narrative of "origins." Beginnings, as

The Encyclopedia of Literary and Cultural Theory   General editor: Michael Ryan
© 2011 Blackwell Publishing Ltd

Said envisages them, fracture the authority of orthodox and dominant systems of thought, presenting a necessary point of departure for intellectual and creative thinking. Beginnings also assert the continuity of a secular history in which human beings are "always-already" immersed and whose narrative they may contest, alter, and revise. In this respect, *Beginnings* initiates Said's critical scholarship as a thinker committed to contesting, altering, and revising narratives of a singular human history.

Published in 1978, Said's *Orientalism* is a touchstone of twentieth-century literary criticism. Its radical exposé of Eurocentric universalism laid the foundations for postcolonial theory. Said argues that Europe colonized the East not only economically, but also discursively and cognitively. Just as the raw materials of the East were appropriated for Western use, so also the detail and texture of Eastern life were absorbed into stereotypical categories that served a useful function in the West's concept of itself. Rather than be a world known for itself, the East became the West's "other," a comparative entity that confirmed Western assumptions of superiority. If the West was industrious, rational, and modern, the East was lazy, emotional, and traditional. Drawing on Foucault's description of discourse, Said paid special attention to the way Western scholarship created a discursive Orient, a body of knowledge that categorized the worlds of the East and subsumed their myriad differences into one totalizing and highly stereotypical picture.

The insights yielded by *Orientalism* inspired a postcolonial criticism committed to illuminating the diversity of other literatures and which continues to implicate the symbolic and territorial violence of colonial power. Yet Said's account also elicited broad criticism. For some, his analysis perversely misread the sympathetic accounts of the East presented by Orientalist

scholarship; for others Said's critique of British imperial power fails to attend similarly to Ottoman and Persian empires. Ironically, critics leveled at Said his own charges of prejudiced and partial representation, accusing his "Orient" of being limited to Palestine and Egypt, and his account guilty of stereotyping Europe in turn. The legacy of Said's critique, though, is a continuing vigilance over the prevailing representations of cultures, and a recognition of the imperial and ideological operations of scholarship, knowledge, and imagination.

In *Covering Islam* (1981), Said channels the insights of *Orientalism* to examine the representations of Islam and Islamic countries by Western media, governments, corporations, and scholarship.

He observes that all sites of cultural and ideological production are complicit in the limited register of Western representations of Islam, which render it synonymous with terrorism, fundamentalism, and religious extremism. The deployment of the terms "terrorism" and "fundamentalism" in the analysis of political conflicts warrants special caution for Said, who identifies them as fearful terms that lack content but assert the moral power and approval of those who yield them. His analysis also extends to examine Islam's representations of itself to itself, observing the ways in which Islamic countries deploy an idea of "Islam" to justify unrepresentative and often repressive regimes. If *Orientalism* exposed the coextension of knowledge and power, *Covering Islam* investigates the representations of Islam (both by others and to itself) as a biased discursive expression, posing the question of whether knowledge and power can be more justly engaged in relation to each other.

In *Culture and Imperialism* (1993) Said investigates the reach of Western imperialism through its cultural productions, arguing that works as diverse as Conrad's

Heart of Darkness, Jane Austen's *Mansfield Park*, and Verdi's *Aida*, knowingly and unknowingly, assert the authority of imperial domination. The essays develop the thesis of *Orientalism* by investigating the intricate relationship between cultural forms and the identities they produce, authorize, and deny. Said traces how European cultural forms not only affirm a right to rule, but also authorize oppression as moral obligation. He defines "culture" as acts of description, communication, and representation (often aesthetic) that are autonomous from economic, social, and political realms, but which can be engaged in the service of political and ideological causes. Imperialism, which refers to the forceful appropriation of land, is a process that is reflected, contested, and decided in the cultural narratives that surround and spring from it. For Said, the implication of this relationship is that the cruelty of colonialism is inseparable from the poetry, music, and philosophy that it also produces. Strikingly, his analysis prescribes only closer and yet more respectful engagement with such texts, rather than rejection, and in this regard his work retains a lingering admiration for the attentive modes of the old "New Criticism" tradition. His reading of Conrad's *Heart of Darkness*, for example, offers a sophisticated alternative to the blanket accusation of racism issued in Chinua Achebe's essay on the same text. Said observes the duality of Conrad's narrative, which demonstrates how imperial excursions are underwritten by an idea of a right to forcefully possess other lands, but also exposes the immorality of a practice that is obscured by the justifications of a self-aggrandizing, self-originating authority. Said recognizes the aesthetic merit of a novel that could be capable both of narrating the practices of imperialism, while exposing the self-deceptions it requires in order to continue do so. The narratives of colonialism, for Said, require this attentive

kind of "contrapuntal" reading, where one reads *punctus contra punctum* – "point against point" – for the differing, dependent, and syncopated parts of a melody. This practice of reading attends to what may have been forcibly or implicitly silenced or excluded, and extends to texts that may not immediately appear colonial or postcolonial. Jane Austen's *Mansfield Park*, for instance, a resolutely English novel, Said reads contrapuntally, noting the quiet inquiries Fanny Price makes to her uncle regarding his business interests in the Antiguan slave trade, and the silence with which they are received. Said argues through *Mansfield Park* that the narratives of imperialism stretch back before the nineteenth-century "scramble for Africa," and that earlier cultural forms might be implicated in the relationship of culture and imperialism. Culture itself is indicted, by Said, as a place of exclusive canonical selection, and he notes that colonialism also elicits narratives of resistance and opposition from sources as diverse as Frantz Fanon, C. L. R. James, and W. B. Yeats. Said argues that the culture of resistance is as powerful as the culture of imperialism, asserting the capacity to reclaim, rename, and reinhabit occupied lands with new assertions and identifications.

In the conclusion to *Culture and Imperialism* Said observes that the practices of critical resistance require safeguarding from institutional and disciplinary cultures of professionalization. While Marxism, structuralism, feminism, and Third World studies emerge in English departments with interrogative rigor, they are also increasingly pacified formations of knowledge, identifiable as academic subspecialties. For Said, if culture is a site of ideological affirmation, then criticism must be vigilantly guarded as an inappropriable and radical interpretative force. Said examines the increasing institutionalization of critical consciousness more closely in the essay collection, *The World, the*

Text, the Critic, analyzing the complacencies of structuralist and poststructuralist traditions. He argues that if modern literary theory seeks to transform the strict disciplinarity and orthodoxies of the traditional university, then its increasing institutionalization threatens to blunt its edge. He critiques too the reflexivity of theories that displace history with arguments of labyrinthine textuality. Instead, he insistently recalls the worldliness of texts, that record or form part of the human lives, social existence, and historical moments in which they are located and interpreted.

Consequently, Said offers a conception of "humanist criticism" which reaffirms these connections while advocating a critical consciousness that remains reflective, alert to its own failings, and skeptical of hermetic systems, even those that might be called "postcolonial." In this respect, Said, following Adorno, acknowledges the singularity of art as a model of resistance to systematic appropriations. The works of Swift, Hopkins, Conrad, and Fanon offer such resistance; Said proposes that their exemplary attention to the singularity of existence is inappropriable to any organization of power or interpretation. Swift, whose prose style is often anarchic, eccentric, and agitational, resists even the appropriations of modern critical theory, eluding readings that could be reducible to doctrine or political position. Said retrieves from his reading of Swift the possibility of alternatives to dominant formations of social organization and the creative capacity for alternative acts of interpretation. In his essay "Traveling theory" (1982; see Bayoumi and Rubin 2000: 195–217), he cautions against the pacification of critical consciousness and the assimilation of theory to dogma, promoting, instead, an idea of mobility where theoretical frameworks are never completed nor ideas exhausted by the models or mantras produced by theory. For Said, the history

of imperialism discloses the consequences of the effort by one culture to comprehend, dominate, or capture another, and he exalts instead the dynamism of a ceaseless critical thinking that eludes this impulse for containment.

For Said, the relation of knowledge and power defines the field of criticism, literary and political, and this is most apparent in his critical writing regarding Palestine. In the issue of Palestinian statehood, Said's literary, musical, and political analysis converge. In 1977, he was elected to the Palestine national council as an independent intellectual, and his diplomatic role included assisting with Arab–English translations of the draft treaty leading to the Oslo Peace Process. Although Said withdrew from this process, rejecting the Oslo Accords as unfairly weighted toward Israeli interest, he was an advocate of the two-state solution, implicitly recognizing Israel's right to exist. For him, the question of Palestine epitomized the necessity of a complex and sensitive contrapuntal thinking which could acknowledge but dissociate the legacy and trauma of the Holocaust from the Palestinian question. *The Question of Palestine* (1992) remains one of Said's most provocative works, demonstrating the rigor of his historical scholarship, critical analysis, and contrapuntal thinking. In it, he explores the collisions of Palestinian and Israeli claims for statehood and tracks their continuing repercussions, considering the complex relationship of occupier and occupied, and examining the role of the West in the Middle East. The study offers a history of the Palestinian people through its literature, and traces the inception of Zionist ideologies through the writings of figures such as Theodor Herzl and Menachem Begin, as well as employing demographic and sociological analyses. For Said, understanding the question of Palestine requires this multitextual and interdisciplinary analysis; comprehending the modern formations of Israel/Palestine and the violence it inspires requires the resources of history and philology.

The publication of *The Question of Palestine* ratified the explicit political bent of the critical function as Said understood it, and it reaffirmed the original insights of *Orientalism* in its understanding of the discursive formation of Palestinian and Israeli identities and the residual colonial logic at work in the claims for nationhood. In his later collaborative project with photographer Jean Mohr, *After the Last Sky* (1998), Said contests the limited register of media representations of Palestinians as murderous terrorists or pitiful refugees, by punctuating Mohr's photographs of daily life with his own commentary and the interleaved poetry of Mahmoud Darwish. Charting the effects of successive dispossessions, Said sought to present a Palestinian identity not limited to exilic status, but fortified by it. His last collaboration with Daniel Barenboim demonstrated again his willingness to experiment with interdisciplinarity and multimedia, but also acknowledged the musical origin of contrapuntal criticism. The conversations between Barenboim and Said, recorded in *Parallels and Paradoxes* (2002), reveal the fluency of Said's own "traveling theory," moving between music, literature, and politics. Rearticulating the Adornian insight that the bristling complexity of music might serve as indictment of reductive systematizations, Said recognizes in art the critique of intractably rigid national allegiance. Music, he insists, is unrepeatable, but also a language for experiences of unique and complex identifications and dislocation. The opening phrases of Beethoven's Fourth Symphony he reads as an articulation of belonging and strangeness; the long sustained notes followed by silence impress upon the listener a harmonic "feeling at home," a feeling of being in no man's land and then finding a way home

once more, necessary for the affirmation of an identity forged by its willingness to encounter difference without violence.

In his last work, *Humanism and Democratic Criticism*, published posthumously in 2004, Said proposes that questioning, challenging, and defending a canon is the work both of a properly humanistic education and the responsibility of a democratic criticism. The philological component of this criticism that requires the critic to penetrate language in order to disclose what might be hidden binds democracy to literature in a special way. Art remains for Said the domain for what might be yet ungrasped, waiting in readiness for articulation but free from imposition. For Said, criticism is a political and humanist practice insofar as it excavates silence and illuminates places of exclusion and invisibility, restoring the testimony of barely surviving itinerant groups that have survived the displacements of colonization in old imperial and new capitalist forms. Said's legacy is his invocation of the intellectual responsibility to further the formulations and expectations of those who might seek social justice and economic equality, where critical consciousness challenges the imposed silences of normalized power, not only identifying situations of crisis but discerning the possibilities for intervention.

SEE ALSO: Adorno, Theodor; Althusser, Louis; Foucault, Michel; Marx, Karl; Orientalism; Rose, Jacqueline

REFERENCES AND SUGGESTED READINGS

Bayoumi, M., & Rubin, A. (2000). *The Said Reader*. New York: Vintage Books.
Said, E. (1978). *Orientalism*. London: Vintage.
Said, E. (1981). *Covering Islam: How the Media and the Experts Determine How We See the Rest of the World*. New York: Pantheon.

Said, E. (1983). *The World, the Text, the Critic*. Cambridge, MA: Harvard.

Said, E. (1985). *Beginnings: Intention and Method*. New York: Columbia University Press.

Said, E. (1992). *The Question of Palestine*. London: Vintage.

Said, E. (1993). *Culture and Imperialism*. New York: Random House.

Said, E., with Mohr, J. (1998). *After the Last Sky*. New York: Columbia University Press.

Said, E. (2000). *Out of Place: A Memoir*. London: Granta Books.

Said, E. (2002). *Parallels and Paradoxes: Explorations in Music and Society*. London: Vintage.

Said, E. (2004). *Humanism and Democratic Criticism*. London: Palgrave Macmillan.

Scholes, Robert

JOE HUGHES

Robert Scholes (b. 1929) has written more than 20 books on topics ranging from contemporary fiction and science fiction, to structuralism and the role of literary theory in the classroom, to the rise of literature as an academic discipline. He is best known for his work in twentieth-century fiction and in particular for his concept of fabulation.

Realism, Scholes argued in *The Fabulators* (1967), was on its last legs. It was challenged by advances in psychology, by the cinema, and by suspicions regarding the abilities of language to reach the real. The further fiction plumbed the depths of the unconscious, the closer it came to archetypes or ideas and thus the closer it came to allegory. The cinema was able to provide far more accurate representations of the real than fiction could, and it too could give them narrative shape (1967: 12). At the same time, philosophers, novelists, and physicists were discovering that their sentences and formulae were fundamentally unable to reach the real. An irreducible gap had emerged between language and reality. "It is because reality cannot be recorded that realism is

dead," Scholes claimed in *Structural Fabulation* (1975: 7). For all of these reasons, realism was, and may still turn out to be, an unviable option for fiction.

In the 1960s, Scholes felt that the critical establishment was unable to come to terms with a new kind of "postrealistic" fiction which responded to this situation, embodied in authors like John Barth, Lawrence Durrell, Iris Murdoch, John Hawkes, and Kurt Vonnegut among others. In 1966, he wrote, with Robert Kellogg:

> [T]wentieth century narrative has begun to break away from the aims, attitudes, and techniques of realism. The implications of this break are still being explored, developed, and projected by many of the most interesting writers of narrative literature in Europe and America. But, by and large, our reviewers are hostile to this new literature and our critics are unprepared for it. (Scholes & Kellogg 1966: 5)

Scholes hoped to provide critics with a mode of access to this new postrealistic fiction. This is what the concept of "fabulation" was supposed to do.

The difficulty of grasping this concept of fabulation, and the reason many critics of the 1960s and '70s missed its importance, was that Scholes was not approaching fiction empirically. "I am something of a Platonist," he wrote in *Fabulation and Metafiction* (1979: 106). This doesn't simply mean that he distinguishes essence from existence. It means that rather than surveying past and currently existing modes of fiction and inducing a general concept, he derives the possibilities of fiction from the very idea of fiction itself – from the idea of something created by the imagination. In *Elements of Fiction* (1968), he outlines a continuum which distinguishes four literary modes according to their distance from reality. Closest to fact is history. Next comes realism, which is followed by romance. Fantasy, a product of pure imagination, occupies the far right of the spectrum (1968: 9). If realism was losing its power (and it doesn't matter from this idealist point of view that Saul Bellow or Philip Roth were still writing compelling realistic fiction) the question for Scholes was where it could go. It could go toward history, but Scholes thought it was already headed toward the right, and he coined the word "fabulation" to designate this "revival of romance."

Scholes chose the word "fabulation" for its proximity to fables. In fact he cites a very specific fable for his inspiration – the eighth fable of Petrus Alphonsus appended to Caxton's 1484 translation of Aesop. There were three characteristics of fables which Scholes hoped to capture with the term: their unapologetic distance from realism, their attention to and delight in design and craft, and their didactic function. Fabulation "means a return to a more verbal kind of fiction. It also means a return to a more fictional kind. By this I mean a less realistic and more artistic kind of narrative: more shapely, more evocative; more concerned with ideas and ideals, less concerned with things" (1967: 12). If postrealistic fiction delights in design and imagination, it still retains a hold on the world. While it isn't realistic, it does create models and patterns of the world in which we live. Thus, in temporarily abandoning life, it allows us to fix our gaze upon it. "All fiction," Scholes claims, "contributes to cognition, then, by providing us with models that reveal the nature of reality by their very failure to coincide with it" (1975: 7). While it was more imaginative than history and realism, fabulation provided a didactic function because the link to reality – through imaginative modeling – was not entirely severed.

It is this emphasis on didactic fabulation that seems to have drawn Scholes to science fiction. Scholes was one of the first critics to give science fiction a serious consideration – the only book-length academic consider-

ation of science fiction before his was Kingsley Amis's New Maps of Hell (1960). In works like Structural Fabulation (1975) and Science Fiction: History Science, Vision (written with Eric S. Rabkin in 1977), Scholes demonstrates the way science fiction develops the literary and didactic potential of the imagination. Science fiction is not unbridled imagination for the fun of it. We do not simply luxuriate in ungoverned imaginings. Rather, writers imagine a world to come, and this world is highly structured. This is what distinguishes "structural fabulation" from simple fabulation: structural fabulation presents us with a well-developed model of a possible world. "That modern body of fictional works which we loosely designate 'science fiction' either accepts or pretends to accept what is not yet apparent or existent, and it examines this in some systematic way" (1975: 102).

Scholes's recent work has tended in two directions. Works such as In Search of James Joyce (1992) and Paradoxy of Modernism (2006) develop his earlier work on James Joyce (1961) and explore the literary and popular aspects of modernism. Works like The Rise and Fall of English (1998) and The Crafty Reader (2001) are concerned with the state and potential of literary studies. In The Crafty Reader he begins to outline various ways of reading. In the same way that the craft of writing can be taught, so too can the craft of reading. Scholes provides various techniques, tools, and "ways of reading" for several different genres.

SEE ALSO: Postmodernism; Semiotics; Structuralism

REFERENCES AND SUGGESTED READINGS

Scholes, R. (1961). The Cornell Joyce Collection: A Catalogue. Ithaca: Cornell University Press.

Scholes, R. (1967). *The Fabulators*. New York: Oxford University Press.

Scholes, R. (1968). *Elements of Fiction*. New York: Oxford University Press.

Scholes, R. (1974). *Structuralism in Literature*. New Haven: Yale University Press.

Scholes, R. (1975). *Structural Fabulation: An Essay on the Future of Fiction*. Notre Dame: University of Notre Dame Press.

Scholes, R. (1979). *Fabulation and Metafiction*. Urbana: University of Illinois Press.

Scholes, R. (1982). *Semiotics and Interpretation*. New Haven: Yale University Press.

Scholes, R. (1992). *In Search of James Joyce*. Urbana: University of Illinois Press.

Scholes, R. (1998). *The Rise and Fall of English*. New Haven: Yale University Press.

Scholes, R. (2001). *The Crafty Reader*. New Haven: Yale University Press.

Scholes, R. (2006). *Paradoxy of Modernism*. New Haven: Yale University Press.

Scholes, R., & Kellogg, R. (1966). *The Nature of Narrative*. New York: Oxford University Press.

Scholes. R., & Rabkin E. S. (1977). *Science Fiction: History, Science, Vision*. New York: Oxford University Press.

Sedgwick, Eve Kosofsky

KOONYONG KIM

Eve Kosofsky Sedgwick (1950–2009) is best known as a key figure in queer theory. She was born in Dayton, Ohio and received her BA from Cornell University in 1971 and her PhD from Yale University in 1975. She taught at Hamilton College, Boston University, and Amherst College before moving to Duke University, where from 1988 to 1998 she, together with her colleagues Jonathan Goldberg and Michael Moon, helped to consolidate queer studies as a new paradigm of literary and cultural theory. On leaving Duke in 1998, she became Distinguished Professor of English at the Graduate Center at the City University of New York.

As befits her description of herself as "a deconstructive and very writerly close reader," Sedgwick's oeuvre from her doctoral thesis, *The Coherence of Gothic Conventions*, onward can be characterized as a series of arduous endeavors to decenter binaristic oppositions upon which our traditional understanding of sexuality and gender is based and to call for a nonregulative and productive cartography of myriad sexual orientations and identity formations. In *Between Men: English Literature and Male Homosocial Desire* (1985), one of the founding texts in the evolution of queer studies, she reads a wide range of British novels from the mid-eighteenth to the mid-nineteenth century and conceptualizes what she calls "homosocial desire." The term "homosocial," as it is used in history and the social sciences, designates social bonds between people of the same sex, usually with no sexual desire attached, and is therefore distinguishable from "homosexual." Nevertheless Sedgwick places "homosocial" back into the realm of desire and hypothesizes a continuum between homosocial and homosexual desire, thereby exploring the general and specific structure of men's relations with other men. More specifically, she draws on René Girard's insistence that in a love triangle, the same-sex bond is no less intense and powerful than the bond either of the two rivals forms with the beloved, and examines the ways in which men's homosocial bonding is structured through triangulated desire involving a woman who simultaneously mediates and averts the possible development of homoeroticism. As she thus attends to the destructive effects of such a routing of men's same-sex bonding through male–female bonds, Sedgwick discusses the asymmetrical way in which there exists a continuum of homosocial and homosexual bonding among women whereas that continuum is radically disrupted and dichotomized for men in homophobic culture. She traces the historically disparate contours of male and female homosociality with a view toward examining the way that "the shapes of sexuality" and "what *counts* as sexuality" are deeply grounded in the inequality of power between men and women.

If *Between Men* ends with a discussion of the radical disruption of the male homosocial continuum and the emergence of discourse on homosexuality at the end of the nineteenth century, Sedgwick's next book, *Epistemology of the Closet* (1990), takes up the history precisely at that moment. Sedgwick insists that any meaningful understanding and knowledge (epistemology) of modern Western culture should grapple with the incoherent and contradictory definitional structure of homo/heterosexuality. In particular, she formulates two interrelated contradictions internal to the modern structure of sexuality and gender. The first is what she refers to as the contradiction between "a minoritizing view" and "a universalizing view," a contradiction revolving around the question of whether homo/heterosexual definition is to be thought of as a critical issue only for a small group of gay or lesbian individuals or whether it pertains to every subject in society. The second concerns the contradiction between seeing homosexuality as "a matter of liminality or transitivity between genders" (i.e., queer people are situated between genders) and seeing it through the lens of "gender separatism" (i.e., queer people too should bond together along the axis of sexual desire and thus be reassimilated to the existing gender dichotomy). Arguing that these incoherences and contradictions in modern homo/heterosexual definition have affected all Western identity and social structure, together with its related dichotomized categories such as knowledge/ignorance, private/public, same/different, active/passive, and in/out, to name but a few, Sedgwick enacts a Derridean critique of such binarisms. In her search for "sites of definitional creation, violence, and rupture," she proposes seven axioms. The most influential

second axiom builds on Axiom 1, namely "People are different from each other," and maintains that although sexuality and gender are inextricably related, the study of sexuality cannot be coextensive with the study of gender. Insofar as feminist inquiry tends to subsume homosexuality under its heterosexist problematic, she claims, its analytic tools cannot fully explain or theorize the far more complex articulations and arrangements of sexual orientations and other possible future sexuality formations.

Prefiguring her later works such as *A Dialogue on Love* (1999), *Tendencies* (1993) experiments with representational forms as varied as prose, poetry, theory, obituary, and autobiography and seeks to investigate innovative ways to map the complexity of gay, lesbian and other sexually dissident identities and activities. Here as elsewhere Sedgwick ingeniously offers an incisive analysis of the extent to which the incoherent and conflicting system of sexuality/gender models pervades even seemingly neutral and natural everyday practices. One such example is her reflection on the family in "Queer and now," in which she defamiliarizes the familial institution by debunking its underlying assumptions. In this manner reminiscent of Louis Althusser's view of the family as one of Ideological State Apparatuses, Sedgwick also enumerate a list of dimensions condensed in the notion of sexual identity, thus striving to demystify our "common sense" about sexuality and gender. Of note in this regard is that Sedgwick, like another prominent theorist in queer studies, Judith Butler, invokes "queer performativity" here in order to delve into the formative relationship certain linguistic utterances possibly have with same-sex desire, and to find a new way in which such linguistic/sexual performativity not only articulates but, rather, *dis*articulates the preexisting sexuality/gender system. In her more recent publication, *Touching Feeling: Affect, Pedagogy, Performativity* (2003), the implications of performativity for sexuality and gender are further explored. In addition, her last personal essays provided rare opportunities to get a glimpse of how her fight with cancer helped her think through many issues as regards the social construction of sexual and gender identities.

SEE ALSO: Althusser, Louis; Derrida, Jacques; Feminism; Gender and Cultural Studies; Queer Theory

REFERENCES AND SUGGESTED
READINGS

Sedgwick, E. (1980). *The Coherence of Gothic Conventions*. New York: Arno Press.
Sedgwick, E. (1985). *Between Men: English Literature and Male Homosocial Desire*. New York: Columbia University Press.
Sedgwick, E. (1990). *Epistemology of the Closet*. Berkeley: University of California Press.
Sedgwick, E. (1993). *Tendencies*. Durham, NC: Duke University Press.
Sedgwick, E. (1994). *Fat Art, Thin Art*. Durham, NC: Duke University Press.
Sedgwick, E. (1999). *A Dialogue on Love*. Boston: Beacon.
Sedgwick, E. (2003). *Touching Feeling: Affect, Pedagogy, Performativity*. Durham, NC: Duke University Press.

Self-Referentiality

DANIEL BURGOYNE

Self-referentiality occurs when something refers to itself, such as a statement or work of art that mentions or points to itself. At the simplest level, this occurs in ordinary speech when a person uses the first-person pronoun ("I"). In postmodernism, self-referentiality has been associated with the roles and limits of subjectivity and systematic knowledge.

Self-referentiality is often used as a synonym for reflexivity. Reflexivity relates to reflection, the process of observing oneself in a mirror. This optical appearance of the self is also used as a metaphor for self-awareness in general. It is important to stress that self-reference has more technical usages in certain areas of study like mathematics, while reflexivity is a generic term for self-awareness in art or other work. Reflexivity is used specifically in fields like sociology for the practice of revealing a researcher's method or point-of-view, or for issues associated with the subjective limitations of studying phenomena that include the observer.

In philosophy and mathematics, self-reference has a long history of association with paradox that became central to debates in the twentieth century. In philosophy, there is a group of paradoxes created by self-reference that include the liar's paradox, Russell's paradox, and Curry's paradox. For example, in the liar's paradox, a sentence refers to itself with apparently contradictory results: "This sentence is false." The circularity created by this type of statement can be described as paradoxical or undecidable.

In 1931 the Austrian-American mathematician Kurt Gödel showed that formal mathematical systems are necessarily incomplete. Gödel's proof of this theorem involves a self-referential mathematical statement akin to the apparently paradoxical sentence, "This sentence is false." Gödel focuses on a type of self-reference called recursion, the repetition of a pattern in such a manner that the repetition is part of the pattern, and the pattern is included in each repetition. Gödel's theorem and the idea of self-referentiality was popularized by the American cognitive scientist Douglas Hofstadter's idea of "strange loops" in his 1979 *Gödel, Escher, Bach: An Eternal Golden Braid*. Hofstadter's example of recursion is the acronym GOD, in which the letters stand for "GOD Over Djinn." GOD is both the acronym and the first word of the phrase that the acronym represents. Each expansion of the acronym reveals another acronym. Thus a recursive statement properly refers to a simpler version of itself. Gödel's theorem suggests inherent limitations in knowledge just as reflexivity in sociology or psychology places obvious constraints on knowledge by showing that the knower can't get outside the phenomena being studied.

In psychoanalysis, especially in the thought of the French psychoanalyst Jacques Lacan, self-referentiality plays a radical role in what Lacan called the mirror stage or mirror phase. Here, self-referentiality works at the psychological level of a child identifying with its image in a mirror in order to create an imaginary wholeness as a means to compensate for incompleteness or lack in the child's identity. In this sense, in the mirror stage, a child develops an idea of "I" by way of its double, a double which is ironically more whole than itself.

Self-reference has been a persistent feature of art and literature since at least the Renaissance, but there are distinctive changes in Romanticism with its preoccupation with subjectivity. For example, in *The Rime of the Ancient Mariner* British poet Samuel Taylor Coleridge includes a telling of the poem itself within the poem. These tendencies may be due to what French philosopher Michel Foucault, in *The Order of Things*, characterizes as the emergence of the human as an object of knowledge from the seventeenth century forward.

In twentieth-century literature, self-referentiality has been predominantly associated with postmodernism in the fiction of writers like Argentine Jorge Luis Borges, Italian Italo Calvino, and American Donald Barthelme. Such fiction is often described as using metafiction, in which the self-referential technique provides a commentary on the act of

writing or reading fiction itself. It has also played a prominent role in poetry, especially for the $L = A = N = G = U = A = G = E$ poets and writers associated with them such as Canadian bpNichol, American Ron Silliman, and French-Canadian Nicole Brossard.

Critical assessment of self-referentiality in art and literature adopted a more concerted political focus with French-American academic Raymond Federman and Canadian literary theorist Linda Hutcheon's work in the late 1980s. Federman and Hutcheon argue that by drawing attention to representation, language, and the act of storytelling itself, postmodern writers provide a means to critique power and domination.

Self-reference has become increasingly common in popular culture, notable in television programs like *Seinfeld* and *The Simpsons* that use self-reference to manipulate the genre. In film, the technique often employs video cameras, as in American film director Michael Almereyda's adaptation of William Shakespeare's *Hamlet* (2000). Such techniques are often a means to produce irony and they often draw attention to the media, the genre, or the simple fact that the work is a representation. For example, American comic artist Art Spiegelman begins *Maus II* with a picture of himself wearing a mouse mask while composing *Maus II*, and this self-referentiality seems to promote reflection on or self-awareness about Spiegelman's act of representation or its inherent limits.

SEE ALSO: Foucault, Michel; Lacan, Jacques; Postmodernism; Subject Position

REFERENCES AND SUGGESTED READINGS

Cornis-Pope, M. (1997). Self-referentiality. In H. Bertens & D. Fokkema (eds.), *International*

Postmodernism: Theory and Literary Practice. Amsterdam: John Benjamins, pp. 257–264.

Federman, R. (1988). Self-reflexive fiction. In E. Elliott (ed.), *Columbia Literary History of the United States.* New York: Columbia University Press, pp. 1142–1157.

Foucault, M. (1970). *The Order of Things: An Archaeology of the Human Sciences.* New York: Vintage.

Hofstadter, D. R. (1979). *Gödel, Escher, Bach: An Eternal Golden Braid.* New York: Basic Books.

Hutcheon, L. (1989). *The Politics of Postmodernism.* New York: Routledge.

Lacan, J. (1977). *Écrits: A Selection* (trans. A. Sheridan). New York: Norton.

Woolgar, S. (1988). *Knowledge and Reflexivity: New Frontiers in the Sociology of Knowledge.* London: Sage.

Semiotics

MARCEL DANESI

Semiotics is defined as the discipline studying and documenting signs, sign behavior, sign creation, and sign functions. It also comes under the rubric of semiology, significs, and even structuralist science, although semiotics is the designation adopted by the International Association of Semiotic Studies during its founding meeting in 1969 and, as a consequence, the most commonly used term. A sign is any physical form – a word, a picture, a sound, a symbol, etc. – that stands for something other than itself in some specific context. A cross figure, for instance, constitutes a sign because it stands for various things, such as "crossroads" and "Christianity." It all depends on who uses it and in what context it is used. Today, semiotics is an autonomous discipline, but it has become a powerful cross-disciplinary methodological tool in the study of such sign-based phenomena as body language, aesthetic products, visual communication, media, advertising, narratives, material culture (fashion, cuisine, etc.), and rituals. One

of its modern-day founders, the Swiss philologist Ferdinand de Saussure, defined it as the science concerned with "the role of signs as part of social life" and "the laws governing them" (1958[1916]: 15).

SIGNS

The first fundamental task of any science is to define its object of study and to classify the phenomena associated with it. In order for "something" to be identified or perceived as a sign, it must have structure – that is, some distinctive, recognizable, or recurring pattern in its physical form. Saussure called this component of sign structure, the signifier. The other component – the concept or referent for which a physical structure stands – he called the signified. The connection between the two, once established, is bidirectional or binary – that is, one implies the other. For example, the word "tree" is a word sign in English because it has a recognizable phonetic structure that generates a mental concept (an arboreal plant). When we say the word "tree," the image of an arboreal plant inevitably comes to mind and, in fact, such an image cannot be blocked; vice versa, when we see an arboreal plant, the word "tree" seems to come also automatically to mind. This model of the sign, incidentally, traces its origin back to the Scholastics in the medieval ages, who also viewed the sign (*signum* in Latin) as an identifiable form composed of two parts – a *signans* ("that which does the signifying") and a *signatum* ("that which is signified"). Although the psychological relation that inheres between signs and the concepts they evoke has come under several terminological rubrics, the term *semiosis* is the preferred one today.

The American pragmatist Charles Sanders Peirce, also a modern-day founder of semiotics, called the sign a *representamen*, in order to bring out the fact that a sign is something that "represents" something else in order to suggest it (that is, "re-present" it) in some way. He defined it as follows:

> A sign, or representamen, is something which stands to somebody for something in some respect or capacity. It addresses somebody, that is, creates in the mind of that person an equivalent sign. That sign which it creates I call the interpretant of the first sign. The sign stands for something, its object not in all respects, but in reference to a sort of idea. (1931–58: 2.228)

A key notion in this definition is that a sign invariably generates another sign, or *interpretant*, which, in turn, becomes itself a source of additional semiosis. This process does not continue indefinitely, however. Eventually it must resolve itself into a set of forms that allow us to classify and understand the world in a relatively stable fashion. This set, Peirce claimed, generates a system of beliefs that guide our actions and shape our behaviors unconsciously.

Peirce also provided the first sophisticated classification of signs. Although he identified 66 species of signs in total, the three that have seeped into the general scientific lexicon of semiotics and its cognate disciplines are icons, indexes, and symbols. These reflect three general psychological tendencies in human semiosis: resemblance, relation, and convention. Icons can be defined simply as signs that have been constructed to resemble their referents in some way. Photographs, portraits, Roman numerals such as I, II, and III are visual icons because they resemble their referents in a visual way. Onomatopoeic words such as "drip," "plop," "bang," and "screech" are vocal icons created to simulate the sounds that certain things, actions, or movements are perceived to make. Peirce termed the referent that is modeled in an iconic way the

"immediate" object, whereas the infinite number of referents that can be modeled in similar ways he termed the "dynamical" objects.

Iconicity is simulative semiosis. It is evidence that human understanding of the world is guided initially by sensory perception and is, thus, sensitive to recurrent patterns of color, shape, dimension, movement, sound, taste, etc. As a "default" tendency, therefore, it reveals that humans tend to model the world as they see, hear, smell, taste, and touch it. The prehistoric inscriptions, cave drawings, and pictographic signs of humanity indicate that iconicity played an important role in the constitution of early sign systems and cultures. Iconicity also marks early learning behaviors. Children invariably pass through an initial stage of imitative gesticulation and imitative vocalism before they develop full verbal language. It is relevant to note that, although the latter eventually becomes the dominant form of communication in humans, the gestural and vocalic modalities do not vanish completely. They remain functional subsystems of human communication throughout life that can always be utilized as more generic forms when linguistic interaction is impossible or limited. Iconicity also shows up in the instinctive desire of children to make scribbles and elemental drawings at about the same time that they utter their first true words. Iconicity is also the source of the construction of diagrams in mathematics and science.

An index is a sign that involves relation or indication of some kind. Unlike icons, which are constructed to resemble things, indexes are designed to put referents in relation to each other, to sign-users, or to the context or contexts in which they occur. A perfect example of an indexical sign is the pointing index finger, which we use instinctively from birth to point out and locate things, people, and events – a sign that emphasizes, again, the importance of the hands in knowledge-making and communication. Many words, too, have an indexical function – for example, "here," "there," "up," "down" allow speakers of English to refer to the relative location of things when speaking about them.

There are four main types of indexes:

1 *Location indexes*: These include manual signs like the pointing index finger; demonstrative words such as "this" or "that," adverbs of place like "here" or "there," figures such as arrows, and maps of all types are common examples of location indexes. Essentially, location indexes allow sign-users to refer to their physical location with respect to something ("near," "far," "here," "there," etc.), or else to indicate the relative location of some referent in spatial terms.

2 *Temporal indexes*: These include adverbs such as "before," "after," "now," or "then," timeline graphs representing points in time, time units (days, hours, minutes, etc.), and dates on calendars. Temporal indexes allow sign-users to refer to time in culturally appropriate ways as a relational construct.

3 *Identification indexes*: These include personal pronouns ("I," "you," "he," "she," "they") and indefinite pronouns (such as "the one," "the other"), and surnames (which identify persons in terms of ethnic and familial membership). Identification indexes relate the participants involved in a specific situation or context to each other or to some culturally appropriate domain.

4 *Organizational indexes*: These allow us to organize, classify, or categorize things in relation to each other or to other things. The arrangement of books in alphabetical order on library shelves is an example of organizational indexicality. In mathematics, an organizational index, such as a number or symbol written as a subscript or superscript, can indicate an operation to be performed, an ordering relation, or the use of an associated expression.

Indexicality is also the psychological force behind several diagramming techniques. For example, flowchart diagrams and the algorithms employed in mathematics and computer science to indicate the procedures required to perform a task are indexical in nature, as are the time-line diagrams used by scientists to portray temporal relations.

A symbol is a sign that stands for something in a conventional way. For example, the cross figure stands for "Christianity," the V-sign for "peace," and so on. Symbols are the building blocks of social systems. Certain symbols serve as shorthand forms for recording and recalling information. Every branch of science has its own symbols – in astronomy a set of ancient symbols is used to identify the sun, the moon, the planets, and the stars; in mathematics, Greek letters are used to represent certain constants and variables; and so on.

Actually, the first definition and classification signs go right back to the ancient Greek physician Hippocrates. Hippocrates argued that the particular physical form that a symptom takes – a *semeion* ("mark") – constitutes a vital clue for finding its etiological source. Shortly thereafter, philosophers started referring to signs as being either *natural* (produced by the body or nature) or *conventional*. Among the first to examine and elaborate this basic typology was St Augustine in his *De Doctrina Christiana*. St Augustine describes natural signs (*signa naturalia*) as forms lacking intentionality, and conventional ones (*signa data*) as forms produced by human intentions. The former include not only symptoms, but also such natural phenomena as plant coloration, animal signals, and the like; the latter include not only words, but also gestures and the various symbols that humans invent to serve their psychological, social, and communicative needs (Deely 2001: 24–56).

MEANING

A major area of investigation for semiotics is determining what meaning is and how it is captured (or even constructed) by signs. To avoid the many ambiguities built into the word "meaning," semioticians prefer to use the terms "semiosis" and "signification." The former refers to the innate ability to produce signs and to engage in sign-based behavior (Fisch 1978: 32, 41); the latter refers to the referents that signs encode. Signification implies two main modalities – "reference" and "sense." The former is the activity and end result of connecting a sign form to a referent; sense is what that form elicits psychologically, historically, and culturally. Signs may refer to the same (or similar) referents, but they have different senses. For example, the "long-eared, short-tailed, burrowing mammal of the family Leporidae" can be called "rabbit" or "hare" in English. Both word forms refer essentially to the same kind of mammal. But there is a difference of sense between the two words – "hare" is the more appropriate term for describing the mammal if it is larger, has longer ears and legs, and does not burrow. Another difference is that a rabbit is often perceived to be a "pet," while a hare is unlikely to be perceived as such (Danesi 2007: 34).

Signification unfolds on two planes simultaneously. One of these is the denotative and the other the connotative plane. Consider, again, the word "rabbit." The word elicits an image of a "creature with four legs, a small tail, furry hair," etc. This is its denotative meaning. As this shows, denotation has a referential function – that is, it allows users of the sign to apply it to a mammal that has the characteristics of a "rabbit." Denotative meaning thus divides the world of reference into "yes–no" domains – something is either a rabbit or it is not. All other meanings of the word "rabbit" are connotative, such as the belief that a rabbit's paw brings about good luck, or that a rabbit is a pet. These meanings are products of the historical associations forged between rabbits and socially significant concepts or processes. Connotation thus connects the world of reference to larger historical-cognitive processes. In 1957, the psychologists Charles Osgood, George Suci, and Percy Tannenbaum showed how this unfolds by using a technique that they called the "semantic differential." This consists in asking a series of evaluative questions to subjects about a particular concept – "Is X good or bad?" "Should Y be weak or strong?" etc. – which they are then told to rate on seven-point scales. The ratings are collected and analyzed statistically in order to sift out any general pattern that they might bear. Suppose that subjects are asked to rate the concept "ideal American president" in terms of the following scales: "Should the president be: (1) young or old? (2) practical or idealistic? (3) modern or traditional? (4) male or female? (5) attractive or bland?" and so on. A subject who feels that the president should be more "youngish" than "oldish" would place a mark toward the "young" end of the top scale; one who feels that a president should be "bland" would place a mark toward the "bland" end of the attractive–bland scale; and so on. Research using the semantic differential has shown that connotation is invariably culture-specific and is constrained by a series of historically sensitive factors involved in signification.

STRUCTURALISM

As mentioned, signs, sign systems, and texts (assemblages of signs) exhibit structure. In music, for example, the arrangement of tones into melodies is felt to be "musically correct" only if it is consistent with harmonic structure; in the domain of fashion, the type and combination of dress items put on the body is felt so be "sartorially correct" only if it is consistent with the rules of dress that are operative in a certain social situation; and so on. Structural appropriateness involves differentiation and combination in tandem. In effect, in order to recognize something as a sign, one must be (6) able to differentiate it from other signs, and (7) know how its component parts fit together. More technically, the former is called "paradigmatic" (differential) and the latter "syntagmatic" (combinatory) structure.

The notion of structure is so central to semiotic theory and practice that, also as mentioned, the term "structuralism" is often used as a synonym for the discipline. The same term is used in linguistics and psychology. The fact that certain forms, such as words and melodies, bear meaning by virtue of the fact that they have a specific type of structure suggests that they probably mirror internal sensory, emotional, and intellectual structures.

What keeps two words, such as "cat" and "rat," recognizably distinct? It is, in part, the fact that the sound difference between initial *c* and *r* is perceived as distinctive in English. This distinctiveness constitutes a paradigmatic feature of the two words. Similarly, a major and minor chord of the same key are perceived as distinct on account of a half-tone difference in the middle note of the chord; and so on and so forth. As such examples bring out, forms are recognizable as meaning-bearing structures in part through a perceivable difference built into some aspect of their physical constitution – a minimal difference in sound, a minimal

difference in tone, etc. The psychological importance of this structural feature was noticed first by the psychologists Wilhelm Wundt and Edward B. Titchener, who termed it "opposition." Saussure also saw opposition as an intrinsic property of linguistic structure. He called it *difference*. And his insight remains a basic one to this day, guiding a large part of semiotic and linguistic analysis. The linguist determines the meaning and grammatical function of a form such as "cat" by opposing it to another word such as "rat." This will show, among other things, that the initial consonants *c* and *r* are important in English for differentiating the meaning of words. From such oppositions the linguist establishes, one or two features at a time, what makes the word "cat" unique, pinpointing what cat means by virtue of how it is different from other words such as "rat," "hat." and so on.

Paradigmatic structure tells only part of the semiotic story of how we recognize signs. The other part is syntagmatic structure. Consider again the words "cat" and "rat." These are legitimate English words, not only because they are recognizable as phonetically distinct through a simple binary opposition of initial phonemes, but also because the combination of phonemes with which they are constructed is consistent with English syllable structure. On the other hand, "mtat" is not recognizable as a legitimate word in English because it violates an aspect of such structure – English words cannot start with the cluster "mt." Syllable structure is an example of syntagmatic structure, which characterizes the constitution of signs in all semiotic systems – in music, a melody is recognizable as such only if the notes follow each other in a certain way (for example, according to the rules of classical harmony); two shoes are considered to form a pair if they are of the same size, style, and color; and so on.

Differentiation co-occurs with combination. When putting together a simple sentence, for example, we do not choose the words in a random fashion, but rather according to their differential and combinatory properties. The choice of the noun "boy" in the subject slot of a sentence such as "That boy loves school" is a paradigmatic one, because other nouns of the same kind – "girl," "man," "woman," etc. – could have been chosen instead, and the overall structure of the sentence would have been maintained. But the choice of any one of these nouns for the same sentence slot constrains the type – "love" vs. "drink" – and form – "loves" vs. "loving" – of the verb that can be chosen and combined with it. Co-occurrence is a structural feature of all systems. A note chosen to make up a major chord, for instance, must be either the tonic, median, or dominant – if it is the tonic, then the other two must be the median and dominant; if it is the median, then the other two must be the tonic and dominant; and if it is the dominant, then the other two must be the tonic and median.

In summary, a sign can thus be considered to be the result of two intersecting semiotic axes, a vertical (paradigmatic) and a horizontal (syntagmatic) one. Like the coordinates that locate points in the Cartesian plane, they underlie recognition of a form as a sign. The Cartesian plane is a plane divided into four quadrants by two axes crossing at right angles, the so-called x- and y-axes. Their point of intersection is known as the origin.

A main tenet of structuralist semiotics is that signs can vary in "size," so to speak. A sign can thus be something "small," such as two fingers raised in a V-form; or it can be something much "larger," such as a mathematical equation, a novel, a painting, a clothing style, and so on. The interpretation of the sign – no matter its size – is "holistic," not "discrete" (decoded in terms of its con-

stituent parts). If asked what $c^2 = a^2 + b^2$ means, a mathematician would say that it stands for the Pythagorean theorem, not for specific digits captured by the letters used (even if this is also true). If we ask someone why he or she is dressed in a certain way, we would get an answer that typically involves how each of the clothing items defines the style; and if we ask someone who has just read a novel what it was all about, we would receive an answer that reveals a perception of the novel as a form containing a singular (holistic) message or purpose. The larger signs are really assemblages of smaller signs (such as words used in constructing a novel). They are called texts. The meanings we extract from them are called messages, rather than just signifieds. In semiotics, therefore, the term text embraces a broad range of signifying phenomena, ranging from conversations, letters, speeches, poems, myths, and novels to television programs, paintings, fashion styles, scientific theories, mathematical equations, musical compositions, and so on. Texts are composite signs (signs made up of smaller signs) that are not interpreted in terms of their constituent parts (the smaller signs), but holistically as single meaning-bearing structures.

Texts function primarily as representation forms, intended to relate, depict, portray, or reproduce some referent that is perceived as having complexity. A rabbit (although complex biologically) is perceived to have a unitary referential status. Consequently, a single word sign is used to refer to it. However, we perceive the use of rabbits as analogues of human personality as a semiotically complex phenomenon. So, we represent the phenomenon in textual ways – through stories, paintings, cartoons, and so on. The construction of texts implies knowledge of how smaller signs cohere into systems or codes that can be used to create texts. To enter into a conversation, for example, one would need to know the language code involved – including its system of sounds, its words, its syntactic rules, etc. Language, dress, music, and gesture, among many other things, are examples of codes. These can be defined, more formally, as systems of signs that can be used over and over for the purposes of representation. There are many kinds of codes. For example, intellectual codes contain signs in them (numbers, words, symbols, etc.) that allow for representational activities of a logical, mathematical, scientific, or philosophical nature. Social codes (dress, gender, food, space, etc.) contain sign-structures for making messages about oneself in socially appropriate ways and for regulating interpersonal activities. Food codes, for example, underlie how people interpret certain foods as signs of various rituals, meanings, etc. It is important to note that once a text is constructed, it takes on its own paradigmatic and syntagmatic properties – that is, it is differentiable from other texts in terms of the kinds of signs that constitute it (verbal, pictorial, etc.), and it is the result of specific syntagmatic properties associated with the code or codes utilized to construct it (language, narrative, and so on). In other words the structure of smaller signs is mirrored in the structure of the larger textual signs.

CRITIQUES OF STRUCTURALISM

As mentioned, to identify forms as meaning-bearing structures, Saussure introduced the notion of *différence*. This was developed theoretically and methodologically by the Prague Circle of linguists in the 1920s and '30s into the technique of opposition. The Prague Circle linguist Nicholas Trubetzkoy [1936, 1968], arguably, was the first to apply the notion of opposition formally to the study of the structure of sound systems using single words such as

cat-versus-*rat*. But it soon became apparent that opposition had a broader utilization. As psychologist Charles K. Ogden, an early promoter of the theory, claimed, opposition offered "a new method of approach not only in the case of all those words which can best be defined in terms of their opposites, or of the oppositional scale on which they appear, but also to *any* word" (1932: 18). In the 1930s and '40s, linguists and semioticians started noticing that oppositional structure was not confined to language. It surfaced in the analysis of nonverbal codes as well – in mathematics, for example, fundamental oppositions include positive vs. negative, odd vs. even, and prime vs. composite; in music, they include major vs. minor and consonant vs. dissonant; and so on (Danesi 2008).

The Prague Circle linguists also claimed that oppositional structure often went beyond the purely binary (Hjelmslev 1939; Jakobson 1939; Benveniste 1946). In mathematics, for example, the addition vs. subtraction opposition is a basic one, while the multiplication vs. division opposition is a derived but related opposition – since multiplication is repeated addition and division repeated subtraction. In effect, there are different levels of orders in oppositional structure. The French semiotician Algirdas J. Greimas later introduced the notion of the "semiotic square" to connect sets of oppositions (Greimas 1987). Given a word such as "rich," Greimas claimed the overall meaning of the word unfolds in terms of its contradictory, "not rich," its contrary, "poor," and its contradictory, "not poor," in tandem. And as already discussed, the work carried out with the semantic differential in the 1950s showed that there are gradations of conceptualization within the binary oppositions themselves. Anthropologist Claude Lévi-Strauss [1958] further expanded opposition theory by showing that pairs of oppositions often cohere into sets forming recognizable units. In analyzing kinship systems, he found that the elementary unit of kinship was made up of a set of four oppositions: brother vs. sister, husband vs. wife, father vs. son, and mother's brother vs. sister's son. Lévi-Strauss suspected that similar sets, or orders, characterized oppositions in other cultural systems.

Almost from the outset, opposition theory was criticized as being a concoction that was inconsistent with human psychology. But already in the 1940s Jakobson (1942) showed empirically that the theory of opposition actually predicts psychological phenomena. For example, he found that the sequence of acquisition of verbal sounds in children follows a pattern – the sound oppositions that occur frequently are among the first ones learned by children, while those that are relatively rare are among the last ones to be acquired by children.

Another early critique of opposition theory was that it did not take into account associative meaning and structure. The study of such structure came, actually, to the forefront in the latter part of the 1970s, becoming a major trend within linguistics itself (Pollio et al. 1977; Lakoff & Johnson [1980, 1999]; Fauconnier & Turner 2002; Danesi 2004). The American linguist George Lakoff and philosopher Mark Johnson are primarily responsible for this paradigm shift within linguists, claiming in 1980 that a simple linguistic metaphor such as "My friend is a pussycat" cannot be viewed as a simple idiomatic replacement for some literal form, but, rather, that it revealed a conceptual systematicity. It is, more specifically, a token of an associative structure that they called a conceptual metaphor. This is why we can also say that Bill or Frida or whoever we want is an animal – a gorilla, snake, pig, puppy, and so on – in attempting to portray his or her personality. Each specific linguistic metaphor ("Bill is a gorilla,"

"Mary is a puppy," etc.) is an instantiation of a more general associative cognitive structure – people are animals. Needless to say, associative structure is a productive source of signification. But is it truly a counterexample of oppositional structure? Conceptual metaphors are formed through image schemata, as Lakoff and Johnson have cogently argued (Lakoff 1987; Johnson 1987). The image schematic source for the "people are animals" conceptual metaphor seems to be an unconscious perception that human personalities and animal behaviors are linked in some way. In other words, it is the output of an ontological opposition: humans-as-animals. It constitutes, in other words, an example of how opposition manifests itself as an associative mechanism, not just a binary or multi-order one (as discussed above). In this case, the two poles in the opposition are not contrasted (as in vs. day), but equated: humans-as-animals. This suggests that oppositional structure operates in a noncontrastive way at the level of figurative meaning.

The most severe critiques of opposition theory have revolved around the relative notion of markedness (Tiersma 1982; Eckman et al. 1983; Andrews 1990, Battistella 1990). In oppositions such as night vs. day, it is a rather straightforward task to say that the "default" pole is day – that is, the notion in the opposition that we perceive as culturally or psychologically more fundamental. This pole is called the unmarked pole, and the other pole, the marked one (since it is the one that stands out). This markedness analysis can be justified, arguably, because it has a source in human biology – we sleep at night and carry out conscious activities in the day. Now, the problem is deciding which pole is marked and unmarked in a socially problematic opposition such as the male vs. female one. The answer seems to vary according to the social context to which the opposition is applied. In patrilineal societies the unmarked form is male; but in matrilineal societies, such as the Iroquois one (Alpher 1987), it appears to be female. Markedness, thus, seems to mirror social realities. But according to some, it may even influence them. This was the view of the late French semiotician-philosophers Michel Foucault and Jacques Derrida. In his own way, and for his own specific reasons, each one claimed essentially that the structuralist approach to sign study, which was based on opposition and markedness, was itself flawed and a potential source of social inequalities (Foucault 1972; Derrida 1976). Their critiques led to the movement known as poststructuralism, which started in the late 1950s and gained prominence in the 1970s. In this movement, the oppositions identified by linguists and semioticians are to be "deconstructed" (as Derrida put it), and exposed as resulting from an endemic logocentrism on the part of the analyst, not the result of some tendency present in the human brain. Saussure claimed that every sign was understandable in terms of its difference from other signs. In contrast to Saussure's idea of *différence*, Derrida coined the word *différance* (spelled with an "a" but pronounced in the same way), to intentionally satirize Saussurean theory. With this term Derrida aimed to show that Saussure's so-called discoveries could be deconstructed into the implicit biases that he brought to the analytical task at hand, because a science of signs or of language cannot succeed since it must be carried out through language itself and thus will partake of the slippage (as he called it) it discovers.

Derrida argued further that all sign systems are self-referential – signs refer to other signs, which refer to still other signs, and so on ad infinitum. The goal of deconstructionism, as he called it, was to make people aware of this circularity and slippage. The concept was subsequently expanded to study narratives and the implicit biases they subsumed, most of which had oppositional structure (good vs. evil, young vs. old). Thus, what appears to be "natural" in a story turns out to be embedded on presuppositions implicit already in the structure and meanings of the forms used to tell the story. Poststructuralism has had a profound impact on many fields of knowledge, not just semiotics and linguistics. Because written language is the basis of knowledge-producing enterprises, such as science and philosophy, poststructuralists claim that these end up reflecting nothing more than the writing practices used to articulate them. But in hindsight, there was (and is) nothing particularly radical in Derrida's diatribe against structuralism. Already in the 1920s, Jakobson and Trubetzkoy started probing the "relativity" of language oppositions in the light of their social and psychological functions. Basing their ideas in part on the work of German psychologist Karl Bühler, they posited that language categories mirrored social ones. The goal of a true semiotic science, they claimed, was to investigate the isomorphism that manifested itself between sign and social systems. In other words, opposition theory was the very technique that identified social inequalities, not masked them.

CONCLUDING REMARKS

Semiotics is a fundamental form of inquiry into how humans shape raw sensory information into knowledge-based categories through sign-creation, no matter what particular orientation is taken to the inquiry (structuralist or poststructuralist). Signs are selections from the flow of information intake allowing us to encode what we perceive as meaningful in it, and thus to utilize it for various intellectual and social purposes. The world of human beings is essentially a *semiosphere*, as the late Estonian semiotician Juri Lotman called it (Lotman 1991). Like the biosphere, the semiosphere regulates human behavior and shapes cultural evolution. But sign systems are never permanent. Unlike most animal signaling systems, they are open to intentionally designed change. This ability to create new signs and textual products, not to mention new codes, is what distinguishes human semiosis from all other kinds. Our literary textual productions, for instance, stimulate us to seek new meanings and new ways of seeing the world, even though they may be completely fictitious. These open up the mind and stimulate freedom of thought. As Charles Peirce often wrote, although we are inclined to "think only in signs," we also are creative producers of signs, and these help us reflect upon the world and carry it around literally "in our heads."

SEE ALSO: Derrida, Jacques; Foucault, Michel; Narratology and Structuralism; Peirce, Charles Sanders; Poststructuralism; Saussure, Ferdinand de

REFERENCES AND SUGGESTED READINGS

Alpher, B. (1987). Feminine as the unmarked grammatical gender: Buffalo girls are no fools. *Australian Journal of Linguistics*, 7, 169–187.

Andrews, E. (1990). *Markedness Theory*. Durham, NC: Duke University Press.

Battistella, E. L. (1990). *Markedness: The Evaluative Superstructure of Language*. Albany: SUNY Press.

Benveniste, E. (1946). Structure des relations de personne dans le verbe. *Bulletin de la Société de Linguistique de Paris*, 43, 225–236.

Bühler, K. (1934). *Sprachtheorie: Die Darstellungsfunktion der Sprache*. Jena: Fischer.

Danesi, M. (2004). *Poetic Logic: The Role of Metaphor in Thought, Language, and Culture*. Madison, NJ: Atwood.

Danesi, M. (2007). *The Quest for Meaning: A Guide to Semiotic Theory and Practice*. Toronto: University of Toronto Press.

Danesi, M. (2008). *Problem Solving in Mathematics: A Semiotic Perspective for Teachers and Educators*. New York: Peter Lang.

Deely, J. (2001). *Four Ages of Understanding: The First Postmodern Survey of Philosophy from Ancient Times to the Turn of the Twentieth Century*. Toronto: University of Toronto Press.

Derrida, J. (1976). *Of Grammatology* (trans. G. C. Spivak). Baltimore: Johns Hopkins University Press.

Eckman, F. R., et al. (eds.) (1983). *Markedness*. New York: Plenum.

Fauconnier, G., & Turner, M. (2002). *The Way We Think: Conceptual Blending and the Mind's Hidden Complexities*. New York: Basic Books.

Fisch, M. H. (1978). Peirce's general theory of signs. In T. A. Sebeok (ed.), *Sight, Sound, and Sense*. Bloomington: Indiana University Press, pp. 31–70.

Foucault, M. (1972). *The Archeology of Knowledge* (trans. A. M. Sheridan Smith). New York: Pantheon.

Greimas, A. J. (1987). *On Meaning: Selected Essays in Semiotic Theory* (trans. P. Perron & F. Collins). Minneapolis: University of Minnesota Press.

Hjelmslev, L. (1939). Note sur les oppositions supprimables. *Travaux de Cercle Linguistique de Prague*, 8, 51–57.

Jakobson, R. (1939). Observations sur le classement phonologique des consonnes. *Proceedings of the Fourth International Congress of Phonetic Sciences*, 34–41.

Jakobson, R. (1942). *Kindersprache, Aphasie und algemeine Lautgesetze*. Uppsala: Almqvist and Wiksell.

Johnson, M. (1987). *The Body in the Mind: The Bodily Basis of Meaning, Imagination and Reason*. Chicago: University of Chicago Press.

Lakoff, G. (1987). *Women, Fire, and Dangerous Things: What Categories Reveal about the Mind*. Chicago: University of Chicago Press.

Lakoff, G., & Johnson, M. (1980). *Metaphors We Live By*. Chicago: Chicago University Press.

Lakoff, G., & Johnson, M. (1999). *Philosophy in the Flesh: The Embodied Mind and Its Challenge to Western Thought*. New York: Basic Books.

Lévi-Strauss, C. (1958). *Structural Anthropology*. New York: Basic Books.

Locke, J. (1690). *An Essay Concerning Human Understanding*. London: Collins.

Lotman, Y. (1991). *Universe of the Mind: A Semiotic Theory of Culture*. Bloomington: Indiana University Press.

Ogden, C. K. (1932). *Opposition: A Linguistic and Psychological Analysis*. London: Paul, Trench, and Trubner.

Osgood, C. E., Suci, G. J., & Tannenbaum, P. H. (1957). *The Measurement of Meaning*. Urbana: University of Illinois Press.

Peirce, C. S. (1931–58). *Collected Papers of Charles Sanders Peirce*, vols. 1–8 (ed. C. Hartshorne & P. Weiss). Cambridge, MA: Harvard University Press.

Pollio, H., Barlow, J., Fine, H., & Pollio, M. (1977). *The Poetics of Growth: Figurative Language in Psychology, Psychotherapy, and Education*. Hillsdale, NJ: Lawrence Erlbaum.

Saussure, F. de (1958). *Course in General Linguistics* (ed. C. Bally & A. Sechehaye; trans. W. Baskin) New York: McGraw-Hill. (Original work published as *Cours de linguistique générale*, 1916.)

Tiersma, P. M. (1982). Local and general markedness. *Language*, 58, 832–849.

Trubetzkoy, N. S. (1936). Essaie d'une théorie des oppositions phonologiques. *Journal de Psychologie*, 33, 5–18.

Trubetzkoy, N. S. (1968). *Introduction to the Principles of Phonological Description*. The Hague: Martinus Nijhoff.

Showalter, Elaine

REBECCA MUNFORD

Elaine Showalter (b. 1941) is an American feminist literary critic and historian who was an active member of the Women's Liberation Movement. Born in Cambridge, Massachusetts, she was educated at Bryn Mawr, Brandeis University, and the University of California, Davis. From 1967 to 1984 she taught English and women's studies at Rutgers University before becoming a Professor of English and, subsequently, Avalon Professor of the Humanities at Princeton University. She is currently Professor Emeritus at Princeton, and is a past president of the Modern Language Association (MLA).

Showalter was a leading figure in Anglo-American feminist literary criticism in the 1970s, and played a vital role in the recovery and celebration of female literary history. Her pioneering study, *A Literature of Their Own: British Women Novelists from Brontë to Lessing* (1999[1977]), which was based on her PhD thesis, mapped out a tradition of nineteenth- and twentieth-century women writers. This placed writers with established literary reputations, such as Virginia Woolf, alongside lesser-known figures, such as Mary Elizabeth Braddon. Eschewing notions of a trans-historical female imagination, Showalter locates women's literature as part of "the female subculture" that emerges from the evolving relationship between women writers and their social context. Importantly, she conceptualizes the development of female literary history in three stages: "feminine" (a phase of imitating the modes of the dominant tradition and internalizing its aesthetic and social values); "feminist" (a phase of protest against these dominant modes and values); and "female" (a final phase of self-discovery and a search for an independent identity).

Showalter's landmark study played an imperative role in recovering a submerged tradition of women's writing. However, it has been criticized for its failure to address the differences between women, and the ways in which experiences of gender intersect with and are shaped by experiences of class, race, sexuality, religion, nationality, and ethnicity. In the second edition of *A Literature of their Own* (1999), Showalter addresses some of the criticisms leveled at the work and incorporates a discussion of the legacy of feminist criticism in the context of women's writing since the 1970s.

A concern with developing a methodology for reading the distinctive traditions of women's writing in relation to women's culture underpins much of Showalter's work. In her 1979 essay "Towards a feminist poetics" she outlines two possible modes of feminist critical practice. The first of these is "feminist critique," which is concerned with the role of "woman as reader," with analyzing literary representations of women, and with the gaps in androcentric constructions of literary history. The second of these is "gynocritics," a term Showalter coins in order to designate a mode of feminist criticism that focuses on "*woman as writer* – with woman as the producer of textual meaning, with the history, themes, genres and structures of literature by women." Showalter aligns gynocritics with feminist research into "muted" female subcultures in the fields of history, anthropology, psychology, and sociology. She is suspicious of "feminist critique" because of its reliance on theory, which she considers to be a "male invention." However, for some feminist critics, gynocritics is problematic because it assumes that texts, and language itself, reflect a preexistent and objective reality. The Norwegian feminist theorist Toril Moi, for example, criticizes Showalter's approach for failing to treat texts as signifying processes that do not simply reflect reality but are constitutive of it. Showalter also edited two collections of feminist essays in the 1980s, *The New Feminist Criticism:Essays on Women, Literature, and Theory* (1985b) and *Speaking of Gender* (1989), which explore a variety of theoretical approaches to women's writing and the relationship between literature and gender.

Showalter's second book, *The Female Malady: Women, Madness, and English Culture, 1830–1980* (1985a), is a historical study of women and psychiatric practice, which illuminates the ways in which cultural ideas about femininity and insanity are constructed through the language of psychiatric medicine. *Sexual Anarchy: Gender and Culture at the Fin de Siècle* (1990) examines cultural fears and fantasies about gender and sexual identity, mapping correspondences between the ends of the nineteenth and twentieth centuries, and their representations in English and American literature, art, and film. An interest in the cultural and historical dimensions of hysteria and millennial panic also informs the controversial *Hystories: Hysterical Epidemics and Modern Culture* (1997). Arguing that epidemics of hysteria are spread through various cultural narratives (including self-help books, mass media, and literary criticism), Showalter anatomizes six syndromes of the 1990s: chronic fatigue syndrome (CFS), alien abduction, Gulf War syndrome, recovered memory, multiple personality syndrome, and satanic ritual abuse.

Although Showalter's work is diverse in its thematic and historical scope, recovering the work of women writers and mapping out female traditions have remained consistent threads. *Sister's Choice: Traditions and Change in American Women's Writing* (1991) uses the motif of quilt-making, borrowed from Alice Walker's *The Color Purple* (1982), as an analogy for the historical continuities and diversities characterizing American women's writing. She has also edited a collection of short stories by "New women" writers, entitled *Daughters of Decadence: Women Writers of the Fin-de-Siècle* (1993). Showalter's most recent study, *A Jury of Her Peers: American Women Writers from Anne Bradstreet to Annie Proulx* (2009), provides a history of American women writers from the seventeenth to the twenty-first century. The author of *Teaching Literature* (2002), *Inventing Herself: Claiming a Feminist Intellectual Heritage* (2001) and *Faculty Towers: The Academic Novel and Its Discontents* (2005), Showalter is also a regular contributor to the *Guardian*, *Times Literary Supplement*, and *London Review of Books*.

SEE ALSO: Feminism.

REFERENCES AND SUGGESTED READINGS

Moi, T. (1985). *Sexual/Textual Politics*. London: Routledge.

Robbins, R. (2000). *Literary Feminisms*. Basingstoke: Palgrave.

Showalter, E. (1979). Towards a feminist poetics. In M. Jacobus (ed.), *Women Writing and Writing about Women*. London: Croom Helm, pp. 22–41.

Showalter, E. (1981). Feminist criticism in the wilderness. *Critical Inquiry*, 8(1), 179–205.

Showalter, E. (1985a). *The Female Malady: Women, Madness, and English Culture, 1830–1980*. New York: Pantheon.

Showalter, E. (ed.) (1985b). *The New Feminist Criticism: Women, Literature, Theory*. New York: Pantheon.

Showalter, E. (ed.) (1989). *Speaking of Gender*. New York: Routledge.

Showalter, E. (1990). *Sexual Anarchy: Gender and Culture at the Fin de Siècle*. New York: Viking.

Showalter, E. (1991). *Sister's Choice: Traditions and Change in American Women's Writing*. Oxford: Clarendon.

Showalter, E. (ed.) (1993). *Daughters of Decadence: Women Writers of the Fin-de-Siècle*. London: Virago.

Showalter, E. (1997). *Hystories: Hysterical Epidemics and Modern Culture*. London: Picador.

Showalter, E. (1999). *A Literature of Their Own: British Women Novelists from Brontë to Lessing*. London: Virago. (Original work published 1977.)

Showalter, E. (2001). *Inventing Herself: Claiming a Feminist Intellectual Heritage*. New York: Simon and Schuster.

Showalter, E. (2002). *Teaching Literature*. Oxford: Blackwell.

Showalter, E. (2005). *Faculty Towers: The Academic Novel and Its Discontents*. Philadelphia: University of Pennsylvania Press.

Showalter, E. (2009). *A Jury of Her Peers: American Women Writers from Anne Bradstreet to Annie Proulx*. London: Virago.

Walker, A. (1982). *The Color Purple*. New York: Harcourt Brace Jovanovich.

Smith, Barbara H.

JOE HUGHES

Barbara Herrnstein Smith has written widely and influentially on almost every major problem of humanistic inquiry. Her earlier work was preoccupied with literary theory and poetics. More recently she has written on cognitive science, the relations between the humanities and the sciences, and the philosophy of biology.

Smith is best known for *Contingencies of Value* (1988), a work in which she re-establishes the theory of value – the theory of what makes a work good or bad – on pragmatic grounds. Rather than asking what characteristics of the work might make it good or bad or what in us might make us predisposed to liking or disliking a certain work, she asks about what we actually do when we make value judgments. She treats evaluation as a form of behavior – one that is not limited solely to works of art, but to the evaluative decisions we make in everyday life from the way we evaluate a person we've just met to deciding which bed is second-best.

Smith outlines three variables which inform this act of evaluation:

> I would suggest, then, that what we may be doing ... when we make an explicit value judgment of a literary work is (a) articulating an estimate of how well that work will serve certain implicitly defined functions (b) for a specific implicitly defined audience, (c) who are conceived of as experiencing the work under certain implicitly defined conditions. (1988: 13).

These three interlinked variables constitute the system in which value judgments are formed: function, audience, and conditions.

By function, Smith means the use we intend to make of the object. In a certain sense this is obvious. If you are looking for something to eat, pizza is almost always a good idea. If you are looking for something to wear, it is not. But often, the functions a work is meant to fulfill remain implicit and unnoticed. They can be caught up, for example, in the conventions of genre. A detective novel is satisfying to the extent that the murderer and his motivations are revealed. When the novel ends with a private-eye who fails to reveal a causal connection between events and instead dissolves into the network of associations, as in Paul Auster's *City of Glass*, we need to invent a new function for the novel to fulfill before we can consider it successful. Thus we call it "meta-detective-fiction," or say that it comments on detective fiction or that is a postmodern detective novel. Smith's claim is that there is a plurality of functions the work can perform from meeting generic requirements to acting as a doorstop.

In her treatment of audience, Smith creates a middle ground between two classical accounts of aesthetic judgment. For many Enlightenment thinkers there seemed to be two possibilities for the aesthetic judgment: either the work is good for me and only me, grounded in my highly personal reaction to it or it is universally valid, good for anybody with a properly cultivated faculty of taste. For Smith the judgment is neither universal nor singular. She maintains that our value judgments are indeed valid for others. "Not *all* others, however, but *some* others" (1988: 13). What constitutes the temporary unity of these groups is not entirely clear, however. Smith suggests that they are people who are similar to us in terms of their physical and mental constitution, their education, and their competencies (41). Her point here is the same: audience is an ever-changing variable. It changes historically, geographically, socially, and so forth. In 1913 Parisians rioted when

they heard Stravinsky's *Rite of Spring*. We now applaud vigorously. Each variously defined group will produce a judgment that other members of that group may find satisfactory but which members of other groups may reject.

In addition to function and audience, Smith emphasizes the various conditions under which a judgment is formed. These conditions can be historical, social, institutional, technological, or merely circumstantial (1988: 41, 78). They define the situation in which an audience encounters an object – and thus these conditions often determine the other two variables (function and audience). Imagine two readers with identical educational backgrounds reading the same work of experimental fiction, one of them in a major publishing house, the other in a graduate seminar on contemporary fiction. Each will reach different conclusions about the work according to the groups they discuss it with and the function they need it to fulfill. If we want to determine the value of any given work, we need to specify these three variables: function, audience, and conditions.

These three aspects taken together constitute value as a dynamic system – a system which is contingent and variable, but not arbitrary. Smith is careful to emphasize that these three variables are indeed variables. They are not constants, constraints, or determinants in any strict sense. Rather, they function as structural positions whose terms are subject to constant and unpredictable change. In fact, it is precisely this view which allows her to demonstrate the genesis of traditional value theory: a universal standard of taste is achieved only by rigidifying one of more of these variables. One must claim that the audience never changes, that the conditions under which an audience meets its objects are stable, or that the function a work can reasonably serve is constant.

"All value," Smith holds, "is radically contingent, being neither a fixed attribute, an inherent quality, or an objective property of things but, rather, an effect of multiple, continuously changing, and continuously interacting variables or, to put it another way, the product of the dynamics of the system, specifically an *economic* system" (1988: 30). We, and our aesthetic judgments, are fundamentally "scrappy."

SEE ALSO: Canons

REFERENCES AND SUGGESTED READINGS

Connor, S. (1992). *Theory and Cultural Value*. Oxford: Blackwell.
Smith, B. H. (1968). *Poetic Closure: A Study of How Poems End*. Chicago: University of Chicago Press.
Smith, B. H. (1978). *On the Margins of Discourse: The Relation of Literature to Language*. Chicago: University Chicago Press.
Smith, B. H. (1988). *Contingencies of Value: Alternative Perspectives for Critical Theory*. Cambridge, MA: Harvard University Press.
Smith, B. H. (1997). *Belief and Resistance: Dynamics of Contemporary Intellectual Controversy*. Cambridge, MA: Harvard University Press.
Smith, B. H. (2005). *Scandalous Knowledge: Science, Truth and the Human*. Edinburgh: University of Edinburgh Press.
Smith, B. H. (2009). *Natural Reflections: Human Cognition at the Nexus of Science and Religion*. New Haven: Yale University Press.

Social Constructionism

MRINALINI GREEDHARRY

Social constructionism is an approach to the analysis of society that originated in the field of sociology, and takes its starting point from the idea that the human reality people experience as objectively true is a socially constructed reality. This is a view which seems commonplace in a postmodern world, but should be understood in its original context as an attempt to theorize specifically how human beings produce the world they inhabit in relation to their biological limits. The foundational book of social constructionism is *The Social Construction of Reality* by Peter Berger and Thomas Luckman, which was first published in 1966 and intended as a theoretical contribution to the subdiscipline of the sociology of knowledge.

It might be surprising to some, given the current understanding of social constructionists as those who do not believe in reality itself, that Berger and Luckmann take their cues for social constructionist analysis from Marx. They identify Marx as undoubtedly the first theorist to give us the idea that we must investigate the dialectic between social reality and individual existence in history if we are to provide any useful study or analysis of social issues (1966: 209). Though they do not want to introduce Marxist formulas into sociological theory, Berger and Luckmann emphasize the importance of renewing Marx's concept of the dialectic between humans and their social reality in order to prevent sociology from carrying out analyses that reify social facts, rather than examine them. For them, social constructionism specifically refers to the approaches that attempt to deal with the paradox "that man is capable of producing a world that he then experiences as something other than a human product" (78). In other words, social constructionism attempts to defamiliarize sociological reality and reveal the reification of existing social structures. It is specifically interested in the sociological reality that has already acquired its status as fact to the ordinary man or woman.

As a result of this interest, social constructionism is an approach found among a range of other approaches and critical traditions invested in defamiliarizing that which goes by the name of "common sense," such as feminist, queer, and race studies. However, properly speaking, social constructionism hits a limit in all of these approaches when the categories of gender, sexuality, and race are not also included as objects for social constructionist analysis. This is a problem that is becoming increasingly urgent as identity-based politics, more or less happy with the essentialism – strategic or otherwise – of its foundational categories, begins to break down. In the sense that social constructionism treats all aspects of human knowledge and reality as productions, it should be obliged to consider the terms of its own critique in the same light that introduces exacting methodological and philosophical standards into the task of providing social analysis. Genuine social constructionism, then, should aim to examine the obvious focal points of its research field. Though she is a historian rather than a sociologist, a good example of a social constructionist analysis in this sense is Joan Scott's "The evidence of experience" (1991), in which she explores the category of experience itself in historical research. Experience is a fundamental unit of any analysis of a reality produced through the social, and yet, as she indicates, it thereby acquires the status of an unquestioned concept itself.

Social constructionism is often linked, in the minds of readers, critics, and practitioners, with the work of Michel Foucault. Though Foucault's work is clearly based on different philosophical and disciplinary grounds than that of Berger and Luckmann, and it aims at different scholarly objectives, there is some overlap in the two approaches. Scholars who have aimed to produce a sociology of scientific knowledge have been particularly influenced by Foucault. For both Foucault and social constructionists the world is a product of the processes

and beliefs of a particular historical moment. However, the two groups differ strongly on their understanding of power and authority, the role of language and methods. For example, Berger and Luckman rely on relatively straightforward culturally Marxist views of how power and hegemony operate in society, whereas Foucault aims to determine the specific network of relations between power and knowledge in any given situation. Perhaps most concretely, *The Social Construction of Reality* outlines a more or less complete sociological theory, whereas social constructionism derived from Foucault is necessarily the interpretation an individual scholar makes of Foucault's historical method of discourse analysis.

INSTITUTIONALIZATION, TYPIFICATION, AND LEGITIMATION

In *The Social Construction of Reality* Berger and Luckmann outline a comprehensive sociological theory that accounts for the general sociological processes according to which any society is likely to be constructed. What is important for subsequent discussions of social constructionism, especially considering its controversial uses in analyses of scientific knowledge, is that Berger and Luckmann emphatically do not theorize a world that is independent of either biological limits (that is aspects of human life that depend upon the biological structure and needs of human beings as biological organisms) or of embodiment (they recognize the embodiment of humans as a factor in the social world he or she produces). What they do emphasize is that society cannot be considered to be simply derived from biology. In their own words, the "social order is not part of the nature of things" (1966: 70). Their theory presupposes a relationship between man, as biological organism, and society, but it is not a determining one. The "causes" of society, then, are to be found by performing a rigorous analysis of man's processes of building and objectifying that social reality. In this sense, a social constructionist analysis of any given institution is not simply a case of showing that practices or beliefs have been produced by humans rather than discovered as facts (this is a given for Berger and Luckmann); rather it is a case of tracking the particular processes through which a whole social world has come to be objectified.

The three main processes through which a social world is produced, according to Berger and Luckmann, are institutionalization, typification of roles, and legitimation. The first requirement for any social world to develop is the presence of at least two social actors who habitually perform actions in reciprocal relation to each other. The nucleus of a social world is contained in this simple relation, but the process of institutionalization is actually only intensified and promoted with the passing of time. As institutionalization continues in time it acquires historicity, and thus becomes objectified for those who encounter the institutionalizations at later stages. Historicity ensures that institutionalizations, which are after all the creations of social actors who are more or less aware that they have been its creators, achieve objectification equal to that of the natural world. As new members of a society, for example younger generations, are introduced into this social world, institutionalized activities cease to be embodied in particular persons, but become sociological realities for all concerned.

Nevertheless, new members in the social world necessitate a second set of processes that Berger and Luckmann describe as legitimation. Though the new generation acquires the institutionalized activity as natural, or objective reality, it also, like the creator generation, recognizes that it may recreate or redefine those activities if there are no sanctions against the freedom to do so. Among the various ways in which legitimation may occur, Berger and Luckmann single out for discussion language transmission, rudimentary theory (folk wisdom), explicit theory (the differentiated knowledge of experts), and the creation of symbolic universes. What is important for the scholar who wishes to carry out a social constructionist analysis is not the particular mode of legitimation, which like the other social processes of production is subject to historical and cultural circumstances, but the fact that for the individual in the society legitimation not only tells him or her which specific actions should be performed but why things are what they are. In Berger and Luckmann's terms, therefore "'knowledge' precedes 'values' in the legitimation of institutions" (111), hence the importance of a sociology of knowledge as the foundation of analysis of any social world.

The typification of roles, that is the habitual performance of certain activities in reciprocal relation to the habitually performed activities of other social actors, is considered crucial to all developments in the objectification of the social world in Berger and Luckmann's theory. This is the means by which they are able to place the dialectic back into the heart of the sociological analysis. The analysis of roles allows the sociologist to examine the ways in which the meanings that have become objectified in that society become subjectively real to specific individuals.

The Social Construction of Reality was intended to further the subdiscipline of the sociology of knowledge, and was thus written in response to certain methodological and theoretical concerns in sociology. Berger and Luckmann, as sociologists of religion, wanted to emphasize that analysis of language and knowledge were not incidental aspects of an analysis of society. Thus, the book is an important moment in the transition from structuralism to poststructuralism in sociology. As they warn fellow analysts, "a purely structural sociology is endemically in danger of reifying social phenomena. Even if it begins by modestly assigning to its constructs merely heuristic status, it all too frequently ends by confusing its own conceptualizations with the laws of the universe" (208).

THE SOCIOLOGY OF SCIENTIFIC KNOWLEDGE

Social constructionism has become widely influential beyond sociology in studies of religion, history, literature, psychology, and management, where it has been used to examine every conceivable aspect of human society. Developments in social constructionist research are therefore produced by changes within disciplines that it would be impossible to summarize here. It may be more useful to think of social constructionism generally as a spectrum. Berger and Luckmann are situated somewhere in the middle ground of this spectrum insofar as they refute the suggestion that society is derived from biology, but do not, for example, question science as an objectified field of human knowledge itself. At the lighter end of the spectrum, we can find scholars who may not always pursue the rigorous analysis of social processes to be found in Berger and Luckmann, but who subscribe to the perceived political effects and implications of social constructionism. Ian Hacking, one of the most careful commentators on the philosophical and methodological contours of this approach, has suggested that in some sense social constructionism often functions less as an indication of actual method and more as a

signal for the scholar's progressive or left-leaning political commitments.

Despite the relative lack of discussion about science as a socially produced form of knowledge in Berger and Luckmann's original theory, science has also come to be treated as a field of knowledge that forms a legitimate object for social constructionist analysis. Scholars who have sought to extend the sociology of knowledge to the sociology of scientific knowledge have been particularly active. In fact, a sociology of scientific knowledge has become the emblematic form of social constructionist analysis in recent years. Historically, sociology has considered the content of science to be a realm of knowledge that may be exempted from sociological analysis. Scientists, as social actors, and the scientific practices those social actors produce have been investigated, but scientific knowledge itself is considered to be a form of knowledge that deals directly in the material, observable world and hence is not susceptible to social production. However, the philosophy of science after Thomas Kuhn, Foucauldian history, and postmodernist theories have all opened the door for sociologists of knowledge to investigate scientific forms of knowledge too.

Scholars such as Bruno Latour, Steve Woolgar, and Michel Callon have been especially influential in the sociology of scientific knowledge. The effect of their work has been to demonstrate that the content of scientific knowledge itself is the result of choices made by the social actors involved, and conditioned by scientific paradigms that are themselves socially produced. For example, Latour's early work focused particularly on the ways in which scientists use what he terms "black boxes." Although, as he claims, these boxes contain what is not known or representable, they constitute core components of the theories built around them since scientists study phenomena in relation to the black boxes. Science as knowledge, in Latour's analysis, consists of relations between these black boxes, and successful scientists are those who work with the greatest number of black boxes. What is inside the black box is not questioned, but since scientists continue to work as though the boxes contain truth the black boxes continue to work unchallenged. In this way, however, Latour argues that even as science appears to make advances in knowledge, it is becoming more and more opaque since one does not and cannot know how the things inside the black box work. Science, then, is no more or less knowledge of the "real" world than other forms of knowledge, since it also produces a world and objects that it then builds theories about.

It is because of this interest in science that social constructionism, considered as part of postmodernism and poststructuralism more generally, has faced fierce criticism in recent years. In 1996 a physicist named Alan Sokal undertook to demonstrate that social constructionist views of science were full of factual errors and imprecise thinking. He submitted an article entitled "Transgressing the boundaries: Towards a transformative hermeneutics of quantum gravity" for publication in the cultural studies journal *Social Text*. The article was purposefully intended as a fraud, and contained quotations from postmodernist scholars such as Jacques Lacan, Luce Irigaray, and Jean Baudrillard on scientific concepts and theories. When the article was duly accepted for publication Sokal published an account of his hoax in a general academic magazine *Lingua Franca* (Sokal 1996) in which he criticized what others have characterized as "left" academia's attack on science. The Sokal affair, as it has become known, generated a lot of attention in the popular press and led to discussions of some version of social constructionism in the pages of serious newspapers as well as academic journals.

In a less polemical vein, perhaps the greatest change in social constructionist research over the past 30 years has more to do with the ways in which it has been mixed and diluted with other theoretical approaches that are often at odds with its stated methods and aims. In sexuality, race, and gender studies, for example, the value of social constructionism in opening up such categories as heterosexuality, whiteness, and masculinity as social constructions rather than biological givens is complicated by the fact that it posits a problem for scholarship underwritten by identity politics (see Gupta 2007 for a careful view of the political and philosophical problems involved as well as some potential solutions).

POST-SOKAL SOCIAL CONSTRUCTIONISM

The Sokal affair and his subsequent publications have triggered serious philosophical and sociological discussions of what actually constitutes social constructionism. It is fair to argue that the philosophical problem of whether scientific knowledge can be exempted from sociological analysis is an ongoing question. Some scholars, such as Latour, have simply distanced themselves from social constructionism in recent years. Together with Michel Callon and John Law, he has instead developed what is known as Actor-Network theory.

For careful, but not unsympathetic commentators, such as Hacking, the question is not whether we should be questioning scientific knowledge or any other kind of knowledge, but the methods that we should use in such analysis. His view of the broad range of studies that go by the name of social constructionism suggests that we should always be asking ourselves what precisely is determined to be socially constructed in an analysis: is it a thing, or the idea that we have formed of the thing that we are trying to subject to analysis? He also reminds scholars that social constructionism must be understood as an ongoing social process, one in which people may become aware that they are classified in certain ways and thus adapt in relation to these classifications (either to escape them or remake them). Thus, when people assess the social construction of X "they are likely talking about the idea, the individuals falling under the idea, the interaction between the idea and the people, and the manifold of social practices and institutions that these interactions involve" (Hacking 1999: 34).

Berger and Luckmann advised their readers that in undertaking the proper analysis of social reality sociologists would find themselves to be "the inheritor of philosophical questions that the professional philosophers are no longer interested in considering" (1966: 211). Hacking's examination of the philosophical implications of various kinds of social constructionist analyses and research objects is a fitting return to these questions. The future of social constructionism, then, will depend largely on the willingness of its practitioners and proponents to pursue the philosophical questions and standards imposed by the original framework.

SEE ALSO: Foucault, Michel; Postmodernism; Poststructuralism; Science Studies

REFERENCES AND SUGGESTED READINGS

Berger, P., & Luckmann, T. (1966). *The Social Construction of Reality: A Treatise in the Sociology of Knowledge*. New York: Anchor.

Bricmont, J., & Sokal, A. (1999). *Intellectual Impostures*. London: Profile.

Foucault, M. (1970). *The Order of Things: An Archaeology of the Human Sciences*. London: Tavistock.

Foucault, M. (1972). *The Archaeology of Knowledge*. London: Tavistock.

Gupta, S. (2007). *Social Constructionist Identity Politics and Literary Studies*. Basingstoke: Palgrave Macmillan.

Hacking, I. (1999). *The Social Construction of What?* Cambridge, MA: Harvard University Press.

Kendall, G., & Wickham, G. (1999). *Using Foucault's Methods*. London: Sage.

Latour, B. (1987). *Science in Action: How to Follow Engineers in Society*. Milton Keynes: Open University Press.

Latour, B., & Woolgar, S. (1986). *Laboratory Life: The Construction of Scientific Facts*. Princeton: Princeton University Press.

Pickering, A. (1984). *Constructing Quarks: A Sociological History of Particle Physics*. Edinburgh: Edinburgh University Press.

Scott, J. W. (1991). The evidence of experience. *Critical Inquiry*, 17(4), 773–797.

Searle, J. (1995). *The Construction of Social Reality*. New York: Free Press.

Smith, D. E. (1990). *The Conceptual Practices of Power: A Feminist Sociology of Knowledge*. Toronto: University of Toronto Press.

Sokal, A. (1996). A physicist experiments with Cultural Studies. *Lingua Franca* (May–June), 62–64.

Specters

GERALD MOORE

The specter is a concept given renewed currency by Jacques Derrida, the French philosopher best known for his critique of Western Metaphysics known as "deconstruction," who used it to characterize the ways in which intellectual, historical, and political legacies come to haunt contemporary thinking. However, it also has an older and wider usage. European Enlightenment sought to banish the supernatural by throwing light over the forces of unreason, cultivating science to replace superstition. Yet the so-called crisis of Western modernity has seen the spectral return as one of the names of the otherness and difference that reason allegedly doesn't so much explain away as deny. We see this in the way the specter comes to designate the point at which fantasy and reality become intertwined, rendered inseparable by the limitations of reason and experience. Earlier thinkers emphasized the possibility of using reason to exorcise or explain away ghostly apparitions. While still denying the existence of supernatural, metaphysical reality, more recent analyses suggest that exorcism is impossible and deploy motifs of spectrality to illustrate the haunting incompleteness of our reality and the constitutive role of the imagination in constructing it.

At the outset of modernity, the French philosopher René Descartes argued that human reason could ward off the supernatural. His *Meditations on First Philosophy* (1641[1997]) forcefully argued that thinking logically about the nature of human consciousness would establish a point of resistance against malevolent demons plotting to infiltrate and disrupt our experience.

Later modern thinkers and writers would go further still in breaking with residually medieval tendencies to grant specters existence. Among these, twentieth-century psychoanalysis has argued that our belief in specters serves as an attempt to explain the reality of an unconscious that we cannot experience. For the Franco-Hungarian psychoanalysts Nicolas Abraham and Maria Torok, writing in the 1960s and '70s, for example, the notion of being repeatedly haunted describes the repetitive structure of the unconscious symptoms of repressed and moreover inherited traumas. The violence of traumatic events is too great for them to be integrated into conscious experience, so they are condemned to exist as fleeting, fragmented, and incoherent. Never properly the object of experience, their existence thus takes the form of a haunting

that looms over and threatens to disrupt the future.

A slightly different psychoanalytic account comes from Jacques Lacan, who traces the origin of trauma to the loss of the object of desire, and in particular, to the point at which we confirm this loss by using language to make present that which is absent. Language thus becomes the "murder" of the object of desire, which we can never have because our access to it is always already mediated by the word. This lost object (*objet petit a*) is what subsequently haunts us, returning in the form of the symptom to the site of its demise, the undead stain of an object that refuses to die, but which nonetheless withdraws from the symbolic reality where human existence is played out. This spectral force is not fantastic but precisely real, the Real, and we resort to the imaginary in an (ultimately unsuccessful) bid to repress it, reconstructing it through fantastic images designed to conceal its truly unrepresentable horror. For Lacan, the psychoanalyst is no longer a type of exorcist, but one who should seek to affirm the more-real-than-reality existence of the undead by trying to give expression to what it is that escapes our consciousness. To traverse the fantasy that masks the Real is to enter the zone between two deaths, suspended between the death of our fantasmically supported symbolic reality and normal biological death.

Contemporary authors have sought to give similar expression to the idea of unresolved trauma. The 1987 novel *Beloved*, written by the African American Nobel prize-winner Toni Morrison, tells the story of a young girl who may or may not be the ghost of a child murdered by her mother to prevent a life of slavery. Morrison's narrative leaves the reader unsure as to whether Beloved is a genuine ghost or simply a child whose language and behavior entail a case of imaginary misrecognition, where a traumatic past returns and unsettles a present in which it finds itself repeated. Whether the child is a ghost or not becomes less important than the traumatic repetition she comes to represent.

Similar themes abound in Jacques Derrida's *Specters of Marx* (1994[1993]). Writing in the aftermath of the collapse of the Soviet Union, Derrida poses the question of what "lives on" of Marx's work after the supposed death of Marxism. His answer is that there is no single legacy of Marx to be inherited, no single soul or specter of Marx that can be recognized as incarnated in his writings, to be teased out and painstakingly reconstructed through the scholarly unveiling of his true identity; nor is there one Marx who can be confirmed dead, consigned to the past by the failures of communism. The author in fact exists only textually, without an existence distinct from the written word, and so is consequently recreated each time we read the texts. Each interpretation constitutes a decision that brings death to innumerable other readings. The ever-present possibility of creating new readings or returning to old ones means that death is never definitive. Alternative readings live on as the specters of what has never "properly" been killed, eternally returning from a past that cannot be closed off to haunt a present that cannot fully experience them. Like many other poststructuralists, Derrida cites Shakespeare's ghost story *Hamlet* to express the impossibility of achieving closure: "This time is out of joint."

SEE ALSO: Deconstruction; Derrida, Jacques; Lacan, Jacques

REFERENCES AND SUGGESTED READINGS

Abraham, N., & Torok, M. (1994). *The Shell and the Kernel: Renewals of Psychoanalysis*, vol. 1 (ed. and trans. N. T. Rand). Chicago: University of Chicago Press.

Derrida, J. (1994). *Specters of Marx: The State of Debt, the Work of Mourning, and the New International* (trans. Peggy Kamuf). London: Routledge. (Original work published 1993.)

Descartes, R. (1997). *Meditations on First Philosophy* (trans. J. Cottingham). Cambridge: Cambridge University Press. (Original work published 1641.)

Lacan, J. (1977). *The Four Fundamental Concepts of Psychoanalysis* (trans. Alan Sheridan). London: Karnac.

Morrison, T. (1987). *Beloved*. New York: Knopf.

Warner, M. (2006). *Phantasmagoria: Spirit Visions, Metaphors and Media into the Twenty-First Century*. Oxford: Oxford University Press.

Žižek, S. (1997). *The Plague of Fantasies*. London: Verso.

Spivak, Gayatri Chakravorty

STEPHEN MORTON

Gayatri Chakravorty Spivak is one of the most influential literary and cultural theorists of the late twentieth century. She is widely regarded as one of the founding figures of postcolonial theory, along with Edward W. Said and Homi K. Bhabha, but she is also a leading translator and commentator on the thought of the French philosopher Jacques Derrida and the Bengali writer Mahasweta Devi, and has made important contributions to debates about the future of comparative literature and the structural inequalities of neoliberal globalization. Born and educated in Kolkata, India, Spivak moved to the United States in the 1960s to study under the American literary critic Paul de Man at Cornell University in Ithaca, New York. Her dissertation was on the poetry of W. B. Yeats. But it was Spivak's English translation of the French philosopher Jacques Derrida's *De la Grammatologie* in 1976 that established her reputation as a deconstructive critic. Spivak went on to write articles on Marxism and deconstruction and French feminist thought in the 1980s for journals such as *diacritics* and *Critical Inquiry*; she subsequently became involved in a critical dialogue with the Subaltern Studies historians, a group of historians who sought to challenge the elitism of South Asian historiography by examining historical events from the standpoint of the subaltern or the socially excluded in South Asian society. One of Spivak's most well known essays is "Can the subaltern speak?" (1995a [1988]), an essay which offers a deconstructive reading of the term "representation" in Marx's *Eighteenth Brumaire of Louis Bonaparte*, and applies this reading to Hindu scriptures and colonial archives on the practice of *sati*-suicide in colonial India. It is perhaps this essay and Spivak's collection of interviews *The Postcolonial Critic* which have established her as a prominent postcolonial critic. Spivak is, however, uneasy with this label, and this uneasiness is signaled in the title of her magnum opus, *A Critique of Postcolonial Reason: Towards a History of the Vanishing Present* (1999), a book that interrogates the emancipatory claims of postcolonial studies in the context of the depredations of global capitalism. More recently in *Death of a Discipline* (2003a), a book of essays based on a lecture series delivered at the University California at Irvine, Spivak has sought to define a political vocation for comparative literature by focusing on subaltern languages as active cultural media for interrupting the corporate agenda of global development.

The literary critic Edward W. Said has argued in *The World, the Text, and the Critic* that "all texts are worldly, even when they appear to deny it, they are nevertheless a part of the social world, human life, and of course the historical moments in which they are located and interpreted" (1983: 4). Like Said, Spivak has also stressed that the

activity of reading literary texts is intimately bound up with the social, political, and economic world. In an essay titled "Reading the world" Spivak has argued that the speculative reason associated with the practice of literary interpretation is crucial to reading the world: "Without the reading of the world as a book, there is no prediction, no planning, no taxes, no laws, no welfare, no war". And yet, as Spivak goes on to explain, the world's politicians and businessmen "read the world in terms of rationality and averages, as if it were a textbook" (1987: 95). For Spivak, what is particularly useful about the act of literary interpretation is its potential to imagine an alternative to the economic rationalization of the world and its resources: "If, through our study of literature, we can ourselves learn and teach others to read the world in the 'proper' risky way, and to act upon that lesson, perhaps we literary people would not forever be such helpless victims" (95). If there appears to be a conceptual resemblance between Said's account of the worldliness of texts and Spivak's political injunction to read the world, it is also important to stress that Spivak takes issue with Said's criticism of Derrida's distinction between textuality and the world. In Said's account, "Derrida's criticism moves us *into* the text, Foucault's *in* and *out*" (1983: 183). For Spivak, however, this "plangent aphorism ... betrays a profound misapprehension of the notion of 'textuality'" (1995a: 87). Like Derrida, Spivak views a text as anything that is based on a system of a signs and codes. In this definition, a text could be a system of government such as democracy or apartheid, an economic division of labor, as well as a work of visual art or a literary text.

Spivak's rereading of value as a deconstructive sign in Marx's economic writings is an interesting example of this.

In "Scattered speculations on the question of value" Spivak traces the ways in which value is an ambivalent sign in Marx's work which always contains a trace of the worker's physical labor power. In the face of arguments that Marx's labor theory of value is no longer relevant to describe contemporary neoliberal economics, Spivak insists that "any critique of the labor theory of value, pointing at the unfeasibility of the theory under post-industrialism, or as a calculus of economic indicators, ignores the dark presence of the Third World" (1987: 167). In so doing, Spivak demonstrates the political significance of deconstruction as a strategy for reading the world. Just as Marx emphasized that the masculine, industrial working-class subject of nineteenth-century Europe is "the source of value" for industrial capitalism, so Spivak argues that the "so-called 'Third World' . . . produces the wealth and possibility of the 'First World'" (1990: 96). In saying this, Spivak also challenges the view of the Third World as a primitive, premodern, or underdeveloped space outside of the circuits of capitalism.

Spivak's invocation of the gendered international division of labor here certainly demonstrates the continuing relevance of Marx's labor theory of value to the gendered and geographical dynamics of contemporary global capitalism. However, the casual and nonunionized conditions of labor for many women (and children) employed in sweatshops and free trade zones, and other forms of subcontracted labor in the global South would seem to make it difficult for such workers to organize and protest against their exploitation, let alone to promote the social redistribution of capital. While Spivak is critical of the international division of labor, she is also skeptical of the transparent claims made by benevolent First World intellectuals to "speak for" subaltern workers in the global South. In A Critique of Postcolonial Reason, for example, Spivak criticizes the "moral imperialism" of "boycott politics" (1999: 415). Focusing on the emergence of a public discourse in the US media during the 1990s around the exploitation of child labor in the Bangladeshi garment manufacturing industry, Spivak criticizes the racism of benevolent liberal reformers, who supported "sanctions against Southern garment factories that use child labor" (416). In common with the liberal reformers, she condemns the exploitation of child labor. However she also questions the efficacy of sanctions against Bangladeshi garment factories that use child labor on the grounds that such sanctions do nothing to redress the broader absence of unionized labor laws or infrastructural reforms in countries such as Bangladesh.

Spivak's critique of the "moral imperialism" associated with "First World" anti-sweatshop campaigns for consumer boycotts of certain commodities that are produced by "Third World" workers under conditions of sweated labor has been taken up in recent critiques of the contemporary anticapitalist movement. The American cultural critic Bruce Robbins, for example, characterizes the "First World" consumer's contemplation of the magnitude of the world economic system and the international division of labor as a contemporary example of Immanuel Kant's theory of the sublime. Robbins acknowledges that there is no guarantee that a "First World" consumer's contemplation of what he aptly calls the "sweatshop sublime" will necessarily lead to their political mobilization; indeed, in many cases, a consumer's experience of the "sweatshop sublime" may lead to political paralysis and inaction. Yet for Robbins, it is precisely the experience of hesitancy, self-questioning, and doubt associated with the sublime which complicates the "tempting simplicity of action."

Significantly, Robbins cites Spivak's *A Critique of Postcolonial Reason* to support his argument. By juxtaposing Spivak's critique of Kant's foreclosure of the native informant in his analytic of the sublime with her critique of the "boycott politics" associated with the North American anti-sweatshop movement and Western human rights discourse, Robbins concludes that in Spivak's *Critique*, "Kant's analytic of the sublime does the same thing that western human rights discourse does when addressed to Bangladeshi sweatshops: it flattens out the complexity and difference of Third World society to suit a First World standard of ethical rationality" (Robbins 2002: 95).

Spivak's criticism of Western human rights discourse is developed further in her writings on human rights and transnational literacy. She first defined what she means by transnational literacy in an essay titled "Teaching for the times." In this essay, Spivak argues that literacy is not simply expertise in another language, but rather "the skill to differentiate between letters, so that an articulated script can be read, reread, written, rewritten" (1995b: 193). More importantly, "literacy allows us to sense that the other is not just a 'voice,' but that others produce articulated texts, even as they, like us, are written in and by a text not of our own making" (193). To clarify this claim, Spivak turns to *Fantasia* (*L'Amour, la fantasia*), a novel by the Algerian feminist writer Assia Djebar, in which the narrator stages the trauma of being denied access to classical Arabic in French-occupied Algeria. In a passage from the third section of the novel entitled "Embraces," the French-educated protagonist attempts to translate *Un Été au Sahara*, a story by the nineteenth-century French orientalist writer Eugène Fromentin, into Arabic for "Zohra, an eighty-year old rural *mujahida* (female freedom fighter)" (197). By translating Fromentin's written text into

an Arabic story, the narrator also retells the story of two Algerian prostitutes, murdered by the French army during a battle. In doing so, Spivak suggests that Djebar's protagonist privileges the perspective of the two Algerian prostitutes in Frometin's text, and that in the act of translation the protagonist undoes her amnesia of the Arabic language. Such an example is significant because it stages the delegitimization of a non-European language by a dominant European language. In doing so, the protagonist also works to legitimize the Arabic language, which she has forgotten as a consequence of French colonial policies. For Spivak, this passage from Djebar's *Fantasia* allows non-Arabic readers to grasp that "the other is not just a 'voice,' but that others produce articulated texts" (193).

Spivak has proceeded to refine what she means by transnational literacy in her claim that subaltern languages, or the subordinate languages of the global South, have restricted permeability, by which she means that subaltern languages are not widely spoken, read, or understood. Spivak develops this point in "Righting wrongs" (2003b), an article that was originally presented at the Oxford Amnesty lectures in 2001. In this article, Spivak argues that "the rural poor and . . . all species of the sub-proletariat" will remain an "object of benevolence in human rights discourse" without the recovering and training of the ethical imagination of such subaltern groups (206–7). To facilitate such training, Spivak proposes a rethinking of the subject of human rights from the standpoint of the rural poor and the sub-proletariat in South Asia. Such a rethinking demands a new pedagogy that is capable of suturing the damage wrought on subaltern groups in South Asia by centuries of class and caste oppression, as well as the transition from colonial modernity to globalization. What is crucial here for Spivak is that such a pedagogy should strive to "learn well one of the languages of the rural poor of the South" (208). In this sense, transnational literacy signals a shift in Spivak's work from the politics of reading the world to an ethical commitment to learn from the subaltern.

SEE ALSO: Bhabha, Homi; Derrida, Jacques; Foucault, Michel; Postcolonial Studies; Said, Edward

REFERENCES AND SUGGESTED READINGS

Morton, S. (2003). *Gayatri Chakravorty Spivak*. London: Routledge.
Morton, S. (2006). *Gayatri Spivak: Ethics, Subalternity and the Critique of Postcolonial Reason*. Cambridge: Polity.
Robbins, B. (2002). The sweatshop sublime. *Publications of the Modern Language Association of America*, 117, 84–97.
Said, E. W. (1983). *The World, the Text, and the Critic*. Cambridge, MA: Harvard University Press.
Sanders, M. (2006). *Gayatri Chakravorty Spivak: Live Theory*. London: Continuum.
Spivak, G. C. (1976). Translator's preface. In J. Derrida, *Of Grammatology*. Baltimore: Johns Hopkins University Press.
Spivak, G. C. (1987). *In Other Worlds: Essays in Cultural Politics*. London: Routledge.
Spivak, G. C. (1990). *The Postcolonial Critic: Interviews, Strategies, Dialogues* (ed. S. Harasym). London: Routledge.
Spivak, G. C. (1995a). Can the subaltern speak? In P. Williams & L. Chrisman (eds.), *Colonial Discourse and Post-Colonial Theory: A Reader*. Hemel Hempstead: Harvester Wheatsheaf, pp. 66–111. (Original work published 1988.)
Spivak, G. C. (1995b). Teaching for the times. In J. N. Pieterse (ed.), *Decolonizing the Imagination*. London: Zed Books, pp. 177–202.
Spivak, G. C. (1999). *A Critique of Postcolonial Reason: Towards a History of the Vanishing Present*. Cambridge, MA: Harvard University Press.
Spivak, G. C. (2003a). *Death of a Discipline*. New York: Columbia University Press.
Spivak, G. C. (2003b). Righting wrongs. In N. Owen (ed.), *Human Rights, Human Wrongs: The Oxford Amnesty lectures, 2001*. Oxford: Oxford University Press, pp. 164–227.

Stiegler, Bernard

ARTHUR BRADLEY

Bernard Stiegler (b. 1952) is a contemporary French philosopher of technology who is most famous for his ongoing book project *La Technique et le temps* [*Technics and Time*]. He is the founder of the group Ars Industrialis, and currently works as the director of the Institute for Cultural Development at the Centre Georges Pompidou in Paris.

First and foremost, Stiegler's philosophy is based on a new concept of "technics" as the fundamental condition of human evolution, culture, and philosophy. According to Aristotle's *Physics*, *techn* is nothing more than a *prosthesis* – a tool – designed for human ends. Yet, it is precisely this influential idea of technology – inert, neutral, a mere human instrument – that Stiegler wishes to challenge. For Stiegler, we cannot oppose humanity and technology as if they were entirely separate entities: each only comes into existence through the other. If we tend to define human nature either biologically (as a particular kind of species) or philosophically (as a soul, mind, or consciousness), he argues that humanity is in fact constituted by our relation to technical systems and structures. In this sense, Stiegler paves the way for a new account of what it means to be human.

It is the legend of Prometheus and his brother Epimetheus that provides the mythological backdrop for this philosophy in the first volume of *Technics and Time* (Stiegler 1998: 185–203). According to Plato's *Protagoras*, the two brothers were ordered by the gods to equip every mortal species with different qualities, but Epimetheus persuades Prometheus to let him do the job himself. However, Epimetheus forgets to allocate any qualities to human beings – leaving them entirely defenseless – and so Prometheus is forced to steal fire and the gift of skill in the arts (*technai*) from the gods by way of compensation for this loss. For Stiegler, this myth of the origin of man contains a crucial insight into the nature of human existence that forms the basis for his own philosophy: humanity is constituted by an originary *lack* of defining qualities, or what he calls a "necessary default" of origin ("le défaut qu'il faut"). What, though, is humanity's way of filling this originary lack?

According to Stiegler, the story of human evolution is the story of a process of "exteriorization" that begins with the carving of the first flint tool and continues to this day. He distinguishes between three different forms of memory: *genetic* memory (which is programmed into our DNA); *epigenetic* memory (which consists of memories acquired during our lifetime and is stored in the central nervous system); and finally, *epiphylogenetic* memory (which is embodied in technical systems or artifacts like tools, cave paintings, archives and so on) (1998: 140). However, Stiegler argues that humans are the only beings who possess this third or "tertiary" form of memory: we alone among all life forms have the ability to record, stockpile, and transmit our experiences to others in the form of technical artifacts. To Stiegler's eyes, then, what defines humanity is nothing other than this process of externalizing life onto non-living apparatuses: we are our own outside. While he pursues this argument in many different ways, the central thesis of *Technics and Time* is that technics is the basis for the human experience of time or *temporalization*: the existence of a technical artifact both embodies knowledge of the past and opens the possibility of the future. Perhaps most importantly, technics also entails an

awareness of human finitude: technical artifacts both enable us to experience historical events that we have never personally lived through, and to preserve our own individual experiences for generations to come. In this respect, technics is not simply the basis for human existence but for culture: we can no more oppose technics to culture than we can to humanity.

For Stiegler, this "originary" technicity is also the basis for a thoroughgoing rereading or "deconstruction" of Western thought. According to *Technics and Time*, the history of Western philosophy is the history of the denial, repression, or Epimethean "forgetting" of its own technical origin. Quite simply, Stiegler sees technics as something that remains essentially unthought, and much of his work is concerned with thinking through the implications of this exclusion. From Greek metaphysics all the way up to the contemporary epoch, Western philosophy transforms the essentially technical constitution *of* temporality into a series of metaphysical oppositions *between* technics and time that relegates the former to a purely incidental or supplemental position. Just as Plato opposes divine recollection (*anamnēsis*) to artificial memory (*hypomnēsis*) in the *Meno*, for instance, so the twentieth-century German phenomenologist Martin Heidegger, too, distinguishes ontological time from what he calls the "vulgar" experience of time in *Being and Time* (1927). If Stiegler's philosophy is clearly influenced by certain key figures in twentieth-century continental theory – Heidegger, Gilbert Simondon, and particularly his intellectual mentor Jacques Derrida – he also claims to detect a certain forgetting of technics at work in their thought (Stiegler 2002). While Derrida's logic of the "supplement" provides the intellectual groundwork for much of Stiegler's work on the prosthesis, Stiegler criticizes a certain abstract dimension in deconstruction: he argues that we need to understand the *history* of specific technical supplements – tools, alphabetic writing, and photography – in order to construct a philosophical *logic* of supplementation (2002: 254). In his recent work, Stiegler's philosophy analyzes the political implications of the technical constitution of the human: *De la Misère symbolique* [Of symbolic poverty] explores the mass industrialization of human memory and desire in the contemporary epoch and the effective reduction of humanity to the status of a mechanical and indiscriminate consumer (Stiegler 2003).

In the Anglophone world, Stiegler's work has received a mixed reception to date. On the one hand, it is frequently criticized for offering a technologically positivist and determinist account of phenomenology, deconstruction, and philosophy in general. On the other, it is praised for offering an original materialist corrective to the residual idealism of contemporary continental philosophy that largely avoids falling into the trap of a crude or reductive empiricism.

SEE ALSO: Deconstruction; Derrida, Jacques; Heidegger, Martin; Phenomenology

REFERENCES AND SUGGESTED READINGS

Derrida, J., & Stiegler, B. (2002). *Echographies of Television* (trans. J.Bajorek). Cambridge: Polity.
Stiegler, B. (1998). *Technics and Time 1: The Fault of Epimetheus* (trans. R. Beardsworth & G. Collins). Stanford: Stanford University Press.
Stiegler, B. (2002). Derrida and technology: Fidelity at the limits of deconstruction and the prosthesis of faith (trans. R. Beardsworth). In T. Conley (ed.), *Jacques Derrida and the Future of the Humanities*. Cambridge: Cambridge University Press, pp. 238–270.
Stiegler, B. (2003). *De la Misère symbolique 1: L'époque hyperindustrielle*. Paris: Galilée.
Stiegler, B. (2004). *Philosopher par accident: Entretiens avec Elie During*. Paris: Galilée.
Stiegler, B. (2005). *Mécréance et discrédit 1: La décadence des démocraties industrielles*. Paris: Galilée.
Stiegler, B. (2007). *Anamnēsis* and *Hypomnēsis*: The memories of desire (trans. A. Bradley & F.-X. Gleyzon). In A. Bradley & L. Armand (eds.), *Technicity*. Prague: Charles University Press, pp. 15–41.

Subject Position

NICK MANSFIELD

The question of the living self, its origins, nature and relationship to the social, cultural and political contexts in which it arises, has been one of the defining themes of modernity. What does the word "I" actually mean? Philosophical modernity is commonly dated from the division by the French philosopher René Descartes of the world between the subject, the thing that thinks, on the one hand, and the multidimensional world of objectivity that is thought about, on the other, between, in short, subject and object. Modernity was founded, then, on the primacy of thinking consciousness and the unified human self. The interrogation of the "modern," commonly denoted as "postmodernity," took as one of its key focuses the questioning of the reality of this individual thinking consciousness, taking the lead from modernist artists, from Arthur Rimbaud to performance art, who saw the self as a fiction, an encumbrance, or even a cruel political device. Indeed, the will to dislocate, deconstruct or destroy coherent human subjectivity is one of the dominant experiments in recent philosophy and culture.

This article will first outline the key features of the "free and autonomous individual," the understanding of the self most dominant since the Enlightenment, and the linchpin of modern liberal political practice and humanist culture. It will then describe the key challenges to this understanding of the subject in the psychoanalytic tradition, running from Sigmund Freud through Jacques Lacan to Luce Irigaray and Julia Kristeva. It will then give an account of the other influential critique of individualism, which runs from Friedrich Nietzsche, through the work of Michel Foucault and Gilles Deleuze and Félix Guattari, to Judith Butler and Giorgio Agamben. Here, the subject is a site of the operation of power. Each of these theories does not only provide an outline of what the human subject is, but, crucially for literary studies, how it emerges in relation to language. In Lacan, for example, the self emerges only in and through language. In Foucault, the subject that is a vehicle of the operation of power emerges through discourses of knowledge. In each of these accounts, texts do not simply represent the subject as much as make or "deploy" it. Literature, therefore, is a key site in which the mechanics by which subjectivity arises and is positioned can be revealed and contested.

THE INDIVIDUAL

The most influential understanding of the human self in modern Western culture is "the individual." To be individual is literally to be that which cannot be divided further, to be, therefore, singular, unified and complete in oneself. The conventional account of modern subjectivity, therefore, emphasizes the self as something homogeneous, autonomous, internally coordinated, and separate from the world around it. To many people, this model of the self is taken for granted. It is certainly the one assumed by almost all of the institutions of liberal society. Yet, this understanding of the self arose at a specific historical moment, and

needed to be formulated by philosophers. In other words, far from being obvious, inevitable, and natural, this understanding of the self is the product of history and culture. What are the key features of this individuality? First, it is dominated by consciousness. Second, it is unified, and finally it is unique. Let us look at the most influential formulations of each of these three aspects of the individual.

Descartes's account of the self emphasized the role of consciousness. In the *Meditations on First Philosophy* (1641), Descartes asked himself what he could possibly be certain of. The senses might deceive; other people might lie and even the revelation of God may be the deceit of an infernal demon. If you could not rely on any of these things, what possible grounds could there be for certainty about anything? His answer was that, if nothing else could be certain, at least he could be sure that he was reflecting on these issues. He was thinking, therefore, and this thinking provided at least some fixity. Descartes famously formulated his conclusion as *cogito ergo sum* (I think therefore I am). Here, Descartes grounded the certainty of all human knowledge in the thinking self. In turn, knowledge was to be taken by modern philosophy as the primary form of human relationship with the world. The importance of the self, therefore, rested in its rational faculties, its awareness of and engagement with the world.

To German philosopher Immanuel Kant, in the *Critique of Pure Reason* (1781), human knowledge of the world was conditioned by the structures of the human mind, through which our perceptions of the outside world reached us. An example of these structures would be the way the human mind divides the world between space and time, or into three dimensions. Human knowledge is governed by these categories. Crucial to this process is the mind's drive to make our different perceptions, or intuitions, converge on one another, to give the impression of the unity of the world. This sense of the unity of the world, therefore, depends on the experience of individual consciousness as a unity. If I experience an object via a variety of my senses – I can look at it, hear it, touch and taste it – why do I get the sense that these different experiences are experiences of the same thing? Because I myself am a unified thing, Kant argues.

The third feature of individuality is its emphasis on the uniqueness of the self. This idea gained prominence in the late eighteenth century, for example in the work of Swiss philosopher Jean-Jacques Rousseau. Rousseau justified the writing of his *Confessions* (1960[1782]) not in the great achievements of his career, or his historical importance. It was the distinctiveness and originality of his individual subjectivity that counted, a distinctiveness all of us could claim. The subsequent romantic cult of sensibility understood this uniqueness of the self as played out in the unshared intensity of personal emotion, or "feeling." This emphasis on feeling as the centerpiece of a distinctive human self has remained powerful in modern and postmodern culture, and was indeed revived as an ideology in the countercultural movements of the 1960s. The contemporary media obsession with how people "feel" after winning a race, witnessing a disaster or losing a loved one descends from this belief that the meaning of experience is grounded in the depth of human emotion.

In sum, then, the individual model of subjectivity that has dominated post-Enlightenment Western culture brings together a set of ideas that are commonly seen to be together, but that are potentially in conflict with one another: consciousness, unity and uniqueness of sensibility. The coordination of conscious knowledge and intense feeling in the one complex would seem to imply conflict, and in Freudian psychoanalysis this tension developed into a new model of the self, one split between the rational conscious mind and an obscure, highly charged and potentially dangerous unconscious.

FREUD: THE DISCOVERY OF THE UNCONSCIOUS

Many of Freud's ideas – for example, the emphasis on sexuality, the unconscious and early childhood experience as determining adult selfhood – have become part of the commonsense popular psychology of Western modernity, largely because of the influence they had on popular culture, especially Hollywood film in the 1940s and '50s. The key breakthrough in Freud's thinking about subjectivity came in his work on dreams. Dreams could not be dismissed as the mere chaotic residue of images left over from daily experience. They at least indicated the existence of some domain in the human mind resistant to conscious understanding, which unsurprisingly Freud chose to name the "unconscious." The intensity of the emotions dreams triggered showed that the unconscious was a site of volatile and pressing investments fundamental to the emotional nature of the individual. What could they mean? To Freud, the unconscious was the domain in which unresolved material from the formation of the subject was stored. The self formed through the process Freud named the Oedipus complex. This process is never completely satisfactorily resolved, and the unconscious is the place where its ambiguous and threatening residue persists.

Freud's account of the Oedipus complex focuses on the experience of boys and his account of female subjectivity is notoriously inadequate. In the Oedipal phase, the boy child becomes anxious about losing his penis, either because he is threatened with castration for playing with it, or because he sees a naked female body, which he inter-prets as a castrated male body. He starts to identify masculine domestic and social power as connected with ownership of the penis, the thing he thinks distinguishes men from women. Yet, he fears his penis may be taken away from him. He becomes desper-ate to identify with his father, the owner of the penis and all its prerogatives. In so doing, he becomes a rival with the father for the mother's affection, because the mother is the sexual object of the father, and someone with whom the boy still feels a strong bond of physical intimacy. This com-petition with the father and sexual longing for the mother contradict all the regulations of social life, and bring on a crisis in the boy's mind. The only way this crisis can be resolved is by opening up a domain in the mind into which the boy's antisocial and violently sexual feelings can be installed. This domain is the unconscious, and the process by which the dangerous emotional material is stored there is repression. Un-conscious material, however, desires to be-come conscious, and through dreams and neuroses, it seeks access to the conscious mind. The function of dreams is to stage an imaginary drama that gives the subject some illusion that his darkest unconscious long-ings have been fulfilled. This process, called "wish-fulfillment," has also been used to explain the intense emotional investment we have in fictional narratives: they play out our deepest unconscious desires and pro-vide some illusion of their satisfaction. Or-thodox Freudian readings of literature, therefore, see it as a restaging of the Oedipal story, in more or less distorted ways.

LACAN AND THE SUBJECT OF LANGUAGE

Since the 1970s, the work of French psycho-analyst Jacques Lacan has been the most influential post-Freudian account of subjectivity in literary studies. Lacan saw the Oedipal drama taking place in language. To Lacan, subjectivity only emerges as the child enters the symbolic order of language. Like Freud, Lacan's account was highly male-centered. The child's first experience of its body is one of fragmentation: the position of the eyes does not allow the child to get a sense of his body as a single whole. This can only be provided by an image received from the outside, perhaps in a mirror, the eye of a carer or in the child's identification with a playmate. This event, which Lacan calls the "mirror-phase," provides the child with a magical sense of the unity, completeness and auton-omy of its body. This imaginary unity, however, does not arise from within, nor does it belong to the child: it comes from outside, from a physical image exterior to the child's body.

The self, then, can no longer be an "individual," because it is no longer self-contained and autonomous. Its image of what it is, its "identity," lies outside of it. It is in language, an alien system of markers that we use to identify and express ourselves, that this process takes place. To Lacan, then, we only assume subjectivity in language, or what he calls the "symbolic order." The symbolic order is outside of us and beyond our control, yet remains the only place in which we can identify and express ourselves. We still aspire in language to that magical sense of unity and oneness that was our first experience of the mirror image. This drive toward "imaginary" unity is unachievable, yet it remains the key cause of the insatiable desire that defines our relationship with the world. Imaginary uni-ty is the quintessence of language. In the same way that the boy in Freud was desperate to ensure his ownership of the penis that represented masculine power, the subject in Lacan dreams of the unifying identity that seems to ensure a unified sense of self. This is not finally achievable. To Lacan, this shows that the order of language is governed by a masculine principle, not the penis per se, but its representation, the phallus, or what he calls the "name-of-the-father."

These psychoanalytic accounts of subjectivity are governed by a clearly masculine-centered perspective. Since the 1960s, feminists have contested this masculine bias. Irigaray has challenged the "phallocentrism," which sees unity, authority, and singularity as key cultural values. In Irigaray's account, feminine subjectivity takes as its defining image not the phallus but the vaginal lips. The lips are never less than two and always in contact with one another in multiple places. The continuity, multiplicity, and difference inseparable from this image of the lips promote, as a challenge to the oppressive authority of masculine unity, an image of subjectivity, aesthetics and identity that celebrates difference, plurality, and possibility.

Kristeva, on the other hand, argues that the disconnected and fragmented sense of the self that preceded the Oedipal continues to influence the growing self. Our sense of our subjectivity is identified with our control over our bodies, our discipline in keeping them "clean and proper," hygienic and contained within their physical perimeters. The problem is that fluids – from food and drink to blood, vomit and excreta – continually cross this imaginary boundary as part of the normal processes of biological life. These "abject" processes are simultaneously a source of horror, because they threaten our sense of unified and controlled selfhood, and of fascination because they seem to offer some possible liberation from logic, order and responsibility. Ambiguity and discontinuity in literary language connect with this feeling of the unfixed boundaries of unified subjectivity.

POWER AND SUBJECTIVATION

These accounts see subjectivity as either a really existing thing or part of a process of the necessary unfolding of language. The other most influential recent account, that centering on the work of French thinker Michel Foucault, and inherited from Nietzsche, sees unified and knowable subjectivity as a fiction created by power in order to maximize control over the human population. Nietzsche believed that life was a struggle for domination between competing human groups. Those who had lost this struggle, the "weak," "slave" or "herd" population were unable to contest the physical superiority of those who had dominated them, so they contrived a system of moral responsibility that made the strong – who, Nietzsche believed, had no choice but to be strong and to dominate – answerable for their strength. This morality relied on a concept of the subject which could be punished. This subjectivity was a kind of straitjacket that reduced, simplified and constrained the multiple forms of drive, desire and energy, what Nietzsche called the "will-to-power," that was human life. The will-to-power should be free to play itself out.

Foucault was not in favor of the unbridled domination of one social group by another, but he did use Nietzsche's understanding of the nature of subjectivity to analyze the way power worked in modern societies. For Foucault, what characterized the modern age was the way subjectivity had become the vehicle of power. In contrast to the Enlightenment view, Foucault did not see the subject as a pre-existing autonomous thing that power oppressed. Instead, he saw the identification and definition of certain types of subjectivity as the key means by which modern power operated. To Foucault, power was not a position or instrument owned by certain people at the top of the social hierarchy to achieve their ends.

Power was part of every human situation. Power operates locally at the extremes of society, in every day-to-day event. Yet, this power is not a power of violence and intimidation in which one person simply dominates another. Modern power operates by defining normal and acceptable forms of behavior, indeed by defining the ways in which human beings are allowed to be subjects. Key social institutions are the key sites where this takes place. Foucault, himself, provided book-length analyses of several institutions, such as the asylum, the clinic, and most influentially, the prison. He argued, however, that his analyses could be extended to schools, workplaces, social welfare bureaucracies and beyond. Indeed, modern life is a life where we pass from one institution to another: born in hospitals, raised in childcare and schools, working in corporations, judged by banks, regulated by the social security apparatus, we are in the hands of the health system when we are sick, the criminal justice system when we are bad, the mental health system when we experience mental illness and the age care system when we are old. We walk in public spaces constantly subject to surveillance, and our personal behavior is constantly measured against what is normal and healthy, from our diet and our way of dressing to our styles of conversation, bodily presentation, and sexual behavior. In each of these contexts, we are expected to take on specific ways of being: to exhibit safe, correct, and healthy behavior. Each institution also has its own sanctions, from medication and ostracism to incarceration and loss of social rights. In some contexts, refusing to conform to normal modes of gender and sexual correctness risks violence, even death.

The key transformation of the modern age was the way in which our personal practices came to be read symptomatically. Once, Foucault argues, a crime or a certain sexual practice was simply something that someone did or did not do. Some of these actions were forbidden and attracted certain consequences. In the modern age, however, our acts became indications of our being certain types of people. The most famous example he gives is of the invention of the homosexual. "Sodomy" was a certain class of sexual acts. People who performed them were merely those who had committed a certain sanctioned act. By the end of the nineteenth century, however, the act was taken to be evidence of a certain type of person, the "homosexual," who was not merely someone who did a specific thing, but a complete species, everything about whom, from their style of speech, their tastes, their moral fitness and even dress sense, was related to their taste in sexual behavior. Modern institutions are only interested in what we do as evidence of the type of person or subject that we are. Their interest, even their whole reason for being, is in judging us as these types.

Where do the categories of human normality these institutions administer come from? It is primarily in the academic domain of the human sciences that the dominant definitions of what it is to be or not be normal emerge. These definitions in turn circulate and are adapted in many domains: government reports, police files, court judgments, case histories, policy documents and institutional procedures all contribute to a generalized model of what acceptable human subjectivity is. Social institutions validate these models of subjective normality as they administer them. Foucault understood this seamless collaboration between research and administration as the perfect coordination of power and knowledge. So interdependent were these two that he believed that the term "power/knowledge" should be considered a single word.

Foucault believed that "power/knowledge" defined the limits in any society of what it was possible for the subject to be, and that these limits should be challenged by an experimentation with selfhood that is fundamentally aesthetic. There is no essential or natural self for us to fall back on as the thing to liberate from the oppressions of power. Our role therefore is to reinvent ourselves in ways that transgress the limits imposed by power/knowledge. Deleuze and Guattari have also argued for a radically experimental self. To Deleuze and Guattari, models of the self, like the psychoanalytic, which rely on a sense of a stable internally structured subjectivity condemn us to a preordained and limited range of possibility. They see this structured sense of self as analogous to the anatomical model of the body as a system of purposefully functioning internal, mutually dependent organs. In contrast, they believe that the subject should be imagined in its relationship to the outside – its "exteriority" – as if it is a "body without organs" (French playwright Antonin Artaud's phrase) situated in a field rich with infinite possibilities of relationship with everything beyond the narrow confines of the single human body. In both of these accounts of the subject, optimism is invested in possibility, plurality, otherness, and the denial of inherited limits.

Foucault's account of the subject has been hugely influential. His account of prisons, for example, drew on the design by English reformer Jeremy Bentham of a model prison, called the Panopticon, in which prisoners' behavior was subject to permanent observation. This image in turn has been taken up as a model of the modern disciplinary society where we are subject to constant surveillance, from security cameras in public places to tracking on the internet. All of this observation, of course, is not aimed at merely observing the body in itself, but as reading its behavior as indicative of the state of our invisible, interior life. Judith Butler has argued that this use of bodily markers as mere signs of an imagined subjectivity shows how dominant gender regimes operate: bodily behavior, from dress and gesture, to sexual practice and body modification are all practices used to indicate a certain abstract and stable gender identity, in conformity with the dominant heterosexual regime. We all work hard to conform to the fixed gender options of our society, because we know the failure to perform these gender norms properly can expose us to ridicule, ostracism, physical violence, and, in some contexts, even death.

Foucault's late work on sexuality argued that in modern culture, social administration had come increasingly to focus on the hygiene of the human population. Genetic inheritance, sexual normality and racial type became the focus of scientific research and social administration. This produced endless government programs to advance collective public health, and indeed, to the present, barely a day goes past without the announcement of the research results of or new public programs to solve social problems from diet and substance abuse, to family relationships, classroom behavior and so on. This is what endures of what Foucault called "biopolitics," the intervention of government policy in the physical life of the human subject. Biopolitics has a history that is far less benign, however, and can be connected with the genocidal policies of the Holocaust, and the forced absorption into the general population – or "breeding out" – of indigenous peoples. Agamben has used Foucault to argue that in the modern era true political "sovereignty" resided in the power to judge who would live and who would die.

The era of modernity has been the era where the human self has come to be seen as the measure of truth and meaning. On the one hand, all events are seen only to have significance in terms of the impact they have on the individual subject – how they make us "feel" – or else the subject has become the primary means for the operation of power. Much modern and postmodern art practice has experimented with going beyond the subject and inventing new horizons of human being. Literary texts have been seen as either reflecting the nature of human subjectivity (as in Freud), remodeling it because literature and subjectivity are made of the same material, language (as in Lacan), or else contributing to the definition of and challenge to what is understood as the norms of subjectivity, gender and biopolitics (as in Foucault, Butler, and Agamben). Whether, as Foucault and more recently Italian philosopher Mario Perniola have argued, the era of the subject is over or not, writing and textual production more generally remain the key sites for the exploration of subjectivity and the radical testing of its limits.

SEE ALSO: Foucault, Michel; Freud, Sigmund; Nietzsche, Friedrich; Psychoanalysis (to 1966); Psychoanalysis (since 1966)

REFERENCES AND SUGGESTED READINGS

Agamben, G. (1998). *Homo Sacer: Sovereign Power and Bare Life* (trans. D. Heller-Roazen). Stanford: Stanford University Press. (Original work published 1995.)
Butler, J. (1990). *Gender Trouble: Feminism and the Subversion of Identity*. New York: Routledge.
Deleuze, G., & Guattari, F. (1977). *Anti-Oedipus: Capitalism and Schizophrenia* (trans. R. Hurley, M. Seem, & H. R. Lane). New York: Viking. (Original work published 1972.)
Descartes, R. (1988). *Selected Philosophical Writings* (trans. J. Cottingham). New York: Cambridge University Press.
Foucault, M. (1987). *History of Sexuality, Volume 1: An Introduction* (trans. R. Hurley). London: Penguin. (Original work published 1976.)
Foucault, M. (1991). *Discipline and Punish: The Birth of the Prison* (trans. Alan Sheridan). London: Penguin. (Original work published 1975.)
Freud, S. (1984). *On Metapsychology: The Theory of Psychoanalysis* (trans. J Strachey). London: Penguin.
Irigaray, L. (1985). *This Sex Which Is Not One* (trans. C. Porter & C. Burke). Ithaca: Cornell University Press.
Kant, I. (2003). *Critique of Pure Reason* (trans. N. Kemp Smith). New York: Palgrave Macmillan. (Original work published 1781.)
Kristeva, J. (1982). *Powers of Horror: An Essay on Abjection* (trans. L. S. Roudiez). New York: Columbia University Press.
Lacan, J. (1977). *Écrits: A Selection* (trans. A. Sheridan). New York: Norton.
Rousseau, J.-J. (1960). *Confessions*. New York: E. P. Dutton. (Original work published 1782.)

Subversion

GAVIN GRINDON

Subversion in literary and cultural theory is usually understood, broadly, as a matter of the reversal of established values, or the insertion of other values into them. The relationship between this mostly cultural or ideological subversion and the actual subversion of existing social relations is a hotly contested topic. Much literary and cultural theory which has developed from a critical standpoint, whether Marxist, feminist or otherwise, has become concerned with debating the extent of subversion's potential, presence or extent. As such, any debate on subversion normally takes place in close relation to a debate on its opposite: containment or recuperation.

Debates on subversion are mostly famously associated with Birmingham School of Cultural Studies. Theorists associated with the school, especially Stuart Hall, emphasized how texts are used subversively. Such a reading stressed the active agency of the subject, focusing on the misuse, appropriation and rereading of texts by supposed "consumers," as well as the production of subcultures and countercultures. This presented a new critical, political approach to culture which didn't simply analyze relations of power or the presence of ideology, which had been the focus of much Marxist scholarship. However, this agency was mostly theorized as present merely in the reception of texts. Other critics came to question how much this internal, private subversion of values could add up to a communal, social subversion of an existing society.

However, as a general theme of cultural theory's debates in the politics of culture, subversion appears again and again in the writing of different critics as a central theme. These theories develop from very different perspectives and all give the idea of subversion quite different meanings and contexts. However, they are often tied to the same debate about the relationship between the subversion of power and its containment or recuperation by power.

Mikhail Bakhtin's writing on carnival was received in the West in light of this developing poststructuralist body of thought, and has become a central reference point on the debate on subversion and its containment. He gives an account of popular medieval carnivals as a utopian subversion of the established values and norms of the Christian church, and suggests the carnivalesque as a means to account for other more contemporary popular cultural subversions. Meanwhile, The Situationist International has also developed a notion of "detournement" close to Bakhtin's analysis of the subjective reorientation of established values. It stands opposed to the recuperation of the capitalist "spectacle."

Later, the poststructuralism of Jacques Derrida, Gilles Deleuze, Félix Guattari, and Michel Foucault has been an important influence on debates on subversion in the late twentieth century. They provide frameworks for thinking about subversion as each of their philosophical frameworks seeks to reveal different forms of subversion (in language, culture and society) by first philosophically subverting the methods and focus of Western philosophy. Deleuze and Guattari, particularly, have provided a number of theoretical models, in concepts such as the "rhizome" and "becoming animal," of a practice of moving between and around fixed power relations. Deleuze and Guattari reverse our normal assumptions about subversion, by emphasizing that the agency and creativity of subversion is always *primary*. Forms of power are not only reliant on subversion's insurgent creativity but also attempt to imitate it. This particular line of argument has been recently developed within a Marxist framework by Michael Hardt and Antonio Negri, who pose a capitalist "Empire" against a subversive "Multitude." Meanwhile, Foucault, though mostly focusing on the analysis of forms of control and discipline, has also written on what he terms spaces of "heterotopia."

The innovations of poststructuralist theory have also been applied to analyze the subversion of gender and racial values in culture at different points. In *The Location of Culture*, Homi Bhabha, for example, has been central to advancing a postcolonial theory of how cultural and racial "hybridity" can be subversive, in that it disrupts the easy operation of disciplinary distinctions between privileged and subaltern cultures and peoples. Similarly in the realm of queer theory, theorists have sought to "queer" normative readings of texts and practices. The most well known of these attempts is Judith Butler's account of gender as a performative relation, which by being performed otherwise by figures such as the Dandy is subverted. More recently, Michel de Certeau has developed these themes in his analysis of the possibility for developing spaces of autonomy in everyday cultural practices.

There is much debate over the content of what is being subverted and contained in these various theories. Marxist critics have contended that for some of these arguments, a purely cultural subversion may be less politically subversive as it is an isolated occurrence or does not affect underlying economic hierarchies and distinctions. However, in an age when culture is increasingly bound up with capitalist work and the commodity form, political subversion has at the same time also taken on a more and more cultural character, evident in recent political texts such as *The Temporary Autonomous Zone* (2003) by Hakim Bey or *The Coming Insurrection* (2009) by The Invisible Committee (a collective and anonymous penname). Meanwhile, some have argued of this entire debate that this whole, often entirely cultural, concern with analyzing and discussing subversion is *itself* implicated in a form of containment, because as it takes place within the university system it moves the language and debate of refusal, subversion and critique away from actual political struggles over these values to the plane of a meticulous but disengaged academic discussion.

SEE ALSO: Bakhtinian Criticism; Bhabha, Homi; Deleuze, Gilles; Derrida, Jacques; Hall, Stuart; Marxism

REFERENCES AND SUGGESTED READINGS

Bakhtin, M. (1984). *Rabelais and His World*. Bloomington: Indiana University Press.

Bey, H. (2003). *The Temporary Autonomous Zone*. New York: Autonomedia.

Bhabha, H. (1994). *The Location of Culture*. New York: Routledge.

Butler, J. (1990). *Gender Trouble: Feminism and the Subversion of Identity*. New York: Routledge.

Certeau, M. de (2002). *The Practice of Everyday Life*. Los Angeles: University of California Press.

Deleuze, G., & Guattari, F. (2003). *A Thousand Plateaus: Capitalism and Schizophrenia*. London: Continuum.

Hall, S. (1997). *Representation: Cultural Representations and Signifying Practices*. London: Sage.

Hardt, M. & Negri, A. (2000). *Empire*. Cambridge, MA: Harvard University Press.

The Invisible Committee (2009). *The Coming Insurrection*. New York: Semiotext(e).

Stallybrass, P. & White, A. (1986). *The Politics and Poetics of Transgression*. New York: Cornell University Press.

Vaneigem, R. (1994). *The Revolution of Everyday Life*. London: Rebel Press.

T

Tel Quel

JOHN MOWITT

Tel Quel, a French journal founded in 1960 and disbanded in 1982, played a major role in the promotion of writers and ideas associated first with structuralism and poststructuralism. The director, Philippe Sollers, was himself an accomplished postmodern writer, and his wife and fellow editorial board member, Julia Kristeva, was a major literary theorist and critic. *Tel Quel* was not strictly an academic journal, although academics served on its various editorial boards and its readership fell largely within the academic intelligentsia. Sollers never held an academic post, and he understood the project of the journal as a sustained challenge to the prevailing academic consensus in such fields as literary study, art history, philosophy, political science, and psychoanalysis. *Tel Quel* became two journals over time. Beginning in 1982, *Tel Quel* became *L'Infini*, a journal with similar ambitions to those of *Tel Quel* that remains in publication to this day. During its heyday in the 1960s and '70s, *Tel Quel* helped spawn several other journals in the humanities and social sciences, such as *Change* and *Cahiers pour l'Analyse*. The book series at Seuil, Collection *Tel Quel* (inaugurated in 1962), published some of the most important monographs of the

period such as *Théorie d'ensemble* (1968), which first introduced Russian formalism and the work of Mikhail Bakhtin to France, as well as germinal books by Roland Barthes, Jacques Derrida, and Julia Kristeva that were highly influential in Anglo-American literary and cultural theory.

Tel Quel differed from its predecessor as France's premier intellectual journal, Jean-Paul Sartre's *Les Temps Modernes*. It reset the terms of debate in the field of cultural politics so as to make all uses of language, whether public or private, fictive or factual, into moments of reflection and, ultimately, revolt. *Tel Quel* succeeded in stimulating a rethinking of both public and literary discourse that attracted enormous attention. Because of its sustained yet fraught dialogue with the French Communist Party (PCF), and notably the journal/magazine *La Nouvelle Critique*, *Tel Quel*'s impact on French intellectual discussion was also articulated in concretely political terms. Indeed, Sollers and the editorial board at *Tel Quel* energetically fostered French Maoism – and specifically its challenge to the emerging alliance between the Communist Party and the Socialist Party of François Mitterrand. Although "*telquelisme*" degenerated into a form of opportunism (what Sollers once characterized as the politics of the "zigzag"), the journal managed, for a time, to articulate an alternative "line"

The Encyclopedia of Literary and Cultural Theory   General editor: Michael Ryan
© 2011 Blackwell Publishing Ltd

or "tendency," one of whose best features is to be found in the current and enormously fecund preoccupations with radical or post-imperial democracy.

The name of the journal, "tel quel" (in English, "as is," or "such as it is"), derives from Paul Valéry's texts of the same name published between 1941 and 1943. Between 1960 and 1982 the editorial collective underwent several purges and reorganizations, all in certain ways expressing the shifting focus of the journal's concerns as expressed in its contracting and expanding subtitle, in effect, from "Science/Literature" to "Literature/Psychoanalysis/Philosophy/Politics/Art." Such a dynamic is certainly not unique to *Tel Quel*, but *Tel Quel* is distinctive in the way it sought to use precisely this sort of heterogeneity to sustain its relevance and impact. The statement published in the immediate aftermath of May 1968, "The revolution here, now: seven points," in which the formation of the Group for Theoretical Study is heralded, makes this point concisely. Put differently, *Tel Quel*, largely under the influence of Derrida's writing, sought to embrace and embody the productivity of difference, if not dissension. During the late 1970s this led it, perhaps predictably, to the theme of dissidence. The journal became increasingly concerned with opposition to state Communism.

This principled instability notwithstanding, *Tel Quel* was always committed to the literary avant-garde. In fact, the Derridean meditation on difference, specifically its challenge to the philosophical ideology of speech and the voice, provided the journal with the theoretical insights by which it proposed to fuse the notion of the literary or aesthetic avant-garde with the notion of the political vanguard. Keenly attuned to everything from Russian Formalism and Socialist Realism to the Expressionist debates of the 1930s and the Sartrean stance of *engagement* ("engaged or activist writing"), the intellectuals affiliated with the journal sought to break with the assumption that the formation of a correct or progressive political tendency required the struggle to bring reality into conformity with a correct analysis of its historical laws, in effect with the right ideas, whether expressed aesthetically or philosophically. Instead, *Tel Quel* labored to establish that the very language in which the right ideas and the concomitant correct analysis were expressed was a proper site for an intervention that was simultaneously aesthetic and political – an achievement understood to have been realized by the likes of Mallarmé, Antonin Artaud, and, later, James Joyce. The literary avant-garde did not follow the political vanguard, but neither did it lead it. Neither, in the end, did it simply travel alongside it. Both leading edges were thought to occur simultaneously, not dialectically in the course of historical struggle, but literally at once. Indeed, it was a commitment such as this that led the journal to Mao and to the concept and practice of "cultural revolution," not as a policy initiative, but as a model for the locus and scale of social transformation.

SEE ALSO: Bakhtin, M. M.; Barthes, Roland; Derrida, Jacques; Kristeva, Julia

REFERENCES AND SUGGESTED READINGS

Debray, R. (1981). *Teachers, Writers, Celebrities: The Intellectuals of Modern France* (trans. D. Macey). London: Verso.
Ffrench, P. (1995). *The Time of Theory: A History of Tel Quel*. London: Clarendon.
Ffrench, P., & Lack, R.-F. (eds.) (1998). *The Tel Quel Reader*. London: Routledge.
Forest, P. (1995). *Histoire de Tel Quel 1960–1982*. Paris: Seuil.

Habermas, J. (1989). *The Structural Transformation of the Public Sphere: An Inquiry into a Category of Bourgeois Society* (trans. T. Burger). Cambridge, MA: MIT Press.

Kaupi, N. (1994). *The Making of an Avant-Garde: Tel Quel.* Amsterdam: Gruyter.

Marx-Scouras, D. (1996). *The Cultural Politics of Tel Quel: Literature and the Left in the Wake of Engagement.* University Park: Pennsylvania State Press.

Mowitt, J. (1992). *Text: The Genealogy of an Antidisciplinary Object.* Durham, NC: Duke University Press.

Textual Studies

FINN FORDHAM

Textual studies are concerned, among other things, with the relations between texts: their multiplicity and singularity, their iterability and corruptibility, their fluidity and monumentality. Given such a wide field of investigation, questions about the status of texts are never far away from developments in literary and cultural theory. Most works of literature – thinking of literature in a broad sense – exist in different, sometimes multiple, versions, and each version may have a different text. This is true of the King James Bible, plays by Aeschylus or Shakespeare, novels by Mary Shelley, Henry James, or James Joyce, poems by Emily Dickinson or John Donne, critical essays by Paul de Man or Coleridge, or studies of evolution by Charles Darwin. Readers often consider works as embodied in a single text – usually the one they are reading – but more often than not, this is a mistake.

A typical set of questions a student of literature might first ask about a given work will include: What does it mean? What did its author mean? How does it relate to other works? How does it relate to the time in which it was written? Is it any good? Beyond or alongside these lie more theoretical questions such as: How is its meaning produced? How is meaning produced? What is "an author"? What is the best theoretical or critical approach to use in interpreting this work? What is "good"? But given the opening statement about multiple versions, these could be supplemented – or preceded – by other questions: Is there more than one version? Why? Which version am I reading? Why? How does it relate to other versions? How is interpretation affected by the form of this edition? How did this work come into being? How was this particular edition arrived at? Is it any good? At an undergraduate level, these questions are less often raised. Answers to them, however, always reveal much about the specific work in question and more generally about literature, culture, and the vicissitudes of both. They also lead easily to theoretical concerns around creation, intention, authority, authorship, authenticity, rights, meaning, interpretation, media, history, and truth.

Attempts at answering such questions (and others) occur in the realm of "textual studies" or "textual scholarship." These terms comprise an increasingly wide and interdisciplinary range of practices and approaches that include or are very closely related to various forms of bibliographical research, paleography, typography, textual criticism, the sociology of texts, genetic criticism, and the history of the book. It not being possible to introduce all of these here, the focus will be on the last four. For introductions to the other practices, the reader is referred to studies by Greetham (1994), Williams & Abbott (1999), Kelemen (2008), and Baker & Womack's (2000) annotated bibliography.

The textual differences between versions of a work can be accounted for in many different ways: they can be the result of intentional or unintentional acts by authors, collaborators, typists, printers, editors, censors, publishers. It has been the business of textual criticism to study these differences and, at least for much of the last century, with a particular goal in view. As defined by a pre-eminent practitioner, Thomas Tanselle, it analyzes "the relationships among the surviving texts of a work so as to assess their relative authority and accuracy" (quoted in Vander Meulen 2009). Such assessment is made traditionally as a prelude to producing an edition of the work in question. These are not trivial practices: in the seventeenth century, the work of biblical textual scholars was condemned and their lives were threatened for suggesting that Moses had not, in fact, written the first five books of the Bible via divine revelation, a hypothesis now universally accepted. Practitioners argue that the study of literature depends on editions of accurate and legible texts, and moreover, that "in order to exist" culture "depends on remaking works" (Grigely 1995).

Recently, however, the same pre-eminent scholar cited above shifted his sense of "textual criticism" when he described it as "an understanding of textual situations rather than taking particular actions based on that understanding" (Tanselle 2005). This is at once a narrowing of the practice – since it passes over both assessing the accuracy of texts and the related goal of editing them – and a broadening of its potential focus, since the phrase "understanding textual situations" is open to extensive interpretation and deployment. Textual criticism can therefore come to include genetic criticism (which studies documents of a work without reference necessarily to some published version), the history of the book (which might for instance examine the archives of publishers and literary institutions), and even phenomenologies of reading (that is, how texts and books are experienced). In this shift, textual criticism is attempting to make its practices appear relevant, as they are, to the field of textual studies and, beyond that, to theories and histories of literature and culture.

Accounting for this shift in purpose leads, in part, to a recognition that in the last 30 years textual criticism has been an area in literary studies of extreme contentiousness, with, on occasion, forms of intellectual warfare being waged involving hostile moves and maneuvers, robust defenses and counterattacks, diplomatic negotiations and retreats. The characterization of such scholarship as practiced by versions of Sir Walter Scott's pedant, Jonas Dryasdust, or George Eliot's Casaubon, is a persistent cliché, a symptom of an enduring binary in the human sciences between practice and theory, scholarship and criticism, historicism and presentism. It ignores and underplays the rigor, precision and humor of the argumentation, and the importance of what can be at stake. A sense of this and of the heat of these conflicts can be gauged from accounts of the Joyce Wars (Rossman 1990) and surveys of the general field carried out by Tanselle (2005).

The conflicts and the separation of a set of practices (examining textual versions of a literary work) from a particular goal (editing a literary work) can be understood as consequences of the various turns that the study of literature has taken in the last 40 or so years: against new criticism and toward theory as embodied in poststructuralism and cultural studies, the turn toward history embodied by the new historicism, and the recent turn toward the archive. Textual studies have often had an uncomfortable relation with literary criticism and with literary theory, as seen in attacks on literary criticism (Bowers 1959), attempts to accommodate theory (McGann 1984; McKenzie 1986; Greetham 1999) or attacks on such accommodation (Lernout 1996; Tanselle 2005). With the turn to theory some of the principles of textual criticism, especially those that helped establish the grounds by which critical texts or scholarly editions were produced, came under attack.

Textual criticism was perceived as the editorial wing of the new criticism, since, in attempting to establish a particular definitive text for an author's work, it attempted to give a work unity and, so it appeared, took a work out of history, both of which had been interpretative aims of new criticism. Cultural studies could argue that the editions also cemented the form of the literary canon. Such editions are still accused of attempting to settle a text's inherent instability, during an era when "text" has been redefined by poststructuralism as "a field of forces: heterogeneous, differential, open and so on" (Derrida 1986). These attacks however ignore the basic editorial principles: they had always been alive to the unstable history of texts, the variety of versions, and the inherent mutability of the work. Moreover the principles themselves were not at fault: they could just as well be applied to noncanonical authors. They have also been attacked for having an idealist conception of the literary work, as something that for its practitioners "begins in the mind of the author" (Williams & Abbott 1999) and for having an "intentionalist" ideology. These were more accurate criticisms since preference was usually given to the intended utterance of an author or "creator" rather than, say, an editor.

Jerome McGann, an editor of the works of Byron, helped bring some of these criticisms to light while seeking to accommodate aspects of new literary theories in order to establish new principles for editorial practice and to think about the sociology of texts. The emphasis on "the autonomy of the isolated author" present in the idea of the author's "final intention" was, he argued, "grounded in a Romantic conception of literary production" (McGann 1983). Author-centered textual criticism was failing to recognize the collaborative and social nature of the production of texts and works.

To achieve an understanding of how a work's history unfolded, the textual variation between versions of a work, and the role of the various producers of such texts needed to be made more apparent. One of McGann's illustrations focused on early editions of Byron's *Don Juan*, first published in an expensive, anonymized and limited edition to protect it from charges of immoralism. However, the edition was soon pirated and thousands of cheap copies were produced and distributed, sometimes illustrated with pornographic plates. There was a moral outcry which became key to the poem's notoriety, its success as a bestseller, critical debate, and thence its canonical status (McGann 1985). Chiming with McGann's work was a program marked out by Don McKenzie, who called for a "sociology of texts," arguing, among other points, that the form of the book and its typography as much as the text could be an "expressive form" (McKenzie 1986). The goal of a textual critic would therefore subsequently be to display the various documents without necessarily evaluating their relative "accuracy." Instead there could be an explanation – perhaps in an apparatus – of the relations between them, or of the semiotics of the "bibliographic code" (the physical features of a book) (McGann 1983). The result of such practice, it was argued, would not be an edition of a work but an archive of documents, gathered together and organized according to a set of principles that were not determined by authorial intention (Tanselle 2005).

Such an archive would be unfeasibly expensive in "codex" (that is "book") form but it has been rendered possible by computer and digitization technology, and both have had an enormous influence on the ways in which textual studies can be practiced, on the objects they produce, and on theories of interpreting texts (see Finneran 1996; Shillingsburg 1996; Siemens &

Schreibman 2007). McGann was an early proponent of using the new technology to produce websites on which materials of particular authors could be displayed and ordered. His choice of the poet and painter Rossetti also meant that textual criticism could broaden out into other forms of cultural production, something that had been argued for by McKenzie (1986). McGann's term for what hypertext promised was "radiant textuality" (2001), a textuality which both glowed on a screen, and radiated in many directions toward a vast intertextual web or, less symmetrically speaking, rhizome. Similar projects have sprung up in the last few years presenting archives of material relating, for instance, to Walt Whitman, Emily Dickinson, Nietzsche, and others. Such hypertexts were once imagined as promoting the idea of a "decentered" text or work since there would no longer be a single authorized or definitive version being given primacy. But material in archives requires various forms of ordering to ease navigation by readers who may be seeking different things. Anxieties are expressed that this ordering may reproduce certain hierarchies. On the other hand, ease of navigation, which digitization contributes to, and which an editor can ensure, actually makes the decentering of texts by readers themselves easier: they are able to construct their own textual routes through the material. But good scholarly editions could always have had this goal. On the other hand, the conservative conception of literary production as issuing primarily from a single named and canonical author remains firmly in place.

The charge of conservatism with respect to the cultural canon has also been aimed at another branch of textual studies, genetic criticism (Davis 2002). Emerging in France during the 1970s, the school focuses, as with the sociology of texts, not on a final product or an author's final intentions, but in the textual processes behind them. It is less interested, however, in the impact of broader social contexts upon a work's dissemination and forms, limiting itself to the textual condition prior to publication, seeking instances of textual movement in what it calls "avant-textes," embodied in the notes, plans, sketches, rough drafts, fair copies, typescripts, and revised proofs of a work and in statements in authors' letters. While genetic criticism places certain limits on its material, it nonetheless comprises a wide and not always compatible range of approaches. For some it makes possible a psychoanalysis of composition (Bellemin-Noel, in Deppman et al. 2004); for others its aim is an impersonalized "science of writing" (de Biasi, in Deppman et al. 2004); while others are interested in the relation between compositional processes and themes within the final or published text (Van Hulle 2004; Fordham 2010). There has been an increasing philological set of approaches concerned with providing genetic editions of material by modern authors such as Flaubert, Proust, Joyce, and Beckett; or with reconstructing writers' libraries, their reading and their use of sources. The forms of such philological work are not particularly original, having been practiced for decades before the appearance of the school; nor is it currently exclusive to genetic criticism, since it is practiced elsewhere. But their results are usually framed in ways that contribute to a theoretical program which destabilizes any sense of a work as unitary, and which sees all texts as intertextual, as "tissues of quotations" in Barthes's well-known phrase.

In the Norton Anthology of Poetry, Shelley declares in *Hymn to Intellectual Beauty* that "the names of Demon, Ghost, and Heaven" are "frail spells." But according to Judith Chernaik, the editor of Shelley's notebooks, Shelley originally said it was "the name of *God* and Ghosts and Heaven" (my italics) which were the frail spells (Chernaik & Burnett 1978). The fear of censorship in the publisher, and perhaps in Shelley too, could not print so open an atheistic statement. Norton's anthology does not indicate the fact of this variation. Genetic criticism would favor an edition showing both because it would reveal a significant movement within textual production. Genetic critics, whether aligned with the French school or not, are convinced of the idea that literature may be more interesting as a process than as a product.

The conservatism of the association with canonical authors should not be surprising: the production of scholarly texts and archives, whether in codex or digital form, are enabled by money, which, being generally public money, requires an investment in relatively safe risks, making use therefore of established authors, established scholars and established methods. This mention of money raises an important issue about the origin of the works of art that is relevant to textual studies: scholarly editions and archives usually involve specialists with years of training, often take a long time to produce and may require extensive resources and funding. Their origins do not therefore lie only in the desirously inquiring mind of a particular scholar, but in the material economic conditions made possible – or, indeed, precarious – by funding bodies, patrons, bankers. This same is true of literary productions: writers generally produce documents; they do not – or very rarely – produce the *books* which are the material means for disseminating those documents. Data about the production of books – about the making and breaking of contracts, copyright, print runs (the number of books a publisher decides to print), the materials and technology used, distribution, booksellers – is gathered and analyzed by historical bibliographers also

known increasingly as "historians of the book." These data emphasize the material and financial dimensions that underpin the entire field of literature: costs in book production, for instance, affect the dissemination of books, which affects a readership or target audience, which in turn helps produce the reputation and certain meanings associated with books. Book history therefore is central to an understanding of how taste and ideas of art are produced, in what Bourdieu influentially called the "field of cultural production" (Bourdieu 1993; repr. in Finkelstein 2006). Book history, which updates historical bibliography, is proving to be perhaps the richest field in textual studies, as illustrated by the optimistic and intellectually acquisitive manifesto in the first volume of a recently established journal: "Our field of play is the entire history of written communication ... We will explore the social, cultural, and economic history of authorship, publishing, printing, the books arts, copyright, censorship, bookselling and distribution, libraries, literacy, literary criticism, reading habits, and reader response" (*Book History*, 1998).

Just as the world, for many literary critics and critical theorists, is made up of perceptions which are produced by texts, so the world of literature – and therefore the world itself – is, for many theorists of textual criticism, made up of versions of texts. The nature of the world's movement seems to be a result of the movement of texts. The fields of cultural and literary theory, on the one hand, and textual studies and theory on the other, are not as polarized as they once were. Both are large and expanding, and they often share a particular activity: both project on to their visions of the world, the very focus of their study.

SEE ALSO: Anglo-American New Criticism; Deleuze, Gilles; New Historicism; Poststructuralism; Presentism

REFERENCES AND SUGGESTED READINGS

Baker, W., & Womack, K. (2000). *Twentieth-Century Bibliography and Textual Criticism: An Annotated Bibliography*. Westport, CT: Greenwood.

Bornstein, G., & Williams, R. G. (eds.) (1993). *Palimpsest: Editorial Theory in the Humanities*. Ann Arbor: University of Michigan Press.

Bourdieu, P. (1993). *The Field of Cultural Production: Essays on Art and Literature* (ed. and trans. R. Johnson). Cambridge: Polity.

Bowers, F. (1959). *Textual and Literary Criticism*. Cambridge: Cambridge University Press.

Chernaik, J., & Burnett, T. (1978). The Byron and Shelley notebooks in the Scrope Davies find. *Review of English Studies*, 29(113), 36–49.

Cohen, P. G. (ed.) (1997). *Texts and Textuality: Textual Instability, Theory, and Interpretation*. New York: Garland.

Davis, O. (2002). The author at work in genetic criticism. *Paragraph*, 25(1), 92–101.

Deppman, J., Ferrer, D., & Groden, M. (eds.) (2004). *Genetic Criticism: Texts and Avant-Textes*. Philadelphia: University of Pennsylvania Press.

Derrida, J. (1986). Critical response: But, beyond . . . (trans. P. Kamuf). *Critical Inquiry*, 13(1), 155–170.

Finkelstein, D., & McCleery, A. (2005) *An Introduction to Book History*. New York: Routledge.

Finkelstein, D., & McCleery, A. (eds.) (2006). *The Book History Reader*, 2nd edn. London: Routledge.

Finneran, R. J. (1996). *The Literary Text in the Digital Age*. Ann Arbor: University of Michigan Press.

Fordham, F. (2010). *I Do I Undo I Redo: The Textual Genesis of Modernist Selves*. Oxford: Oxford University Press.

Greetham, D. C. (1994). *Textual Scholarship: An Introduction*, 2nd edn. London: Garland.

Greetham, D. C. (1999). *Theories of the Text*. Oxford: Oxford University Press.

Grigely, J. (1995). Textualterity: Art, Theory, and Textual Criticism. Ann Arbor: University of Michigan Press.

Kelemen, E. (2008). *Textual Editing and Criticism: An Introduction*. New York: Norton.

Lernout, G. (1996). *Review of Textual Studies and the Common Reader* (ed. A. Pettit). *Text: An Interdisciplinary Annual*, 14, 45–65.

McGann, J. (1983). *A Critique of Modern Textual Criticism*. Chicago: University of Chicago Press.

McGann, J. (1984). Shall these bones live? *Text: An Interdisciplinary Annual*, 1, 21–40.

McGann, J. (1985). *The Beauty of Inflections*. Oxford: Oxford University Press.

McGann, J. (2001). *Radiant Textuality: Literature after the World Wide Web*. New York: Palgrave.

McKenzie, D. F. (1986). *Bibliography and the Sociology of Texts* London: British Library.

Rossman, C. (1990). The "Gabler Ulysses": A selectively annotated bibliography. *Studies in the Novel*, 22(2), 257–269.

Shillingsburg, P. (1996). *Scholarly Editing in the Computer Age*, 3rd edn. Ann Arbor: University of Michigan Press.

Siemens, R., & Schreibman, S. (2007). *A Companion to Digitial Literary Studies*. Oxford: Blackwell.

Tanselle, G. T. (2005). *Textual Criticism since Greg: A Chronicle, 1950-2000*. Charlottesville: Bibliographical Society of the University of Virginia.

Van Hulle, D. (2004). *Textual Awareness: A Genetic Study of Late Manuscripts by Joyce, Proust, and Mann*. Ann Arbor: University of Michigan Press.

Vander Meulen, D. L. (2009). Bibliography and other history. *Textual Cultures: Texts, Contexts, Interpretations*, 4(1), 113–128.

Williams, W. P., & Abbott, C. S. (1999). *An Introduction to Bibliographical and Textual Studies*, 3rd edn. New York: Modern Language Association of America.

WEBSITES

http://graduate.engl.virginia.edu/oralsonline/TextualStudies.htm
www.whitmanarchive.org/
www.rossettiarchive.org/
www.emilydickinson.org/
www.tei-c.org/index.xml

JOURNALS

Book History
Génésis: Manuscrits, Recherche, Invention: Revue Internationale de Critique Génétique Studies in Bibliography
Text: An Interdisciplinary Annual of Textual Studies
Textual Cultures: Texts, Contexts, Interpretations

Trauma and Memory Studies

ANNE WHITEHEAD

Trauma and memory studies together represent a field which has witnessed a dynamic growth in interest and popularity, particularly since the early 1990s. Trauma and memory studies represent complementary and interrelated fields of study, and trauma can usefully be considered in this context as a pathological form of remembering. For the purposes of this entry, then, trauma studies will be considered as a subset of the broader field of memory studies. Trauma and memory studies represent a field which is highly contested and subject to vigorous debate, in part because of the recent explosion of interest in this area which currently continues unabated.

Trauma studies emerged as a distinct area of interest in the late twentieth century, following the official recognition of post-traumatic stress disorder (PTSD) by the American Psychiatric Association in the *Diagnostic and Statistical Manual* of 1980. This was connected in turn to the aftermath of the Vietnam War, as returning soldiers campaigned for recognition of their traumatic symptomatology. Particular interest in trauma arose at Yale University. Literary scholar Cathy Caruth edited the volume *Trauma: Explorations in Memory* (1995), which is notable for a definition of trauma that makes it applicable across a wide range of events. Caruth provides an influential structural model of trauma, in which the very immediacy of the experience precludes its registration so that it exceeds the individual's capacity for understanding. The traumatic experience can only be registered belatedly and so is characterized by a temporal latency or delay. Interest in trauma at Yale centered particularly on the Fortunoff Video Archive Project, led

by psychoanalyst Dori Laub and literary critic Geoffrey Hartman, which recorded the videotestimonies of Holocaust survivors. A second prominent publication to emerge from Yale in the early 1990s was *Testimony: Crises of Witnessing in Literature, Psychoanalysis and History*, co-authored by Laub and literary scholar Shoshana Felman (Felman & Laub 1992). Although ranging beyond discussion of the Holocaust, this study nonetheless conveys something of the close intertwining of trauma studies and Holocaust studies through its partial basis in the videotestimony archive.

There have been numerous responses to the founding work on trauma that emerged from Yale. Historian Dominick LaCapra (2004) articulated concern that, following Caruth's volume, the study of trauma had become too encompassing. He made a case for distinguishing between what he termed "historical trauma," which referred to specific natural or human-made historical catastrophes, and "structural trauma," which encompassed such originary losses as entry into language or separation from the mother. Although both categories are traumatic for LaCapra, they are so in different ways. Humanities professor Ruth Leys (2000) contested Caruth's reliance on the neurobiological model of PTSD, which suggested that traumatic memory was encoded in the brain in a different way from normal memory. The validity of this approach to trauma remains a key point of contestation in the field. Anthropologist Allan Young (1997) has analyzed PTSD as a construct or invention, pointing out that it is embedded in culturally and historically contingent ideas about memory and the self. Young's work has opened up important new directions in trauma studies which question the extent to which PTSD, based on the Western model of the individual self, can be applied in non-Western contexts, for example as it is exported through humanitarian aid projects. For Young, then, as for LaCapra, there is a sense that trauma studies should define its terms precisely and attend carefully to conceptual limits or boundaries.

Allan Young's positioning of PTSD as a historically contingent memory practice serves as a useful reminder that all conceptualizations of memory are historically situated and that ideas of memory have transformed over time. Two seminal works in the field of memory studies make a particular contribution to our understanding of how early-modern conceptions of memory in the West differed from, but provided a key foundation for, our own ideas about memory. British historian Frances Yates published *The Art of Memory* (1966), a study of early-modern memory practices that were, in turn, inherited from ancient Greek and Roman sources. Yates emphasizes that in the early-modern period, remembering was concerned not so much with reviving personal recollections but rather with the efficient storage and retrieval of information. She outlined, in particular, the "place system" of remembering, in which a specific location, typically a building with many rooms, was internalized in the mind; the objects to be remembered were placed in the different rooms and were recalled by the individual mentally walking through the building until the desired object had been retrieved. Through the "place system," Yates's study establishes visualization and order as the key components of successful recollection. The second important study was *The Book of Memory* (1990) by literary scholar Mary Carruthers, which studied the workings and function of memory in the medieval period. Carruthers emphasizes that the rise of the book at this time did not fundamentally transform memory practices inherited from the ancient world. Reading was thus regarded as an activity of memory and the medieval book was designed to facilitate memory

with visual cues and aids. The written page itself was understood to be a memory device and Carruthers explores how mnemonic techniques such as the "place system" and visualization affected literary composition, and indeed, helped to define the very form of the book. Together, Yates and Carruthers make clear that memory was a faculty prized above all others in the period stretching from antiquity through to the Renaissance, and their work shows that, while there are clear affinities with contemporary practices of remembering, ideas of memory at this time were also quite distinct from our own.

One of the affinities that can be seen across early-modern and contemporary memory practices is the close association between memory and place. Late twentieth-century interest in the intersection of place and memory was particularly evident in the scholarly attention paid to sites of memorialization in the 1990s. These sites of memory also often commemorated traumatic events, making visible the close interrelation of trauma and memory studies. American literary scholar James Young published the highly influential *The Texture of Memory* (1993), which studied a range of Holocaust memorials across Germany, Israel, Poland, and the United States. Young concluded that the memorials, like the memory of the events they commemorated, were contingent on the time and place in which they were created. He identified a close intertwining of Jewish and national iconography in the memorials that he studied, and emphasized that every nation remembers the Holocaust according to its own traditions, ideals and experiences. Young's study was quickly followed by British historian Jay Winter's *Sites of Memory, Sites of Mourning* (1995), which looked at the collective remembrance of World War I across Europe. Alongside war memorials, Winter also focused on poetry, art, film, and spiritualism as key "sites of memory" for the war dead. Counter to Young's analysis of Holocaust memorials, Winter proposed that World War I memorials were not predominantly national in character but were simultaneously local, based in villages and towns, and transnational, drawing on traditional tropes of mourning that both transcended and connected European nations. Together, Young and Winter helped to define memorials as an important and underdeveloped area of memory studies. Both emphasized that the work of memorialization is shaped by the interests of the present and that the memory of catastrophic events is formed by groups, although they differed in their sense of what exactly constituted the memory community.

The work of Young and Winter was crucially underpinned by important recent developments in the study of collective memory. The translation into English of *The Collective Memory* by the French-Jewish sociologist Maurice Halbwachs in 1980 provided an important impetus to subsequent work in this area. Originally published posthumously in 1950, after the death of Halbwachs during World War II in the German concentration camp of Buchenwald, the volume argued that memory is not an individual act but is always framed by social structures of remembering. In contrast to history, which Halbwachs regards as universal, memory is more contingent and multiple, and requires the support of a group which is delimited in space and time. Halbwachs pays close attention to a number of different memory groups, including the family, the workplace, and religious communities (particularly Christianity), and he is sensitive to the role of place in collective remembering. The translation of his study has provided a conceptual basis for more recent work on commemoration and public memory. In particular,

Halbwachs' ideas were developed by French historian Pierre Nora in his multivolume collaborative project on the national memory of France, *Les Lieux de mémoire* (1984–92), selections from which were translated into English as *Realms of Memory* (1996–8). Nora extended Halbwachs's theories by looking specifically at the French nation as a collective and identifying the "sites of memory" that were particularly important in this context; these included places such as Versailles, the Louvre or the Eiffel Tower, but also events, for example Bastille Day or the Tour de France, and objects or symbols like the French flag and "liberty, equality, fraternity." His phrase "sites of memory" consciously drew on Frances Yates's "memory places," at once suggesting an affinity with earlier memory practices and updating or transforming them. Importantly, Nora's work was identified by a pronounced nostalgic tendency. In his introduction to the project, he argued that "sites of memory" represent deliberate rather than spontaneous acts of commemoration and characterize the industrialized and secularized modern world. For him, then, we inhabit a "fallen" and amnesiac modernity, which contrasts unfavorably with an idealized but lost peasant culture in which memorial activities occurred naturally. In addition to its elegiac character, Nora's project is also problematic in terms of the "sites of memory" that it omits; these include the less comfortable aspects of the French past, for example its colonial history and "dirty wars."

Nora's work relates to James Young's study in suggesting that the nation represents the most natural vehicle for collective memory. Other theorists have, however, called into question this prioritizing of the nation. Jewish historian Yosef Hayim Yerushalmi's *Zakhor* (1996) explores Jewish collective memory. He places memory at the heart of the Jewish faith and tradition, and traces the evolution of Jewish memory across four distinct historical periods: biblical and rabbinical origins, the Middle Ages, after the Spanish expulsion, and in our own times. He emphasizes that the priest or prophet rather than the historian assumes the role of master of memory in Judaic culture, although his work, like Nora's, has been criticized for constructing too rigid a division between history and memory and adopting a similar nostalgic tone. In taking the Jews as a collective, however, Yerushalmi implicitly questions how collective memory is transmitted and sustained across a diasporic rather than a national community. More recently, sociologists Daniel Levy and Natan Sznaider (2002) have questioned whether, in relation to the Holocaust specifically, we can now speak of a cosmopolitan or global memory, so that the Holocaust acts as a universal icon of atrocity and genocide. Although their theory takes into account the impact of globalization on memory communities, it conflicts with James Young's emphasis on the ways in which the memory of the Holocaust is contingent on time and place, and it fails to address sufficiently the problem that a cosmopolitan model of memory will almost inevitably prioritize Western over non-Western experiences. Other interventions into collective memory have similarly indicated the important political questions of who does the remembering and what gets inscribed into the archive; American feminist theorists Marianne Hirsch and Valerie Smith (2002) have thus critiqued cultural memory studies from a gender perspective, but similar arguments could be made in relation to, among other positions, class and race.

More extensive criticisms of memory studies have been made by a number of historians. In an influential article, Charles S. Maier (1993) argued that the current obsession with memory, and especially with the memory of World War II and the Holocaust, represents a retreat from transformative politics. He noted in particular the tendency for group memories to compete with one another, producing a narrow focus on ethnicity. Contrasting history and memory, he contended that history searched for understanding while memory was productive of a potentially disabling melancholic emotion. Maier's critique was followed by that of Kerwin Lee Klein (2000), who argued that too often in current memory discourse, memory was assumed to have the status of a historical agent, leading scholars to overlook the important political question of precisely who was doing the remembering and the forgetting. Klein also indicated dissatisfaction with the vague theological or spiritual connotations which he identified as pervading the discourse of memory studies. More recently, Wulf Kansteiner (2002) suggested that too much attention has been paid in memory studies to the memorial or material artifact, without sufficiently addressing the ways in which it is received and interpreted by those who interact with it. Again, this issue of reception brings to light the crucial political question of who actually identifies with these representations. Kansteiner also called for a more precise definition of collective remembering, which is often discussed simply by misapplying the terminology of individual memory processes. Finally, Kansteiner, like Maier, drew attention to the close interrelation between memory studies and identity politics, pointing out that historically crises of memory have tended to coincide with crises of identity.

The work of these historians is salutary and indicates some important areas for future development in the field of memory studies. Some of the most interesting work to emerge most recently in memory studies has, however, been concerned to assert the importance and necessity of memory work, especially in the context of ethics. Central to this trend was the last work of French philosopher Paul Ricoeur. Ricoeur (2004) addressed the question of the relation between individual and collective remembering, seeking to reconcile the division between the two by arguing that individuals remember, but that all individuals are essentially relational. For Ricoeur, then, individual and collective remembering have a reciprocal relationship and neither should take priority over the other. Ricoeur likewise seeks to collapse the binary of history and memory, pointing out that memory, in the form of testimony, is the foundation or bedrock of history and the ground on which it must inevitably rest. Perhaps most interesting, however, is the final section of Ricoeur's work, which is devoted to the subject of forgetting. In the context of ethics, and influenced by his own Christian beliefs, Ricoeur questions the value of forgetting and forgiving. Distinguishing between forgetting in reserve, where a memory of the injury can still be called to mind, and total forgetting, Ricoeur seems to incline toward the former, although the discussion is not decisive and leaves the reader suspended between amnesty and amnesia. Israeli scholar Avishai Margalit (2002) covers similar ground to Ricoeur, drawing a parallel distinction between two types of forgiveness: forgiveness as blotting out the sin, so that it is entirely forgotten, and forgiveness as covering it up, which equates to Ricoeur's forgetting in reserve. More decisively than Ricoeur, Margalit concludes that there is a value in disregarding the sin rather than entirely forgetting it. Together, Ricoeur and Margalit suggest a future direction for memory studies in asserting forgetting as integral part of memory. Both also urge us to consider the relationship between forgetting and forgiving. This seems an important focus for the present, as both individuals and political communities are confronted with the problem of how to live with, and move on from, a range of violent, disruptive and traumatic histories.

SEE ALSO: Caruth, Cathy; Felman, Shoshana

REFERENCES AND SUGGESTED READINGS

American Psychiatric Association (1980). *Diagnostic and Statistical Manual of Mental Disorders*. Washington, DC: American Psychiatric Association.

Carruthers, M. J., (1990). *The Book of Memory: A Study of Memory in Medieval Culture*. Cambridge: Cambridge University Press.

Caruth, C., (ed.) (1995). *Trauma: Explorations in Memory*. Baltimore: Johns Hopkins University Press.

Eaglestone, R. (2004). *The Holocaust and the Postmodern*. Oxford: Oxford University Press.

Felman, S., & Laub, D. (1992). *Testimony: Crises of Witnessing in Literature, Psychoanalysis, and History*. New York: Routledge.

Halbwachs, M. (1980). *The Collective Memory* (trans. F. J. Ditter & V. Y. Ditter). New York: Harper and Row. (Original work published 1950.)

Hirsch, M., & Smith, V. A. (2002). Feminism and cultural memory: An introduction. *Signs: Journal of Women in Culture and Society*, 28(1), 3–12.

Kansteiner, W. (2002). Finding meaning in memory: A methodological critique of memory studies. *History and Theory*, 41, 179–197.

Klein, K. L. (2000). On the emergence of *memory* in historical discourse. *Representations*, 69, 127–150.

LaCapra, D. (2004). *History in Transit: Experience, Identity, Critical Theory*. Ithaca: Cornell University Press.

Levy, D., & Sznaider, N. (2002). Memory unbound: The Holocaust and the formation of cosmopolitan memory. *European Journal of Social Theory*, 5(1), 87–106.

Leys, R. (2000). *Trauma: A Genealogy*. Chicago: University of Chicago Press.

Maier, C. S. (1993). A surfeit of memory: Reflections on history, melancholy and denial. *History and Memory*, 5(2), 136–152.

Margalit, A. (2002). *The Ethics of Memory*. Cambridge, MA: Harvard University Press.

Nora, P. (ed.) (1996–8). *Realms of Memory: Rethinking the French Past* (ed. and Foreword L. D. Kritzman; trans. A. Goldhammer), 3 vols. New York: Columbia University Press. (Original work published 1984–92.)

Ricoeur, P. (2004). *Memory, History, Forgetting* (trans. K. Blamey & D. Pellauer). Chicago: University of Chicago Press.

Whitehead, A. (2004). *Trauma Fiction*. Edinburgh: Edinburgh University Press.

Winter, J. M. (1995). *Sites of Memory, Sites of Mourning*. Cambridge: Cambridge University Press.

Yates, F. A. (1966). *The Art of Memory*. London: Routledge and Kegan Paul.

Yerushalmi, Y. H. (1996). *Zakhor: Jewish Memory and Jewish History*. Seattle: University of Washington Press.

Young, A. (1997). *The Harmony of Illusions: Inventing Post-Traumatic Stress Disorder*. Princeton: Princeton University Press.

Young, J. E. (1993). *The Texture of Memory: Holocaust Memorials and Meaning*. New Haven: Yale University Press.

V

Virilio, Paul

IAN JAMES

Best known as a thinker of speed and of the impact of technologies of speed on social and political development, Paul Virilio (b. 1932) engages with a very wide range of disciplines and critical issues: with questions of war and military strategy, with the history of cinema, the nature of modern media and telecommunications, and with the state of contemporary cultural and artistic production. His work touches on politics, international relations theory and war studies, on media and social theory, aesthetics, urbanism and environmental thinking. Within this broad range of concerns the question of technology has played a central and determining role. His work critically explores how and why technology has been, and will continue to be, fundamental to the shaping of human experience and historical development.

Heavily influenced by early twentieth-century thinkers such as Walter Benjamin, by gestalt psychology, and by the phenomenological thought of Edmund Husserl and Maurice Merleau-Ponty, Virilio's key concern is with perception and embodiment and with the way in which technological forms shape individual and collective modes of perceiving and apprehending the world. Often seen as rather negative or pessimistic

with regard to technology, Virilio's thinking aims to uncover the hidden negative impacts of technological development. In particular he aims to explore the way in which the accelerated speeds of modern modes of transport and communication have led to an increasing virtualization of experience, that is to say, to a loss or diminution of situated, embodied engagement with our worldly surroundings. This critical approach to technological development can also be related to Virilio's Catholic and nonconformist left orientated political commitments. He was involved in the French worker-priest movement in the 1950s and was closely associated with figures such as Abbé Pierre. His political orientation is also marked by the influence of personalism, a movement founded by Emmanuel Mounier in the 1930s which emphasized the primacy of the individual person in the organization of society, and set itself against both liberal industrial capitalism and totalitarian forms on the right and the left.

Virilio's elaboration of what he comes to call the science of speed, or dromology, begins with his early major works of the 1970s. In these works he develops his argument that political activity has its origin in the capacity of war to shape geographical terrain into geopolitical territory. In his first work, *Bunker Archeology* (1994[1975]), he argues that the concrete fortifications of World War II mark a historical threshold. These fortifications, rendered redundant by the advent of systematic aerial bombing of urban centers, testify to a transformation in the geopolitical significance of territorial frontiers. Throughout these early works Virilio develops the fundamental thesis which will inform all his subsequent work, namely that the speeds and mode of transmission afforded by military weapons systems are key to the forging of geopolitical space and with that the development of the stare and the space of politics interior to it. Virilio's thinking in this area is developed throughout his career and, most notably, he is the author of seminal work on the way in which new technologies transformed warfare during the first Gulf War in 1991.

While maintaining this interest in military technology, Virilio becomes increasingly preoccupied with contemporary modes of transportation, communication, and with modern visual media. In this context he argues that the accelerated speeds of transmission afforded by these technologies precipitate a decline of lived spatial existence and a crisis in our collective representations of the world. His focus on the phenomenology of perception allows him to highlight, for example, the manner in which the images of cinema and television are "telepresent," that is to say, present at a distance or in their absence. Telepresence, according to Virilio's account, brings with it a privileging of the instant of transmission at the expense of an experience of material or spatial extension. The "real time" of telepresence is one in which the being of sensible forms is altered: the virtual comes to dominate over the actual, the exposure of the calculated instant dominates over the richness and diversity of embodied temporality or duration. Virilio suggests that

modern visual media have invented an entirely new way of seeing, that is, vision as mediated through the transmission of radio waves or electronic pulses and that this "wave optics" has the potential to transform the manner in which we are conscious of ourselves and of the world. The world of vision machines and wave optics is one in which diverse aspects of cultural and political life can be altered in fundamental ways.

If Virilio's early work can be said to be preoccupied with questions of military, urban, and political space, it might be fair to say that the shift toward questions of virtualization and the decline of situated, sensible experience brings with it greater preoccupation with the question of time and the new modes of temporal experience associated with "real time" technologies and quasi-instantaneous means of communication. More recently Virilio has focused his critique of virtualization around the question of contemporary art. He has developed his overall questioning of technology in the context of a theory of the technological accident. In this context he argues that the existence and necessary occurrence of accidents is fundamental to the hidden logic of technology. The invention of a specific technology inevitably brings with it a new mode or possibility of an accident, one whose catastrophic proportions will be determined by the power of the technology itself. What Virilio is suggesting with this theory of the accident is that technological progress can never be cast in simply or straightforwardly positive terms.

While originally orientated toward the military, political, and international relations implications of his thinking, reception of Virilio's work is increasingly focused on questions of visual media and film. From such a diverse thinker, however, his writing is likely to continue to influence a wide variety of disciplines in the future.

SEE ALSO: Benjamin, Walter; Husserl,
Edmund; Merleau-Ponty, Maurice

REFERENCES AND SUGGESTED
READINGS

Armitage, J. (ed.) (2000). *Paul Virilio: From Mod-
ernism to Hypermodernism and Beyond*. London:
Sage.
James, I. (2007). *Paul Virilio*. London: Routledge.
Virilio, P. (1986). *Speed and Politics* (trans. M.
Polizzotti). New York: Semiotext(e). (Original
work published 1977.)
Virilio, P. (1990a). *Popular Defense and Ecological
Struggles* (trans. M. Polizzotti). New York: Semi-
otext(e). (Original work published 1978.)
Virilio, P. (1990b). *Polar Inertia* (trans. P. Camiller).
London: Sage.
Virilio, P. (1992). *L'Insécurité du territoir* [The
insecurity of territory], 2nd edn. Paris: Galilée.
(Original work published 1976.)
Virilio, P. (1994). *Bunker Archeology* (trans. G.
Collins). New York: Princeton Architectural
Press. (Original work published 1975.)
Virilio, P. (2000). *Art and Fear* (trans. J. Rose).
London: Continuum.
Virilio, P. (2005a). *Negative Horizon* (trans. M.
Degener). London: Continuum. (Original
work published 1985.)
Virilio, P. (2005b). *Desert Screen: War at the Speed of
Light* (trans. M. Degener). London: Continuum.
(Original work published 1991.)

Vizenor, Gerald

MICHAEL SNYDER

Gerald Robert Vizenor (b. 1934) is a prolific
and influential Native American novelist,
poet, critic, theorist, editor, and professor
of mixed Anishinaabe (Ojibwe), French,
and Scandinavian ancestry. With much sophistication, his work has deconstructed the
semiotics of the Indian and Indianness,
analyzed Native American literature and
culture, critiqued visual and textual representations of Native Americans, and

examined social, political, and legal issues
affecting them. A practitioner of what he
calls "trickster discourse," he has theorized
and celebrated what he has termed the
"crossblood," emphasizing qualities of positive fluidity and Native transmotion over
tragic tropes of the mixedblood found in
American literature and film. He has theorized Native survivance, a sustained and
complex indigenous cultural continuance,
against notions of tragic victimry.

An enrolled member of the Minnesota
Chippewa (Anishinaabe) Tribe, White
Earth Reservation, Vizenor presently teaches in the American Studies department
at University of New Mexico. His father,
Clement Vizenor, a mixedblood Ojibwe
laborer, was born on the White Earth Reservation and moved to Minneapolis, where
Gerald was born on October 22, 1934.
Gerald was not yet 2 years of age when his
father was murdered, and he experienced a
tumultuous childhood, raised by various
relatives. At age 16, he misrepresented his
age to join the military, serving in Japan,
where he was influenced by the nation's
culture, literature, and recent traumatic history enough to author several books of
haiku poetry and, much later, his 2003 novel
Hiroshima Bugi: Atomu 57. After remaining
in Japan following his military service, he
returned to the United States in the early
1950s and studied at New York University,
Harvard University, and University of Minnesota. Vizenor's early career included positions as a social worker with the Minnesota
State Reformatory and Department of Cor-
rections. From 1964 to 1968 he became a
community organizer and director of the
American Indian Employment Center in
Minneapolis. As a staff writer and a contributing editor in the late 1960s and 1970s,
Vizenor wrote trenchant pieces for the *Minneapolis Tribune* raising questions of justice,
racialism, and representation, including his

iconic work on the Thomas White Hawk murder case and a series on the American Indian Movement (AIM). He then embarked on a prodigious academic career during which he published copious works of fiction, criticism, and poetry. Vizenor has taught at Lake Forest College, Bemidji State University, University of Minnesota, University of California, Berkeley, and University of Oklahoma. He served as Acting Provost at Kresge College, University of California, Santa Cruz and taught at University of California, Santa Cruz. In 1983 Vizenor traveled to China to become visiting professor at Tianjin University, which influenced the creation of his "trickster novel" *Griever: An American Monkey King in China* (1987). He was an editor for University of Oklahoma's American Indian Literature and Critical Studies Series.

Vizenor is unique among Native American intellectuals in his enthusiasm for continental critical theory, chiefly deconstruction, poststructuralism, and postmodern theory. From the 1970s through the 1990s, he increasingly engaged such theory in his analyses of tribal history, culture, and identity. Much of his work has deployed these theories to critique representations and self-representations of the *Indian* and *Indianness*. Vizenor fights the reification of the term "Indian" and renounces usage of the term itself. He fears that many Natives' notions of what "Indian" means have been externally invented and imposed, and internalized by many without critical irony. These outmoded ideas unintentionally preserve ossified definitions of Natives as static if noble victims. These rigid ideas, terminal creeds, de-emphasize tribal specificity and make essentialist claims. Thus the Indian has become a simulacrum, in Jean Baudrillard's sense of the word, a copy of something that never existed in the first place: the simulation of the Indian equals the absence of the Native. Contrastingly,

Vizenor emphasizes and cites tribally specific – Anishinaabe – stories, humor, and philosophy, but also endorses individual dynamism in the service of survivance. Vizenor argues that terminal creeds should be eschewed in favor of a "postindian" identity, an identity that arrives after the simulation. Postindian identity is a means of survivance, of adapting to historical change, and avoiding a victimist, fatalist, or tragic mentality. The postindian, while postmodern in Vizenor's special sense of the word, is also premodern, invested in traditional narratives and tribal humor, and also resistant to what Vizenor sees as the modernism of anthropological and structuralist approaches to consuming native cultures. Vizenor utilizes deconstruction and poststructuralist theory with the goal of liberating native thought from belief in terminal creeds. Emphasizing the fluid and slippery nature of language, poststructuralist theory in his view allows writers, storytellers, and tribal tricksters to use language to innovate new concepts of what it means to be Native. Vizenor endorses the application of theory to indigenous literatures, and denigrates the preceding structuralist approach with its emphasis on scientism and underlying structures as reductive and inattentive to the accomplishments of individual artists. To Vizenor, Native American literatures have been overburdened by readings based on structuralism and other social science theories that to him replicate incoherent foundational representations of indigenous experience.

Vizenor's attitude toward theory evolves over time and becomes more embracing. Beginning in the late 1970s and continuing through the 1990s, Vizenor increasingly engages French critical thinkers such as Jacque Derrida and Roland Barthes. By the end of the 1980s, continental postmodern critics and critics of the postmodern such as Jean Baudrillard, Jean-François

Lyotard, and Umberto Eco become sources. Such sources interweave with an abundance of Native American materials such as histories, autobiographies, and Ojibwe tribal tales. By the mid-1990s, Vizenor's nonfiction prose style had become markedly postmodern, evincing a strategy of collage and striking juxtaposition. In *Manifest Manners* (1999) he prescribes postmodern strategies and renounces structuralism. Theory has informed Vizenor's ideas seeking to promote and further Native American postindian survivance. Vizenor makes use of the poststructuralist free play of language to endorse outrageous humor and tribal trickster discourse to oppose the tragic attitude of static victimization.

SEE ALSO: Barthes, Roland; Baudrillard, Jean; Deconstruction; Derrida, Jacques; Eco, Umberto; Lyotard, Jean-François; Postmodernism; Poststructuralism

REFERENCES AND SUGGESTED READINGS

Blaeser, K. M. (1996). *Gerald Vizenor: Writing in the Oral Tradition*. Norman: University of Oklahoma Press.

Lee, A. R. (ed.) (2000). *Loosening the Seams: Interpretations of Gerald Vizenor*. Bowling Green, OH: Popular Press.

Lee, A.R., & Madsen, D. (eds.) (2010). *Gerald Vizenor: Texts and Contexts*. Albuquerque: University of New Mexico Press.

Madsen, D. (2009). *Understanding Gerald Vizenor*. Columbia: University of South Carolina Press.

Velie, A. (1982). *Four American Indian Literary Masters: N. Scott Momaday, James Welch, Leslie Marmon Silko, and Gerald Vizenor*. Norman: University of Oklahoma Press.

Vizenor, G. (1972). *The Everlasting Sky: New Voices from the People Named the Chippewa*. New York: Macmillan.

Vizenor, G. (1987). *Griever: An American Monkey King in China*. Minneapolis: University of Minnesota Press.

Vizenor, G. (ed.) (1989). *Narrative Chance: Postmodern Discourse on Native American Indian Literatures*. Albuquerque: University of New Mexico Press.

Vizenor, G. (1994). *Shadow Distance: A Gerald Vizenor Reader*. Hanover, NH: Wesleyan University Press.

Vizenor, G. (1998). *Fugitive Poses: Native American Indian Scenes of Absence and Presence*. Lincoln: University of Nebraska Press.

Vizenor, G. (1999). *Manifest Manners: Narratives on Postindian Survivance*. Lincoln: University of Nebraska Press.

Vizenor, G. (2003). *Hiroshima Bugi: Atomu 57*. Lincoln: University of Nebraska Press.

Vizenor, G. (ed.) (2008). *Survivance: Narratives of Native Presence*. Lincoln: University of Nebraska Press.

Vizenor, G. (2009). *Native Liberty: Natural Reason and Cultural Survivance*. Lincoln: University of Nebraska Press.

Vizenor, G., & Lee, A. R. (1999). *Postindian Conversations*. Lincoln: University of Nebraska Press.

White, Hayden

DEIRDRE RUSSELL

Hayden White (b. 1928) is a prominent American historian whose work has had a decisive impact on thought about historiography and substantial influence among literary critics. White gained his BA degree in 1951 from Wayne State University, and his MA in 1952 and PhD in 1955, both from the University of Michigan. After holding positions at Wayne State (1955–8), the University of Rochester in New York (1958–68), University of California, Los Angeles (1968–73), and Wesleyan University in Connecticut (1973–8), in 1978 White went to the University of California, Santa Cruz, where he was later appointed Professor Emeritus of the History of Consciousness, in addition to serving as Professor of Comparative Literature at Stanford University.

Following early co-authored essays and edited collections on European intellectual history, White published his first major, and still most influential, work in 1973: *Metahistory: The Historical Imagination in Nineteenth-Century Europe*. Influenced especially by the Italian philosopher Giambattista Vico, the literary critic Kenneth Burke, and narratology, the book constitutes a detailed analysis of the narrative strategies employed by nineteenth-century historians. White argues that historians do not write objective accounts of the past from disinterested positions, but create stories by approaching events according to certain "interpretive principles" and symbolic modes, determining, for example, how they decide what matters. History, White contends, is above all linguistic and poetic in nature. He describes a historian's particular style as emerging from a combination of different conventional modes of "argumentation," "emplotment," and "ideological implication." These are ultimately subordinate to a fourth, deeper, element: poetic linguistic structure. This is White's theory of tropes (the most influential aspect of *Metahistory*) in which the way a historian "prefigures" their materials is associated with four poetic tropes (figures of speech) – metaphor, metonymy, synecdoche, and irony – which have typical ways of organizing information into a narrative.

The key implications of this theory, foregrounding the historian's selection processes and subjectivity, concern its assertion of the unscientific character of historiography, demonstrated by how different accounts and interpretations of the same events can appear equally plausible. White concludes that the historian's approach is ultimately chosen on aesthetic or moral grounds, rather than derived from factual historical evidence. His intention is to encourage self-reflection on the part of historians as to how their perspectives are predetermined. Furthermore, White alleges the basic sameness of fiction and historiography in how events are made meaningful above all through their narrative representation. For White, given that rhetorical choices already pervade their work, historians should embrace the literariness of their craft and learn from developments in modern art and intellectual debate, rather than continuing to draw on nineteenth-century realism and objectivity, long abandoned by other realms.

Metahistory's interrogations of academic history were predictably heavily criticized by traditional historians. They objected to the correspondence of history and fiction and the refutation of meaningfulness of historical evidence and neutrality. The work was attacked especially on grounds of formalism (the schematic categorization of modes) and relativism (how, if events' meanings are not intrinsic but emerge from emplotment, no history is more "true" than another). *Metahistory* has nonetheless had a vital impact on thought about history writing. Scholars whose work is sympathetic to or in some ways consonant with White's include the American intellectual historian Dominick LaCapra, the Dutch historian Frank Ankersmit, the French philosopher Paul Ricoeur, and the American philosopher Richard Rorty. But while *Metahistory* sparked considerable debate among historians, White's subsequent publications have been largely ignored by the mainstream of the discipline. Scholars in other fields, particularly literary criticism (e.g., Perkins 1992; Grossman 1998) have however continued to engage with his work, variously adopting him as a structuralist, poststructuralist and postmodernist.

Much of White's subsequent work refines and develops his thesis regarding the literariness of historiography while responding to his critics. Many of his essays (this being his favored form) are published in three collected volumes. Several of those featured in the first of these, *Tropics of Discourse: Essays in Cultural Criticism* (1978), continue to clarify the territory broached in *Metahistory*. Among the most significant of these is "The historical text as literary artifact," where White unequivocally states the nature of historical narratives as "verbal fictions."

White's influence on literature scholars grew markedly with the "narrative turn" in the humanities, matched by White's own increasing concern with issues of narrativity and literary theory (drawing on, among others, the French poststructuralists Roland Barthes, Michel Foucault, and Jacques Derrida). His following collection, *The Content of the Form: Narrative Discourse and Historical Representation* (1987), addresses the ideological dimensions of narrative history and the suppression of what White calls the "historical sublime" (the chaos, uncertainty and meaninglessness of history). "The politics of historical interpretation: Discipline and de-sublimation" and "The value of narrativity in the representation of reality" have been especially influential.

In the essays collected in *Figural Realism: Studies in the Mimesis Effect* (1999), White engages with modernist literature and responds to charges of relativism, notably in reference to historical representations of Nazism in "Historical emplotment and the problem of truth in historical representation." Here he argues that the Holocaust can be historically rendered, but as a "modernist event" requires a modernist style of representation.

SEE ALSO: Barthes, Roland; Derrida, Jacques; Foucault, Michel; Master Narrative;

Narratology and Structuralism;
Rorty, Richard

REFERENCES AND SUGGESTED
READINGS

Grossman, M. (1998). *The Story of All Things: Writing the Self in English Renaissance Narrative Poetry*. Durham: Duke University Press.

Jenkins, K. (1995). *On "What is History?": From Carr and Elton to Rorty and White*. London: Routledge.

Perkins, D. (1992) *Is Literary History Possible?* Baltimore: Johns Hopkins University Press.

White, H. (1973). *Metahistory: The Historical Imagination in Nineteenth-Century Europe*. Baltimore: Johns Hopkins University Press.

White, H. (1978). *Tropics of Discourse: Essays in Cultural Criticism*. Baltimore: Johns Hopkins University Press.

White, H. (1987). *The Content of the Form: Narrative Discourse and Historical Representation*. Baltimore: Johns Hopkins University Press.

White, H. (1999). *Figural Realism: Studies in the Mimesis Effect*. Baltimore: Johns Hopkins University Press.

Wittig, Monique

ABIGAIL RINE

Monique Wittig was a novelist, theorist, and feminist activist, known primarily for her fictional works and theorization of feminism from a materialist, lesbian perspective. Wittig was a central figure in the feminist movement in France, and her writings on heterosexuality and the oppression of women have greatly influenced feminist thought and queer theory.

Wittig was born in Dannemarie, France on July 13, 1935. In 1964, after studying language and philosophy at the Sorbonne, Wittig published her first novel, *The Opoponax* (1966[1964]), which garnered critical praise and was awarded the Prix Médicis. Wittig was involved in the student uprisings of May 1968 and produced her second novel, *Les Guérillères* (1972[1969]), in this climate of radical activism. During the 1970s, Wittig was a leading activist in the radical French feminist movement and involved in founding several activist groups, such as the Petites Marguérites and the Féministes Révolutionnaires. Wittig also participated in the 1970 protest march to the Arc de Triomphe, during which French and American feminist activists laid a wreath on the Tomb of the Unknown Solider, commemorating the soldier's unknown wife. In 1976, after publishing her third novel, *The Lesbian Body* (1975[1973]), Wittig immigrated to the United States and held visiting professorships at various universities. Wittig earned her doctorate in 1986 and joined the University of Arizona faculty, where she produced her most well-known theoretical work, a collection of essays entitled *The Straight Mind* (1992). On January 3, 2003, Wittig died from a sudden heart attack in Tucson, Arizona, at the age of 67.

There is no clear divide between Wittig's theoretical works and her fiction, as ideas introduced in her novels are given explicit treatment in her nonfiction works. Within Wittig's theories, language is what connects the conceptual realm with material reality, and therefore any change to the social order is necessarily mediated through language. In this light, writing becomes a political force, and any distinction between Wittig's political activism and her writing is likewise problematic, as all of her works, fiction and nonfiction, are deeply political and fundamentally concerned with combating women's oppression. As reflected in her feminist epic *Les Guérillères*, the revolution Wittig calls for is a conceptual one, an overthrow of categories that are steeped in patriarchal assumptions. A self-described materialist feminist, Wittig argues that the notion of sexual difference masks the social and political forces that segregate the sexes, and the very categories of "man" and "woman" create a supposedly natural justification for social oppression. In other words, according to Wittig, it is the system of oppression that establishes sex/gender categories, not vice versa. Drawing on Marx, Wittig views the struggle between the sexes as a class struggle, one that cannot be resolved until all sex/gender categories are abolished.

In her essay "The straight mind," Wittig extends the feminist critique of patriarchy to include heterosexuality, which she condemns as a political regime that universalizes and perpetuates the oppression of women. Wittig asserts that the concept of "woman" is defined by the obligatory heterosexual contract, an analysis that leads to Wittig's famous and controversial statement: "Lesbians are not women" (1992: 32). Wittig upholds lesbians as uniquely positioned outside the system of patriarchy and heterosexuality, and therefore not encompassed in the category "woman." Distinguishing lesbians from women and deeming "woman" inextricable from patriarchy, Wittig calls for the total abolishment of "woman" as a class and as a concept. In her novel *The Lesbian Body*, Wittig portrays her deconstruction of "woman" by figuratively dismantling the female body as traditionally conceived and refiguring it from a lesbian perspective.

Wittig's technique of invoking the universal viewpoint from a minority, specifically lesbian, perspective provides another method of challenging dominant patriarchal concepts. In her essay, "The point of view: Universal or particular?" (in Wittig 1992), Wittig asserts that marginalized writers can only effect change by universalizing the minority experience. Wittig's fiction consistently subverts traditional narrative perspective and is characterized by unconventional use of pronouns. In *The Opoponax*, her experimental novel about the progression from childhood to adolescence, Wittig conflates the universal with the particular through her use of the French collective pronoun *on*, which is alternately translated as *one*, *we*, and *you*. In this way, the voice of a single girl becomes the voice of anyone, and through portraying one female coming-of-age, Wittig evokes the development of all human identities and perceptions.

Wittig's emphasis on language and its influence on material reality have encouraged some critics to draw parallels between Wittig and Hélène Cixous, particularly in the context of *écriture féminine*. Wittig herself, however, disavows any connection with so-called feminine writing, on the grounds that such a concept reinforces women's marginal subject position. She is careful to distinguish herself from other French feminists who celebrate sexual difference, referring to these perspectives as a backlash against the feminist trend of questioning gendered categories. Parallels have also been drawn between Wittig and Adrienne Rich, whose essay "Compulsory heterosexuality and lesbian existence" (1980) was published in the same year as "The straight mind." Rich's critique of heterosexuality closely mirrors Wittig's, but Rich distinguishes between lesbianism as an erotic choice and lesbianism as conscious identification with women. Though Rich leaves room for women to adopt a lesbian perspective without necessarily adopting homosexual behavior, Wittig asserts that, in order for social transformation to occur, the heterosexual contract must be completely broken and the marginal category of "woman" abolished.

SEE ALSO: Cixous, Hélène; *Ecriture Féminine*; Feminism; Gender Theory; Marxism; Queer

Theory; Social Constructionism;
Subject Position

REFERENCES AND SUGGESTED READINGS

Rich, A. (1980). Compulsory heterosexuality and lesbian existence. *Signs*, 5(4), 631–660.

Shaktini, N. (2005). *On Monique Wittig: Theoretical, Political, and Literary Essays*. Champaign: University of Illinois Press.

Wittig, M. (1966). *The Opoponax* (trans. H. Weaver). London: Peter Owen. (Original work published 1964.)

Wittig, M. (1972). *Les Guérillères* (trans. D. Le Vay). Boston: Beacon. (Original work published 1969.)

Wittig, M. (1975). *The Lesbian Body* (trans. D. Le Vay). Boston: Beacon. (Original work published 1973.)

Wittig, M. (1992). *The Straight Mind and Other Essays*. New York: Harvester Wheatsheaf.

Y

Yale School

MARTIN MCQUILLAN

The "Yale School" is the term commonly used to describe the work of five outstanding scholars – Harold Bloom, Paul de Man, Jacques Derrida, Geoffrey Hartman, and J. Hillis Miller – located in the departments of French and Comparative Literature, and of English, at Yale University between 1972 and 1986. It is often referred to as the Yale School of deconstruction or even as "American deconstruction" in general. While de Man used the term "deconstruction" and both Derrida and Miller remained aligned with this term throughout their writing, the connection between Bloom and Hartman and deconstruction is less obvious. Three broad factors, however, link these critics and thinkers. First, this grouping of scholars represented a profoundly influential opening in literary theory and criticism in North America at this time, through which French-influenced poststructuralist theoretical inquiry came to be accepted, albeit contentiously, in the US humanities, although their reading strategies circled much more within the ambit of Derrida than any other French thinker. Second, and more subtly, what the Yale scholars have most in common is a shared interest in European Romanticism, from Derrida's frequent sorties into eighteenth-

century philosophy, de Man's work on Rousseau, to Hartman's many commentaries on English Romantic poetry. As commentators on eighteenth-century and early nineteenth-century thought, the Yale School might be thought of as representing the reopening of Enlightenment thought through deconstructive reading. Finally, their influence is perhaps most keenly felt in the impressive array of graduate students who passed through the Yale comparative literature doctoral program at the time and who subsequently came to dominate literary and cultural theory in the United States for a generation. Accordingly, the Yale School might be more meaningfully thought of as identifying this pedagogical legacy with the expanded graduate diaspora being more worthy of the title "Yale School" than the five original scholars. The only significant volume produced by the Yale quintet together is the collection of essays *Deconstruction and Criticism* (Bloom et al. 1979), in which each critic contributes an essay on Shelley's "The triumph of life."

De Man, Miller, and Derrida had first met at the 1966 conference "The languages of criticism and the sciences of man" at Johns Hopkins University in Baltimore, where structuralism initially gained a foothold in the American academy, even though (almost without exception) the French visitors, including Roland Barthes and Jacques

---

The Encyclopedia of Literary and Cultural Theory   General editor: Michael Ryan
© 2011 Blackwell Publishing Ltd

Lacan, all spoke of the movement of work beyond structuralism in France. Paul de Man (1919–83) joined Yale, as Sterling Professor of French, from Cornell in 1970 and in 1979 he became the Sterling Professor of Comparative Literature and French. He served variously as the chair of the French department and the comparative literature program. His essays were considered groundbreaking, combining a critical discourse on criticism itself with a new philosophical vocabulary for literature. *Blindness and Insight* appeared in 1971, with a revised edition in 1983 after its significance for deconstruction became apparent. Here de Man argues, in the absence of deconstructive terminology, that all critical texts are blind to that which they are most insightful about, and equally insightful about that which they recognize the least. While he was interested in the relation between literature and philosophy, having written extensively on Heidegger and phenomenological critics, he had not yet fully developed his mature rhetorical reading strategy or "linguistics of literariness" which he identified with "deconstruction" in *Allegories of Reading* (1979). Years of significant theoretical endeavor followed with a range of important essays, which were later published posthumously in works such as *The Resistance to Theory* (1986) and *The Rhetoric of Romanticism* (1984); *Aesthetic Ideology*, which appeared in 1996, contains de Man's late and unfinished essays on ideology and politics. De Man died in 1983 at the height of his powers and was mourned by colleagues and students alike, from Derrida's *Mémoires: For Paul de Man* (1986) to the collection "The lesson of Paul de Man" (Brooks et al. 1985). In 1987 a Belgian PhD student, Ortwin de Graef, currently Professor of Literary Studies at Leuven University, discovered while researching de Man that he had written for the collaborationist press in wartime Belgium. Several of

the articles he wrote represent a cause for concern despite de Man's age at the time and the mitigating circumstances of war in occupied Europe. The fallout from this revelation split the semblance of coherence around the Yale School. While some like Derrida and Miller defended de Man's reputation against unreflective media attacks, Bloom was ever after estranged from Derrida as a result of his defense of their one-time mutual friend.

Harold Bloom (b. 1930 in New York) had been at Yale since 1955, having completed a PhD there under the great American literary critic M. H. Abrams. Bloom's most notable contributions to literary theory came before the Yale School coalesced around the appointment of Derrida. His *The Anxiety of Influence* (1973) offers a theory of literary inheritance (influenced by his own critical predecessor T. S. Eliot) that suggests that a great writer must creatively "misprision" his generational forebear in order to produce innovative and distinctive new work. Subsequent works such as *Kabbalah and Criticism* (1975), *The Breaking of the Vessels* (1982), and *Ruin the Sacred Truths* (1989) combine a polemical response to theoretical approaches to literature with a secularized affiliation to Judaic culture. Bloom later became a great champion of traditional aesthetic approaches to literature, publishing *The Western Canon* in 1994. His witty and erudite writing combines a considerable readerly sensibility with an almost shameless embrace of the politically incorrect, constituting a singular independent voice in literary criticism today.

Geoffrey Hartman was born in Germany in 1929 and came to the United States in 1946. He gained his PhD from Yale in 1953. He was a scholar of Wordsworth who became attuned to the new criticism working its way across the American humanities. His retrospective mid-career collection, *Beyond Formalism: Literary Essays 1958–1970*

(1970), published during the Yale School years, charts a similar progress to de Man, in that his work moves from American new criticism toward a more challenging engagement with the philosophy of language and ultimately deconstruction. His time at Yale is best characterized by the volumes *Criticism in the Wilderness: The Study of Literature Today* (1980) and *Saving the Text: Literature/Derrida/Philosophy* (1981), which demonstrate a profound appreciation of the Romantic inheritance combined with a subtle inquiry into the difference between literature and literary commentary. The later book represents a considerable critical engagement with Derrida's *Glas*. Following the posthumous revelations concerning de Man's wartime journalism, Hartman chose to defend de Man, proposing that while de Man's juvenilia should be roundly condemned, the American academy and media, unable to challenge deconstruction intellectually, had exploited the real horror of the Holocaust to attack deconstruction institutionally and sensationally. Hartman displayed a subsequent interest in Holocaust studies, such as his 1996 work, *The Longest Shadow: In the Aftermath of the Holocaust*. He went on to found the Jewish Studies program at Yale and the Yale Archive for Holocaust Testimony. He has published a memoir of *A Scholar's Tale: Intellectual Journey of a Displaced Child of Europe* (2007) in which he details his friendship with de Man and others.

J. Hillis Miller (b. 1928) joined Yale from Johns Hopkins University in Baltimore in 1972 and taught there for 14 years before moving to University of California, Irvine. Miller is an extraordinary reader of nineteenth-century literature with a keen sensibility for innovation and critique within literary studies. Like Hartman and de Man, his career might be characterized as a journey from the traditions of American formalism toward the phenomenology of

literature and consequently deconstruction. He and de Man frequently intersected as part of an emerging North American new criticism before the arrival of Derrida at Yale. His work ranges from considerations of metatheoretical topics such as narrative and theology to close inspections of literary oeuvres such as that of Dickens and Henry James. His time at Yale is best characterized by theoretically informed literary criticism such as *Fiction and Repetition* (1982) and *The Linguistic Moment* (1985). He published his contribution to the Wellek Lectures series, *The Ethics of Reading: Kant, de Man, Eliot, Trollope, James, and Benjamin*, in 1987. Significantly, such a publication suggests an interest in ethics and the responsibilities of reading a full year (longer given the date of the lectures) before the so-called de Man affair, suggesting that the subsequent "ethical turn" in literary theory after the affair is, on the one hand, spurious and, on the other hand, an articulation of an understanding already present in deconstruction itself. Miller's *Versions of Pygmalion* (1990) and *Ariadne's Thread: Story Lines* (1992) are the work of a mature theorist able to synthesis literary erudition with theoretical capability. The volumes *Theory Now and Then* (1991) and *Topographies* (1995) gather together essays which demonstrate the increasing influence of Derrida and de Man on Miller's writing and his growing importance as a critical interlocutor for both. His work continues to be identified by innovation and a spectacular clarity in his exposition of the most abstruse French theory, exemplified in recent texts such as *Black Holes* (1999) and *For Derrida* (2009). Miller has been perhaps the most "institutionally" influential of the Yale School, counting among his professional achievements presidency of the Modern Languages Association.

Jacques Derrida (1930–2004) taught on the Yale comparative literature program as a visiting professor from 1975 for 12 years before following Miller to the University of California, Irvine in the wake of the de Man affair. Throughout the period of his affiliation with Yale he held appointments in Paris at the École pratique des hautes études and the École des hautes études en sciences sociales. When visiting Yale, Derrida would offer a version of his Paris seminar for his American audience. At this time Derrida always taught in French; it was not until he moved to Irvine in 1989 that he began to offer a hastily improvised English-language version of his seminar. The term "deconstruction" is most commonly associated with Derrida and it would take an entry of considerably greater length to offer a reasoned account of all its complexities. However, it would be a mistake to imagine that all of the influence between Derrida and his American interlocutors was a one-way traffic. His time at Yale is characterized by a profound engagement with the question of literature and one can frequently see in Derrida a marked difference in his treatment of literature and philosophy. At Yale, Derrida also opened up an appreciative English-language audience beyond the prejudicial hierarchies of the French academy, making deconstruction and Jacques Derrida a profoundly American phenomenon. Derrida's American audience frequently dictated the direction of his philosophical interests, such as his late work on legal theory as well as theology. His publications during his Yale years include the texts which make up La Carte postale (1980), notably his polemic with Lacan, "The purveyor of truth," and the text "Envois" which uses Yale as one of the "fictional" backdrops for its love story; Eperons (1978); and Singéponge (1984). Notable English-language translations appeared during this time helping to cement Derrida's reputation in the Anglo-Saxon academy and securing his English-speaking audience, they include:

Of Grammatology (1976), Dissemination (1981), and Margins of Philosophy (1982). When Derrida and Miller moved to UCI, the hegemony of the Yale School in American critical culture and popular imaginary had been surpassed by the latest turns on theory and the eclipse of deconstruction by the de Man affair. In California, so-called American deconstruction opened up a new frontier, leading Derrida to comment (in no way frivolously) that the state of California was the state of theory, given its immanent divisibility and its hybrid historicity.

SEE ALSO: Bloom, Harold;
Deconstruction; Derrida, Jacques;
de Man, Paul; Miller, J. Hillis

REFERENCES AND SUGGESTED
READINGS

Bloom, H. (1973). The Anxiety of Influence: A Theory of Poetry. New York: Oxford University Press.
Bloom, H. (1975). Kabbalah and Criticism. New York: Seabury.
Bloom, H., Derrida, J., Miller, J. H., de Man, P., & Hartman, G. (1979). Deconstruction and Criticism. New York: Continuum.
Bloom, H. (1982). The Breaking of the Vessels. Chicago: University of Chicago Press.
Bloom, H. (1989). Ruin the Sacred Truths. Cambridge, MA: Harvard University Press.
Bloom, H. (1994). The Western Canon: The Books and School of the Ages. New York: Harcourt, Brace.
Brooks, P., Felman, S., & Miller, J. H. (eds.) (1985). The lesson of Paul de Man [special issue]. Yale French Studies, 69.
Derrida, J. (1976). Of Grammatology (trans. G. C. Spivak). Baltimore: Johns Hopkins University Press.
Derrida, J. (1978). Writing and Difference (trans. A. Bass). London: Routledge.
Derrida, J. (1981). Dissémination (trans. B. Johnson). Chicago: University of Chicago Press.
Derrida, J. (1982). Margins of Philosophy (trans. A. Bass). Chicago: University of Chicago Press.
Derrida, J. (1986a). Glas (trans. J. P. Leavey, Jr. & R. Rand). Lincoln: University of Nebraska Press.

Derrida, J. (1986b). *Mémoires: For Paul de Man* (trans. C. Lindsay, J. Culler, & E. Cadava). New York: Columbia University Press.

Derrida, J. (1987). *The Post Card: From Socrates to Freud and Beyond* (trans. A. Bass). Chicago: University of Chicago Press.

Hartman, G. (1970). *Beyond Formalism: Literary Essays, 1958–1970.* New Haven: Yale University Press.

Hartman, G. (1980). *Criticism in the Wilderness: The Study of Literature Today.* New Haven: Yale University Press.

Hartman, G. (1981). *Saving the Text: Literature/ Derrida/Philosophy.* Baltimore: Johns Hopkins University Press.

Hartman, G. (1996). *The Longest Shadow: In the Aftermath of the Holocaust.* Bloomington: Indiana University Press.

Hartman, G. (2007). *A Scholar's Tale: Intellectual Journey of a Displaced Child of Europe.* New York: Fordham University Press.

de Man, P. (1979). *Allegories of Reading: Figural Language in Rousseau, Nietzsche, Rilke, and Proust.* New Haven: Yale University Press.

de Man, P. (1983). *Blindness and Insight: Essays in the Rhetoric of Contemporary Criticism,* 2nd rev. edn. Minneapolis: University of Minnesota Press. (Original work published 1971.)

de Man, P. (1984). *The Rhetoric of Romanticism.* New York: Columbia University Press.

de Man, P. (1986). *The Resistance to Theory.* Minneapolis: University of Minnesota Press.

de Man, P. (1988). *Wartime Journalism, 1939–1943* (ed. W. Hamacher, N. Hertz, & T. Keenan). Lincoln: University of Nebraska Press.

de Man, P. (1996). *Aesthetic Ideology.* Minneapolis: University of Minnesota Press.

Miller, J. H. (1977). The critic as host. *Critical Inquiry,* 3(3), 439–447.

Miller, J. H. (1982). *Fiction and Repetition.* Cambridge, MA: Harvard University Press.

Miller, J. H. (1985). *The Linguistic Moment.* Princeton: Princeton University Press.

Miller, J. H. (1987a). *The Ethics of Reading: Kant, de Man, Eliot, Trollope, James, and Benjamin.* New York: Columbia University Press.

Miller, J. H. (1987b). Presidential address 1986: The triumph of theory, the resistance to reading and the question of the material base. PMLA, 102, 281–291.

Miller, J. H. (1990). *Versions of Pygmalion.* Cambridge, MA: Harvard University Press.

Miller, J. H. (1991). *Theory Now and Then.* Durham, NC: Duke University Press.

Miller, J. H. (1992). *Ariadne's Thread: Story Lines.* New Haven: Yale University Press.

Miller, J. H. (1995). *Topographies.* Stanford: Stanford University Press.

Miller, J. H. (1999). *Black Holes.* Stanford: Stanford University Press.

Miller, J. H. (2009). *For Derrida.* New York: Fordham University Press.

Young, Robert

SHAHIDHA BARI

Robert Young's *White Mythologies: Writing History and the West* was published in 1990 and has since undergone several reprints, having swiftly established itself as a touchstone text for postcolonial criticism. *White Mythologies* offers an investigation into the privileged conception of "history" that is often posed in antagonism to "theory" and whose "reality" is considered a sober counter to theory's textuality. Rather than pose poststructuralism as a theoretical alternative to history, Young (b. 1950) identifies the complicity of theory and history in the long and ongoing narrative of European colonialism, which continues to determine the formations of knowledge that extend beyond the academy. In *White Mythologies* Young examines a range of theoretical thinkers in order to uncover the totalizing logic of their own thought. Signaling the Eurocentrism of writers usually affiliated with the materialist projects of independence and emancipation such as Marx, Althusser, Sartre, and Foucault, Young sketches the possible futures of postcolonial criticism through the work of Said, Bhabha, and Spivak. *White Mythologies* questions the limits of Western knowledge and opens up a continuing line of inquiry in postcolonial criticism.

Young notes that the limited single world history provided by Marx is unthinkingly replicated by later emancipatory writers. For Young, the problems of a class-based Marxism became apparent in the May 1968 protests, where Marxism struggled to incorporate anticolonial criticism. Young argues that even Sartre, who inspired Fanon, invokes a radical politics that operates on a European schema. Although Althusser criticizes the singular, general history of Marxist theory, Young notes how Althusser nonetheless fails to articulate the disjunctive and plural identities of gender, race, and sexuality alongside his analysis of class. Foucault too, who offers a remorseless critique of totalizing forms of history, and who posits genealogy in place of "general" history, Young perceives as continuing to privilege Western history as teleology and event. Young recognizes the complicity of general history with radical theory as a serious epistemological problem, traceable back to the Hegelian dialectic where the other is appropriated as knowledge. Young observes that this epistemic appropriation is replicated in the project of nineteenth-century imperialism. The geographical and economic absorption of the non-European world by the West mimics the violence of knowledge that is constructed through the expropriation and incorporation of the acceptable other. Knowledge is complicit in the dialectic of domination that limits difference to a homogeneous identity. Young argues that politics and knowledge continue to work according to the logic of a Hegelian dialectic; Marx's conception of an authoritative revolutionary history mimics European colonial annexations, just as Freud's characterization of femininity as a "dark unexplored continent" mirrors the appropriative racism of Orientalist scholarship.

Young's critique of the complacent Eurocentrism of leftist and redistributive political theory is acutely made, and he modifies the premise of a silenced subaltern to implicate instead a dominant tradition incapable of listening. The outstanding question for Young is that of how to acknowledge accounts of different histories and cultures in a critical field limited for so long to its white, European, and bourgeois parameters. One of the possibilities that Young poses is the idea of a "tricontinental socialism" which might extend to include Latin America, Africa, and Asia, offering a more equitable understanding of the global power structures. Maoism too is flagged by Young as a dissident form of Marxism capable of countering the Eurocentrism of Marx's single world class analysis. Maoism that specifically acknowledges the role of culture in revolutionary change might also challenge cultural orthodoxies with its emphasis on development through cultural learning. In the last sections of *White Mythologies*, Young evaluates the work of emergent postcolonial thinkers engaged in the ethico-political project of establishing forms of knowledge that do not simply turn the other into the same. In Said, Young sees the exploration of the problematic of historicist forms of knowledge forcibly linked to the question of European imperialism. In Bhabha, Young recognizes the critique of Said's own Oriental–Occidental polarity, in place of which Bhabha posits a theory of dissonance, capable of dislocating the Western paradigm of coherence and univocality. Young recognizes in Bhabha's work the discursive conditions of a postcolonialism that might undermine colonial authority, where mimicry and hybridity become forms of resistance and intervention. Spivak, too, flags for Young the discontinuities of a heterogeneous and plural subaltern, whose prolific difference raises politico-theoretical difficulties and which requires a critical approach that is vigilant to the hidden perpetuations of totalizing structure and system. For Young, the possibilities of postcolonialism criticism posed by Said,

Bhabha, and Spivak are sobered by his own vigilant criticism that recognizes how resistance also operates inside of power.

In his 1996 *Torn Halves*, Young attends to the hybridity of poststructuralism itself, noting how it consists of an improper mixture of many discursive practices – psychoanalysis, semiotics, history, anthropology – which are translated into a philosophical hybrid that elicits accusations of illegitimacy. For Young, though, poststructuralism's hybridity renders it a discourse of "torn halves" that neither adds up nor raises cause for concern. The impropriety of multidisciplinary and intercultural boundary crossing renders poststructuralism resolutely political, insofar as it abstains from staking a position and signals instead a state of difficulty that allows conflict with neither deletion nor resolution of differing terms. In *The Idea of English Ethnicity*, Young considers this problem more locally in the context of English national identity and its problematic relationship with ethnicity. He offers a historical analysis that traces this difficulty to the English–Irish Act of Union of 1800. Observing that the origins of English identity compelled it to sustain an inclusive remit (from Irish union to a larger commonwealth) without specification of race or place, Young proposes that this principle of broad inclusivity has facilitated the multiculturalism of modern Britain.

SEE ALSO: Althusser, Louis; Bhabha, Homi; Foucault, Michel; Marx, Karl; Said, Edward; Spivak, Gayatri Chakravorty

REFERENCES AND SUGGESTED READINGS

Young, R. (1990). *White Mythologies: Writing History and the West.* London: Routledge.

Young, R. (1995). *Colonial Desire: Hybridity in Culture, Theory and Race.* London: Routledge.

Young, R. (1996). *Torn Halves: Political Conflict in Literary and Cultural Theory.* Manchester: Manchester University Press.

Young, R. (2008). *The Idea of English Ethnicity.* Oxford: Blackwell.

Z

Žižek, Slavoj

ARIS MOUSOUTZANIS

Slavoj Žižek (b. 1949) is a Slovenian philosopher whose work has been increasingly popular and widely discussed since the publication of his first book in English, *The Sublime Object of Ideology*, in 1989, primarily for two reasons. The first is Žižek's unique ability to combine discussions on psychoanalysis, philosophy, and politics, and provide original reinterpretations of the work of intellectual figures such as the French psychoanalyst Jacques Lacan and the German philosopher G. W. F. Hegel. The second is his very characteristic and idiosyncratic writing style, which manages to combine references to "high theory" and popular culture, obscene jokes and Continental philosophy, personal anecdotes and political theory. A text by Žižek will easily move from a discussion of psychoanalysis to the video clips of Michael Jackson, from the nature of totalitarianism to the differences between European lavatories, and from German idealism to Marlboro ads. There has always been an iconoclastic element in his work and a tendency to challenge and subvert dominant assumptions about his topic, an attitude that has been seen as related to his own personal and professional background. For Terry Eagleton, for instance, it is the fact that Žižek comes from a former Communist country that explains his concern with challenging authority and the establishment: "No acolyte of Lacan from Paris or Pittsburgh would have anything like Žižek's political nous, a faculty you develop spontaneously in a place where the political is the color of everyday life" (Eagleton 2003: 201). Tony Myers, on the other hand, has seen Žižek's intellectual development as always characterized by "a distance or heterogeneity to the official culture within which he works": "He has always been a stain or point of opacity within the ruling orthodoxy and is never fully integrated by the social or philosophical conventions against which he operates" (Myers 2003: 10).

Žižek was born in Ljubljana, in former Yugoslavia, now Slovenia. His upbringing within the political environment of the 1970s was formative for his work as he started studying at a time when the Communist regime was becoming more liberal, which allowed him to collaborate with dissident intellectuals and publish articles in journals such as *Praxis*, *Tribuna*, and *Problemi*, which he was also editing. The fairly liberal climate also allowed him to familiarize himself with the popular culture of the West that was later to become an important source of material for his discussions. At that period, he also became affiliated with one of a group of Slovenian intellectuals based at the Institute of Philosophy in

The Encyclopedia of Literary and Cultural Theory   General editor: Michael Ryan
© 2011 Blackwell Publishing Ltd

Ljubljana who were particularly focused on the work of Jacques Lacan. It was also there that he obtained his PhD in German Idealism at the University of Ljubljana in 1981. Between 1981 and 1985 he studied psychoanalysis at the University of Paris VIII with Lacan's son-in-law Jacques-Alain Miller, who was to become a major influence on Žižek. With him, Žižek undertook a second doctorate on Hegel, Marx, and Kripke from the perspective of Lacanian psychoanalysis, and this was to provide a lot of the material of Žižek's first two books, *The Sublime Object of Ideology* (1989) and *For They Know Not What They Do: Enjoyment as a Political Factor* (1990). In the late 1980s, Žižek returned to Slovenia where he got involved in politics even more actively, as he ran for president in the first free elections of the Republic of Slovenia in 1990, finishing fifth for the four-person presidency. He has been a very prolific and versatile writer, with countless articles and lectures and more than 40 books since the late 1980s. He has also been the topic of two films, *Slavoj Žižek: The Reality of the Virtual* (2004) and *Žižek* (2005) and wrote the documentary *A Pervert's Guide to Cinema* (2006). Currently he holds various academic posts such as that of international director of the Birkbeck Institute for the Humanities at Birkbeck, University of London, senior researcher at the Institute of Sociology, University of Ljubljana, and professor of the European Graduate School, among others.

Žižek was initially perceived as primarily a popularizer of the theory of Jacques Lacan, whose rewriting of the work of Sigmund Freud from the perspective of structuralist linguistics is often considered to be inaccessible to the point of obscurantism. For psychoanalysis, humans are primarily creatures of pleasure. "Desire," to use Lacan's term, is what defines human identity after the individual's transition from what Lacan discusses as the prelinguistic "register" (or

"order") of the imaginary in which the newborn infant finds itself to the register of the symbolic. Unlike the imaginary, which is the register of "wholeness" where the child does not perceive itself as distinct from its mother or the environment, the register of the symbolic is the register of absence and lack, which the child experiences after the entry into language. Language brings about the sense of absence, because words, "signifiers," stand for things, "signifieds," which are *not there*. "Through the word," as Lacan himself puts it, "which is already a presence made of absence, absence itself comes to be named" (Lacan 2001: 65). Once the individual enters the symbolic, everything is perceived and experienced in a mediated way, through language and signification, and "reality" itself is nothing but a fantasy, "a fragile, symbolic cobweb that" however "can at any moment be torn aside by an intrusion of the real" (Žižek 1991: 17): there is always something that is left out that cannot be assimilated or symbolized, something that threatens to collapse the fantasy of reality, which is what the third register of the real refers to, something that always returns to erupt within the symbolic order "in the form of a traumatic return, derailing the balance of our daily lives" (1991: 29). Žižek's reading and reworking of Lacanian theory has been original primarily in three ways. First, unlike previous approaches to Lacan's work, which were mostly focusing on the interactions between the registers of the symbolic and the imaginary, Žižek placed increasing emphasis on the significance of the dynamic between the symbolic and the real. In fact, it is probably *the* central concept around which Žižek's entire oeuvre oscillates, not least because it encapsulates a central premise of Žižek's philosophy, the argument that within any system there exists an element that threatens its disruption and yet is a prerequisite for its existence. Accordingly,

Žižek has relied on this concept as a central point of reference in various of his discussions and identified the real with sexual difference (1994), capital (1999), and Christian grace – as opposed to symbolic law (2000). It is for this reason that he has been described as "the philosopher of the Real."

Apart from the "turn to the Real", there is a second sense in which Žižek has provided a novel interpretation of Lacan's work, and this is in relation to the work of the German idealist philosopher G.W.F. Hegel. The novelty of Žižek's combined reading of the two theorists lies in his identification of Hegel's concept of the dialectic with Lacan's register of the real. Hegel's idealism relies on the founding premise that new ideas are formed out of the interaction of previously existing ones. According to the Hegelian dialectic, a given statement, a "thesis," will interact with a conflicting or opposite statement, its "antithesis," in order to form a new, more encompassing statement, a "synthesis." The synthesis, in turn, forms a new thesis to be subjected to the same process, until the final achievement of an Absolute Idea that will enable the true understanding of the world in its "totality." One may already identify a shared interest in the function and interaction of tripartite systems in both Hegel and Lacan; Lacan himself had acknowledged his indebtedness to the German philosopher. But he had also launched a severe critique of Hegelianism, as its belief in resolution and wholeness was in conflict with the psychoanalytic vision of a symbolic universe of conflict and split (see Lacan 2001). Žižek's interpretation of Hegel, however, has challenged the dominant view of his theory as one of synthesis and totality and focused on the significance of antithesis and negation, which he identified with the real. The dialectic process, for Žižek, does not eliminate contradiction for the sake of totality but rather foregrounds the existence of contradiction *within* totality, or, in Lacanian terms, the eruption of the real within the symbolic universe. The dialectic, for Žižek, is never finally resolved but rather its incessant development suggests, according to him, that once something reaches its identity it instantly turns into its opposite and thus confirms the existence of difference within identity. Žižek has always been fascinated with the dialectic inversion of something into its opposite to such an extent that he reproduces it in his writings. Often he will start by discussing a film, novel, theory, or anecdote; then he will proceed by offering the usual approach or interpretation to be expected toward the specific topic; and finally he will invert this interpretation, often with a negative interrogative sentence, in order to provide a different insight to the topic in question. The structure of his texts may therefore be seen as reproducing the dialectic process.

The third sense in which Žižek's rereading of Lacan has been considered to be original is the way in which he has combined psychoanalysis with Marxism in order to provide critiques of capitalism, racism, nationalism, and totalitarianism. In this way Žižek added a political twist to psychoanalysis, despite Lacan's own disdain for politics. This aspect of his work has been evident from the very beginning of *The Sublime Object of Ideology*, where he identifies structural analogies between Freud's theory of the dream-work and Marx's theory of the commodity-form, in order to suggest that capitalism is a pathological system of exploitation. More important, in this respect, however, is his project to reinterpret traditional Marxist conceptions of ideology from the perspective of psychoanalysis. The traditional Marxist definition of ideology as "false consciousness" refers to a set of beliefs, values, morals, and assumptions that are presented as "natural" and "commonsense" to citizens of a society when in reality they serve the interests of the dominant social groups. For Žižek, ideology functions through the social organization of what Lacan referred to as the transgressive experience of *jouissance*, the sexual enjoyment individuals have an irresistible urge toward yet have to compromise once they enter the socio-symbolic order. For Žižek, political regimes will only perpetuate their ideology by organizing their subjects' relations to *jouissance* (for example, through music, drugs, alcohol, festivals, etc.). His discussions of popular culture therefore acquire a further meaning through this argument.

During the last few decades, several theorists have suggested that the concept of ideology is outdated in a world where citizens generally demonstrate a certain cynicism toward political authorities and public institutions. But Žižek has always been persistent in underlying its enduring currency. He sees this cynicism as deeply ideological in itself and perfect proof of the pervasiveness of ideology. From the days of *The Sublime Object*, he was relying on the German political theorist Sloterditj in order to suggest that the formula to convey the function of ideology is not "they do not know it, but they are doing it," as Marx himself had put it, but "they know it, but they are doing it anyway" (Žižek 1989: 29). But from the late 1990s onward, the political aspect of his writings has become much more pronounced, as, for instance, in one of his most widely discussed books, *The Ticklish Subject* (1999), where he has examined the nature of totalitarianism, nationalism, capitalism, and globalization. In these writings, Žižek has increasingly emphasized the

importance of what he calls "the act," the action whereby individuals may escape from the confines of ideology and achieve a political version of what, in psychoanalysis, is termed "traversing the fantasy" of everyday life and perceive its illusory nature that hides the real, and therefore manage to build "reality" again. In this sense, his work has become even more relevant politically, especially as he has provided theoretical interventions on debates of events such as 9/11 and the Iraq War, among others.

SEE ALSO: Dialectics; Ideology; Imaginary/ Symbolic/Real; Lacan, Jacques; Marx, Karl; Psychoanalysis (to 1966); Psychoanalysis (since 1966)

REFERENCES AND SUGGESTED READINGS

Eagleton, T. (2003). Slavoj Žižek. In *Figures of Dissent*. London: Verso, pp. 196–206.
Lacan, J. (2001). *Ecrits: A Selection* (trans. A. Sheridan). London: Routledge.
Myers, T. (2003). *Slavoj Žižek*. London: Routledge.
Žižek, S. (1989). *The Sublime Object of Ideology*. London: Verso.
Žižek, S. (1990). *For They Know Not What They Do: Enjoyment as a Political Factor*. London: Verso.
Žižek, S. (1991). *Looking Awry: An Introduction to Jacques Lacan through Popular Culture*. Cambridge, MA: MIT Press.
Žižek, S. (1994). *The Metastases of Enjoyment: Six Essays on Woman and Causality*. London: Verso.
Žižek, S. (1999). *The Ticklish Subject: The Absent Centre of Political Ontology*. London: Verso.
Žižek, S. (2000). *The Fragile Absolute: Or Why the Christian Legacy Is Worth Fighting For*. London: Verso.